ENTERED JAN 1 4 2003

Encyclopedia of Japanese Descendants in the Americas

Encyclopedia of Japanese Descendants in the Americas

An Illustrated History of the Nikkei

Akemi Kikumura-Yano, Editor

Japanese American
National Museum

Foreword by
Senator Daniel K. Inouye

Introduction by
Gary Y. Okihiro

A Division of
ROWMAN & LITTLEFIELD PUBLISHERS, INC.
Walnut Creek • Lanham • New York • Oxford

970 E56k

Encyclopedia of Japanese
descendants in the Americas

Published with the assistance of a grant from

The Nippon Foundation

A Division of Rowman & Littlefield Publishers, Inc.
1630 North Main Street, Suite 367
Walnut Creek, CA 94596
www.altamirapress.com

Rowman & Littlefield Publishers, Inc.
4720 Boston Way
Lanham, MD 20706

12 Hid's Copse Road
Cumnor Hill, Oxford OX2 9JJ, England

Copyright © 2002 by Japanese American National Museum

All rights reserved. No part of this publication may be reproduced, stored in a retrieval system, or transmitted in any form or by any means, electronic, mechanical, photocopying, recording, or otherwise, without the prior permission of the publisher.

British Library Cataloguing in Publication Information Available

Library of Congress Cataloging-in-Publication Data

Encyclopedia of Japanese descendants in the Americas : an illustrated history of the Nikkei / [compiled by] Akemi Kikumura-Yano.
    p. cm.
    Includes bibliographical references and index.
    ISBN 0-7591-0149-3 (alk. paper)
    1. Japanese—America—History. 2. Immigrants—America—History. 3. Children of immigrants—America—History. 4. Japan—Emigration and immigration—History. 5. America—Emigration and immigration—History. 6. Japanese—America—History—Pictorial works. 7. Immigrants—America—History—Pictorial works. 8. Children of immigrants—America—History—Pictorial works. I. Kikumura-Yano, Akemi.

E29.J3 E53   2002
970.004'951—dc21   2002001959

Printed in the United States of America

∞™The paper used in this publication meets the minimum requirements of American National Standard for Information Sciences—Permanence of Paper for Printed Library Materials, ANSI/NISO Z39.48–1992.

Contents

Foreword Daniel K. Inouye, U.S. Senator	xi
Acknowledgments	xiii
Introduction Akemi Kikumura-Yano	1
Glossary	7
Turning Japanese Americans Gary Y. Okihiro	9
Worldwide Distribution of Nikkei, 1993	28
Nikkei World Demography	29

Chapter 1: Japanese Migration — 31
Developed in Collaboration with the Imin Kenkyukai

Historical Overview of Japanese Emigration, 1868–2000, by Eiichiro Azuma	32
An Overview of Japanese Migration Studies, 1905–1998, by Masako Iino, Kenji Kimura, and Tadashi Sugiura	49
Annotated Bibliography of Japanese Migration, compiled by Imin Kenkyukai	52
Supplementary Materials, compiled by Masayo Ohara and Eiichiro Azuma	63
Map 1.1 Japanese Prewar Emigration by Prefecture, 1899–1941	64
Map 1.2 Japanese Postwar Emigration by Prefecture, 1952–1993	65
Table 1.1 Japanese Prewar Emigration by Prefecture, 1899–1941	66
Table 1.2 Japanese Postwar Emigration by Prefecture, 1952–1993	66
Table 1.3 Japanese Immigration to the Americas, Southeast Asia and Oceania, and Asian Continent: Prewar, Wartime, and Postwar	67
Japanese Emigration Timeline, 1868–1998, by Eiichiro Azuma	68

Chapter 2: Japanese Argentines — 71
Developed in Collaboration with the Centro Nikkei Argentino and the Asociación Universitaria Nikkei

Japanese Argentine Historical Overview, by Isabel Laumonier	72
Japanese Argentine Bibliographic Essay, by Isabel Laumonier	83
Japanese Argentine Annotated Bibliography, compiled by Isabel Laumonier	85
Supplementary Materials, compiled by Cecilia Onaha, Isabel Laumonier, and Jorge Higa	89
Map 2.1 Argentina Provinces with Nikkei Populations	90
Table 2.1 Japanese Emigration to Argentina by Prefecture of Origin in Japan, 1906–1993	91

Table 2.2 Japanese Argentine Community Population … 91

Table 2.3 Number of Descendants, Estimated in 1986 … 91

Table 2.4 Japanese Immigrants in Argentina by Place of Origin, Japan National Census Data of 1940 … 92

Table 2.5 Japanese Immigrants in Argentina by Place of Origin, 1948–1970 … 92

Table 2.6 Regional Distribution of Japanese Argentines … 92

Table 2.7 Educational Achievement of Japanese Descendants by Percentage, 1986 Survey of Descendants Fifteen Years and Older … 92

Table 2.8 Occupational Areas of Japanese Immigrants and Their Descendants by Percentage … 93

Table 2.9 Religion of Japanese Immigrants and Their Descendants by Percentage, 1995 Questionnaire Survey … 93

Chapter 3: Japanese Bolivians … 95
Developed in Collaboration with the Presencia Japonesa en el Continente Americano at Keio University and the Federación Nacional de Asociaciones Boliviano Japonesas

Japanese Bolivian Historical Overview, by Iyo Kunimoto … 96

Bibliographic Essay on the Japanese Migration to Bolivia and Nikkei Society, by Iyo Kunimoto … 105

Japanese Bolivian Annotated Bibliography, compiled by Iyo Kunimoto … 107

Supplementary Materials, compiled by Federación Nacional de Asociaciones Boliviano Japonesas, Toshio Yanaguida, and Kozy Amemiya … 111

Map 3.1 Japanese Bolivian Settlements … 112

Table 3.1 JICA-Sponsored Japanese Emigration to Bolivia by Prefecture of Origin in Japan, 1952–1993 … 113

Table 3.2 Regional Distribution of Japanese Bolivians, 1955–2000 … 113

Table 3.3 Japanese Bolivian Gender Breakdown by Percentage, 1955–2000 … 113

Table 3.4 Educational Level of Japanese in Bolivia by Percentage, 2000 … 114

Table 3.5 Occupational Fields of Japanese Bolivian Heads of Household by Percentage, 2000 … 114

Table 3.6 Occupational Fields of Japanese Bolivian Population of Wives and Children by Percentage, 2000 … 114

Table 3.7 Religion of Japanese Bolivians by Percentage, 2000 … 114

Chapter 4: Japanese Brazilians … 115
Developed in Collaboration with the Museu Histórico da Imigração Japonesa no Brasil

Japanese Brazilian Historical Overview, by Masato Ninomiya … 116

Bibliographic Essay of Japanese Immigrants and Their Descendants, by Masato Ninomiya and Naomi Hoki Moniz … 127

Annotated Bibliography of Japanese Brazilians, compiled by Masato Ninomiya and Naomi Hoki Moniz … 130

Supplementary Materials, compiled by John Mizuki, Masato Ninomiya, and Hironobu Kai … 143

Map 4.1 Locations of Nikkei Populations in Brazil … 144

Table 4.1 Japanese Emigration to Brazil by Prefecture of Origin in Japan, 1906–1993 … 145

Table 4.2 Total Population of Japanese Brazilians, 1923–2006 (Projected) — 146

Table 4.3 Male/Female Ratio of Japanese Immigrants in Brazil on Arrival, 1908–1962 — 146

Table 4.4 Regional Distribution of Japanese Brazilians, 1923–1974 — 146

Table 4.5 Education of Japanese Immigrants and Their Descendants by Percentage, Ages Fifteen Years and Older in 1958 — 147

Table 4.6 Nisei Enrolled in Higher Education in the City of São Paulo by Percentage, 1967 — 147

Table 4.7 Occupational Areas of Japanese Brazilians by Percentage — 147

Table 4.8 Religion of Japanese Brazilians by Percentage, Ages Seven Years and Older in 1958 — 147

Chapter 5: Japanese Canadians — 149
Developed in Collaboration with the Japanese Canadian National Museum

A Brief History of Japanese Canadians, by Audrey Kobayashi and Midge Ayukawa — 150

Japanese Canadian Bibliographic Essay, by Audrey Kobayashi and Midge Ayukawa — 162

Japanese Canadians Annotated Bibliography, compiled by Audrey Kobayashi and Midge Ayukawa — 164

Supplementary Materials, compiled by Audrey Kobayashi, Midge Ayukawa, Kathleen Wilson, and Michael Pacey — 171

Map 5.1 Locations of Nikkei Populations in Canada — 172

Table 5.1 Japanese Emigration to Canada by Prefecture of Origin in Japan, 1899–1993 — 173

Table 5.2 Total Population of Japanese Canadians (Showing Single and Multiple Responses by Sex) — 173

Table 5.3 Total Population of Japanese Canadians (Showing Age–Sex Distribution), 1996 — 173

Table 5.4 Regional Distribution of Japanese Canadians by Sex (Showing Single and Multiple Responses) — 174

Table 5.5 Total Population of Japanese Canadians (Showing Age–Sex Distribution), 1996 — 174

Table 5.6 School Attendance of Japanese Canadians, Ages Fifteen Years and Older, 1996 — 174

Table 5.7 Highest Level of Schooling of Japanese Canadians, Ages Fifteen Years and Older, 1996 — 175

Table 5.8 Labor Force Activity of Japanese Canadians, Ages Fifteen Years and Older, 1996 — 175

Table 5.9 Industry Divisions of Japanese Canadians, Ages Fifteen Years and Older Who Worked since January 1, 1995 (Showing Sex Distribution), 1996 — 176

Table 5.10 Japanese Canadians, Ages Fifteen Years and Older Who Worked since January 1, 1995, by Occupation (Showing Sex Distribution), 1996 — 176

Chapter 6: Japanese Chileans — 177
Developed in Collaboration with the Sociedad Japonesa de Beneficencia, "Nikkei-Chile"

Japanese Immigrants and Nikkei Chileans, by Ariel Takeda — 178

Japanese Chilean Bibliographic Essay: General Historical Perspective, by Naomi Hirose, María Teresa Senda, and Ariel Takeda — 192

Annotated Bibliography of Japanese Chileans, compiled by Naomi Hirose, María Teresa Senda, and Ariel Takeda — 194

Supplementary Materials, compiled by Naomi Hirose, María Teresa Senda, and Ariel Takeda — 197

Map 6.1 Geographic Distribution of Nikkei Populations in Chile — 198

Table 6.1 Japanese Emigration to Chile by Prefecture of Origin in Japan, Pre-1940 — 199

Table 6.2 Japanese Population in Chile, 1875–1940 — 199

Table 6.3 Distribution of Japanese Population by Province, 1907–1940 — 200

Table 6.4 Nikkei Population by Gender and Regional Distribution, 1992 — 200

Table 6.5 Nikkei Families by Income, 1992 — 201

Document 6.1 Survey of Nikkei Families, December 1999 — 202

Chapter 7: Japanese Mexicans — 203
Developed in Collaboration with the Asociación México Japonesa, A.C.

Japanese Mexican Historical Overview, by Jesús K. Akachi, Carlos T. Kasuga, Manuel S. Murakami, María Elena Ota Mishima, Enrique Shibayama, and René Tanaka — 204

Japanese Mexican Bibliographic Essay, by Jesús K. Akachi, Carlos T. Kasuga, Manuel S. Murakami, María Elena Ota Mishima, Enrique Shibayama, and René Tanaka — 222

Annotated Bibliography of Japanese Mexicans, compiled by Jesús K. Akachi, Carlos T. Kasuga, Manuel S. Murakami, María Elena Ota Mishima, Enrique Shibayama, and René Tanaka — 223

Supplementary Materials, compiled by Jesús K. Akachi, Carlos T. Kasuga, Manuel S. Murakami, María Elena Ota Mishima, Enrique Shibayama, and René Tanaka — 225

Map 7.1 Locations of Japanese Mexican Populations in the Historical Overview — 226

Table 7.1 Japanese Emigration to Mexico by Prefecture of Origin in Japan, 1890–1949 — 227

Table 7.2 Total Japanese Mexican Population and Male/Female Ratio, 1950–1990 — 227

Table 7.3 Regional Distribution of Japanese Mexicans, 1950–1990 — 227

Table 7.4 Educational Level of Japanese Mexicans, 1950–1990 — 227

Table 7.5 Educational Level of Japanese Mexicans by Primary, Secondary, and College Education, 1950–1990 — 228

Table 7.6 Occupational Areas of Japanese Mexicans by Percentage, 1950–1990 — 228

Table 7.7 Religion of Japanese Mexicans, 1950–1990 — 228

Chapter 8: Japanese Paraguayans — 229
Developed in Collaboration with the Centro Nikkei Paraguayo

Japanese Paraguayan Historical Overview, by Emi Kasamatsu — 230

Bibliographic Essay on Themes of the Japanese and Nikkei of Paraguay, by Emi Kasamatsu — 239

Annotated Bibliography of Japanese Paraguayans, compiled by Emi Kasamatsu — 241

Supplementary Materials, compiled by Emi Kasamatsu — 243

Map 8.1 Locations of Nikkei Populations in Paraguay — 244

Table 8.1 Japanese Emigration to Paraguay by Prefecture of Origin in Japan, 1921–1993 — 245

Table 8.2 Nikkei Population in Paraguay by Ethnic Categories in 1991 — 245

Table 8.3 Japanese-Language Education in Asunción — 245

Table 8.4 Japanese-Language Education of Two Japanese Paraguayan Settlements — 246

Table 8.5 Occupational Fields of Japanese Paraguayans by Percentage — 246

Table 8.6 Religion of Japanese Paraguayans by Percentage — 246

Chapter 9: Japanese Peruvians — 247
Developed in Collaboration with the Fundación Cultural Nikkei del Perú and the Museo Conmemorativo de la Inmigración Japonesa en el Perú

Japanese Immigrants and Their Descendants in Peru: 1899–1998, by Amelia Morimoto — 248

Peruvian Japanese Bibliographic Essay, by Raúl Araki and Jorge M. Nakamoto — 258

Annotated Bibliography of Japanese Peruvians, compiled by Raúl Araki — 262

Supplementary Materials, compiled by Amelia Morimoto — 271

Map 9.1 Important Locales in the History of Japanese Peruvians — 272

Table 9.1 Japanese Emigration to Peru by Prefecture of Origin in Japan, 1906–1923, and 1989 — 273

Table 9.2 Total Population and Gender Breakdown of Japanese Immigrants and Their Descendants in Peru — 273

Table 9.3 Regional Distribution of Japanese Peruvians by Percentage — 274

Table 9.4 Educational Level of Japanese Peruvians by Generation in 1989 — 274

Table 9.5 Occupational Fields of Japanese Peruvians by Percentage, 1934–1989 — 274

Table 9.6 Religion of Japanese Peruvians in 1989 — 274

Chapter 10: Japanese Americans — 275
Developed in Collaboration with the Center for Oral History and Social Science Research Institute at the University of Hawai`i at Mānoa and the Asian American Studies Center at the University of California at Los Angeles

Japanese American Historical Overview, 1868–2001, by Eiichiro Azuma — 276

Japanese American Bibliographic Essay, by Brian Niiya and Eiichiro Azuma — 293

Annotated Bibliography of Japanese Americans, compiled by Brian Niiya, Michiko Kodama-Nishimoto, and Eiichiro Azuma — 295

Supplementary Materials, compiled by Eiichiro Azuma, Marie Masumoto, Toshiko McCallum, and Sharon Yamato — 307

Map 10.1 Location of Sites of Incarceration during World War II — 308

Table 10.1 Japanese Emigration to Hawai`i and the Continental United States — 309

Table 10.2 Total Japanese American Population by Decade and Gender Breakdown, 1900–2000 — 310

Table 10.3 Regional Distribution of Japanese Americans, 1900–2000 — 310

Table 10.4 Japanese American Population by State, 1900–2000 — 311

Table 10.5 Educational Level of Japanese Americans, 1950–1990 — 311

Table 10.6 Occupational Breakdown of Japanese Americans, 1920–1990 — 311

Contributors — 313

Index — 317

Foreword

DANIEL K. INOUYE
U.S. SENATOR

There were profound changes during the latter half of the 19th century as the forces of modernization spread throughout the world. Reacting to the impact of the industrial nations of the West, Japan quickly moved out of the era of feudalism. The push and pull of economic forces led to the emigration of Japanese seeking new opportunities in the Americas. Hawai`i, operating within a context of an international market economy, sent officials to actively recruit Japanese for the sugar plantations. In 1868, the first year of Japan's Meiji era, an unauthorized group of laborers, known as the *gannenmono*, initiated the overseas migration.

My own family's immigration history to Hawai`i began soon after as emigrants left in increasing numbers, mainly from prefectures along Japan's Inland Sea. My grandfather was a part of this migration as he set out from his Fukuoka village in Kyushu to work in the cane fields of Hawai`i. In the following decades, the Issei embarked for North, Central and South America, established families and communities, and contributed to the development of the nations where they settled.

This encyclopedia is an important contribution to the study of the Nikkei, the descendants of the Japanese, who settled in the various countries of the Americas. Nikkei in their respective countries who wrote about their own history and experiences developed each of the chapters in this volume. The compilation of their histories into one volume allows for a reexamination of the meaning of community and the process of identity formation among those who consider themselves Nikkei.

Today, globalization is becoming increasingly a common parlance. The seeds of this process were sown some years ago but in recent times, changes have amplified its complexity and have placed the individual histories of Nikkei communities into a broader context. This encyclopedia of Nikkei in the Americas allows for comparisons and thereby increases our own understanding of the process of becoming functional citizens in each of our countries. Furthermore, the forces of globalization have established new relationships between the Nikkei communities, their home nations, and Japan, as a large number of Nikkei Latin Americans have sojourned to Japan and have established Nikkei communities in the land of their ancestors.

It is important to examine the interdependency and interconnections among people in our high tech universe. Our shared knowledge of experiences help to bridge the understanding across nations, cultures, and generations. We need to promote cross-cultural understanding if we are to achieve the best possible world for all in the future.

I commend the Japanese American National Museum and The Nippon Foundation for making this encyclopedia of the Nikkei in the Americas available to the general public through this important publication. This is the first work of its kind that provides an overview of the Nikkei communities in North, Central, and South America. I hope that this volume is just the beginning of comparative studies of the Nikkei in the world. Further documentation and analyses will provide the coming Nikkei generations with the wherewithal to make informed, rational life choices for themselves in the future.

Acknowledgments

THERE ARE MANY WHO NEED SPECIAL RECOGNITION FOR the enormous work we have accomplished here. First, Francis Y. Sogi deserves special credit for his vision, leadership, and involvement with Nikkei communities in the Americas, work that helped to open doors for the International Nikkei Research Project's (INRP) exploration into Nikkei cultures and histories. Second, without the institutional support and guidance provided by the National Museum's executive director and president, Irene Hirano, this project never would have moved beyond the early concept and development phase. To the INRP's chief advisor, James Hirabayashi, we are most indebted for the critical role he played in the development of the project's research framework, and to the senior advisors Richard Kosaki and Lloyd Inui, we are forever grateful for the valuable input and feedback they provided on a range of project matters concerned with concepts, organization, and direction. While the chapter contributors and institutional partners are prominently acknowledged on a separate page, let us give special recognition here to the many consultants and volunteers who provided their time, expertise, and services to complete this volume. They include Yuki Ono, Sharon Yamato, Mariko Nagoshi, John Mizuki, Mika Tanner, Melanie Goodman, Antonia Green, Louis Medina, Urara Nakada, Marisa Shirasuna, Jerrine Konami, Kiyoshi Yano, Yanco Inone, Tomoko Ozaza, Translation Services, Bob Uragami, and Its Endo. The INRP team based on-site at the Japanese American National Museum deserve special thanks; it includes Toshiko McCallum, Cameron Trowbridge, Tami Kaneshiro, Claudia Sobral, and Tawney Lee. We are grateful to Alison Kochiyama, who temporarily assumed responsibility for the project's general coordination. Our deepest appreciation is extended to Satomi Takeda, project coordinator, who helped to hold together the work of our many partners, in multiple languages, in different locations. This project and its research were conducted in four languages, different continents, and time zones, and it brought in many disciplines. Without the outstanding scholarship and involvement of Eiichiro Azuma, we could not have completed this volume within the three-year limitation. Paramount recognition must be given to Masayo Ohara, whose outstanding research and language skills in Japanese, Spanish, and English, as well as her coordination of the work compiled in this volume, helped to keep the multiple tracks on course, in sync, and on time. Finally, without the generous support of The Nippon Foundation, this ambitious work could never have been realized.

Akemi Kikumura-Yano, Editor

Introduction

AKEMI KIKUMURA-YANO

Nikkei (PEOPLE OF JAPANESE DESCENT AND THEIR descendants) who have settled in the Americas are the focus of this encyclopedia. Featured in this volume are countries with the oldest and largest Nikkei populations reported in 1993; they include Argentina, Bolivia, Brazil, Canada, Chile, Mexico, Paraguay, Peru, and the United States of America. The encyclopedia is organized alphabetically by country, with each chapter containing four primary fields of information: historical overview, bibliographic essay, annotated bibliography, and supplementary materials mainly containing demographic information. Contributing authors address common themes of work and recreation, family and community life—from early immigration up to the present. Each chapter is highlighted with historical images made available by the participating institutions in each country.

Two important essays precede these individual country chapters and provide us with a broader historical context and deeper understanding into our subject. Who are the Nikkei? Why did they leave Japan? What are the historical events, special circumstances, and individual and collective choices that shaped the course of Nikkei experiences and community formations? The first essay, written by Professor Gary Y. Okihiro, helps us to appreciate the unique histories and diversity of cultures between Nikkei in the Americas by drawing from the actual words of those who lived these experiences. The second essay, written by Professor Eiichiro Azuma, provides a historical overview of Japanese migration from 1868 to 2000, focusing on the Japanese government's perspective on the role of emigration over the course of time. Azuma's analysis gives insight into how the changing landscape of national priorities, shaped by global events and internal social economic forces, influenced the geographic patterns of Japanese emigration, as well as the origin, destination, and characteristics of its emigrants.

THE INTERNATIONAL NIKKEI RESEARCH PROJECT

This encyclopedia is one of the many outcomes that were developed as a result of the International Nikkei Research Project (INRP), a collaborative three-year research project that began on April 1, 1998. An important companion piece that complements this volume is *New Worlds, New Lives: Globalization and People of Japanese Descent in the Americas and from Latin America in Japan* (Stanford University Press, 2002), an anthology of eighteen original essays written by distinguished experts in the field and edited by Lane Ryo Hirabayashi (senior editor) and James Hirabayashi and myself (co-editors). The general purpose of the research project was to explore Nikkei communities and identities in the Americas, as well as the transformative processes involved in "becoming Nikkei." The Japanese American National Museum served as the coordinator of this innovative project, which assembled an impressive multidisciplinary and multinational research team of fourteen institutions and numerous scholars located in ten different countries. Without a doubt, research of this scope could not have been done without the generous support of The Nippon Foundation.

The collaborative approach utilized to compile the work gives this encyclopedia its uniqueness. In each of the countries highlighted in this volume, great effort was made to involve scholars, research groups, and institutions based in the specific Nikkei community of each country included in this volume. Great attention and consideration were given to finding contributors who could deploy the "insider's" experiences and viewpoints in their work. Contributors to each chapter are directly connected to the experiences they write about, not only by virtue of birth and training in many cases but also in terms of firsthand participation in community-based organizations. A complete listing of the participating institutions and contributing scholars and committee members who worked on the individual chapters of this volume is provided at the end of this volume.

The occasions that brought members of the research team together made us acutely aware of our different perspectives and experiences. What emerged from our dialogues and the work of scholars and community-based researchers and institutions was a fascinating, multifaceted portrait of people of Japanese descent in the Americas. But more importantly, there evolved among us a greater understanding of who we are and how we are linked together—as individuals, families, and communities—especially in an increasingly global framework. The project underscored the need for greater comparative research covering a variety of topics and issues. Ultimately it served as a catalyst in the creation of long-lasting friendships, affiliations, and networks between scholars, museums, research groups, historical societies, universities, and community-based institutions.

METHODOLOGY AND SUGGESTED GUIDELINES TO THE ENCYCLOPEDIA

One of the most challenging and difficult parts of the INRP involved the identification of experts in the field of Nikkei Studies and the institutional participants who were willing to commit one-to-three years of their time in developing various components of the country chapters. Many of the contributors/participants were selected based on the National Museum's previous working relations with the individuals and groups or through recommendations made by reliable sources. Other contacts were made during the X COPANI, the tenth convention of the Pan-American Nikkei Association, held in Santiago, Chile, on July 28–31, 1999. At the conference we met with community representatives from various countries throughout the Americas (mainly Latin America) to discuss the details of our project, particularly with institutional participants from Bolivia, Chile, and Mexico.[1] A separate visit to Argentina and a meeting with thirty members of the Buenos Aires community resulted in our partnership with Centro Nikkei Argentino and the Asociación Universitaria Nikkei.

Each of the country chapters was to include the same components: a brief historical overview, timeline, bibliographic essay, annotated bibliography, demographic data, community directory, and photographic images with caption information.[2] Initially, the chapters for Brazil, Canada, Japan, Peru, and the United States contained many more references in the bibliography than are included in this encyclopedia. However, total page-length and publication costs were major considerations in trimming the number of bibliographic entries and other components.

The suggested guidelines to the encyclopedia evolved over the course of the three-year project.[3] The guidelines provided general instructions in regard to content and specific requirements relating to format, page length, and procedures. The Nikkei community was the primary focus of the study, and the concept of "culture building" was a significant part of our inquiry. General topics offered as suggestions included work and recreation, family and community, early immigration, the Pacific War, and contemporary issues and activities. Given these guidelines and instructions, the distinctive approach that each of the participating institutions and contributors took in writing their respective chapters, and the special facets of their experiences that they chose to highlight—or exclude—are very telling in and of themselves with respect to the unique perspectives, histories, and cultures of the Nikkei in the Americas. Clearly, each of the chapters in this volume deserves a book-length treatment. Nonetheless, the compilation of ten countries represented in this volume allows for a comparative perspective on this numerically small but important group of immigrants who have transformed their lives and, in the process, forever changed the history and culture of the countries where they settled. Readers who want to explore any of the countries in greater depth will find many resources included in this book with which to pursue their venture.

TRANSLATION

A word about the process of translation is important, since our work involved ten countries and four languages (English, Spanish, Portuguese, and Japanese). All verbal and written communications were either in English, Japanese, or Spanish. The project team worked closely with professional translation services or with museum staff, friends, and acquaintances who were fluent in one or more of these languages. The team was most fortunate to have the expertise of Masayo Ohara, a native of Japan who received her bachelor's degree in Spanish and a Ph.D. in political science from Columbia University. English was the language most utilized in all modes of verbal and written communications, Japanese was second, Spanish third; although Portuguese is the national language of Brazil, the participants from this country either wrote or spoke in English or Japanese. Throughout the course of the project, we became increasingly aware of the fact that language is a dynamic means of communication influenced by the social, cultural, and historical context in which it is used and that "translation" is not simply a process of "changing one language into another." On a number of occasions, it was vital to get the input of "native speakers" who were familiar with the syntax and special terms of a country's language in order to achieve an accurate rendering of the author's intent. Furthermore, knowledge of the insider's worldview or the writer's discipline was important, since word usage and meaning could vary from one context to the next. For example, the meaning of the Japanese word "Nikkei" (persons of Japanese descent and their descendants) holds different meanings for the Nikkei situated in different countries of the Americas (see definition below). Mindful of the many problems presented by the translation and editing process, all participating institutions and contributors received numerous drafts of their chapter components and have played an active role in reviewing, correcting, and revising the final text that appears in this volume.

COMMON TERMS AND DEFINITIONS

The contributors to each of the chapters provide their own definition of terms within the text. However, readers can refer to the glossary for a listing of terms that appear in many of the chapters. "Nikkei," the subject of this encyclopedia, is treated below in greater depth, since the nuances of this term cannot be encapsulated into a brief phrase. In addition, the historical and contemporary dimensions of the term *dekasegi* are briefly discussed, since the word/concept appears frequently in all chapters of this volume.

Nikkei

At the heart of each of the chapters is the question, what does it mean to be Nikkei in the Americas? Certainly, the word's meaning has changed with each succeeding generation, each country of settlement, and each historical time frame. Also, the subtle connotations and implicit understanding of the term take on complex shapes and nuances depending on gender, context, situation, and locale. At the first project conference, held at the Japanese American National Museum and attended by scholars who represented countries included in this volume, the seemingly "simple" question, "What is a Nikkei?" prompted lively debate and dialogue that probed the center and margins of our query. Is "being Nikkei" a matter of blood, kinship and descent? Is it a matter of self-identification and affiliation? Is it a matter of retaining key cultural values rooted in Japanese traditions? Or is it grounded to the land and a matter of geographical and community ties? How does generation impact the experiences of being "Nikkei"? Does it diminish with each passing generation? What about the impact of mixed descent? Does "Nikkei-ness" mean the same thing to men as well as women? At the end of the conference, it was clear that the term "Nikkei" included "processes," "constructions," and "characteristics" that represented a complex set of meanings for scholars from different countries and backgrounds.

Ethnic groups in immigrant settings initially were defined in terms of ascribed characteristics. Cultural traditions from the societies of origin were said to have been transmitted through "genetic ties." Geographic variables and regional characteristics were thought to have a very strong influence and to affect social forms and patterns in the new settings. Change was recognized, but it was usually conceptualized in a linear fashion, with the culture of origin at the starting point of the continuum and the culture of the "new society" at the other end.

The definition of *Nikkei* used in this volume is comprehensive and inclusive. The term refers to all Japanese emigrants and their descendants who, while acknowledging their Japanese ancestry, have created unique communities within various national contexts throughout the Americas. The term also includes persons of mixed racial descent who identify themselves as Nikkei, as well as those who have returned to Japan but retain identities separate from the native Japanese.

The notion of transformations is central to the concept of Nikkei. Nikkei culture and identity is not a static entity that determines the behavior of its members at any given time. Rather, it is a symbolic social, historical, and political construction that involves a dynamic process of selection, reinterpretation, and synthesis of cultural elements set within the shifting and fluid contexts of contemporary realities and relationships. Its "construction" is characterized by diversity, ambiguity, flexibility, and soft boundaries. Our study has revealed that "Nikkei-ness" is also a dynamic cultural resource, especially in Latin America, where "being Nikkei" is not a matter of "race" per se but rather "a pragmatic ethnic network of potential opportunities." One of the most significant contextual relationships is the interactive relationship between the Nikkei community, the "home nation" (or place of settlement), and Japan. These relationships have had a long history and have intensified within the current context of global capitalism.

Dekasegi

For the sake of uniformity, we use the English spelling of this Japanese term, though it is written as *dekasegui* (in Spanish) or *dekassegui* (in Portuguese). In brief, it refers to a practice of leaving one's home place for another location for temporary work to supplement family income. Rural Japanese farmers had engaged in this type of labor since before the Meiji period (1868 to 1912), but after the start of government-contract migration to Hawai`i in 1885, the practice of dekasegi came to have international application. The movement of dekasegi laborers from Japan to overseas destinations was meant to be only temporary from the outset. Therefore the term conceptually differs from the orthodox definition of "immigration," which refers to the movement of persons whose intent is to settle permanently.

As the "historical overviews" of all countries in this volume reveal, the early Japanese usually entered the Americas as dekasegi laborers but decided to prolong their stay in their host societies, under different circumstances and for a variety of reasons. Since the 1980s, the economic difficulties faced by Latin American countries have motivated many people of Japanese ancestry to seek temporary work in Japan. As was the case in the initial Japanese "immigration" into the Americas at the beginning of the twentieth century, this phenomenon has caused a number of Nikkei Latin Americans to extend their stay in Japan beyond a few years. The topic of dekasegi Latin Americans working and living in Japan is covered by the scholars of the INRP. Prolonged residency in the ancestral land has produced new Nikkei communities and businesses in different parts of Japan, and it has revealed the ongoing fluidity of Nikkei populations, the elusive nature of Nikkei identity, and the transnational dimensions of their community formations.

NOTES ON THE BIBLIOGRAPHY

Every chapter in this volume has an annotated bibliography, and every bibliography has entries in at least two languages. In general, the criteria for selecting the recommended readings in the bibliographies were quality and availability.[4] The bibliographic essay that precedes each bibliography discusses some of the more important works and trends in the development of the literature in that particular country. The works cited in this essay have numbers that correspond to their placement in the bibliography. Since the bibliographies contain more than one language, the first letter of each language—E (English), J (Japanese), P (Portuguese), S (Spanish)—appears before the number.

The process of establishing a "standard" system for the citation of works in this volume was very complex, since it involved four languages and ten countries, with differing rules and, in some cases, inaccessible publication histories or bibliographic information. Many adjustments were made in this volume to accommodate these variations. The result is a hybrid styling system, loosely based on the *Chicago Manual of Style* and the current U.S. library cataloguing system.

Bibliographies of materials written in languages other than English follow the custom of the original languages. For example, Japanese, Spanish, and Portuguese book titles are not capitalized. When the material is published in Japanese, macrons (-) are added to the long vowels (ā, ē, ī, ō, ū) in English transliteration. However, when a Japanese author's work is published in Western languages, macrons do not appear in his or her name or the title. The word order of Japanese authors' names that appear in Japanese-language materials does not follow the *Chicago* style convention of first name followed by last name for second or third authors. The place of publication for titles in all languages is noted the same as indicated in the original book. For example, Portuguese books published in São Paulo are written as São Paulo, while Japanese books published in São Paulo are written as San Pauro. Also, depending on the Japanese spelling of terms, such words such as "Bolivia" may be written as either "Boribia" or "Borivia." In general, the word "Hawai`i" appears with a "glottal stop" (`) unless the original publication or name of organization spells it "Hawaii" without the glottal stop.

NOTES ON DEMOGRAPHIC INFORMATION

Demographic information on Nikkei populations in the Americas is rare. The most comprehensive census was taken by the Japan International Cooperation Agency (JICA) in 1993. Since then, there has been no global census taken that could serve as a comparative basis. The weakness of the JICA census is that it lacks detailed information, such as regional distribution, occupational information, education, and religion within each country. Some countries, such as Peru and Brazil, have conducted large-scale censuses of their own, gathering more detailed information of their Nikkei populations. Other countries also have collected some statistics on their Nikkei population, if not as comprehensively. These statistics are shown in the individual chapters. They provide rich information on the Nikkei population of each country; however, they have little comparative value, since methodologies are all different. For example, the basic definition of such terms as "Nikkei" varies from one census to another.

Another constraint due to lack of information is that we were unable to cover some major segments of the Nikkei population. For example, in reference to prewar Japanese emigrants, the only reliable data available were those of the Ministry of Foreign Affairs and the Colonial Ministry. They were based on the number of passports issued to legally sanctioned "emigrants." Therefore, a significant number of people who left Japan with other types of passports or without one were not included. A similar bias occurs with the statistics of postwar Japanese emigrants. The reliance on the statistics gathered by the JICA—the semigovernmental agency that organized emigration to South America—excludes the most typical postwar emigrants, such as students and holders of labor visas who later permanently settled in these home nations. Reliance on statistics gathered by the foreign ministry on the basis of the issuance of emigrant passports creates the same problem of biases and reliability in regard to emigrant statistics to North America. An important future agenda would be to incorporate these emigrants into our focus of examination.

NOTES

1. Lane R. Hirabayashi and James Hirabayashi also attended this conference. We each attended separate workshops and

recorded our notes and reflections, which are infused in the INRP anthology *New World, New Lives*.
2. The timeline and community directory are not included in this volume but are available on the Japanese American National Museum's website at www.janm.org.
3. Suggested guidelines to the encyclopedia (originally referred to as the "Educational Resource Guide") are available at the Japanese American National Museum.
4. Many English, Japanese, Portuguese, and Spanish titles listed in the annotated bibliographies of this volume have been deposited at the Hirasaki National Resource Center at the Japanese American National Museum.

Glossary

Colonia: Spanish term used in this volume to refer to Nikkei settlement and/or community or colony.

Dekasegi: Dekasegui (in Spanish) or dekassegui (in Portuguese). The term refers to a practice of leaving one's home place for another location for temporary work to supplement family income (see introduction for further definition of term).

Gosei: Fifth generation, children of the Yonsei.

Imin: The term means both emigrants and immigrants as a group of people, and both emigration and immigration as a process or phenomenon.

INRP: International Nikkei Research Project.

Issei: First generation of Japanese to emigrate from Japan and settle permanently in a new country.

JICA: Japan International Cooperation Agency.

Kachi-gumi: Believers in Brazil of Japanese victory after World War II.

Ken-jin: Person from the same prefecture in Japan.

Kenjin-kai: Prefectural association.

Kibei: Second generation, children of the Issei, born in the country of settlement and educated in Japan.

Make-gumi: Believers in Brazil of Japan's defeat after World War II.

Nikkei: People of Japanese descent and their descendants (see introduction for further definition of term).

Nisei: Second generation, children of the Issei, born in the country of settlement.

Sansei: Third generation, children of the Nisei.

Shin Issei: "New Issei," post–World War II immigrants.

Yobiyose: Migrants/immigrants called over by friends or relatives to home nations.

Yonsei: Fourth generation, children of Sansei.

Turning Japanese Americans

GARY Y. OKIHIRO

I can only imagine the immensity of the Pacific Ocean. Sailing across its girth, countless voyagers must have filled their days and nights marking its expanse by the positions of heavenly bodies.[1] Polynesians pointed northward, Europeans rushed toward the west, and Asians were conveyed eastward, making landfall on distant shores, in novel climes, and astride moving currents of history. Conquerors and subjects, settlers and sojourners alike left their marks on those environments, which in turn wrought their changes on those who visited them. And although their trails might be tracked to places of origin, trans-Pacific travelers confused those identities by making claims upon their destinations.

The central figures of this book, the *Nikkei*, are both united by their ports of departure and divided by the transformations of their arrivals. Although they might all have been "Japanese," they have turned into "Japanese Americans" in the broad sense of "Nikkei" and "Japanese" in the Americas. I thus begin my reflections by rooting their experiences within the native soils of their diverse national histories.

ARGENTINA

The late nineteenth century was typified by political leaders who prized order and progress over democracy and freedom amidst great upheavals and mass movements of peoples. From 1879 to 1880, the state waged a war against the Indians to seize pampas lands; that led to land speculation and consolidation, and a rise in the production of cattle and wheat. Millions of European, mainly Italian and Spanish, immigrants were recruited for agricultural labor, but they failed to prosper in the land boom, which was dominated by big landowners. Instead, they flocked to the cities, like Buenos Aires, to work in the meatpacking plants, factories, and railroads. That infusion of European immigrants created pools of surplus labor, resulting in long hours for workers, low wages, strikes, and deportations of "foreign agitators."[2]

Unlike those European immigrants, Asians—a few Chinese and more Japanese—entered Argentina mainly as "indirect migrants," migrants who went first to places like Peru and Brazil and from there moved to neighboring Argentina. Although the Argentine constitution of 1853 and immigration laws did not restrict Asians, their application became increasingly stringent, and the state consistently favored European over Asian immigrants. During the period 1914–1930, Argentina allowed its resident Japanese to call their relatives and friends to join them, but from 1930 to 1941, calling was limited to immediate relatives, from spouses to first cousins. Most of the migrants were men, and during the early 1920s some of them sent for "picture brides," but these were few in number because of administrative controls. In contrast to its small Japanese population during those decades, Argentina's trade with Japan, begun when they signed the Treaty of Friendship, Commerce, and Navigation in 1898, exceeded that of other Latin American countries, reaching a peak in 1935–1936.[3]

The beginnings of Japanese settlement in Argentina reveal a diversity that typified the national experience. Kinzo Makino, who arrived in Buenos Aires in 1886, was the first permanent resident in the country and was among the earliest Japanese settlers in Latin America as a whole. Over the next two decades, two students, four businessmen, and a sailor joined Makino, constituting Argentina's incipient Japanese community. G. Yoshio Shinya, the sailor, was employed at the age of thirteen as a cabin boy on board the Argentine frigate *Presidente Sarmiento* when the vessel visited Yokohama in 1899. He arrived in Buenos Aires the following year, settled in Argentina and gained citizenship, married an English woman, and established a career as a journalist.[4] Japanese remigrants from Brazil and Peru joined the small group of Japanese in Argentina between 1906 and 1910; they included Seizo Hoshi and his wife, the first Japanese woman to settle in Argentina, and Seijitsu Chinen who, called his fellow Okinawans from Brazil to join him. In 1910, sixty-eight Okinawans from Brazil and seven from Peru swelled Argentina's Japanese population to about three hundred. Okinawans, thus, constituted a substantial portion of Argentina's Japanese; by 1924 they nearly equaled the number of *Naichi* (mainland) Japanese. In the 1930s they exceeded them.[5]

Japanese women who migrated as picture brides found both hope and despair in their lots as women and migrants. Chie Sokei refused an offer of marriage from a man in Argentina. For a year and a half she resisted his proposal, only to discover later that her parents had agreed to her marriage to another man in Argentina. Sokei argued with her parents, ran away from home, and thought seriously about suicide. She finally submitted to her parents' decision, and then became even more frightened when she heard from a man who had returned from Argentina that the country was "a living hell." Yoshi Higa and Yuki Agarie, on the other hand, dreamed of wealth and a better life in Argentina and went willingly as picture brides. Going abroad, thought Higa, was a wonderful and respectable thing to do, and Agarie noted that Okinawans who returned from overseas sojourns had nice houses and that their children were well educated.[6]

A few Japanese Argentines, like Magojiro Hira, led uncommon lives. Hira was a teacher in Naha, Okinawa, and a womanizer. He fell in love with a gangster's mistress, impregnated her, and fled the country when the boss put a contract on his head. He chose Argentina because it was the farthest place from Okinawa of which he could think. In Buenos Aires, Hira first sold curios on the streets, then gained employment in a large department store. With those experiences he opened a variety store, which failed, despite the booming economy, and finally began a laundry—which succeeded, because he stole business secrets from Argentine laundries that employed the latest technologies. He was a generous man, and he housed, fed, and employed Japanese remigrants from Brazil and Peru. Before long he had several laundries, and because he loved to dance, especially the tango, he opened a dance studio. He became the president of an Okinawan organization and was a frequent guest at the Japanese consulate. Hira married a blond Spanish woman in 1932 but died two years later, at the age of forty-eight.[7]

Seijitsu Chinen was an actor who played in both Japanese plays and *Othello;* he promoted a play in Hawai`i in 1929. He arrived in Argentina in 1908, opened the first Japanese café in Buenos Aires in 1912, and was a founder of the Okinawa *kenjin-kai,* or prefectural association.[8] Senshu Yamanuha, an eighteen-year-old teenager, arrived in Brazil in 1908 as a contract farm laborer. Because of the harsh work and living conditions, he and other contract laborers fled. Their pursuers tracked them, cut them with huge knives, and even killed a few of them. Yamanuha was lucky to escape to Argentina, where he worked in a sugar factory and as a dishwasher and later cook in a Buenos Aires café. During his final years, Mamanuha worked on various vegetable farms and drank heavily; he died alone.[9]

In 1922, with Okinawa's economy in decline, Kiho Kishimoto migrated to Argentina to join his brother, Kamezo. The brothers worked on their farm from dawn to dusk. By 1926, Kamezo was able to send for a bride, Matsu, who helped on the farm and bore two daughters and a son. In 1932, Kiho called for a bride. Kama Higa's parents urged her to marry him. Kama refused, but her parents insisted, so she left for Argentina in the company of a Mr. Nakamura, who had been in Argentina. Kama knew nothing of the place and was shocked upon her arrival to see the vastness of the countryside; she was homesick whenever she heard the cows mooing. She had a difficult time adjusting to the language and culture; her sister-in-law, Matsu, died within a year of her arrival and left her three children to rear. Besides working on the farm and caring for her nieces and nephew, Kama bore and reared thirteen children of her own. She recalled that the rigors of farm life and the family's extreme poverty led her to blame her parents and to frequent thoughts of suicide.[10]

World War II had little effect on the Japanese in Argentina, mainly because of the pro-Axis sympathies of the government. However, on March 27, 1945, the government of Gen. Edelmiro Farrell declared war against Japan and Germany; consequently Japanese and Germans became "foreigners under vigilance" and were subjected to a series of restrictions. The state required them to register with and report periodically to the police, receive permission to travel, and close their foreign-language newspapers and their language schools and social organizations. Japanese businesses suffered, and some lost many of their customers.[11] All of the state's restrictions were lifted in 1947.

Gisuke Anzai remembered how the Argentine Japanese were devastated by news of Japan's surrender. Most of the Japanese, he recalled, lived in shanties near Buenos Aires and worked hard just to survive. They had dreamed of returning home to a better life in Japan, but when its defeat shattered the dream, they awakened to the fact that Argentina would be their permanent home.[12] Chie Sokei told how she and her husband stopped speaking Japanese in their home after the war because they thought that they would never return to Japan and that Japanese would hinder the acquisition by their children of the Spanish language.[13]

After the war, the Argentine government issued its Five Year Plan, which promoted the immigration of laborers for agriculture and industry. Most of those migrants came from Europe, but Japan was a key source, because of favorable attitudes toward the Japanese among Argentina's political leadership and because of redevelopment and population pressures in postwar Japan and Okinawa. After Japan regained its sovereignty in 1952, its government assisted emigrants with loans for passage and resettlement and facilitated the process of emigration. As a result of those incentives, 2,736 Okinawans and about six hundred *Naichi* arrived in Argentina during 1948–1960.[14] Disincentives included Argentina's tight land market and its immigration laws, which limited in-migration among Japanese to those called to work.

Argentina has been both opened and closed to its Japanese. The state restricted immigration but remains generous with naturalization. Its landholding pattern limited farming, while its urban centers welcomed workers and entrepreneurs. Its European peoples, many of whom were immigrants in the early twentieth century like the Japanese, both discriminated against the Nikkei and intermarried with them. Fumiko Agarie recalled how white children taunted Japanese children at school, and a Japanese observed that the British were more likely to hold racist views of the Japanese than were Spaniards or Italians. Children threw stones at the Japanese and called them "chino."[15] Despite their exclusions from full participation in Argentine society, the Japanese have made the country their home and share in its past and future. During the Malvinas War of 1982, seven thousand Nikkei marched in support of the war. Included among the signs they carried was: "*Con la cara japonesa pero con el corazón Argentina*" (with a Japanese face but an Argentine heart).[16]

BOLIVIA

Bolivia, part of Upper Peru in the colonial period, generated vast amounts of wealth for the Spanish empire, especially through its Potosí silver mines. Named for "the liberator," Simón Bolívar, despite his ambition for a confederation of states in the area, Bolivia declared its independence from Spain and separated itself from Peru in 1825. The nation's geography tends to divide its peoples among the arid *altiplano* highlands, the lush intermountain valleys, and the eastern lowlands, with their tropical rainforests. In the War of the Pacific (1879–1883), Chile took away from Peru and Bolivia the mineral-rich coastal strip and cut off Bolivia's access to the sea.

Bolivia's government was ruled by a succession of dictators and generals until 1880, when civilian political parties replaced military strongmen. Political influence centered on the old landed aristocracy and new mining elite, constituting a plutocracy based upon the production of tin. Racially, whites ruled over a nation of mainly Indians and *mestizos*. The worldwide depression of the 1930s brought down Bolivia's tin prices and with it the Bolivian economy, because of its near total dependence upon tin exports. To compound the problem, in 1931 Bolivia severed diplomatic relations with Paraguay over disputed land, the Gran Chaco territory, and waged a war from 1932 to 1935 over that claim. In the Chaco War, Bolivia lost about sixty thousand lives, its debt soared, and its defeat fostered discontent. Class conflict divided the country, and the military resisted reforms that threatened its powers.

World War II and U.S. interests in Bolivia's strategic metals led to greater U.S. influence over Bolivia's internal affairs. The United States bought Bolivia's tin and extended loans to Bolivia's financially strapped government; Bolivia in turn renewed payments on debts to U.S. banks. The political opposition accused the government of selling out to the United States. In July 1941 the U.S. ambassador accused the opposition of conspiring with Nazi Germans to seize power in La Paz. Although fabricated, the allegation prompted the Bolivian government to expel the German ambassador and harass and arrest many Germans. In 1942, Bolivia broke off diplomatic relations with the Axis nations, declaring war on them the following year. Civil and political unrest continued throughout the 1940s, involving coups, strikes by miners, military interventions, and a civil war in 1949. The revolution of 1952 instituted nationalization of the mines, land reform, and an extended suffrage, marking a radical departure from the past. But in 1964 Bolivia saw a return to military rule that continued for the most part through the 1980s.

During the period 1900 to 1915, the rubber industry was the principal instigator of Japanese migration to Bolivia, and its demands rose and fell with the worldwide market for rubber from the Amazon basin. Japanese companies supplied most of these migrants, and most came through Peru. The Japanese laborers in eastern Bolivia numbered less than five hundred, with no more than ten women among them. The American Rubber Company hired the majority of that group, although Bolivian, German, and Swiss rubber companies also employed Japanese workers. After the collapse of the rubber boom some Japanese returned to Japan, and others went to Peru; those who remained in Bolivia moved to towns like Riberalta and Trinidad, in the eastern part of the country. There, some opened grocery stores, barber and tailor shops, and bazaars, and a large number went into small farming, producing garden crops for the local market.[17]

The life of a rubber gatherer or *seringero* was arduous and lonely. The day normally began at 4 A.M., when the seringero started his round of eighty to 150 rubber trees. He placed cups on the trunks to collect the sap, gathered wood to make a fire and the nuts that made the white smoke needed to cure the rubber, and cooked the milky fluid, taking care to keep rainwater from diluting and thus spoiling the batch. Seringeros commonly stayed in the forest for three or four months at a time before returning to outposts to deposit their accumulations of crude rubber and to restock their stores of food, ammunition, utensils, and other supplies. They lived in one-room huts made of logs and thatched with leaves, and they usually planted gardens for their vegetables and hunted and fished for their meat. During the heavy rainy season, from November through April, most seringeros left the forests for the towns, where they worked on nearby farms.[18]

Pedro Shimose noted the memorial tower built in Riberalta to commemorate the early Japanese migrants in area. Many of those immigrants married Bolivians, Shimose stated, and worked to gain the respect of their fellow Bolivians. His father worked for the railroads and taught him, despite hard times, "always [to] look forward." During World War II, Bolivians vandalized German and Japanese property, and Shimose was ashamed to be the child of a Japanese man. But his father persisted in his love for Bolivia, and Shimose pointed to the symbolism of names that combined Japanese and Spanish for the formation of singular, harmonious identities as both Japanese and Bolivians.[19]

Tatsuo Makabe recalled listening occasionally to Japan's overseas shortwave radio broadcasts during World War II to follow the course of the war. On May 4, 1944, police arrested Makabe and took him to a police station, which was crowded with Germans and Japanese. At night, they took the twenty-nine Japanese and eighty Germans to La Paz's airport; three days later, U.S. military planes landed with armed American soldiers, who loaded the prisoners onto the planes and took off.[20] "We all looked so down and depressed," remembered Makabe. "Without being able to bid farewell to La Paz where I had lived for so long, to Mt. Ilimani that stood so majestically in the blue sky, and to my best friend Don George and others, I only shouted in my mind, 'Adios.'" The United States interned Makabe for one year and seven months at Camp Kenedy, in Texas, before exiling him to Japan in December 1945.[21]

The United States and its occupation government promoted the emigration of Okinawans to Bolivia during the 1950s to reduce the postwar problems of high unemployment and poverty, land shortages caused in part by the U.S. military's displacement of civilians, and social unrest. Because of its economic dependence on the United States, Bolivia agreed to the U.S.-sponsored program, although immigration also coincided with Bolivia's plans to develop lands along its eastern frontier.[22]

"I wanted to leave Okinawa at any cost," remembered Matsusuke Kinjo (Kinjono). "It was right after the war and Okinawa was so poor." The year was about 1951, and Kinjo saw a newspaper advertisement calling for emigrants with farm experience. He applied, was interviewed, and waited. "I cannot forget how happy I felt when I learned that I had been accepted." Kinjo's ship landed at Port Santos, Brazil, where, much to his surprise, a group of local Okinawans greeted the migrants, gave them food and money, and put them on a train bound for Bolivia. Along the way, Brazilian Okinawans gave them food, sweets, and fruit. "I still remember their kindness today," he noted gratefully. Yoshiko Toma's family arrived in Bolivia after sunset. Although an earlier group of immigrants greeted them, noted Toma, "I still recall feeling so lonely." She gathered branches and leaves to make their beds and fended off the swarms of mosquitoes that attacked them. "I really regretted coming to such a remote country . . . deep in the forest," she admitted. "I sighed and sighed."[23]

Life was difficult for the colonists. Masako Tamashiro remembered: "We came full of hope to this unknown country, but it was in the middle of a jungle and I got all sorts of skin problems. It was like hell." She and her husband labored to clear fields from the forest and would return home exhausted. "It was such a tough life that I could not remember how many times I cried." Things got more difficult when her baby was born. Tamashiro had to work in the fields and tend to a baby at the same time. Besides the work demands, Tamashiro missed her mother and her brothers and sisters, and she felt alienated from everything around her. "I felt unbearably lonely," she admitted.[24]

About a year after they arrived, a mysterious illness called the "Uruma disease" struck the settlers, afflicting about half of them and leaving fifteen dead. "Those were depressing days," recalled Yoshiko Toma. "As a wife and mother, I swore that I would protect my family. I prayed to god." Sono Higa's thirteen-year-old son lay down and died within three days. "I never imagined that he would die in three days," Higa grieved. Gensho Nema lost his wife to the sickness. Her death completely shattered his "dream for the new land," and he thought seriously of returning to Japan with his children. "Fortunately," he continued, "I remarried a good person who reared the children as her own. That is why I am still here."[25] To escape the illness, the settlers moved from Uruma to Palometia, where they stayed for two years before returning to Uruma.

Despite those dislocations and losses, the colonists persisted and continued to build a community. They began a school for their children, established a Women's Association, and reclaimed the forest from the monkeys, snakes, armadillos, anteaters, and deer. It was like "a war," observed Yoshiko Toma, but it was also immensely satisfying to see the fruits of their labor. In fact, she declared, all of their struggles helped to bequeath to the second generation "strong minds." She summed up her years of toil and sorrow: "It is strange, but even though my house is in the middle of nowhere, I now feel no pain because I consider it my home."[26]

BRAZIL

Great landowners—the aristocracy and elites—dominated much of Brazil's politics and economy throughout the nineteenth century. Slavery thus retained its hold as long as the landed aristocracy required that form of labor for their plantations. The sugar and coffee growing regions of the country especially resisted manumission until 1888, when the parliament formally ended the system of slavery. The following year Brazil became a republic, having been a monarchy; the new government, led by the state of São Paulo, encouraged European immigration to supply the labor needs of its growing industries and export sectors. São Paulo's population swelled from 6,600 in 1885 to ninety thousand just three years later; whereas Brazil supplied about 56 percent of the world's coffee from 1880 to 1889, it produced about 76 percent of that crop by 1900 to 1904.

European immigrants arrived at the rate of over a hundred thousand each year, and many settled in cities, where they encountered poor working conditions and wages in the textile mills and food-processing plants. They resorted to union organization and strikes. The ruling class became divided between the older rural plantation oligarchy, which was often split between sugar and coffee interests, and the newer urban business elite, but both shared a distrust of the masses and favored a dictatorial republic to achieve their ideals of modernity, order, and progress. Workers, too, varied between a large rural peasantry and an urban proletariat. Police repression of workers, socialists, and anarchists followed the labor struggles and strikes of the early 1900s, as did the roundup of union leaders and deportations of "agitators."[27]

Social stratification was not simply a matter of class but also of race. Most members of the elite were white, while those on the bottom were black. People of mixed race occupied middle positions. Studies showed a correlation between race and income, but the social structure was neither fixed nor unchanging. Even as the elite sought to rid Brazil of blackness, an ideal called "bleaching," it allowed some degree of racial mobility, and marriage across color lines was common.

The military played a key role in governing Brazil during much of its history. For instance, a plot led by Marshal Deodoro da Fonseca toppled the monarchy of Dom Pedro II in 1889 and instituted the republic; also, top military commanders deposed President Washington Luís in October 1930 and installed Getúlio Vargas as president. In 1937, Vargas, backed by the military, dissolved Congress and assumed a dictatorship that lasted until 1945. During his rule Vargas steered Brazil toward the United States in trade and military alliance, and his security forces repressed dissent by routinely employing torture and censorship. A shift toward populism and the Left inspired a military intervention that deposed him in October 1945. The military was instrumental in Vargas's rise and also his demise; authoritarian regimes, headed by generals, ruled Brazil from 1964 to 1985.

Perhaps more fundamental to Brazilian history than the vicissitudes of political rule was the country's changing economy, which shaped the society and the relations among its social classes. Like most colonial economies, Brazil exported raw products to the centers of capital and industry in Europe and the United States. It was thus economically dependent upon those markets, and their booms and busts, for the prices set on its few exports—chiefly sugar, rubber, and coffee. After independence in 1822, sugar, produced on large plantations with slave labor, continued to dominate exports until its decline during the nineteenth century. Rubber production, begun in the early nineteenth century, experienced a steep rise in the early twentieth century, when it amounted to about one-third of all exports, but British production in the East Indies undermined and ended that boom. Coffee provided the most sustained stimulus to economic growth, and it became a central feature of Brazilian life, rising and falling with the tide of the world market. Although blessed with ample agricultural land and excellent growing conditions, Brazil suffered from its colonial economy and perennial shortage of labor.

African slaves and European immigrants offered solutions to Brazil's labor needs; in addition, as early as the mid-nineteenth century, during the reign of Dom Pedro II, Brazil sought Chinese migrant workers. After the antislavery law of 1871, which freed all children born of slave mothers (though owners retained the labor of those children until the age of twenty-one), the government ordered its consul general in the United States to investigate the possibilities of Asian labor migration to Brazil. After emancipation in 1888 the government dispatched a special mission to China to negotiate the importation of Chinese workers, and in 1896 Brazil discussed labor migration with Japan. Brazil's mediations to secure migrant workers and the insistence of its coffee growers led to the organized importation of Japanese contract laborers.

A Japanese emigration company tried to send contract workers to Brazil in 1898, but large-scale migration began only after the state of São Paulo signed an agreement in 1907 with a Japanese colonization company, the Kokoku Shokumin Kaisha, represented by Ryu Mizuno.[28] The company agreed to send three thousand Japanese workers and their families over the course of three years; the state was to settle them on coffee plantations and along the Brazilian Central Railroad. The first contingent of migrants arrived in June 1908, but the Kokoku Shokumin Kaisha declared bankruptcy, and the experiment failed. Other emigration companies stepped into the breach, especially after World War I, and by 1930 they had sent about seventy-three thousand Japanese to Brazil. The 1924 Exclusion Act in the United States was a key factor in directing Japanese migrants southward, away from North America to Latin America and Brazil. Likewise, Brazil's increasingly restrictive immigration laws, such as a 1934 law that severely reduced the number of immigrants allowed into the country, regulated and constricted the migrant flow. The Vargas government during the late 1930s initiated regulations against unassimilated aliens, mainly Japanese and Germans, to restrict their freedoms and movements. Those regulations led to the closing of Japanese schools and community organizations in 1938. Thus, where in 1933 24,494 Japanese had entered Brazil, by 1939 the number had declined to 1,411.[29]

Contrary to the seductive advertisements spread by emigration companies of quick wealth and easy living in Brazil, Japanese migrants commonly confronted poverty and harsh living and working conditions. "I heard there was an opportunity for extensive farming [in Brazil]," remembered Sadao Okuma. "I also heard success stories. I really wanted to try my luck farming in Brazil . . . rather than remaining in Okinawa, which has very limited land." But after arriving in Brazil, "I felt surprised; at the same time, I felt disappointed. It was quite different from what I had heard in Okinawa." Machinery, he explained, was scarce, and farmers had to rely on draft animals.[30] Seijun Yamashiro recalled life on a coffee plantation. "After I came to Brazil, I lived in a stable with horses for about six months," he began. "One of my friends was forced to sleep right next to the toilet. I worked at a coffee farm; work was tough. I continued to work from 5 A.M. to dark. It was so hard that I felt like taking a nap rather than having a tea break." Because of the harsh regimen, Yamashiro reported, many workers tried to escape their contracts by fleeing to Japan; hard times led to family quarrels, breakups, and even murders. Although food, especially meat, was plentiful compared to Okinawa, noted Tsuruko Ginoza, "food could not ease our sense of loneliness. There was no recreation, and neighbors all lived far away. I could not go to see my friends, because their houses were so far away." On their rare visits to town, Ginoza recalled, her children beamed with joy. "I cannot forget their faces, such happy faces."[31]

Although Japanese immigration and capital investments in Brazil were small compared to those of Europeans and the United States, some anti-Asianists saw those advances as sinister, representing master plots by Japan's government for hemispheric influence and domination.[32] When President Vargas, following his reckoning that the United States and not Nazi Germany provided the best opportunity for modernization, trade, and access to military hardware, opted for the Allies during World War II, Brazil's Japanese were a conspicuous target for patriots and racists.

"I lived along a railroad line," recalled Sadao Okuma of this period. "It was a relatively safe place and we suffered nothing serious. But because we were Japanese, we were discriminated against badly and oppressed hard. Brazil was hostile to Japan, so all the diplomats returned to Japan. Those Japanese who were left behind in Brazil felt that they were abandoned."[33] The poet Masami Tanaka recorded this apprehension, which materialized as violence against Brazil's Japanese.

> At table conversation I spill coffee
> The rumor of mob attacks in northern Brazil
> Burning Japanese houses and stores
> In reaction to the sinking of a Brazilian ship.[34]

The police found and arrested alleged spies and military and naval officers among Japanese farmers and fishermen, and confiscated contraband equipment; the press reported supposed Japanese conspiracies plotted by colonists in São Paulo and claimed that they had deliberately settled in a ring to surround the port of Santos.[35] The government expelled Santos's Japanese, like Natsumi Tanaka, the daughter of Masami Tanaka, who wrote on July 1943:

> Japanese residents
> Exiled from their community
> Only their persons
> Put into railroad cars.[36]

The war and its aftermath were destructive of Japanese property, rights, and social standing, and they shattered the dream of quick success in Brazil and of a return to Japan. Coming to terms with the recognition of their permanence occupied many of Brazil's Japanese after the war and through the 1950s. Japan's devastation, as reported by relatives in Japan and the postwar Japanese migrants who entered Brazil from 1953, affirmed their identity as Brazilians, and the processes of acculturation and generational change, including intermarriage, strengthened their claims as Japanese Brazilians. Exiled in Japan as one of

Brazil's *dekasegi* in the 1990s, Rafael Masahiro Atsumi mirrored some of the sentiments of Japanese pioneers in Brazil: "Often, it is hard for me and I long for my home in São Paulo"; Alfonso Maeda added, "I really miss the friendliness of my home country."[37]

CANADA

Nearly all Japanese Canadians, according to the 1941 census, lived in British Columbia. Vancouver Island had become a British colony in 1849 under the threat of U.S. interest in the area, and on the mainland the British had created the colony of British Columbia in 1858, after the discovery of gold on the Fraser River that year. The colonies joined in 1866 as British Columbia. Chinese miners from California and China arrived in British Columbia during the 1860s, as did the thousands of other migrants who poured into the colony in search of gold and fortunes. Agriculture, coal mining, and the timber industry grew with the gold economy, and by the 1870s, lumbering replaced gold as the colony's economic mainstay. In 1866, the colony's governor reported over 30,000 native Indians, 3,070 whites, and 1,705 Chinese on the mainland.[38]

Although equal under the law, the colony's Chinese felt the sting of racism from white employers, who saw them as at best a necessary evil, useful laborers; they were, in the words of a newspaper, "inferior to Europeans and Americans in energy and ability, and hostile to us in race, language and habits, and may remain among us a Pariah race." White workers, some of whom carried their prejudices from California and Australia, castigated the Chinese as "mere slaves" under the control of wealthy merchants and "a swarm of locusts" intent only on devouring the colony's wealth.[39] The British rejected local proposals for special taxes exacted on the Chinese, but confederation in 1871, by which British Columbia became a province of Canada, with responsible government, opened the door to discriminatory legislation against the Chinese and Asians generally.

Over the next several decades, certain classes of white British Columbians pursued an anti-Asian campaign to restrict Asian immigration and curtail their activities. To preserve British Columbia as "a white man's province," they warned against the "overwhelming" tide of Chinese and later Japanese, Korean, and Asian Indian migration, and they railed against Asians who thrived under the protection of "our laws" while living in "a world of their own." British Columbia denied Asians, both alien and citizen, the vote from 1885 to well past World War II; and in 1885 the federal government imposed a head tax on Chinese immigrants and excluded them entirely in 1923. As early as 1897, the province passed laws that discriminated against the Japanese, including a ban on Japanese labor on public works projects and an exclusion of Japanese migrants; the federal government struck these down under pressure from the British, who did not want to offend Japan.

On September 4, 1907, in Bellingham, Washington, a few miles south of the Canadian border, whites rioted against and expelled some 250 Sikh lumber-mill workers, many of whom retreated to British Columbia, where they had first landed in North America. The Asiatic Exclusion League had formed in Vancouver that summer with the assistance of U.S. anti-Asianists; on September 7, 1907, following a parade and mass meeting organized by the league, a white mob descended on the city's Chinese and Japanese quarters. It caused substantial property damage and inflicted and sustained several injuries.[40] The Canadian federal government, anxious to preserve the good relations between Japan and Britain, investigated the riot, paid Japanese and Chinese damage claims, and negotiated for a limit on Japanese immigration. While insisting on the validity of its treaties allowing freedom of entry and residence between Britain and Japan and their dominions, Japan consented, in a "gentlemen's agreement" in 1908, to limit emigration to Canada. Canada in that same year passed a continuous-voyage act that limited immigration to those on a direct passage from the migrant's country of birth, effectively excluding Asian remigrants from Hawai`i and Latin America and most passages from Asia. Asian Indians challenged that law unsuccessfully when the *Komagata Maru* arrived in Vancouver in 1914 with Punjabi Sikh passengers.[41]

"My family is from Hiroshima, but since my father was a military man, I was born in Kumamoto, where he was stationed," began Tami Nakamura, a "picture bride." Schooling for girls, she remembered, was simply "a bride's education," in that girls were expected to become wives and mothers and not have careers outside the home. She felt ugly because of her face and "frizzy hair," Nakamura confided, and thought that no one would marry her in Japan, so she thought about going abroad. One of her classmates had gone to Hawai`i, and that planted in her the dream of going to America. Her mother's friend told her about a man in Canada who was looking for a bride. He was a farmer, she said, who was doing well. Seeing marriage as a ticket out of Japan and thinking that "any husband will do," Nakamura agreed to the arrangement.

Nakamura's husband had grown up on the coast near Hiroshima and had left to work on the sugar plantations of Hawai`i before moving to Canada in 1907. There he had worked on road construction and in the sawmills, saved his money "by practically starving," and bought twenty acres of land after three years. But he was still "very, very poor" by the time Nakamura arrived; he had cleared only some of the land and planted a few strawberries. She left on the *Sado Maru* from Kobe in the company of many other brides, and the happy women, she recalled, had fun and "made a lot of commotion." One of her shipboard friends built up her husband so much in her imagination that when she saw him she was bitterly disappointed that he was in reality "an old man."

Her husband greeted her in Victoria. "When I saw him for the first time," noted Nakamura, "I thought his face was quite a bit nicer than in the photos. He was smiling a big smile. . . . As for me, I wasn't especially glad. I didn't think the marriage was good or bad. I thought, 'Well, this is the man I've married.'" Her husband, though, proved to be "a nice man and I had nothing to complain about," she added in retrospect. "My husband has a good character; he's gentle. He does everything he can for the children, and for his workers, too. He doesn't drink or smoke, and he's sincere. . . . He has no hobbies; he's never cared about anything but working in the fields, and he was there from morning to night."

The farmhouse was in Mission, in the mountains on the Fraser River about forty miles from Vancouver. During winters, with less farm work, Nakamura moved to the city to work as a domestic servant to white families, and to earn wages, learn English, and enjoy seeing "how white people lived." By February, with farm work picking up, Nakamura returned to the country. Pregnant and suffering from morning sickness, she found the strawberry season months of "war." "I was busy, busy every day and I had no spare time at all." The family hired field workers—Indians, Chinese, whites, and Japanese—and a cook, but washing, cooking, and directing the operation required getting up at four in the morning and working till late at night. "I wonder how I held out, being pregnant so often," she reflected. "Every year it was the same work, and come to think of it, we did it for twenty-five years, so we must have done pretty well. Even now, when Mission people get together, they always talk about those days. The women say that just thinking about it gives them the shivers. It was the same hard life for all the housewives."

Nakamura gave up the idea of making money and returning to Japan, because they were always in debt. "I wanted to see my mother and brothers and sisters," she explained, "but every year, I felt more and more resigned, and I got used to feeling like that. I had baby after baby, and Japan seemed further and further away." Nakamura bore seven children.

When World War II came to Canada, "it was horrid." "When the order came for us to leave Mission," remembered Nakamura, "I was amazed. Spring had come, and we had started taking care of the fields as usual. The boxes for the strawberries had arrived. We went away in a hurry, leaving the fields and the house just as they were." Most of her friends and neighbors applied to work on the sugar beet fields of Alberta. "They were forced to leave their land and houses behind and move," explained Nakamura.

Her family carried only its bedclothes, Nakamura recalled sadly. "We got on the train, the last family to leave Mission. It was June 1942. The train passed in front of our house, and I nearly cried." She was comforted by the hope that she would return home, but the government gave her house to returning veterans instead. Living in a bunkhouse on a sugar beet farm, working in the fields, and getting thirty cents an hour broke both the spirit and the body. "It was very hard labour, absolutely the worst, and it wore me down to skin and bones," she testified. Displaced to Montreal after the war, Nakamura received five thousand dollars for her farm from the government. Her life's work gone, Nakamura chose to bury the past. "I don't remember much about that time," she said simply, "and I don't talk about it to my husband."

After about ten years in Montreal, Nakamura moved to southwestern Ontario to start a new farm. "My husband couldn't rest easy unless he owned some land," she explained. Her husband worked the land, and she raised chickens and hogs. To soften some of the anti-Japanese resentment that still remained, her husband reassured the white neighbors, the family joined the church "right away," and they "tried hard to melt into the community." Over time, the farm prospered, and they passed it on to their second son when they retired. "The children live in places all over the map, so we traveled here and there, visiting them," Nakamura noted. "They don't give us any worry, and once a year they come to visit us here, so I'm grateful."

"When all's said and done," concluded Nakamura, "I can't forget how hard it was in Mission. I wonder I was able to go through with it. . . . I'm the thin type and maybe because I grew up in the city I'm not strong. You need strength to be a farmer. . . . My husband has a strong constitution and he likes farming, it suited his character. He's really crazy about farming. He says he's had a life without regrets. It's been interesting to farm together." Nakamura brought her story to a close: "I got to like it, too. If I were reborn, I'd probably come to Canada and be a farmer."[42]

CHILE

A distant outpost of the Spanish empire, Chile sustained itself on agriculture and mining. The Indian population decimated by Spanish warfare and diseases, Chile's people emerged from the colonial period largely mestizo, although most claimed a European or white ancestry. Chile won independence from Spain in 1818, but political instability typified the first decades of national life. The major forces involved, first, powerful landowners in the country's fertile central valley, where the vast estates produced agricultural products, mainly fruit and grain, for Chile's cities as well as for export to Peru and to the west coast of Spanish America. The other power center was the Catholic Church, with its privileges in education and finances, and its alliances with an element of the landowning elite.

Independence and protectionist policies reduced Chile's agricultural trade with the rest of Spanish America, though the California gold rush boosted its agricultural exports to the United States for a brief period during the 1850s, until California could produce grains for its own needs. Chile's decisive victory over Peru and Bolivia in the War of the Pacific (1879–1883), however, and its resulting acquisition of Peru's nitrate mines led to an economic boom and infusion of foreign investors, especially British, who owned and exploited the nitrate fields. Silver and especially copper mining accompanied the export of nitrates; copper eclipsed nitrates as the engine of Chile's economy after the marketing of synthetic nitrates in the early twentieth century. American companies controlled the copper industry, and most of their profits went to the United States.

The landed aristocracy extended their influence by forming ties with the mining and business elite, although foreign investors were a conspicuous and persistent presence. The working class consisted of rural peasants and urban workers who were mostly all native born. Unlike other Latin American countries, Chile did not require, and hence did not recruit, large numbers of foreign laborers. In fact, the rural system of landed estates, led by a patrician class of white families and worked by numerous Indian and mestizo peons, resisted the intrusion of outsiders. It was a closed circle, predicated on stability and built on a hierarchy of race and class. A line was drawn well into the mid-twentieth century between the white, respectable class and the mass of people of color, who worked with their hands and had little hope of social improvement. "The weakness of our agricultural production," the 1919 Assembly of Landowners heard, "is the consequence of mental retardation produced in Chile and in all Spanish America, by the crossing of the conquistador with the aboriginal race." When thousands of peons left Chile for work in Peru during the late nineteenth century, a suggestion to import Chinese "coolies" to replace them was greeted by the government with horror.[43]

In 1906, a government bulletin noted that certain "distinguished Chilean citizens" had "gone so far as to advocate the excellent aspects of Japanese emigration, arguing that the Japanese are different from the Chinese.... Nevertheless, when it comes to immigration—in other words, when you are talking about inoculating against a new germ, that germ being other people who come to stay, to mix their blood, customs, ideas, tendencies with ours—the Chinese and the Japanese turn out to be the same: the Yellow Race with their physical inconveniences and their moral aberrations."[44] Chileans drew lessons from the anti-Japanese movement in the United States, observing how "California farmers watched in alarm as the Japanese gradually took away their livelihood and took over their lands." "When they are outside of their native land," the bulletin declared, "the Japanese show their true character, which is obviously unacceptable to the European social and moral order. Japanese are little or not at all respectful, and above all, very deceitful."[45] Even after World War II, anti-Japanese attitudes persisted, as was voiced in the Chilean senate in reference to a proposal for a Japanese whaling station in Chile: "Here is what the Japanese plan to do: they plan . . . to restructure the fishing industry. This would be an economic invasion akin to what happened in Korea and Manchuria, in Peru and Brazil, all of which experienced the sprouting up of racial conflicts with minorities and great disruption in international harmony."[46]

As a consequence, few Japanese were drawn to Chile, and those who did migrate there found a society, both in the city and countryside, steeped in rural values imposed by white masters over nonwhite workers. But those who settled in Chile, like Joichi Kamei, made for themselves fulfilling lives. "I dared and I won, but one needs to be ready to sacrifice a lot," a friend of Kamei's family once said after returning to Japan from years of labor in Chile. That example encouraged Kamei to follow in his footsteps, so at the age of nineteen he left Japan for Chile. He arrived in 1930 and, like his family friend, became a barber. Others like Kaoru Yamada moved to Chile from Bolivia. On a vacation trip in 1942, Yamada explained simply, "I arrived in Chile and I fell in love with the country."[47]

MEXICO

On the Yucatán Peninsula, in Guatemala and southern Mexico, arose the Mayan civilization around 500 B.C.E. Renown for its achievements in architecture, astronomy, mathematics, and chronology, that complex society of independent city-states collapsed, suffered invasion, and then absorption from the thirteenth through sixteenth centuries, at the hands of Toltec invaders from the central Mexican highlands. From the north of the Toltecs came the Aztecs, who waged war against them, in turn, subduing all of the peoples of the central valley and building the Aztec empire, which reached its peak around the time of Columbus's landing on America's shores. Having built a highly stratified and militarized society, the Aztecs fought against but by 1521 were ultimately defeated by the Spaniards' guns, diseases (for which they had no immunity), and non-Aztec allies. Conquest led to a drastic decline in the Indian population, because of smallpox, measles, and influenza, and the harsh conditions of life and labor under the Spaniards.[48]

In 1810, a Catholic priest, Miguel Hidalgo y Costilla, rallied an army of Indians and mestizos to abolish Indian tribute and slavery and to institute agrarian reform. His successor, José Maria Morelos, another priest, added the right of all citizens to choose their form of government. In 1813, the Congress of Chilpancingo declared Mexico's independence and an end to slavery, and it installed the Catholic Church as the state's religion. But Spain refused to relinquish control of Mexico; by 1815 Morelos had been captured and executed and the crown had reclaimed its powers. That control was short lived, however, and from 1821 to 1860, Mexico was ruled by numerous presidents, most of whom were the heads of military regimes. The U.S. annexation of Texas, a territory of Mexico, in 1845 was an act of war, but despite its resistance, the divided and weak Mexican nation could not repulse its northern neighbor. The U.S. prevailed in the Treaty of Guadalupe Hidalgo of 1848, which ended the war but gave Texas and California to the United States for a mere fifteen million dollars.

During the many wars of the nineteenth century, precipitated by power struggles and the U.S. invasion, poverty persisted among the masses of Mexico's peoples, many of whom were peasants who worked on haciendas as virtual serfs, furnishing labor for the agricultural sector. Because of that large pool of surplus labor and a virulent antiforeign sentiment, the government did not encourage immigration. In addition, since the Spanish conquest, Mexico's ruling class had installed a hierarchy of color that valued whiteness and denigrated Indians and darker-skinned *mestizos*. Racism and a claim of unfair economic competition prompted the Spanish barbers of Mexico City to petition the viceroy to expel Chinese barbers from the city, where they had lived since 1635.[49]

In 1876, after a brief period of republican rule, the dictator Porfirio Díaz assumed the presidency and accelerated the liberal program of modernization and economic development, inviting foreign investment and immigration. That opening, along with the passage of the 1882 Chinese Exclusion Act in the United States, made Mexico an attractive destination for Chinese migrants, who sought employment and a staging place for illegal migration into the United States. Mexican supporters of Chinese migrants saw them as useful laborers for the country's emerging farms, mines, and railroads, while its detractors depicted them as threats to the nation's health—displacing Mexican workers, spreading immorality and diseases, and encouraging prostitution. President Díaz appointed a commission to study the question of Asian immigration, and in 1904 it issued its report. The Chinese, the commission's chairman declared, as had been shown by the U.S. experience, endangered Mexico because they were an inferior race, unassimilable and immoral; nonetheless, they supplied beneficial labor. He thus recommended a controlled migration that regulated the Chinese and their labor, and precluded full integration into Mexican society. The Chinese, according to the chairman, were unlike the Japanese, who had adopted the forms of Western civilization and had become a world military power.[50]

Although some of Mexico's rulers might have distinguished between "inferior" Chinese and "superior" Japanese, the position of Japanese laborers in Mexico resembled the lot of Chinese workers in the mines and fields and on the railroads. A Japanese diplomat reported on the condition of Japanese migrants along the Mexico and Texas border in 1908. He found about forty Japanese in one location working for Mexicans for wages that barely allowed them subsistence; they were "always hungry and thirsty." "They live like cattle on the mudfloors, eating pieces of mouldy bread, barely hanging onto their frail lives. I don't have any words in my vocabulary to describe their misery," he wrote. The group had gathered there to await a chance to get into the United States, but that was impossible, the diplomat noted, after a 1908 presidential order cutting off Japanese migration to the United States from Hawai`i, Canada, and Mexico. He asked the men why they chose not to return to their former places of employment as farm workers and miners. "Even if we went back to those jobs," they replied, "we could not stand the slave-driving of the Mexican bosses, the low salaries and the harsh punishment. Since we don't know any other way, we would rather die of hunger here."[51]

In truth, many apparently died trying to get into the United States. A priest, Teiryo Sawada, who made frequent visits along the Mexico and U.S. border around 1926, found "many Japanese smuggling-in to the States from Mexican territory. I also learned that many couldn't make it to America, collapsing in the desert country and dying in their tracks. . . . Those who tried to steal in from Mexico literally risked their lives. Hundreds of Japanese were scattered over that area just waiting for a chance to cross the border."[52]

Fukuhei Saito was one of the men who entered the United States through Mexico. He sailed from Kobe in December 1906; while at sea, about fifty of the men who had signed three-year contracts to work in Mexican coal mines resolved to flee instead to the United States because of the physical risks of mining. Soon after landing at Salina Cruz, the men left their luggage, took only what they could carry, and headed for the border. Food the men stole from the gardens of Mexicans, but water was more difficult to find. "It was a dry, torrid area, and if one has no water in such a hot desert place, he suffers pains as severe as death," Saito explained. They survived by catching sandy rain in empty cans or bottles and by sucking water left standing in animal prints after a shower. It took the men two weeks to get to Eagle Pass, Texas, where a twenty-dollar fee gained them entry into the United States. "Now that I look back on it," Saito reflected, "it was a flight at the risk of all our necks."[53]

Although many Japanese, like the Chinese before them, used Mexico as a transit stop en route to the United States, many more stayed in Mexico to live and build communities. Hisao Ito left Japan when he was seventeen years old, in 1925. He left a father who was dying and a mother who stood alone as he walked away. He regretted not heeding his father's plea to await his death before leaving, and his mother's departing words haunted him: "You will know how hard life is," she told him, "when you leave home." For the next decade in Mexico, Ito remembered, he worked from six in the morning until nine at night and took only two days off each year. But he never gave up. He hated working on a farm; eventually he started a store in Ciudad Juarez, where about a fourth of his customers were Americans from across the border in El Paso, Texas. Like many of his fellow Mexicans, admitted Ito, he disliked the "gringos" intensely, in his case because of their history of anti-Japanese exclusion. "They made me sick to my stomach," he declared. In 1937, at the prompting of his brother-in-law, he married a "picture bride," Hatsuko Kikuchi. "We didn't have a honeymoon," Ito lamented. "As usual, we had to work from early in the morning till late at night." When World War II began, "many Mexicans helped the Japanese," recalled a grateful Ito, but American and Mexican officials, who behaved like Americans, arrested and held him, searched his house, and confiscated his papers. That night, he and others were jailed in a military barracks, with armed soldiers outside; Ito worried about his future and his family. "We all huddled together," Ito noted, "trembling from anxiety and the December chill all through the night." The authorities forcibly evicted about fifty Japanese families from Juarez. As the Japanese left their homes for Mexico City, their Mexican neighbors gathered and shouted: "Viva Japón. Viva México. Muera [death to the] gringo!" Of his fellow Mexicans Ito wrote, "I was so grateful for their goodwill that I cried. At a time when no one came to the defense of the Japanese, they extended their helping hand to us. I will never forget their kindness for the rest of my life."[54]

Kikuko Saiki described her love for Mexico. Her husband, Mario, had been in Mexico for decades and had married and lost two previous wives—the first a Mexican and the second a Japanese. They met in Osaka, and within a month they got married. Although she had studied Spanish in Japan and had hoped to go to Latin America, Saiki was disappointed when she first arrived in Mexico. The land, she said, seemed so barren. But Mario's children from his former marriages and their grandchildren brought joy to her life, and they tried to teach her to become Mexican. She began cooking Mexican food and learned to make Japanese dishes with Mexican ingredients. "I experienced alternately the joy and disappointment of creation," she recalled playfully. She made pickled vegetables, miso, and tofu, and used a Mexican purple bean to make the fillings for Japanese sweets. She satisfied her craving for *natto* (fermented soy beans) by wrapping beans in a dried cornhusk used to make tamales and placing the bundle in a warm place. The husks, she explained, helped to ferment the beans. Her cooking, Saiki reported, was like a balance, alternating between chiles and tomato sauce, and soybeans and soy sauce. Then she began craving spicy Mexican foods; eventually she contributed recipes to a Mexican cookbook intended for the Japanese. Their son married a Mexican woman, who on her visits with her, Saiki proudly reported, asked to learn to cook Japanese food. "I am truly happy to have moved to Mexico," she concluded.[55]

PARAGUAY

The Paraguay River forms a boundary between the vast plains of the Gran Chaco to the west and the variable and better-watered landscape to the east. The country's geography and climate has affected the limits of human habitation and economic activity. Although its winters are mild, frost prevents the cultivation of tropical products, and despite adequate rainfall, droughts are recurrent and threaten crop failures. Guaraní Indians once populated Paraguay almost exclusively, but the Spanish invaders mixed with them so thoroughly that by 1600, there were far more mestizos than Spaniards; two centuries later that mixture, which included African slaves introduced by the Spaniards, became the predominant group. In 1811, Paraguay won its independence from Spain and Argentina, thereby becoming the first independent South American nation.

A backwater of the Spanish empire because of its landlocked remoteness and lack of resources, independent Paraguay continued its isolation under a series of dictators. That solitude was broken by the disastrous War of the Triple Alliance (1864–1870), which pitted Paraguay against the Triple Alliance of Brazil, Argentina, and Uruguay. After the war Paraguay, saddled with debt, moved gradually into world trade; it finally allowed immigration in 1903. The immigration law, however, excluded Asians and Africans until 1924, when Paraguay opened the country to Asian migration. Paraguay won the Chaco War (1932–1935) against Bolivia, but the aftermath brought an end to the Liberal government in 1936 and the beginning of more than fifty years of military rule. Japanese migration to Paraguay took place within that context of political turmoil, but only after Brazil imposed a quota system restricting Asians in 1934. The first group of Japanese migrants arrived in Paraguay in May 1936.

The Japanese pioneers, accepted by Paraguay as an experiment, established the colony of La Colmena, some eighty miles southeast of the capital, Asunción. The few Paraguayans who lived on that land were given the option to purchase lots; several chose to stay among the colony's approximately 138 Japanese families, most of whom had come from Japan, though a few were remigrants from Brazil. The colony's problems included the facts that less than half of the migrants were experienced farmers, that the timing of their arrival in October precluded a full growing season for their first plantings, and that the settlers had to contend with political unrest, a weak national economy, and undeveloped transportation and communication systems. The La Colmena Company allocated land to the Japanese and owned the warehouses and mills, and its store dispensed tools, fertilizer, seeds, utensils, clothing, and Japanese goods. Colonists fretted under company direction and control, and some made their own decisions and pursued their own goals.[56]

Fujio Moritani remembered moving from Brazil to Paraguay as a young boy. At the time, he noted, Paraguay was devastated by its recent war with Bolivia, and the country was less developed than Brazil. But he discovered that Paraguay's people were good natured and kind. Life at La Colmena, however, was made especially difficult by locust invasions that plagued the colony periodically throughout the 1930s and 1940s. Millions of locusts, Moritani recalled, darkened the skies, cutting off the sunlight; their weight broke the branches of trees. The locusts, which devastated the crops, were so overwhelming that farmers simply watched the destruction.[57]

During World War II, the United States assumed an active role in Paraguay's affairs and pressed the nation, which had been openly sympathetic to Germany, to join the war effort against the Axis. To enlist U.S. economic aid, Paraguay assured the United States of its support of the Allies (while ignoring commitments to restrict Axis activities in the country). As the tide turned against the Axis powers in late 1943, however, Paraguay's government imposed restrictions on the nation's Germans and Japanese.[58] The police took over La Colmena from 1943 to 1947, closed its Japanese-language school, prohibited meetings among the Japanese, and restricted their movement. Cut off from Japan, the company's funds dried up, and in 1944 La Colmena was incorporated into the Paraguayan administration as a *distrito*. A bloody, five-month civil war erupted in 1947, adding to the instability of life in Paraguay; from 1936 to 1957, nearly half of the country's Japanese left for Japan, Brazil, or Argentina. Meanwhile, Paraguayans moved into La Colmena seeking work on Japanese farms and settling on available land. By the 1950s, the colony had more Paraguayans than Japanese, although the Japanese, many of whom had been born in Paraguay, were still important to the settlement's economy.

In 1953, a group from La Colmena, concerned with their isolation, formed the Compañía Nipo-Paraguayo de Colonización to explore the possibility of a new stream of Japanese migration to Paraguay and to reawaken Japan's interest in those Japanese already in Paraguay. As a result of those efforts, 137 Japanese families arrived in 1955 to begin the Colonia Presidente Chávez, and two years later a Japanese colonization company started Colonia Fram with several hundred families. Some groups of second-wave immigrants joined the Japanese at La Colmena. In 1959, Paraguay and Japan signed an immigration agreement that allowed eighty-five thousand Japanese into Paraguay over a thirty-year period, although by 1989 there were only about seven thousand Japanese Paraguayans.

On the fiftieth anniversary of Japanese settlement in Paraguay, a new generation of Japanese Paraguayans reflected on the past and their present circumstance. Shuzo Yamanaka expressed his appreciation for the struggles of the Issei who transformed the wilderness into a human habitation, and he observed that the future depended upon the labors of his generation. He saw himself as both Paraguayan and Japanese, stating that he should strive to retain and acquire only the good and not the bad elements of both cultures. Fumiko Abe pondered the meaning of being a Japanese Paraguayan when she felt she was a stranger in her native land. How could she, Abe wondered, contribute to both Paraguayan and Japanese societies? Chiyoko Kanazawa remembered her eighty-eight-year-old grandmother and her hard life. La Colmena, she claimed with pride, had achieved national recognition because of the labor of Japanese like her grandmother. That legacy, she declared, should never be forgotten. Perhaps that remembrance can be best celebrated, she felt, through lives of service to others. Fumiko Abe's desire to be a teacher was motivated by that desire, and Miho Miyasato became a physician because she was inspired to help those who suffered and were in need. As Abe put it, the most important thing is to have a kind heart.[59]

PERU

A major center of Spain's American empire largely because of its rich silver mines, Peru has three geographical regions, a division that explains much of the nation's society and history. Its arid coastal area, dominated by the city of Lima, gave rise to commercial agriculture and fishing. Its sierra, the Andean mountain range, supplied minerals; its peaks and valleys fed livestock and provided niches for subsistence agriculture. Its *montaña* reaches on the eastern slopes of the Andes are the headwaters of the Amazon River and the site of dense tropical forests, as well as of their products, including rubber, coffee, and fruit.

Peru remained a stronghold of the Spanish crown despite the winds of independence blowing through the rest of Spanish America. Independence was achieved only after the march of José de San Martín and his army across the Andes from Argentina to Chile and the southern coast of Peru. The Spaniards evacuated Lima in July 1821, and San Martín proclaimed Peru's independence. Still, the Spaniards relinquished its formal hold over Peru only after their decisive defeats at Junín in 1824 and Ayacucho in 1826. Coups, countercoups, and fighting during the 1820s left Peru's government in limbo, its cities and estates in ruins, and its treasury depleted. With its economy in shambles and a growing foreign debt, Peru pinned its recovery on the guano trade.

Formed from bird droppings on islands off Peru's coast, guano was abundant and, because it was rich in nitrogen, an excellent source of fertilizer. The first guano shipment reached Liverpool in 1841, and by the early 1860s the government relied upon the export for about 80 percent of its total revenues. Guano required sizable investment, however, in mining equipment, warehouses, ships, and labor. Because of the nature of the labor—harsh, unremitting, brutal, and toxic—guano companies relied upon the bound, exploitable worker that the Chinese coolie represented. After largely unsuccessful efforts to induce migration from Europe and Hawai`i, the government passed the "Chinese law" in 1849, granting funds and exclusive rights to Domingo Elías and Juan Rodríguez to import Chinese laborers into Peru.

Chinese were commonly captured in raids, deceived into signing contracts, or forced to board ships, called "floating hells," where mortality rates sometimes soared to over 30 percent during the middle passage. Because of the notoriety of the traffic, Peru's government canceled the monopoly given to Elías and Rodríguez when it expired in 1853 and terminated the "Chinese law" three years later. Although diminished, the trade in Chinese labor continued throughout the 1850s, and it accelerated after the Peruvian congress passed a new "Chinese law" in 1861 and approved in 1875 an annual subsidy of 160,000 *soles* to any shipping company that carried Chinese indentures to Peru. The insatiable appetite of Peru's industries for Chinese workers continued to propel the coolie trade, and only the War of the Pacific (1879–1883), in which Peru and Bolivia suffered devastating losses to Chile, interrupted and then practically brought to an end the human traffic. By then, more than a hundred thousand Chinese had entered Peru.[60]

Like the Chinese, the Japanese were recruited for their labor by Peru's coastal landowners who had relied upon African slaves and Chinese indentures to supply their chronic need for cheap, efficient workers. The first Latin American country to establish diplomatic relations with Japan in 1873, Peru instructed its agent to promote trade and migration that would assist in the development of Peruvian agriculture. The envoy had been prompted by the *María Luz* incident of 1872, in which Japan charged a Peruvian ship anchored in Yokohama harbor with slave trafficking and had freed its cargo of Chinese coolies.

On February 28, 1899, 790 Japanese migrants sailed from Yokohama to Callao on the *Sakura Maru*. On April 3, the ship arrived at Callao, and the next day it sailed along Peru's coastline, stopping to unload its cargo of laborers at eleven plantations. Barely three months later, Japan's minister to Mexico received word of trouble among the workers.[61] The planters felt that the Japanese got "angry about little things," were "lazy," and failed to obey regulations and orders. Japanese workers objected to the monopoly of plantation company stores, preferring to buy from Chinese merchants, and refused to work under overseers who were abusive, threatened them with whips, and treated them like slaves. By August, the number of Japanese who had fled or been expelled from plantations reached 321. They gathered in Callao, seeking alternative employment or remaining in town—where native workers, who saw the Japanese as competitors, shouted abuse and threw stones at them. Protests and runaways continued. By the end of October 1900, because of diseases and work and living conditions, 124 of the original group had died.[62]

In 1923, Peru and Japan agreed to end contract labor migration, and many of those under contract, after the expiration of their terms of service, left the plantations for the cities, especially Lima and Callao. There they worked as domestic servants or day laborers; a few established small businesses, frequently buying Italian and Chinese shops. Like the Chinese before them, Japanese economic mobility fostered suspicion and enmity among certain classes of Peruvians, who generally made no distinction between the Chinese and Japanese, viewing them both as "Asiatics"—an inferior race—and as such as undesirable. According to Seiichi Higashide, whenever there was a political crisis mobs commonly ransacked Chinese and Japanese-owned stores.[63]

A series of events brought matters to a head during the 1930s. The worldwide depression underscored Peru's vulnerability to international economic forces, and a wave of nationalism surged under the activist presidency of Oscar R. Benavides. In 1935, the influential Asociación de Comercio e Industrias de Arequipa petitioned Benavides for protection against Japanese and Chinese immigration and economic "invasion." The government passed an exclusion law aimed at Japanese immigration in 1936, adding strict regulations the following year.[64] A 1937 law removed from Japanese Peruvians born in the country the status of citizen and in 1940 did the same to those who went to Japan and returned to Peru.[65]

On May 13, 1940, mobs in Lima and Callao, acting on a false rumor that firearms had been found in Japanese Peruvian homes, attacked and beat Japanese and sacked their businesses and homes. According to a report, the riots caused damage to eight hundred businesses; many Japanese suffered wounds, two or three were killed, and one was raped.[66] Despite government redress to some of the riot victims, anti-Japanese attitudes persisted, as was evidenced in leaflets toward the end of 1940 that accused Peru's Japanese of espionage and concealing firearms.[67] The *Peru Jiho*'s editor tried in a letter published in the *El Universal* on December 6, 1940 to counter the charges. "The Japanese who reside here have no desire to return to their place of origin," he pleaded. "Here they work, here they have their homes and here they are planning to die. . . . [T]hey love Perú as their second country."[68]

One day after Japan's attack on Pearl Harbor, President Manuel Prado joined in a U.S.-led program for the common defense of the continent; he began by freezing Japanese Peruvian assets. Peru severed relations with Japan in January 1942, but it declared war on Japan only in February 1945. Peru nonetheless passed measures that authorized the forced sale and expropriation of Japanese land, shops, and businesses to Peruvians. As a result, according to a December 1945 letter, Japanese Peruvians suffered losses of 326 property holdings, with a value of 41,960,982.87 *soles,* or roughly $6.5 million.[69]

Besides economic losses and the collapse of Japanese Peruvian business activity, Japanese-language newspapers ceased publication, the government shut down Japanese language schools, and Japanese community clubs, societies, and associations closed. At the bidding of the United States, Peru sent more than six hundred Germans, a few Italians, and 2,118 Japanese for internment in the United States. The Japanese Peruvian internees constituted 80 percent of all Japanese sent from Latin America to the United States.[70] In fact, President Prado had hoped to deliver all of Peru's Japanese to the United States for internment and "repatriation" to Japan, a desire frustrated only by a shipping shortage and Washington's reluctance to take on so many Japanese.[71] After the war, the United States tried to remove all enemy aliens brought from Latin America to Germany, Japan, and Italy. Peru refused to take back its expelled Japanese; in the immediate postwar years only seventy-nine, mainly wives and children, were admitted back into Peru.[72]

Despite their government's rejection of them, Japanese Peruvians have claimed the country as their own. During the 1990s, *dekasegi* Pamela Shimabukuro found life difficult in Japan and admitted, "I miss Peru a lot. Although Peru has many economic and political problems, I think the people there are really warm and friendly." Luís Nicho Hiraoka memorialized his homeland in a poem entitled "Nostalgia at the Foot of Mount Fuji." "Near the slopes of Japan's sacred mountain," Hiraoka began, "many Peruvians work." A letter from home conjures memories of Peru's mountains, Lake Titicaca, historical places, "our national heritage." Beautiful is "my land," he declares. He summed up his feelings in Japan:

> We find sadness
> Because we miss
> our families,
> our customs
> our Peru.[73]

UNITED STATES

Native peoples, called uniformly "Indians" by Europeans, were actually a widely diverse collection of societies across the coasts, woodlands, plains, and deserts of North America—not "India," as Spain's Christopher Columbus mistakenly believed. They were the original tillers and caretakers of the waters and lands that became the United States; they were conquered, despite sharp resistance, and removed by Europeans who encroached on them beginning in the sixteenth century. Spaniards pursued their quest for wealth from their bases in the Caribbean into Florida, Mexico, and New Mexico; Indians fell to the invaders' sword but especially to their infections, like smallpox, influenza, and measles, for which they had no immunity. Entire peoples were decimated by waves of epidemics that washed over the Caribbean islands and American mainland. Millions died in this holocaust. Indians, however, did not vanish but played central roles in the making of the United States.

Europeans, mainly Portuguese at first, conveyed Africans to the Americas in the sixteenth century to work on their sugar plantations as slaves. The British settled North America in 1607 and the French the following year. In 1609, the Dutch arrived in New York. Sailing up the river that would bear his name, Henry Hudson, like his fellow Europeans, was seeking a water route to Asia, where he believed he would acquire a fortune and great wealth. Asia fired the imagination of Europeans, who steered their ships westward to the Americas and beyond.

As the European colonies grew, they developed cultures that differed from their European roots and from one another. The interactions of Indians, Africans, and immigrants from England, Scotland, Ireland, and the European continent linked the lives of those peoples, despite strenuous attempts to separate Europeans from Indians and Africans and to distinguish men from women. Ultimately, the regional differences would dissolve into union when faced with a common enemy—the colonizer, Britain—but many of those differences, bounded by inscriptions of geography, race, and gender, would remain long after independence. By the 1770s, relations between the colonies and Britain reached a breaking point because of both long-standing and immediate grievances. In 1773, the British East India Company's exemption from colonial taxes on its tea imports angered local merchants and triggered a mass mobilization and consumer boycott of that product across the colonies. On the evening of December 16, 1773, white men cross-dressed as Mohawk Indians boarded three ships in Boston Harbor and dumped the company's tea, produced in Asia, into the water.

Armed rebellion flared up in 1775, and on July 2, 1776, the Continental Congress voted in favor of independence from Britain; two days later it approved the Declaration of Independence. In 1783, the Treaty of Paris established U.S. independence, and four years later a new government (replacing the postwar Articles of Confederation) was formed under the Constitution of the United States. But the republic and its constitution were works in progress, often created through conflict, as the nation expanded its borders westward and debated the meanings of its laws and the composition of its peoples. Indian tribes, for instance, were recognized as sovereign entities but subject to the United States and as such both foreign and domestic; slaves were property without the rights of citizens; in 1790 the United States limited naturalization to "free white persons" and thereby excluded from citizenship immigrants who were neither free nor "white."

In 1784, the *Empress of China* slipped its moorage and sailed from New York for China. It was as if the tea steeped in Boston's harbor at the nation's founding had whetted Yankee appetites for the "fabulous East," needs that lay at the heart of America's "discovery" and the westward march of the United States. From Asia, conveyed like tea, spices, porcelain, and silks on those U.S. and European vessels, came men—principally as sailors and servants. South Asians arrived along the eastern seaboard as early as the 1780s, and Malays, Chinese, and Japanese in 1785. As U.S. ships traversed the oceans, pioneer wagons and prairie schooners plied the valleys, plains, and deserts of the North American interior, as if manifestly destined to reach the Pacific shore. The purchase of Louisiana in 1803 and a war with Mexico that ended in 1848 extended the United States "from sea to shining sea." With its iron warships, the United States "opened" Japan to commerce in 1854 and helped stimulate Japan's eager embrace of Westernization and modernity. Not content with its continental settlement limits, the United States embarked on expansion overseas beyond its shores, to Cuba and Puerto Rico to its south and to the Philippines and Hawai`i to its west in 1898.

Hawaiians helped sail U.S. ships in the Pacific trade. It began in Hawai`i, where the ships were outfitted and took on cargoes of sandalwood; the vessels proceeded to the Pacific Northwest, where they acquired pelts and furs from Indians, and then sailed to China for the goods that had motivated the trade. Chinese sailed on those ships to Hawai`i, where some experimented in sugar cane production and engaged in business, and many others, having signed contracts, worked on American and European plantations. With the discovery of gold in 1849, the Chinese and Hawaiians, like many Europeans and Latinos, were drawn to the rivers and mines of California to seek their fortunes. Like the Indians and Latinos, the Chinese and Hawaiians encountered discriminatory laws and physical violence from European Americans.

Those same forces of recruitment and attraction impelled the movement of Japanese to Hawai`i and the United States. When the Civil War cut off the South's sugar from the North, Hawai`i experienced an economic boom because of the high price of, and demand for, its sugar. In 1865, the kingdom's foreign minister asked an American businessman in Japan to supply laborers for Hawai`i's expanding sugar plantations. As a result, 149 Japanese recruited from Yokohama's streets sailed for the islands in 1868, setting a pattern for Japanese labor migration to Hawai`i and the U.S. mainland. In 1869, a group sent to California by a feudal lord displaced in the Meiji restoration established an outpost, the Wakamatsu Tea and Silk Farm Colony. The venture, like the earlier effort at labor recruitment, failed, but it established a pattern of migration that depended upon Japanese initiative and the lure of new opportunities in the United States.

Japanese women migrants were often both driven by necessity and lured by extravagant dreams. Onatsu Akiyama was born in Hiroshima, where her father delivered rice by wagon. She enjoyed a close and special relationship with her father, Akiyama recalled, but it was her mother who was most influential in her life as a child. "My mother was a very able woman," Akiyama revealed. "She could do anything that a man could do." Sickly and the only daughter, Akiyama was pampered. "I was such a spoiled girl!" she exclaimed. "Later on, when I came to America, I really regretted the fact that I was so spoiled because I had a difficult time adjusting." Akiyama graduated from eighth grade, attended sewing school for a year, and worked as a dressmaker.

One winter's day a matchmaker arrived with a marriage proposal. "I didn't want to get married," she remembered, "because I had heard that it was a very difficult life." Unlike her peers, Akiyama had resisted marriage and was then almost twenty-one and still single. But this proposal came from a man in the United States. "Going to America was very attractive to me," Akiyama admitted, as a way to escape a bride's service to her in-laws, which was lifelong and commonly contentious and oppressive. In addition, she dreaded a life of labor and sought to avoid "all those tiresome things." She thus agreed to the marriage.

The ship left Yokohama, stopped briefly in Hawai`i, and arrived in San Francisco. Contrary to her expectations of luxury, Akiyama experienced years of toil. "As soon as we arrived in Florin," she recalled, "I started working hard. We worked and worked and were in the depths of poverty. Carrying our blanket rolls and moving from one camp to another, we worked as farm laborers for three years. . . . It was very difficult for us but I didn't regret the fact that I came to this country. I really wanted to come here."

Race, Akiyama believed, bore scant relevance to her everyday life. "I never had any unpleasant experiences with white folks," she remembered. But Japan's attack on Pearl Harbor led to curfews, frozen bank accounts, and travel restrictions. "Then the FBI came and took my husband around the end of April [1942]," Akiyama recounted. The FBI whisked her husband away to the Sacramento jail and an internment camp. She didn't see her husband again for two years.

"We were really afraid," Akiyama admitted, when they were forcibly evicted from their homes. "We went to the Fresno Assembly Center first. . . . When we lined up in front of the mess hall, many people fainted because of the extreme heat. . . . I was only there for five months." From the assembly center, Akiyama and her children went with thousands of others to a concentration camp erected at Jerome, Arkansas. In the camp, Akiyama received the distressing news from a white friend that her house had been burned completely. "Camp for two years was very difficult," she commented tersely. In the third year, the family was reunited at the internment camp in Crystal City, Texas.

After the war's end, Akiyama chose to return to Japan. One of her sons had been in Japan during the war, and she was anxious to find him, explained Akiyama. "Besides, our house in Florin had been burned to the ground and we had no home to return to." Although governments frame certain choices as simple questions of patriotism, citizens frequently have more personal motivations. As his family languished in American concentration camps, Akiyama's son, born in the United States, had trained as a pilot for Japan's army. When asked why he had volunteered to serve in the Japanese military, he replied that he wanted to fly to the United States to liberate his parents.

Japan's destruction depressed her spirit, but seeing her son again was uplifting, Akiyama related. It was a struggle, though, merely to find enough to eat. The family borrowed money and eventually opened a noodle shop. Their third son returned to the United States to attend school and join the U.S. Army. His army earnings helped to pay for his parents' return to America after thirteen years in Japan.

"It was very fortunate that the United States government allowed us to return," Akiyama concluded. "You see, Papa had a slight stroke in Japan, and he could not work anymore because he had lost his coordination. He must have been relieved to return and be close to his sons once again. He died three years later. That was fourteen years ago."[74]

COMPARATIVE THOUGHTS
Conceptualizing a "Japanese" diaspora can result in narrow thinking. Such a focus could follow the migrants

from Japan to their destinations in straight lines; the sum of those mainly east-west filaments would constitute the global diaspora. The reality, however, is messier, in that migrants moved east and west but also north and south, and they settled, acculturated, and reproduced in particular countries. They became, over generations, local. Further, their transformation was shaped by the nation's history and society, including the relations of production and of race, beyond the singular "Japanese" diaspora. They were affected by histories that preceded their arrival; many learned and spoke Spanish, Portuguese, and English; and some married non-Japanese spouses and produced multiracial offspring.

Borders elicited national experiences, but remigrations and international relations exceeded those constraints. Perhaps the originating impetus was Europe's search for a passage to Asia. That ambition led to the "discovery" of the Americas by Europeans, their conquest of native peoples, and their implantations of colonies that evolved into nation-states. Because of their thirst for laborers, those colonies and postcolonial states—like Brazil, Peru, and the United States—drew Europeans, Africans, and Asians to their shores. When the United States restricted and excluded Asians, the traffic moved to Brazil and Mexico. When Brazil restricted Asians in 1934, Japanese migration flowed into Paraguay. Japanese moved from Brazil and Peru to Argentina, from Brazil to Paraguay, from Peru to Bolivia, from Bolivia to Chile, and from Mexico and Canada to the United States. The anti-Asian movement in the United States inspired similar sentiments in Canada, Chile, and Mexico, including exclusion laws and mob violence.

Wars between nations affected the patterns of migration and settlement. Paraguay incurred huge debts following its defeat in the War of the Triple Alliance (1864–1870) at the hands of Argentina, Brazil, and Uruguay, and as a consequence it opened its doors to trade and immigration. Chile gained access to mines after its victory over Bolivia and Peru in the War of the Pacific (1879–1883), destroying their economies and virtually ending Peru's coolie traffic. During World War II, the United States exercised its powers over Bolivia, Brazil, Mexico, Paraguay, and Peru, trading economic and military aid for what it said was hemispheric security. As a result, governments restricted mainly Germans and Japanese, and Nikkei faced expulsion and internment in Bolivia, Brazil, Mexico, and Peru. Canada and the United States devised the most comprehensive programs for the control of their Nikkei. Peru saw the war and U.S. initiatives as its opportunity to rid itself completely of its Nikkei. Even pro-Axis Argentina and Paraguay eventually fell in line with the United States and imposed restrictions on their Nikkei, even after Japan's surrender.

After the war, the U.S. occupation of Japan and Okinawa and its cold war waged against China sought outlets for impoverished and displaced Japanese in the Americas. Using U.S. influence, the U.S. and later Japanese governments supervised the migration and settlement of Japanese and larger numbers of Okinawans to Argentina, Bolivia, and Paraguay. In a reverse migration, with Japan's economy booming and in need of service workers but Latin America's in decline, Nikkei Latina/os sojourned in Japan as dekasegi, who changed Japan even as they and their forebears had transformed the Americas.

While economic forces and wars influenced migration patterns, relations of race, gender, and class shaped the more discrete experiences of Japanese in the Americas. White dominance and the notions of white supremacy in Argentina, Canada, Chile, Peru, and the United States restricted the freedoms of racialized minorities. The colonial legacies and hierarchies of color in Bolivia, Brazil, Mexico, and Paraguay achieved both similar and different effects, because of smaller numbers of Europeans and greater mixtures among Indians, Europeans, Africans, and Asians. The position of Asians in Brazil, Canada, Mexico, Peru, and the United States was largely determined by the reception accorded the Chinese, who generally preceded the Japanese, but it also depended upon the nature of the wider racial formation. The predominance, in numbers and power, of Nikkei men over women, as well as heterosexuality, led to the sexual harassment of women, the "picture bride" practice, and intermarriage. Some women sought marriage as an escape; others found it a prison. Employers might have welcomed Asian laborers, but workers who perceived them as threats to their jobs and wages sought their exclusion. Comparable sentiments greeted Nikkei Latina/os in Japan.

In the end, despite the overarching forces of international and economic relations and national governments under democracy or dictatorship, I am impressed with the quiet lives forged by those who might identify themselves as Nikkei. Reading their accounts, I find evidence of opportunities afforded and constraints imposed by nation-states. But I also perceive the pervasive power of individuals to shape their destinies for themselves and their future. They hold these in common within and without the "Japanese" diaspora—the cycles of birth, maturity, and death, a life of labor, failures, and achievements, and a reminiscence of times past and places trod.

Kamado Miyasato's husband left Okinawa for Argentina and later called her to join him there. In the country's hinterland, Miyasato cooked for the landowner, lived in a house with dirt floors, and harbored a deep fear of the Indian workers whose houses lined the river's edge. When her baby was due, Miyasato had to rely on an Indian midwife despite her prejudice. The midwife hanged a rope from the ceiling, instructed her to hold onto the rope while squatting, and told her to push. The pain was unbearable, Miyasato remembered, and the midwife screamed at her to bear down. Suddenly her body felt light and she heard the baby's cry. "I cannot forget that moment," she noted.[75]

Miyoji Fujita told how ordinary Mexicans helped him and his comrades escape their work contracts and make it into the United States. As a sixteen-year-old, Fujita signed with the Continental Emigration Company to work on a Mexican railroad. Laborers, he noted, lived "like cattle" in sheds made of millet stalks, and the bosses threatened the men with guns. One night six men ran away from camp and slept in the woods, and traveling only in the dark to elude their pursuers. Fujita fell ill with dysentery, but kindly Mexicans housed the men and hired a physician to nurse Fujita back to health. He was delirious and ate nothing for four days, and he thought he would die. After he regained his health, Fujita and his companions offered to pay their Mexican hosts but the hosts refused to accept their ten-dollar gold piece. So instead, the men left them things they had brought from Japan—picture cards, handkerchiefs, wooden clogs and sandals, and a fan. "I thought there wasn't any barrier between human beings," Fujita concluded.[76]

Poets crystallize lifetimes in luminous verse.

> The *kimonos* that we brought from Japan
> Replaced by western clothes one after another
> The fewer they become with the passing years.[77]

> Holding my first grandchild in my arms
> Reflecting on my old days
> I only feel lonely
> My fifty years here.[78]

> After trials and errors
> This wide green field
> Our fertile farm
> Planted by parents
> Raised by children
> The fruits of immigration
> Enjoyed by grandchildren.[79]

NOTES

1. Masayo Ohara and Eiichiro Azuma translated all of the Japanese-language sources used in this essay. I would like to thank them for their kind labor, without which this chapter would be palpably weaker.
2. Benjamin Keen, *A History of Latin America* (Boston: Houghton Mifflin, 1992), 221–26.
3. James Lawrence Tigner, "The Ryukyuans in Argentina," *Hispanic American Historical Review* 47:2 (May 1967): 204, 217.
4. See the interview with his daughter, Violeta Shinya, in Aruzenchin Takushoku Kyodo Kumiai, *Takushokou* 6 (Soritsu 45-shunen Kinenshi) (c.1998).
5. Tigner, "Ryukyuans," 204–06.
6. *Historia de la Immigracion de Nago Chojin en la Argentina* (Kyu Nago Chojin Aruzenchin Ijushi).
7. Zaia Okinawa Kenjin Rengokai, *Aruzenchin no Uchinanchu Hachiju-nenshi* (Buenos Aires, 1994), 26–29.
8. Zaia Okinawa Kenjin Rengokai, *Aruzenchin no Uchinanchu Hachiju-nenshi*, 50–52.
9. Shintoku Agarie (ed.), *Kyu Nago Chojin Aruzenchin Ijushi* (Buenos Aires, 1994), 87–88.
10. Shintoku Agarie (ed.), *Kyu Nago Chojin Aruzenchin Ijushi*, 147–51.
11. Zaia Okinawa Kenjin Rengokai, *Aruzenchin no Uchinanchu Hachiju-nenshi*.
12. Aruzenchin Takushoku Kyodo Kumiai, *Takushokou* 6.
13. Shintoku Agarie (ed.), *Kyu Nago Chojin Aruzenchin Ijushi*.
14. Tigner, "Ryukyuans," 221, fn. 55
15. Shintoku Agarie (ed.), *Kyu Nago Chojin Aruzenchin Ijushi*, 420; and Zaia Okinawa Kenjin Rengokai, *Aruzenchin no Uchinanchu Hachiju-nenshi*, 78.
16. Tetsuzo Oshiro, *Nihon Imin Hassho no Chi Korudoba: Aruzenchin Korudoba Shu Nihonjin Hyakuju-nenshi* (Córdoba, 1997).
17. James Lawrence Tigner, "The Ryukyuans in Bolivia," *Hispanic American Historical Review* 43:2 (May 1963): 206–09.
18. Tigner, "The Ryukyuans in Bolivia," 210–11.
19. *Nihonjin Iju 100 Shunenshi, Boribia ni Ikiru* (Santa Cruz: Federación Nacional de Asociaciones Boliviano-Japonesas, 2000), 47–49. The Bolivian government pledged its support of the United States after Pearl Harbor, broke off relations with the Axis in January 1942, and declared a state of war with the Axis powers in April 1943. During the war, the government required the Japanese to register their firearms, refrain from using cameras or possessing Japanese-language newspapers and magazines, get permission to travel, and disband all of their organizations. Still, enforcement of those regulations was lax. Tigner, "The Ryukyuans in Bolivia," 215, fn. 24, 216.
20. According to a report, the United States requested 120 Germans and 40 Japanese, but the Bolivian government could not fill the quota and only sent 50 Germans and 28 Japanese. Tigner, "The Ryukyuans in Bolivia," 215.
21. *Nihonjin Iju 100 Sunenshi, Boribia ni Ikiru*, 42–46.

22. For studies of these migrants, see Stephen I. Thompson, "Separate but Superior: Japanese in Bolivia," in *Ethnic Encounters: Identities and Contexts*, edited by George L. Hicks and Philip E. Leis (North Scituate, Massachusetts: Duxbury Press, 1977), 89–101; and Stephen I. Thompson, "Religious Conversion and Religious Zeal in an Overseas Enclave: The Case of the Japanese in Bolivia," *Anthropological Quarterly* 41:4 (October 1968): 201–08.
23. *Boribia Koronia Okinawa Nyushoku 25 Shunenshi* (1979), 79, 80, 89–91, 146. On mosquitoes, see the essay, "The Mosquitoes of Bolivia," by Seitoku Toyama, in Gary Mukai and Rachel Brunette, *Japanese Migration and the Americas: An Introduction to the Study of Migration* (Stanford, Calif.: Institute for International Studies, 1999), 76–77.
24. *Boribia Koronia Okinawa Nyushoku 25 Shunenshi*, 164.
25. *Boribia Koronia Okinawa Nyushoku 25 Shunenshi*, 75, 77, 147.
26. *Boribia Koronia Okinawa Nyushoku 25 Shunenshi*, 147.
27. Keen, *History of Latin America*, 244–46.
28. Referred to as "Ryu Minumo" by Normano and Gerbi (see note 29), but I refer to him as "Ryu Mizuno."
29. J. F. Normano and Antonello Gerbi, *The Japanese in South America: An Introductory Survey with Special Reference to Peru* (New York: Institute of Pacific Relations, 1943), 21–23, 34.
30. Kinchoshi Hensan Iinkai (ed.), *Kinchoshi*, v. 1 (Kincho, Okinawa: Kinchoshi Hensan Iinkai, 1996), 350.
31. Kinchoshi Hensan Iinkai (ed.), *Kinchoshi*, 302, 304, 439.
32. See e.g., Normano and Gerbi, *Japanese in South America*, 56–58; Ciro Alegria and Alfredo Saco, "Japanese Spearhead in the Americas," *Free World* 2:1 (February 1942): 81–84; and John W. White, "Japan's Amazon Dream," *Asia and the Americas* 43:10 (October 1943): 580–83.
33. Kinchoshi Hensan Iinkai, *Kinchoshi*, 295.
34. Masami Tanaka, *Burajiru ni okeru Katei Tankakai* (Tokyo: Shinsei Shobo, 1957), 61, 95.
35. Normano and Gerbi, *Japanese in South America*, 57–58.
36. Tanaka, *Burajiru ni okeru Katei Tankakai*, 96.
37. Mukai and Brunette, *Japanese Migration*, 35, 39.
38. Patricia E. Roy, *A White Man's Province: British Columbia Politicians and Chinese and Japanese Immigrants, 1858–1914* (Vancouver: University of British Columbia Press, 1989), 5.
39. Roy, *A White Man's Province*, 7, 8.
40. For details of this riot, see Howard H. Sugimoto, "The Vancouver Riots of 1907: A Canadian Episode," in *East across the Pacific: Historical and Sociological Studies of Japanese Immigration and Assimilation*, edited by Hilary Conroy and T. Scott Miyakawa (Santa Barbara, Calif.: ABC-Clio, 1972), 92–126.
41. On the *Komagata Maru* incident, see Joan M. Jensen, *Passage from India: Asian Indian Immigrants in North America* (New Haven, Conn.: Yale University Press, 1988), 121–38.
42. As told in Tomoko Makabe, *Picture Brides: Japanese Women in Canada* (Toronto: Multicultural History Society of Ontario, 1995), 125–49.
43. Arnold J. Bauer, *Chilean Rural Society from the Spanish Conquest to 1930* (Cambridge, England: Cambridge University Press, 1975), 153, 163.
44. Bulletin No. 32 of the National Agricultural Service, 1906.
45. *Social Bulletin for Industrial Advancement* (Santiago) 31:7 (July 1914).
46. *Senate Session Journal* (Santiago), 9th Session, July 2, 1959.
47. Unpublished oral histories collected by the Sociedad Japonesa de Beneficencia "Nikkei-Chile," Japanese American National Museum, Los Angeles.
48. Thomas E. Skidmore and Peter H. Smith, *Modern Latin America* (New York: Oxford University Press, 2001), 20.
49. Evelyn Hu-DeHart, "Racism and Anti-Chinese Persecution in Sonora, Mexico, 1876–1932," *Amerasia Journal* 9:2 (1982): 2.
50. Hu-DeHart, "Racism and Anti-Chinese Persecution in Sonora, Mexico, 1876–1932," 4–6.
51. Quoted in Kazuo Ito, *Issei: A History of Japanese Immigrants in North America*, translated by Shinichiro Nakamura and Jean S. Gerard (Seattle: Japanese Community Service, 1973), 65.
52. Kazuo Ito, *Issei*, 65–66.
53. Kazuo Ito, *Issei*, 67–68.
54. Hisao Ito, "Eiji Shuta Don Rauru no Iko: Nichibei no Kokkyo no Machi de no Shinkusa o Koete," in *Meishin*, edited by Ryuhei Kato (Mexico City: Meishinkai, 1996), 25–61. That same solidarity was expressed in 1906, reported Miyoji Fujita, when Mexican villagers shouted "Banzai! Banzai!" to the Japanese because of Japan's victory in the Russo-Japanese War. Ito, *Issei*, 68, 69.
55. Kikuko Saiki, "Mario ni Sasagu: Ningen Banji Saio ga Uma no Uta"; and Masaru Saiki, "Gojunoto Gojukki no Mokei Kansei o Mezashite: Mekishiko Zaiju Rokuju Shichinen no Kyuju-o no Kaiso" in Kato, *Meishin*, 93–105, 106–24.
56. For a study of La Colmena undertaken in 1958, see Norman R. Stewart, *Japanese Colonization in Eastern Paraguay* (Washington, D.C.: National Academy of Sciences, 1967).
57. Fujio Moritani, "Shoki no Omoide: Ra Korumena Ijuchi," in *Paraguay Nihonjin Iju 50 Nenshi* (Asunción, 1987), 120–24.
58. Paraguay severed diplomatic relations with the Axis powers in 1942, but only declared war against Germany and Japan on February 1945.
59. Shuzo Yamanaka, "Bokutachi no Sekinin: Issei no Jisseki o Mamoritai"; Fumiko Abe, "Watashitachi no Kadai: Omoiryari no Kokoro o Taisetsu ni"; Chiyoko Kanazawa, "Hyakunensai o Mezashite Ganbaro"; and Miho Miyasato, "Kono Kinen no Toshi ni Ishi no Masseki o Ete," in *Paraguay Nihonjin Iju 50 Nenshi*, 54–58.
60. On the horrors of the coolie trade, see Watt Stewart, *Chinese Bondage in Peru: A History of the Chinese Coolie in Peru, 1849–1874* (Durham, N.C.: Duke University Press, 1951); and Eugenio Chang Rodríguez, "Chinese Labor Migration Into Latin American in the Nineteenth Century," *Revista de Historia de América* 46 (December 1958): 375–97.

61. Toraji Irie, "History of Japanese Migration to Peru, Part I," translated by William Himei, *Hispanic American Historical Review* 31:3 (August 1951): 445.
62. For a detailed accounting of these early years, see Irie, "History, Part I," 437–52; and Toraji Irie, "History of Japanese Migration to Peru, Part II," translated by William Himei, *Hispanic American Historical Review* 31:4 (November 1951): 648–64.
63. Seiichi Higashide, *Adios to Tears: The Memoirs of a Japanese-Peruvian Internee in U.S. Concentration Camps* (Honolulu: E&E Kudo, 1993) 61, 62.
64. Normano and Gerbi, *Japanese in South America*, 76–77, 79.
65. Edward N. Barnhart, "Japanese Internees from Peru," *Pacific Historical Review* 31:2 (May 1962): 169–70; and Normano and Gerbi, *Japanese in South America*, 116.
66. Mischa Titiev, "The Japanese Colony in Peru," *Far Eastern Quarterly* 10:3 (May 1951); 238–39. For details of the 1940 riots and their aftermath, see Higashide, *Adios*, 105–12.
67. Normano and Gerbi, *Japanese in South America*, 79–80, fn. 36.
68. Normano and Gerbi, *Japanese in South America*, 80–81, fn. 37. I am grateful to Johnny Roldán-Chacón for this translation.
69. Titiev, "Japanese Colony," 239–40, fn. 53.
70. Barnhart, "Japanese Internees," 172. Cf., Titiev, "Japanese Colony," 240, who claims that only 510 Japanese Peruvian men were expelled, along with their wives and children.
71. C. Harvey Gardiner, *Pawns in a Triangle of Hate: The Peruvian Japanese and the United States* (Seattle: University of Washington Press, 1981), 18, 19, 20, 52–53. For details of life in Peru and the U.S. internment camps, see Gardiner, *Pawns*, 52–111; and Higashide, *Adios*, 113–75.
72. Barnhart, "Japanese Internees," 173, 174.
73. Mukai and Brunette, *Japanese Migration*, 38, 40–41.
74. Onatsu Akiyama's account is in Eileen Sunada Sarasohn, *Issei Women: Echoes From Another Frontier* (Palo Alto, Calif.: Pacific Books, 1998), 50–55, 64–68, 120–33, 173–77, 207–14.
75. Zaia Okinawa Kenjin Rengokai, *Aruzenchin no Uchinannchu Hachiju-nenshi*, 110–14.
76. Ito, *Issei*, 68–69.
77. Masami Tanaka, in Tanaka, *Burajiru ni okeru Katei Tankakai*, 66.
78. Miyakoji, in *Nichiboku Koryushi*, 1007.
79. Yoshi Kamiya, in *Boribia Koronia Okinawa Nyushoku 25 Shunenshi*, 62.

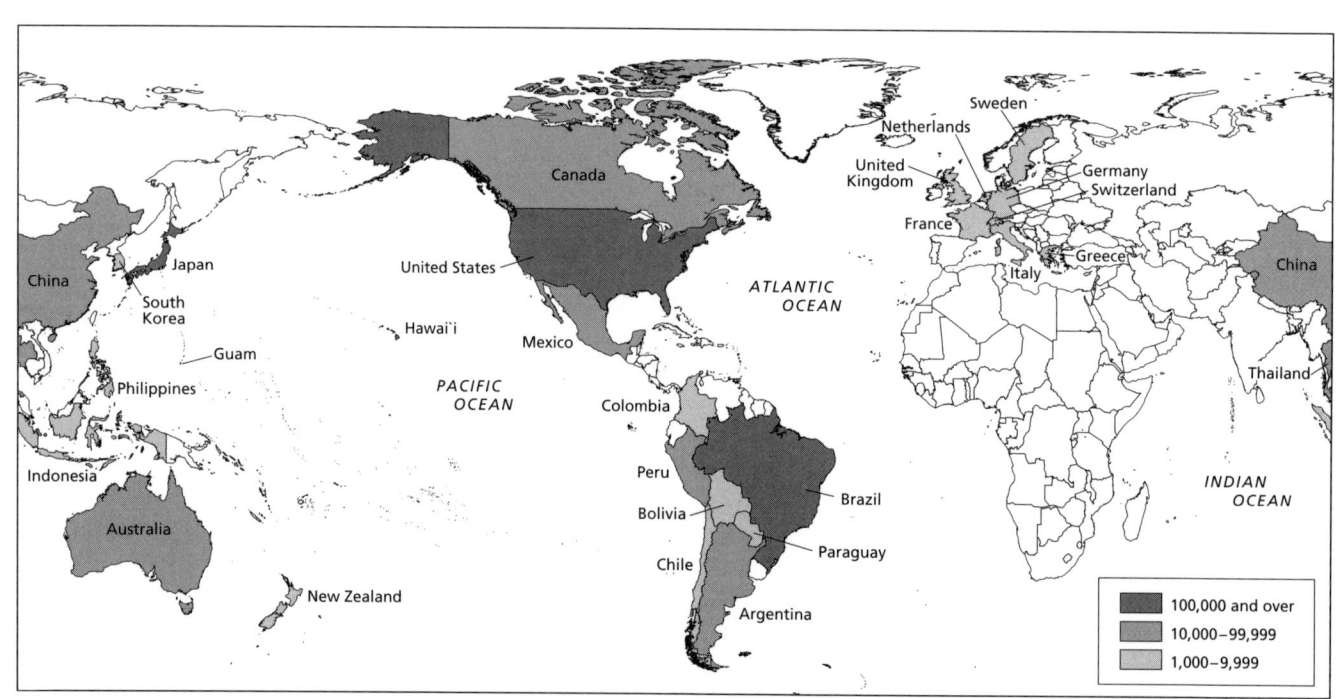

Worldwide Distribution of Nikkei, 1993

Nikkei World Demography

Countries with Over 50 Nikkei (1993)[1]

ASIA
Burma	70
China, People's Republic of	29,859
Hong Kong	872
India	142
Indonesia	2,979
Korea, South	7,440
Malaysia	466
Pakistan	197
Philippines	4,959
Singapore	568
Taiwan	493
Thailand	10,240

PACIFIC
Australia	10,915
Guam	2,338
New Zealand	1,847
Pacific Islands (Trusted to U.S. by UN)	1,063

NORTH AMERICA
Canada	55,111
U.S.	760,916

CENTRAL AMERICA
Costa Rica	57
Cuba	842
Dominican Republic	583
Guatemala	113
Mexico	11,926

SOUTH AMERICA
Argentina	29,262
Bolivia	7,986
Brazil	620,370
Chile	2,292
Colombia	1,106
Ecuador	152
Paraguay	6,054
Peru	55,472
Uruguay	436
Venezuela	828

WESTERN EUROPE
Austria	620
Denmark	699
Finland	275
France	2,832
Germany	3,296
Great Britain	3,886
Greece	1,220
Ireland	61
Italy	1,110
Netherlands	1,177
Norway	508
Spain	464
Sweden	1,412
Switzerland	2,875

EASTERN EUROPE
Poland	53
Russia	503

MIDDLE/NEAR EAST
Iran	66
Israel	103
Kuwait	51
Turkey	163

AFRICA
Egypt	120

JAPAN, REVERSE MIGRATION FROM SOUTH AMERICA (1997)[2]
Argentina	3,300
Bolivia	3,337
Brazil	233,254
Paraguay	1,466
Peru	40,394

Sources:

[1] Japan International Cooperation Agency, *Kaigai ijū Tōkei (FY 1952–FY 1993)* (Tōkyō, 1994), 124–125. The data were originally collected by the Ministry of Foreign Affairs of Japan and reported in *Kaigai zairyū hōjinsū chōsa tōkei*. The number includes the permanent resident and Nikkei population. Nikkei is defined as those who do not have Japanese citizenship but are descendant of the Japanese (naturalized Issei, Nisei, and Sansei etc.).

[2] Compiled by Marcelo Higa from Nyūkoku Kanrikyoku (eds.). *Zairyū gaikokujin tōkei*, 1998.

CHAPTER 1

Japanese Migration

DEVELOPED IN COLLABORATION WITH THE IMIN KENKYUKAI

STARTING WITH THE DEPARTURE OF FORTY LABORERS FOR HAWAI`I AND GUAM in 1868, Japanese overseas migration underwent different phases in accordance with both domestic and international changes. Between 1885 and 1907, a vast majority of emigrants from rural Japan, who had fallen victim to the development of a capitalistic economy, headed for Hawai`i and North America, as well as South Pacific islands, to work temporarily as manual laborers—a practice known as dekasegi. With the rise of the anti-Japanese exclusion movements in the United States and Canada, Brazil emerged as the main destination for labor emigrants. Meanwhile, Imperial Japan brought under its colonialist control Taiwan, Korea, southern Sakhalin, Micronesia, and parts of northern China, where thousands of Japanese settlers moved. After the mid-1930s, Manchuria, in particular, served as the chief magnet for state-sponsored agricultural settlers through the early 1940s, while other regions, including Latin America, began to shut the door to Japanese immigration. The fall of the Japanese empire in 1945 meant the sudden end to Japanese emigration until after 1952, when Japanese emigration to South American countries resumed under the bilateral treaty arrangements. Unlike their prewar counterparts, these postwar emigrants were mostly agriculturists or skilled specialists, who intended to become permanent settlers. From the 1950s, growing numbers moved to North America and other areas, for a variety of reasons, including marriage, education, and business. In recent years, economic difficulties in Latin America have caused tens of thousands of Nikkei to seek temporary work in a more prosperous Japan. Backed by favorable changes in Japanese immigration laws, these Nikkei have formed sizable ethnic communities throughout Japan today.

Historical Overview of Japanese Emigration, 1868–2000

EIICHIRO AZUMA

THE OVERSEAS MIGRATION OF JAPANESE STARTED WITH the opening of the island nation to the rest of the world and its entry into modernity in 1868.[1] Becoming a part of the international network of labor, capital, and transportation, the Japanese suddenly found themselves in the middle of rapid socioeconomic change, thereby creating a rural population ready for domestic and international migration. Furthermore, the development of modern medicine and public hygiene, contributed to the mounting pressure of the post-1868 population growth on the new nation, with its very limited resources.

The availability of relatively cheap labor in Japan drew attention from Western merchants, who scrambled to the country for new business opportunities. The transportation of Chinese "coolies" to work on plantations in Hawai`i and South America was in full motion at that time, and these merchants viewed the Japanese in a similar light. In 1868, the first year of Meiji, American trader Eugene Van Reed recruited a group of approximately 150 Japanese to work on sugar plantations in Hawai`i and another forty people for Guam. This unauthorized shipment of laborers, known as *gannen-mono*, marked the beginning of Japanese labor migration overseas.

However, for the next two decades the Meiji government forbade the departure of any more groups of emigrants, due to the slavelike treatment that the first Japanese migrants had received in Hawai`i and Guam. In their quest to forge a modern nation-state equal to those in

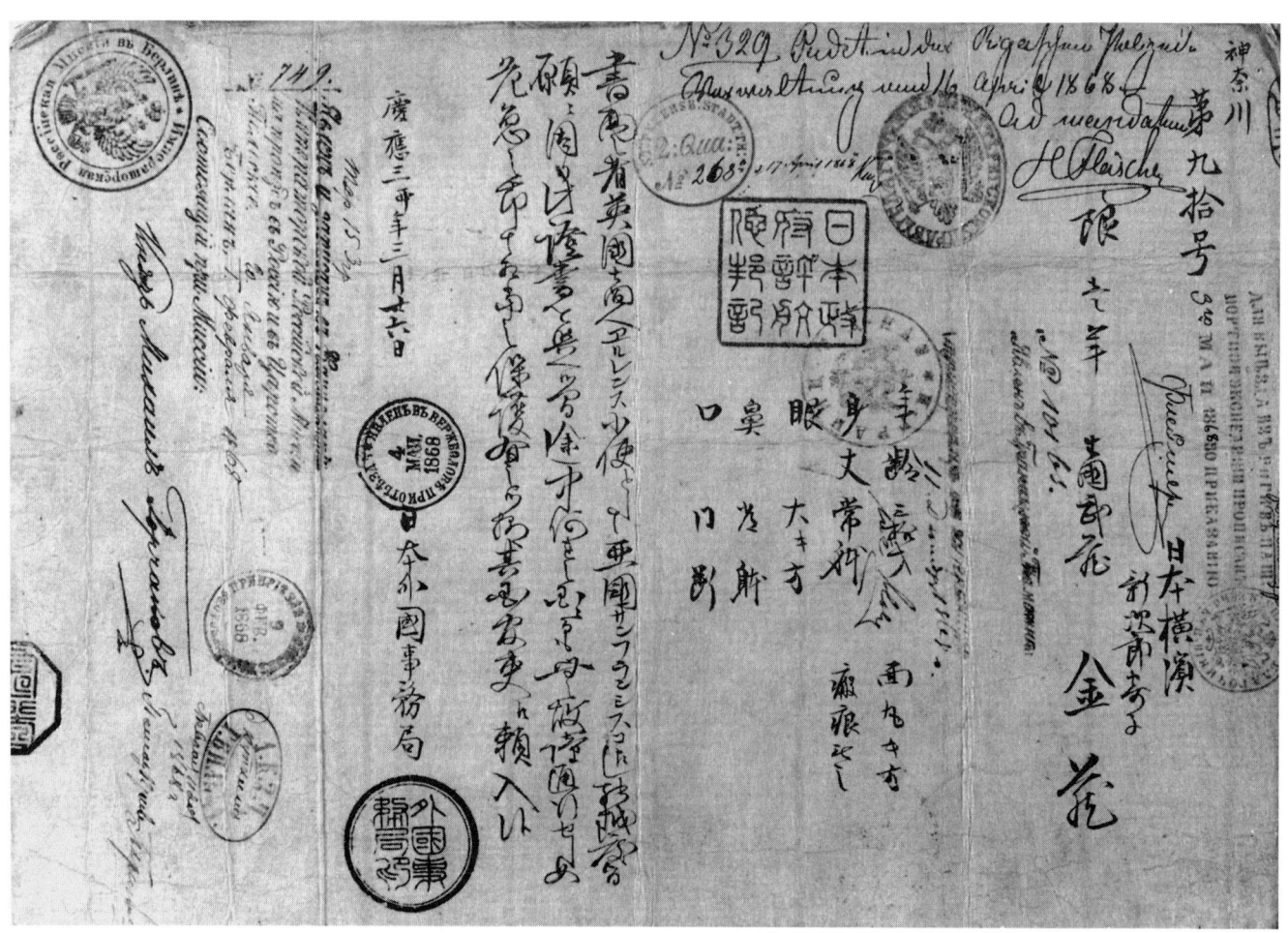

Passport issued to a Japanese citizen traveling to San Francisco and accompanying a British merchant, Ernst, Yokohama, Japan, March 1868. (Collection of Ministry of Foreign Affairs Diplomatic Record Office)

The Meiji emperor, who assumed his reign from 1868 to 1912. This photograph was taken in the 1870s. (Collection of National Diet Library of Japan)

Western Europe and the United States, Meiji leaders wanted to avoid a situation in which Japan's "imperial subjects" were treated like Chinese "coolies" and African "slaves." Hence, instead of going abroad, many Japanese were recruited for the development of Hokkaido, Japan's northernmost island.

BEGINNINGS OF OVERSEAS EMIGRATION

It was not until 1885 that the massive emigration of Japanese began. In that year, the governments of Japan and Hawai`i concluded the Immigration Convention, under which approximately twenty-nine thousand Japanese (known as kan'yaku emigrants) traveled to Hawai`i for the next nine years to work on sugar plantations under three-year contracts. In the wake of severe rural depression and social turmoil, the Meiji government found it beneficial to provide gainful employment for Japan's farming population and to enrich the country with American dollars through their remittances from Hawai`i.

Meiji leaders thought that the possibility of abuse and poor treatment of Japanese laborers in the host country—a potential embarrassment for Japan—could be minimized by close government supervision. To pursue this crucial point, the Japanese government enacted the Emigrant Protection Ordinance *(Imin Hogo Kisoku)* when the Immigration Convention with Hawai`i expired in 1894. Two years later, the Emigration Protection Act *(Imin Hogoho)* was passed to regulate the activities of emigration companies, which usually assumed the recruitment of contract laborers.

With the lifting of the de facto government ban on labor emigration and the systematization of emigration laws, thousands of Japanese departed for Thursday Island, New Caledonia, Australia, Fiji, and other South Pacific destinations for a variety of contract work. Starting in 1903, contract laborers also went to the Philippines, where they were involved in construction of a major highway. Other Southeast Asian regions attracted Japanese laborers and business people as well. The migration of contract laborers to Latin America began in 1899, when a group of 790 Japanese were recruited to work on Peruvian plantations. In essence, most of these "emigrants" were not settlers but dekasegi laborers, planning to return home with money after a few years of hard labor in a foreign land.

Because the initial recruitment of Hawai`i-bound kan'yaku emigrants was carried out in the Chugoku and Kyushu areas of southwestern Japan, the majority of early dekasegi laborers originated from such prefectures as Hiroshima, Yamaguchi, Fukuoka, Kumamoto, and Wakayama. In the context of economic difficulty and Meiji colonial domination after the turn of the century, Okinawa started to send thousands of laborers overseas. Joining the ranks of common Japanese laborers, Okinawan immigrants often found themselves subject to inferior treatment within the Japanese immigrant communities, mirroring the status of their native land relative to other prefectures in Japan. Because local networks based on family connections and word of mouth among friends and neighbors aroused emigration fever, overseas migration was notably a phenomenon of southwestern Japan until the beginning of Manchurian colonization during the 1930s.

Although most Japanese emigrants were dekasegi laborers, Meiji leaders usually viewed overseas emigration within the framework of Japan's colonial development and expansion rather than in terms of family economics or personal opportunities. Ever since the opening of Japan to the West, the introduction of modern ideas had induced the development of colonialist thought in the intellectual circles of Meiji Japan. Western powers had embarked on their own colonial expansion throughout the

The original Immigration Convention of 1886 between Japan and Hawaiian Kingdom, which provided some protection to Japanese immigrants and even granted them the right to vote. The Bayonet Constitution of 1887 abrogated key provisions. (Collection of Ministry of Foreign Affairs Diplomatic Record Office)

world, and many educated Japanese believed that Japan should do the same. From the early 1890s, this line of thought became very popular; it formed a background for the Sino-Japanese War of 1894–1895 and the sudden boom of colonial "studies" and "explorations" among Japan's urban elites. Some intellectuals looked at Micronesia and the Philippines as possible realms of Japanese expansion (*nanshinron*: argument for southward advancement), while others were more interested in Korea and the Asian continent. In addition, there was a group of people who advocated for the Japanese entry into Latin America.

In this context, a coalition of Japanese government officials, politicians, and journalists organized the Colonization Society (Shokumin Kyokai) in 1893, calling for an overseas development of Japanese "colonies" through emigration. Often referring to the Malthusian theory,

they argued that Meiji Japan would need to expand externally in order to obtain larger markets to export its "surplus" population and commercial goods. The society's pet project of 1897 was to attempt to establish an agricultural colony in Chiapas, Mexico. Known as the Enomoto Colony, it did not succeed, but some of its settlers remained in Chiapas, where they intermarried local women and established the first Japanese settlement community in Latin America.

EXODUS TO NORTH AMERICA

The entry of Japanese people into the U.S. mainland started in the 1880s. Initially, the early arrivals consisted mostly of sailors who "jumped" ship, prostitutes, anti-Meiji government activists, and indigent students. Around the turn of the century, more and more young men left Japan to get an education in the United States, for

Okinawan picnic in Hawai`i, 1920s. (Gift of the Roy Yonahara family. Japanese American National Museum [96.331.17])

the opportunities in Japan had become increasingly limited. Some were fortunate enough to get funding to attend prestigious universities on the East Coast, but most congregated in cities like San Francisco, Portland, and Seattle. Often known as "school boys," they attended school while performing domestic duties for white families in exchange for room and board.

In the meantime, with the legalization of labor emigration, there was a large number of common laborers who entered along the Pacific Coast, both in the United States and British Columbia, Canada. Under the leadership of former "school boys," who could speak some English, these dekasegi laborers worked in farms, sawmills, salmon canneries, and on railroads. When the U.S. annexation of Hawai`i ended contract labor in 1899, many plantation workers in Hawai`i joined this growing ethnic labor force on the West Coast, until the migration of Japanese from the islands to the mainland was banned by the U.S. government in 1907.

The increase of common dekasegi laborers resulted in organized anti-Japanese movements in Hawai`i and the Pacific Coast states. When the Japanese crossed the Pacific, the tradition of anti-Asian racism had been already firmly established in the local political scenes, and coalitions of white labor unions and opportunistic politicians had rallied to ensure the passage of the Chinese Exclusion Act in 1882. It did not take long for anti-Asian prophets to define the Japanese as the next "menace" from the Orient. In 1905 the Japanese-Korean Exclusion League was formed in San Francisco; it engaged in fierce exclusionist propaganda, in tandem with local newspapers.

There was a major riot against the Japanese in Vancouver, Canada, in 1907. The first major anti-Japanese incident, however, had occurred in 1906, when the San Fran-

"Going to America," by Issei artist Henry Sugimoto, who was born in Wakayama, Japan, in 1900. Sugimoto came to the United States at the age of nineteen to join his parents in Hanford, California. He was a versatile and prolific artist whose works were widely exhibited in both the United States and Europe. (Gift of Madeleine Sugimoto and Naomi Tagawa, Japanese American National Museum)

cisco Board of Education ordered the segregation of Japanese students from white pupils. As Japan's victory over Russia in 1905 had convinced Japanese leaders of their equality with the West, the discriminatory treatment of Japanese subjects by American officials was unacceptable to them. Therefore, this local issue developed into a major international controversy, involving both the Japanese and U.S. governments in the general question of Japanese immigration.

The resultant settlement between the two countries was known as the Gentlemen's Agreement of 1907–1908. On the one hand, the San Francisco Board of Education agreed to cancel its segregation order, and the federal government prohibited the entry of Japanese laborers into the U.S. mainland via Canada, Mexico, and Hawai`i. On the other hand, Japan agreed to prevent the departure of new labor emigrants to the United States. Canada followed suit with the Hayashi-Lemiuex Gentlemen's Agreement in 1908. Likewise, anti-Japanese exclusion in the United States, combined with the domestic turmoil during the Mexican Revolution after 1910, virtually killed Japanese emigration to Mexico until the mid-1920s; Mexico had attracted several thousand people aspiring to enter the United States across the border.

Consequently, North America ceased to be the major destinations of dekasegi laborers from Japan. Under the 1907–1908 agreement, only bona fide immigrant residents in the United States and their family members (except tourists, merchants, students, and diplomatic officials) could legally depart for the United States. This drastically changed the characteristics of incoming Japanese immigrants to that country after 1908, as more newcomers were young wives (including "picture brides") and children (yobiyose) than single male laborers. In Canada, the trend was the same, although its agreement with Japan still admitted annually a maximum of four hundred Japanese laborers and domestic servants.

Thereafter, Japanese immigrant societies in the United States and Canada became increasingly family-based, which slowly changed the basic mode of social orientation from temporary sojourning to permanent settling. The entry of new Japanese immigrants into both countries was later curtailed further. In 1924, the United States completely terminated Japanese immigration, while four years later Canada reduced the annual quota to only 150, which included family members.

TO LATIN AMERICA AND BEYOND

With North America shutting its doors to immigrants from Japan, other countries and areas absorbed the growing number of Japanese immigrants. Latin America emerged as the primary destination of Japanese emigrants after the Gentlemen's Agreements. The most important regional country in this regard was Brazil, where the first group of Japanese emigrants arrived in 1908. The recruitment of contract laborers to Peru, which happened only haphazardly between 1900 and 1906, resumed and intensified after 1907. Hundreds of Japanese laborers in Peru subsequently went to Chile, thereby establishing a very fluid community of mining and plantation workers near the Peruvian border. Some migrated from Peru to Bolivia to work on rubber plantations in Bolivia. Argentina had its first group of Japanese immigrants via Brazil in 1909. Starting five years later, the country allowed direct immigration of Japanese, particularly those from Okinawa.

With an eye to promoting Japanese emigration to the region further, the Japanese government started to get involved, albeit indirectly. In 1917, it urged existing emigration companies to merge themselves into one firm called the Overseas Development Company (Kaigai Kogyo),

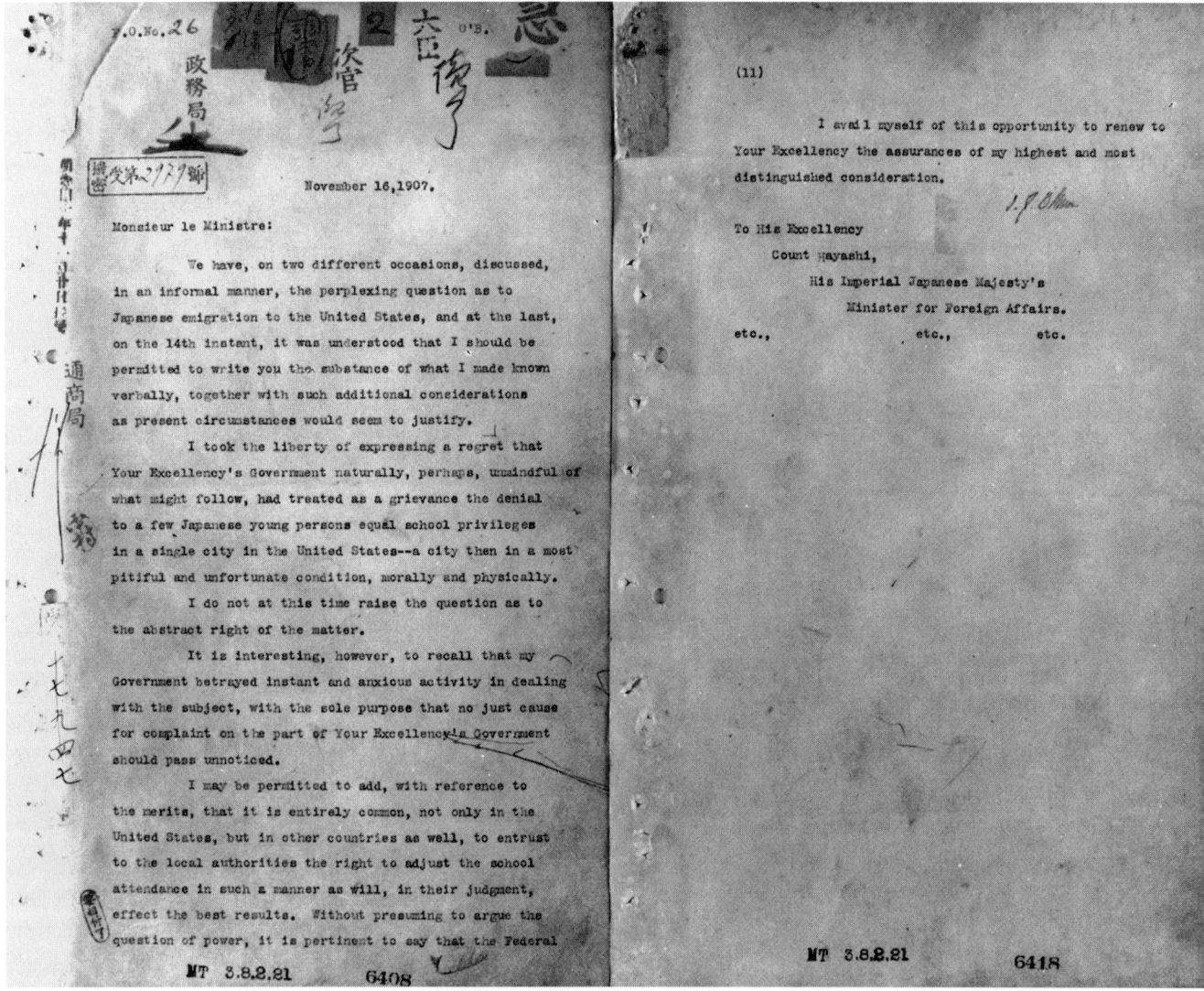

A letter sent by Thomas J. O'Brien (U.S. State Department official) to the Japanese foreign minister, Count Tadasu Hayashi, on November 16, 1907. This is a part of the exchanges between the U.S. and Japanese governments that resulted in Gentlemen's Agreement of 1908. From the text: "[I]t was claimed that the incoming Japanese work people had wage disturbing characteristics very demoralizing to existing labor standards." (Collection of Ministry of Foreign Affairs Diplomatic Record Office)

which streamlined the process of recruitment and aftercare for emigrants. In the midst of the post–World War I recession, the government decided to shore up the operation of the company through annual subsidies. After the Great Kanto Earthquake of 1923 induced the government to sponsor the travel of the victims to Brazil free of charge, the policy of direct financial assistance to all Brazil-bound emigrants became official in 1925. Two years later, the Japanese government enacted the Overseas Emigration Cooperative Act, which provided the legal basis of the formation of the semi-official Overseas Emigration Cooperative Federation. This organization was expected to encourage the building of large-scale Japanese agricultural settlements in Brazil and in other countries.

In the sphere of policy making and governmental structure, overseas emigration came to hold a more significant place during the latter half of the 1920s. In 1926, the Home Ministry incorporated overseas emigration into the social policy of the state, defining it as a useful solution to Japan's urban and rural poverty and the worsening problem of "surplus population." Then, with the increase of the Japanese population abroad, the government realized the need to "guide" its overseas residents under one institutional umbrella rather than to divide a range of responsibilities among multiple ministries. Therefore, in 1929, the Ministry of Colonial Affairs (Takumusho) was established. Although jurisdictional contradictions and interministerial rivalries continued to exist, especially in

Japanese Migration 37

Mitsu Suzawa (third row, second from left) attended the Kensei Gijuku in Hotaka, Nagano Prefecture, along with other "picture brides" to learn English before leaving Japan to marry her future husband—Shungo Hirabayashi who lived in Seattle, Washington, ca. 1913. (Gift of the Hirabayashi family. Japanese American National Museum [98.150.24])

relation to the Foreign Ministry, the Colonial Ministry managed to consolidate much of the key bureaucratic functions pertaining to overseas emigration and colonial development, and it rendered the residents a useful service in such areas as education. Yet because Japanese officials, who were always concerned about the activities of anti-Japanese agitators in North America, considered it diplomatically inappropriate and misleading to establish direct connections with Japanese residents in the United States and Canada, the Colonial Ministry dealt only with those in Latin America, Southeast Asia, and other non-Western countries.

In addition to these regions, the rapid colonial expansion of imperial Japan had prompted the dispersal of its "subjects" throughout the empire. Although Latin America ranked as one of the most preferred destinations, the increase of new colonial territories offered Japanese people other choices for migration. Following a series of foreign wars, including World War I, the Japanese empire had steadily acquired colonial territories in the surrounding areas and Micronesia. Taiwan became a formal colony as early as 1895, after Japan's victory over China, while Korea was officially annexed in 1910, as a result of the Russo-Japanese War. Japan took over Micronesia from Germany in 1914; it became a Japanese mandate after 1919. These regions, combined with portions of Sakhalin, Manchuria, and Kwangtung Province in northern China, became a locus of "Japanese development" where tens of thousands of "immigrants" settled and displaced local populations. Though many of these so-called immigrants shared similar socioeconomic backgrounds with their counterparts in the Americas, the former group essentially comprised colonizers protected by the military power of Japan, whereas the latter tended to become targets of social and legal discrimination in "host countries."

STATE-SPONSORED EMIGRATION AND ANTI-JAPANESE CONTAINMENT

In the mid-1930s, after forming a puppet government in Manchuria, Japan officially made overseas emigration a part of its colonialist policy. Except for the government-contract labor migration to Hawai`i and the travel subsidy for emigrants to South America, the Japanese government had not been directly involved in the recruitment and management of emigrants, a service that was usually provided by emigration companies. However, the colonization of Manchuria in the 1930s involved the state-sponsored emigration of impoverished farm families in a highly systematic fashion.

Following the Great Depression, the Japanese economy struggled, losing much of its international trade. The rural agricultural economy was hit especially hard, for the silk export to the United States had decreased drastically. Unemployment soared, and many people in the farm areas were on the verge of starvation by the mid-1930s. Within this context, the Manchurian development came to be seen as a major solution to the nation's economic and social problems. At first, neither emigration to Manchuria nor agricultural development there seemed promising. Shortly after the establishment of "Manchukuo" in 1932, the Colonial Ministry sent the first group of armed immigrants to the region, followed by several other groups. However unfamiliar farming conditions and severe weather, combined with the presence of Chinese guerrillas, deterred any further influx of settlers. In order to shore up the colonization scheme, the government thus had to play a progressively bigger role in the business of emigration and settlement.

Bridal photo of Mrs. Mitsu Suzawa (née) Hirabayashi in her wedding gown, Seattle, Washington, 1914. (Collection of the Hirabayashi Family)

In 1935, under the auspices of the governments of Japan and Manchukuo, the Society for Manchurian Emigration (Manshu Imin Kyokai) and the Manchurian Colonization Company (Manshu Takushoku Kaisha) were set up in the capitals of two countries for the purpose of facilitating the relocation of colonists from Japan to Manchuria. The following year, the Colonial Ministry proposed a plan to send one million Japanese families (or five million people) to the region in the ensuing two decades. The Japanese parliament endorsed the proposal, thereby starting the first five-year program. While the two organizations established in 1935 merged to form an official governmental agency, a total of six thousand agricultural families were to enter Manchuria in 1937.

The direct involvement of the state brought a change to the geographic patterns of Japanese emigration. Because central and northern Japan experienced the most severe economic depression, much of the recruitment for the Manchurian development occurred in these areas,

Japanese passport issued April 15, 1872 (Meiji 5) to Kishiro Saito, who settled in Peru. (Collection of Museo Conmemorativo de la Inmigración Japonsa en el Perú)

Japanese Migration   39

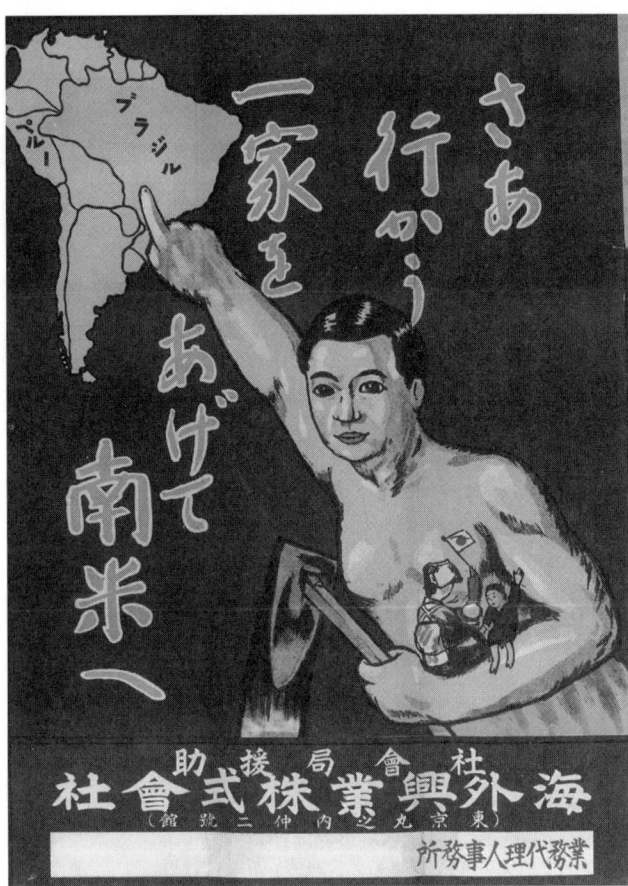

A recruitment poster promoting Japanese emigration to South America, ca. 1925. Recruitment was conducted by the Overseas Development Company (Kaigai Kogyo Kabushiki Kaisha), established in 1917 to cope with the severe restrictions imposed on Japanese immigration to the United States. (Collection of Ministry of Foreign Affairs Diplomatic Record Office)

Japanese "settlers" standing in front of the agricultural processing facility in Rikko village in Shinkyo, Manchuria. Rikko was established in 1938 and lasted until the end of the Pacific War. (Collection of Nippon Rikkokai)

Photograph of Kishi Okino (second from right), his wife, two children, and his two younger brothers, taken in Manchuria after the war just before their return to Japan in August 1945. (Collection of Nippon Rikkokai)

thereby mitigating the existing concentrations in southwestern Japan. This new geographical trend in the origins of overseas Japanese transformed emigration from a matter of specific regions to one involving the whole nation.

However, in terms of the social background of Manchurian settlers, very little had changed. As in the case of the kan'yaku to Hawai`i or "colonists" to South America and Micronesia, the majority of state-sponsored emigrants derived from the economically disadvantaged classes of the rural population, although there were some entrepreneurs and white-collar workers, including professionals and bureaucrats in the service of Japan's puppet empire. This suggests that most Manchurian settlers, like their predecessors elsewhere, were acting upon their individual (or family) interests and concerns, not simply responding to the state's expansionist ideology. In a macroeconomic sense, and despite their privileged position

Kadori Naruse, first consul of Japan in Paraguay, 1937. (Collection of Centro Nikkei Paraguayo)

Pastor Nakamura (right) and Mr. Nagata of Rikkōkai (left), standing in front of the Badan Textile Extension in Java, 1942. Malaysian hemp production was a major industry in which the Japanese immigrants in Southeast Asia were engaged. (Collection of Nippon Rikkokai)

relative to colonized peoples in Manchuria, many Japanese emigrants simultaneously filled the increasing need for labor in the scheme of Japan's colonial development in Manchuria, supported by the military and big capital.

The expansion of Japanese colonialism in Asia contributed to the rise of anti-Japanese sentiments elsewhere. The United States was particularly worried about its decreasing control over northern China, and its animosity toward Japan influenced the neighboring countries in the Western Hemisphere. Between the 1920s and the mid-1930s, Japanese immigrants had entered Cuba (1924), Panama (1928), Columbia (1929), and Paraguay (1936), but the rise of Japanese militarism quickly soured Tokyo's relations with Latin American countries. In 1934, Brazil enacted a new constitution that limited an annual number of Japanese immigrants to 2,849, and Japanese land rights in Amazonia were repealed two years later. Likewise, the Peruvian government severely restricted Japanese immigration and their commercial activities. On May 13, 1940, Lima's Japanese residents became the target of a race riot that resulted in the destruction of some six hundred businesses and residences. Less than a year later, prewar Japanese immigration to South America came to an end with the departure of the *Buenosu Airesu Maru* from Kobe.

A major community of Japanese immigrants at Davao, in the Philippines, also fell victim to anti-Japanese exclusion in the 1930s. Under U.S. colonial rule, the local government tended to follow the discriminatory policies of the United States toward the Japanese. In 1918, for instance, it enacted a land law that disallowed the "foreign" acquisition of public lands for agriculture, legislation similar to that enacted by California and other western U.S. states at about the same time. Japanese residents in Davao

Japanese emigrants waiting to board the Santos Maru, bound for Brazil at Kobe Port, 1956. (Collection of Nippon Rikkokai)

A Japanese flag signed by students, staff, and officials "wishing health and happiness" to emigrants departing for Bolivia in 1958. (Collection of Federación Nacional de Asociaciones Boliviano Japonesas)

managed to go around the law to enlarge their flax cultivation there, which generated a thriving community of over fourteen thousand by the mid-1930s. Starting in 1935, however, the Philippine government completely prohibited the "foreign" acquisition of private land, while outlawing Japanese subtenancy, a prevailing form of farming in Davao. On the eve of the Pacific War, very few countries or areas, except in Manchuria and Japan's colonial territories, welcomed the Japanese.

PACIFIC WAR AND MASSIVE RETURN MIGRATION

Eventually, imperial Japan opted to force its way militarily through Southeast Asia and the Pacific. The wartime years from 1941 to 1945 saw the rapid growth of Japanese populations in these regions. Both civilian and military personnel moved around within the realm of the empire, although it shrank day by day after 1943. Though no exact figure is available, several millions of Japanese are considered to have resided outside of the Japanese islands in this period.

In the meantime, the war placed the Japanese immigrants and their descendants living in the Americas in extremely difficult situations. In the United States and Canada, people of Japanese descent were treated as enemies, regardless of their citizenship status; they were put into concentration camps or under tight scrutiny. While most of Latin American countries severed diplomatic relations with Japan by January 1942, their treatment of Nikkei residents differed to a considerable degree from that of the United States. Located adjacent to the United States, Mexico moved the Japanese from the northern border regions and coastal areas to Mexico City and Guadalajara, while Peru, Bolivia, and Central American countries were pressured by the U.S. government to round up leading Nikkei individuals and families and send them to the American camps as hostages. Hundreds of Japanese in these areas repatriated to Japan during the war under a civilian exchange arranged between Japan and the United States. In South America, the governments of Brazil, Paraguay, Chile, and Argentina did not declare war on Japan until the final months of the Pacific War. Therefore, most Japanese residing in these countries did not experience mass internment or removal. Nonetheless, they were still put under certain restrictions, including the ban on Japanese-language education and sociocultural activities. With the termination of the war, the Japanese of the Americas had to start all over again.

Japan's defeat in 1945 caused a massive reverse migration of former colonial settlers, soldiers, and repatriates back to Japan, a process that involved tragedies of family separation, starvation, and death. Between 1945 and 1950, a total of over 6.2 million people managed to return to the main Japanese islands, but many children and women were left behind in Manchuria, Micronesia, the Philippines, and other Asian regions, where some were taken in by local people.

POSTWAR RESUMPTION OF OVERSEAS EMIGRATION

While struggling to recover from total destruction, war-devastated Japan was faced with an imminent need to disperse its growing population, which exceeded the domestic supply of food and other limited resources. During the Allied occupation no emigration was permitted, but an exception was made for "war brides," who entered the United States, Canada, and Australia, among others, with their Nikkei and non-Nikkei husbands after 1947. In 1952, the United States repealed the twenty-eight-year-old prohibition on Japanese immigration and admitted

The sixth group of Japanese immigrants who came on board the ship M.S. Ruys *in Amsterdam and settled in colonies of the Itapúa Department, 1955. (Photograph by Ishii Studio—Kobe. Collection of Centro Nikkei Paraguayo)*

185 Japanese per year, followed by over a thousand "refugees," mainly from Kagoshima, between 1953 and 1955. Meanwhile, as it had been placed under direct American rule, Okinawa received different treatment from the mainland Japan. In fact, family members of Okinawan immigrants were able to leave for Peru, Brazil, and Argentine from around 1948, a factor that contributed to the postwar increase of the Okinawan population in local Japanese communities.

The end of the Allied occupation enabled Japan to resume overseas mass emigration. The new constitution of Japan explicitly acknowledged the right of the people to emigrate at will, and the Japanese government started to contemplate the ways to facilitate the process shortly after the San Francisco Peace Treaty of 1951 granted Japan sovereignty and reentry into the international community. Brazil emerged as the first major destination of postwar mass emigration. In 1952, two immigrant leaders, one of whom had become a member of the Japanese parliament due to his part-residency in Japan, successfully negotiated with the Brazilian president for the immigration of five thousand Japanese families to the country. Backed by financial support from the Japanese government, these and several thousand more family settlers left Japan for Brazil in the ensuing years. Until Japan and Brazil entered into a bilateral treaty in 1960, Japanese immigration basically occurred through the agency of intermediaries—usually successful immigrant entrepreneurs, who obtained special permissions from the Brazilian government to invite laborers to farms and colonies.

Bolivia was the second Latin American country that drew postwar Japanese immigrants. In 1953, a newly established Okinawa Colony in Santa Cruz successfully petitioned the Bolivian government to permit the entry of agricultural settlers from Okinawa, then still under the American rule. Starting in 1954, an ambitious ten-year plan was aimed at bringing a total of three thousand families, or twelve thousand immigrants, to the colony. With an eye to ameliorating the overpopulation problem in resource-poor Okinawa, the Ryukyu government and the U.S. representative office there enthusiastically supported the venture, setting up a special "emigration fund" (over $243,000). Although the return of Okinawa to Japan had to wait until 1972, the bureaucratic jurisdictions over the matter of overseas migration from Okinawa to Bolivia and other countries were handed over to the Japanese government in 1967; thereafter, Okinawan emigrants carried Japanese passports.

Parallel to the Immigration Convention of 1886 with Hawai`i, the Japanese and the Bolivian governments es-

People standing in front of the emigrant training center in Kobe, where films, lectures, and education on opportunities abroad were presented, ca. 1950s. (Collection of Nippon Rikkokai)

tablished a basic pattern of postwar Japanese emigration to Latin America. In 1955, only one year after the Okinawan scheme, another Japanese agricultural colony in Bolivia invited fourteen families, marking the resumption of Japanese immigration to the country from the Japanese mainland. In 1956, the two countries concluded the first postwar immigration treaty, which consolidated recruitment, education and training, supervision, and after-care in the hands of special authorized agencies. What distinguished this postwar treaty from the prewar kan'yaku emigration practice to Hawai`i was that the former had been intended to promote the permanent settlement of Japanese agriculturists in the host country. This arrangement also was beneficial to Latin American nations, which had plenty of undeveloped land.

Like Bolivia, Paraguay also first allowed the entry of postwar Japanese immigrants in 1953. Groups ranged from several families to a few dozens; some groups joined existing Japanese settlements, while others entered the country as tenant farmers hired by American firms. In 1956, the Japan Emigration Promotion Cooperation set up in Asunción a representative office that obtained thousands of acres for agricultural development. Japanese arrivals peaked in the years 1956 and 1957. The official immigration treaty between Japan and Paraguay was concluded in 1959. Meanwhile, two other preferred destinations with bilateral treaties, the Dominican Republic and Argentina, accepted the first postwar immigrants in 1956 and in 1957, respectively, along with Brazil in 1960.

While overseas emigration became a business of the state, the Japanese foreign ministry established a new emigration bureau in 1955, and a special committee was organized directly under the office of the prime minister to achieve the emigration of ten thousand Japanese per year. The committee recommended that the government define the basic goals of this new policy, as appropriate for "peace-loving," democratic Japan. Among other goals, the policy was: to give Japanese citizens an opportunity for constructive activities overseas; to bring into full play their latent ability in working frontier land; to contribute

Takeaki Hidaka (foreground) operating a rice-planting machine in his rice paddy, located in the Jarabacoa settlement of La Vega, Dominican Republic, ca. 1970s. (Collection of Japan International Cooperation Agency)

to the development of host countries and the welfare of the world; and to uplift the international reputation of Japan and the Japanese. Because Japan's wartime aggression had made the Asia and Pacific region extremely hostile to it, and North America and Australia were still strongly anti-Asian in terms of their immigration policies, Latin America was the only "new world" that was willing to accommodate Japanese people and appreciate their role in national development.

With the basic agenda set in clear terms, a well-coordinated emigration campaign swept Japan. In cooperation with local governments, the federation of prefectural overseas associations conducted grassroots education on opportunities abroad through films and lectures, and emigration companies energetically recruited prospective emigrants. In 1963, the Japanese government consolidated all the functions into the newly established Overseas Emigration Agency (Kaigai Iju Jigyodan). With training centers in Kobe and Yokohama, it had representative offices in all the domestic prefectures and in major Latin American cities. Later, when Canada (1966) and Australia (1978) began to admit professionals and skilled specialists, the agency became responsible for them, too.

Although postwar emigration to Latin America was generally a national phenomenon, specific regions of southwestern Japan were still responsible for a disproportionately large number of emigrants. Okinawa was particularly prominent, as it sent a total of 7,164 people to Latin America between 1952 and 1993. Kumamoto and Fukuoka were second, with 4,392 and 4,368, respectively. Notable exceptions were Hokkaido (4,354 emigrants) and Tokyo (4,263), the areas that had had large numbers of internal transplants from other prefectures since before the war. Some from Tokyo might have suffered total losses due to the American firebombing of the city in 1945, while others in Hokkaido found cold weather not suitable for agriculture. Whatever the reasons, thousands of the people from these prefectures saw new opportunities in the agricultural lands of Latin America. On the contrary, due to the highly selective nature of Japanese immigration to Canada and Australia, the origins of professional and skilled emigrants were concentrated in the Kanto and Kansai metropolitan areas, where Japan's leading educational institutions are located.

Hidetoshi Takeda (twenty-seven years old) teaching in a Japanese-language school in Monte Alegre, in the Amazon region of Brazil, 1988. He participated in the third Youth for Development Abroad Program (Kaihatsu Seinen), administered by Japan International Cooperation Agency. (Collection of Japan International Cooperation Agency)

A NEW PHASE

Despite the continuing support of the Japanese government, the postwar emigration fever had virtually died down by the mid-1960s, when the people of Japan found their national economy recovering at a miraculous pace. Domestic industries started to suffer from serious labor shortages, which not only pushed up wages but weakened support for mass emigration as a national policy. The annual statistics of emigrants showed the sharp drop from 6,262 to 2,201 between 1961 and 1962. From the next year on, the number never exceeded two thousand, and the post-1973 years saw only six hundred or less. What contributed to this trend was the disastrous failure of emigration to the Dominican Republic under a treaty arrangement. The host government promised to provide prospective settlers with dwellings, basic furniture and household items, planting-ready land, and financial assistance until the first harvest, but the fall of the dictatorial government there caused many of these obligations to be unfulfilled. By 1961, the discontent of immigrant settlers grew to the extent that a group of twenty-two families demanded the Japanese government enable them to return to Japan at once. Flabbergasted, Japanese officials quickly made special arrangements with the governments of Brazil, Argentina, and Bolivia to allow these settlers to remigrate from the Dominican Republic. Since 1961, a total of seventy families (736 people) have availed themselves of this option, and 133 families (611 people) have gone back to Japan. In Japan, reports of their "tragic" return and the failure of the state-supported treaty system cooled emigration fever and put into question the prevailing optimism and inflated expectations. The consequent decline of enthusiasm induced the Foreign Ministry to abolish its Central-South America Emigration Bureau in 1968.

Eventually, the Japanese government was faced with the need to redefine the role of emigration in the changing national agenda. The focus was shifted from sending emigrants to providing after-care for overseas residents in the areas of technical support, capital and human investment, and cultural exchange. As Japan emerged as one of the developed nations, the government combined immigrant care with the new policy of "official development assistance" (ODA) to third-world nations. In 1974, the Overseas Emigration Agency was thus reorganized into

Shin Issei Satomi Takeda (far left) enjoying a chat with a Japanese student (second from left), Eddie Kurushima (a Nisei veteran), and Naoko Nawamura during the Nisei Week Festival in Los Angeles, August 16, 1998. (Japanese American National Museum)

the Japan International Cooperation Agency (JICA). In addition to dispatching young volunteers and a wide variety of specialists to both Nikkei communities and other countries, the JICA also sponsored diverse projects, ranging from agricultural improvement to infrastructure development, and from Japanese language education to technical training programs.

By the 1970s, the era of mass emigration was over, and the exodus of Japanese people took place increasingly in the context of family reunions, "brain (or skill) drain," education, and work transfers. In the post–mass emigration years, the United States emerged as a preferred destination of these new emigrants. The enactment of the 1965 Immigration Act, which completely eliminated racial quotas, had opened doors to Japanese professionals and people with certain skills, as well as to family members of bona fide American residents. The global expansion of Japan's export economy increased the number of business people and their family members in the United States and other countries. The economic recovery of Japan also enabled Japanese youths to pursue education in the United States and Canada, and to a lesser extent, Europe and Australia. Although a majority of these people returned to Japan after the completion of temporary work assignments or higher education, their presence has not only revitalized existing Japanese communities but created new ones. The need to serve these new groups of Japanese residents has also induced individual entrepreneurs to start locally based small businesses. These settlers are often called the *Shin Issei* (new first-generation immigrants, as opposed to the prewar immigrants).

Japan's rise as an economic power also accompanied another new phenomenon: dekasegi migration of Nikkei Latin Americans to Japan. Since the mid-1980s, many second- and third-generation Nikkei have come to the country of their ancestors, where they could earn much better wages than in their economically troubled homelands. Changes in the Immigration Control and Refugee Recognition Act in 1990 has enabled descendants of Japanese emigrants from Latin America to stay and work legally in Japan and avail themselves of basic social services, including national medical insurance and public education. En-

Brazilian dekasegi *taking part in Carnival festivities in Kobe, Japan, 1997. (Photograph by Internal Press. Collection of Museu Histórico da Imigração Japonesa no Brasil)*

couraged by this change and Japan's booming "bubble" economy, the number of Nikkei residents in Japan increased dramatically. By the end of the 1990s, there were 230,000 registered Brazilians, forty thousand registered Peruvians, and thousands more from other Latin American countries, the majority of them estimated to be Nikkei workers and their spouses and children. Underlying the changes in the immigration law was the serious labor shortage in Japan at the time and the presumed familiarity, compared to other foreigners, of Nikkei workers with Japanese culture. Although the movement of Japanese immigrants has never been a one-way stream since the departure of gannen-mono in 1868, the process of migration and remigration has increased exceedingly, because of the changing relations between Japan and host countries, and with the world itself.

Indeed, while the era of mass migration may be over, the movement of Japanese people in the world still continues in different and more complex forms, modes that defy simple characterizations based on labor or economic necessities. The development of global transportation and communication has made the world smaller, while at the same time it has expanded the realm of Japanese economic, cultural, and social activities even further. In 1993, there was a total of 1,650,285 Nikkei and Japanese permanent residents in the countries other than Japan. Among them, 816,034 resided in North America, while 737,642 lived in Latin America. Asia had a population of 58,395; Europe had 21,179; Oceania, 16,235; and Africa and the Middle East, 796. Wherever they have settled or stayed temporarily, Japanese have contributed to the development of multicultural societies, not only in their "host countries" but also in their country of origin, Japan.

NOTE

1. Professor Kenji Kimura provided valuable input in the development of this essay.

An Overview of Japanese Migration Studies, 1905–1998

MASAKO IINO, KENJI KIMURA, AND TADASHI SUGIURA

The following annotated bibliography consists of "The Top One Hundred Works of Japanese Migration Studies in Japan." It was compiled by the Imin Kenkyukai, Tokyo, a group of scholars in the field of migration studies. The term *imin* means both emigrants and immigrants as a group of people, and both emigration and immigration as a process or phenomenon. Therefore, the members of the Imin Kenkyukai include those whose major academic interests are emigration in addition to those who are interested in immigrants and their processes of settlement in the receiving countries. It follows that members of the Imin Kenkyukai are of various disciplines: anthropology, economics, geography, history, linguistics, literature, political science, psychology, sociology, as well as cultural studies, ethnic studies, international relations, media studies, philosophy, religion, and others. Recently, research in the fields of gender studies, medicine, social welfare, and gerontology also address imin. The research of the Imin Kenkyukai members deals with imin and their descendants in various areas as well: United States, Canada, Brazil, Peru, Bolivia, Paraguay, Philippines, China (Manchuria), and the South Sea islands. This variety is particularly important and valuable for the group, as the research in the field of imin studies draws from a wide range of perspectives, disciplines, and geographic areas. Thus the bibliography compiled by Imin Kenkyukai deals with the various aspects of imin from diverse perspectives.

The books cited in the bibliography were selected from the following sources of data: (1) *Nihon no imin kenkyū: dōkō to mokuroku* (Imin Kenkyukai ed., Imin Studies in Japan: Trends and Annotated Bibliography) (1994: J-17); (2) Data Base of the National Center for Science Information System (NACSIS—whose name was changed in April 2000 to National Institute of Information, or NII), and keyword retrieval; and (3) latest publication information sources.

The criteria for selecting the entries were as follows. (1) Major book-length works published in Japan between World War II and December 1998 were given greater emphasis. Books published before World War II were included in the list, though only those that are important as pioneer works and have served as basics for researchers in the field. (2) Academic works, which deal with specific themes of imin and pay attention to the historiography of the field, in addition to complete notes or bibliographies, were included. (3) Books original in their methodology and pioneering in their themes were preferred. (4) Attention was paid to the geographic areas where Japanese imin have settled to ensure that these areas were covered. (5) Translated works, research reports, literatures, and documentaries were not included.

The oldest book in the bibliography, Ōkohira (1905: J-61), shows that imin studies in Japan have a century-long history. In the early period, however, imin studies focused on emigration, without placing much emphasis on examining the immigrants' experiences and the histories of the places where they settled. Given this background, Irie's work (1938: J-20) is of special importance due to its comprehensive overview of Japanese imin, though as the title indicates, the book sees the imin process as part of Japan's overseas expansion. It is after World War II that imin studies in Japan became comprehensive and interdisciplinary and started to produce consistently useful academic works.

The numbers of the listed books for five-year periods after World War II are as follows: none (1946–1950), two (1951–1955), six (1956–1960), two (1961–1965), three (1966–1970), six (1971–1975), eleven (1976–1980), eight (1981–1985), fifteen (1986–1990), twenty (1991–1995), and eighteen (1996–1998). These numbers indicate that Japanese imin studies became particularly active and started to produce results in the latter half of the 1970s. This perception is supported by the fact that an interdisciplinary association for imin studies, Nihon Imin Gakkai (or the Japanese Association for Migration Studies), was organized in 1991. Although several small, local associations of imin studies had been in existence by then, it was the first time that a nationwide association of this field was founded. In the 1990s, many general or comprehensive works were published; examples included Kodama (1992: J-29), Yagasaki (1993: J-92), Takezawa (1994: J-76), Kumei (1995: J-31), Yoshida (1995: J-99), Maeyama (1996: J-35), Iino (1997: J-16), and Ishikawa (1997: J-21).

Imin studies can be roughly divided into two major categories: emigration studies and immigration studies. Twenty-nine books listed in the bibliography fall into the first category. The rest of the bibliography generally contributes to the understanding of imin or of imin communities in the receiving countries, such as the United States, Canada, Brazil, or Peru. Many of the works in emigration studies, written by scholars in such fields as Japanese history, economics, and geography, analyze the push-factors in certain areas of Japan. Naturally, major attention has been paid to the areas that produced a large number of emigrants, such as Hiroshima, Yamaguchi, Okinawa, Wakayama, and Shiga Prefectures. Among the books on emigration studies, Kodama (1992: J-29) and Ishikawa (1997: J-21) are of great importance, due to their scope and intensive examination of primary sources. The former deals with mainly Japanese emigrants to Hawai`i and the mainland United States; the latter concentrates on those to South America. Researchers in the field of imin consider these works basics for the experiences of imin in various countries.

Although research focusing on emigrants has the longest history within imin studies and has resulted in a large number of books and papers in Japan, discussion on emigration policy has been insufficient. Research on imin as a whole, including international relations and domestic policies as well as civilian organizations related to imin, is needed.

Regarding the research of imin in receiving countries, the plurality of works deal with the continental United States: for example, Wakatsuki (1972: J-87), Tsuruki (1976: J-82), Tsurutani (1977: J-84), Togami (1986: J-79), Murakawa (1987: J-44), Murayama (1989: J-45), Kitamura (1992: J-27), Takezawa (1994: J-76), Yoshida (1995: J-99), Miwa (1997: J-43), and Kurokawa (1998: J-34). The works on Hawai`i follow: Shimaoka (1978: J-66), Yanagawa and Morioka (1981: J-94), Nakano (1983: J-48), Maeyama (1986: J-36), Takagi (1992: J-71), and Okita (1997: J-59; 1998: J-60). The themes covered in these works include the history of immigration and settlement; immigration policies of the United States; the acculturation of Japanese immigrants, from the perspective of religion, ethnic identity, and community; economic activities; and the treatment of Nikkei people during World War II. Among these, the treatment of Nikkei people during the war has been one of the most popular themes of published books, articles, papers, and translated works. Many of these works deal with the experiences of Nikkei during the war and analyze the government's decisions concerning Nikkei people. Some works cover the resettlement and the redress movement of Nikkei in the United States and Canada; examples are Shimada (1995: J-65) and Iino (1997: J-16).

Works on Japanese immigrants in Brazil have not been as numerous as those on immigrants in North America, although their history is long and the number of Japanese imin is the largest in the world. Major academic accomplishments that focus on the Japanese Brazilian experience have been made in the field of anthropology; they include the works of Izumi (1957: J-24), Saitō (1960: J-62; 1978: J-63), and Maeyama (1981: J-37). Research on imin to other countries in South America other than Brazil has recently increased. Takayama (1986: J-74), Tsunoyama (1986: J-81), and Ueno (1994: J-86), for example, deal with imin to Mexico, while Wakatsuki (1987: J-88) deals with imin to Bolivia, Takahashi (1987: J-73) to the Dominican Republic, and Yanagida (1997: J-96) to Peru.

Since the 1980s, the focus of research on imin and Nikkei people in both North America and South America has shifted. A major research theme is the hardship experienced by imin due to economic obstacles and racism. It was, at first, considered necessary to introduce to the Japanese readers the existence of imin and their situations. More recent trends of imin studies in Japan are as follows. (1) Many works dealing with imin and Nikkei people in the receiving countries pay close attention to the conditions in Japan that produced imin. (2) Many works deal with imin and Nikkei within the broader context of interactions with other ethnic groups in the countries where they have settled. (3) Some works compare the Nikkei experiences in various countries. (4) A large number of them deal with Nikkei people in the context of ethnicity.

Ethnicity has been the central theme of a great number of publications, dealing with Nikkei in both North America and South America; see Takezawa (1994: J-76), Maeyama (1982: J-38; 1996: J-35), Kurata (1997: J-33), and Yamamoto (1997: J-93). Takezawa (1994: J-76) examines the changes in ethnic identity of Nikkei in the United States through their internment experiences during World War II and the recent redress movement. Maeyama (1996: J-35) analyzes the changing ethnicity of Nikkei people in Brazil. It is noteworthy that the viewpoint of ethnicity has broadened the interdisciplinary approaches and perspectives to imin studies in Japan. Miwa (1997: J-43) and Iino (1997: J-16) deal with Nikkei people in Canada, comparing their experiences with Nikkei in the United States, trying to avoid seeing them only as victims of racism but in the context of systems and international relations—a new perspective.

Research on imin to and in Asian countries has recently produced a great deal. In the past, imin to Asian countries were not included in the framework of imin studies, since most of them were not labor immigrants but were engaged in commerce, agriculture, and the fishing industry in Japan's colonies or in areas under Japan's colonial sphere of influence. However, a more recent trend points to the commonalities between imin to Asian countries and those to North and South America. Reports about the children left behind in China after World War II have directed attention to the process of emigration to Asian countries and to the cultural conflict experienced by those who returned to Japan. Manshū Iminshi Kenkyūkai (1976: J-41) analyzes the policy, background, and impact on imin to Manchuria; Takahashi (1997: J-72) analyzes the case of a farming village that sent imin to Manchuria; Araragi (1994: J-2) deals with the post–World War II experiences of those who returned from Manchuria. Kimura (1989: J-26) deals with commercial imin to Korea in the Meiji period, and Matayoshi (1994: J-42) describes the complex situation of Okinawan people in Taiwan. Wakatsuki (1991: J-89) makes clear the process of Japanese people who returned from those areas after Japan was defeated in the war.

As for the imin to and in Southeast Asia, Hara (1986: J-11) depicts the situation of reclamation work and fisheries on the Malay Peninsula, while Hayase (1989: J-12) deals with imin who worked in Benguett Road construction in the Philippines. Kataoka (1991: J-25) shows that the Japanese imin who were fishermen in the South Sea were related to Japan's advance to the area.

The geographical approach to the imin processes is now considered important, as it expands the perspectives of imin studies. Four books in the bibliography fall into the category of geographical studies. Two of them are written by many authors, including geographers, Okinawa-ken Kyōiku Iinkai (1974: J-58) and Togami (1986: J-79). The remaining two, Yagasaki (1993: J-92) and Ishikawa (1997: J-21), are important works from the viewpoint of geography. The former examines the geographical aspects of Japanese immigrant agriculture—namely, their agricultural productions and the marketing systems in prewar days and their changing features in California after World War II. The latter is an extensive study of Japanese emigrants from the geographical viewpoint.

These two works can be considered as major contributions made by geographers to imin studies in Japan.

It should be noted that the geographical approaches to imin have broad possibilities; their methodological problems should be further examined. The geography of migration can be divided into two major categories, the geography of emigration and that of immigration. The former comprises various themes. A few are delimitation of the regions from which emigrants came, examination of socioeconomic and regional characters of those regions, and consideration of geographical backgrounds of emigration. The latter can be reorganized as the geography of ethnicity or ethnic geography. Several cultural geographers have discussed the methodology and themes of ethnic geography. Five main themes of the geographical approaches to immigrant ethnic groups are: (1) formation and historical development of ethnic groups and geographical dimensions; (2) residential patterns and segregation; (3) formation and changing characters of ethnic territories; (4) ethnicity and regional sociocultural integration; and (5) ethnic cultural landscapes. It is important to note that these five themes are structurally interrelated in the settlement process of an immigrant ethnic group.

Since the revision of the Immigration Control and Refugee Recognition Act of Japan in 1990 and the increase in the number of Nikkei immigrants to Japan from South America, more research than ever before has been conducted on their employment and settlement in Japan. Also, an increasing number of young scholars and students are becoming interested in imin studies and are more aware of its importance in understanding the socioeconomic and sociocultural nature of imin in the evolution of modern Japan and for international relations. A great many articles, papers, and theses dealing with imin are being published in Japan to complement the present bibliography, and they should be of great use in understanding the development of the imin studies in Japan.

Annotated Bibliography of Japanese Migration

COMPILED BY IMIN KENKYUKAI

ENGLISH

1. Adachi, Nobuhiro. *Linguistic Americanization of Japanese-Americans in Hawaii.* Osaka: Kyoiku Tosho, 1996.
   Conducts research on the language policies of the federal and state governments and their influence on the culture, senses of value and identities of Japanese Americans in Hawai`i.

JAPANESE

1. Akashi, Norio, and Masako Iino [明石紀雄 and 飯野正子]. *Esunikku Amerika: taminzoku kokka ni okeru tōgō no genjitsu* [エスニック・アメリカ: 多民族国家における統合の現実]. Tōkyō [東京]: Yūhikaku [有斐閣], 1997.
   Analyzes the processes in which people with different racial and cultural backgrounds arrived in the U.S. and integrated into American society to form a nation. Describes the state of American society, which contains diverse ethnic groups.

2. Araragi, Shinzō [蘭信三]. *"Manshū imin" no rekishi shakaigaku* [「満州移民」の歴史社会学]. Kyōto-shi [京都市]: Kōrosha [行路社], 1994.
   Focuses on the Japanese immigration project to Manchuria, its inception in 1932, and the period after the project collapsed. Emphasizes their subjective experiences in Manchuria during and after the war from a sociological standpoint.

3. Burajiru Nikkeijin Jittai Chōsa Iinkai [ブラジル日系人実態調査委員会], ed. *Burajiru no Nihon iming kijutsu hen* [ブラジルの日本移民. 記述編]. Tōkyō [東京]: Tōkyō Daigaku Shuppankai [東京大学出版会], 1964.
   Investigates the actual conditions of Brazilian Nikkei between 1958 and 1964 commemorating the fiftieth anniversary of the establishment of the Brazilian Nikkei community. Consists of two parts: (1) the present condition of the immigrants and their descendants (demographic and economic aspects, social life and acculturation), and (2) the historical background (conditions upon arrival and migration after arrival).

4. Doi, Yatarō [土井弥太郎]. *Yamaguchi-ken Ōshima-gun Hawai iminshi* [山口県大島郡ハワイ移民史]. Tokuyama-shi [徳山市]: Matsuno Shoten [マツノ書店], 1980.
   Revised version of the author's article, "History of Immigrants in Hawai`i from Ōshima, Yamaguchi," written in 1957 and published by Yamaguchi University. Includes many documents related to immigrants to Hawai`i, found in the author's house, and other basic information related to Ōshima. Also refers to the history of immigrants from Ōshima to Hawai`i between the period of contract immigrants and the 1970s, and relations between the people in Hawai`i and Ōshima.

5. Dōshisha Daigaku Jinbun Kagaku Kenkyūjo [同志社大学人文科学研究所], ed. *Hokubei Nihonjin Kirisutokyō undōshi* [北米日本人キリスト教運動史]. Tōkyō [東京]: PMC Shuppan [PMC出版], 1991.
   Illustrates activities of Japanese Christian churches in Hawai`i, the mainland U.S., and Canada, which contributed to the Japanese immigrant community between the 1870s and 1930. Wide-ranging topics include missionary activities by the Japanese Christians, education, employment references, medical activities, enlightenment movements to prevent anti-Japanese movements, and more.

6. Dōshisha Daigaku Jinbun Kagaku Kenkyūjo [同志社大学人文科学研究所], ed. *Zaibei Nihonjin shakai no reimeiki* [在米日本人社会の黎明期]. Tōkyō [東京]: Gendai Shiryō Shuppan [現代史料出版], 1997.
   Examines various aspects of *Fukuin Kai* (Gospel Society), the first Japanese organization in the U.S., utilizing *Fukuin Enkaku Shiryō* [福音沿革資料] and related historical sources. Also examines its relations to other Japanese organizations in the U.S., its attitudes toward racial issues, U.S.-Japan relations and Japanese migration issues and its position on Japan's modernization, in addition to analyzing its activities and membership.

7. Ebihara, Hachirō [蛯原八郎]. *Kaigai hōji shinbun zasshishi: fu kaigai hōjin gaiji shinbun zasshishi* [海外邦字新聞雑誌史: 附海外邦人外字新聞雑誌史]. Tōkyō [東京]: Meicho Fukyūkai [名著普及会 or 學而書院], 1980.
   Discusses the content and the process in which Japanese-language newspapers and magazines (and also local languages) were launched in various countries. Also introduces the lives of intellectuals abroad. The figures and chronological table of first publications are of great value.

8. Fujisaki, Yasuo [藤崎康夫]. *Dekasegi Nikkei gaikokujin rōdōsha* [出稼ぎ日系外国人労働者]. Tōkyō [東京]: Akashi Shoten [明石書店], 1991.
   Observes that the Nikkei community was significantly affected by the dekasegi phenomenon that started in the 1980s and the revision of the restrictive immigration laws of Japan. Considers Nikkei from different countries as "affiliated races" with similar cultural traits, different from the Japanese and foreigners. Also criticizes Japan's disinterest in them.

9. Fukutake, Tadashi [福武直]. *Kaigai imin ga boson ni oyoboshita eikyō: Wakayama-ken Hidaka-gun Mio-mura jittai*

chōsa [海外移民が母村に及ぼした影響：和歌山県日高郡三尾村実態調査]. Tōkyō [東京]: Mainichi Shinbunsha Jinkō Mondai Chōsakai [毎日新聞社人口問題調査会], 1953.

Conducts research on Mio village in Hidaka, Wakayama, which is called *Amerika-mura* (America Village). A large-scale investigation on the entire aspects of village life from the pre-migration period to 1951 uncovers the social and economic motives for emigration within a historical context and examines the influence emigration had on the village.

10. Gaimushō Ryōji Ijūbu [外務省領事移住部]. *Waga kokumin no kaigai hatten: ijū hyakunen no ayumi* [わが国民の海外発展：移住百年の歩み]. Tōkyō [東京]: Gaimushō Daijin Kanbō Ryōji Ijūbu [外務省大臣官房領事移住部], 1971.

Contains various data on migration abroad, published by the Ministry of Foreign Affairs to commemorate the hundredth anniversary of Japanese migration. Consists of a main volume and a reference volume. The former addresses the significance of foreign migration, history, patterns of migration and government migration organizations. The latter contains data including the number of passports issued in the pre- and postwar period, and statistics on postwar migrants and immigration laws of various countries.

11. Hara, Fujio [原不二夫]. *Eiryō Maraya no Nihonjin* [英領マラヤの日本人]. Tōkyō [東京]: Ajia Keizai Kenkyūjo [アジア経済研究所], 1986.

At its peak, a little less than nine thousand people migrated to English Malaya in 1928, 1929, and 1940. This book presents the history and legal status of Japanese immigrants to English Malaya in part I and to English Borneo in part II, and conducts field studies to examine the actual state of the immigrants.

12. Hayase, Shinzō [早瀬晋三]. *"Bengetto imin" no kyozō to jitsuzō: kindai Nihon, Tōnan Ajia kankeishi no ichi kōsatsu* [「ベンゲット移民」の虚像と実像：近代日本・東南アジア関係史の一考察]. Tōkyō [東京]: Dōbunkan Shuppan [同文舘出版], 1989.

Examines misperceptions and realities of the Japanese construction workers of Benguet Road in Baguio, Philippines that opened in 1905, from the viewpoint of Japanese-Philippine relations. The observation poses concern for Japan in the modern world and the loss of identity among the Japanese.

13. Higashide, Seiichi, and Yukinori Koyama [東出誓一 and 小山起功], eds. *Namida no Adiosu: Nikkei Perū imin, Beikoku kyōsei shūyō no ki* [涙のアディオス：日系ペルー移民、米国強制収容の記]. Tōkyō [東京]: Sairyūsha [彩流社], 1995.

An autobiography of Seiichi Higashide, who emigrated to Peru in 1930 at the age of twenty-one. Describes his hardships before, during, and after the Pacific War. Mainly focuses on his forced internment in a concentration camp in the U.S. and the redress issues after the war.

14. Hiroshima-ken [広島県], ed. *Hiroshima-ken ijūshi, tsūshi hen* [広島県移住史．通史編]. Hiroshima-shi [広島市]: Hiroshima-ken [広島県], 1993.

Contains six chapters, including the introduction and conclusion. Provides a general overview of immigrants' history from Hiroshima since the Meiji period. Depicts the summary of lives of immigrants from Hiroshima and all over the world. Also analyzes economic and social conditions of the areas that sent many immigrants, and international conditions, in an attempt to incorporate immigration history into Japanese modern history. Above usual prefectural migration history.

15. Hosokawa, Shūhei [細川周平]. *Sanba no kuni ni enka wa nagareru: ongaku ni miru Nikkei Burajiru iminshi* [サンバの国に演歌は流れる：音楽にみる日系ブラジル移民史]. Tōkyō [東京]: Chūō Kōronsha [中央公論社], 1995.

Examines the history of Nikkei communities in Brazil through music. The author insists that the lives and perspectives of the immigrants are best understood in the particular situation in which a song is sung.

16. Iino, Masako [飯野正子]. *Nikkei Kanadajin no rekishi* [日系カナダ人の歴史]. Tōkyō [東京]: Tōkyō Daigaku Shuppankai [東京大学出版会], 1997.

Examines the settlement history of Japanese Canadians and Canadian policies toward Japanese Canadians, in comparison with those in the U.S. Regards Japanese Canadians not so much as victims facing discrimination in Canadian society but as people helplessly caught between the national interests of Japan and Canada.

17. Imin Kenkyūkai [移民研究会], ed. *Nihon no imin kenkyū: dōkō to mokuroku* [日本の移民研究：動向と目録]. Tōkyō [東京]: Nichigai Asoshiētsu [日外アソシエーツ], 1994.

A comprehensive compilation of migration studies of diverse methodologies. Consists of three parts: (1) studies on the country of origin; (2) studies on the recipient country; and (3) international relations. Includes bibliography updated to the first half of 1992.

18. Imin Kenkyūkai [移民研究会], ed. *Sensō to Nihonjin imin* [戦争と日本人移民]. Tōkyō [東京]: Tōyō Shorin [東洋書林], 1997.

Nikkei specialists in various fields examine different aspects of how World War II affected the Japanese immigrants throughout the world in terms of their lives, social and cultural activities, and language. Also examines the impact of the war upon Japanese immigrants/Nikkei population, by observing how they dealt with the war.

19. Inoue, Nobutaka [井上順孝]. *Umi o watatta Nihon shūkyō: imin shakai no uchi to soto* [海を渡った日本宗教：移民社会の内と外]. Tōkyō [東京]: Kōbundō [弘文堂], 1985.

Shows how Japanese religions arrived in Hawai`i with Japanese immigrants and took root in the settlement community by using concrete cases. Focuses on new sects along with preexisting sects of Japanese religions.

20. Irie, Toraji [入江寅次]. *Hōjin kaigai hattenshi* [邦人海外発展史]. Tōkyō [東京]: Imin Mondai Kenkyūkai [移民問題研究會], 1938.

One of the most fundamental resources to study Japanese migration history. Covers all ranges of migrants, between *gannen-mono* (first-year people) and immigration restriction in Brazil, including immigrants not only to Hawai`i, North America, and South America, but also to Siberia, Manchuria, and the Pacific islands. Utilizes documents of the Japanese Ministry of Foreign Affairs.

21. Ishikawa, Tomonori [石川友紀]. *Nihon imin no chirigakuteki kenkyū: Okinawa, Hiroshima, Yamaguchi* [日本移民の地理学的研究：沖縄・広島・山口]. Okinawa-ken Ginowan-shi [沖縄県宜野湾市]: Yōju Shorin [榕樹書林], 1997.

    Adapted from the author's dissertation submitted to Hiroshima University in 1982 with additional field research in North and South America. Discusses the purpose, objectives, methodology of the study, and the historiography of Japanese migration in the introduction. Also discusses major Asian migrants (Chinese, Indians and so on), Japanese migrants (focusing on periodization, geographical distribution, and typology), and immigration companies in the general introduction. Chapters consist of study of the villages in the Setouchi coastal area in Hiroshima and Yamaguchi, which produced mostly contract migrants, villages in Okinawa, which produced mostly free migrants, and the history and present condition of Japanese immigrants in recipient countries such as Hawai`i, Brazil, Peru, Argentina, and Bolivia.

22. Itō, Kazuo [伊藤一男]. *Hokubei hyakunen-zakura* (2 vols.) [北米百年桜（正・続２巻）]. Tōkyō [東京]: Nichibō Shuppansha [日貿出版社], 1973.

    History of Japanese immigrants and their communities in Seattle, Tacoma, Portland, Spokane, and Vancouver in the past hundred years. The research is based on a great amount of primary sources and the author's own interviews with the Issei and Nisei who still live in the areas. The two volumes give vivid pictures of the lives of Japanese immigrants.

23. Iyotani, Toshio, and Tōru Sugihara [伊豫谷登士翁 and 杉原達], eds. *Nihon shakai to imin* [日本社会と移民]. Tōkyō [東京]: Akashi Shoten [明石書店], 1996.

    Examines contemporary issues of receiving foreign workers and their settlement in Japan within a wider framework of foreigners and emigration during the formation and development of a modern nation-state and reevaluates Japan as a modern state. Includes nine articles, attempting to conduct empirical research on the relations among Japan, Asia and the U.S., and theorizes international labor migration.

24. Izumi, Seiichi [泉靖一]. *Imin: Burajiru imin no jittai chōsa* [移民：ブラジル移民の実態調査]. Tōkyō [東京]: Kokon Shoin [古今書院], 1957.

    A compilation of case studies on colonies and local small towns, conducted in Brazil between 1952 and 1956. Mainly focuses on anthropological and sociological studies on assimilation in the Japanese colonies and postwar Japanese immigrants.

25. Kataoka, Chikashi [片岡千賀之]. *Nan'yō no Nihonjin gyogyō* [南洋の日本人漁業]. Tōkyō [東京]: Dōbunkan Shuppan [同文舘出版], 1991.

    Analyzes the role and significance of "deep-sea fishery" and Japan's fishing industry since the Meiji era especially in the Southern Seas in relation to fishing in foreign territories and foreign migration. It is unique in taking multiple viewpoints of the original fishing village and fishing destination; in using periodization based on international affairs, in categorizing fishing types; and in focusing on relations between the fishermen and the fishing industry.

26. Kimura, Kenji [木村健二]. *Zaichō Nihonjin no shakaishi* [在朝日本人の社会史]. Tōkyō [東京]: Miraisha [未来社], 1989.

    Focuses on the Japanese in Korea that had the largest Japanese population in 1910. Mainly examines economic, social, and historical aspects. Compared to the policies toward U.S. immigrants, migration policies to Korea were protective and promoted by the government. Motives to migrate to Korea were created by shipping industries under unstable economic conditions and immigrants organized Japanese associations and chambers of commerce in their settlement and lobbied for trade-promoting policies.

27. Kitamura, Takao [北村崇郎]. *Issei to shite Amerika ni ikite* [一世としてアメリカに生きて]. Tōkyō [東京]: Sōshisha [草思社], 1992.

    Includes Interviews conducted in the mid-1970s with Henry Sugimoto, Torakichi Nanbu, Masato Ueda, Sam Wada, Mitsuyori Kawashima, Shichinosuke Asano, Hisago Ōta, Kunisada Kiyasu, Kenji Muraoka, Tōyō Miyatake, Shōryū Kariya, Haru Kishimoto, Yoshio Fujii, Shinobu Matsuura, Masahide Imai, Shima Jessy, and Mitsuru Nakayama.

28. Kobayashi, Tadao [小林忠雄]. *Nyū Karedoniatō no Nihonjin: keiyaku imin no rekishi* [ニュー・カレドニア島の日本人：契約移民の歴史]. Tōkyō [東京]: Karuchā Shuppansha [カルチャー出版社], 1977.

    A report on a nickel mine in New Caledonia, which began its operation in 1883 and hired six hundred contract immigrants as industrious workers in 1890. The author, who actually worked in the mine, compiled his own experiences and interviews. Includes such topics as licensing contracts, transportation, working conditions, and the condition of the Japanese after World War II.

29. Kodama, Masaaki [児玉正昭]. *Nihon iminshi kenkyū josetsu* [日本移民史研究序説]. Hiroshima-shi [広島市]: Keisuisha [渓水社], 1992.

    Consists of three parts and twelve chapters. The first part deals with contract immigration; the second, relations between immigrants and the host society; and the third, Japanese immigrants to the mainland U.S. during the 1900s. Utilizes basic primary sources, examines relations between sending countries and international affairs from socioeconomic and historical viewpoints, and presents the push-factors that shifted from period-to-period and actual conditions.

30. Kojima, Masaru [小島勝]. *Dainiji Sekai Taisen zen no zaigai shitei kyōikuron no keifu* [第二次世界大戦前の在外子弟教育論の系譜]. Kyōto-shi [京都市]: Ryūkoku Gakkai [龍谷學會], 1993.

    Analyzes approaches to the education of Japanese students abroad in the prewar period. Divides periods into the beginning, first period of colonial education, second period of colonial education, period of colonial development, and period of Asian prosperity. Concludes that what promoted these classifications were the execution of nationalist education, population problem, ethnic culture, and military invasion.

31. Kumei, Teruko [粂井輝子]. *Gaikokujin o meguru shakaishi: kindai Amerika to Nihonjin imin* [外国人をめぐる社会史: 近代アメリカと日本人移民]. Tōkyō [東京]: Yūzankaku Shuppan [雄山閣出版], 1995.

    Mainly focuses on the formation of the Japanese communities in the U.S. Examines how Japan and the U.S. were involved in the process as sending and receiving countries, and discusses, from a social historic viewpoint, the problems encountered between different cultures created by international migration.

32. Kurahashi, Masanao [倉橋正直]. *Shimabara no karayukisan: kisō Hirota Gonshō to Daishidō* [島原のからゆきさん: 奇僧・広田言証と大師堂]. Tōkyō [東京]: Kyōei Shobō [共栄書房], 1993.

    Consists of two parts. Part I introduces the life and activities of Genshō Hirota, who developed his activities in Shimabara and was respected by Japanese *karayuki* prostitutes. Their donations contributed greatly to the development of the great temple that Hirota built. Part II presents the finding of the author's field research and introduces the great temple as having close connections with *karayuki* prostitutes. Emphasizes the necessity for objective studies of these women.

33. Kurata, Washio [倉田和四生]. *Hokubei toshi ni okeru esunikku mainoriti: taminzoku shakai no kōzō to hendō* [北米都市におけるエスニック・マイノリティ: 多民族社会の構造と変動]. Kyōto-shi [京都市]: Mineruva Shobō [ミネルヴァ書房], 1997.

    Examines the lives and transformation of ethnic minorities and the formation and development of ethnic communities in American and Canadian cities, in relation to urban issues. Reexamines preconceived ideas about ethnicity in the two countries.

34. Kurokawa, Katsutoshi [黒川勝利]. *Amerika rōdō undō to Nihonjin imin: Shiatoru ni okeru haiseki to rentai* [アメリカ労働運動と日本人移民: シアトルにおける排斥と連帯]. Okayama-shi [岡山市]: Daigaku Kyōiku Shuppan [大学教育出版], 1998.

    Examines American labor unions within the framework of American labor union history and the cooperation among the Japanese in Seattle by mainly focusing on the Seattle General Strike, which started from the ship builders' strike in 1919. Also mentions the International Labor Conference, which was held in Washington, D.C., in 1919, and Ototaka Yamaoka, and *Search Light*, a pro-Japan Black magazine in Seattle. Detailed footnotes and commentaries.

35. Maeyama, Takashi [前山隆]. *Esunishiti to Burajiru Nikkeijin: bunka jinruigakuteki kenkyū* [エスニシティとブラジル日系人: 文化人類学的研究]. Tōkyō [東京]: Ochanomizu Shobō [御茶の水書房], 1996.

    Contains major findings of the author's anthropological research on Japanese Brazilians carried out over more than thirty years. Includes various studies concluded from acculturation to personal life stories, based on the anthropological theory of individualism and subjectivity.

36. Maeyama, Takashi [前山隆]. *Hawai no shinbōnin: Meiji Fukushima imin no kojinshi* [ハワイの辛抱人: 明治福島移民の個人史]. Tōkyō [東京]: Ochanomizu Shobō [御茶の水書房], 1986.

    A life history of a "person with perseverance," who emigrated from Fukushima to Hawai`i, worked hard to achieve his goals, faced a society that culturally and racially differed from him, and adjusted with flexibility.

37. Maeyama, Takashi [前山隆]. *Hi sōzokusha no seishinshi: aru Nikkei Burajirujin no henreki* [非相続者の精神史: 或る日系ブラジル人の遍歴]. Tōkyō [東京]: Ochanomizu Shobō [御茶の水書房], 1981.

    Constructs the spiritual history of an ordinary person by presenting a personal history of the second son of a farm villager who went to Brazil as a dekasegi immigrant with great dreams of success and hopes to return home. Describes how he gradually develops his life, ethics, and worldview, while caught between his home and alien culture.

38. Maeyama, Takashi [前山隆]. *Imin no Nihon kaiki undō* [移民の日本回帰運動]. Tōkyō [東京]: Nihon Hōsō Shuppan Kyōkai [日本放送出版協会], 1982.

    Focuses on immigrants' Japanism during the postwar movements by *kachi-gumi* (those who believed the victory of Japan) by tracing the spiritual history of Japanese immigrants in Brazil. Examines the adaptability of the Japanese abroad to an alien society and culture from the viewpoint of individual identities and strategies. Applies the movement to a general anthrolopogical framework.

39. Makabe, Tomoko [真壁知子]. *Shashinkon no tsumatachi: Kanada imin no joseishi* [写真婚の妻たち: カナダ移民の女性史]. Tōkyō [東京]: Miraisha [未来社], 1983.

    Transcription of interviews with five Japanese women who were born during the Meiji period and went to Canada as picture brides. An added chapter introduces Nikkei history to explain the background of their stories.

40. Mamiya, Kunio [間宮國夫]. *Saibara Seitō kenkyū* [西原清東研究]. Kōchi-shi [高知市]: Kōchi Shimin Toshokan [高知市民図書館], 1994.

    A biographical study of Seitō Saibara, who went to the U.S. in 1903. The first half describes his achievement in Japan. The second half describes his motives to move to the U.S., based on the increased interest in rice growing among the Japanese immigrants, encouraged by the U.S. Agricultural Department. Also discusses a study published in Japan on a promising rice-growing business in Texas, and Nishihara's farm management as a pioneer rice grower in the U.S. Illustrates the decline of rice growing due to various factors, including labor shortage, excess supply, and anti-Japanese sentiment.

41. Manshū Iminshi Kenkyūkai [満州移民史研究会], ed. *Nihon teikoku shugika no Manshū imin* [日本帝国主義下の満州移民]. Tōkyō [東京]: Ryūkei Shosha [龍渓書舎], 1976.

    Examines migration to Manchuria in regards to the sending of human resources for colonial domination under Japanese imperialism. Addresses agricultural and migration policy-making and relevant organizations, plans of selected migration, conditions of the immigrants' villages of origin, agricultural management in Manchuria, anti-Japanese movements by the Chinese, and conditions of the Koreans in Manchuria.

42. Matayoshi, Seikiyo [又吉盛清]. *Taiwan shihai to Nihonjin: Nisshin Sensō 100-nen* [台湾支配と日本人：日清戦争100年]. Tōkyō [東京]: Dōjidaisha [同時代社], 1994.

    Focuses on the relations between Taiwan and Okinawa and studies the military affairs in both areas, "Imperialization" policies, and migration patterns, in order to understand the relations between Taiwan and modern Japan through colonial domination. Emphasizes the fact that "Okinawans" were used as a tool for Japan to advance into Taiwan and insists that Taiwanese-Okinawan relations be reconsidered as a "negative legacy" of colonial dominance.

43. Miwa, Kimitada [三輪公忠], ed. *Nichi-Bei kiki no kigen to hainichi iminhō* [日米危機の起源と排日移民法]. Tōkyō [東京]: Ronsōsha [論創社], 1997.

    Presents eighteen articles written by specialists of various fields. Examines Japanese relations with the U.S. and other countries of the Pacific Rim with the main focus on the (anti-Japanese) Immigration Act of 1924. Contains diverse topics including diplomatic history, immigration policy, naturalization rights, redress, and Japanese literature.

44. Murakawa, Yōko [村川庸子]. *Amerika no kaze ga fuita mura: utasebune monogatari* [アメリカの風が吹いた村：打瀬船物語]. Matsuyama-shi [松山市]: Ehime-ken Bunka Shinkō Zaidan [愛媛県文化振興財団], 1987.

    Investigates push-factors of the areas of Yawatahama City, Ehime where most of the emigrants to the U.S. resided. Attempts to understand emigration from every aspect. Examines changes in the social and economic foundation during the Meiji and Taishō periods. Interviews emigrants and their families in order to understand their knowledge and image of the U.S. prior to emigration.

45. Murayama, Yūzō [村山裕三]. *Amerika ni ikita Nihonjin imin: Nikkei issei no hikari to kage* [アメリカに生きた日本人移民：日系一世の光と影]. Tōkyō [東京]: Tōyō Keizai Shinpōsha [東洋経済新報社], 1989.

    Examines Japanese immigrants mainly in Washington, from the 1880s, the pioneering period of Japanese immigration to 1942, when forced removal was executed. Analyzes wages and incomes encompassing economic methods and presents a number of letters and interviews.

46. Nagai, Matsuzō [永井松三], ed. *Nichi-Bei bunka kōshōshi [5]. Ijū hen* [日米文化交渉史[5]．移住編]. Tōkyō [東京]: Yōyōsha [洋々社], 1955.

    A history of Japanese immigrants in the mainland U.S. and Hawai`i. Begins with the focus on drifters, moves on to immigration, settlement, anti-Japanese movements, assimilation, and finally, various aspects of the prewar Japanese communities in the U.S. (education, religion, literature, and newspapers).

47. Nakamaki, Hirochika [中牧弘允]. *Nihon shūkyō to Nikkei shūkyō no kenkyū: Nihon, Amerika, Burajiru* [日本宗教と日系宗教の研究：日本・アメリカ・ブラジル]. Tōkyō [東京]: Tōsui Shobō [刀水書房], 1989.

    Analyzes Japanese religions and those of Japanese immigrants and their descendants from a viewpoint of comparative studies of civilizations based on intensive research. An excellent source to understand how Nikkei religions developed in Japan, the U.S., and Brazil.

48. Nakano, Takashi [中野卓]. *Nikkei josei Tachikawa Sae no seikatsushi: Hawai no watakushi, Nihon de no watakushi, 1889–1982* [日系女性立川サエの生活史：ハワイの私・日本での私、1889-1982]. Tōkyō [東京]: Ochanomizu Shobō [御茶の水書房], 1983.

    A life history of Sae Tachikawa, a Japanese woman who moved to Hawai`i in 1911, married and devoted her life to the Japanese education of the second generation Japanese Americans. Mainly focuses on the interviews of immigrants' Japanese-language education collected by the founder of "Tachikawa Women's School."

49. Nichi-Boku Kyōkai Nichi-Boku Kōryūshi Henshū Iinkai [日墨協会日墨交流史編集委員会], ed. *Nichi-Boku kōryūshi* [日墨交流史]. Tōkyō [東京]: PMC Shuppan [PMC出版], 1990.

    Provides a comprehensive history of Japan-Mexico relations, which extends beyond the migration history of the Japanese to Mexico. In parallel with Mexican domestic and social history, it describes the development of Japan-Mexico relations in various aspects, including the history of Japanese immigration, economic and cultural exchange.

50. Nihon Bunka Kenkyūjo [日本文化研究所], ed. *Amerika, Kanada ni okeru Nikkeijin kōreisha no fukushi mondai: chōsa kenkyū repōto* [アメリカ・カナダにおける日系人高齢者の福祉問題：調査研究レポート]. Tōkyō [東京]: Nihon Bunka Kenkyūjo [日本文化研究所], 1980.

    Conducts field research on the welfare of the older generation (Issei and Nisei) of the Nikkei population in the U.S. and Canada. Analyzes and reports the results along with the welfare system, the social status of the Nikkei population, and the social and cultural conditions of the two countries.

51. Nihon Kaigai Kyōkai Rengōkai [日本海外協会連合会], ed. *Kaigai ijū no kōka: sono keizaiteki kanten yori no kōsatsu* [海外移住の効果：その経済的観点よりの考察]. Tōkyō

[東京]: Nihon Kaigai Kyōkai Rengōkai [日本海外協会連合会], 1957.

Examines the effect of postwar overseas migration through economic records. The appendix presents case studies in Wakayama, changes in the migration budget, and comparisons with domestic migration and settlement patterns.

52. Nihon Kaigai Kyōkai Rengōkai [日本海外協会連合会], ed. *Muragurumi shūdan ijūgo ni okeru boson no jōtai (Kōchi-ken Taishō-machi)* [村ぐるみ集団移住後における母村の状態（高知県大正町）]. Tōkyō [東京]: Nihon Kaigai Kyōkai Rengōkai [日本海外協会連合会], 1960.

Focuses on Taishō-machi in Kōchi that sent collective migrants to Paraguay in order to relieve the problems of excess population due to the people returning from Manchuria and Mongolia, and the overcutting of forest resources, which the town heavily relied upon. Analyzes the process of collective migration, and stratification of the immigrants, and its impact on the original town, and their lives in the countries of settlement. A small, but important book on a sending village.

53. Nihonjin Aruzenchin Ijūshi Hensan Iinkai [日本人アルゼンチン移住史編纂委員会], ed. *Nihonjin Aruzenchin ijūshi* [日本人アルゼンチン移住史]. N.p., 1971.

Focuses on the Japanese immigrants in Argentina where most of the immigrants were Caucasians, in the context of political, economic, and cultural history. Observes the Japanese immigrants between 1910 and World War II, difficulties they faced, characteristics in each period, and contributions they made to create economic and social foundations. Divided into: I. Background; and II. History—(1) beginning, (2) development and prosperity, (3) adversity, and (4) postwar new era.

54. Nihonjin Borivia Ijūshi Hensan Iinkai [日本人ボリヴィア移住史編纂委員会]. *Nihonjin Borivia ijūshi* [日本人ボリヴィア移住史]. Tōkyō [東京]: Nihonjin Borivia Ijūshi Hensan Iinkai [日本人ボリヴィア移住史編纂委員会], 1970.

Published by the Committee on the Compilation of Japanese Bolivian History, formed by officials of the Japanese Ministry of Foreign Affairs and local parties. Consists of an introduction of Bolivian history, geography, society and economy, the history of Japanese immigrants in both pre- and postwar periods, and interviews with the Japanese immigrants in Bolivia.

55. Nihonjin Perū Ijūshi Hensan Iinkai [日本人ペルー移住史編纂委員会], ed. *Perūkoku ni okeru Nihonjin ijūshi* [ペルー国における日本人移住史]. N.p. Nihonjin Perū Ijūshi Hensan Iinkai [日本人ペルー移住史編纂委員会], 1969.

An immigration history of Peru, compiled by Minoru Izawa, Masaki Yodogawa, Eiji Kawasaki, Yoshirō Masuda, Gorō Yokose, Toraji Irie, and others. Offers a thorough overview based on primary sources. However, some materials were omitted due to the position of the committee, mainly comprised of officials of the Ministry of Foreign Affairs.

56. Nishikawa, Daijirō [西川大二郎]. *Dourādosu ni okeru Nihonjin shūdan nyūshoku-chi no shakai keizaiteki kenkyū* [ドウラードスにおける日本人集団入植地の社会経済的研究]. Tōkyō [東京]: Kokusai Ijū Kenkyūkai [国際移住研究会], 1960.

Investigates "Matsubara immigrants," who was settled in Dourados, Mato Grosso in Brazil, an immigration frontier, after World War II. Analyzes the developments in the settlement, various conditions for stratification, and relations between social rivalry and various economic issues.

57. Nozoe, Kenji [野添憲治]. *Umi o watatta kaitaku nōmin* [海を渡った開拓農民]. Tōkyō [東京]: Nihon Hōsō Shuppan Kyōkai [日本放送出版協会], 1978.

Focuses on Taishō-machi in Kōchi, where a selected partial migration policy was carried out during the Great Depression of 1929 based on the national policy on Manchurian-Mongolian development. Migration to Paraguay after World War II was an attempt to resolve financial difficulties and excessive population due to migrants returning from abroad. Describes in detail the harsh lives of immigrant farmers in remote areas such as Manchuria and Paraguay, fully utilizing migration data and interviews with immigrant farmers.

58. Okinawa-ken Kyōiku Iinkai [沖縄県教育委員会], ed. *Okinawa kenshi. Dai 7-kan Kakuron hen 6. Imin* [沖縄県史 第7巻．各論編6．移民]. Naha-shi [那覇市]: Ryūkyū Seifu [琉球政府], 1974.

Several geographers and economic historians discuss emigration/dekasegi within Okinawa and from Okinawa to other parts of Japan or abroad. Arranged chronologically beginning from the early Meiji period to the end of World War II and by destination. Shows the distribution of immigrant-producing prefectures and social backgrounds including push-factors by utilizing statistical data.

59. Okita, Yukuji [沖田行司]. *Hawai Nikkei imin no kyōikushi: Nichi-Bei bunka, sono deai to sōkoku* [ハワイ日系移民の教育史：日米文化、その出会いと相剋]. Kyōto-shi [京都市]: Mineruva Shobō [ミネルヴァ書房], 1997.

Consists of two parts: (1) the education philosophy of prewar Japan; and (2) the establishment and developments in the Japanese schools in Hawai`i. Part 1 is further divided into three time periods: the period of nationalism, development abroad, and internationalism. Part II focuses on the debate of whether or not Japanese schools should be discontinued.

60. Okita, Yukuji [沖田行司], ed. *Hawai Nikkei shakai no bunka to sono hen'yō: 1920-nendai no Mauitō no jirei* [ハワイ日系社会の文化とその変容：1920年代のマウイ島の事例]. Kyōto-shi [京都市]: Nakanishiya Shuppan [ナカニシヤ出版], 1998.

A comprehensive analysis of the Japanese American community on the island of Maui in Hawai`i during the 1920s. Mainly utilizes Japanese American *Maui Shimbun* (newspaper) with other primary and secondary sources. Its main focus is the history of education and acculturation in the multicultural society of Hawai`i.

61. Ōkohira, Takamitsu [大河平隆光]. *Nihon iminshi* [日本移民史]. Tōkyō [東京]: Bunbudō [文武堂], 1905.

    A full-scale immigration study published after the Russo-Japanese War. Reflects Japan's expansionist international position and mounting anti-Japanese sentiments. The author presents his own position on migration, after examining domestic and international colonial policies and immigration policies of each country. The author also investigates the actual conditions of Japanese immigrants in South and North America, Australia, and the Pacific Islands and concludes that the most adequate destination for Japanese migration was to South America, especially Brazil and Argentina. Reveals expansionist tendency, reflecting the date of publication.

62. Saitō, Hiroshi [斉藤広志]. *Burajiru no Nihonjin* [ブラジルの日本人]. Tōkyō [東京]: Maruzen [丸善], 1960.

    Analyzes migration and settlement in the recipient country (Brazil). Compilation of the author's research findings since 1952. The first half analyzes the historical background and adaptation to local life styles, including their diet and housing. The second half analyzes the economic and social structures.

63. Saitō, Hiroshi [斎藤広志]. *Gaikokujin ni natta Nihonjin: Burajiru imin no ikikata to kawarikata* [外国人になった日本人：ブラジル移民の生き方と変わり方]. Tōkyō [東京]: Saimaru Shuppankai [サイマル出版会], 1978.

    Introduces acculturation of Japanese Brazilians (especially the first generation) from various viewpoints. Useful for the Japanese, who tend to be easily trapped in fixed perceptions, to become aware of the reality that the Nikkei people are different from the Japanese.

64. Satō, Tsutae, and Hanako Satō [佐藤伝 and 佐藤英子]. *Nikkei Kanadajin no Nihongo kyōiku* [日系カナダ人の日本語教育]. Tōkyō [東京]: Nichibō Shuppansha [日貿出版社], 1976.

    An autobiography of the Satōs, who were dedicated to the education of the children of Japanese immigrants mainly in the Japanese school in Vancouver, Canada. Vividly describes the Nikkei community at that time as the background. Also useful as a reference to the Nikkei history of education in Canada and community studies.

65. Shimada, Noriko [島田法子]. *Nikkei Amerikajin no Taiheiyō Sensō* [日系アメリカ人の太平洋戦争]. Tōkyō [東京]: Rīberu Shuppan [リーベル出版], 1995.

    A historical survey regarding the internment and resettlement of the Japanese Americans. Focuses on issues that have been neglected so far, such as the comparative experiences of Nikkei in the Americas during the war, the relations between the American society and Nikkei society, and American groups that were critical of the anti-Japanese movements.

66. Shimaoka, Hiroshi [島岡宏]. *Hawai imin no rekishi: shintenchi o motometa kunan no michi* [ハワイ移民の歴史：新天地を求めた苦難の道]. Tōkyō [東京]: Kokusho Kankōkai [国書刊行会], 1978.

    Focuses on gannen-mono, who moved to Hawai`i in the first year of Meiji, historically situating the emigrants at the beginning of modern Japan. Also deals with the history from drifters to Hawai`i in the pre-Meiji era to contract immigrants, analyzing Van Reed and Japanese-Hawaiian relations.

67. Shinoda, Satae, and Iwao Yamamoto [篠田左多江 and 山本岩夫]. *Nikkei Amerika bungaku zasshi kenkyū: Nihongo zasshi o chūshin ni* [日系アメリカ文学雑誌研究：日本語雑誌を中心に]. Tōkyō [東京]: Fuji Shuppan [不二出版], 1998.

    Comments on eight literary magazines of the Japanese Americans published in the Japanese language between the 1930s and 1970s. Explains their reasons for establishment, the contents, characteristics of the authors and historical backgrounds, and discusses their roles and significance. Uncovers the full story behind these magazines and compares the literature written by the Issei, Kibei, and postwar immigrants.

68. Shinpo, Mitsuru [新保満]. *Kanada imin haisekishi: Nihon no gyogyō imin* [カナダ移民排斥史：日本の漁業移民]. Tōkyō [東京]: Miraisha [未来社], 1985.

    Introduces the life of a fisherman and describes the Nikkei communities as a background to his life. Insists that Nikkei fishermen were treated in the cruelest manner among all immigrants in Canada. Describes the "tragic" Nikkei history in the pre–World War II period from the victim's point of view.

69. Shinpo, Mitsuru [新保満]. *Nihon no imin: Nikkei Kanadajin ni mirareta haiseki to tekiō* [日本の移民：日系カナダ人に見られた排斥と適応]. Tōkyō [東京]: Hyōronsha [評論社], 1977.

    Describes the establishment and developments in the Nikkei communities and their experiences during and after World War II in order to understand changes in the Canadian society including the Nikkei. Attempts to historically and sociologically analyze Nikkei communities.

70. Suzuki, Jōji [鈴木譲二]. *Nihonjin dekasegi imin* [日本人出稼ぎ移民]. Tōkyō [東京]: Heibonsha [平凡社], 1992.

    Insists that Japanese immigrants were dekasegi immigrants who moved around in search of higher wages. From this perspective, an overview of Japanese immigrants in Hawai`i, Australia, and South and North Americas, from the end of the Edo era to the eve of World War II, is presented, utilizing such sources as "Japanese Diplomatic Documents." Also refers to illegal immigrants, remittance to Japan, and dekasegi immigrants after World War II.

71. Takagi, Mariko [高木眞理子]. *Nikkei Amerikajin no Nihonkan: tabunka shakai Hawai kara* [日系アメリカ人の日本観：多文化社会ハワイから]. Kyōto-shi [京都市]: Tankōsha [淡交社], 1992.

    Shows the footsteps of the first, second, and third generations of Japanese Americans in Hawai`i, and their feelings toward "Japan," relying on oral history collections. Also suggests what the Japanese should learn from the history of Japanese Americans in Hawai`i.

72. Takahashi, Yasutaka [高橋泰隆]. *Shōwa senzenki no nōson to Manshū imin* [昭和戦前期の農村と満州移民]. Tōkyō [東京]: Yoshikawa Kōbunkan [吉川弘文館], 1997.

    Examines international migration from modern Japan and the characteristics of agricultural policies in Manchuria, and the situation of agricultural villages in prewar Japan that triggered Manchurian agricultural immigration with the main focus on Nagano.

73. Takahashi, Yukiharu [高橋幸春]. *Karibukai no "rakuen": Dominika imin sanjūnen no kiseki* [カリブ海の「楽園」: ドミニカ移民三十年の軌跡]. Tōkyō [東京]: Ushio Shuppansha [潮出版社], 1987.

    A story of Japanese immigrants in the Dominican Republic, where immigrants encountered much worse conditions than what they had been told, reminding them that emigrants were like a group of abandoned people. Accuses the Japanese government for sending immigrants without sufficient research and satisfactory follow-ups while attributing the failure to domestic conditions.

74. Takayama, Tomohiro [高山智博]. *Mekishiko ni kakeru yume: Ogita Masanosuke to Nikkei imin no sekai* [メキシコにかける夢: 荻田政之介と日系移民の世界]. Tōkyō [東京]: Heibonsha [平凡社], 1986.

    A biography of Tomohiro Takayama (1898–1976), who settled in Mexico via Peru and, while working as a dentist, interacted with other intellectuals—both Japanese and non-Japanese—and studied indigenous cultures. Based on interviews, his diary, and letters.

75. Takeshita, Thomas K., and Kaname Saruya [トマス・K・タケシタ and 猿谷要]. *Yamatodamashii to seijōki: Nikkei Amerikajin no shiminken tōsōshi* [大和魂と星条旗: 日系アメリカ人の市民権闘争史]. Tōkyō [東京]: Asahi Shinbunsha [朝日新聞社], 1983.

    Focuses on legal conflicts and legislative movements regarding the citizenship of Japanese Americans after World War II. Takeshita writes based on his own experience and historical materials, and Saruya edits and adds the history of Japanese Americans and recollections from the redress movement. An earlier version of the same title was published in 1967.

76. Takezawa, Yasuko [竹沢泰子]. *Nikkei Amerikajin no esunishiti: kyōsei shūyō to hoshō undō ni yoru hensen* [日系アメリカ人のエスニシティ: 強制収容と補償運動による変遷]. Tōkyō [東京]: Tōkyō Daigaku Shuppankai [東京大学出版会], 1994.

    Focuses on Seattle, Washington and analyzes how the ethnic identities of the second and third generation Japanese Americans transformed because of the internment during World War II and the redress movement since the 1970s.

77. Tamura, Norio [田村紀雄]. *Seigi wa ware ni ari: zaibei Nikkei jānarisuto gunzō* [正義は我に在り: 在米・日系ジャーナリスト群像]. Tōkyō [東京]: Shakai Hyōronsha [社会評論社], 1995.

    Examines the battle and defeat against racism and overcoming cultural differences in U.S.-Japan relations by studying actual cases and the activities of Japanese American journalist. Searches for a place for Japanese Americans in American society, where the Japanese sense of justice collides with Western ideology.

78. Tamura, Norio, and Shigehiko Shiramizu [田村紀雄 and 白水繁彦], eds. *Beikoku shoki no Nihongo shinbun* [米国初期の日本語新聞]. Tōkyō [東京]: Keisō Shobō [勁草書房], 1986.

    A compilation of articles that focuses on Nikkei publications for the entire century beginning in 1886, when *Shinonome* magazine was first published in San Francisco. Mainly focuses on the early periods until the Immigration Act of 1924. A history of intellectuals revolving around newspapers.

79. Togami, Muneyoshi [戸上宗賢], ed. *Japanīzu Amerikan: ijū kara jiritsu e no ayumi* [ジャパニーズ・アメリカン: 移住から自立への歩み]. Kyōto-shi [京都市]: Mineruva Shobō [ミネルヴァ書房], 1986.

    Analyzes, from the viewpoint of humanity and social sciences, the Japanese immigrants to the U.S. from their departure to achieving independence and overcoming many hardships. Uniquely interprets the Japanese enterprises that conducted business in the U.S. as enterprise migration.

80. Tsuji, Shin'ichi [辻信一]. *Nikkei Kanadajin: Redressing the Past* [日系カナダ人: Redressing the Past]. Tōkyō [東京]: Shōbunsha [晶文社], 1990.

    Conducts interviews with eleven first and second generation Japanese Americans and examines Japanese Canadian identities; especially focuses on people who began to speak up during the redress movement.

81. Tsunoyama, Yukihiro [角山幸洋]. *Enomoto Takeaki to Mekishiko shokumin ijū* [榎本武揚とメキシコ殖民移住]. Tōkyō [東京]: Dōbunkan Shuppan [同文舘出版], 1986.

    Examines the failure of Takeaki Enomoto's attempt to establish a Japanese colony in Mexico to support Japan's (economic) development with migration settlement enterprises. Concludes that the root cause of his failure was ironic. Enomoto had to work as an individual without organized support, despite his high position in the Japanese government.

82. Tsuruki, Makoto [鶴木真]. *Nikkei Amerikajin* [日系アメリカ人]. Tōkyō [東京]: Kōdansha [講談社], 1976.

    Describes the history of Japanese Americans, who overcame such hardships as exclusion and internment during World War II and attained a "middle-man position." Examines the consciousness of Japanese Americans by focusing on issues such as assimilation of each generation in Hawai`i and on the mainland, and their search for ethnic identity.

83. Tsurumi, Kazuko [鶴見和子]. *Sutebusuton monogatari: sekai no naka no Nihonjin* [ステブストン物語: 世界の中の日本人]. Tōkyō [東京]: Chūō Kōronsha [中央公論社], 1962.

    Conducts field work on the Nikkei community in Steveston, Canada, which was formed as a result of the collective immigration from Mio village, Wakayama. Shows that the community maintained its own community and culture, while interacting with Canadian citizens. Comparatively examines the transformation of the consciousness of the Issei (from dekasegi to permanent settlement) and that of the Nisei.

84. Tsurutani, Hisashi [鶴谷寿]. *Amerika Seibu kaitaku to Nihonjin* [アメリカ西部開拓と日本人]. Tōkyō [東京]: Nihon Hōsō Shuppan Kyōkai [日本放送出版協会], 1977.

    Consists of five chapters. Presents valuable primary sources (including an interview with Mr. Kumagaya, an Issei in Wyoming), and uncovers the actual condition of railroad workers and miners in the remote areas (including Wyoming) in the early periods, and, more importantly, of immigration agents and companies as a major factor promoting immigrants' advancement into these regions.

85. Ueki, Teruyo, and others. [植木照代他]. *Nikkei Amerika bungaku: sansedai no kiseki o yomu* [日系アメリカ文学: 三世代の軌跡を読む]. Ōsaka-shi [大阪市]: Sōgensha [創元社], 1997.

    Selects sixteen Nisei and Sansei writers and introduces their English works with commentaries and analyses of the authors. Also provides a summary of the history of Japanese American literature and historical background for each work. The discussion of literary works by Issei writers revolves around short poems.

86. Ueno, Hisashi [上野久]. *Mekishiko Enomoto shokumin: Enomoto Takeaki no risō to genjitsu* [メキシコ榎本殖民: 榎本武揚の理想と現実]. Tōkyō [東京]: Chūō Kōronsha [中央公論社], 1994.

    Traces Takeaki Enomoto's failed colonial enterprise in Chiapas, Mexico, the hardships, and the how they overcame problems and started their own enterprise—Japanese-Mexican Cooperation Company—establishing the foundation for future Japanese-Mexican relations.

87. Wakatsuki, Yasuo [若槻泰雄]. *Hainichi no rekishi: Amerika ni okeru Nihonjin imin* [排日の歴史: アメリカにおける日本人移民]. Tōkyō [東京]: Chūō Kōronsha [中央公論社], 1972.

    A basic overview of Japanese immigrant history for a general audience. Covers thirteen aspects, including social, economic, political, and diplomatic developments between Japan and the U.S. Focuses on the Nikkei soldiers in European front in World War II, and history of anti-Japanese movements in the U.S.—beginning in the 1880s, developing to the anti-Japanese Immigration Act of 1924, climaxing in the 1930s, and declining due to the 1965 Immigration Act.

88. Wakatsuki, Yasuo [若槻泰雄]. *Hatten tojōkoku e no ijū no kenkyū: Boribia ni okeru Nihon imin* [発展途上国への移住の研究: ボリビアにおける日本移民]. Tōkyō [東京]: Tamagawa Daigaku Shuppanbu [玉川大学出版部], 1987.

    Studies immigration to Bolivia using Japanese immigrants as case studies. Includes diverse topics, but mainly focuses on San Juan in Santa Cruz to illustrate the characteristics of Japanese immigrants in the recipient country, through studies on the formation of the Nikkei, social and economic circumstances, lives of the immigrants, and their adaptations and identities.

89. Wakatsuki, Yasuo [若槻泰雄]. *Sengo hikiage no kiroku* [戦後引揚げの記録]. Tōkyō [東京]: Jiji Tsūshinsha [時事通信社], 1991.

    Regards *hikiage* (returning home) phenomenon of the 3.5 million Japanese abroad after World War II as a unique case of migration. Observes the movement. Includes personal stories, which official documents of the Ministry of Welfare lack, and domestic and international legal matters.

90. Wakatsuki, Yasuo, and Jōji Suzuki [若槻泰雄 and 鈴木譲二]. *Kaigai ijū seisaku shiron* [海外移住政策史論]. Tōkyō [東京]: Fukumura Shuppan [福村出版], 1975.

    Focuses on Japanese migration to South and Central America in the postwar period. Examines the government's policies and the patterns of migration, motives, process of settlement, and circumstances after settlement. Analyzes relevant organizations.

91. Wakayama-ken [和歌山県], ed. "Kaigai imin [海外移民]." In *Wakayama-ken iminshi* [和歌山県移民史], 947–1027. Wakayama-shi [和歌山市]: Wakayama-ken [和歌山県], 1957.

    Presents a historical overview of emigration from Wakayama, where pioneering emigrants left for Hokkaidō and ventured to Hawai`i, North America, Australia, Central and South America, and Asia. Explains the background that promoted emigration, including the significance of pioneers, immigration companies and related activities by local dignitaries, strong preference for foreign migration, and economic factors.

92. Yagasaki, Noritaka [矢ヶ崎典隆]. *Imin nōgyō: Kariforunia no Nihonjin imin shakai* [移民農業: カリフォルニアの日本人移民社会]. Tōkyō [東京]: Kokon Shoin [古今書院], 1993.

    An economic analysis of the Nikkei communities from a cultural geographic standpoint. Situates the Nikkei agricultural activities in the agricultural development of California. Focuses on the establishment of production and distribution systems in the vegetable and flower industries of Japanese immigrants in Southern California before World War II, and the role of financial institutions. Also examines the interruption of agricultural activities of the Japanese (due to forced relocation) and its resumption and transformation after the war.

93. Yamamoto, Takeo [山本剛郎]. *Toshi komyuniti to esunishiti: Nikkeijin komyuniti no hatten to hen'yō* [都市コミュニティとエスニシティ: 日系人コミュニティの発展と変容]. Kyōto-shi [京都市]: Mineruva Shobō [ミネルヴァ書房], 1997.

    Traces the formation and development of the Japanese American and Japanese Canadian communities and examines issues of discrimination, prejudice, and ethnicity. Also examines Japan's internationalization, the state of ethnic communities and their future.

94. Yanagawa, Keiichi, and Kiyomi Morioka [柳川啓一 and 森岡清美]. *Hawai Nikkeijin shakai to Nihon shūkyō: Hawai Nikkeijin shūkyō chōsa hōkokusho* [ハワイ日系人社会と日本宗教: ハワイ日系人宗教調査報告書]. Tōkyō [東京]: Tōkyō Daigaku Shūkyōgaku Kenkyūshitsu [東京大学宗教学研究室], 1981.

    Provides detailed descriptions of how religions that originated in Japan were incorporated and adapted on the islands of Hawai`i. Examines the characteristics of each religion and the role of the religions in the lives of Japanese Americans in Hawai`i.

95. Yanagida, Toshio [柳田利夫], ed. *Amerika no Nikkeijin: toshi, shakai, seikatsu* [アメリカの日系人: 都市・社会・生活]. Tōkyō [東京]: Dōbunkan Shuppan [同文舘出版], 1995.

    Presents the research results of the "Research Project on the Japanese in the American Continent" by the Precencia Japonesa en el Continente Americano (PJECA) group. Participating historians, anthropologists, political scientists, epidemiologists, linguists, and sociologists conducted individual studies on Nikkei communities in Honolulu, Lima, São Paulo, New York, and Vancouver.

96. Yanagida, Toshio [柳田利夫], ed. *Rima no Nikkeijin: Perū ni okeru Nikkei shakai no takakuteki bunseki* [リマの日系人: ペルーにおける日系社会の多角的分析]. Tōkyō [東京]: Akashi Shoten [明石書店], 1997.

    A collection of articles written during the "Comprehensive Investigation of Nikkei Society in Lima," conducted by Presencia Japonese en el Continente Americano (PJECA) in 1995. Examines the formation processes and the actual state of Nikkei communities in Lima from the viewpoint of history, linguistics, theology, sociology, political science, epidemiology, psychology, and physical anthropology.

97. Yano, Tōru [矢野暢]. *"Nanshin" no keifu* [「南進」の系譜]. Tōkyō [東京]: Chūō Kōronsha [中央公論社], 1975.

    Insists that individual Japanese and enterprises moving into Southeast Asia were more important than the official policy of the Meiji government in building the foundation for Japan's military advancement into that region during the Pacific War.

98. Yoshida, Hideo [吉田秀夫]. *Nihon jinkōron no shiteki kenkyū* [日本人口論の史的研究]. Tōkyō [東京]: Kawade Shobō [河出書房], 1944.

    Examines Japan's ideology on migration, developments in Hokkaidō, and dekasegi to Hawai`i in relation to the problem of excessive population, by applying Malthus' Population theory. Also traces the history of Japan's population censuses.

99. Yoshida, Ryō [吉田亮]. *Ameirika Nihonjin imin to Kirisutokyō shakai: Kariforunia Nihonjin imin no haiseki, dōka to E. A. Sutōji* [アメリカ日本人移民とキリスト教社会: カリフォルニア日本人移民の排斥・同化とE・A・ストージ]. Tōkyō [東京]: Nihon Tosho Sentā [日本図書センター], 1995.

    Examines the development of the Japanese Christian churches in California in 1877 when the Gospel Society was established in San Francisco, until 1924, when the Immigration Act ending the Japanese immigration was enacted. Focuses on E. A. Sturge as a case study and observes the historic relations between the church and Japanese immigrants from the viewpoint of an American missionary.

Supplementary Materials

COMPILED BY MASAYO OHARA AND EIICHIRO AZUMA

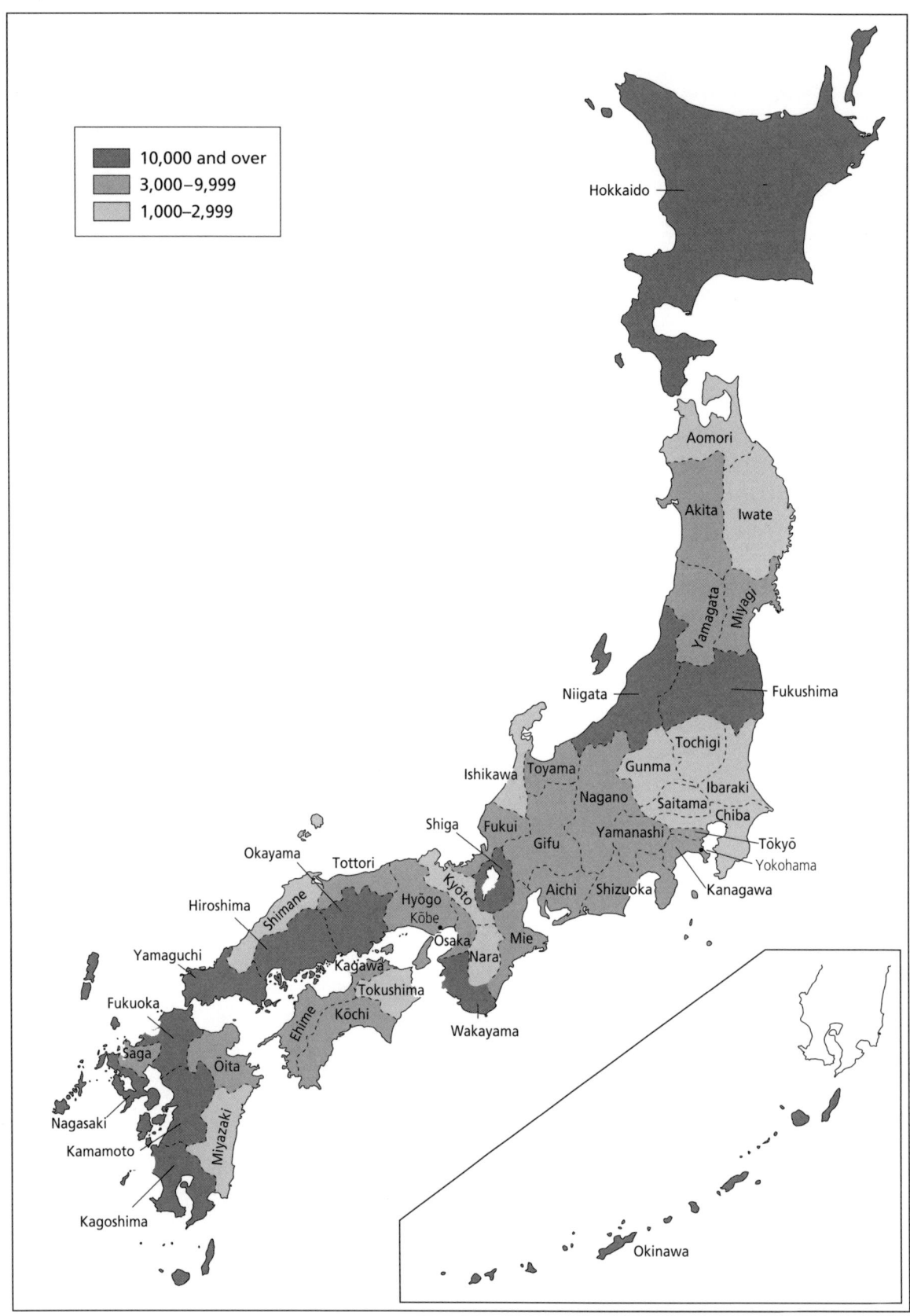

Map 1.1 Japanese Prewar Emigration by Prefecture, 1899–1941

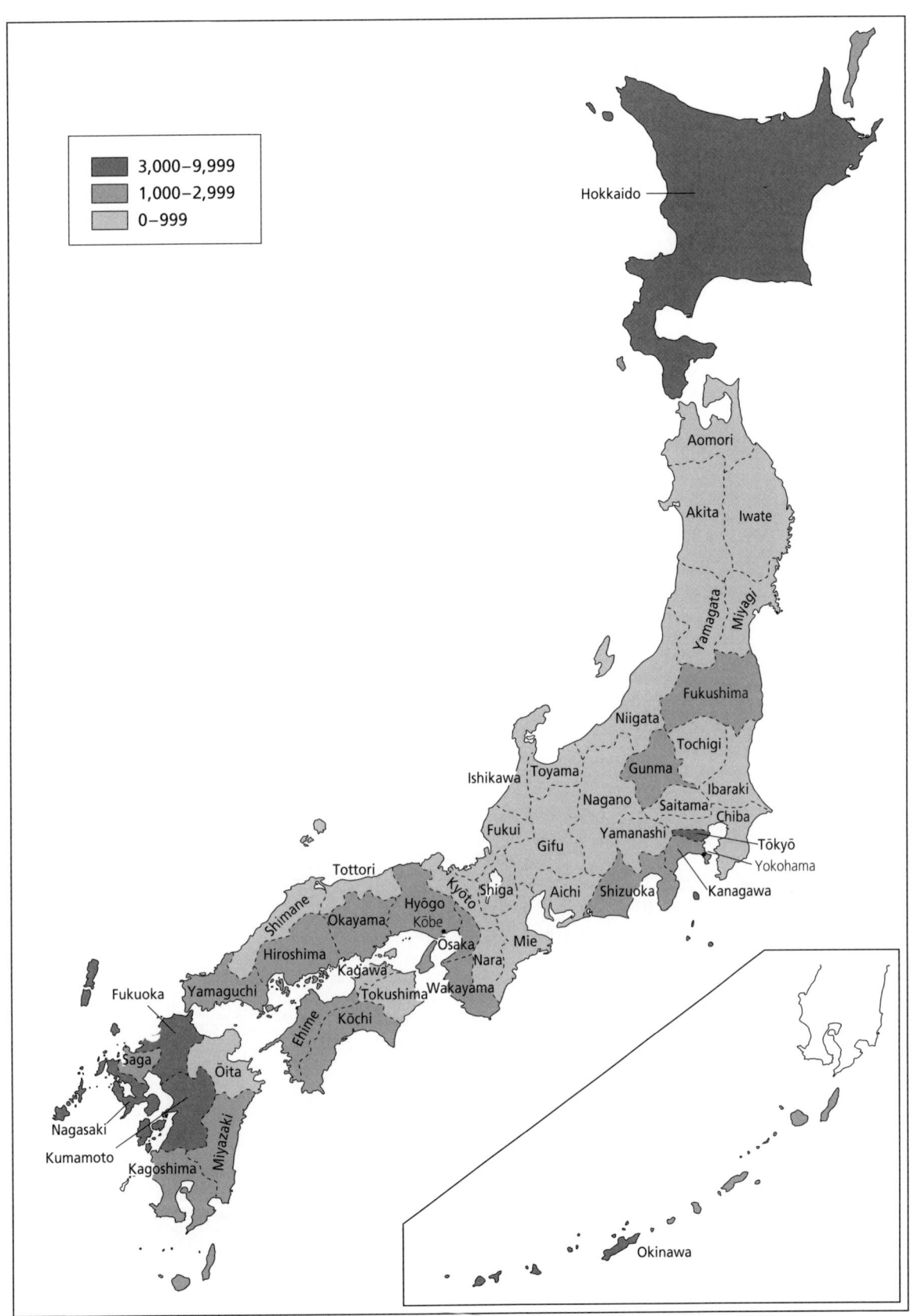

Map 1.2 Japanese Postwar Emigration by Prefecture, 1952–1993

Table 1.1 Japanese Prewar Emigration by Prefecture, 1899–1941

Prefecture	Number of Emigrants	Prefecture	Number of Emigrants
Hiroshima	96,848	Fukui	5,988
Okinawa	72,227	Nagano	5,942
Kumamoto	68,245	Yamanashi	4,557
Fukuoka	51,240	Yamagata	4,305
Yamaguchi	45,223	Kagawa	4,296
Wakayama	30,980	Tottori	4,221
Fukushima	25,923	Ōita	4,054
Hokkaidō	22,674	Toyama	3,182
Okayama	20,839	Akita	3,158
Nagasaki	19,331	Gifu	3,002
Niigata	15,633	Shimane	2,704
Kagoshima	14,085	Iwate	2,685
Shiga	13,246	Gunma	2,405
Saga	9,382	Ibaraki	2,352
Shizuoka	9,296	Ishikawa	2,047
Kōchi	9,044	Miyazaki	1,975
Ehime	8,714	Chiba	1,948
Tōkyō	8,468	Aomori	1,889
Hyōgo	8,442	Kyōto	1,815
Kanagawa	8,389	Tokushima	1,536
Aichi	7,855	Saitama	1,435
Miyagi	7,805	Tochigi	1,321
Ōsaka	7,696	Nara	1,225
Mie	6,025	Unknown	9

Source: Japan International Cooperation Agency (JICA), *Kaigai ijū tōkei* (*FY 1952–FY 1993*) (Tōkyō, 1994), 133.

Table 1.2 Japanese Postwar Emigration by Prefecture, 1952–1993

Prefecture	Number of Emigrants	Prefecture	Number of Emigrants
Okinawa	7,227	Nagano	877
Tōkyō	6,002	Iwate	849
Fukuoka	4,536	Yamagata	849
Hokkaidō	4,487	Saitama	784
Kumamoto	4,454	Aomori	680
Nagasaki	3,877	Ibaraki	650
Kōchi	2,723	Kagawa	615
Kagoshima	2,618	Mie	564
Fukushima	2,616	Ōita	552
Kanagawa	2,364	Gifu	543
Yamaguchi	2,207	Kyōto	502
Hiroshima	2,127	Akita	463
Wakayama	1,939	Shimane	448
Ehime	1,851	Yamanashi	438
Miyazaki	1,670	Niigata	427
Ōsaka	1,446	Fukui	422
Gunma	1,265	Tokushima	355
Hyōgo	1,249	Tochigi	351
Saga	1,124	Ishikawa	302
Shizuoka	1,084	Tottori	298
Okayama	1,025	Nara	276
Miyagi	941	Toyama	263
Chiba	906	Shiga	215
Aichi	882	Unknown	692

Source: Japan International Cooperation Agency, 25.

Table 1.3 Japanese Immigration to the Americas, Southeast Asia and Oceania, and Asian Continent: Prewar, Wartime, and Postwar

	Prewar (1868–1941)	Wartime (1941–1945)	Postwar (1945–1989)	Total (1868–1989)
Latin America				
Brazil	188,985	-	71,372	260,357
Peru	33,070	-	2,615	35,685
Mexico	14,667	-	671	15,338
Argentina	5,398	-	1,206	6,604
Paraguay	709	-	9,612	10,321
Bolivia	222	-	6,357	6,579
Dominican Rep.	-	-	1,390	1,390
Cuba	616	-	-	616
Chile	538	-	14	552
Panama	456	-	-	456
Others	1,305	-	168	1,473
Total	**245,966**	**-**	**93,405**	**339,371**
North America				
United States	338,459	-	134,842	473,301
Canada	35,777	-	11,226	47,003
Total	**374,236**	**-**	**146,068**	**520,304**
Southeast Asia & Oceania				
Philippines/Guam	53,115	-	-	53,115
Malay/Singapore	11,809	-	-	11,809
Dutch East Indies	7,095	-	-	7,095
New Caledonia	5,074	-	-	5,074
Hong Kong/Macao	3,815	-	-	3,815
Australia	3,773	-	1,525	5,298
New Zealand	1,046	-	-	1,046
Northern Borneo	2,829	-	-	2,829
Others	1,880	-	-	1,880
Total	**90,436**	**-**	**1,525**	**91,961**
Asian Continent				
China	95,508* (1938)	-	-	95,508
[China		497,000 (1945)][1]		497,000
Siberia/USSR	56,821	-	-	56,821
India	1,885	-	-	1,885
Europe	2,807* (1938)	-	-	2,807
Africa	213* (1938)	-	-	213
Japanese Colonies				
Korea		753,000* (1942)		
South Sakhalin		398,838* (1942)		
Taiwan		385,000* (1942)		
Kangtung		222,652* (1942)		
Total		**1,759,490**		
Areas under Japanese Rule				
Manchuria		874,348* (1942)		
[Emigrants to "Manchukuo"		270,007 (1932–1945)][2]		
Micronesia		96,000* (1942)		
Total		**970,348**		

Sources: Mark R. Peattie, *Nan'yo: The Rise and Fall of the Japanese in Micronesia, 1885–1945* (Honolulu: University of Hawai`i Press, 1988), 334, n. 6. Wakatsuki Yasuo, *Sengo hikiage no kiroku* (Tōkyō: Jiji Tsūshinsha, 1995), 16–17, 85. JICA, *Kaigai ijū tōkei* (Tōkyō, 1994), 122, 126–27.

Notes: Prewar emigration figures were compiled by the Ministry of Foreign Affairs and the Colonial Ministry, based on the numbers of passports issued to legally sanctioned "emigrants." It should be emphasized that there were many people who went to the Americas, as well as other destinations, with other types of passports, or even without one. These people were not accounted for in the statistics reported here. Therefore, actual number of emigrants is much higher than the figures shown here.

Postwar emigration figures to Latin America are based on statistics collected by the Japan International Cooperation Agency—the semi-governmental agency that took charge of sending emigrants under the bilateral treaties with the host countries. North American figures were derived from the Foreign Ministry data based on the issuance of emigrant passports. It is more than likely that large numbers of Japanese were unaccounted for due to their passport status. For example, spouses of American, Canadian, or Australian citizens are not part of the statistics. Nor are students, holders of labor visas, and so on, many of whom remained in host societies.

Asterisk (*) indicates the number of Japanese living in a given locale, in the year designated in parentheses. Because the Japanese government did not record the statistics of Japanese departing to its colonial possessions and controlled areas, the population of Japanese residents in these areas is given as a reference for rough comparison to actual emigration figures.

1. With Japan's invasion into China after the Marco Polo Bridge Incident of July 1937, tens of thousands of Japanese moved to newly occupied areas in the northern and coastal regions of China. The big jump in the number of Japanese residents in China from 1938 to 1945 underlined the rapid expansion of Japanese military, followed by the influx of civilian emigrants—a pattern also common in other places of Japanese military deployment throughout Asia and the Pacific.

2. Manchuria had attracted a number of Japanese entrepreneurs and farmers since the end of the Russo-Japanese War in 1905, which resulted in Japan's acquisition of the Southern Manchurian Railway and parts of Kangtung Province. "Manchukuo," established in 1932, was the destination of state-sponsored emigrants between 1932 and 1945. The figure, 270,007, refers to these colonists—the number included in the total of 874,348.

Japanese Emigration Timeline, 1868–1998

EIICHIRO AZUMA

1868 -Meiji Restoration marks the beginning of Modern Japan.

*Eugene Van Reed, an American businessman, sends 153 Japanese to Hawai`i for work on a sugar plantation without government permission. They are commonly known as the *gannen-mono*.

+Van Reed also sends forty Japanese for work in Guam.

1869 *Edward Snell, a Dutch businessman, takes some forty Japanese from Fukushima to Gold Hill, California, to establish an agricultural colony known as the "Wakamatsu Colony." The project fails in a year, and the members disperse.

1885 *The first group of 943 government-sponsored Japanese immigrants *(kan'yaku imin)* enters Hawai`i under the treaty between the governments of Japan and the Hawaiian Kingdom. They work on sugar plantations under three-year contracts. In all there are twenty-six groups until the termination of government-sponsored immigration in 1894.

1886 +An English businessman sends forty Japanese laborers to the Thursday Island in the Pacific.

+A group of one hundred Japanese departs for a sugar plantation in Queensland, Australia.

1889 *There are 2,039 Japanese living in the continental United States. They are mostly students and political activists.

1892 +A total of six hundred Japanese leaves for New Caledonia to work in a nickel mine.

1893 **About 130 Japanese workers in Hawai`i enter Guatemala.

-The Colonization Society is formed in Tokyo, under the leadership of ex-Foreign Minister Takeaki Enomoto.

1894 + More than 305 Japanese go to Fiji.

-The Japanese government issues the Emigrant Protection Ordinance (Imin Hogo Kisoku), which relegates the basic function of emigrant recruitment to emigration companies.

+The Sino-Japanese War begins. Many Japanese enter Korea and Manchuria.

1896 -The Japanese government passes the Emigrant Protection Act (Imin Hogoho), which regulates the activities of emigration companies and protects the interests of emigrants. This law does not attempt to promote emigration, however.

1897 **The first group of twenty-eight Japanese enters Chiapas, Mexico, to establish an agricultural colony. It is often called "the Enomoto Colony," since it is organized by the former foreign minister, Takeaki Enomoto.

1899 **The first group of 790 Japanese immigrates to Peru. Among this group, ninety-one immigrants, along with two immigration supervisors, migrate to the rubber forest of Bolivia.

1903 +Over three thousand Japanese go to the Philippines to engage in a highway construction.

**Over 120 Japanese leave for Chile to work as coal miners.

1904 +Some 150 Japanese enter Davao, in the Philippines. The settlement later becomes the largest Japanese community in the country.

+The Russo-Japanese War begins; it results in virtual Japanese control of Korea and of Manchuria along the South Manchurian Railroad. Subsequently, thousands of Japanese enter the region.

1907–08 *The Gentlemen's Agreement between Japan and the United States in 1907–1908, and the Hayashi-Lemiuex Agreement between Japan and Canada in 1908, decrease the entry of Japanese laborers into these countries. Instead, thousands head for Mexico, through which they attempt to migrate illegally into the United States. Others seek alternative destinations, including South America and East and Southeast Asia.

1908 **The first emigrants leave Japan for Brazil.

1909 **Some 160 Japanese remigrate from Brazil to Argentina. In 1914, the first group of Argentina-bound emigrants leaves Japan.

1910 -Japan officially colonizes Korea, prompting the displacement of Korean farmers.

1914 -World War I begins.

+Japan occupies Micronesia after defeating the German fleet there. The region becomes a de facto colony of the empire; thousands of Japanese migrate there until the mid-1940s.

1924 *The termination of Japanese immigration into the United States prompts many Japanese to head for South America—particularly Brazil.

1925 **The Japanese government starts to subsidize transportation for the emigrants bound for Brazil.

1927 -The Japanese government enacts the Overseas Emigration Cooperatives Act, which provides a background for the formation of the Overseas Emigration Cooperatives Federation. This organization promotes the establishment of Japanese agricultural settlements in Brazil and other countries.

1928 *Severe restrictions are put into effect on the entry of Japanese to Canada.

1929 -The Ministry of Colonial Affairs (Takumusho) is established within the Japanese government.

**A group of twenty-five Japanese enters Columbia.

1931 -The Manchurian Incident marks the beginning of the Japanese invasion of China.

1932 +The establishment of "Manchukuo." The Japanese Colonial Ministry sends the first group of armed immigrants to the region to establish a Japanese agricultural settlement.

1935 -The Society of Manchurian Emigration (Manshu Imin Kyokai) and the Manchurian Colonization Company (Manshu Takushoku Kabushiki Gaisha) are set up in the capitals of Japan and "Manchukuo" to facilitate the migration of Japanese colonialists there.

1936 **The first Japanese immigrants enter Paraguay.

1937 +The Japanese government starts a five-year program to promote Japanese migration into Manchuria, a step that marks the beginning of the state-sponsored emigration policy. Under the first-year plan, a total of six thousand agricultural families will enter the region. Thousands of others depart, mainly from impoverished farm regions in central and northern Japan, until the defeat of Japan.

1938 **Brazil enacts a new immigration law that severely restricts the entry of Japanese.

1940 **An anti-Japanese riot erupts in Lima, Peru.

1941 -The Pacific War begins. Until the defeat of Japan, thousands of Japanese move from their homeland to Southeast Asia, Micronesia, and China, and immigration to South America ends.

1945 -Japan surrenders.

1947 *Japanese "war brides" are allowed to enter the United States under a special law.

1950 -A total of 6,249,000 Japanese, including soldiers, return to Japan, mostly from former colonial territories and occupied areas.

1951 -San Francisco Peace Treaty ends the occupation of Japan by the Allied powers.

1952 **The government of Brazil approves a plan to bring nine thousand families for agricultural development in northern and central Brazil. The first group of fifty-four Japanese leaves for the South American country, marking the beginning of postwar Japanese immigration to South America.

*The United States allows the entry of 185 Japanese per year, under the Walter-McCarran Act.

1954 **The first postwar immigrants (eighteen people) to Paraguay leave Japan.

1955 **The Japanese foreign ministry establishes the new Emigration Bureau, which oversees the departure and treatment of Japanese immigrants in host countries.

*Under a new refugee act, a total of 1,006 Japanese are granted entry to the United States by October 1956. Most of them are from Kagoshima Prefecture.

1956 **The first immigrants (185) to the Dominican Republic leave Japan.

+Short-term mining laborers leave for West Germany under a bilateral treaty.

1957 **The first postwar immigrants (159) to Bolivia leave Japan.

1961–62 **A total of 595 Japanese return to Japan from the Dominican Republic, while many others remigrate to other South American countries. News of miserable living conditions and the general growth of Japanese economy prompt the end of mass Japanese immigration to South America.

1963 -A semigovernmental agency affiliated with the Foreign Ministry takes over the recruiting and sending of emigrants to Latin America. The agency later becomes the Japan International Cooperation Agency.

1965 *A new U.S. immigration law abolishing the national quota system becomes effective.

1966 *The emigration of Japanese professionals and skilled laborers to Canada begins.

+Australia repeals the "white Australian" policy by opening the door to Asian immigrants.

**Venezuela repeals its white-only immigration policy.

1978 +The Japan International Cooperation Agency starts sending Japanese professionals and skilled laborers to Australia.

1988 **The dekasegi migration of Japanese Brazilians to Japan becomes a conspicuous social phenomenon. Subsequently, many Nikkei workers also come to Japan from other Latin American countries, including Peru, Argentina, Bolivia, and Paraguay.

1990 -The Japanese government amends the immigration law, which enables Nikkei laborers to stay and work legally in Japan. Combined with the "bubble" economy of Japan, this change prompts more Japanese Latin Americans to come to Japan.

Legend:

* United States (including Hawai`i) and Canada

** Central and South America (including Mexico)

+ Other

- General

CHAPTER 2

Japanese Argentines

DEVELOPED IN COLLABORATION WITH THE CENTRO NIKKEI ARGENTINO AND THE ASOCIACIÓN UNIVERSITARIA NIKKEI

JAPANESE ARGENTINE HISTORY BEGAN IN 1908–1909 WITH THE ARRIVAL OF immigrants from Okinawa and Kagoshima—the major prefectural origins of Argentine Nikkei. The first Japanese entered the country via Brazil, and succeeding groups of immigrants tended to reach Argentina through the neighboring nations. In the prewar years, Nikkei were concentrated in urban small businesses, especially dry cleaning and cafes in Buenos Aires, while some worked as domestic servants, factory workers, and longshoremen. A minority of Japanese also engaged in horticulture, floriculture, and fishery. In regions with a substantial Japanese population, institutions such as prefectural associations and Japanese language schools were established and served as loci of Nikkei community formations and ties. During the U.S.-Japanese conflict, Argentina remained neutral until 1943, which limited the impact of war on the lives of Nikkei. However, restrictions included the ban on meetings, Japanese education, newspaper publication, as well as a freeze on Japanese assets—which remained effective between 1944 and 1946. Meanwhile, Japanese residents strove to become more integrated into society and to make Argentina their permanent home. Between 1960s and 1970s, the influx of new immigrants rejuvenated the Nikkei community. Many were attracted by the economic opportunities in agriculture. The postwar years witnessed the upward mobility of the Argentine-born generations, many of whom received higher education and believed in the Catholic faith. With the growing popularity of white-collar employment, the career choices of younger Japanese Argentines are now more diversified, although some Nisei and Sansei decided to work in Japan, reflecting domestic recessions since the 1980s.

Japanese Argentine Historical Overview

ISABEL LAUMONIER

INTRODUCTION

Since the end of the nineteenth century there have been Japanese in Argentina, but these have been isolated individuals that cannot be included in the category of "immigration." However, the Japanese population in Argentina has been always low in relation to the huge influx of foreigners who arrived on these shores during the thirty-year period after the enactment of the Law of Immigration in 1867.

Japanese immigration to Argentina officially began in 1908–1909 with the arrival of Japanese from Okinawa and of families from Kagoshima Prefecture. This first wave of settlement occurred indirectly, since they originally immigrated to Brazil before migrating to Argentina. These early arrivals constituted the greater part of Japanese immigrants who came to this country. Those immigrants settling in Peru or in countries bordering Argentina decided to move when their contracts expired, in search of better opportunities. In this way "links" were formed by those who first established themselves and made the necessary arrangements for the subsequent arrival of family members and neighbors.

EARLY BUSINESSES AND OCCUPATIONS

During the first years of their stay in the country, patterns became apparent that would characterize the employ-

Japanese immigrants making the difficult trek through the Andes Mountains to enter Argentina after arriving in Chile in 1915. (Collection of Asociación Japonesa en Argentina)

ment of different groups. For example, like many immigrants of other nationalities, the early arrivals found work loading or unloading goods in the port of Buenos Aires or in adjacent areas. At the end of the nineteenth century the first factories of importance were built on or near waterfronts. Factory personnel records—of Alpargatas or Bagley, for example—show a significant number of Japanese workers, as do the personnel records of the country's first cold-storage warehouses, located around Riachuelo in Boca and Barracas.

In the early twentieth century, wealthy Buenos Aires society tended to employ domestic servants of Japanese origin, in particular chauffeurs and gardeners. But working for others gradually gave way to self-employment. The early formation of associations, like the first *kenjin-kai* (prefectural association) from the Kagoshima Prefecture, which began in 1911, contributed to the creation of small independent businesses. For decades, these enterprises

Driver's license of Ryoko Miyagui, which he had to obtain in order to be a chauffeur, July 25, 1921. (Collection of Asociación Universitaria Nikkei)

Women workers at a metallurgical plant of Pedro Vesena & Sons Ltd., 1919. (Collection of Asociación Japonesa en Argentina)

In the 1920s, the dry cleaning business was highly popular among Japanese residents. The Japanese owner of the "Kioto" drycleaners located at 2047 Lavalle, in Buenos Aires, arrived in Argentina in 1914. (Collection of Sato Family)

Café Tokio, located in Junín province of Buenos Aires, was owned by Yoichi Miura, who arrived in Argentina in 1926. A "ladies orchestra" performs on the elevated stage. (Collection of Asociación Universitaria Nikkei)

Interior of the Japanese antique shop, La Maison Satsuma, owned by Kenkichi Yokohama, Buenos Aires, Argentina, 1917. Japanese art was known in Argentina before the arrival of Japanese immigrants. (Collection of Asociación Universitaria Nikkei)

gave employment to a large part of the Japanese community in urban areas. That is how the first laundries were formed, which later became dry cleaners, a phenomenon synonymous in Argentina with the Japanese community. The "Japanese dry cleaner" still exists in the national imagination.

At the end of the first decade of the twentieth century, another area of employment became important—the café. Japanese cafés flourished in all of the country's large cities. They could be found in Entre Ríos, Córdoba, Corrientes, and of course Buenos Aires. The most important of these cafés had "ladies' orchestras," and others were meeting places for the Bohemian society.

In addition to small or medium-sized businesses within the urban centers, we must also include Japanese importers and businessmen (a group distinct from those already mentioned), who had settled early in Argentina. Within three years of their arrival, their famous Japanese bazaars—"Casa Togo" in Florida Street, "El Nuevo Japón" in Carlos Pellegrini, and "Bazar Tokyo" in Flores—were well established in the heart of the city. There were also import houses for trade from Yokohama and Kobe.

Another branch of the community chose nonurban occupations. In 1919, a Japanese immigrant from Kagoshima established a fishing trade. However, most rural Japanese worked in horticulture and floriculture. Over the years a great number of nurseries were established in the city of Buenos Aires, in Greater La Plata, extending outward in a radius of sixty kilometers from the capital and throughout the province of Buenos Aires. It can be said that the current Nikkei population in Argentina is the result of these early commercial or factory enterprises.

SETTLEMENT PATTERNS

In the country's interior, the number of Nikkei residents was always small. One of the oldest settlements is probably Córdoba, a province in which the first Japanese settler in Argentina, Kinzo Makino, bought land in 1890. Although his arrival does not mark the beginning of Japan-

The Hisaki family was one of the first families to settle in the Escobar province of Buenos Aires and cultivate flowers, 1929. (Collection of Sato Family)

Railroad worker's union card belonging to Kinzo Makino, the first Japanese settler in Argentina, who moved to the province of Córdoba in 1890 and was employed by the Central Argentine Railroad as a machinist in 1900. (Collection of Asociación Japonesa en Argentina)

ese immigration to Argentina, his employment as a machinist in the Central Argentine Railroad enabled him to help many of his countrymen. This fact was acknowledged by the emperor of Japan in a decoration awarded to Kinzo Makino by the Count Nakamura in 1910 "for his contribution to the progress of immigrants." In the capital of Córdoba province, the Japanese owned some of the most famous and flourishing cafés.

The northern provinces of Tucumán and Jujuy were settled early by Japanese immigrants from Bolivia and Peru who worked in the sugar industry. The few who bought real estate in these areas were exposed to greater exogamy and tended to intermix with the local population.

Another center where immigrants settled was the province of Mendoza, especially in General Alvear. These early settlers came on the first trans-Pacific crossings in 1916. They landed in Chile and crossed the cordillera by mule train.

A few Japanese families also settled in the northeastern province of Misiones, cultivating rice, *yerba mate* (tea), and producing silk. From the 1930s, Japanese settlers arrived from Paraguay, and in 1959 they established the Garuhapé Colony.

Kinzo Makino and his wife, Amalia Rodriguez, with their sons, Armando, Roger, Pedro, and Jose, at the zoo in Córdoba, 1915. (Collection of Asociación Japonesa en Argentina)

Members of a Japanese agricultural settlement in Chaco province, Argentina, 1926. (Collection of Asociación Japonesa en Argentina)

In all the regions where Japanese families settled, they quickly formed prefectural associations; in the case of immigrants from Okinawa, who constituted the largest group, these associations were formed according to the town of origin. Through the end of World War II, they represented 57 percent of all immigrants from Japan. In 1916, the Japanese Argentine Association (Asociación Japonesa Argentina, or AJA) was established as a center of community activity. Immigrant communities also founded institutions dedicated to the teaching of the Japanese language (with classes usually held on Saturdays), such as the Japanese-Argentine Bilingual Academy, founded in 1938.

The first Argentine Nisei was born in 1911. However, despite the birth of the second generation on Argentine soil, the general intent of the Japanese immigrant was to return to Japan. In order to facilitate the return to their country of origin, many families used to send their eldest sons to study in Japan.

THE IMPACT OF WORLD WAR II ON THE JAPANESE COMMUNITY

When World War II began, a great number of Japanese wanted to return to Japan. But for the most part, the Japanese community demonstrated their ability to adapt to and integrate themselves into Argentine society. At the time, the Japanese represented the only Asian ethnic minority in Argentina; immigration policies tended to favor Europeans. In 1938, approximately six thousand Japanese were living in Argentina among a total of nearly six million foreigners. In spite of their small numbers, they stood out from the rest because of their unique physical characteristics. Even though the Nisei were born in Argentina and citizens by birth, they were labeled "Japanese." Fur-

The Nihongo Gakko, a Japanese-language school located at 840 Patagones Street, was closed after Argentina declared war on Japan and Germany in 1945. This photo of teachers and students was taken circa 1936. (Collection of Asociación Japonesa en Argentina)

thermore, Japanese were concentrated in certain employment sectors, which made them more identifiable.

In general, there were no overt manifestations of racism among Argentines, who came themselves from all over the world, due to the great wave of immigration at the start of the twentieth century. The Japanese were on the whole recognized as hard working, honest, and discreet. However, there were a few isolated cases, such as the one recorded at a meeting of the Dry Cleaners' Council, which warned that the massive entry of Japanese into the professional association could create undesirable competition.

Argentina was neutral during World War II. In January 1944, it ceased to have diplomatic relations with Germany and Japan, suspending banking and business trade with both countries, and cutting off all telegraphic, telephone, and radio communications. In March 1945, Argentina declared war on Japan and Germany. In April, the Japanese ambassador, Baron Shu Tomii, and his family were transferred by presidential train to La Falda, in the province of Córdoba, and lodged in the region's best hotel. Some businesses were seized, and the three Japanese-language newspapers were closed.

In general, the Japanese community did not suffer from any major signs of hostility, but meetings were forbidden; also, as a form of control, the Japanese had to present themselves regularly at the police stations corresponding to their respective places of residence. Some Nisei still remember the Japanese classes offered secretly on Saturdays, as well as the pain caused by the closure of the bilingual school on Patagones Street in Buenos Aires. Births of Nisei born during this period could not be registered in the families' registry *(koseki)* in Japan via the Japanese consulate. In 1947, all prohibitions and embargos against Japanese capital and goods were lifted, the newspapers were reinstated, the building on Patagones Street was reopened, and Japanese community institutions regained their legal status.

This period coincided with a time of great dynamism and economic prosperity for the Japanese already estab-

President Juan Domingo Perón (seated in the middle, front row) was the first Argentine president to visit the Asociación Japonesa en la Argentina (Japanese Association in Argentina) in 1953. (Collection of Asociación Universitaria Nikkei)

lished in Argentina, as well as for those who emigrated after the war. Relations with local authorities were strengthened. Gen. Juan Perón, president of Argentina during these years, facilitated the repatriation of those Japanese Argentines who had gone to Japan to study and who, due to the war, had found themselves unable to return to Argentina. The María Eva Duarte de Perón Social Aid Foundation sent several tons of provisions and goods to Japan to help alleviate the scarcity of supplies in the period following the war, an effort that owed a great deal to the hard work of Japanese residents of Argentina.

But the most significant change in the Japanese community was its members' acceptance that their stays in Argentina were not temporary but permanent. Many Nisei had been educated at good secondary schools and had gone to university. They were participating in sports and club competitions in greater numbers; they had strengthened the preexisting associations (cleaners' and florists' associations, for example). The cafés, however, were disappearing, due to tax pressures and the lack of laborers.

The majority of the Nisei were baptized in the Catholic faith. Many in the Japanese community made annual pilgrimages to the sanctuary of the Virgin of Luján in the Buenos Aires province. This period coincided with a time of economic prosperity for Argentina, with a certain political stability, in great contrast to the difficult postwar conditions in Japan. Thus, the conditions for immigration to Argentina were favorable; the flow peaked in 1961, when 1,228 new immigrants arrived, a high not reached again thereafter.

TRANSFORMATIONS AND CHANGES

The 1960s were a time of change for the Japanese community. A significant number of the Nisei, descendants of the first and second waves of Issei, who had come to Argentina before World War II and in the decade following, were attending universities or already had earned university degrees. Japanese immigrants had deliberately kept a low profile. Quietly settled in the community, they were recognized for their honorableness and dedication to

The "Japanese Catholic Circle" founded in 1936, still meets at "Nuestra Señora de las Victorias." (Collection of Asociación Universitaria Nikkei)

their work. Their social lives unfolded mainly within their own circles, and for the most part they did not participate in national politics.

Now, however, the Nisei from the colonies of greater Buenos Aires who studied at the University of La Plata, and also those who studied at the University of Buenos Aires, began to question not only the national political situation but especially their own identity. Periodicals of very short duration were published (such as *Horizonte*). Associations were formed, and ideological issues were debated. Ten years later, the Nisei suffered as a result of the loss of democracy and the ensuing repression within Argentina. Amnesty International has reported that fourteen Nikkei "disappeared" (by this date there were approximately 8,800 Japanese families living in Argentina). In addition, the Nikkei declared their support for Argentina in 1982 when the country went to war with England over the Falkland Islands. The first assembly of Nisei took place in 1980, in Rosario (Santa Fe). In 1985, the Nikkei-Argentine Center (Centro Nikkei Argentino) was founded, creating an institutional space for the descendants of Japanese in Argentina.

From the mid-1970s, Japan's prosperity contrasted markedly with the fluctuating situation in Argentina. This was due more to politics than to economic problems. Immigration began to drop, but at the same time certain Japanese institutions, such as the Japan International Cooperation Agency (JICA), were developed and consolidated. From 1960 to 1970 agricultural communities were formed (Garuhapé Colony, and various others in the so-called belt of Greater La Plata), as well as other institutions such as La Plata Association of Nipponese Academics (Asociación Nipona de Universitarios de La Plata, or ANULP). In 1984, the bilingual school of Nichia Gakuin was reopened.

A 1986 census of the Japanese community carried out by the National Board of Immigration shows that it then had forty-five thousand members, of which eight thou-

The Japanese garden, located in one of the most valued areas of the city, the Palermo zone of the federal capital, is the pride of the Japanese residents. Conferences and events related to the diffusion of Japanese culture are held in the Cultural Pavilion. (Collection of Asociación Universitaria Nikkei)

sand were Issei, twenty thousand Nisei, ten thousand Sansei, and seven thousand Yonsei and Gosei. In general, their socioeconomic situation was fairly prosperous and consisted in large part of family-owned businesses. Endogamy continued to be an important value (only 4 percent of married Japanese had spouses not belonging to their ethnic group). Most Nikkei were settled in Buenos Aires and in the surrounding twenty-five districts—that is, the First and Second Tiers of the province of Buenos Aires, as well as in communities somewhat farther away. These areas account for 65 percent of Japanese immigrants and their descendants. Outside of these locations, there were small nuclei of Japanese settled in the provinces of Santa Fe, Córdoba, Mendoza, Neuquén, Corrientes, Misiones, and Tucumán, although it was possible to find Japanese settlers throughout the entire country.

According to the census, the grandchildren of Japanese immigrants (Sansei) were more diversified in their choice of occupation than their elders and more likely to be in salaried positions; the immigrants and their children predominated in independent employment, such as family-owned businesses. Finally, the census noted "although on a small scale, the Japanese immigrants and their children have begun to return or emigrate to Japan, for stays of short or long duration." Evidently this was the beginning of the dekasegi phenomenon.

EVENTS OF THE LAST TWO DECADES

The phenomenon of returning to Japan noted in the report of the National Board of Emigration was accentuated at the end of the 1980s. Currency fluctuations, inflation, and recession had strong impacts on the country and on the Japanese community. Japanese florists suffered from a shortage of imports and at the same time were obliged to pay back loans tendered in dollars or in yen with the Argentine peso, which had lost most of its value. The dry cleaning business, a middle-class occupation, became less

A celebration parade held along the central avenues of Buenos Aires on August 1998, commemorating the hundredth anniversary of the Friendship, Commercial and Navigation Treaty between Argentina and Japan, signed in 1898. (Collection of Asociación Universitaria Nikkei)

profitable and suffered from a shortage of labor as the Nisei, who had always worked for their parents, became with the passage of time full-time professionals. Faced with a series of problems such as these, many Nikkei became temporary workers (*dekasegi*) in Japan, with various results. The number of those resettled in Japan is not available. Nevertheless, this exodus, the slow process of attrition of the ageing Issei, and the lack of new immigration to Argentina have reduced the size of the Japanese community.

Japanese Argentine Bibliographic Essay

ISABEL LAUMONIER

IN ARGENTINA, BIBLIOGRAPHIC MATERIALS RELATED TO the Nikkei experience are scarce, due either to the small number of Japanese immigrants or to the low profile assumed by the Japanese community itself from the beginning of Japanese settlement in the country (see table 2.2). The first figures that can be obtained are from reports related in general to Issei employment in agricultural work, dry cleaning establishments, bars, and factories. From the beginning of the twentieth century the Nikkei community organized its networks of *yobiyose* (the calling over of relatives) and mutual aid entirely by its own efforts. Immigration occurred in a trickle, as immigrants who faced difficult experiences in other countries opted for a second chance and migrated to Argentina. However, these early immigrants did not have the backing of an immigration policy on the part of either Japan or Argentina.

The majority of Issei planned to stay in Argentina for a short time and return to Japan. However, their return to Japan was postponed indefinitely, perhaps due to the economic difficulties assailing Okinawa, the place of origin for most of the immigrants. The figures for this first stage of immigration, which lasted until the early 1940s, come from the *Boletín de la Cámara de Tintoreros* (Bulletin of the Dry Cleaners' Association), from the records of the florists' association, and from sporadic publications produced by various groups formed by prefecture.

At the end of the Second World War, after a short break in diplomatic relations, the Japanese immigrant community entered a period of relative prosperity, unlike the situation in other American countries. The bibliographic materials dealing with the consequences of war for the Nikkei are not significant. Relations with the political power, the government of Argentina, which had always sympathized with the Axis, were strengthened (Higa: S-18). The Nisei began to enter various professional or university careers. They published twenty-four issues of the journal *Horizonte,* one of the first attempts by descendants of Japanese immigrants to establish a space for their self-expression. However two decades would pass before they again took up the printed word. The Issei, for the most part, were involved with small publications, generally anniversaries of the *kenjin-kai* (prefectural associations) or genealogical lists of immigrant families (Uehara: S-42).

The voices of the youngest Nikkei are also heard, thanks to the creation of associations such as the La Plata Association of Nipponese Academics (Asociación Nipona de Universitarios de La Plata, or ANULP), which provided funding for Nikkei students and was sponsored and financed by the Japan International Cooperation Agency (JICA). In 1981, ANULP produced an annual bulletin. Later, the Nikkei Argentine Center was created; in 1986 it produced the publication *Nikkei Argentino.* There are various other publications, such as the newspaper *Somos Nisei* and the journal *Sekai,* linking the Argentine and Japanese communities.

The pages of all these publications contain a handful of common themes: identity, generational problems, and what it means for a Nisei/Sansei "to be Argentine" (Nizen: S-35). These are themes that the Japanese community had to face daily during the "lead years" (the military regime of 1976–1983), during which time fourteen Nikkei "disappeared," and when they unanimously took a pro-Argentina stance during the nation's war with Britain over the Falkland Islands (1982). As an integral part of the nation, the Nikkei suffered equally the economic blows of inflation and recession. The dekasegi problem, at first rarely discussed, became a regular feature of the official Japanese news organ (*La Plata Hochi:* S-1).

In 1989, the Okinawa Center celebrated the eightieth anniversary of the arrival of the first immigrants from that prefecture, who formed the majority of all Japanese settled in Argentina. A group of professionals formed a new association, the Association of University Nikkei (Asociación Universitaria Nikkei, or AUN), and began to publish a journal (total of fourteen issues from 1993 to 1998). Some of its members had been part of the group that published the aforementioned *Horizonte* in the mid-1960s. Current issues of general interest were discussed, including the history of the Japanese community.

These publications made the mindset of the second- and third-generation descendants more widely known. With few exceptions (Jorge Higa: S-15, S-16; Marcelo Higa: S-18, S-19, S-20, S-21), the topic of Japanese immigration was explored by *gaijin* (non-Nikkei) researchers (Laumonier: S-25, S-26, S-27, S-28, S-29, S-30, S-31; Lépore: S-32; Maletta: S-33; Sabarots: S-37; Muñoz: S-38). One work that collected the greatest amount of information about the Nikkei community was the census undertaken by the National Board of Immigration in 1986–1987 (S-33), financed by JICA. Unfortunately, some of the works on this topic undertaken by the city of Córdoba, the Greater La Plata Colonies, and the Garahupé Colony are available only in private libraries. The surveys conducted in Japanese homes in Buenos Aires mobilized the community through the young Nisei and Sansei who helped to complete them. However, research of a sociological and historical nature was immobilized during the 1970s and was resumed only shortly before democracy was reinstated in 1983, largely due to institutions such as the Museo Roca, the Institute of Economic and Social Development (Instituto de Desarrollo Económico y Social, or IDES), and the Latin American Center for Immigration Studies (Centro de Estudios Migratorios de América Latina, CEMLA).

Issues concerning generational problems or racism have also been explored through the eyes of the gaijin (non-Nikkei); see Laumonier (S-25) and Sabarots (S-37, pages 147–65). Those dealing with women or health and psychology have found space in the publications of the Pan American Nikkei Conventions.

Traditionally, the children and grandchildren of Japanese immigrants have entered careers in the sciences. Lately, this seems to hold true also for the social sciences (anthropology, sociology, history); consequently, it might be expected that the Japanese community will acquire the greater introspection necessary to produce research, and attendant publications, on Nikkei issues.

Japanese Argentine Annotated Bibliography

COMPILED BY ISABEL LAUMONIER

ENGLISH

1. Higa Marcelo. "The Emigration of Argentines of Japanese Descent to Japan." In *New Worlds, New Lives: Globalization and People of Japanese Descent in the Americas and from Latin America in Japan*, edited by Lane Ryo Hirabayashi, Akemi Kikumura-Yano, and James Hirabayashi. Stanford, Calif.: Stanford University Press, 2002.
2. National Migration Bureau of the Argentine Republic, Department for the Study and Promotion of Immigration. "A Study of the Japanese Community in Argentina." Buenos Aires, August 1985.

    An official memorandum submitted to the Japan International Cooperation Agency.
3. Tigner, James Lawrence. "Japanese Immigration into Latin America." *Journal of Interamerican Studies and World Affairs* 21, no. 4 (November 1981), 457–82.
4. Tigner, James Lawrence. "The Ryukyuans in Argentina." *Hispanic American Historical Review* 47, no. 2 (May 1967), 203–24.

    A study, sponsored by the collaborative Ryukyuan Emigration Project, of Okinawan migration to Argentina from 1909 to the 1960s. Topics include a history of immigration, social organizations, acculturation, economic activity, World War II, and Argentina's immigration policies.

JAPANESE

1. Akoku Sensengyō Kyōdō Shōhi Kumiai [亜国洗染業協同消費組合], ed. *Zaia Nihonjin sensengyō 50-nen no ayumi* [在亜日本人洗染業50年の歩み]. Buenos Aires: Akoku Sensen Kurabu [亜国洗染クラブ], 1968.

    Summary of one of the principal labor activities of the community. Fiftieth anniversary of the Japanese dry cleaners in Argentina.
2. Gashū, Kuhei [賀集九平]. *Aruzenchin dōhō gojūnenshi* [アルゼンチン同胞五十年史]. Tōkyō [東京]: Seibundō Shinkōsha [誠文堂新光社], 1956.

    Information of the settlement and development of the Japanese in rural Argentina.
3. Irie, Toraji [入江寅次]. *Hōjin kaigai hattenshi* [邦人海外発展史]. Vol. 1. Tōkyō [東京]: Imin Mondai Kenkyūkai [移民問題研究會], 1938.

    History of the Japanese development abroad.
4. Irie, Toraji [入江寅次]. *Hōjin kaigai hattenshi* [邦人海外発展史]. Vol. 2. Tōkyō [東京]: Imin Mondai Kenkyūkai [移民問題研究會], 1942.

    A study of the settlement of immigrants before World War II.
5. Ishikawa, Tomonori [石川友紀]. "Aruzenchin ni okeru Okinawa-ken shusshin jiyū imin no shokugyō hensen ni tsuite [アルゼンチンにおける沖縄県出身自由移民の職業変遷について]." *Ryūkyū Daigaku Hōbun Gakubu Kiyō* 琉球大学法文学部紀要] (1986).

    The transformations suffered by Okinawan immigrants through eight decades.
6. Mori, K. "Kasato maru ijusha Komaki Karu san ni kiku." *La Plata Hochi* Feburary, nos. 1, 6 (1979).

    Discussion of the first wave of Japanese migration to Argentina. This article appeared in two parts in the newspaper *La Plata Hochi*. Odyssey of the migrants viewed from the perspective of a Japanese woman.
7. Nihonjin Aruzenchin Ijūshi Hensan Iinkai [日本人アルゼンチン移住史編纂委員会], ed. *Nihonjin Aruzenchin ijūshi* [日本人アルゼンチン移住史]. Tōkyō [東京]: Raten Amerika Kyōkai [ラテンアメリカ協会], 1971.

    Immigration history of the Japanese in Argentina.
8. Nihonjin Kaki Engei Kumiai Rengōkai [日本人花卉園藝組合聯合會], ed. *Akoku no kaki engei* [亞國の花卉園藝]. Buenos Aires: Nipparu Kaki Sangyō Kumiai [ニッパル花卉産業組合], 1941.

    Information of the first years of development of the Japanese floriculture in Argentina.
9. Sato, Amelia L. "Nikkeijin shakai ni okeru shijo no nihongo kyōiku." *Universidad de Tsukuba, Asociación de estudios de literatura y lengua nacional. (Idioma y literatura japonesa)* 2 (1982): 171–183.

    This article is an offprint of the thesis by the author about the education of the Japanese language.
10. Terashima. "Akoku teichaku zairyū hōjin no katsudō jōkyō [亜国定着在留邦人の活動状況]." *Imin johō* [移民情報] 8–3 (1936): 43–45.

    An early exposition of the Japanese dekasegi in Argentina in their early era.
11. Uehara, Kyotomi. *La historia del pueblo de Nakijin en Argentina*. Buenos Aires: Akoku Nippo, 1974.

    The history of Nakijin Village in Argentina. Text in Japanese illustrated with photographs.

SPANISH

1. "Emigración y crisis." *La Plata Hochi* (March–May 1989).

    Ten articles referring to the dekasegi problem in South America.
2. Alsina, Juan. *La inmigración en el primer siglo de la independencia*. Buenos Aires: Felipe S. Alsina, 1910.

    Basic text that shows political trajectory of the immigration in Argentina.
3. Aranzazu, Mara R. "Realización de prácticas y adies-

tramiento en las técnicas de la Antropología Socio-Cultural llevadas a cabo entre un grupo de estudiantes universitarios japoneses residentes en La Plata." (May 1997). Unpublished monograph. Faculty of Ciencias Naturales y Museo, Universidad Nacional de La Plata.

Information regarding the scholarship in training (in consultation with the Department of Ethnography).

4. Asato, Angel. *Historia de la colectividad japonesa en la Provincia de Córdoba*. N.p. Asociación Japonesa de Córdoba, 1997.

Discussion of the Nikkei community in the province of Córdoba, region of settlement of the first Japanese immigrants in Argentina.

5. Asociación Japonesa Argentina (AJA). *Guía de la colectividad japonesa en la Argentina*. Buenos Aires: AJA, 1967.

A guide of notable families and individuals of the community. Bilingual text, illustrated with photographs.

6. Asociación Kuba, Cultural y Deportiva. *Pro-ingreso de agricultores japoneses en Argentina, 25 aniversario*. Buenos Aires: n.p., 1963.

Pamphlet published by the Kuba Association. Mimeographic version. Copy in the archives of Centro Nikkei Argentino.

7. Bossio, Jorge. *Los cafés de Buenos Aires*. Buenos Aires: Plus Ultra, 1994.

Japanese presence in traditional cafés in Buenos Aires.

8. Cárdenas, Isabel L. *El servicio doméstico en barrios prestigiosos de Buenos Aires 1895–1985. De Ramona a la computadora*. Buenos Aires: Búsqueda, 1986.

Documents the presence of the Japanese community in domestic service in the first decades of the century.

9. Cazaux, Silvia, Alicia Gómez, and Isabel Laumonier. *Los japoneses Vol. III: Colonia Luján-Garuhapé*. Buenos Aires: Dirección Nacional de Migraciones de la República Argentina (DNM): Agencia de Cooperación Internacional del Japón (JICA), 1987.

Complete information of the results of the census of the Japanese community, with fieldwork conducted in the provinces of Buenos Aires, Córdoba, and Misiones during 1986 and 1987.

10. Centro Okinawense en la Argentina. *Okinawenses en la Argentina-90 aniversario de la inmigración*. Buenos Aires: Centro Okinawense en la Argentina, 1999.

Summary of the presence of the Okinawans, the most populous among the Japanese immigrants in Argentina. Shows their activities in Argentina and celebrates the tenth anniversary of the new building of the Okinawan Center in Argentina.

11. Círculo Cultural Bella Flor. *30 aniversario del Club de Bella Flor*. Buenos Aires: Círculo Cultural Bella Flor, 1982.

Text written in Japanese contains photographs.

12. Erb, Hebe, and others. "La inmigración japonesa en la República Argentina." *Separata del Boletín de estudios geográficos* 58, no. XV (January–March 1968).

One of the first works covering the history of Japanese immigration in Argentina, statistical data, and graphics. Analysis of various Japanese settlements established in Argentina.

13. Forn Domecq García, Manuel. "Manuel Domecq García, 1859–1946. Forjando los destinos de la Patria." In *Argentina y Japón se conocieron en el violento amanecer del mundo moderno*. Edited by Francesca Arena de Tejedor, H. Forn, P. Falconi, and C. Fraguio. Buenos Aires: Instituto de Publicaciones Navales, 1992.

Biographical sketch of Admiral Domecq García, documents the shipment of the battleships *Moreno* and *Rivadavia* to Japan during Russo-Japanese War. Analysis of Admiral's intervention as observer of the war.

14. Gashu, Kuhei. *XV aniversario de Ataku*. Buenos Aires: Akoku Nippo, 1970.

Books with photographs and a map of the Ataku Society, dedicated to the settlement.

15. Higa, Jorge. "Hace cincuenta años terminaba la II Guerra Mundial." *Cuadernos de A.U.N.* 5 (May 1995).

Discussion of an Okinawan student and his return to Argentina after the war.

16. Higa, Jorge. "La historia vista con ojos oblicuos." *Todo es historia* 316 (1993): 60–80.

Perspective of Japanese immigration from its beginning.

17. Higa, Jorge, and Isabel Laumonier. *La otra inmigración*. Buenos.Aires: A.U.N. (Asociación Universitaria Nikkei), 1990.

The book includes a chronology of Japanese immigration, from its beginning to the 1990s. Includes life history of one of the pioneer Okinawan immigrants in Argentina.

18. Higa, Marcelo G. "Desarrollo histórico de la inmigración japonesa en la Argentina hasta la Segunda Guerra Mundial." *Estudios migratorios latinoamericanos (CEMLA)* 10, no. 30 (August 1995): 471–512.

The historical development of Japanese immigration in Argentina up until World War II.

19. Higa, Marcelo G. "Inmigrantes de otros puertos. Los japoneses en Buenos Aires hacia 1910." Unpublished. (September 1995).

The inclusion of the first Japanese immigrants in the perspective of growing capital.

20. Higa, Marcelo G. "Notas sobre la inmigración japonesa en Argentina. Aspectos del desarrollo histórico de la inmigración y las características ocupacionales de los inmigrantes." Unpublished (September 1994).

Result of the fieldwork conducted for the Toyota Foundation.

21. Higa, Marcelo G. "La problemática identificatoria de los inmigrantes japoneses y sus descendientes en Argentina." Unpublished. Work presented in las V Jornadas sobre colectividades. CEMLA-Museo Roca-IDES-UNICEN-UNCLU (October 1995).

Conference proceedings on the Conference about communities, especially deals with the Okinawan problem.

22. Imai, Keiko. "Los inmigrantes japoneses en Argentina: historias personales de empresarios pioneros." *Estudios migratorios latinoamericanos (CEMLA)* 10 (August 1995): 453–70.

    Research conducted among Japanese entrepreneurs with comparative and statistical frameworks.

23. Kagami, Norma. *El idioma japonés en la Argentina.* Tokyo: Work presented to the Human Academy, 1993.

    A survey and its results conducted among Argentine residents in Japan. Unpublished in Argentina.

24. Kyoiku Rengo Kai. *Educación del idioma japonés en Argentina.* N.p.: Zai Nihongo, 1994.

    An analysis of the efforts made by both academia and schools in order to conserve the Japanese language in Argentina.

25. Laumonier, Isabel. "La casa de mi madre. Mi casa." In *Los relatos de vida. El retorno a lo biográfico*, compiled by M. Chirico, Buenos Aires: CEAL, 1992.

    Discussion of acclimatization/acculturation through the life history of a pioneer. Also reviews the changes that happened in the receiving country.

26. Laumonier, Isabel. "La colectividad japonesa: una ruptura, una adaptación." *Revista sekai* 3, no. 24 (February 1984): 3–34.

    The magazine *SEKAI* was published between 1981 and 1989. Its copies can be found in the Centro Nikkei Argentino. A special issue dedicated to the publication of bachelor's thesis.

27. Laumonier, Isabel. "Japoneses, esa otra inmigración." *Todo es historia.* 263 (May 1989): 62–91.

    A historical overview of the Japanese community.

28. Laumonier, Isabel. *Los japoneses Vol. II: panorama histórico de la colectividad japonesa.* Buenos Aires: Buenos Aires Dirección Nacional de Migraciones de la República Argentina (DNM): Agencia de Cooperación Internacional del Japón (JICA), 1987.

    Complete information about the results of the census of the Japanese community, with fieldwork conducted in the provinces of Buenos Aires, Córdoba, and Misiones during 1986 and 1987.

29. Laumonier, Isabel. *Los japoneses Vol. IV: Colonias El Pato, Urquiza y La Plata.* Buenos Aires: Dirección Nacional de Migraciones de la República Argentina (DNM): Agencia de Cooperación Internacional del Japón (JICA), 1987.

    Complete information about the results of the census of the Japanese community, with fieldwork conducted in the provinces of Buenos Aires, Córdoba, and Misiones during 1986 and 1987.

30. Laumonier, Isabel. *Los japoneses Vol. V: Ciudad de Córdoba.* Buenos Aires: Dirección Nacional de Migraciones de la República Argentina (DNM): Agencia de Cooperación Internacional del Japón (JICA), 1987.

    Complete information about the results of the census of the Japanese community, with fieldwork conducted in the provinces of Buenos Aires, Córdoba, and Misiones during 1986 and 1987.

31. Laumonier, Isabel. "Panorama histórico de la colectividad japonesa en Argentina." *Revista sekai* 7, no. 69 (May 1988).

    A special edition of the magazine dedicated to the publication of Research Project conducted by the DNM (Department of Study and Promotion of the Immigration).

32. Lépore, Silvia, and others. *Los japoneses Vol.1: imagen de una colectividad: los japoneses y sus descendientes en la Argentina.* Buenos Aires: Dirección Nacional de Migraciones de la República Argentina (DNM): Agencia de Cooperación Internacional del Japón (JICA), 1987.

    Complete information about the results of the census of the Japanese community, with field work conducted in the provinces of Buenos Aires, Córdoba, and Misiones during 1986 and 1987.

33. Maletta, Héctor, and Maletta, Silvia. "La colectividad japonesa en la Argentina." *Estudios migratorios latinoamericanos (CEMLA)* 5, nos. 15–16 (1990): 425–521.

    Summary and commentary of the first census about Japanese communities conducted by the National Board of Immigration. Financed by JICA (Japan International Cooperation Agency).

34. Nichia Gakuin. *70 años. Historia del Instituto Privado Argentino—Japonés.* Buenos Aires: n.p., 1997.

    A detailed discussion of the Nichia Gakuin, from its first classrooms to the completion of the second cycle. Photographs of the institution and various promotions.

35. Niizen, Jorge. "Búsqueda de las raíces perdidas." *Somos Nisei* 9 (1984): 20–21.

    Article that appeared in the newspaper *Somos Nisei* (*We Are Nisei*), from the perspective of a Nisei and his identity problem. *Somos Nisei* was published between 1984 and 1985. The majority of the copies can be found in the Centro Nikkei Argentino.

36. Onaha, Cecilia. "Inmigración de japoneses en Argentina previa a la II Guerra Mundial." Monograph presented during the VIII Congreso Internacional de ALADAA. Viña del Mar, Chile (1995).

    A case study of free immigrants and *yobiyose* immigrants who were invited by their relatives. The presentation studies the model of the migratory chain, usually observed among the immigrants living in Argentina. Contains graphics.

37. Sabarots, Horacio. "La identidad étnica en los migrantes japoneses de la denominada zona Sur, (Prov. de Bs.As.)." In *Procesos de contacto interétnico.* Buenos Aires: Bermejo, 1987.

    The research studies a particular situation of the Japanese who live in settlements and certain cases of discrimination. Deals with a fieldwork conducted among residents of the Japanese settlements in the area south of Gran La Plata and the situations of prejudice between communities.

38. Sanchis Muñoz, Jos R. *Japón y la Argentina: historia de sus relaciones.* Buenos Aires: Sudamericana, 1997.

    A study richly documented about the history of the Japanese community in Argentina. Also in Japanese version. An exhaustive research about the relations between Argentina and Japan from the perspective of an ambassador in Japan. Contains the list of the treaties and special accords between both countries.

39. Shinya, Violeta. "Yoshio Shinya." *Anuario La Plata Hochi* (1968).

    Life history of the first documented Japanese who entered Argentina on board *Fragata Sarmiento*. His daughter, Ms. Violeta Shinya, summarizes the work of cultural diffusion that her father worked on through communication both with the Japanese and the Argentines.

40. Tejedor, Francesca Arena de. "Argentina en el contexto internacional, 1868–1946. Sus primeros vínculos con el Japón," edited by Tejedor, et al., Buenos Aires: Instituto de Publicaciones Navales, 1992.

41. Tejedor, Francesca Arena de, and others. *Argentina y Japón se conocieron en el violento amanecer del mundo moderno.* Buenos Aires: Instituto de Publicaciones Navales-Centro Naval, 1992.

    A comparative study of Argentina and Japan entering into modern times.

42. Uehara, Kyotomi. *La historia del pueblo de Nakijin en Argentina.* Buenos Aires: Akoku Nippo, 1974.

    The history of Nakijin Village in Argentina. Text in Japanese illustrated with photographs.

43. Uehara, Kyotomi. *Quién es quién de la colectividad japonesa en la Argentina.* Buenos Aires: La Plata Hochi, 1968.

    Contains brief biographies and photographs of distinguished members of the community.

44. Zakimi, Alberto, comp. *Las dos vertientes del Nikkei.* Buenos Aires: Centro Nikkei Argentino, 1988.

    Messages, lectures, and works presented in the IV Pan-American Nikkei Convention. Chapter 5, Theme A, "The Third Era." (several authors.)

Supplementary Materials

COMPILED BY CECILIA ONAHA, ISABEL LAUMONIER, AND JORGE HIGA

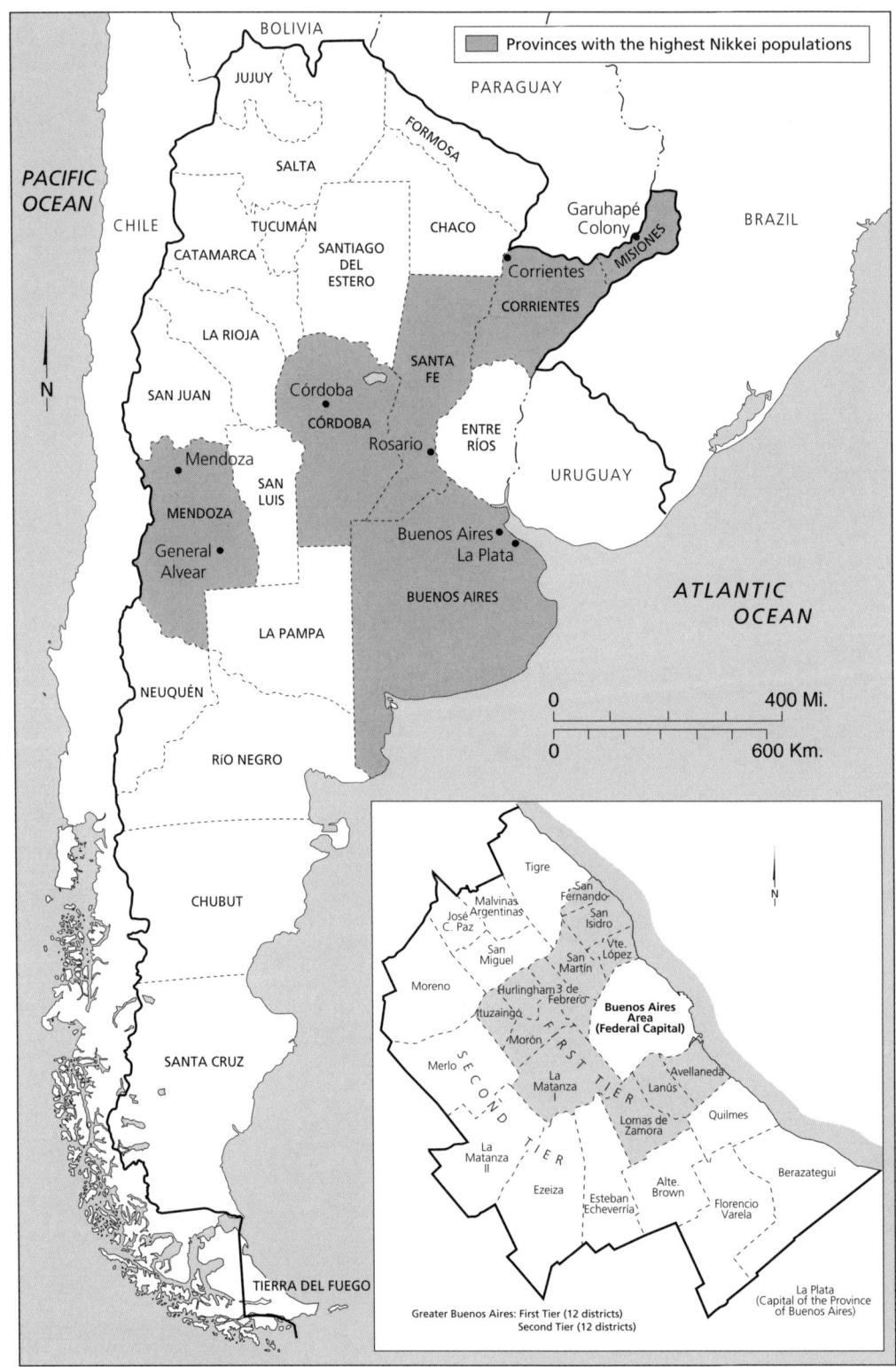

Map 2.1 Argentina Provinces with Nikkei Populations

Japanese Argentine Demographic Information

Table 2.1 Japanese Emigration to Argentina by Prefecture of Origin in Japan, 1906–1993

	1906–'10	'11–'15	'16–'20	'21–'25	'26–'30	'31–'35	'36–'41	Total
	4	195	612	350	1,750	1,049	1,438	**5,398**

	1952–'55	'56–'60	'61–'65	'66–'70	'71–'75	'76–'80	'81–'85	'86–'90	'91–'93	Total*
Okinawa	-	4	164	396	129	54	35	6	4	**792**
Tōkyō	4	15	44	57	87	40	18	8	1	**274**
Hokkaidō	29	52	67	20	19	6	5	2	-	**200**
Kanagawa	-	22	49	23	16	20	19	9	2	**160**
Ōsaka	7	7	14	34	30	12	6	1	2	**113**
Total*	119	328	687	760	432	198	154	69	13	**2,760**

Sources: Figures for 1906–1941 were taken from Gaimushō Ryōji Ijūbu. *Waga kokumin no kaigai hatten: ijū hyakunen no ayumi (shiryō hen)* (Tōkyō, 1971), 140. Figures for 1952–1993 were taken from Japan International Cooperation Agency, *Kaigai ijū tōkei (FY 1952–FY 1993)* (Tōkyō, 1994), 32–33.

Note: *Total includes other prefectures.

Table 2.2 Japanese Argentine Community Population

Year	Males	Females	Total
1914	860	147	1,007[1]
1920	1,561	395	1,959[1]
1922	1,745	436	2,181[1]
1930	2,959	1,068	4,027[2]
1940	3,977	1,861	5,838[1]
1947	3,682	1,510	5,192[1]
1960	4,544	3,062	7,606[1]
1980	4,049	3,558	7,607[3]
1985	-	-	15,660[3]
1990	-	-	12,663[3]
1995	-	-	11,709[3]
1997	-	-	11,364[4]
1998	-	-	11,457[4]

Sources:
[1] Nihonjin Aruzenchin Ijūshi Hensan Iinkai. *Aruzenchin no nihonjin ijūshi*, 1971, 265; S. Lépore and H. Maletta. "La colectividad japonesa en la Argentina." In *Estudios migratorios latinoamericanos*, 5: 15–16, 1990, 453.
[2] Prime Minister's Cabinet. Office of Statistics. *55th Statistic Annual of Japanese Empire*, 1936, Table 47: Japanese Living Abroad, by sex and work—data based on October 1, 1930, National Census, 76.
[3] Statistic Bureau. Management and Coordination Agency. 39th Japan Statistical Yearbook, 1989, 46 (data from 1975 to 1985); 44th Japan Statistical Yearbook, 54, (data of 1990); 49th Japan Statistical Yearbook, 2000, 54. (data from 1995–1997).
[4] Japan, Ministry of Foreign Affairs. Home page (data of 1998).

Table 2.3 Number of Descendants, Estimated in 1986

Descendants who live with Japanese national relatives	11,500
Those who cohabitate with other Japanese nationals	2,500
Those who don't cohabitate with Japanese nationals	15,500
Those who have no living Japanese national relatives	10,300
Total	**39,800**

Source: S. Lépore, 438–43.

Table 2.4 Japanese Immigrants in Argentina by Place of Origin, Japan National Census Data of 1940

Prefecture	Males	Females	Total
Okinawa	1,424	407	1,831
Kagoshima	265	61	326
Hiroshima	128	60	188
Kumamoto	121	62	183
Fukushima	106	30	136
Hokkaidō	86	42	128
Tōkyō	69	25	94
Saga	57	24	81
Nagano	52	16	68
Akita	50	13	63
Ehime	41	18	59
Hyōgo	42	13	55
Fukuoka	33	21	54
Kōchi	33	21	54
Others	571	164	735
Total	**3,078**	**977**	**4,055**

Source: Nihonjin Aruzenchin Ijūshi Hensan Iinkai, 116–17.

Table 2.5 Japanese Immigrants in Argentina by Place of Origin, 1948–1970

Years	Japan	%	Okinawa	%	Total
1948/1970	1,857	34	3,657	66	**5,514**

Source: Nihonjin Aruzenchin Ijūshi Hensan Iinkai, 264.

Table 2.6 Regional Distribution of Japanese Argentines

Region	1914	%	1947	%	1960	%	1980	%
Capital	541	54	1,933	37	2,017	27	5,824	33
Buenos Aires	122	12	2,211	42	4,119	54	9,567	54
Córdoba	26	3	302	6	317	4	531	3
Santa Fe	119	12	255	5	309	4	220	1
Misiones	(*)	-	129	2	402	5	694	4
Jujuy	122	12	19	0	10	0	(*)	-
Mendoza	14	1	51	1	95	1	105	1
Río Negro	(*)	-	(*)	-	(*)	-	191	1
Others	63	6	311	6	337	4	635	4
Total	**1,007**	**100**	**5,211**	**100**	**7,606**	**100**	**17,767**	**100**

Sources: Nihonjin Aruzenchin Ijūshi Hensan Iinkai, op.cit. (from 1914 to 1947), 265;
S. Lépore, op.cit. (1980 data includes descendants), 453.
Notes:
(*) Data included in "Others."
In 1882, the province of Buenos Aires ceded its ancient capital, the city of Buenos Aires, to the nation, and it became the Federal Capital as an independent district. The province established its new capital in the county of La Magdalena, in the city founded especially for that purpose: the city of La Plata. Since then, the Argentine statistical census data has dealt with the city of Buenos Aires (Federal Capital) separately from that of the province of Buenos Aires. There is a group of districts in between both jurisdictions that surround the Federal Capital and form what is known as the "Gran Buenos Aires" (Greater Buenos Aires); however, politically they are part of the province.

Table 2.7 Educational Achievement of Japanese Descendants by Percentage, 1986 Survey of Descendants Fifteen Years and Older

Level	Japanese	Descendants
None	0.95	0.22
Primary (incomplete)	4.25	0.53
Primary	37.85	18.82
Middle (incomplete)	16.92	14.85
Middle	33.43	44.79
Higher (incomplete)	0.87	1.75
Higher	5.56	18.36
Other	0.17	0.68
Total	**100**	**100**
(n)	1,194	1,313

Source: S. Lépore, 455.

Table 2.8 Occupational Areas of Japanese Immigrants and Their Descendants by Percentage

Year	Agriculture*	Industry	Commerce	Services	Others	Total
1920	15.3	43.8	19.2	20.4	1.3	100.0[1]
1929	24.5	17.7	41.5	9.5	6.7	100.0[1]
1935	30.3	33.2	25.9	7.4	3.2	100.0[2]
1969	30.4	2.5	61.9	0.5	4.7	100.0[1]
1980	23.3	11.0	21.4	37.2	7.1	100.0[3]

Sources:
[1] Nihonjin Aruzenchin Ijūshi Hensan Iinkai, 67–69 (1920); 86 (1929); 216–17 (1969).
[2] Keiko Imai. "Aruzenchin no nihonjin imin shi- Nikkei genchi kigyō no sōgyōshatachi." (In: *Gaikokugo gakubu kiyō*, Tōkyō, Jōchi Daigaku, 24, 92).
[3] S. Lépore, 458.

Notes:
*Includes cattle raising and fishery.
For more detailed data about occupational distribution of Japanese immigrants in general and Okinawans in particular, see Tomonori Ishikawa, "Changes in Occupational Structure among Okinawan Immigrants in Argentina." (In: *Ryūkyū daigaku hōbun gakubu kiyō: shigaku-chirigaku hen,* 26, 57–125), 1986.

Table 2.9 Religion of Japanese Immigrants and Their Descendants by Percentage, 1995 Questionnaire Survey

Religion	Japanese	Descendants
Christian Catholic	17.7	62.6
Christian Other	4.6	7.5
Other Nontraditional	0.0	0
Buddhist	35.8	0.4
Shintoist	1.5	0
Other Traditional	0.0	0.9
Atheist	34.4	24.8
NA	6.0	3.8
Total	100.0	100.0
(n)	67	214

Source: Cecilia Onaha. *Aruzenchin ni okeru nihonjin imin no rekishi. Jiyū imin to nikkei shakai keisei.* Ph.D. dissertation (Sōgō Kenkyū Daigakuin Daigaku, 1996). These rates correspond to the data about Nikkei who answered a questionnaire on perceptions on human relations, 1995, Appendix, 309–10.

Note: The religion professed by Japanese and their descendants was not considered in the 1986 survey or in the report published by Silvia Lépore. For other references on this subject, see F. Pages Larraya, "Síndrome de aculturación oriental en Buenos Aires." In: *Publicaciones del seminario de investigaciones sobre antropología psiquiátrica*. Buenos Aires: CONICET, second year, 1991, which includes data from a survey of over 113 Japanese. Also see Tomonori Ishikawa, et al. *Research Report on the Okinawan Immigrants in Latin America* (Okinawa: The University of the Ryukyus, Department of Geography, 1981), which includes data of 214 Okinawans in Argentina.

CHAPTER 3

Japanese Bolivians

DEVELOPED IN COLLABORATION WITH THE PRESENCIA JAPONESA EN EL CONTINENTE AMERICANO PROYECTO AT KEIO UNIVERSITY AND THE FEDERACIÓN NACIONAL DE ASOCIACIONES BOLIVIANO JAPONESAS

PRIOR TO THE 1950S, MOST JAPANESE ENTERED BOLIVIA AS COMMON LABORERS through Peru. In 1899, the Mapiri River region in La Paz witnessed the first entry of ninety-one Japanese laborers to work on rubber plantations. Thereafter, the highland Andes attracted a few hundred more Japanese, who found employment in mining and railroad construction. The inland Amazon emerged as the second major destination for the workers, who also came through Peru to work on rubber plantations, in northwestern Bolivia. The end of World War I and the Great Depression displaced Japanese laborers in the rubber and mining industries respectively. Only the capital city of La Paz and the town of Riberalta survived the economic changes, becoming the centers of Japanese commercial activities. In the 1930s, many Japanese brought wives from Japan, while others married local women—a distinction that often divided the ethnic community. With the exception of twenty-nine deportees to the United States, World War II had little impact on the lives of Nikkei residents in Bolivia, especially since the government did not adopt anti-Japanese measures. Treaty arrangements after 1954 ushered in a new chapter of Bolivian Nikkei history and a massive influx of agricultural settlers from U.S.-controlled Okinawa and Japan. The necessity of transplanting surplus populations in war-torn Japan met the Bolivian government's desire to develop the eastern lower lands in Santa Cruz Department. With the financial assistance of the Japanese government, the Colonia Okinawa and Colonia San Juan de Yapacaní were established; the two settlements formed distinctive communities—with separate identities, one Okinawan and the other Japanese—that are currently in transition from the immigrant to the Bolivian-born generation.

Japanese Bolivian Historical Overview

IYO KUNIMOTO

INTRODUCTION

In a total Bolivian population of 7.5 million, the Nikkei population is quite significant. In 1998, the current Japanese Bolivian population was estimated to be 13,500, according to the National Federation of Japanese Bolivian Associations. However, if persons with a fraction of Japanese blood are taken into account, the Nikkei population could be as many as thirty to sixty thousand. The highly regarded Nikkei community is more visible than its actual numbers would indicate, however, because of the great contributions that the postwar immigrants have made in the cultivation of primeval forests, their establishment of medium-scale mechanized farming, and their prolific production of soy beans, rice, and chicken eggs.

The pre– and post–World War II Japanese migrants to Bolivia differed greatly in their purposes of emigration and their places of settlement. Before World War II, the vast majority of Japanese immigrants came to Bolivia as individuals, in pursuit of personal goals. The Amazon and the Andes were the two major areas where the prewar Japanese immigrants settled. The two areas communicated little with each other and developed two different types of Nikkei societies. Some Japanese migrated to the deep forest region along the Amazon River in the northwestern part of Bolivia, attracted by the economic boom of rubber production in the early twentieth century. Others moved to urban areas in the highland Andes and became engaged in commercial activities. They all embarked on private initiatives without official support. However, after World War II, most of the postwar emigrants responded to the government's recruitment of collective agricultural settlers. The Bolivian government provided them with land, without compensation, and the Japanese government supported their efforts to establish medium-scale mechanized agricultural settlements.

Prewar immigrants almost completely assimilated into the Bolivian society, except for those in La Paz, who had a very strong Japanese identity. However, postwar immi-

Man sawing down almendrillo tree at San Juan de Yapacaní. (Collection of Federación Nacional de Asociaciones Boliviano Japonesas)

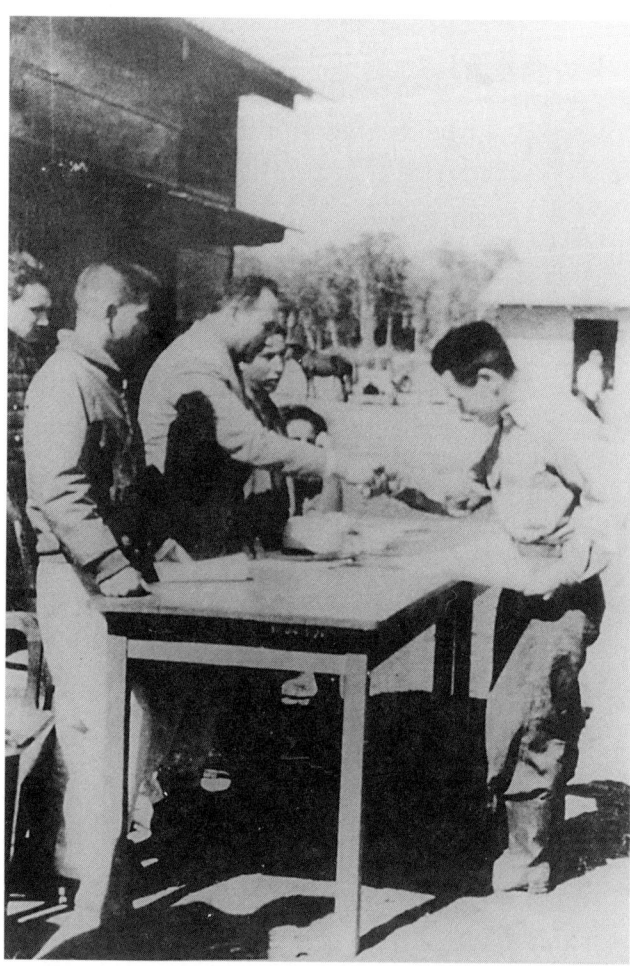

Transfer of land title to Okinawan settlers, Tetsu Nagayama (far right) by Mr. Cuellar (center), head of the Santa Cruz office of the Bolivian Reform Bureau. (Collection of Federación Nacional de Asociaciones Boliviano Japonesas)

Japanese Society of La Paz, 1928. (Collection of Federación Nacional de Asociaciones Boliviano Japonesas)

grants who left their initial collective settlements and moved to Santa Cruz have formed a strong Japanese society that is still active today. In La Paz and Santa Cruz, a deep cleavage exists between the first generation, which emphasizes the Japanese language and culture, and the younger generations, which live in Bolivian society as Bolivians. The generational conflicts are serious, and the differences in opinions are great.

THE JAPANESE OF THE HIGHLAND ANDES

The first Japanese who entered Bolivia were a part of the original 790 immigrants who arrived in Callao, Peru, on April 3, 1899. Due to the poor treatment they received from their employers, breach of contracts, and the unfamiliar environment, many immigrants escaped the sugar plantations and gathered in Callao. Teikichi Tanaka, the local representative of the Morioka Company, found employment for them in the promising rubber production area along the Mapiri River, east of the Andes in Bolivia. Thus, on August 31, 1899, ninety-one Japanese immigrants led by two supervisors Fujikuma Aoki and Takeo Miyazaki left the port of Callao bound for Bolivia. Their arduous journey lasted many weeks before they arrived on foot at the assigned area deep in the Amazon. However, they soon discovered that work in the Bolivan rubber forest was just as hard as the labor on the sugar plantations in the coastal area of Peru.

The Japanese who entered Bolivia following this first group of emigrants were dispersed from the capital city of La Paz to the mining towns of Oruro, Uncía, Potosí, Uyuni, and Cochabamba. Many were engaged in commercial activities, but a significant number worked on railway construction. The mining and railroad construction sites in the Andes each had the capacity to hire five to six thousand Japanese laborers, according to an investigative report written in 1911 by Ryōji Noda, a diplomat who worked at the Japanese consulates of Peru, Bolivia, and Brazil in the early twentieth century (see annotated bibliography, J-30). At the time of Noda's report, the Meiji Emigration Company was negotiating wages with a rail-

La Paz Japanese Society Tennis Club, Second Anniversary commemorative photo, July 16, 1929: (back row, from right to left) Kaneyoshi Oku, Tomisuke Oishi, Monjiro Noda, Yoshio Kawamura, Tamotsu Fujiike; (front row, left to right) Flores, Kozo Suematsu, Keiryo Komori, Keiji Terasawa, Tokutaro Shimaru. (Collection of Federación Nacional de Asociaciones Boliviano Japonesas)

Family photo of Mr. Yoshinori Yoshida of La Paz. (Collection of Federación Nacional de Asociaciones Boliviano Japonesas)

Sawaya Store, 1932. (Collection of Federación Nacional de Asociaciones Boliviano Japonesas)

road company. However, the negotiation failed, and no collective emigration of Japanese workers to the highland Andes was realized.

The areas with the greatest concentration of the Japanese population in Andes were La Paz and Oruro. According to a census taken right after diplomatic relations were established between Bolivia and Japan in 1914, approximately two hundred Japanese were reported in La Paz and Oruro, and in their suburbs. In 1922, the Japanese Society was established in La Paz, the center of Bolivian politics, economy, and culture. The activities of the Japanese Society centered on those who succeeded in commercial activities. By 1930 its membership had grown to eighty.

During the 1920s and 1930s, many single youths came to La Paz, invited by the Japanese who had succeeded in their business. In the 1930s, the number of young "immigrant brides" increased. Many Japanese males in La Paz married Japanese women. This was one of the reasons that the Japanese Society in La Paz had maintained a strong Japanese identity, a fact that had caused conflicts within the Nikkei society between the inmarried and mixed-marriage groups.

During the Chaco War, from 1932 to 1935 (a territorial conflict between Bolivia and Paraguay), business opportunities increased due to inflation and a shortage of goods. At that time, the Germans, Italians, French, British, Americans, and Arabs were the groups most actively engaged in the commercial activities of La Paz. However, the Japanese also were enormously successful, forming the Japanese Commercial Union in 1935. The Japanese operated fifteen stores in the highest-earning business district on Comercio and Potosí Streets. Almost all the Japanese of La Paz were engaged in commercial activities, according to Hisashi Ono, who arrived in La Paz in 1935 as the first participant of the Overseas Commercial Intern Program, administered by the Japanese Ministry of Foreign Affairs. The Komori Company, which was the largest and most successful Japanese enterprise, owned a shirt factory (established in 1937) and a textile factory (established in 1940). At its peak, the company hired as many as 1,200 workers (see J-1 in the Japanese Bolivian annotated bibliography).

Until the 1920s, the Japanese community of Oruro flourished commercially as much as that in La Paz due to the mining industry, which was at the center of Bolivia's economic prosperity until the Great Depression of 1929.

Suárez Co., Cachuela Esperanza. (Collection of Federación Nacional de Asociaciones Boliviano Japonesas)

The Japanese population of Oruro was fifteen in 1917, according to the Japan's Ministry of Foreign Affairs. It increased to thirty-seven in 1921 and recorded its highest number of forty in 1923. Many Japanese of Oruro first worked at a railroad construction site, saved money, and then opened stores. Japanese societies were apparently organized in Oruro and Potosí, and economic activities were vigorous. However, little information is available on the Japanese in the Andean zone—Oruro or Potosí, Uyuni, Uncía, and Cochabamba.

Meanwhile, the towns located deep within the Amazon region had become isolated inland villages with the decline of rubber by the end of World War I. Many *barracas* (rubber-gathering locations) along the rivers were abandoned. Moreover, the economy in the highland Andes, which had experienced the economic boom of mining and railway construction, had also collapsed. Given these circumstances, the Japanese who were settled in various areas became assimilated into the local society, with little mutual communication. The only exception was La Paz.

THE JAPANESE OF THE AMAZON RIVER

The inland Amazon area of Bolivia was first revealed to Western civilization during the quinine boom in the mid-nineteenth century and the rubber boom that started in the 1880s. The first group of Japanese came at the height of the rubber boom. Until 1920, approximately two thousand Japanese were believed to have come to this area, located in the northwestern part of Bolivia. Many worked for a few years as rubber tappers. Then they left the jungle and settled in the cities of Pando and Beni Departments, creating the foundation for Nikkei society in inland Bolivia.

Except for the first ninety-three Japanese who approached the Mapiri River area through Lake Titicaca, the Japanese rubber workers entered northwestern Bolivia through Maldonado, Peru. The majority had entered Peru as contract workers, worked there for a while, and then moved to Bolivia. At the beginning of the twentieth century, the rubber boom shifted to the area around Madre de Díos River, one of the major streams in the Amazon re-

The Japanese of Riberalta celebrating the Emperor's birthday (Tenchōsetsu), *ca. 1936. (Collection of Federación Nacional de Asociaciones Boliviano Japonesas)*

gion. The rubber-growing area of Bolivia could be reached through Maldonado, Peru. The trip from Maldonado to Bolivian territory took one day by raft on the Madre de Dios River. The riverside was studded with *barracas*. Many belonged to the Suárez Company, owned by Nicholás Suárez, known as the "rubber king," who hired many Japanese as rubber tappers. Also, several dozen Japanese worked in various capacities in Cachuela Esperanza, where numerous facilities, such as hotels, schools, drug stores, a hospital, and a theater, were supported by the Suárez Company.

Many locales in the northwestern part of Bolivia, such as Riberalta, Guayaramerín, Cobija, Porvenir, and Sena, grew rapidly during the rubber boom and became destinations for new Japanese immigrants. Riberalta was where most Japanese rubber workers finally settled. At the end of the twentieth century, there were over ten thousand Japanese descendants, 15 percent of Riberalta's population, which made Riberalta the biggest Nikkei city in Bolivia.

The first Japanese in Riberalta is believed to have arrived around 1907. When Sentei Yagi came in 1914 and wrote about the lives of early Japanese immigrants in Bolivia and Peru in *Gojūnen zengo no omoide* (Memories of about Fifty Years Ago) (J-47), there were eight Japanese living in Riberalta from Maldonado, Peru. In 1914, Denju Horiuchi reported in *Seibo kahan no jūrokunen* (*Sixteen Years at Madre de Dios River*) (J-6) that the total population of Riberalta was about 3,500. The streets were organized in checkerboard fashion and lined with tiled-roof houses. Jackets were required on the street. Seventy-three Japanese lived in the city. Their occupation varied from hired employees, such as store clerks and waiters, to owners of grocery stores and cafés, of a tailor shop, laundry and barbershop, an ice vender, cider producer, and contractor. In addition, some were in specialized occupations—carpenters, woodcutters, and steamboat conductors. Meanwhile, a total of 148 Japanese were engaged in farming on fifty-six Japanese-owned farms: twenty-five along Beni River above Riberalta, nineteen below Riberalta, and twelve along Madre de Dios River. These Japanese were already very important to Riberalta, because they were feeding the population. Horiuchi interviewed the head of Riberalta, who stated: "Thanks to the Japanese, the residents here can obtain inexpensive foods." The population of Riberalta increased rapidly, and the Japanese quickly entered the agricultural field to meet the growing demand. In 1915, 166 attended a ceremony establishing the Japanese Society. During that period, approximately three hundred Japanese who lived in Riberalta and its suburbs were engaged in diverse occupations.

Traces of the Japanese past can be found in other areas too. In the rubber-growing region in the northwestern part of Pando Department, along the Tahuamanu, Orthon, and Acre Rivers, are locales known as Mukden, Yokohama, Tokio, and Japón. These areas, around which the Japanese lived, were registered points for mail delivery. It is also known that in such locales as Carmen, Sakata, and Sena, located along Madre de Dios River, there were significant numbers of Japanese. In Sena, a Japanese Society was organized around 1916. However, as the rubber boom declined, the Japanese moved to bigger towns and then gathered in central cities, such as Cobija and Riberalta. Some moved even farther, to Trinidad, the capital of Beni Department, and vicinity, in the southern part of Beni. According to the report written by Ryōji Noda during his investigative trip in 1931 (J-32), there were fifty-nine Japanese settlers in Trinidad. However, very few moved farther south to Santa Cruz. Only a dozen or so settlers lived there when the collective immigrants arrived after World War II.

THE JAPANESE IN BOLIVIA BEFORE AND DURING WORLD WAR II

Looking back at the paths taken by the Japanese who entered Bolivia before the war, almost all originally entered Bolivia from the shoreline of Peru as contract immigrants, or entered as rubber workers in the northwest of Bolivia. They were drawn to the Riberalta area in Bolivia because it was the collection point for rubber workers. As the rubber business declined, some remained as farmers, leasing and operating small farmlands on the shore of the Beni River. Some moved into towns and worked as small-business owners or provided various services. Others moved to bigger towns in search of greater business opportunities.

When Japanese moved to larger towns after achieving success in their businesses, they usually turned their enterprises over to another Japanese, such as their sales clerk, or left it in the general charge of their employees.

The celebration of Mr. Tamiichi Komori's return to Japan: (from right to left) Tsunesaburo Wada (age 20), Shinyemon Komori (age 34), Toichi Nakamura (age 34), Yoshio Kawamura (age 20), Tatsuzo Mori (age 19), Tamiichi Komori (age 26), Tamotsu Fujiike (age 22), La Paz, April 1923. (Collection of Federación Nacional de Asociaciones Boliviano Japonesas)

Though its numbers were not comparable to the Japanese immigrant communities in Brazil or Peru, the Japanese community in Bolivia established roots in its own way. Gradually, a sense of solidarity arose among the people who were successful in business. Moreover, when an issue of great importance in their homeland occurred, it seems that their solidarity grew even stronger. From the 1930s, successful Japanese immigrants in various cities of Bolivia brought their human resources directly from Japan. These were different types of immigrants from the ones who worked for the rubber. When the Japanese who were brought in directly from Japan joined with Japanese in Bolivia, their interests in Japan intensified.

Ryōji Noda, who observed the Japanese in Bolivia, reported in his book (see J-32), "There were no Imperial Government authorities nor institutions or facilities that would help or support them since the area was quite remote; however, compatriots stood together as a single body, helped and encouraged by one another faithfully, and together they found their way out of the difficulty and found a peaceful place to live in a foreign land millions of miles away from home. If they were given material support, that would increase their dependency and weaken their independent and courageous spirits." Furthermore, Noda concluded, "the compatriots living in this region are different from the compatriots who are concentrated in certain areas. They would not dream of receiving relief money. They are determined to be independent and quite

Oruro Japanese Society, ca. 1941: (front row, left to right) Carlos Noda, Mr. Omoya, Mr. Koriyama, Dr. Pinto (holding a picture which may be Emperor Jinmu, the first Emperor of Japan), Mr. Kugimiya, Victor Yamamoto, Mr. Manabe; (second row, left to right) first two men unknown, Tatsuzo Mori, Mr. Uchino, Mr. Shojima, Shinobu Tsuchiya, unknown man, Kajo Higa, Riokichi Higa. (Collection of Federación Nacional de Asociaciones Boliviano Japonesas)

General meeting of the first immigrants approximately one week after their arrival at Uruma Colony, August 1954. (Collection of Federación Nacional de Asociaciones Boliviano Japonesas)

unique masculine figures." Instead, Noda requested donations of old magazines and books. Noda's request was aimed at maintaining the identity of Japanese imperial citizens.

Bolivia, as an ally of the United States, terminated its diplomatic relationship with Japan on January 28, 1942, and declared war on Japan. Upon request of the U.S. government, Bolivia sent twenty-nine Japanese who lived in Bolivia to internment camps in Crystal City, Texas, and Santa Fe, New Mexico. However, the Bolivian government was more lenient than that of Peru and did not actively adopt anti-Japanese measures. Some of the Japanese merchants volunteered to become citizens and tried to keep their assets from being frozen. Others had many local friends and could continue their life uninterrupted under their protection. Aside from barbershop and restaurant owners, who escaped the freeze, all Japanese business activities were essentially stopped. However, Japanese who were operating *chacos* (small farm lands) were not impacted, since the seizure of their real estate was not enforced. Consequently, some of the businessmen decided to purchase land and returned to being farmers.

After the war, out of the twenty-nine Japanese who were sent to the internment camps in the United States, twenty-four went back to Japan; only five returned to Bolivia. Among the Japanese who returned to Japan, only one person went back to Bolivia.

POST–WORLD WAR II EMIGRATION AND TWO COLLECTIVE SETTLEMENTS

The postwar immigrants developed the third kind of Nikkei society, formed by collective immigration to two settlements in the Santa Cruz region: Colonia Okinawa and Colonia San Juan de Yapacaní. These two settlements differed from previous immigration patterns in terms of their process of establishment and the type of Japanese who participated.

After the war, the Okinawans in Bolivia, mainly in Riberalta, wanted to help the Okinawans in their homeland, which had been devastated by war. Therefore, plans were made for some of them to start new lives in Bolivia. Land was purchased, an agricultural cooperation was formed (in 1950), and preparations were made for their arrival. Concomitantly, the U.S. government's plan to expand military bases in Okinawa caused many residents to lose their homes and required resettlement. The two plans were mutually compatible. This is how Colonia Okinawa was established.

Tenth-anniversary celebration of Colonia Okinawa, September 23, 1964. (Collection of Federación Nacional de Asociaciones Boliviano Japonesas)

Classroom in Colonia Okinawa with teacher Chosho Yara, ca. 1960. (Collection of Federación Nacional de Asociaciones Boliviano Japonesas)

Just before the San Francisco Peace Treaty, which allowed Japan to rejoin the international society as an independent country, became effective, Professor James Tigner of Stanford University visited Latin American countries in order to find a good place for Okinawans to resettle. The trip had been commissioned by the People's Welfare Bureau of the U.S. Occupation Army in Okinawa and the Pacific Council in California. Tigner became familiar with the efforts of the Okinawan immigrants in Bolivia and recommended Bolivia as the place for resettlement. Thus, the United States took the initiative in negotiations with the Bolivian government.

Fortunately, the new revolutionary government, established as a result of the Bolivian Revolution of 1952, had a plan to institute land reforms and develop the eastern lower lands. These plans were another harmonious match. As a result, the collective immigration of the Okinawan residents to primeval forests of Bolivia became a reality. Detailed historical processes of the Colonia Okinawa settlement can be found in their commemorative publications on its tenth, twenty-fifth, thirtieth, and fortieth anniversaries.

Before Okinawa was returned to Japan in 1972, the jurisdiction of Colonia Okinawa was transferred to the Japanese government. Colonia Okinawa and Colonia San Juan de Yapacaní became beneficiaries of strong support from the Japanese government, consequently developing into two of the best soybean producers in Bolivia. Furthermore, the Okinawan municipal government has supported the Colonia Okinawa community in recent years. This has caused the residents of the settlement to develop their identity as "Okinawan." Colonia Okinawa is divided into three villages, but they are all usually known as "Colonia Okinawa" and exist as Japanese or Okinawan villages that maintain the Japanese language and Okinawan traditional culture.

The second collective settlement is Colonia San Juan de Yapacaní, which consists of applicants and their families who had responded to the recruitment by the Japanese prefectures, excluding Okinawa, under the guidance of the Japanese government. As in the case of Colonia Okinawa, the establishment of Colonia San Juan de Yapacaní was a marriage between two emigration plans. One plan involved the emigration policy of the Japanese government. Japan needed to release some of its population, people were suffering extreme poverty as a result of the World War II. Six million people who had lived in lands occupied by Japan in the prewar period had returned, adding a severe burden on the economy. Few countries were willing to accept Japanese citizens as immigrants, but Bolivia was an exception. In 1956, an immigration pact was signed between Bolivia and Japan. The pact allowed a thousand Japanese families (six thousand people) to migrate to Bolivia in the following five years.

Toshimichi Nishikawa initiated the other emigration plan, for the purpose of establishing a sugar enterprise. Nishikawa's plan was carried out by fourteen families (eighty-eight people) before the signing of the 1956 immigration pact. Prior to World War II, Nishikawa had been engaged in the production of sugar in Southeast Asia. Based on the advice given to him by Japan's Ministry of Foreign Affairs, he tried to restart the business in Bo-

Wedding photo of newlyweds in San Juan de Yapacaní, 1963. (Collection of Federación Nacional de Asociaciones Boliviano Japonesas)

Nishikawa immigrants of San Juan de Yapacaní, ca. 1956. (Collection of Federación Nacional de Asociaciones Boliviano Japonesas)

livia after the war, purchasing land in Bolivia and recruiting Japanese families as sugar farmers. Thus, Japanese emigration to Bolivia took advantage of Nishikawa's ongoing project.

Despite the preferential treatment and the fifty hectares of free land given to the immigrants, the challenge of cultivating primeval land was overwhelming, and life was harsh. It took about twenty-five years for the farming enterprise to become successful and for the Japanese government's support to bear fruit. At the end of the twentieth century, Colonia San Juan de Yapacaní mainly depended on rice, soybean, and poultry. In addition, the settlers were engaged in citrus fruit production and livestock farming, using medium-scale mechanized farming methods. Although the first generation is now retiring, most meetings are conducted in Japanese, and traditional Japanese culture is deeply rooted. The settlers also communicate frequently with Japan. The name "Japanese village" is not just rhetoric here.

San Juan de Yapacaní kindergarten class, 1973. (Collection of Federación Nacional de Asociaciones Boliviano Japonesas)

It is just a matter of time before the management of economic and social affairs will be passed on to the second generation both in Colonia Okinawa and Colonia San Juan de Yapacaní. At this historical juncture, they are facing difficult issues. How will the "Japanese village" function as a municipality in Bolivia? Will the two settlements, which have relied heavily on the support of the Japanese government, be able to survive in the twenty-first century as the wave of globalization destroys the conventional social and economic structure? This issue is particularly serious since the settlements are engaged in agriculture, where the effect of globalization is most significant.

Bibliographic Essay on the Japanese Migration to Bolivia and Nikkei Society

IYO KUNIMOTO

THE HISTORY OF JAPANESE BOLIVIAN IMMIGRATION AND SOCIETY

The most useful overview of Japanese immigration to Bolivia is *Boribia ni ikiru* (Living in Bolivia), which was published in commemoration of the hundredth anniversary of Japanese immigration (J-1). This publication, containing 332 pages, has three parts. The first part is titled "The Celebration of the Hundredth Year Anniversary and the Prospect for the Twenty-first Century." It contains congratulatory messages from political leaders and presidents of various organizations of both Japan and Bolivia, which are indispensable to this kind of publication. The second part, "Living in Bolivia: Testimonies and Proposals of Nikkei People," contains thoughts and experiences of some representative people from the first, second, and third generations. The third part, which is approximately two-thirds of the entire book, is entitled "One hundred-year History of Japanese Immigration to Bolivia"; it has eight chapters. It presents the process of formation of Nikkei societies in various areas of Bolivia. Each chapter identifies the name of the author, which shows their attempt to record histories of Nikkei societies in these areas as objectively as possible, assigning responsibility for content. There are some differences in the amount of description from chapter to chapter. Still, there is no doubt that it is the most useful publication for the history of Japanese immigration and the overall situation of Nikkei societies in Bolivia at the end of the twentieth century.

Other publications that provide an overview are *Nihonjin Borivia ijūshi* (History of Japanese Immigration to Bolivia) (J-29), *Colonia japonesa en Bolivia* by Parejas (S-3), and *La inmigración japonesa en Bolivia: estudios históricos y socio-económicos,* by Wakatsuki and Kunimoto (S-4). *Nihonjin Borivia ijūshi* (J-29) is important because it was the first publication on the history of Bolivia's immigration, which utilized primary sources. The second half of this publication is especially valuable as a research source because it records, without editing, the discussions among prewar immigrants and individual interviews conducted during field research at the end of the 1960s. *Colonia japonesa en Bolivia* (S-3) is written by a Bolivian historian. It is a short book that presents a brief history of Japanese immigration to Bolivia. Japanese and Bolivian researchers formed the Investigative Group of the Bolivian Nikkei and conducted a field research funded by the Japanese Ministry of Education. The results were published as *La inmigración japonesa en Bolivia: estudios históricos y socio-económicos* (S-4). Each member of the group wrote a research essay on the history of immigration, economic and social conditions, and changes in Nikkei societies.

RECORDS OF IMMIGRATION BEFORE WORLD WAR II

There are some unpublished primary sources, such as proceedings and diaries of the Japanese associations in different areas. Information about these sources can be found in the reference section of *Boribia ni ikiru* (Living in Bolivia) (J-1). In addition, reports from local consulates found in *Nihon gaikō bunsho* (Japan Diplomatic Record) and *Imin chōsa hōkoku* (The Report on Immigrants) are valuable primary sources (J-30, J-31). Among others, Ryōji Noda, the author of these reports, described the Japanese in Bolivia and their societies in the 1930s in his book *Nanbei no kakushin ni funtō seru dōhō o tazunete* (Visiting Fellow Japanese Working Hard in the Heart of South America) (J-32). He was a diplomat with abundant practical experience. While working at Japanese consulates in Peru, Bolivia, and Brazil in the early twentieth century, part of his responsibility was to visit and conduct investigations on many Japanese who lived throughout South America. He wrote various research reports.

Some authors wrote about their individual experiences. Especially valuable are *Seibo kahan no jūrokunen* (Sixteen Years at Madre de Dios River) (J-6), by Denjū Horiuchi, and *Gojūnen zengo no omoide* (Memories of about Fifty Years Ago) (J-47), by Sentei Yagi. Denjū Horiuchi (J-6) lived in various areas in the Amazon region, traveling by canoe, during the 1910s. His diary and letters to his family, in which he wrote about his experiences, were published posthumously by his surviving family. Sentei Yagi's book (J-47) is also a record of his experiences. However, the author actually did not write the book until the 1960s, fifty years after his travel. Therefore, as the title "memories" suggests, the record is not as vivid as Horiuchi's (J-6).

There are reasonably abundant secondary sources on the prewar Japanese migration, especially the many academic essays that trace the Japanese who left Peru and entered the Amazon area in Bolivia (J: 5, 9, 24, 34, 36). In addition, the essays, reports, and travel diaries of references cited in J-14, J-15, J-26, and J-33 provide good overviews of the Japanese who settled in the northwestern part of Bolivia during the "rubber boom," and of their lives thereafter. However, there are very limited sources on the Japanese who settled in the highland Andes, including the city of La Paz. "Ra Pasu Nihonjinkai" (Japanese Society in La Paz) (J-37) is the only available reference. There are few sources that provide information on the lives and migration patterns of the Japanese who were engaged in commercial activities in the cities in the highland Andes.

THE HISTORY AND CURRENT CONDITIONS OF JAPANESE IMMIGRATION AFTER WORLD WAR II

On this topic, *Hatten tojōkoku e no ijū no kenkyū* (A Study on Emigration to Developing Countries) (J-46) critically analyzes the emigration policy of the Japanese government. Emigration after World War II was concentrated in Colonia Okinawa and Colonia San Juan de Yapacaní, which involved group migration and settlement. There are a number of sources available on these two *colonias* (settlements). Many internal reports were generated by the Japan International Cooperation Agency (JICA)—including its former body, the Overseas Emigration Agency (Kaigai Iju Jigyodan)—which was involved in the management and support of the two colonias. Some of them can be viewed at the reference room of the JICA in Tokyo. The agency also compiles detailed data on agricultural management with information updated yearly. Some personnel at the JICA have written essays in a private capacity, which are also valuable. Examples of such essays are Japanese 7, 15, 35, 43, and 44, all of which can be found in one of the thirty-three volumes of JICA's periodical, *Ijū kenkyu* (Migration Research), which was continued until 1996.

These two colonias published detailed records themselves in the form of anniversary publications. Colonia Okinawa has published a tenth-anniversary issue (J-16), a twenty-fifth-anniversary issue (J-17), a thirtieth-anniversary issue (J-18), and a fortieth-anniversary issue (J-19). The editors of fortieth anniversary issue (J-19) made an especially serious effort to make the book historically useful; therefore, it provides the most comprehensive information. In addition, Cooperativa Agropecuaria Integral Colonias Okinawa (CAICO), the colonia's agricultural cooperative, independently compiled mostly economic aspects of its activities (J-2). James Tigner (E-6) and Kanchō Gushi (J-3) both wrote about the history of Okinawan immigrants in Bolivia. In Colonia San Juan de Yapacaní, a fifteenth-anniversary issue (J-38), thirtieth-anniversary issue (J-39), and fortieth-anniversary issue (J-40) have been published. There is also a fortieth-anniversary publication of their agricultural cooperative CAISY (Cooperativa Agropecuaria Integral San Juan de Yapacaní Ltd.) (J-41). Among these issues, the thirtieth-anniversary issue (J-39) traces all the settlers' migration records for the past thirty years, which is extremely valuable.

The two colonias have been a focus of academic research. Research conducted by geographers include the doctoral dissertation of Mario Hiraoka submitted to the University of Wisconsin (E-2) and works written by Professor Tomonori Ishikawa of the Ryūkyū University (J-9, J-10, J-11, J-12). Ishikawa exclusively focuses on Colonia Okinawa. On the other hand, Hiraoka's work (E-2) has a wider focus, including both colonias, and it discusses them within the context of their geographic environment and their developmental history in the lowlands of eastern Bolivia. The doctoral dissertation by the cultural anthropologist Stephen Thompson (E-5) focuses on Colonia San Juan de Yapacaní. Also, *Boribia no Nihonjin-mura* (Japanese Village in Bolivia) (J-21), by Iyo Kunimoto, focuses on Colonia San Juan de Yapacaní. It was also published in Spanish (S-1) with support from the Japan Foundation.

Okinawa ijūchi (Colonia Okinawa) (J-4), and *Imin konjō* (Immigrants' Spirit) (J-13) were both written by immigrants in Colonia Okinawa. These two books show the agonies of the leaders in the colonia and the hopes and aspirations of the Issei (first generation). Not included in this list of recommended readings are many field research reports issued by agricultural, medical, educational, and other kinds of organizations. However, they can be viewed in such places as in the reference room of the JICA in Tokyo.

Among those reports on the current condition of the Nikkei society, "Nikkei Boribiajin no seikatsu to ishiki" (J-25) presents the current situation of Nikkei societies in six areas of Bolivia, on the basis of an on-site questionnaire survey conducted in Bolivia by an academic investigative group. Japanese 8, 20, 23 and 33 are reportage or travel diaries, describing the Nikkei societies. Some are based on limited information, such as hearsay and observation during short stays. They offer some fresh points of view, but at times they completely misinterpret situations, and in some cases their approaches to issues are problematic. Even so, they are valuable in that they deal with the Japanese immigrants and Nikkei societies in Bolivia—subjects that receive little attention.

Japanese Bolivian Annotated Bibliography

COMPILED BY IYO KUNIMOTO

ENGLISH

1. Amemiya, Kozy. "The 'Labor Pains' in Forging a Nikkei Community: A Study of the Santa Cruz Region in Bolivia." In *New Worlds, New Lives: Globalization and People of Japanese Descent in the Americas and from Latin America in Japan*, edited by Lane Ryo Hirabayashi, Akemi Kikumura-Yano, and James Hirabayashi. Stanford, Calif.: Stanford University Press, 2002.

2. Hiraoka, Mario. "Pioneer Settlement in Eastern Bolivia." Ph.D. diss., The University of Wisconsin, 1974.

    A study of Okinawa and Colonia San Juan de Yacataní by a geographer. Discussed in the context of the geographical environment and developmental history of the eastern lowlands of Bolivia.

3. Hiraoka, Mario. "Structural Variation among Dwelling in the Japanese Colony of San Juan de Yapacaní, Bolivia." *Association of Pacific Coast Geographers Yearbook* 34 (1980).

4. Thompson, Stephen Ide. "Religious Conversion and Religious Zeal in an Overseas Enclave: The Case of the Japanese in Bolivia." *Anthroplogical Quarterly* 41, no. 4 (1968).

5. Thompson, Stephen Ide. "San Juan Yapacaní: A Japanese Pioneer Colony in Eastern Bolivia." Ph.D. diss., University of Illinois, 1968.

    The Ph.D. dissertation by an anthropologist focuses on Colonia San Juan de Yacataní.

6. Tigner, James Lawrence. "Ryukyuans in Bolivia." *Hispanic American Historical Review* 43, no. 3 (1983).

    A history of Okinawan immigrants to Bolivia.

JAPANESE

1. Boribia Nihonjin 100-shūnenshi Hensan Iinkai [ボリビア日本人100周年誌編纂委員会], ed. *Boribia ni ikiru: Nihonjin ijū 100-shūnenshi* [ボリビアに生きる：日本人移住100周年誌]. Santa Kurusu [サンタ・クルス]: n.p., 2000.

    Published to commemorate the hundredth anniversary of the Japanese immigration to Bolivia. The most useful and valuable publication to learn the history of Nikkei in Bolivia.

2. CAICO 20-shūnen Kinen Hensan Iinkai [CAICO20周年記念誌編集委員会], ed. *CAICO sōritsu 20-shūnen kinenshi: Boribia Koronia Okinawa Nōboku Sōgō Kyōkai Kumiai 20-nen no ayumi.* [CAICO創立20周年記念誌：ボリビア・コロニア沖縄農牧総合協会組合20年の歩み]. N.p., 1993.

    The twentieth anniversary publication of CAICO (Co-operativa Agropecuaria Integral Colonias Okinawa), the agricultural cooperative of Colonia Okinawa.

3. Gushi, Kanchō [具志寛長]. "Boribia imin no kigen: Uruma Nōsangyō Kumiai shi [ボリビア移民の起源：ウルマ農産業組合史]." *Yūhi* [雄飛] 37 (1981).

    An essay on the origin of postwar Okinawan immigrants to Bolivia, written by one of the greatest contributors to the establishment of Colonia Okinawa.

4. Gushiken, Kōtei [具志堅興貞]. *Okinawa ijūchi: Boribia no daichi to tomoni* [沖縄移住地：ボリビアの大地とともに], edited by Yutaka Terui [照井裕]. Naha-shi [那覇市]: Okinawa Taimususha [沖縄タイムス社], 1997.

    An essay on personal experiences, written by a leader of the Okinawan immigrants' group.

5. Honma, Takeo [本間剛夫]. "Boribia no Nihonjin [ボリビアの日本人]." *San Pauro Jinbun Kagaku Kenkyūjo Kenkyū Repōto* [サンパウロ人文科学研究所・研究レポート] (1968).

    A research on the Japanese migration to the Amazon area in the prewar period based on secondary sources.

6. Horiuchi, Denjū [堀内傳重]. *Seibo kahan no jūrokunen: Horiuchi Denjū ikō* [聖母河畔の十六年：堀内傳重遺構]. Horiuchi, Denjū [堀内傳重], 1926.

    A diary and letters written by the author who traveled and lived in the deep Amazon area in the 1910s.

7. Imaizumi, Shichirō [今泉七郎]. "Boribia, Nikkei ijūchi no einō tenkai: nōgyō kikaika no sokumen kara [ボリヴィア・日系移住地の営農展開：農業機械化の側面から]." *Ijū kenkyū* [移住研究] 30 (1993).

    Study on the agricultural mechanization of the postwar Japanese settlements in Bolivia. Written by a personnel of the Japan International Cooperation Agency.

8. Ishida, Jintarō [石田甚太郎]. *Boribia imin kikigaki: Andesu no kanata no Okinawa to Nihon* [ボリビア移民聞書：アンデスの彼方の沖縄と日本]. Tōkyō [東京]: Gendai Kikakushitsu [現代企画室], 1986.

    A reportage on the Nikkei society in Santa Cruz, Bolivia.

9. Ishikawa, Tomonori [石川友紀]. "Boribia ni okeru Nihon imin no chiikiteki bunpu to shokugyō kōsei no hensen: Dainiji Sekai Taisen zen o chūshin ni [ボリビアにおける日本移民の地域的分布と職業構成の変遷：第二次世界大戦前を中心に]." *Ryūkyū Daigaku Hōbun Gakubu kiyō, shigaku, chirigaku hen* [琉球大学法文学部紀要・史学・地理学編] 35 (1992).

    A research on the Japanese migration to the Amazon area in the prewar period based on secondary sources includes regional distribution and occupational structure.

10. Ishikawa, Tomonori [石川友紀]. "Boribia, Okinawa ijūchi keisei e no Ryūkyū Seifu keikaku imin no keii: shonendo imin o jirei toshite [ボリビア・オキナワ移住地形成への

琉球政府計画移民の経緯：初年度移民を事例として]." *Ryūkyū Daigaku Hōbun Gakubu kiyō, chiiki, shakai kagakukei hen* [琉球大学法文学部紀要・地域・社会科学系編], [創刊号] [Sōkangō] (1995).

    A study by a geographer on the first group of Okinawan immigrants to Colonia Okinawa, planned by the Okinawan government.

11. Ishikawa, Tomonori [石川友紀]. "Boribiakoku koronia Okinawa imin no saiijū ni kansuru jisshōteki kōsatsu [ボリビア国コロニア沖縄移民の再移住に関する実証的考察]." *Okinawa chiri* [沖縄地理] 1 (1986).

    An empirical study by a geographer on the resettlement of immigrants to Colonia Okinawa.

12. Ishikawa, Tomonori [石川友紀]. "Okinawa ijūchi hatten no rekishi o furikaeru: shonendo imin o chūshin ni [オキナワ移住地発展の歴史を振り返る：初年度移民を中心に]." *Kaigai ijū* [海外移住] 557 (1994).

    An essay by a geographer on the development of Colonia Okinawa mainly focuses on the first immigrants.

13. Ishū, Chōki [伊集朝規]. *Imin konjō: Nanbei no daichi ni ikite* [移民根性：南米の大地に生きて]. Naha-shi [那覇市]: Hirugisha [ひるぎ社], 1987.

    An essay on personal experiences, written by a leader of the Okinawan immigrants' group.

14. Itō, Kazuo [伊藤一男]. "Watashitachi wa aruite Andesu o tōhashita: Boribia ni teichakushita 'nagare imin' no kaisō [私たちは歩いてアンデスを踏破した：ボリビアに定着した「流れ移民」の回想]." *Kikan kaigai Nikkeijin* [季刊海外日系人] 7 (1980).

    A memoir edited by a journalist based on interviews with Japanese immigrants who crossed the Andes on foot from Peru to Bolivia in the early period.

15. Kawaji, Ken'ichirō [川路賢一郎]. "Amazon jōryū ni Nihonjin o tazunete: Boriviakoku Benishū, Pandoshū [アマゾン上流に日本人を訪ねて：ボリヴィア国ベニ州、パンド州]." *Ijū kenkyū* [移住研究] 19 (1982).

    A reportage on the prewar Japanese immigrants in the Amazon area.

16. Koronia Okinawa Nyūshoku 10-shūnen Kinen Saiten Iinkai [コロニア沖縄入植10周年記念祭典委員会], ed. *Koronia Okinawa 10-nen no ayumi* [コロニア・オキナワ10年の歩み]. N.p., 1964.

    The tenth anniversary publication of Colonia Okinawa.

17. Koronia Okinawa Nyūshoku 25-shūnen Kinen Saiten Iinkai [コロニア沖縄入植25周年記念祭典委員会], ed. *Koronia Okinawa nyūshoku 25-shūnen kinenshi* [コロニア沖縄入植25周年記念誌]. N.p., 1980.

    The twenty-fifth anniversary publication of Colonia Okinawa.

18. Koronia Okinawa Nyūshoku 30-shūnen Kinen Saiten Iinkai [コロニア沖縄入植30周年記念祭典委員会], ed. *Koronia Okinawa 30-nen no ayumi* [コロニア・オキナワ30年の歩み]. N.p., 1984.

    The thirtieth anniversary publication of Colonia Okinawa.

19. Koronia Okinawa Nyūshoku 40-shūnen Kinen Saiten Iinkai [コロニア沖縄入植40周年記念祭典委員会], ed. *Uruma kara no tabidachi: Koronia Okinawa nyūshoku 40-shūnen kinenshi* [うるまからの出発：コロニア・オキナワ入植40周年記念誌]. N.p., 1995.

    The fortieth anniversary publication of Colonia Okinawa.

20. Kunimoto, Iyo [国本伊代]. "Boribia Nikkei shakai no genjō to mondai [ボリビア日系社会の現状と問題]." *Kikan kaigai Nikkeijin* [季刊海外日系人] 24 (1989).

    An essay on the current condition and problems of Nikkei society in Bolivia.

21. Kunimoto, Iyo [国本伊代]. *Boribia no Nihonjin-mura: Santa Kurusu-shū San Fuan ijūchi no kenkyū* [ボリビアの日本人村：サンタクルス州サンフアン移住地の研究]. Tōkyō [東京]: Chūō Daigaku Shuppanbu [中央大学出版部], 1989.

    A study on the Colonia San Juan de Yacapaní. Also published in Spanish. See S-1.

22. Kunimoto, Iyo [国本伊代]. "Boribiakoku San Fuan ijūchi: jittai to ishiki chōsa ni yoru Nihonjin-mura no sobyō [ボリビア国サンフアン移住地：実態と意識調査による日本人村の素描]." *Ijū kenkyū* [移住研究] 21 (1984).

    A research on the current conditions of Colonia San Juan de Yacapaní.

23. Kunimoto, Iyo [国本伊代]. "Borivia Nikkei shakai no ima: genchi shisatsu no tabi kara [ボリヴィア日系社会の今：現地視察の旅から]." *Kaigai ijū* [海外移住] 550 (1994).

    Reportage on the Nikkei society in Bolivia.

24. Kunimoto, Iyo [国本伊代]. "Nihonjin Boribia shoki imin ni kansuru ichi kōsatsu [日本人ボリビア初期移民に関する一考察]." *Imin kenkyū nenpō* [移民研究年報] 6 (1999).

    A research on the Japanese migration to the Amazon area in the prewar period based on secondary sources.

25. Kunimoto, Iyo [国本伊代]. "Nikkei Boribiajin no seikatsu to ishiki: 1983-nen ankēto chōsa yori [日系ボリビア人の生活と意識：1983年アンケート調査より]." *Ijū kenkyū* [移住研究] 22 (1985).

    An analytical research essay based on the survey conducted by an academic investigation team in six Nikkei societies in Bolivia.

26. Kunimoto, Iyo [国本伊代]. "Riberaruta no Nikkei shakai: Borivia Nikkeijin chōsa no tabi kara [リベラルタの日系社会：ボリヴィア日系人調査の旅から]." *Kaigai ijū* [移住研究] 429 (1984).

    Reportage on the Nikkei community in Riberalta.

27. Nakano, Mikio [中野幹雄]. *Oku Amazon no nikkeijin: Perū kudari to akuma no tetsudō* [奥アマゾンの日系人 — ペルー下りと悪魔の鉄道]: Kōmyakusha [鉱脈社], 1998.

    Reportage tracing the Japanese who were involved in the construction of Madeira Railroad during the first half of the 1910s.

28. Nakayama, Mitsuru [中山満]. "Boribia, Okinawa ijūchi no kiroku to teigen: ima Koronia Okinawa ni nani ga okotte iru no ka [ボリビア・沖縄移住地の記録と提言：今コロ

ニア・オキナワに何が起こっているのか]." *Yūhi* [雄飛] 31–32 (1974–1975).

Reportage on the problems of Colonia Okinawa.

29. Nihonjin Borivia Ijūshi Hensan Iinkai [日本人ボリヴィア移住史編纂委員会], ed. *Nihonjin Borivia ijūshi* [日本人ボリヴィア移住史]. Tōkyō [東京]: Nihonjin Borivia Ijūshi Hensan Iinkai [日本人ボリヴィア移住史編纂委員会], 1970.

A history of Japanese emigration to Bolivia. Very valuable.

30. Noda, Ryōji [野田良治]. "Arika, Ra Pasu tetsudō fusetsu chihō shisatu hōkoku [アリカ、ラ・パス鉄道敷設地方視察報告]." *Imin chōsa hōkoku 1* [移民調査報告 第1回].

A useful primary source. Noda reports on the condition of the local railroad construction site between Arica and La Paz.

31. Noda, Ryōji [野田良治]. "Borivia kyōwakoku shisatu hōkokusho [ボリヴィア共和国視察報告書]." *Imin chōsa hōkoku 1* [移民調査報告 第1回].

A useful primary source. Noda reports on the Bolivian Republic.

32. Noda, Ryōji [野田良治]. *Nanbei no kakushin ni funtō seru dōhō o tazunete* [南米の核心に奮闘せる同胞を訪ねて]. Hakubunkan [博文館], 1931.

A useful primary source. Noda reports on his investigative travel through South America. Includes his report on Japanese society in Bolivia in the 1930s.

33. Noro, Yoshimichi [野呂義道]. "Maboroshi no ijūchi: Borivia no Nihonjin-machi [まぼろしの移住地: ボリヴィアの日本人町]." *Ushio* [潮] 6 (1984).

A travel diary tracing the Japanese in the deep Amazon area.

34. Ono, Motoo [小野基雄]. "Andesu o koeta hitobito: Boribia Nihonjin no senkusha [アンデスを超えた人々: ボリビア日本人の先駆者]." *Ijū kenkyū* [移住研究] 6 (1970).

A research essay on the Japanese migration to the Amazon area in the prewar period based on secondary sources.

35. Oshimoto, Naomasa [押本直正]. "Boribia no Okinawa ijūchi: sono settei no keii o chūshin toshite [ボリビアの沖縄移住地: その設定の経緯を中心として]." *Ijū kenkyū* [移住研究] 7 (1970).

A study on the establishment of Colonia Okinawa. Written by a personnel of the Japan International Cooperation Agency.

36. Ōtsuka, Makoto [大塚真琴]. "Aragaki Yōei to Borivia tōbō imin [新垣庸英とボリヴィア逃亡移民]." *Ijū kenkyū* [移住研究] 29 (1992).

A research essay on the Japanese migration to Amazon area based on Yōei Aragaki's diary.

37. Ra Pasu Nihonjinkai Shoki Kōhōbu [ラ・パス日本人会書記広報部], ed. "Ra Pasu Nihonjinkai [羅巴斯日本人会]." *Ijū kenkyū* [移住研究] 24 (1987).

Published by the La Paz Japanese Association. A rare record on the Japanese immigrants in the Andes area.

38. San Fuan 15-nenshi Hensan Iinkai [サンフアン15年史編纂委員会], ed. *San Fuan 15-nenshi* [サンフアン15年史]. N.p., 1971.

The fifteenth anniversary publication of Colonia San Juan de Yacapaní.

39. San Fuan Ijūchi Nyūshoku 30-shūnen Kinen Jigyō Suishin Iinkai [サンフアン移住地入植30周年記念事業推進委員], ed. *San Fuan ijūchi 30-nenshi: Nanbei no genshirin ni idonda Nihonjin no kiroku* [サンフアン移住地30年史: 南米の原始林に挑んだ日本人の記録]. N.p., 1986.

The thirtieth anniversary publication of Colonia San Juan de Yacataní.

40. San Fuan Nichi-Bo Kyōkai [サンフアン日ボ協会], ed. *Midori no kagayaku daichi: San Fuan Nihonjin ijūchi nyūshoku yonjisshūnen kinenshi* [緑の輝く大地 : サン・フアン日本人移住地入植四十周年記念誌]. N.p., 1997.

The tenth anniversary publication of Colonia San Juan de Yacataní.

41. San Fuan Nōboku Sōgō Kyōdō Kumiai [サンファン農牧総合共同組合]. *San Fuan Nōboku Sōgō Kyōdō Kumiai yonjūnen no ayumi* [サンファン農牧総合共同組合四十年の歩み], 1998.

The forty-year history of San Juan Agricultural Cooperative, self-published.

42. Tamashiro, Bigorō [玉城美五郎]. "Okinawa kara mita Okinawa ijū 20-nen no ayumi [沖縄からみた沖縄移住20年の歩み]." *Yūhi* [雄飛] 31–32 (1974–1975).

A twenty-year history of Okinawan Immigration to Bolivia, from the viewpoint of Okinawa.

43. Tomizu, Yasuji [戸水康二]. "Boribiakoku Okinawa ijūchi no watasaku [ボリビア国オキナワ移住地の綿作]." *Ijū kenkyū* [移住研究] 9 (1973).

A study on the cotton production in Colonia Okinawa. Written by a personnel of the Japan International Cooperation Agency.

44. Uehara, Seiki [上原盛毅]. "Santa Kurusu chihō no kindaika: Nihonjin ijū ukeire no rekishiteki haikei [サンタクルス地方の近代化 : 日本人移住受け入れの歴史的背景]." *Ijū kenkyū* [移住研究] 18 (1981).

A research essay providing historical background on the reception of Japanese immigrants in Santa Cruz.

45. Wakatsuki, Yasuo [若槻泰雄]. " 'Gengo' o ushinaikakeru 2, 3-sei: Boribia no Nihon imin no kyōiku [「言語」を失いかける2・3世: ボリビアの日本移民の教育]." *Asahi Shinbun* [朝日新聞] (1983).

A critical essay on the educational problem of the second and third generations of Japanese immigrants in Bolivia.

46. Wakatsuki, Yasuo [若槻泰雄]. *Hatten tojōkoku e no ijū no kenkyū: Boribia ni okeru Nihon imin* [発展途上国への移住の研究: ボリビアにおける日本移民]. Tōkyō [東京]: Tamagawa Daigaku Shuppanbu [玉川大学出版部], 1987.

A critical study of the immigration policies by the Japanese government in the postwar era, using Bolivia as a case study.

47. Yagi, Sentei [八木宣貞]. *Gojūnen zengo no omoide* [五十年前後の思い出]. Unknown, 1963.

The author reports fifty years later on his personal experiences in Bolivia during the 1910s.

SPANISH

1. Kunimoto, Iyo. *Un pueblo japonés en la Bolivia tropical: Colonia San Juan de Yapacaní en el Departamento de Santa Cruz.* Santa Cruz: Casa de la Cultura, 1990.

    A study of Colonia San Juan de Yacataní. Originally published in Japanese. See J-21.

2. Mitsuhashi, Toshimitsu. "Los problemas educativos de los jóvenes descendientes japoneses en Bolivia." *Bulletin of Nagoya Holly Spirit Junior College* 2 (1986).

    A research essay on educational problems of the young Japanese descendants in Bolivia.

3. Parejas Moreno, Alcides. *Colonia japonesa en Bolivia.* N.p. Colegio de Don Bosco, 1981.

    A book edited by the Bolivian historian that contains a short history of Japanese immigration to Bolivia.

4. Wakatsuki, Yasuo, and Iyo Kunimoto, eds. *La inmigración japonesa en Bolivia: estudios históricos y socio-económicos.* Tokyo: Chuo Universidad, 1985.

    A collaboration between Bolivian and Japanese researchers. An academic book that contains essays on the history of immigration, economic, and social condition of Nikkei society and its transformation.

Supplementary Materials

COMPILED BY FEDERACIÓN NACIONAL DE ASOCIACIONES BOLIVIANO JAPONESAS, TOSHIO YANAGUIDA, AND KOZY AMEMIYA

Map 3.1 Japanese Bolivian Settlements

Japanese Bolivian Demographic Information

Table 3.1 JICA-Sponsored Japanese Emigration to Bolivia by Prefecture of Origin in Japan, 1952–1993

	1952'–'55	'56–'60	'61–'65	'66–'70	'71–'75	'76–'80	'81–'85	'86–'90	'91–'93	Total*
Nagasaki	42	437	289	4	-	4	1	-	-	**777**
Okinawa	-	-	-	66	19	46	12	9	-	**152**
Fukuoka	7	60	71	5	1	3	-	1	-	**148**
Tōkyō	20	45	3	9	9	7	1	2	5	**101**
Kumamoto	6	79	-	-	-	4	1	-	-	**90**
Total*	94	1,162	400	90	36	86	25	15	11	**1,919**

Source: Japan International Cooperation Agency, *Kaigai ijū tōkei (FY 1952–FY 1993)*, (Tōkyō, 1994), 34–35.
Note: *Total includes other prefectures.

Table 3.2 Regional Distribution of Japanese Bolivians, 1955–2000

Year	San Juan¹	Okinawa²	La Paz³	Santa Cruz	Total
1955	88	400	-	-	488
1960	771	-	251	474	1,496
1970	-	-	115	446	561
1980	1,344	1,265	114	622	3,345
1990	857	1,050	134	617	2,658
2000	754	828	213	665	2,460

Source: Survey conducted by the Federación Nacional de Asociaciones Boliviano-Japonesas, based on data provided by Japanese associations in four settlements, 2000.
Notes:
¹ San Juan: The first year of settlement was 1955. Between 1957 and 1960, there were 722 settlers, 60 births and 11 deaths; between 1961 and 1979, there were 846 settlers, 665 births, and 138 deaths. The reason for the decrease in population between 1980 and 1990 is due to the inflation that started around 1982 and accelerated rapidly, lasting until about 1986. Concomitantly, Japan was experiencing an economic boom. As a result, many returned to Japan or went to work there as dekasegi. Due to the decrease of younger populations, the birth rate has declined and has not recovered. The population for 2000 is based on the survey of the Japanese in Bolivia on October 1, 2000.
² Okinawa: The reason for the decrease in the population between 1990 and 2000 may be due to the dekasegi boom and longer stay (or permanent settlement) in Japan.
³ La Paz: Source unknown for the population of 1960. Population figures for 1970, 1980, 1990, and 2000 are numbers provided by the members of the Japanese Association. The populations of 2000 include family members.

Table 3.3 Japanese Bolivian Gender Breakdown by Percentage, 1955–2000

	San Juan		Okinawa		La Paz		Santa Cruz	
Year	Male	Female	Male	Female	Male	Female	Male	Female
1955	56.8	43.2	-	-	-	-	-	-
1960	-	-	-	-	-	-	52.1	47.9
1970	-	-	-	-	-	-	50.2	49.8
1980	51.0	49.0	52.9	47.1	92.9	7.1	49.0	51.0
1990	49.9	50.1	51.2	48.8	84.3	15.7	48.2	51.8
2000	50.0	50.0	50.3	49.7	59.1	40.9	49.9	50.1

Source: Federación Nacional de Asociaciones Boliviano Japonesas, 2000.

Table 3.4 Educational Level of Japanese in Bolivia by Percentage, 2000

Age	NA	None	Grade School (incomplete)	Grade School (complete)	Junior High	Senior High	College (2 & 4yrs.)	
San Juan								
20–23 (20)	15.0	-	-	-	5.0	80.0	-	
24–34 (58)	7.0	-	-	3.0	15.0	59.0	17.0	
35–44 (89)	6.0	-	-	2.0	32.0	50.0	9.0	
45–54 (98)	5.0	-	1.0	9.0	68.0	13.0	2.0	
Over 55 (179)	10.0	-	-	4.0	33.0	14.0	3.0	
Okinawa (no data available for Okinawa)								
La Paz								Professionals
25–34 (55)	4.0	-	2.0	-	5.0	18.0	53.0	18.0
35–44 (31)	6.0	-	-	-	10.0	10.0	45.0	29.0
45–54 (52)	8.0	-	2.0	-	17.0	27.0	35.0	11.0
Over 55 (41)	2.0	-	-	-	24.0	27.0	32.0	15.0
Santa Cruz								Others
25–34 (99)	7.0	0	-	-	-	38.0	50.0	4.0
35–44 (84)	1.0	0	-	-	3.0	36.0	51.0	8.0
45–54 (105)	5.0	0	-	3.0	12.0	47.0	30.0	5.0
Over 55 (120)	11.0	0	-	7.0	27.0	39.0	12.0	4.0

Source: Federación Nacional de Asociaciones Boliviano Japonesas, 2000.

Note: Grade school (complete) includes junior high school students and dropouts. Junior high school includes senior high school students and dropouts. Senior high school includes college students and dropouts.

Table 3.5 Occupational Fields of Japanese Bolivian Heads of Household by Percentage, 2000

	Agriculture	Japanese Service	Org.	Company	Bolivian Service	Multi-Corp.	Business	Other	Total
San Juan	77.0	5.0	-	5.0	0.0	-	4.0	8.0	**189**
Okinawa	75.0	6.0	-	1.0	0.4	-	3.0	14.0	**235**
La Paz	0.0	0.0	0.6	19.0	0.2	15.0	34.0	24.0	**80**
Santa Cruz	13.0	2.0	4.0	2.0	0.0	2.0	47.0	30.0	**160**

Source: Federación Nacional de Asociaciones Boliviano Japonesas, 2000.

Table 3.6 Occupational Fields of Japanese Bolivian Population of Wives and Children by Percentage, 2000

	Agriculture	Japanese Public Service	Nikkei Org.	Japanese Company	Bolivian Public Service	Multi-national Corp. (MNC)	Business	Housewife	Student	Other	Total
San Juan	10.0	3.0	-	4.0	-	-	-	64.0	5.0	14.0	**220**
Okinawa	5.0	2.0	0.5	0.3	-	-	0.5	32.0	32.0	26.0	**593**
La Paz	-	-	4.0	-	4.0	1.0	7.0	19.0	42.0	23.0	**210**
Santa Cruz	2.0	2.0	1.0	-	0.4	0.4	8.0	20.0	49.0	17.0	**447**

Source: Federación Nacional de Asociaciones Boliviano Japonesas, 2000.

Table 3.7 Religion of Japanese Bolivians by Percentage, 2000

	Christian	Buddhist	Others	None	NA	Total
San Juan	60.0	22.0	5.0	4.0	7.0	**237**
Okinawa	-	-	-	-	-	-
La Paz	79.0	15.0	-	5.0	-	**97**
Santa Cruz	45.0	21.0	-	19.0	14.0	**496**

Source: Federación Nacional de Asociaciones Boliviano Japonesas, 2000.

CHAPTER 4

Japanese Brazilians

DEVELOPED IN COLLABORATION WITH THE MUSEU HISTÓRICO DA IMIGRAÇÃO JAPONESA NO BRASIL

JAPANESE IMMIGRANTS FIRST CAME TO BRAZIL IN JUNE 1908. THESE FAMILIES worked on coffee plantations under contract labor to coffee planters in search of cheap labor. After the United States closed its door to Japanese immigration in 1924, the Japanese government facilitated the accelerated immigration of Japanese into Brazil. However, life was so unbearable that most Japanese left the plantations for urban areas, suburbs, or new Japanese farm settlements. São Paulo city and its surrounding areas were the main areas of concentration. By the 1930s, the Brazilian government had become increasingly wary of Japanese residents, culminating in the introduction of a quota system for immigration in 1935 and a ban on Japanese education three years later. The Pacific War added more restrictions on the lives of Issei, including a ban on meetings and traveling without permits. Some residents in the coastal areas and downtown São Paulo were forcibly removed. The war also caused a deep rupture between two factions in the immigrant society—one believing that Japan had triumphed and the other accepting its defeat. It was not until 1954 that the conflict finally subsided and a new chapter of Brazilian Nikkei history began, with the influx of postwar immigrants between 1953 and 1973. While the prewar Nikkei households left the rural areas for the cities, the postwar settlers revived Japanese agriculture in Brazil. In the 1990s, 250,000 Nikkei in the prime of their lives went to Japan for *dekasegi* work, due to the recession. Today, with an estimated population of 1,228,000 in Brazil, the Brazilian Nikkei community is faced with a host of new issues, including the care for the elderly and the relative indifference of the younger generations to Nikkei community affairs.

Japanese Brazilian Historical Overview

MASATO NINOMIYA

INTRODUCTION

They came anxiously to work on coffee plantations they had never seen before, with plans to become rich and return to their home country in triumph. It is said that on their first night in Brazil, while still in the seaport of Santos, they thought the fireworks in the sky were honoring their arrival. Later, they discovered that the fireworks display had been part of the traditional parties held in June called "*festas juninas*."

This was not the only disappointment experienced by the Japanese immigrants in Brazil since their first arrival in June 18, 1908, on the steamship *Kasato Maru*. By contract, they comprised families with at least three members who were fully capable of working. Emigration was a way out of Japan, a country faced with deep social, economic, and demographic problems. Excited by the promises made by the agents of emigration companies, they dreamed of returning to Japan in five years with enough money to start independent lives. Approximately 7 percent of the 188,000 Japanese immigrants that came before World War II were able to achieve this dream. However, spurred on by their hopes, they were able to face the worst conditions in life.

According to their labor contracts, the Japanese immigrants were to work on the coffee plantations as laborers for two or three years. Not everyone followed the contract to the letter. Disenchanted by the working conditions, some escaped from the coffee plantations and made their way to the cities. Others changed farms with the consent of their employers.

While the immigrants were seeking riches, the coffee employers were after a cheap workforce. After the end of black slavery in 1888, the coffee farmers of São Paulo State turned to the European immigrant population, especially Spanish and Italian, as a source of labor. However, with their labor problem still unsolved, they decided to bring Japanese; during the first stage of Japanese immigration from 1908 to 1925, the coffee producers and the São Paulo State government subsidized their trips. Because of problems of adaptation, however, the project was abandoned. For example, among the 781 immigrants who first came to Brazil under contract, only 191 remained at the same place nine months after their arrival.

In the beginning of emigration, the Japanese government made efforts to send its subjects to the United States. However, after the United States passed the 1924 Immigration Act, which prohibited the entry of Japanese into the United States, the Japanese government increased and subsidized the program of immigration to Brazil. Japanese immigration to Brazil increased quickly; it decreased only after 1935, when the Brazilian constitution established a quota limiting foreign immigrants. In 1941, the

Kasato Maru, *the ship that brought the first group to Japanese immigrants to Brazil in 1908. (Collection of Museu Histórico da Imigração Japonesa no Brasil)*

These women were among the first Japanese immigrants to arrive in Brazil on the ship Kasato Maru *on June 18, 1908. (Collection of Museu Histórico da Imigração Japonesa no Brasil)*

Gheisha cleaning service of Shugo Ouchida on Teixeira de Mello Street, Rio de Janeiro, in the early 1930s. (Collection of Museu Histórico da Imigração Japonesa no Brasil)

migratory movement was interrupted and diplomatic relations between the two countries were ruptured with the start of World War II.

On April 28, 1952, the San Francisco Peace Treaty reestablished diplomatic relations between Japan and the Allies; immigration to Brazil resumed the following year. Over more than twenty years, ships brought approximately fifty-five thousand Japanese immigrants to Santos and other seaports in Brazil. Unlike in the previous stage, many of the postwar immigrants were specialized technicians who came to work in the industries of Brazil.

The period from 1958 to 1962 was the peak of Japanese immigration to Brazil. Thereafter, the numbers decreased year after year. The precarious conditions that had stimulated emigration in postwar Japan had disappeared, including unemployment among people who had returned from territories in Asia occupied by the Japanese before and during World War II. In the mid-1960s, Japan became a fully industrialized nation.

At the end of the 1950s, Japanese companies started to

A father and his two children have lunch in the pioneer frontier of the 1930s, where Japanese immigrants cleared the forests to start coffee plantations. (Collection of Museu Histórico da Imigração Japonesa no Brasil)

Japanese Brazilians   117

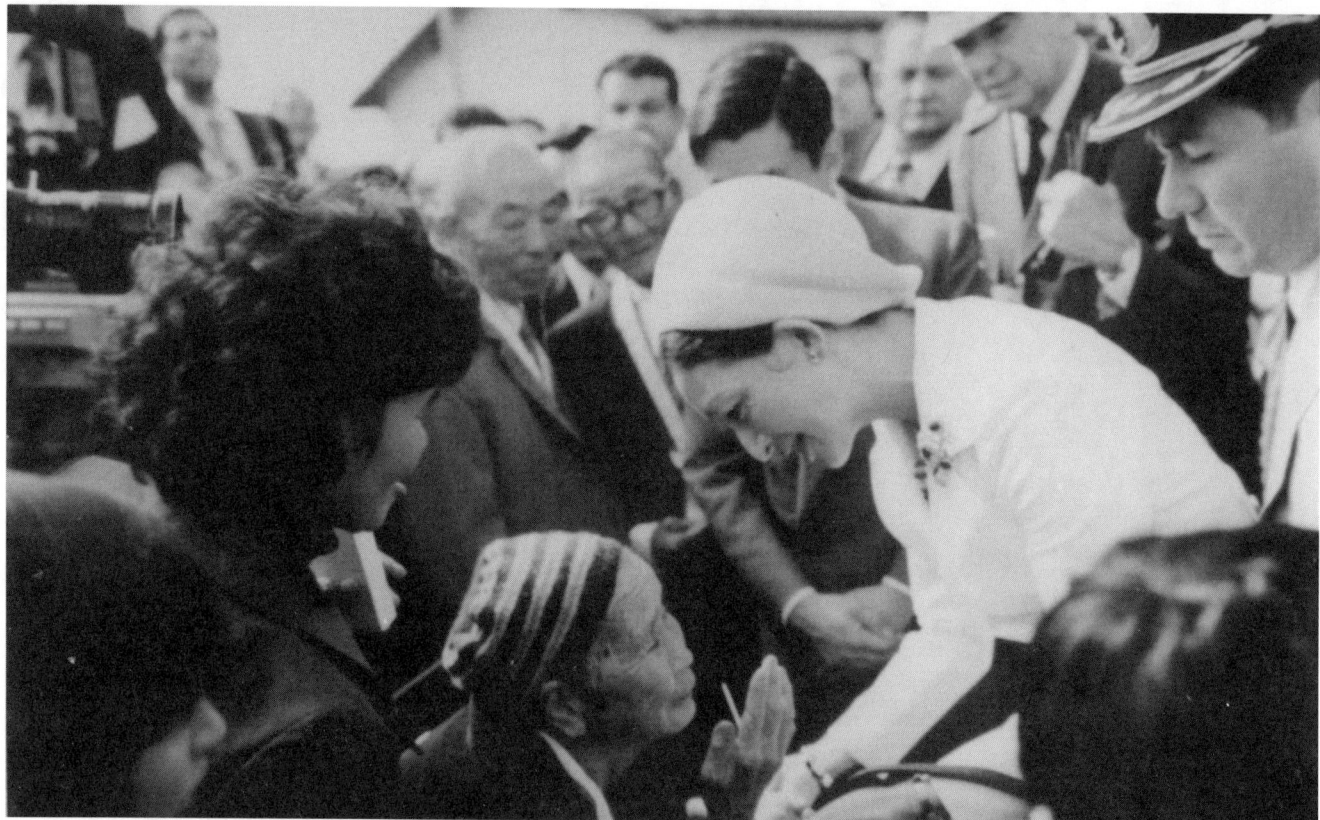
Princess Michiko of Japan comforts an old Japanese immigrant woman on her second visit to Brazil in 1978. (Collection of Museu Histórico da Imigração Japonesa no Brasil)

invest in Brazil. Trade between the two countries diversified, especially with the export of Brazil's agricultural products to Japan. In 1957, the Usinas Siderúrgicas de Minas Gerais (USIMINAS), a steel mill complex, was constructed in Minas Gerais State, with the cooperation of Japanese and Brazilian government and private investments. In 1959, the Ishibras (Ishikawajima do Brasil Estaleiros S.A.) shipyard was established in Rio de Janeiro.

Over the years, Japanese business interests increased. In the second half of the 1970s, more than five hundred Japanese companies from different fields opened their subsidiaries or offices, with representatives in Brazil. It was still a very productive decade, with important national projects supported by Brazilian and Japanese governmental and by private investment, such as the Companhia Siderúrgica de Tubarão (steel mill), the Albras-Alunorte complex (manufacture of aluminum and alumina), Cenibra (manufacture of pulp), and PRODECER (agricultural projects in the Cerrado region located in the central part of the country).

The "Brazil boom" suffered a great crash when the country centralized the exchange rate through its Central Bank in the middle of 1983, an action that was tantamount to a declaration of moratorium. The 1980s witnessed a cooling in the bilateral economic relations between Brazil and Japan, while at the same time a different movement emerged as the sons and daughters of Japanese immigrants left Brazil for jobs in Japanese companies. Today, approximately half of the Japanese companies and industries that were in Brazil in the 1970s remain, though not with the same vitality.

JAPANESE COLLECTIVE SETTLEMENTS IN BRAZIL

Until the 1940s, the main destinations for the contract workers were the Japanese collective settlements located in the coffee plantation zone along the Mogiana, Paulista, and Araraquara Railroads in São Paulo State. Some contract workers also went to the rice-growing areas in the region called Triangulo Mineiro (close to the Minas Gerais State and São Paulo State frontier). Others went to the coastal region along the Ribeira Valley. In the lands along the Noroeste, Alta Paulista, and Alta Sorocabana Railroads, the first collective settlements of small independent farms started to emerge.

Few of the immigrants decided to remain after their two-to-three-year contracts ended on the farms, which

Bananas were largely cultivated by the Japanese immigrants in the Ribeira River Valley (southern part of São Paulo) in the 1930s. (Collection of Museu Histórico da Imigração Japonesa no Brasil)

Oil painting by Tomoo Handa of Japanese immigrants working on the coffee plantation, 1958. (Collection of Museu Histórico da Imigração Japonesa no Brasil)

offered them chances to develop their own crops between the coffee trees. The majority decided to live independently in the urban regions or suburbs, or on new land.

Tomoo Handa, an artist and writer of many books about the daily life and history of the Japanese immigrants, points out three basic kinds of settlement centers. The first type was conceived and implemented by the emigration companies and subsidized by the Japanese government. Prospective dwellers were able to buy their properties directly in Japan. In São Paulo State, the main collective settlements were: Iguape and Registro in the south; Aliança, Tietê (now Pereira Barreto), and Bastos in the central and northwestern regions; and Três Barras (now Assaí), located in Paraná State.

The second kind of settlement was formed by a leader who gathered inhabitants of coffee farms. In the northwestern region of São Paulo there were the Hirano, settlement established by Umpei Hirano (close to Cafelândia County), and the Uetsuka settlement, formed by Shuhei Uetsuka (now Promissão County). Both were located alongside the Noroeste do Brasil Railway.

The third kind of settlement was formed as a result of the sale of land to immigrants by private enterprises, such as the settlement in Biriguí (located alongside Noroeste do Brasil Railway), the São Paulo State southern coastal settlements situated alongside the Santos-Juquiá Railway, and those in the north of Paraná State.

THE BREAKDOWN OF JAPANESE IMMIGRANT ORGANIZATIONAL STRUCTURES

In all collective settlements, especially in the latter two kinds listed above, the inhabitants themselves were responsible for the development of organizational struc-

A six-year coffee plantation completely in flower in the 1930s. (Collection of Museu Histórico da Imigração Japonesa no Brasil)

tures to solve their local problems. As soon as a settlement (usually called a "colony") was established, it created an association of Japanese *(Nihonjin-kai)*, the central pillar of the community. The Nihonjin-kai, represented by the heads of the family, promoted social-cultural activities, such as the emperor's cult, New Year's commemoration, weddings, and other activities; it also supported and coordinated local development and projects, like the construction of bridges and the repair of the roads.

A top priority of the Nihonjin-kai was to construct and maintain a Japanese-language school. After all, the immigrants planned to return one day to their home country; they had to preserve their original culture and ensure their children's education in the Japanese tradition. However, the educational goal was to make them good subjects of

Professor Tatsuo Ishihara with students in Nambu Japanese School in Juqueri City, on the outskirts of São Paulo, 1930. (Collection of Museu Histórico da Imigração Japonesa no Brasil)

Japan rather than to form future citizens of Brazil who would contribute to their adopted country. According to research conducted in 1932, the Society to Diffuse Japanese Language Education in Brazil (Sociedade de Difusão de Ensino de Japones no Brasil) encompassed 187 schools with a total of ten thousand registered students.

In many locales, the Nihonjin-kai constructed schools and offered them to the state government, which assumed responsibility for providing instructors to teach Portuguese and other subjects. In addition, the Nihonjin-kai recruited teachers for Japanese classes. These schools were fully operational until the beginning of World War II. However, in 1938 all the Japanese, Italian, and German schools were closed. In 1941, newspapers written in foreign languages were suspended in Brazil. After Japan's attack on Pearl Harbor and the consultative meeting of Chancellors of Inter-American States held in Rio de Janeiro on January 1942, diplomatic relations were disrupted between Japan and Brazil, as well as with many Central and South American countries. Thereafter, the Japanese in Brazil suffered numerous restrictions, such as prohibition of meeting, travel by permit only, freezing of assets, and compulsory relocation of the Japanese who lived on the coast and in downtown São Paulo. It is important to mention, however, that legal restrictions were not imposed on Brazilian nationals of Japanese descent, unlike the case in the United States with Japanese and their descendents who lived on the West Coast.

Isolated from the greater Brazilian society, the Japanese experienced a crucial period in their history. Without access to trustworthy sources of information, the immigrants believed that Japan was gaining the victory. Before the end of the war, radical movements erupted within the immigrant society. Groups boycotted Issei silkworm breeders and also spearmint producers, charging that silk and spearmint were used to produce parachutes and explosives to be employed against Japan. These accusations

Tribuna *newspaper of Santos City, São Paulo, reporting about the move of the Japanese from the coastal region, July 10, 1943. (Collection of Museu Histórico da Imigração Japonesa no Brasil)*

served as justification for setting fire to warehouses full of such products.

Japan's final surrender caught the immigrants by surprise. During the first months after the war, the great majority could not believe that their home country had been defeated. Overzealous *kachi-gumi* (people who believed that Japan had won the war) acted fiercely against the *make-gumi* (those who acknowledged Japan's defeat), accusing them of betrayal of their home country. There were approximately a hundred incidents, in which twenty-three make-gumi were murdered.

Even months later, after contradictory and erroneous information had been corrected, the *kachi/make* division remained, revealing on one side an extremist conservative group and on the other a pacifist group. The former insisted on continuing to be "loyal subjects to the emperor" no matter what, and the latter tried to become part of the adopted country. The conflict was officially resolved by Japanese participation in São Paulo's Fourth Centennial Foundation in 1954. With the surplus of capital raised as a result of the centennial, two entities were created: the Sociedade Paulista de Cultura Paulista, previously known as the Sociedade Brasileira de Cultura Japonesa (Brazilian Society of Japanese Culture), and the Aliança Cultural Brasil-Japão (Brazil-Japan Cultural Alliance).

JAPANESE IMMIGRANT: A SYNONYM FOR FARMER

Japanese immigrants contributed to the development of agriculture, not only in productivity but also in the introduction of new agricultural cultures. Today, although the great majority of Japanese Brazilians live in cities (90 percent) and are involved in other kinds of jobs, they still are respected as capable farmers.

A census of the Japanese population conducted by Professor Teiichi Suzuki in 1958 revealed that in 1912 the vast majority of Japanese had been dedicated to coffee (92.6 percent), with a much smaller percentage involved in rice (2.5 percent), cotton (1.2 percent), and growing fruits and vegetables and raising poultry in the suburbs (0.6 percent).

In 1922, coffee cultivation decreased to 52.2 percent, in contrast to the increase in rice production (to 17.6 percent), cotton (12.1 percent), and suburban farming (10.2 percent). A decade later there were visible changes in the Nikkei community; cotton production increased to 14 percent, coffee to 59 percent, and suburban farming to 13 percent, while rice production decreased to 8.3 percent.

Before World War II, the peak of Japanese immigration to Brazil occurred in the second half of the 1920s and the first half of the 1930s. Some of these immigrants headed to the north of Paraná State, due to a drastic decrease in international coffee prices and a prohibition of planting new coffee trees in São Paulo State. At the same time, Japanese companies became interested in cotton production. As a result, there were increased activities related to this commerce—the processing of cotton, its import and export, and financing. The production statistics of 1942 indicated a similar trend, with coffee production decreasing to 24.3 percent and rice to 4.5 percent, while cotton increased to 39.2 percent and suburban farming to 19.9 percent.

Once the war was over, more changes took place. The dream of returning home became impossible with Japan's defeat, and it became essential to restructure future lives in Brazil. A great majority of immigrants chose to live in the cities. They believed that college degrees would guarantee their children's well-being and social ascent. Some decided to go into commercial activities, and others remained in agricultural production close to the cities.

Professor Teiichi Suzuki's census indicated that in 1952 the suburban cultivation of vegetables, fruits, and poultry raising had assumed the leading role (34.1 percent)

The Sakuragumi Teishintai, a unit of the kachi-gumi *group, marching in the streets of São Paulo in 1955 and demanding repatriation of the Japanese. (Collection of Museu Histórico da Imigração Japonesa no Brasil)*

among the agricultural activities of Japanese immigrants. Coffee production decreased to 27.5 percent, cotton to 20.5 percent, and rice production to 3 percent. This urbanization process created new collective settlements, to the detriment of the old. São Paulo's suburban area was one of the destinations for these immigrants, transforming cities like Mogi das Cruzes, Suzano, Santo André, Cotia, Vargem Grande, and Ibiúna into what Brazilians call the "green belt," which supplied the state capital and other states with vegetables, fruits, and poultry in the 1950s. Today, industrialization has invaded these locales, pushing the "green belt" farther out.

In 1953, Japanese emigration to Brazil resumed, contributing to an increase in agricultural production, especially the production of vegetables, fruits, poultry raising, and floriculture. Immigrants who decided to live in the cities worked as employees or started their own small businesses, such as grocery stores, cafes, general stores, and street markets and vendors, while others worked in

Members of the kachi-gumi *group being processed for public disturbance in the city of Tupã in 1947. (Collection of Museu Histórico da Imigração Japonesa no Brasil)*

Japanese farm family that began producing cotton after the coffee plantation prohibition, ca. 1930s. (Collection of Museu Histórico da Imigração Japonesa no Brasil)

the service trades, such as in hair salons, tailor shops, barbershops, and laundries. In general, these were activities that employed familial work, which made it possible for the children to study but help their parents during their free time. It should be emphasized that among the immigrants who continued to farm, some remained on the traditional fertile fields of the southeastern zone, and others went to Brazil's west and central regions to develop new agricultural frontiers.

A census conducted by the Japanese-Brazilian Studies Center (Centro de Estudos Nipo-Brasileiros) in 1988 estimated the Japanese population at 1,228,000 (including immigrants and their descendents), of which 72.2 percent lived in São Paulo State. The census indicated that 90 percent of Japanese-Brazilians resided in the urban region and that 25.8 percent dedicated their time to commercial activities, 15.4 percent to agriculture, 15.3 percent to the industrial sector, 13.9 percent to service enterprises, and 10.2 percent to social services. More than ten years have passed since this census. Though the current situation is not known precisely, the tendency toward urbanization seems to persist, as does the increase in the commercial and service sectors.

THE DIFFICULTIES OF DEALING WITH CHANGES

One important phenomenon that was not surveyed by the census was the Nikkei movement to Japan, currently known as *dekasegi*, which, according to Japanese-Brazilian Studies Center, started around 1985. In the beginning, the majority of the dekasegi were Issei (persons born in Japan) who, faced with unemployment and economic difficulties, chose to find work in Japan's booming economy, which was experiencing labor shortages in certain sectors.

Farmers, businessmen, employees, and retired people, among others, left for Japan to find employment in the nonspecialized labor force that performed the "three Ks"—*kiken* (dangerous), *kitsui* (hard), and *kitanai* (dirty)

Pig breeding in the 1930s. (Collection of Museu Histórico da Imigração Japonesa no Brasil)

work. Although this kind of work was despised by many local Japanese workers, it guaranteed good wages for the Japanese-Brazilians. In the early 1990s, a dekasegi factory worker could receive monthly wages of between three and four thousand U.S. dollars, which included long overtime hours. This salary was equivalent to the salaries of executives of major companies in Brazil.

Word of the wage opportunities in Japan spread rapidly throughout Brazil and other countries of Latin America, such as Peru, Paraguay, and Bolivia. It is estimated that in 1985 about 13,800 Japanese Brazilian descendents went to work in Japan. In June 1990, Japan's Immigration Control and Refugee Recognition Act was changed, allowing the second and third generations of Brazilians of Japanese descent to stay in Japan with long-term resident visas, without restrictions on their activities. The result was an increase in the dekasegi trend, from 67,300 going to Japan in 1990 to 96,300 the following year. According to statistics gathered by Japan's minister of justice in December 1999, there were approximately 224,000 Brazilians staying in Japan, including the non-Japanese Brazilians living with Japanese Brazilian spouses. Not included in these figures were people with dual nationalities and Japanese nationals holding permanent resident status in Brazil. Adding these two categories gives a total of about 250,000 people—the same number of Japanese that immigrated to Brazil before and after World War II.

Originally, a great number of the dekasegi were retired people. However, over time the age group became younger, and entire families started to go to Japan. Increasingly, high school–aged students choose to work in Japan and earn money fast, rather than attend school. This exodus generated a series of changes in the community. Suddenly, the Japanese associations found themselves with reduced memberships. In the both old and new settlements alike, only children and elders were left. While the departure to Japan represented a way out of

Headquarters of Cooperativa Agrícola de Cotia (Cotia Agricultural Cooperative), founded by the producers of potatoes of Cotia (outskirts of São Paulo) in 1927 and located in Largo da Batata (Potato Square) in the Pinheiros district of São Paulo City. (Collection of Museu Histórico da Imigração Japonesa no Brasil)

Japanese Brazilian worker in Japan, 1997. (Photograph by International Press. Collection of Museu Histórico da Imigração Japonesa no Brasil)

Two men chatting in Liberdade Square in downtown São Paulo, 1988. (Photograph by Edson Komiya. Collection of Museu Histórico da Imigração Japonesa no Brasil)

Traditional Japanese dancing is enjoyed by the residents of Assistencia Social Dom José Gaspar (Ikoi no Sono), a home for the elderly in São Paulo, 1980. (Photograph by Yuji Kusuno. Collection of Museu Histórico da Imigração Japonesa no Brasil)

economic problems, it created a complex set of social-cultural concerns.

With more than ninety years of history and five generations of descendants, the Japanese-Brazilian community faced other existential problems as well. Aging was one of them. It is estimated that the longevity of Japanese-Brazilians is close to the Japanese life span—77 years for men and 83.5 for women.

The Ikoi-no-Sono rest home, managed by the Dom José Gaspar Association, is one of the most traditional and important care facilities for the elderly. It is always full and has a long waiting list. In addition, there is an increasing number of elderly stricken by Alzheimer's disease. Specialized care and more homes for the elderly are urgently needed. When then–Prime Minister Ryutaro Hashimoto visited Brazil in June 1996, the Japanese Brazilian Beneficence of São Paulo (Beneficência Nipo-Brasileira de São Paulo) presented a plan to construct a house for the elderly with specialized treatment. The Japanese-Brazilian Geriatric Care Center (Centro Geriátrico Nipo-Brasileiro) was opened December 19, 1999, with assistance given by the Japanese government through the Japan International Cooperation Agency (JICA). Its capacity at this writing is fourteen persons, male or female, sixty-five years of age or older. By March 2002, the capacity will be increased to fifty persons.

Change is inevitable. The Issei who founded and have

Three generations of Japanese Brazilians dancing at Tanabata Festival, a tourist attraction and celebration held every year in the Liberdade district of downtown São Paulo, 1998. (Collection of Museu Histórico da Imigração Japonesa no Brasil)

maintained the Japanese associations are constantly looking for successors. In many cases, older Nisei have assumed this responsibility. However, many Nisei prefer to live outside the community's limits.

Today, Nisei also need to find their successors. The Sansei, the children of the Nisei, are open to criticism because of their constant refusal to support Japanese associations. The fact is that many are not interested in the continuation of the traditional structures and prefer to seek out other groups and alternative forms of social life. However, this behavior does not always mean withdrawal from Nikkei friends.

Bibliographic Essay of Japanese Immigrants and Their Descendants

MASATO NINOMIYA AND NAOMI HOKI MONIZ

INTRODUCTION

This annotated bibliography on Japanese immigrants and their descendants in Brazil consists of works in English, Japanese, and Portuguese.[1] Preference is given to more recent studies, since most of the earlier materials are already annotated in Robert Smith et al. (E-44). The word "biblio [book] graphy [written]" is expanded here to include materials in different media, such as movies or documentaries. Works of fiction are included in the bibliography as an important source that brings insight into the creative, psychological, and symbolic dimensions of individual and collective experiences. The goals of this annotated bibliography are to provide diverse perspectives by including works produced in different formats by authors of various nationalities (mainly Japanese, Brazilian, or American), and to list representative works that illustrate the manner in which Nikkei studies has evolved alongside historical changes in Brazil and other Latin American countries, as well as in Japan.

ENGLISH-LANGUAGE MATERIALS: BY NAOMI HOKI MONIZ

Brazil boasts of the largest population of Japanese descent in any country outside of Japan, entering the new millenium with over a million, not counting those quarter-million who are presently in Japan as *dekasegi* guest workers. Today, they are, in general, a very prosperous community, with Nikkei achieving remarkable acceptance in society as farmers, industrialists, and professionals. They have been nominated to high government positions in the past three decades, including three ministries, the directorship of the Central Bank, and as finance secretary of São Paulo State. Some of them have been elected as representatives in federal, state, and municipal legislative branches, or to mayoralties, such as in Curitiba, the capital city of Paraná State.

However, this road was not easy for the first generation, which faced disease, physical hardship in a tropical climate, anomie due to cultural and language barriers, different food habits, and a social and political climate that bordered often on hysteria against them—especially in the 1920s, during World War II, and soon after. This is a tale of hardship and tenacity, of a group image from the Eurocentric/American/Brazilian perspective that has evolved from "the yellow peril to that of the model minority." Very few people realize that in 1946, but for one vote—the chairman's—the Brazilian Constitutional Assembly would have enacted a law that excluded Japanese immigration to Brazil, as had the U.S. Immigration Act of 1924. A glimpse into the works selected for this bibliography reveals how various racial identities, expressed often in forms of stereotypes, have been constructed for the Japanese and, consequently, how the Nikkei have negotiated their identity as members of the Brazilian society, often adjusting to or challenging the canonic model of national identity (see E-25, E-26).

In general, the selections may be divided into two major categories: before World War II and after. Before the war, the Japanese emigration to Brazil can be characterized as having four stages: (a) 1908–1920, a period for which most studies find the rationale in the Japanese government's settlement of its population surplus, along with its search for new sources of raw materials in Brazil, and in the Brazilian government's search for a new source of labor (E: 4, 18, 21, 26, 31, 32, 33, 35); (b) 1924–1932, the period that saw the largest migration of Japanese to Brazil, giving rise to many charges—by official, institutional, and private voices, influenced by American sources leveled against the presence of Japanese in Brazil (E-1, E-15, E-53); (c) 1932–1938, the prewar period of Japanese expansion in Southeast Asia and Manchuria, which led to a tendentious and almost hysterical reaction to the "invasion" by a Japanese fifth column of Latin America, and eventually to the 2 percent rule, sharply curtailing Japanese immigration to Brazil (E: 7, 8, 15, 16, 26, 53); and (d) 1938–1945, the war period, when the Axis nationals living in Brazil suffered restrictions, especially the German and Japanese (E: 2, 12, 14, 23). Emilio Willens produced the first real scholarship on these two ethnic groups (E-54, E-55).

After the war, the Japanese community of Brazil underwent considerable changes due to Japan's defeat. First, return to the homeland was less achievable and desirable since the country was destroyed by the war. Second, the community's children were going to schools and becoming integrated into the mainstream Brazilian society. Finally, the division of groups into *make-gumi* (who accepted Japan's defeat) and *kachi-gumi* (believers in victory by Japan) led to a deep schism in the community and serious rethinking about the future of Japanese in the New World (E-24, E-51). In the 1950s, the majority of the studies were concerned with the "assimilation and integration" of the Japanese into Brazilian society (E: 6, 9, 13, 22, 28, 34, 38, 40). The offering of a Japanese pavilion to the city of São Paulo during its four-hundred-year celebration in 1954 was the turning point in the evolution of the immigrants' presence, their contributions to Brazilian agriculture, and the opening of frontiers in the northwestern states of São Paulo, Paraná, and Pará (E-37, E-46).

As Japan expanded into a major economic world power, studies were concerned with technology transfer, enterprise investments, and economic ties linked to Brazil's growing economy (E: 10, 19, 41, 42, 43, 52). However, as Brazil ended its economic miracle years and entered a period of economic "stagflation" in the 1980s and 1990s, a new phase began for members of the Nikkei community who "returned" to Japan as guest workers. Brazil, itself, had experienced two fundamental changes: redemocratization and a radical economic transformation, from a state-centered economy to one focused on privatization, market exchange, and globalized competition. All this, in the context of the end of the Cold War, led to significant shifts in the country. Also, because of its unemployment, Brazil for the first time became an exporter of emigrants—the *brazucas* (Brazilian nationals moving to the United States) and the dekasegi (mostly ethnic Brazilian Japanese, who were given favored visa status to work in Japan as foreigners). They became the focus of many studies on the transnationals, the members of the so-called masscapes of the new globalized economy (E-39, E-50, E-52). Many of the Nikkei, who considered themselves Japanese in Brazil, discovered a new identity in Japan, an identity forged in their construction of a Brazilian identity, not based on race or ethnicity but on culture—that of Brazilians, who drink the Brazilian national drink, *guaraná*, who dance the samba, and wear costumes as Brazilian Indians or black *Baianas* (Brazilian women from Bahia). Likewise in Brazil, *mestiços* of Japanese ancestry choose to assert a Japanese identity, practicing Japanese martial arts, flower arrangement, or Japanese religions, and performing in *noh* plays, Japanese-inspired dance, or writing haiku poetry (one of the favored genres in Brazil today). Thus, they are creating a hybridism that goes beyond the hegemonic, patriarchal white dominant concept of the founding "three races"—black, Indian, Portuguese "*lusotropicalismo mestiço*"to a more multicultural and polyphonic culture (E: 3, 11, 20, 27, 40, 54).

JAPANESE- AND PORTUGUESE-LANGUAGE MATERIALS: BY MASATO NINOMIYA

The selected bibliography in the Japanese and Portuguese language is divided in eight areas: (1) history; (2) sociology and anthropology; (3) biographies, testimonies, and autobiographical accounts; (4) agriculture and economy; (5) dekasegi; (6) culture; (7) politics; and (8) bibliographies and symposia. These areas reflect the works of academics and others interested in Japanese immigration and its history.

History

A wide range of works on the history of Japanese in Brazil is included in this bibliography. Many were written to commemorate special anniversary celebrations that marked the beginning of Japanese immigration (J-43; P-1, P-4) and Japanese-Brazilian relations (J-42, J-63, P-33). Others chronicled the histories of cultural and community organizations (J: 3, 12, 37, 38, 44, 81; P: 1, 4, 17), commercial enterprises and economic associations (J-27, J-31, J-41), Japanese education in Brazil (J-6), and the histories of Japanese settlements (J-28, J-34; P-33). Teijiro Suzuki presents an historical overview of Japanese immigration history (J-69) and offers statistics related to the Japanese community in Brazil (J-68), while the famous painter Tomoo Handa draws upon his personal experiences and insights to depict the history and cultural characteristics of Japanese immigrants in Brazil (J-8). Works written in Portuguese by Nogueira provide a brief history of Japanese immigration to Brazil (P-16) and Brazil-Japan relations from 1908 to 1922 (P-17).

Sociology and Anthropology

Selections in these two fields include books and articles that analyze the different ways in which the Japanese immigrants and their descendants have integrated themselves into Brazilian society (J-62, J-70, J-71). The works of Hiroshi Saito, written in both Japanese (53, 54, 55) and Portuguese (23, 24, 25), analyze Japanese immigration and the process of settlement and integration into Brazilian society. Toshirō Takagi (J-70) focuses on the World War II–era conflict between the kachi-gumi (believers in Japan's victory) and make-gumi (believers in Japan's defeat) to get at the question, "What is Japanese?" Issues of acculturation and identity are further examined in *Nihon bunka denshō no mondai* (J-62). Anthropologist Ruth C. Leite Cardoso's doctoral dissertation analyzes the characteristics of Japanese Brazilian immigrant society (P-2); it has been translated into both Japanese and English (see E-9, J-4).

Biographies, Testimonies, and Autobiographical Accounts

Materials in this category are by far the most numerous. Most of these pay tribute to the lives and contributions of important persons (J: 1, 11, 14, 23, 24, 25, 29, 38, 52, 56, 60, 67, 74, 75, 76, 78; P-6, P-21). Biographical and first-person accounts written by or about Japanese diplomats give special insight into the Japanese Brazilian experience in terms of the events that occurred during their tenures (J-17, J-50, J-66). One of the most outstanding works was written by Ryōji Noda (J-49), who worked as an interpreter for the Japanese embassy in Brazil for eighteen years. These personal accounts (J-26, J-35; P-8, P-19, P-31) provide rich social and historical context for the events and processes of integration into Brazilian society.

Agriculture and Economy

The works gathered in these fields can be divided into pre-war and postwar titles on agriculture and economy. Hiroshi Saito's works focus on the Cooperativa Agrícola de Cotia (P-24) and the contributions made by Japanese and their descendants to agriculture and Brazilian society (P-23). For a discussion of postwar economic developments see Japanese 2, 21, 31, 80.

Dekasegi

Starting in the 1980s, Brazil witnessed the movement of Japanese immigrants and their descendants back to Japan. For references discussing this phenomenon see Japanese (45, 46, 48, 51) and Portuguese (12, 13) listings.

Culture

References listed here specifically refer to works in the field of art, especially literature and fine art (paintings, drawings, and sculpture). See J: 18, 19, 24, 32, 33, 65, 79 and P-12.

Politics

This field has few authors compared to the other fields in the social sciences, despite the fact that a large number of Japanese descendants have worked in the legislative and executive branches of government since the end of the war. See J-42, J-53 and P-33.

Bibliographies and Symposia

Many scientific meetings have been organized to focus on the Japanese in Brazil, and they have resulted in publications. See Japanese 45, 46 and Portuguese 13, 14, 20, 21, and 27 for symposia; see J-30 for bibliographies.

NOTE

1. Naomi Hoki Moniz dealt with English-language materials; Masato Ninomiya dealt with Japanese and Portuguese-language materials.

Annotated Bibliography of Japanese Brazilians

COMPILED BY MASATO NINOMIYA AND NAOMI HOKI MONIZ

ENGLISH

1. "Booming Brazil in Japan." *Literary Digest* 8 (January 1927).

    The period of highest migration of Japanese to Brazil.

2. "Brazil Warned for the Treatment of Immigrants." *Journal Chronicle and Japan Mail* (September 27, 1947).

3. "International Press Makes Life Easier for Brazilians in Japan." *Japan Quarterly Magazine* 19, no. 3 (1996): 28–29.

    This article features *International Press*, published in Portuguese with a circulation of fifty-five thousand, which serves the dekasegi Brazilian population in Japan.

4. "Reports of Immigration Commission," Senate Document Number 761, 1911, Washington, D.C.: Government Printing Office.

    See section titled "The Immigration Situation in Brazil," 209–29.

5. Avila, Fernando Bastos. *Economic Impacts of Immigration: The Brazilian Problem*. Westport, Conn.: Greenwood Press, 1970.

    Preface by A. Camillo de Oliveira and Julius Isac.

6. Bastide, Roger, and Pierre Van Den Berghe. "Stereotypes, Norms and Interracial Behavior in São Paulo, Brazil." *American Sociological Review,* 22, no. 6 (December 1957): 689–94.

    A study of anti-Negro prejudice among various ethnic minorities and the "white" population of São Paulo. Those of Japanese descent were found to be much less prejudiced than the general sample. Sample: all white and university students.

7. Beals, Carleton. *The Coming Struggle for Latin America*. New York: J.B. Lippincontt, 1938.

    General conditions and problems of Latin American countries, focuses on trans-Pacific relations. Relations with Japan and problems arising from Japanese immigration to Latin America are discussed on pages 13–14.

8. Beals, Carleton. "Japan invades Latin America." *Foreign Affairs* (October 1935): 299–306.

9. Cardoso, Ruth Corrêa Leite. *Family Structure and Social Mobility*. São Paulo, Brazil: Ed. Kaleidos-Primus, 1998.

    Trilingual edition: English, Japanese, and Portuguese. See P-2 and J-4.

10. Cohen, Roger. "Ethnic Japanese in Brazil Look to Tokyo." *The Wall Street Journal* (Wednesday, March 15, 1989): A4.

    The subtitle, "Cultural Ties and Huge Market Lure Japanese Investment," sums up the article.

11. Deiró, Carlos, Cine/TV. *Ai no ko—The Children of Love*. Curitiba, Paraná, 1998.

    Subsidized by the Prefecture of Curitiba and the Paraná State Government. Very useful documentary about the history of Japanese immigration from the first arrival in 1908 to 1998. The phrase *ai-no-ko* is used negatively to refer to the children of the marriage of love instead of the arranged marriage *o-miai-kekkon*–between Japanese and Brazilians. However, the title is used as a positive metaphor for the blending of both Brazilian and Japanese cultures and races. Shot in some historical locations of the immigrants' early days, photos, old films, interviews with different personalities of the Japanese community, such as the only living member of the *Kasato Maru*, some politicians, academics, artists, third- and fourth-generations as well as dekasegi. English narration and subtitles.

12. Diffie, Baily W. "Some Foreign Influences in Contemporary Brazilian Politics." *Hispanic American Historical Review*, no. 20 (August 1940): 410.

13. Fujii, Yukio, and Lynn T. Smith. *The Acculturation of the Japanese Immigrants in Brazil*. Latin American Monographs Number 8. Gainesville, Florida: University of Florida Press, 1959.

    General study of the Japanese in Brazil, with brief history to 1957, demography, ecology, sociocultural evolution. Based on published sources, it contains useful statistical tables analyzed from other works and a short bibliographical note.

14. Fukunaga, Patrick. "The Brazilian Experience: The Japanese Immigrants during the Period of Vargas' Regime and the Immediate Aftermath." Ph.D. diss, University of California, Santa Barbara, 1983.

    During Vargas' dictatorship increasing restrictions against the Axis powers were implemented. The Germans, the Japanese, and the Italians, to a lesser extent, suffered the prohibition of the teaching and use of their languages.

15. Hall, Robert King. "Foreign Colonies of Brazil—A North American View." *Inter-American Quarterly* 3, no. 1 (January 1941): 5–19.

    Examines German and Japanese settlements in Brazil, and includes useful review of charges presented against the Japanese by Brazilians opposed to their immigration.

16. Hauser, Henri. "Japanese Immigration in Brazil." *The New Mexico Quarterly Review* 12, no. 1 (February 1942): 5–17.

    Original French manuscript was written in 1936. Only English version was published. A clear, well-informed analysis of the mechanisms, rates, and political consequences of Japanese immigration, set against the perspective of Brazil's general immigration issues. It presents the Japanese favorably, compared to other foreign groups, in the agricultural sector. Great footnotes give insightful information on pre–World War II conditions. Additional footnotes by Richard F. Beherendt.

17. Hosokawa, Fumiko. *The Sansei: Social Interaction and Ethnic Identification among Third Generation Japanese.* San Francisco: R&E Research Associates, 1978.

    Useful study of the seldom-covered Sansei generation.

18. Idei, Seishi. "Japan's Migration Problem." *International Labor Review* 22, no. 6 (December 1930): 773–89.

    Author analyzes emigration as an unpromising solution to Japanese population problem, which is caused by industrial growth. Reviewing the history of Japanese overseas migration, he finds a reluctance to move abroad along with declining material incentives in host countries, combining to reduce emigration.

19. Inoue, Tadakatsu. "Overseas Operations of Japanese Business Enterprises in Brazil." *Kobe Economic and Business Review* 12 (1965 Annual Report): 39–45.

    A survey of types of businesses opened in Brazil, owned and managed by Japanese. It separates firms established by immigrants and branches of companies in Japan. These overseas branches receive major attention, with emphasis on their impact on the Brazilian economy and prospects for establishment of new investments in terms of the conditions of the labor force and government regulations.

20. Insdorf, Annete. "Gaijin—A Portrait of the Outsider." *The New York Times* (Sunday, June 14, 1981).

    A review of the film by the Japanese-Brazilian movie director Tizuka Yamazaki examines the issues around the idea of who is the outsider, the *gaijin*, in Brazilian society as experienced by the director's grandmother in the 1910s on a coffee plantation.

21. Ishii, Ryoichi. *Population Pressure and Economic Life in Japan.* London: P.S. King, 1936.

    Contains brief references to the history of Japanese emigration to Brazil, especially page 199, dealing primarily with emigrants from the viewpoint of the larger problem of prewar population pressures in Japan.

22. Izumi, Seiichi. "Acculturation among the Japanese agricultural immigrants in Brazil." *Proceedings of the World Population Conference, Rome, August 31–September 10, 1954* 2: 467–78.

23. Kirk, Betty. "War on Hidden Japanese." *Inter-American* 2, no. 1 (January 1943): 14–16.

24. Kumusaka, Y., and H. Saito. "Kachigumi: A Collective Delusion among Japanese and Their Descendants." *Canadian Psychiatric Association Journal* 15, no. 2 (April 1970): 167–75.

    Study of the two factions in Brazil, claiming the victory of Japan in the World War II.

25. Lesser, Jeffrey. "Asians in South America." In *Encyclopedia of World Cultures, Vol. 7, South America.* New York: G.K. Hall/MacMillan, 1995.

26. Lesser, Jeffrey. *Negotiating National Identity. Immigrants, Minorities, and the Struggle for Ethnicity in Brazil.* Durhan & London: Duke University Press, 1999.

    Lesser examines the role that ethnic minorities from China, Japan, Middle East, and North Africa have played in the construction of a national identity. Most of the book is about the Japanese immigrants: Chapters 4): "Searching for a Hyphen"; 5) " Negotiations and New Identities"; 6) "Turning Japanese" (pp. 81–165). Indispensable reading, very informative footnotes.

27. Linger, Daniel. "Brazil Displaced: Restaurante 51 in Nagoya, Japan." *Horizontes Antropológicos 5*, Porto Alegre: 1997, 181–203.

    Linger analyzes the way Brazilian *dekasegi* have constructed a new Brazilian cultural identity in Japan as it is symbiotically represented in the eatery as a "little Brazil."

28. Loftin, Marion T. "The Japanese in Brazil: A Study in Immigration and Acculturation." Ph.D. diss., Vanderbilt University, 1952.

29. Maeyama, Takashi. "Ethnicity, Secret Societies and Associations: The Japanese in Brazil." *Comparative Studies in Society and History* 21, no. 4 (1979): 589.

    Recent study on the role of the ethnic based associations in the Japanese communities.

30. Maeyama, Takashi. "Japanese Religions in Southern Brazil: Change and Syncretism." In *Latin American Studies,* 6, Tsukuba: Japan, 1983.

    Interesting study about how syncretism functions between Japanese and Brazilian traditions, mainly about *Seichō no ie*.

31. Normano, João F. "Japanese Emigration to Brazil." *Pacific Affairs*, no. 7 (March 1934): 42–61.

    An insightful review of the patterns and mechanisms of Japanese immigration. In the author's view, the primary policy motive behind immigration to south central Brazil was displacement of surplus agrarian population, whereas in the northern area (Amazonia), it was agrarian resettlement associated with development of virgin areas and capital investment. Contrary to prevalent opinion at the time, the author doubts that the Japanese government had a conscious and organized policy in Brazil.

32. Normano, João F., and Gerbi. "Japanese Emigration to Latin America." *Genus* 3, no. 1–2 (May 1938): 47–90.

    As in the study above (E-31) the author sees no ulterior motives in the trade and emigration policies by the Japanese government. He does not see emigration as a solution to Japan's population problem.

33. Ogoshima, Toru. "Japanese Emigration." *International Labor Review* 34, no. 5 (November 1935): 618–51.

    An excellent overview of the formal organizational structure (both public and private), and the legal framework of sponsored overseas migration of the Japanese from the Japanese viewpoint. Reviews the history of Japan's interest in emigration, procedures for recruiting, transportation and resettlement of emigrants, with special attention given to Brazil and other Latin American countries.

34. Reichl, Christopher. "Stages in the Historical Process of

Ethnicity: The Japanese in Brazil, 1908–1988." *Ethnohistory* 42, no. 1 (Winter 1995): 42.

35. Rickey, Carrie. "Gaijin—A Brazilian Journey." *The Village Voice* (June 24–30, 1981).

    The film critic Rickey discusses Tizuka Yamazaki's ideas about the word *gaijin*: foreigners in their own language. He explores the issues of exclusion from the mainstream society of different groups in Brazil, with focus on the Japanese immigrants' story narrated from the perspective of the main character Titoe, a woman who immigrated to Brazil in 1908.

36. Saake, Guilherme Wilheim. "The Forty-Year-Old Japanese Colony in Registro, Brazil." *ICMC News (International Catholic Migration Commission)* 4, no. 11 (1955): 3–5.

    The immigrant settlements in the Vale da Ribeira, south of São Paulo are some of the oldest Japanese colonies in Brazil. This study by Swiss Catholic missionaries is a valuable source of information to study the manner in which concessions to the Japanese Government Colonization Company "KKKK" developed agricultural and mineral resources to supply Japan with raw materials, creation of economic ties in Brazil, as well as resettlement of surplus population.

37. Sakamoto, Tatsuki. "Three Problems of Post-War Emigration from Japan." *Migration News* 8, no. 1 (1959): 22–24.

    This study claims that the Japanese made substantial contributions to the agricultural development of countries in which they settled and that, with the end of World War II, there are no longer problems of assimilation based on patriotic, ultra nationalistic sentiments.

38. Sasaki, John. *Japanese Emigrants in Brazil: A Study of the Integration of Japanese People.* Rio de Janeiro: Serviço Social da Indústria, Departmento Nacional.

    A very brief survey of the history of Japanese immigration to Brazil, with comments on the linguistic and religious aspects of assimilation. Most of the data presented are derived from published materials.

39. Sellek, Yoko. "Nikkeijin: The Illusion of Homogeneity." In *Japan New Minorities*, edited by Michael Weiner, 178–210. London: Routledge, 1997.

    An interesting analysis of the much-romanticized idea of the homogeneity of Nikkei, examines different groups and alliances.

40. Simons, Marlise. "Japanese Gone Brazilian: Unhurried Workaholics." *New York Times* (Sunday, June 1978): A-14.

    During the celebration of seventy years of Japanese immigration to Brazil, held on June 18, 1978, Simons examines the presence of Japanese Brazilians as the "bridge between East and West" in Brazil and their economic and social achievements with a blend of Japanese efficiency and Brazilian tropical easiness.

41. Sims, Harold D. "Japanese Postwar Migration to Brazil: An Analysis of the Data Presently Available." *International Migration Review* 6, no. 3 (Fall 1972): 246–66.

    Of the very few Japanese who moved to Brazil after the war, many were bureaucrats of Japanese companies with no intention of settling in the country.

42. Sims, Harold D. *Japanese Postwar Migration to Brazil: An Analysis of Data Presently Available.* Pittsburgh: University of Pittsburgh, Center for Latin American Studies, 1973.

43. Smith, Charles. *Japanese Technology Transfer to Brazil.* Ann Arbor, Michigan: UMI Research Press, 1981.

    A new slant in the contribution of Japan to Brazil, a product of the Japanese miracle and growth as a world economic power.

44. Smith, Robert, and Hiroshi Saito. *The Japanese and Their Descendants in Brazil: An Annotated Bibliography.* São Paulo: Centro de Estudos Nipo-Brasileiros, 1967.

    Very comprehensive, useful, and informative bibliography up to 1967.

45. Smith, T. Lynn. *Brazil: People and Institutions.* Baton Rouge: Louisiana State University Press, 1963.

    Study on Brazilian rural sociology. The chapter that deals with the Japanese population is not very favorable to them. See: Chapter V, "Some other population characteristics," pages 75–96; Chapter VIII "Immigration," pages 391–427. Deals with immigration history, patterns of settlement, land use practices, agricultural economics, and demography.

46. Staniford, Philip. *Pioneers in the Tropics: The Political Organization of Japanese in an Immigrant Community in Brazil.* New York: Humanities Press, 1973.

    Very interesting anthropological study of Tomé-Açu in the 1960s.

47. Suzuki, Teiichi. *The Japanese Immigrant in Brazil.* Tokyo: University of Tokyo Press, 1964.

    Complete statistical data of the situation of Japanese immigrants in Brazil, collected and researched by the Census Committee of the Japanese Community in 1958.

48. Suzuki, Teiichi. *The Japanese Immigrant in Brazil: Narrative Part.* Tokyo: University of Tokyo Press, 1969.

    The Japanese Community Census Report, published in 1958 on the occasion of the fiftieth anniversary of Japanese immigration to Brazil.

49. Suzuki, Teiichi. "Japanese immigrants in Brazil." *Population Index* 31, no. 22 (April 1964): 117–38.

    A selective report of results of the census reported fully in No. 24, by the head of the Commission for the Census of the Japanese Community. Four sections: I. Present State of Immigrants and their Descendants; II. Background of Immigrants; III. Conditions on Arrival in Brazil; and IV. Mobility.

50. Tigner, James Lawrence. *The Okinawans in Latin America: Investigations of Okinawan Communities in Latin America with Exploration of Settlement Possibilities.* Strategic Investigations, Ryukyu Islands, Number 7. Washington, D.C.: Pacific Science Board, National Research Council, 1953.

    Very important study of a group that is often lumped together with the Japanese mainlanders. Okinawans have a distinctive history and culture from them and see themselves as such despite the tendency to be viewed as Japanese in the host countries. They form one of the most cohesive groups even today and very successful in many areas, and notably in Brazilian politics. Tigner presents a comprehensive report, based on literature in Portuguese, Spanish, English, and Japanese, including government documents, and on interviews by the author on the history, economy, and society of Ryukyuan immigration to Brazil, Bolivia, Argentina, Peru, and Mexico, with secondary attention to Japanese immigration. Great source of documents, photos, and interviews.

51. Tigner, James Lawrence. "Shindo Remmei: Japanese Nationalism in Brazil." *Hispanic American Historical Review* 41, no. 4 (November 1961): 515–32.

    Report on Japanese separatism and ethnic nationalism before, during, and after World War II. Reviews the postwar activities of the Shindo-Remmei (Riga do Caminho dos Vassalos), founded in 1944.

52. Ueki, Hideo. *Report on the Promotion of Industrial Development by Japanese Investment in the State of Minas Gerais.* Tokyo: Japan International Cooperation Agency, 1980.

    An interesting document for the period of major Japanese investments in Brazil.

53. White, John W. "Japan's Amazon Dream." *Asia and the Americans* 43, no. 10 (October 1944): 582–83.

    R. Smith (see E-44) summarizes this text as: "A classic of the genre. The author imputes ambitions of world conquest to Japan with the Amazon Basin as a major military target. His argument is based on evidence of programmed immigration colonization, extensive economic concessions, and the heavy inflow of technical specialists to the area. Stresses sinister interlocking ties between immigration organizations, Japanese diplomatic agents, and clandestine military cadres disguised as settlers and technicians."

54. Willens, Emílio. "The Japanese in Brazil." *Far Eastern Survey* 18, no. 1 (January 12, 1949): 6–8.

    General review of the Japanese situation in interior southern Brazil, based chiefly on the author's field studies in the Ribeira Valley, and Mogi das Cruzes, both with heavy concentrations of Japanese immigrants in the state of São Paulo. Examines the assimilation of students through schools, the problems concerning marriage and the way ultra nationalistic movement played a part in the division of the "Colonia" into two groups, i.e., the assimilationists and the traditionalists.

55. Willens, Emílio. "Some Aspects of Cultural Conflict and Acculturation in Southern Rural Brazil." *Rural Sociology* 7, no. 4 (December 1942): 375–84.

    A review of cultural conflicts between the indigenous "folk" populations and immigrant groups in Brazil, based on the author's field studies of the Japanese in the Ribeira Valley, state of São Paulo, and the Germans in Itajaí-Mirim, state of Santa Catarina. Contends that, after industrialization, foreign immigrants are the major source of social stress in Brazilian rural society. The Japanese appear to undergo the more severe strain, with the growth of individualistic relationships at the expense of traditional patriarchal family ties attributed mostly to a clash between Japanese and Brazilian viewpoints about the educational process.

56. Yamanaka, Keiko. "Factory Workers and Convalescent Attendants: Japanese Brazilian Migrant Women and Their Families in Japan." In *International Female Migration and Japan Networking, Settlement and Human Rights.* Tokyo: International Peace Research Institute, Meiji Gakuin University, 1996.

57. Yamanaka, Keiko. "Return Migration of Japanese Brazilians to Japan: The Nikkeijin as Ethnic Minority and Political Construct." *Diaspora* 5, no. 1 (Spring 1991): 65–97.

    The dekasegi in Japan as members of the transnational communities in a globalized economy carve out their identity as ethnic minority and research for workers' rights and political space.

58. Yamashita, Karen Tei. *Brazil Maru.* Minneapolis: Coffeehouse Publishing House, 1992.

    A novel by a Japanese American writer who lived for a few years in Brazil and wrote a story based on true facts, about an utopic settlement of a Christian group in the northwest of São Paulo State in the first decades of the past century.

59. Yamashita, Karen Tei. *Through the Arc of the Rain Forest.* Minneapolis: Coffeehouse Publishing House, 1990.

    This book reads like a Garcia Marques Japanese gone tropical, magic realism reigns in the Amazon forest. It is narrated by a satellite dangling above the head of a naïve character named Kazumasa who, by fate of destiny, becomes the lightning rod to disastrous events that involve industrial espionage, miracles, Amazonian xamans, big money, miracles, and Armageddon. Parodying the soap opera genre ubiquitous in Brazil, the Novela, this is an entertaining and foreboding tale of the topsy-turvy world beyond the arc of the rain forest.

JAPANESE

1. Aiba, Shin'ichi, and Michiko Aiba [相場真一 and 相場道子]. *Aiba Yoshinari no shōgai* [相場美成の生涯]. San Pauro [サンパウロ]: San Pauro Shinbunsha Insatsubu [サンパウロ新聞社印刷部], 1992.

    A compilation of contributions that the deceased made to the colony with recollections by those who knew him.

2. Aoki, Hiroshi [青木公]. *Yomigaeru daichi Serādo: Nihon to Burajiru no kokusai kyōryoku* [甦る大地セラード：日本とブラジルの国際協力]. Tōkyō [東京]: Kokusai Kyōryoku Shuppankai [国際協力出版会], 1995.

    "Cerrado" is denominated as a large area in the central part of Brazilian midland, similar to "savannah." It is a heavy clay and acid soil, practically abandoned owing to its difficulty on agricultural use. As of the 1970s, the Brazilian government sought Japan cooperation in order to improve the soil and to develop the agriculture. It became a successful project and today Brazil is one of the biggest exporters of soybeans in the international market.

3. Bunkyō Yonjūnenshi Hensan Iinkai [文協四十年史編纂委

員会]. *Bunkyō yonjūnenshi* [文協四十年史]. San Pauro [サンパウロ]: Burajiru Nihon Bunka Kyōkai [ブラジル日本文化協会], 1998.

　　Describes forty years of history of the Brazil-Japan Cultural Association that was established in 1955 and has been active as the central organization of local Japanese associations.

4. Cardoso, Ruth Corrêa Leite. *Kazoku kōzō to shakaiteki idōsei: San Pauro-shū ni okeru Nihonjin no kenkyū* [家族構造と社会的移動性：サンパウロ州における日本人の研究]. São Paulo: Kaleidos-Primus Consultoria e Comunicaçao Integrada S/C Ltda, 1998.

　　Originally a dissertation by the wife of Brazilian president, published in Japanese, Portuguese, and English. It investigates and analyzes the characteristics of the Japanese immigrants and accurately indicates the direction of the Japanese-Brazilian society. See also E-9 and P-2.

5. Daigo, Masao [醍醐麻沙夫]. *Mori no yume* [森の夢]. San Pauro-shi [サンパウロ市]: San Pauro Shinbunsha [サンパウロ新聞社], 1979.

　　A novel about Umpei Hirano. It describes the tragedy of colonial management haunted by malaria. See also P-6.

6. Hakkoku Nichigo Gakkō Rengōkai [伯国日語学校連合会]. *Ikusanga* [幾山河]. San Pauro [サンパウロ]: Paurisuta Insatsu [パウリスタ印刷], 1966.

　　A history of Japanese education in Brazil. An edited compilation of reports and articles that Japanese teachers all over Brazil wrote on the Japanese language education for Nikkei students.

7. Handa, Tomoo [半田知雄]. *Burajiru imin no seikatsu: Handa Tomoo gabunshū* [ブラジル移民の生活：半田知雄画文集]. Akita-shi [秋田市]: Mumyōsha Shuppan [無明舎出版], 1986.

　　The author, also a famous painter, explains his works to tell the reality of immigrants' lives based on his personal experiences.

8. Handa, Tomoo [半田知雄]. *Burajiru Nihon imin/Nikkei shakai shi nenpyō (kaitei zōhoban)* [改訂増補版 ブラジル日本移民・日系社会史年表]. San Pauro [サンパウロ]: Toppan Press Insatsu Shuppan [トッパン・プレス印刷出版], 1996.

　　Originally published by Tomoo Handa in 1976. The Japanese-Brazilian Social Science Study Center in São Paulo significantly revised it with additional data for the one-hundredth anniversary of the Japanese-Brazilian relations. It is the most reliable timeline currently available.

9. Handa, Tomoo [半田知雄]. *Ima nao tabiji ni ari: aru imin no zuisō* [今なお旅路にあり：ある移民の随想]. San Pauro [サンパウロ]: Taiyōdō Shoten [太陽堂書店], 1966.

　　The author, famous painter, wrote down what came to his mind while sketching. In the second half, he ponders the future of the Nikkei society.

10. Hayashi, Hisao [林寿雄]. *Burajiru Rikkōkai zenshi* [ブラジル力行会全史]. San Pauro [サンパウロ]: Toppan Puresu Insatsu Shuppan [トッパン・プレス印刷出版], 1992.

　　Describes the seventy-five years of activities of Brazil Rikkōkai, its effort on regional agricultural development, ideology (Christianity), the 4H movement, interns, Japanese language students, and youth organizations that visited Japan.

11. Hayashi, Hisao, Shūhei Yagi, and Hisashi Nagata [林寿雄, 八木修平, and 永田久]. *Nihon to Burajiru ni kaketa hashi: Nagata Shigeshi no shōgai to shisō* [日本とブラジルにかけた橋：永田稠の生涯と思想]. São Paulo: Nippaku Nōson Bunka Shinkōkai [日伯農村文化振興会], 1986.

　　The life and ideology of Shigeshi Nagata, a president of Rikkōkai Association, who became a bridge between Japan and Brazil and had contributed to build the Aliança Settlement in the Northwestern part of São Paulo State.

12. Hironaka, Chikako [弘中千賀子]. *Inochi oriori* [いのち折々]. San Pauro [サンパウロ]: Nippaku Mainichi Shinbunsha [日伯毎日新聞社], 1994.

　　Published as part of celebration for fifty-fifth anniversary of *Japanese-Brazilian Mainichi Daily*. A compilation of essays that describes sentiments of immigrants called "semi-Nisei," in one form of immigrant literature. Simultaneously published in Portuguese.

13. Hoshino, Hōsaku [星野豊作]. *Takkon 100-nen* [拓魂100年]. Tōkyō [東京]: Shūsakusha [秀作社], 1990.

　　A history of Japanese immigrants, recorded mainly through interviews. Focuses on some persons within the Japanese community of Brazil during the period of confusion after World War II.

14. Hosoe Shizuo Sensei to Sono Igyō Kankō Iinkai [細江静男先生とその遺業刊行委員会]. *Hosoe Shizuo Sensei to sono igyō* [細江静男先生とその遺業]. San Pauro [サンパウロ]: Asami, Hironari [浅海護也], 1995.

　　A compilation of memorial writings by friends of Mr. Hosoe, who made a great contribution as a physician in the colonies in the inland Amazon. Doctor Hosoe graduated from Keio University in medicine. He came to Brazil to help immigrants but he had to study again at the University of São Paulo, Medical School, and to become a naturalized citizen of Brazil in order to practice in this country. He was one of the founders of Caramuru Boy Scout Association and also contributed in bringing to Brazil the so-called "Boy Scout Immigrants." Resumé of twenty-three pages in Portuguese.

15. Hosokawa, Shūhei [細川周平]. *Shinema-ya Burajiru o yuku* [シネマ屋ブラジルを行く]. Tōkyō [東京]: Shinchō Sensho [新潮選書], 1999.

　　This is a story of people engaged in movie screenings in the Japanese settlements and mainland area of São Paulo State mainly before World War II. These groups gradually disappeared after installment of permanent movie theatres that specialized in Japanese movies in São Paulo and other cities.

16. Ijū Jigyōshishi Hensan Iinkai [移住事業私史編纂委員会]. *Ijū jigyōshishi* [移住事業私史]. N.p., 1999.

Compilation of seventy-seven people who worked at the JICA and were engaged in other activities concerning the emigration to the South America.

17. Ishii, Itarō [石射猪太郎]. *Gaikōkan no isshō* [外交官の一生]. Tōkyō [東京]: Chūō Kōronsha [中央公論社], 1986.

    Author's memoirs as a diplomat in the important period of prewar Japan. The author was appointed to ambassador in several countries, including Brazil where he had been from November 1940 to July 1942. He was in Rio de Janeiro at the start of World War II and the rupture of diplomatic relations between Japan and Brazil in January 1942.

18. Ishikawa, Tatsuzō [石川達三]. *Sōbō* [蒼氓]. Tōkyō [東京]: Shinchōsha [新潮社], 1939.

    The author accompanied poor immigrants from Tōhoku region to Brazil, from immigrant preparation center to departure, on board to arrival in Brazil, and life on the plantation, and tells sad stories experienced by immigrants. It was awarded the prestigious Akutagawa award in Japan.

19. Iwanami Kikuji Kashū Kankō Iinkai [岩波菊治歌集刊行委員会]. *Iwanami Kikuji kashū* [岩波菊治歌集]. San Pauro [サンパウロ]: Paurisuta Insatsu [パウリスタ印刷], 1959.

    Compilation of the works a settler and famous poet, Kikuji Iwanami, wrote between 1918 and 1952. Also includes experiences and memoirs as an immigrant.

20. Izumi, Seiichi, and Hiroshi Saitō [泉靖一 and 斎藤廣志]. *Amazon: sono fūdo to Nihonjin* [アマゾン：その風土と日本人]. Tōkyō [東京]: Kokin Shoin [古今書院], 1954.

    Introduces geography and climate of Amazon, and life style of Indians and native tribes there. Also traces footsteps that Japanese immigrants left in the region.

21. Jitsugyō no Burajirusha [実業のブラジル社], ed. *Burajiru Nikkei kigyō nenkan* [ブラジル日系企業年鑑]. São Paulo: Jitsugyō no Burajirusha [実業のブラジル社], 1998.

    Reference of the Japanese corporation and Nikkei corporation and business prospect of major two hundred Japanese corporations in 1998.

22. "Kibō no Ie" Sōritu 25-shūnen Kinenshi Kankō Iinkai Henshūbu [「希望の家」創立25周年記念誌刊行委員会編集部]. *Koetekita shihanseiki* [超えて来た四半世紀]. San Pauro [サンパウロ]: "Kibō no Ie" Fukushi Kyōkai [「希望の家」福祉協会], 1995.

    A story of people who helped handicapped children and were dedicated to difficult welfare enterprises.

23. Kitahara Chikazō Tsuiokushū Kankōkai [北原地價造追憶集刊行會], ed. *Kitahara Chikazō Tsuiokushū: Ariansa ijūchi no chichi* [北原地價造追悼集：アリアンサ移住地の父]. San Pauro [サンパウロ]: Kitahara Chikazō Tsuiokushū Kankōkai [北原地價造追憶集刊行會], 1972.

    A memorial writing for late Chikazō Kitahara, who was called "father of Aliança Settlement." His friends contributed essays.

24. Kiyotani, Masuji [清谷益次]. *Iwanami Kikuji: tanka ni tadoru ichi imin no kokoro no kiseki* [岩波菊治：短歌に辿る一移民の心の軌跡]. San Pauro [サンパウロ]: San Pauro Jinmon Kagaku Kenkyūjo [サンパウロ人文科学研究所], 1993.

    Kikuji Iwanami, who was called "father of Colonia Tanka," lived a fifty-four-year life filled with financial difficulties, which brought pain and fretfulness to his emotional life.

25. Kiyotani, Masuji [清谷益次]. *Nakazawa Gen'ichirō: hito to gyōseki* [中沢源一郎：人と業績]. San Pauro [サンパウロ]: Nanpaku Nōkyō Chūōkai Sōritsu 60-shūnen Kinen Kankō Iinkai [南伯農協中央会創立60周年記念刊行委員会], 1990.

    A profile, written by more than twenty writers, of late Gen'ichiro Nakazawa (Nacazawa), who lived his life as a top leader of Japanese Brazilians as the president of Cooperativa Agricola Sul-Brasil, Beneficencia Nipo-Brasileira de São Paulo, and Sociedade Brasileira de Cultura Japonesa.

26. Kiyotani, Masuji [清谷益次]. *Tōi hibi no koto* [遠い日々のこと]. San Pauro [サンパウロ]: Kiyotani Masuji [清谷益次], 1985.

    The author, who was a "child immigrant," describes his memory from youth. It includes a commentary of immigration history in *tanka* verse.

27. Kochia Sangyō Kumiai Chūōkai [コチア産業組合中央会]. *Kochia Sangyō Kumiai Chūōkai rokujūnen no ayumi* [コチア産業組合中央会六十年の歩み]. San Pauro [サンパウロ]: Kochia Sangyō Kumiai Chūōkai [コチア産業組合中央会], 1987.

    History of Cotia Industrial Cooperation Central Association between 1927 and 1987. Topics include how it was established, postwar immigration, and tax reform, and the cooperation's crisis.

28. Kochia Seinen Ijū Yonjisshūnen Kinenshi Henshū Iinkai [コチア青年移住四十周年記念誌編集委員会]. *Kochia seinen ijū yonjisshūnen kinenshi* [コチア青年移住四十周年記念誌]. San Pauro [サンパウロ]: Kochia Seinen Renraku Kyōgikai [コチア青年連絡協議会], 1995.

    Fortieth anniversary edition of "Cotia Youth Immigration." The book traces the footsteps of immigrants in different regions.

29. Kodama, Shōichi [児玉正一]. *Burajiru imin no chichi, Uetsuka Shūhei* [ブラジル移民の父、上塚周平]. San Pauro [サンパウロ]: Nanbei Jiji Shinbunsha [南米時事新聞社], 1950.

    A biography of Shūhei Uetsuka, who was famous as the father of Japanese immigrants to Brazil. The book depicts his personality.

30. Kokuritsu Kokkai Toshokan Senmon Shiryōbu [国立国会図書館専門資料部], ed. *Imin kankei shiryō mokuroku: Kokuritsu Kokkai Toshokan Tokubetsu Shiryōshitsu-shozō* [移民関係資料目録：国立国会図書館特別資料室所蔵]. Tōkyō [東京]: Kokuritsu Kokkai Toshokan [国立国会図書館], 1997.

    A bibliographic collection of various data on Nikkei immigrants in Hawai`i, and Central and South America.

31. Kokusai Kyōryoku Jigyōdan [国際協力事業団]. *Jamikku Jemisu gyōsekishi* [ジャミック・ジェミス業績史]. São Paulo: n.p., 1988.

JAMIC Company and JEMIS Financial Company were long-time, active Brazilian corporations established by Japan International Cooperation Agency and forced to dissolve by the Brazilian government. This book is a complete record of the two companies and of the postwar immigration.

32. Koronia Geinōshi Hensan Iinkai [コロニア芸能史編纂委員会]. *Koronia geinōshi* [コロニア芸能誌]. São Paulo: Koronia Geinōshi Hensan Iinkai [コロニア芸能史編纂委員会], 1986.

    Authorities in fourteen Japanese public entertainment fields, such as Minyō, Rōkyoku, and movies, which comforted and revitalized people in Nikkei settlements, discuss secret and funny stories, reflecting their golden ages.

33. Koronia Man'yōshū Kankō Iinkai [コロニア万葉集刊行委員会]. *Koronia Man'yōshū* [コロニア万葉集] [English title: Colonia Man'yoshu, anthology of tanka poems, written by Japanese immigrants in Brazil]. San Pauro [サンパウロ]: Koronia Man'yōshū Kankō Iinkai [コロニア万葉集刊行委員会], 1981.

    Includes tanka verses which were poetic forms written by Japanese immigrants to express their happiness and sadness. Divided into prewar and postwar parts. One thousand three hundred and seventy eight authors contributed 6,634 verses in this monumental work of colonia tanka verses.

34. Kosaka, Makoto [小坂誠]. *Itakēra koronia shichijūnen no ayumi* [イタケーラ・コロニア七十年のあゆみ]. San Pauro [サンパウロ]: Itakēra Nikkei Kurabu [イタケーラ日系クラブ], 1998.

    A history of Itaqueira Colony, known as "Peach Village," since the first immigrants who settled there provided vegetables and fruits to São Paulo.

35. Kōyama, Rokurō [香山六郎]. *Kōyama Rokurō kaisōroku: Burajiru daiikkai imin no kiroku* [香山六郎回想録: ブラジル第一回移民の記録]. São Paulo: San Pauro Jinmon Kagaku Kenkyūjo [サンパウロ人文科学研究所], 1976.

    An autobiography covering fifty years of life of the first immigrant who arrived on the *Kasato Maru*. The author wrote in his twilight years, while suffering from hearing and sight loss.

36. Maeyama, Takashi [前山隆]. *Dona Marugarīda Watanabe: imin, rōjin fukushi no gojūsannen* [ドナ・マルガリーダ・渡辺: 移民・老人福祉の五十三年]. Tōkyō [東京]: Ochanomizu Shobō [御茶の水書房], 1996.

    This is Mrs. Margarida Watanabe's biography who arrived in Brazil at the age of eleven, and dedicated fifty-three years of her life assisting elderly people from the Japanese-Brazilian community, through the nursery home, Ikoi no sono.

37. Maringa Bunka Taiiku Kyōkai 40-nenshi Hakkan Iinkai [マリンガ文化体育協会40年史発刊委員会]. *Asema 40-nenshi* [アセマ40年史]. Burajiru Parana-shū Maringa [ブラジルパラナ州マリンガ]: Bunka Taiiku Kyōkai [文化体育協会], 1988.

    A record of forty years of history of the Maringa Cultural and Athletic Association, its establishment and direction.

38. Masuda, Hidekazu [増田秀一]. *Emeboi jisshūjōshi* [エメボイ実習場史]. San Pauro [サンパウロ]: Emeboi Kenkyūjo [エメボイ研究所], 1981.

    History of the Emeboi Practice Center for immigrants, which affected the Colonia society greatly.

39. Mizumoto, Mitsuto [水本光任]. *Kiku no shita mizu: Wada Shūichirō den* [菊のした水: 和田周一郎伝]. San Pauro [サンパウロ]: San Pauro Shinbunsha [サンパウロ新聞社], 1984.

    A biography of Shūichirō Wada, who was disappointed by devastated Japan, and moved to Brazil to settle in Uetsuka colony. It recollects the confusion and special attack unit of the *kachi-gumi* during the immediate postwar period and depicts Wada's personality.

40. Nagata, Hisashi [永田久]. *Burajiru Rikkōkai sōritsu hachijisshūnen kinenshi* [ブラジル力行会創立八十周年記念誌]. San Pauro [サンパウロ]: Nippaku Nōson Bunka Shinkō Insatsujo [日伯農村文化振興印刷所], 1999.

    Rikkōkai association described by people who have been involved in its activities and its member's list.

41. Nanbei Ginkō Gojūnenshi Henshū Iinkai [南米銀行五十年史編集委員会]. *Nanbei Ginkō gojūnenshi* [南米銀行五十年史]. San Pauro [サンパウロ]: Nanbei Ginkō [南米銀行], 1994.

    Fifty-year history of Nanbei Ginkō, established in 1940. It reports how it conquered the difficulties during the war. Originally, it was Brazil Colonial Bank, established in 1937.

42. Nihon Burajiru Kōryūshi Henshū Iinkai [日本ブラジル交流史編集委員会]. *Nihon Burajiru kōryūshi: Nippaku kankei 100-nen no kaiko to tenbō* [日本ブラジル交流史: 日伯関係100年の回顧と展望]. Tōkyō [東京]: Nihon Burajiru Shūkō 100-shūnen Kinen Jigyō Soshiki Iinkai [日本ブラジル修好100周年記念事業組織委員会], 1995.

    Hundred-year history of the Japanese-Brazilian relations. More than twenty experts in various fields discuss topics including diplomacy, immigration, economy, cultural exchange, present conditions, and the future.

43. Nihon Imin Hachijūnenshi Hensan Iinkai [日本移民八十年史編纂委員会]. *Burajiru Nihon imin hachijūnenshi* [ブラジル日本移民八十年史]. San Pauro [サンパウロ]: Imin Hachijūnensai Saiten Iinkai [移民八十年祭祭典委員会], 1991.

    Published to commemorate the eightieth-year anniversary of the first group of immigrants who arrived on the *Kasato Maru*. A detailed record of immigrants' history, their beginnings as contract laborers on coffee plantations, their offspring, and how they have become what they are now. See P-4 for Portuguese-language translation.

44. Nihonjin Kyōryokukai [日本人協力会]. *San Pauro 400-nensai: Sei-shi yonhyakunen saiten* [サンパウロ400年祭: 聖市四百年祭典]. N.p.: Nihon Shashin Insatsu Kabushiki Kaisha [日本写真印刷株式会社], 1957.

History of the Japanese Cooperation Society compiled and published by the Nikkei community as part of the celebration for the 400th anniversary of the establishment of São Paulo City. The society was later developed into the Brazil-Japan Cultural Association.

45. Ninomiya, Masato [二宮正人], ed. *"Dekasegi" genshō ni kansuru shinpojūmu hōkokusho* [「出稼ぎ」現象に関するシンポジューム報告書]. São Paulo: Burajiru Nihon Bunka Kyōkai [ブラジル日本文化協会], 1993.

    Report on the symposium among Brazilian and Japanese experts on the dekasegi phenomenon, who discuss pros and cons of dekasegi labor in Japan, now deeply in recession, and search for the future adjustment. See P-14 for Portuguese-language translation.

46. Ninomiya, Masato [二宮正人], ed. *Dekasegi, sono 10-nen no rekishi to shōraizō* [「出稼ぎ」その10年の歴史と将来像]. São Paulo: Kokugai Shūrōsha Jōhō Engo Sentā [国外就労者情報援護センター], 1998.

    Record of the celebration for the fifth anniversary of the establishment of Information and Support Center for Brazilian Workers Abroad, and of the Symposium: "Ten Years of Dekasegi History and Its Future." Bilingual edition in Portuguese/Japanese. See P-13.

47. Ninomiya, Masato [二宮正人], ed. *"Nikkei Komyunitīno shōrai" shinpojūmu hōkokusho* [「日系コミュニティーの将来」シンポジューム報告書]. São Paulo: Burajiru Nihon Bunka Kyōkai [ブラジル日本文化協会], 1995.

    Record of symposium held as part of celebration for the eighty-fifth anniversary of Japanese immigration. Its main theme deals with the younger generations who identify less and less with the Nikkei society and the future direction of the Japanese Brazilians. See P-15 for Portuguese-language translation.

48. Ninomiya, Masato, and Rōdōshō Shokugyō Anteikyoku Gyōmu Chōseika [二宮正人 and 労働省職業安定局業務調整課]. *Nihon, Burajiru ryōkoku ni okeru Nikkeijin no rōdō to seikatsu* [日本・ブラジル両国における日系人の労働と生活]. Tōkyō [東京]: Nikkan Rōdō Tsūshinsha [日刊労働通信社], 1994.

    Compares Nikkei dekasegi workers of today with Japanese immigrant workers to Brazil in the early period and describes current condition of Japan.

49. Noda, Ryōji [野田良治]. *Jissa jūhachinen Burajiru jinkokuki* [實査十八年ブラジル人國記]. Tōkyō [東京]: Hakubunkan [博文館], 1926.

    A masterwork on Brazilian situation in 1925, based on author's experiences as interpreter for the Japanese Embassy in Brazil for eighteen years. The author foresees great prospects for the development of Japanese society in Brazil.

50. Ōkuchi, Nobuo [大口信夫]. *Gaikōkan yūkaisaru* [外交官誘拐さる]. Tōkyō [東京]: Daiamondosha [ダイアモンド社], 1989.

    In March 1970, six months after assuming the position of Consul General of Japan in São Paulo, Nobuo Ōkuchi was kidnapped and, after five days, five political prisoners (among them was Mário Ozawa, a Nikkei) were released in exchange for the consul's release. After ten years, Ōkuchi returned to Brazil, this time as Ambassador of Japan by his own wishes. In this book, written in 1989, he remembers details of the episode, the backstage, and provides us with an ample view about the left wing groups that were fighting against the military regime in the 1970s. See P-18 for Portuguese translation.

51. Ōmiya, Tomonobu [大宮知信]. *Dekasēgī: gyakuryū suru Nikkei Burajirujin* [デカセーギー：逆流する日系ブラジル人]. Tōkyō [東京]: Sōshisha [草思社], 1997.

    The author is a journalist who describes the emerging problems endured by more than 200,000 Brazilians who go to Japan as dekasegi, including problems of discrimination against them.

52. Paurista Shinbunsha [パウリスタ新聞社]. *Nihon Burajiru kōryū jinmei jiten* [日本・ブラジル交流人名辞典]. Tōkyō [東京]: Satsuki Shobō [五月書房], 1996.

    Who's who widely covering pioneers and contributors in the Nikkei community for the past hundred years. Also includes many Brazilians who were deeply involved with Japanese immigrants.

53. Saitō, Hiroshi [斎藤広志]. *Atarashii Burajiru: genchi kara no tokubetsu hōkoku* [新しいブラジル：現地からの特別報告]. Tōkyō [東京]: Saimaru Shuppankai [サイマル出版会], 1974.

    Describes the current situation in Brazil, mainly from an economic viewpoint, and examines the future relations with Japan.

54. Saitō, Hiroshi [斎藤広志]. *Burajiru to Nihonjin: ibunka ni ikite 50-nen* [ブラジルと日本人：異文化に生きて50年]. Tōkyō [東京]: Saimaru Shuppankai [サイマル出版会], 1984.

    The last essays in which the author, who had tried to be the bridge between Japan and Brazil, wrote about Japanese and Brazilian culture.

55. Saitō, Hiroshi [斎藤広志]. *Gaikokujin ni natta Nihonjin: Burajiru imin no ikikata to kawarikata* [外国人になった日本人：ブラジル移民の生き方と変わり方]. Tōkyō [東京]: Saimaru Shuppankai [サイマル出版会], 1978.

    Describes the process in which the Japanese assimilate to Brazil, while staying tightly together among them.

56. Saitō, Hiroshi [斎藤広志]. *Hachiya Sen'ichi* [蜂谷専一]. San Pauro [サンパウロ]: San Pauro Jinmon Kagaku Kenkyūjo [サンパウロ人文科学研究所], 1983.

    Biography of Sen'ichi Hachiya, a magnate in the colonial business world. After his death, enormous amounts of his writings were compiled and descriptions by his relatives were added to show the personality of the deceased who had been a distinguished person in the colonial society.

57. San Pauro Gakuseikai [サンパウロ学生会]. *Arumonia gakuseiryō "25-nen no ayumi"* [アルモニア学生寮「25年の歩み」]. San Pauro [サンパウロ]: Nihon Bijutsu Insatsu Shuppan Gōshikai [日本美術印刷出版合資会], 1978.

    Published to celebrate the twenty-fifth anniversary of

the establishment of Harmonia Student Dormitory, which has been managed by São Paulo Student Association. Describes the full aspects of the dormitory today.

58. San Pauro Jinmon Kagaku Kenkyūjo [サンパウロ人文科学研究所]. *Burajiru Nihon imin, Nikkei shakaishi nenpyō* [ブラジル日本移民・日系社会史年表]. San Pauro [サンパウロ]: San Pauro Jinmon Kagaku Kenkyūjo [サンパウロ人文科学研究所], 1996.

    Originally published by Tomoo Handa in 1976. Japanese-Brazilian Social Science Study Center in São Paulo significantly revised with additional data for the hundredth anniversary of the Japanese-Brazilian relations. It is the most reliable timeline currently available.

59. San Pauro Jinmon Kagaku Kenkyūjo [サンパウロ人文科学研究所]. *Burajiru no Nikkei shinshūkyō* [ブラジルの日系新宗教]. San Pauro [サンパウロ]: Toppan Puresusha [トッパン・プレス社], 1985.

    Examines the influence of Nikkei religion on Brazilian society.

60. San Pauro Jinmon Kagaku Kenkyūjo [サンパウロ人文科学研究所]. *Hyōhensuru Burajiru Nikkei shakai: Nakao Kumayoshi tsuitō kinen ronshū* [豹変するブラジル日系社会: 中尾熊喜追悼記念論集]. San Pauro [サンパウロ]: Toppan Puresusha [トッパン・プレス社], 1977.

    A memorial writing for Kumayoshi Nakao. Also ponders the future of the Nikkei community.

61. San Pauro Jinmon Kagaku Kenkyūjo [サンパウロ人文科学研究所]. *Jinmonken No.1* [人文研]. San Pauro [サンパウロ]: San Pauro Jinmon Kagaku Kenkyūjo [サンパウロ人文科学研究所], 1998.

    Reports on research results conducted by the Japanese-Brazilian Social Science Study Center in São Paulo. The first report was on the "current condition of the Japanese-language education in Brazil."

62. San Pauro Jinmon Kagaku Kenkyūjo [サンパウロ人文科学研究所]. *Nihon bunka denshō no mondai* [日本文化伝承の問題]. San Pauro [サンパウロ]: Toppan Puresusha [トッパン・プレス社], 1980.

    Examines the transmission of culture and Japanese identity.

63. San Pauro Nikkei Kyōryoku Iinkai [サンパウロ日系協力委員会]. *Nihon Burajiru shūkō 100-shūnen kinen jigyō* [日本ブラジル修好100周年記念事業]. San Pauro [サンパウロ]: Toppan Puresu [トッパン・プレス], 1996.

    Published as part of the celebration of the hundredth anniversary of the Japanese-Brazilian relations. Activity report by São Paulo Nikkei Cooperation Committee.

64. San Pauro Nippaku Engo Kyōkai [サンパウロ日伯援護協会]. *Enkyō 40-nenshi* [援協40年史]. N.p., 1999.

    This book was published in both Japanese and Portuguese. This book traces the trajectory of an institution with more than ten thousand members and working in the Japanese community in the area of hospital and care for the elderly with emphasis on those in economic need. See also P-29.

65. Satō, Nenpuku [佐藤念腹]. *Kokage zatsuei senshū: kushū* [木蔭雑詠選集: 句集]. Tōkyō [東京]: Nagata Shobō [永田書房], 1979.

    A collection of *haiku* verses. From fifty-seven thousand that had been published in *Kokage* (Brazilian *haiku* magazine) between 1948 and 1965, 2,489 verses were selected and divided into seasonal topics.

66. Sawada, Toshio [澤田壽夫]. *Sawada Setsuzō kaisōroku: ichi gaikōkan no shōgai* [澤田節蔵回想録: 一外交官の生涯]. Tōkyō [東京]: Yūhikaku [有斐閣], 1985.

    A biography of a diplomat who was assigned to different missions. He was appointed as Japanese ambassador to Brazil between 1934 to 1938, a time when Japanese immigration was very difficult because of the 1934 Brazilian Constitution, which severely restricted Japanese immigration to Brazil.

67. Shimomoto Kenkichi Henshū Iinkai [下元健吉編集委員会]. *Shimomoto Kenkichi: hito to sokuseki* [下元健吉: 人と足跡]. San Pauro [サンパウロ]: San Pauro Jinmon Kagaku Kenkyūjo [サンパウロ人文科学研究所], 1979.

    A biography of Kenkichi Shimomoto, a strong leader who founded the Great Cotia Industrial Cooperation. Many people examined and analyzed his life from unique viewpoints of dictatorship and cooperation management.

68. Suzuki, Teiichi. *The Japanese Immigrant in Brazil*. Tokyo: University of Tokyo Press, 1964.

    Complete statistical data of the situation of Japanese immigrants in Brazil, collected and researched by the Census Committee of the Japanese Community in 1958.

69. Suzuki, Teijirō [鈴木貞次郎]. *Umoreyuku takujin no sokuseki* [埋もれ行く拓人の足跡]. San Pauro [サンパウロ]: Suzuki, Teijirō [鈴木貞次郎], 1969.

    Presents an overview of immigration history, based on the examination of the people with whom the author had been acquainted.

70. Takagi, Toshirō [高木俊朗]. *Kyōshin: Burajiru Nihon imin no sōran* [狂信: ブラジル日本移民の騒乱]. Tōkyō [東京]: Farao Kikaku [ファラオ企画], 1991.

    A non-fiction book which describes the bloody conflict between *kachi-gumi* (believers of Japan's victory in World War II) and *make-gumi* (believers of Japan's defeat), arising from lack of accurate information, in the Japanese immigrant community in Brazil. It poses the question: "What is Japanese?"

71. Tamiya, Torahiko [田宮虎彦]. *Burajiru no Nihonjin* [ブラジルの日本人]. Tōkyō [東京]: Asahi Shinbunsha [朝日新聞社], 1975.

    The author, who stayed in Brazil as a visiting professor of the Institute for Japan Cultural Study at São Paulo University, observes the situation and future of the Brazilian Nikkei community sixty years after the start of Japanese immigration to Brazil.

72. Tsunoda, Fusako [角田房子]. *Amazon no uta: Nihonjin no kiroku* [アマゾンの歌: 日本人の記録]. Tōkyō [東京]: Chūō Kōronsha [中央公論社], 1976.

73. Tsunoda, Fusako [角田房子]. *Burajiru no Nikkeijin: shintenchi ni ikiru chi to ase no kiroku* [ブラジルの日系人: 新天地に生きる血と汗の記録]. Tōkyō [東京]: Ushio Shuppansha [潮出版社], 1979.

    A collection of short stories that deal with Nikkei people living in Brazil.

74. Tsunoda, Fusako [角田房子]. *Miyasaka Kunito den* [宮坂國人伝]. São Paulo: Nanbei Ginkō [南米銀行], 1985.

    A biography of Kunito Miyasaka, who overcame many difficulties as a pioneer immigrant in Peru and the Philippines, managed the four settlements in Brazil Colonial Enterprises, and established and managed Nanbei Ginkō (Bank of South America). Those who were acquainted with Miyasaka talk about his life without pretense.

75. Ueno, Antonio Yoshio [上野アントニオ義雄]. *Ueno Yonezō den* [上野米蔵伝]. Kōbe-shi [神戸市]: Kōbe Besuto [神戸ベスト], 1978.

    Series of testimonies about Yonezō Ueno, made by his sons and friends, uncovering many episodes of his life related to immigration history.

76. Wako Shungorō-shi Tsuitōki Kankō Iinkai [輪湖俊午郎氏追憶記刊行委員会]. *Hibi aratanariki: aru takujin no shōgai* [日々新たなりき: ある拓人の生涯]. San Pauro [サンパウロ]: Teikoku Shoin [帝国書院], 1967.

    A memorial writing for Shungorō Wako. His friends recollect his memories and personality. Also includes the essays that Wako himself had written.

77. Yamada, Michio [山田迪生]. *Fune ni miru Nihonjin iminshi: Kasato Maru kara kurūzu kyakusen e* [船にみる日本人移民史: 笠戸丸からクルーズ客船へ]. Tōkyō [東京]: Chūō Kōronsha [中央公論社], 1998.

    This is a history of all immigration ships starting from the *Kasato Maru*, the first steamship to carry immigrants to Brazil until the last steamship *Nippon Maru*, which came to Brazil in 1973. After this ship the immigrants began to come by airplane in small numbers.

78. Yamamoto, Kiyoshi [山本喜誉司]. *Utsurikite gojūnen: Burajiru no Nikkeijin* [移り来て五十年: ブラジルの日系人]. Tōkyō [東京]: Raten Amerika Chūōkai [ラテンアメリカ中央会], 1957.

    The author, who was the first president of the Brazilian Society of Japanese Culture (*Sociedade Brasileira de Cultura Japonesa*), describes the condition of the Colonia at that time, which was facing the most confusing period in its fifty years of Japanese immigration history.

79. Yashinoki Gōdō Kashū Kankō Iinkai [椰子樹合同歌集刊行委員会]. *Ikusanga no fu* [幾山河の賦]. San Pauro [サンパウロ]: Yashinoki Gōdō Kashū Kankō Iinkai [椰子樹合同歌集刊行委員会], 1996.

    Published as part of the celebration of the hundred-year anniversary of Japan-Brazil relations. One hundred and forty members present *tanka* verses, an art form brought to Brazil by the Japanese immigrants, which express immigrants' sentiments and lives.

80. Yokota, Pauro [横田パウロ]. *Sengo no Nippaku keizai kankei* [戦後の日伯経済関係], translated by Masato Ninomiya, [二宮正人]. São Paulo: Primus Consultoria e Comunicação Integrada, 1997.

    A detailed report on the postwar economic relations between Japan and Brazil, which extend from trade and industry to agriculture. Also covers wider cultural relations. See P-33 for Portuguese translation.

81. Zaidan Hōjin Akama Gakuin [財団法人赤間学院]. *Zaidan Hōjin Akama Gakuin sōritsu gojūnenshi* [財団法人赤間学院創立五十年史]. San Pauro [サンパウロ]: Toppan Puresu [トッパン・プレス], 1985.

    A pictorial history published as part of the celebration for the fiftieth anniversary of the establishment of the Akama Gakuin.

PORTUGUESE

1. Aramasa, Taku. *Pioneiros imigrantes japoneses: portraits*. São Paulo: MASP, 1988.

    An album that celebrates the eightieth anniversary of Japanese immigration in Brazil with photographs of pioneer immigrants taken by Aramasa.

2. Cardoso, Ruth C. Leite. *Estrutura familiar e mobilidade social*. São Paulo, Brasil: Ed. Kaleidos-Primus, 1998.

    This is a doctoral dissertation, published in trilingual editions—Portuguese, Japanese, and English—written by the Brazilian first lady when she was a graduate student at the University of São Paulo. It investigates and analyzes the characteristics of Japanese immigrants concerning their interests in the education of children and accurately indicates the direction of Japanese-Brazilian community. The author made her research in the 1960s and the dissertation was approved in 1972. See also E-9 and J-4.

3. Cardoso, Ruth C. Leite. *O papel das associações juvenis na aculturação dos japoneses*. São Paulo: Centro Regional de Pesquisas Educacionais de São Paulo, 1959.

    One of the early works of the author who is an anthropologist and did an interesting study of the development of the *seinen-kai* (youth organizations) in São Paulo.

4. Comissão de Elaboração da História dos 80 Anos de Imigração Japonesa no Brasil. *Uma epopéia moderna: 80 anos da imigração japonesa no Brasil*. São Paulo: HUCITEC: Sociedade Brasileira de Cultura Japonesa, 1992.

    The "Eightieth Anniversary of Japanese Immigration to Brazil Special Issue" includes several articles by Brazilian and Nikkei researchers. See also J-43.

5. Comitê Organizador da III Convenção Panamericana Nikkei. *O Nikkei e sua americanidade: temas apresentados na III Convenção Panamericana Nikkei*. São Paulo: Massao Ohno Editor, 1986.

    Essays by researchers analyzing themes related to the

descendants of Japanese immigrants in the American continent. Includes a text of a lecture by then-Senator Fernando Henrique Cardoso.

6. Daigo, Massao. *A mata das ilusões*. São Paulo: Aliança Cultural Brasil-Japão, 1997.

   Tells the saga of Umpei Hirano and the tragedy of the first immigrants to arrive in Brazil in 1908; contains episodes of the pioneer struggle in Cafelandia, in the state of São Paulo. See also the J-5.

7. Handa, Tomoo. *O imigrante japonês: história de sua vida no Brasil*. São Paulo: T.A Queiroz Editor: Centro de Estudos Nipo-Brasileiros, 1987.

   History of Japanese immigrants in Brazil, focusing on the habits and cultural characteristics of that community from 1908 to 1968.

8. Handa, Tomoo. *Memórias de um imigrante japonês no Brasil*. São Paulo: T. A Queiroz Editor, 1980.

   A memoir. The author was both a writer and a painter. He describes the early daily life experiences of Japanese immigrants in São Paulo between 1908 and 1927.

9. Hatanaka, Maria L. E. "O processo judicial da 'Shindo-Remmei': um fragmento da história dos imigrantes japoneses no Brasil." São Paulo: PUC-SP, 1993.

   Master's thesis on the lawsuit against Shindo-Remmei, a nationalist association that believed in the victory of Japan and perpetrated terrorist acts against those who preached the truth, i.e., the defeat of Japan in World War II.

10. Maeyama, Takashi. "O imigrante e a religião: estudo de uma seita religiosa japonesa em São Paulo." São Paulo: mimeograph copy, 1967.

    Master's thesis of the author. A brief introduction to the religious life of the Japanese community in Brazil. The study focuses mainly on the *Seichō no ie* sect.

11. Morais, Fernando. *Corações Sujos*. São Paulo: Companhia das Letras, 2000.

    This is the story concerning the fanatic institution called "Shindo-Remmei" (League of Loyal Subjects) whose members did not believe in Japan's defeat in World War II. They organized "killer groups" who attacked other Japanese immigrants who accepted Japan's capitulation. During 1946 and 1947, twenty-three people were killed, and more than two hundred were wounded. It constitutes one of the darkest pages of history of Japanese immigration to Brazil.

12. Museu de Arte de São Paulo Assis Chateaubriand. *Vida e arte dos japoneses no Brasil*. São Paulo: MASP: Banco América do Sul, 1988.

    The book provides an overview of the Nikkei's artistic world and shows the trajectory and manifestation of its cultural movements.

13. Ninomiya, Masato. *Dekassegui: Dez anos de história e suas perspectivas futuras*. São Paulo: CIATE, 1998.

    Minutes of the symposium in celebration of the fifth anniversary of the Support and Information Center for Workers Abroad. See J-46 for Japanese translation.

14. Ninomiya, Masato, org. *Dekassegui: palestras e exposições do Simpósio sobre o Fenômeno Chamado Dekassegui*. São Paulo: Estação Liberdade: Sociedade Brasileira de Cultura Japonesa, 1992.

    Report on lectures and exhibits presented at the symposium "A Phenomenon Named Dekasegi" that initiated many support activities on behalf of the Japanese-Brazilians who went to work in Japan. See J- 45 for Japanese translation.

15. Ninomiya, Masato, org. *O futuro da comunidade nikkey: palestras, painéis e debates do simpósio comemorativo dos 85 anos de imigração japonesa no Brasil*. São Paulo: Editora Mania do Livro, 1996.

    Minutes of the symposium celebrating the eighty-fifth anniversary of Japanese immigration to Brazil. See J-47 for Japanese translation.

16. Nogueira, Arlinda R. *Imigração japonesa na história contemporânea do Brasil*. São Paulo: Centro de Estudos Nipo-Brasileiros: Massao Ohno Editor, 1984.

    A brief history of Japanese immigrants in Brazil based on a course presented at the University of São Paulo.

17. Nogueira, Arlinda R. *A imigração japonesa para a lavoura cafeeira paulista (1908–1922)*. São Paulo: Instituto de Estudos Brasileiros: USP, 1973.

    The author elaborates on Brazil-Japan relations and the reasons that brought Japanese immigrants to Brazil (1908–1922).

18. Oi, Célia Abe, and Federação Paulista de Beisebol e Softbol. *Beisebol: histórias de uma paixão*. São Paulo: Federação Paulista de Beisebol e Softbol, 1996.

    The book is a summary of fifty years of history of the Baseball and Softball Federation of São Paulo, its main clubs and championships.

19. Okuchi, Nobuo. *O seqüestro do diplomata: memórias*, translated by Masato Ninomiya. São Paulo: Estação Liberdade: Primus, 1991.

    Memoirs of Nobuo Ōkuchi, former consul general of Japan in São Paulo, kidnapped by the guerrilla in the 1970s. See J-50 for Japanese translation.

20. Paula, Eurípedes S. de. *Anais do I Colóquio Brasil-Japão, 25–27 de julho de 1966*. São Paulo: Gráfica da Faculdade de Filosofia, Ciências e Letras da Universidade de São Paulo, 1967.

    Minutes of the symposium held at University of São Paulo in 1966, contains papers and lectures by several researchers and scholars.

21. Paula, Eurípedes S. de, org. *O japonês em São Paulo e no Brasil*. São Paulo: Centro de Estudos Nipo-Brasileiros, 1971.

    Minutes of the symposium held at the University of São Paulo in 1968 in celebration of the sixtieth anniversary of Japanese immigration to Brazil.

22. Rezende, Tereza Hatue de. *Ryu Mizuno: saga japonesa em terras brasileiras*. Curitiba: Instituto Nacional do Livro, 1991.

    A brief history of the life of Ryo (Ryu) Mizuno, who signed the first Japanese immigration permission contract with the Government of the State of São Paulo in 1907, and who was responsible for the arrival of the first immigrant groups on ship *Kasato Maru* in 1908.

23. Saito, Hiroshi. *Assimilação e integração dos japoneses no Brasil*. Petrópolis: Editora Vozes, 1973.

    A compilation of several articles and essays on social and cultural aspects of Japanese immigrants in Brazil.

24. Saito, Hiroshi. *O cooperativismo e a comunidade*. São Paulo: Editora Sociologia e Política, 1964.

    A social-historic study of the structure of Japanese cooperative system in Brazil, taking the Cotia Cooperative as an example.

25. Saito, Hiroshi. *A integração e participação de japoneses e descendentes na sociedade brasileira*. São Paulo: Centro de Estudos Nipo-Brasileiros, 1977.

    A summary of the contribution of Japanese immigrants and their descendants to Brazilian society, focusing mainly on agriculture.

26. Saito, Hiroshi. *O japonês no Brasil*. São Paulo: Editora Sociologia e Política, 1961.

    A pioneer and classical study of the Japanese in Brazil. The author works with the subjects of assimilation and cultural adaptation of the Japanese immigrant in Brazil.

27. Saito, Hiroshi, org. *A presença japonesa no Brasil*. São Paulo: T. A. Queiroz: Editora da Universidade de São Paulo, 1980.

    Minutes of the symposium on Japanese presence in Brazil organized by University of São Paulo in 1978 with the participation of great scholars in the immigration field.

28. Sakurai, Célia. *Romanceiro da imigração japonesa*. São Paulo: FAPESP: IDESP, Editora Sumaré, 1993.

    The author elaborates on the imaginary in Japanese immigrants' culture in Brazil, based on women writers and their work.

29. San Pauro Nippaku Engo Kyōkai. *Enkyō 40-nenshi*. N.p., 1999.

    This book, published in both Japanese and Portuguese, traces the trajectory of an institution with more than ten thousand members, working in the Japanese community in the area of hospital and care for elders with emphasis on those in economic need. See also J-64.

30. Vieira, Francisca Isabel Schurig. *O Japonês na frente de expansão paulista: o processo de absorção do japonês em Marília*. São Paulo: Livraria Pioneira Editora: Editora de Universidade de São Paulo, 1973.

    A profile of the Japanese community in the city of Marilia in the hinterland of the state of São Paulo.

31. Yamamoto, Katsuzo. *Toda uma vida no Brasil*, translated by José Yamashiro. São Paulo: Editora Mania do Livro, 1994.

    A selection of articles and essays written by Yamamoto between 1962 and 1993; an overview of the economic, social, and cultural situation in Brazil as seen through the eyes of an immigrant who became a successful entrepreneur.

32. Yamashiro, José. *Trajetória de duas vidas: uma história de imigração e integração*. São Paulo: Aliança Cultural Brasil-Japão: Centro de Estudos Nipo-Brasileiros, 1996.

    The work is based on the memoirs of the author who was born in Okinawa, and tells the history of Japanese immigration using his own experience and autobiography and that of his fathers as recorded in his translated diary.

33. Yokota, Paulo, ed. *Fragmentos sobre as relações nipo-brasileiras no pós-guerra*. Rio de Janeiro: Bolsa de Mercadorias & Futuros: Topbooks, 1997.

    A selection of articles written by scholars and researchers analyzing the Brazilian-Japanese relations in the post-World War II period.

34. Yoshioka, Reimei. "Por que migramos do e para o Japão: os exemplos dos bairros das Alianças e dos atuais dekasseguis." Ph.D. diss., Department of Geography, University of São Paulo, 1995.

    The first part of the book focuses on the history of the "Colônia das Alianças" (Colony of Alliances), settlements of Japanese immigrants which became the city of Mirandopolis, 600 km northwest of São Paulo City. The second part is a study of the dekasegi profile.

Supplementary Materials

COMPILED BY JOHN MIZUKI, MASATO NINOMIYA, AND HIRONOBU KAI

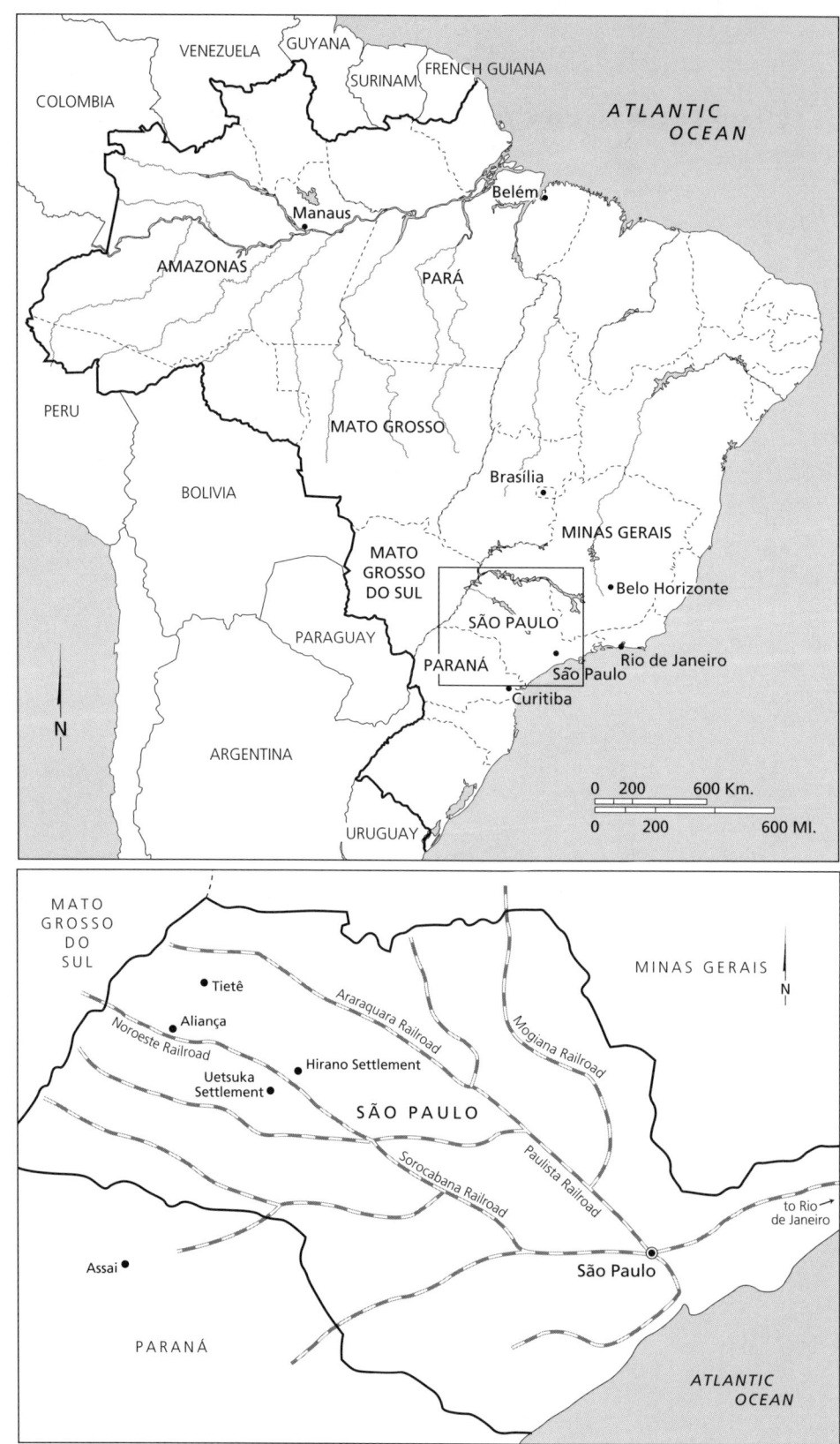

Map 4.1 Locations of Nikkei Populations in Brazil

Japanese Brazilian Demographic Information

Table 4.1 Japanese Emigration to Brazil by Prefecture of Origin in Japan, 1906–1993

	1906–'10	'11–'15	'16–'20	'21–'25	'26–'30	'31–'35	'36–'41	Total
	1,714	13,371	13,576	11,350	59,564	72,661	16,750	**188,986**

	1952–'55	'56–'60	'61–'65	'66–'70	'71–'75	'76–'80	'81–'85	'86–'90	'91–'93	Total*
Okinawa	5	3,985	1,405	444	146	135	47	11	-	6,178
Kumamoto	970	2,151	497	98	16	24	5	10	-	3,771
Tōkyō	247	1,477	777	336	445	183	70	45	10	3,590
Fukuoka	587	2,224	584	51	44	46	11	3	-	3,550
Hokkaidō	413	1,719	825	117	76	43	28	6	1	3,228
Nagasaki	279	1,931	577	48	33	23	3	4	-	2,898
Fukushima	648	1,508	120	25	11	14	11	3	1	2,341
Yamaguchi	504	1,109	220	60	28	7	5	1	-	1,934
Kagoshima	80	1,221	215	57	31	4	8	-	-	1,616
Wakayama	707	800	65	22	2	12	4	3	-	1,615
Miyazaki	260	898	153	107	14	11	11	10	-	1,464
Kanagawa	90	438	282	213	208	167	29	8	9	1,444
Kōchi	189	981	133	31	5	12	-	1	1	1,353
Hiroshima	208	696	245	90	57	32	2	8	4	1,342
Ehime	144	954	107	21	10	12	10	2	-	1,260
Gunma	307	625	76	35	43	18	4	2	-	1,110
Saga	43	672	246	15	7	10	7	-	-	1,000
Total*	**7,715**	**29,727**	**9,488**	**2,753**	**1,992**	**1,352**	**411**	**171**	**48**	**53,657**

Sources: Figures for 1899–1941 were taken from Gaimushō Ryōji Ijūbu. *Waga kokumin no kaigai hatten: ijū hyakunen no ayumi (shirō hen)* (Tōkyō, 1971), 140. Figures for 1952–1993 were taken from Japan International Cooperation Agency, *Kaigai ijū tōkei (FY 1952–FY 1993)* (Tōkyō, 1994), 28–29.

Note: *Total includes other prefectures.

Table 4.2 Total Population of Japanese Brazilians, 1923–2006 (Projected)

Year	Total
1923	39,249
1932	133,358
1940	205,850
1958	430,151
1976	800,000
1986	1,075,133
1996	1,444,889
2006	1,941,810

Source: Figures for 1923, 1932, 1940, and 1958 are taken from John Mizuki, *The Growth of Japanese Churches in Brazil* (Pasadena: William Carey Library, 1978), 10, 142.

Notes:
1. Regarding the Brazilian population, there are great discrepancies among various population statistics. The Japanese Ministry of Foreign Affairs presents the following figures: 705,489 (1973), 807,372 (1980), 642,200 (1986), and 620,370 (1993) (*Kaigai zairyū hōjinsū chōsa tōkei*, Tōkyō: Ministry of Foreign Affairs, 1974, 1981, 1987, 1994). San Pauro Jinmon Kagaku Kenkyūjo (Japanese-Brazilian Social Science Study Center in São Paulo) conducted its own survey in 1988 and recorded 1,228,000. See *Burajiru Nihon imin hachijūnen-shi* (São Paulo: Imin Hachijūnen Saiten Iinkai, 1996), 259. These discrepancies are most likely the result of their different methodologies. The decrease in numbers by the Ministry of Foreign Affairs is probably due to the dekasegi phenomenon, in which an estimated 250,000 left Brazil to work in Japan. For further details, please contact each organization.
2. Figures for 1976, 1986, 1996, and 2006 are estimated based on the population of mid-1970s with 3 percent annual growth rate of the Japanese Brazilian population. The projected figures above by Mizuki do not reflect the emigration of the Brazilian Japanese to Japan as temporary workers (*dekasegi*). The decrease in numbers of the Ministry of Foreign Affairs shows this emigration trend in the past decade. According to Mizuki, the number of emigrants is estimated at 250,000.

Table 4.3 Male/Female Ratio of Japanese Immigrants in Brazil on Arrival, 1908–1962

Period	Males per 100 Females
1908–12	152.4
1913–17	139
1918–22	141.3
1923–27	122.2
1928–32	120.2
1933–37	120.2
1938–41	108.5
1952–58	153.3
1958–62	141.8

Source: Suzuki, Teiichi, *The Japanese Immigrant in Brazil: Narrative Part* (Tokyo: University of Tokyo Press, 1969), 184.

Table 4.4 Regional Distribution of Japanese Brazilians, 1923–1974

Year	São Paulo	Paraná	Minas Gerais	Mato Grosso	Rio de Janeiro
1923	34,707	2,126	1,012	1,143	261
1932	120,285	3,967	1,997	2,337	389
1940	193,364	4,300	1,922	3,710	1,191
1958	325,899	77,846	2,885	8,926	5,805
1974	535,356	133,368	4,799	13,855	5,356

Source: Figures for 1923, 1932, 1940, 1958, and 1974 are taken from John Mizuki, *The Growth of Japanese Churches in Brazil* (Pasadena: William Carey Library, 1978), 10.

Table 4.5 Education of Japanese Immigrants and Their Descendants by Percentage, Ages Fifteen Years and Older in 1958

Immigrants	Primary	Secondary and Above
15–19 Years	65.40	34.1
20–24	50	47.3
25–29	72.3	20.5
30–34	81.4	11.2
35–44	83.1	14.2
45–54	75.1	23.4
55 and Over	82.6	13.2

Descendants	Primary	Secondary and Above
15–19 years	60.9	37.8
20–24	68.5	29.2
25–29	75.8	20.9
30–34	78.7	16.9
35–44	78.7	12.2
45 and over	69.6	14.2

Source: Suzuki, 47.

Table 4.6 Nisei Enrolled in Higher Education in the City of São Paulo by Percentage, 1967

Medicine, Dentistry, Veterinarian, Pharmacy, and Public Health	13.9
Engineering, Architecture, and City Planning	13.1
Law	3.5
Economic and Business Administration	17.7
Philosophy, Letters, Social Service, Journalism, and Arts	8.7
Total	**10.1**

Source: Mizuki, 15.
Note: Concerning the interpretation of the above statistics, Mizuki comments: "Considering that in the State of São Paulo, the percentage of the Japanese is only 3 percent of the total population, we may say that they are comparatively speaking highly educated" (Mizuki, 15).

Table 4.7 Occupational Areas of Japanese Brazilians by Percentage

Year	Agriculture	Industry	Commerce
1932	93.60	2.20	4.20
1958	57.30	7.80	34.90
1967	50.00	12.00	38.00

Source: Mizuki, 14.

Table 4.8 Religion of Japanese Brazilians by Percentage, Ages Seven Years and Older in 1958

	Issei	Nisei	Sansei/Yonsei
Buddhist	70.60	29.20	19.00
Catholic	15.50	58.70	70.00
Other	13.90	12.10	11.10
Total	**100**	**100**	**100**
Number	**136,694**	**184,510**	**29,383**

Source: Mizuki, 17.

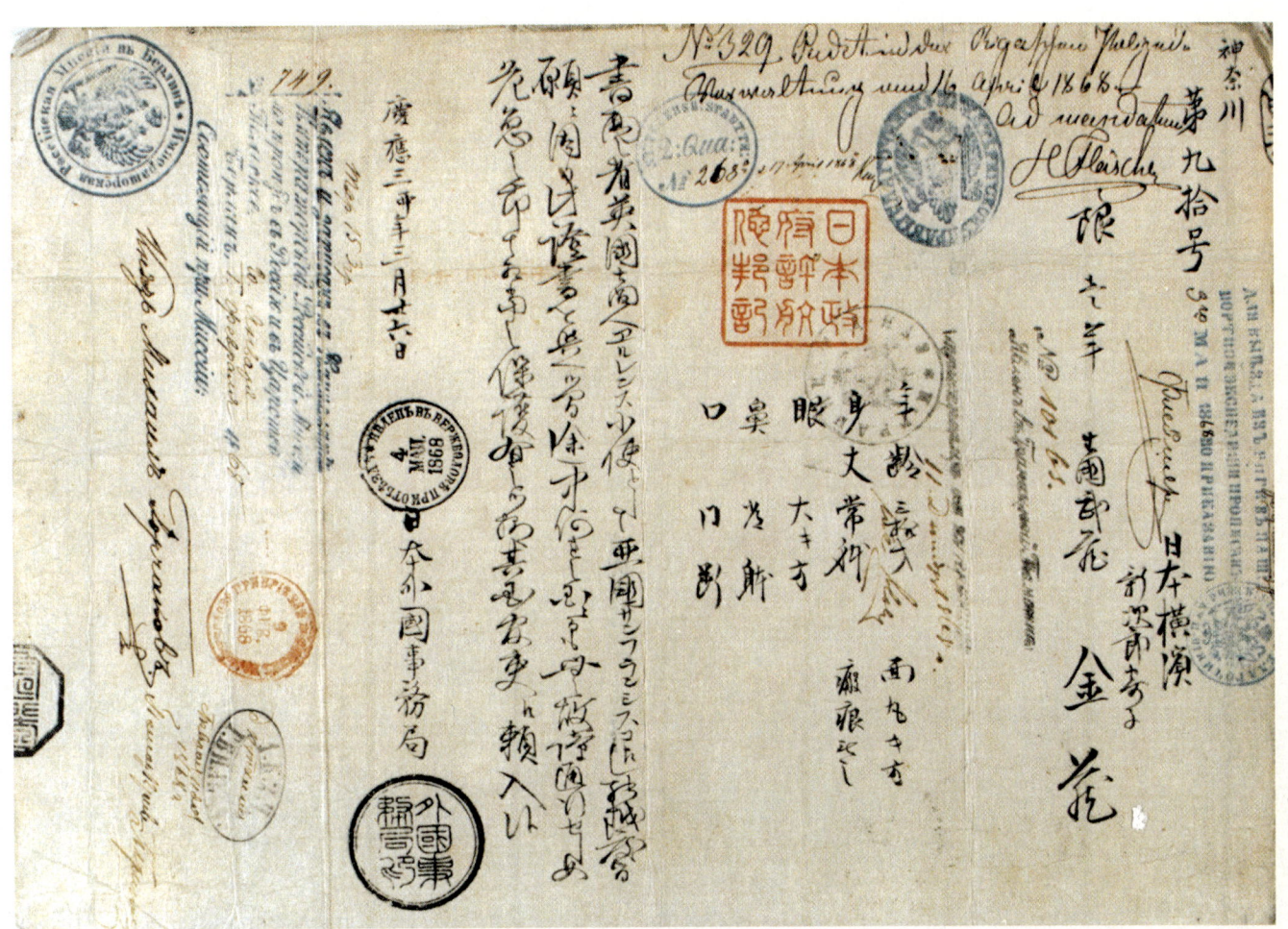

Passport issued to a Japanese citizen traveling to San Francisco and accompanying a British merchant, Ernst, Yokohama, Japan, March 1868. (Collection of Ministry of Foreign Affairs Diplomatic Record Office)

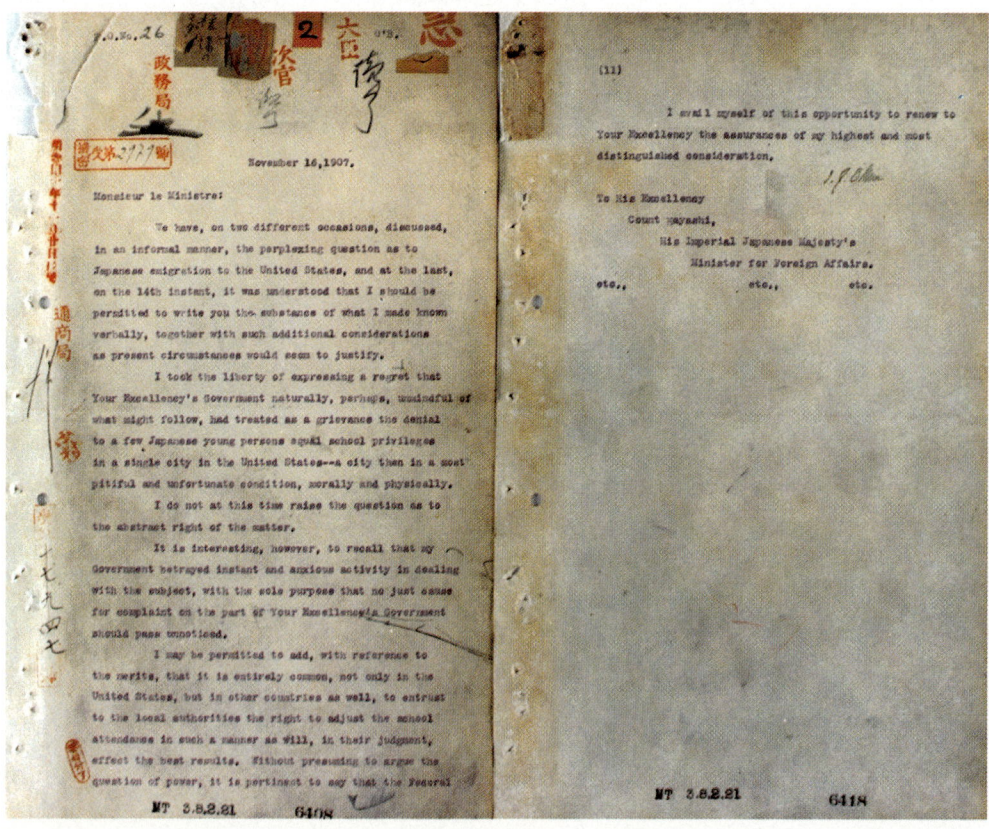

The original Immigration Convention of 1886 between Japan and Hawaiian Kingdom, which provided some protection to Japanese immigrants and even granted them the right to vote. The Bayonet Constitution of 1887 abrogated key provisions. (Collection of Ministry of Foreign Affairs Diplomatic Documents Office)

A letter sent by Thomas J. O'Brien (U.S. State Department official) to the Japanese foreign minister, Count Tadasu Hayashi, on November 16, 1907. This is a part of the exchanges between the U.S. and Japanese governments that resulted in Gentlemen's Agreement of 1908. From the text: "[I]t was claimed that the incoming Japanese work people had wage disturbing characteristics very demoralizing to existing labor standards." (Collection of Ministry of Foreign Affairs Diplomatic Documents Office)

"Going to America," by Issei artist Henry Sugimoto, who was born in Wakayama, Japan, in 1900. Sugimoto came to the United States at the age of nineteen to join his parents in Hanford, California. He was a versatile and prolific artist whose works were widely exhibited in both the U.S. and Europe. (Gift of Madeleine Sugimoto and Naomi Tagawa, Japanese American National Museum)

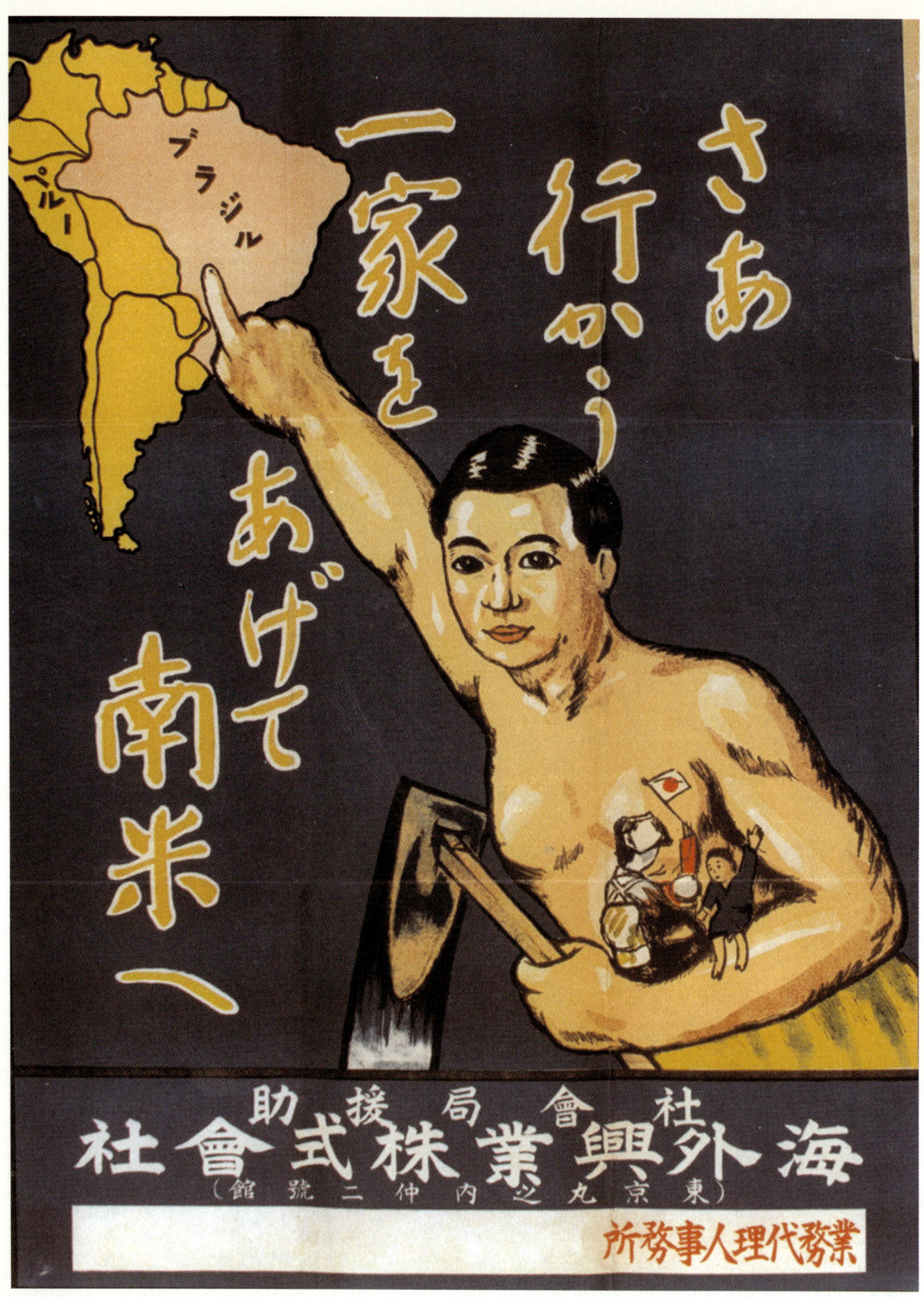

A recruitment poster promoting Japanese emigration to South America, ca. 1925. Recruitment was conducted by the Overseas Development Company (Kaigai Kogyo Kabushiki Kaisha), established in 1917 to cope with the severe restrictions imposed on Japanese immigration to the United States. (Collection of Ministry of Foreign Affairs Diplomatic Record Office)

A Japanese flag signed by students, staff, and officials "wishing health and happiness" to emigrants departing for Bolivia in 1958. (Collection of Federación Nacional de Asociaciones Boliviano Japonesas)

Takeaki Hidaka (foreground) operating a rice-planting machine in his rice paddy, located in the Jarabacoa settlement of La Vega, Dominican Republic, ca. 1970s. (Collection of Japan International Cooperation Agency)

Hidetoshi Takeda (twenty-seven years old) teaching in a Japanese-language school in Monte Alegre, in the Amazon region of Brazil, 1988. He participated in the third Youth for Development Abroad Program (Kaihatsu Seinen), administered by Japan International Cooperation Agency. (Collection of Japan International Cooperation Agency)

Shin Issei Satomi Takeda (far left) enjoying a chat with a Japanese student (second from left), Eddie Kurushima (a Nisei veteran), and Naoko Nawamura during the Nisei Week Festival in Los Angeles, August 16, 1998. (Japanese American National Museum)

Brazilian dekasegi taking part in Carnival festivities in Kobe, Japan, 1997. (Photograph by Internal Press. Collection of Museu Histórico da Imigração Japonesa no Brasil)

A celebration parade held along the central avenues of Buenos Aires on August 1998, commemorating the hundredth anniversary of the Friendship, Commercial and Navigation Treaty between Argentina and Japan, signed in 1898. (Collection of Asociación Universitaria Nikkei)

The Japanese garden, located in one of the most valued areas of the city, the Palermo zone of the federal capital, is the pride of the Japanese residents. Conferences and events related to the diffusion of Japanese culture are held in the Cultural Pavilion. (Collection of Asociación Universitaria Nikkei)

San Juan de Yapacaní kindergarten class, 1973. (Collection of Federación Nacional de Asociaciones Boliviano-Japonesas)

Princess Michiko of Japan comforts an old Japanese immigrant woman on her second visit to Brazil in 1978. (Collection of Museu Histórico da Imigração Japonesa no Brasil)

Oil painting by Tomoo Handa of Japanese immigrants working on the coffee plantation, 1958. (Collection of Museu Histórico da Imigração Japonesa no Brasil)

Tribuna newspaper of Santos City, São Paulo, reporting about the move of the Japanese from the coastal region, July 10, 1943. (Collection of Museu Histórico da Imigração Japonesa no Brasil)

Two men chatting in Liberdade Square in downtown São Paulo, 1988. (Photographer, Edson Komiya. Collection of Museu Histórico da Imigração Japonesa no Brasil)

Japanese Brazilian worker in Japan, 1997. (Photograph by International Press. Collection of Museu Histórico da Imigração Japonesa no Brasil)

Sumiko Kawashima, Issei woman who contributed twenty-five years of her life (1971–1996) to the diffusion of Japanese culture in the community, Santiago, Chile. Deceased in 1996. (Collection of Sociedad Japonesa de Beneficencia)

Family photo of Sansei Kimio Naito and his wife María Galleguillos, her mother Berta Guajardo, and their children Hasuko, Kimiko, and Takeshi in Antofagasta, 1999. (Collection of Sociedad Japonesa de Beneficencia)

Nikkei delegates from throughout the Americas gather at the closing dinner of the Pan-American Nikkei Association's Tenth Conference held in Santiago, Chile, Saturday, July 31, 1999; (seated) James Hirabayashi (far right), Akemi Kikumura-Yano (second from right); (standing) Emilio Higa (second right). (Photograph by Marilyn Alquizola)

María Isabel Vergara Kimura is among other Nikkei Chilean dekasegi working in Nagoya, Seki, and other areas, who actively participates in the diffusion of Chilean artisan culture in Japan. Photo taken in Seki in 1994. (Collection of Sociedad Japonesa de Beneficencia)

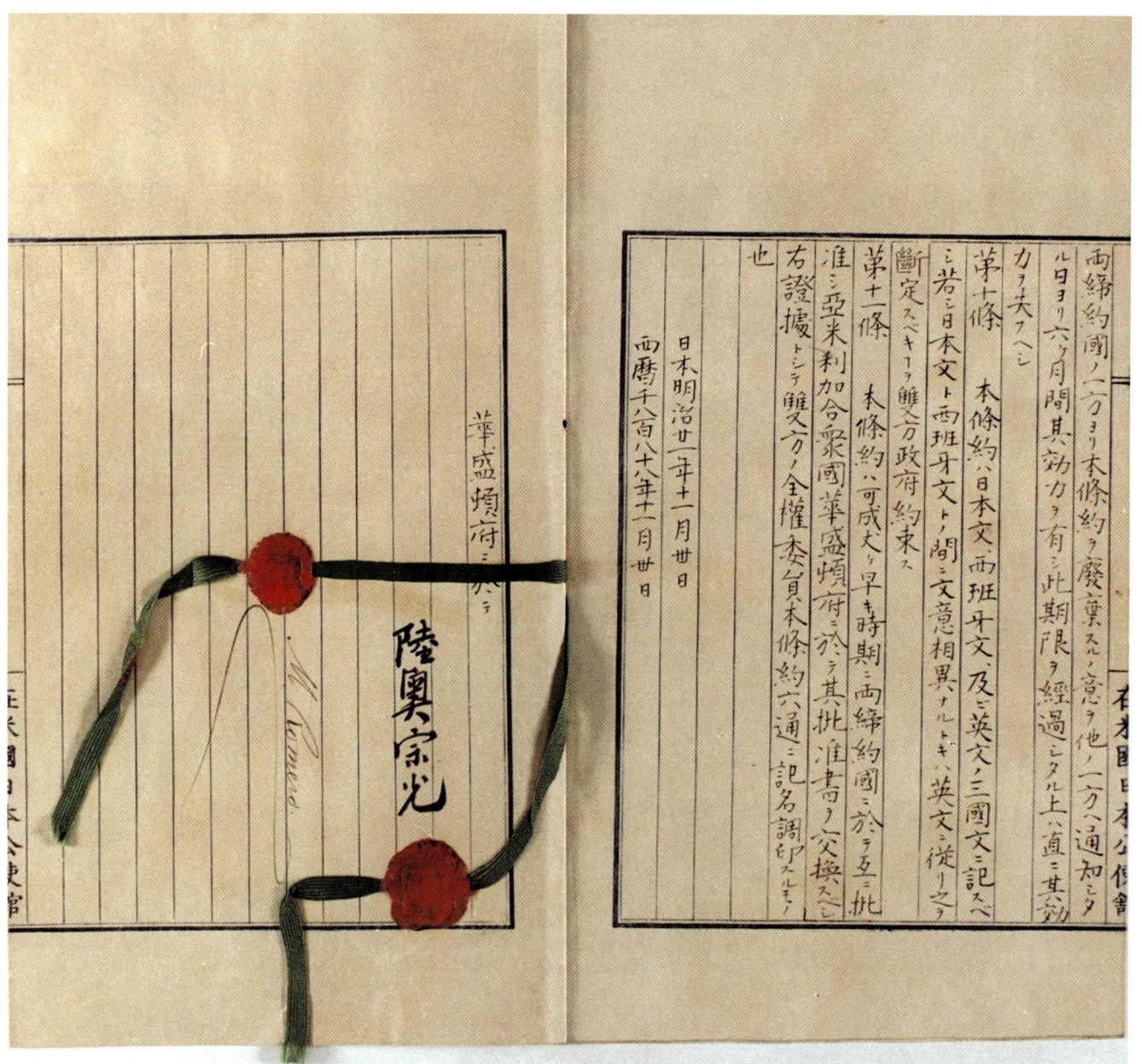

The Treaty of Amity and Commerce between Japan and Mexico, signed on November 30, 1888, between Japanese Ambassador to the United States, Munemitsu Mutsu, and Mexican ambassador to the United States, Matias Romero. This treaty was unusual in that it did not impose unequal conditions on Japan. (Collection of Ministry of Foreign Affairs Diplomatic Record Office)

Partial view of the Japanese Mexican Association (Asociación México Japonesa, A.C.) building in Mexico City. (Collection of Asociación México Japonesa, A.C.)

President Luis Echeverria (third from right) and his family at the home of Carlos Kasuga, head of the Society of the Japanese Mexican New Leaders (Nichiboku Seinenkai), and his friends, 1971. (Collection of Asociación México Japonesa, A.C.)

Reception hosted by students at the Universidad La Salle attended by Prince Haruhito (center), June 30, 1993. (Collection of Asociación México Japonesa, A.C.)

Two brothers on a pig farm in Paraguay, ca. 1961. (Collection of Centro Nikkei Paraguayo)

The first State visit to Japan of Alfredo Stroessner, president of Paraguay, greeted upon his arrival by Emperor Hirohito, April 1972. (Photograph by Kajima Projections Ltd., Japan. Collection of Emi Kasamatsu [Mrs. Desiderio Enciso, former ambassador to Japan])

The imperial highnesses of Japan signing official document commemorating the fiftieth anniversary of Japanese immigration to Paraguay, September 1986. (Collection of Emi Kasamatsu)

The inauguration of Centro Nikkei Paraguayo in February 1996, with the president of Paraguay, Juan Carlos Wasmosy (third from left), the ambassador of Japan (second from left), Emi Kasamatsu (fourth from left), and members of the Comisión Directiva of the Centro Nikkei Paraguayo. (Photograph by Japan Color. Collection of Centro Nikkei Paraguayo)

On August 10, 1988, President Ronald Reagan signs the redress law, H.R. 442 (Gift of Norman Y. Mineta, Japanese American National Museum [96.370.16A])

A joyous birthday celebration for Ryan Hanami (six years old, seated on floor, center left) with a taiko drum demonstration held at the Japanese American National Museum, November 23, 2000. (Photograph by Clement Hanami)

Asian American performance artist Nobuko Miyamoto Betserai (center) with her husband Tarabu Betserai (left), son Kamau Ayubbi, and granddaughter Asiyah Ayubbi. Los Angeles, California, November 29, 1998. (Gift of Nobuko Miyamoto. Japanese American National Museum [98.363.2])

CHAPTER 5

Japanese Canadians

**DEVELOPED IN COLLABORATION WITH
THE JAPANESE CANADIAN NATIONAL MUSEUM**

MOST NIKKEI IMMIGRATED TO CANADA BETWEEN THE 1890S AND THE 1920S, although the first Japanese in Canada was recorded in 1877. Early immigrants worked in the lumber and mining industries, and in the fisheries and agriculture in British Columbia. Japanese immigration peaked between 1905 and 1907, a trend that exacerbated anti-Japanese racism. The demand for Japanese exclusion led to the Hayashi-Lemieux "Gentlemen's Agreement" of 1908, which reduced the yearly admission of Japanese laborers to four hundred. Subsequent years saw the influx of "picture brides," since the immediate family members of Nikkei residents were still allowed to immigrate into Canada. However, by 1928 Japanese immigration was limited to 150 per annum. The emergence of families stabilized the community, but the Pacific War destroyed its foundation. The confiscation of properties and the internment of Nikkei in inland concentration camps soon followed. Under the War Measures Act, the internees, most of whom were Canadian citizens, were forced either to move permanently to the east or renounce their citizenship and leave for Japan after the war. Until 1949, Japanese Canadians were not able to return to British Columbia or fully regain their civil rights. The postwar years thereafter, however, saw the rapid integration of Japanese Canadians into the mainstream society. Most who lived in Toronto and Vancouver were highly educated, and had married non-Japanese spouses. The redress movement for the wartime internment and its eventual success in 1988 offered a common cause around which the Canadian Nikkei could unite. Today, the Nikkei community has witnessed an unprecedented creation of community infrastructure and networks, despite its internal diversity.

A Brief History of Japanese Canadians

AUDREY KOBAYASHI AND MIDGE AYUKAWA

THE EARLY YEARS

Nikkei history in Canada began when Japanese immigrants established a niche within the system of primary industries that supported the British Columbia economy during the late nineteenth century. Japan had maintained limited contact with Canada during the Tokugawa Period, when foreign travel was strictly forbidden, although numerous Japanese sailors and fishermen are known to have been shipwrecked along what was to be the British Columbia coast during the first half of the nineteenth century. Although international emigration was not officially allowed until after 1885, the first immigrants (Issei) to Canada arrived unofficially during the 1870s, soon after the establishment of the Meiji government. The first immigrant of record was Manzo Nagano, who jumped ship in New Westminster in 1877 and later ran a general store in Victoria. The anniversary of his arrival was celebrated as the Japanese-Canadian centenary in 1977; however, he was probably one of many who arrived on fishing boats, as stowaways, or across the border from the United States.

The early Issei left a country undergoing massive economic, social, and political change. The Meiji Restoration had created a modern state with a rapidly growing economy, a strong military, and a literate society with raised material expectations and strong motivations. The foundation of the new society was agriculture, constructed ideologically as an exalted profession whose honorable social customs, based on former samurai ideals, defined the norms of Meiji society. The honor afforded to farmers, however, did not stop the government from taxing them at a debilitating rate in order to finance development of the new state. The costs of modernization were thrust upon the peasants, who made up approximately 80 percent of the population. The lofty claims of the Meiji government encouraged the values of a liberal economy but hid the reality of poverty resulting from the vagaries of economic development, deflationary fiscal policies, and uneven crop yields, combined with increased population growth. As it became clear throughout the 1880s that the rewards promised by the new era would not be easily achieved, ambitious households, anxious to continue the lines of their ancestors, did what they could to secure a viable farming interest, including sending available members—women and men—to work under contract in industrial jobs in urban areas. This practice became known as *dekasegi*, meaning to "go out to work."

EMIGRATION AS DEKASEGI

Emigration to Canada was an extension of this transformation from an agrarian to an industrial labor force, a new form of dekasegi. In 1885, the government allowed emigration to Hawai`i for three-year work terms. As the influx of money became noticeable in the villages, emigration increased, now to *"Amerika,"* which comprised the United States and Canada. While emigration often made possible a return to the village under enhanced circumstances for those who owned or inherited land, the

The first Japanese male to take up permanent residence in Canada was Manzo Nagano (center), shown here with his family, Victoria, B.C., 1910. (Collection of Japanese Canadian National Museum [94/85.001a-b])

Stumps, such as those shown here, had to be removed to clear land for farming, location unknown, ca. 1910. (Collection of Japanese Canadian National Museum [94/85.017a-c])

The "Sun Bun" Tamura building is located at Powell and Dunlevy Streets, in the neighborhood of what was the major settlement area for prewar Japanese Canadians, Vancouver, B.C., ca. 1935. (Collection of Japanese Canadian National Museum [95/102.1.001a-b])

vaunted agrarian life could not provide for everyone. Second and third sons and others who did not stand to inherit property usually moved permanently. Conditions in *Amerika* were better than in one of the growing Japanese cities, where wages were low and employment unreliable.

The major employment for the Issei in Canada was in the sawmills. In about 1883, there is a record of a Takizo (surname unknown) who is believed to have been the first Issei to work at the Hastings Mill in Vancouver. He died in 1889, the first recorded Issei death. By then, the Issei crew at Hastings Mill numbered two hundred; it was headed by Yasukichi Yoshizawa, later to be known as "Indian Yasu," because he bought and sold salmon from the aboriginal people on the Skeena River. Over the next two decades, Issei grew to become the largest ethnic group in British Columbia's sawmills.

The second-largest source of employment was the fishing industry. In 1887, Gihei Kuno, from the impoverished village of Mio in Wakayama, visited the West Coast. Seeing the potential for salmon fishing, he arranged for others from the village to come to Canada, and the village of Steveston, at the mouth of the Fraser River, became their new home. Although conditions were often difficult and they were constantly opposed by the white unions, the Nikkei working in fishing and canning industries spread out along the coast of British Columbia and thrived until their uprooting during World War II.

Japanese labor migration to Canada was well organized, and it consisted almost exclusively of men. The Issei entrepreneurs, known as *bosu* (bosses), traveled to Japan or worked through agents to recruit contract labor. Each contractor recruited mainly in a specific area of Japan, with the result that workers from the same districts, or even the same villages, were regrouped in the Canadian workplace. In 1891, a group of one hundred contract workers from Hiroshima came to work the mines at Cumberland on Vancouver Island. Seventy-three experienced miners from Fukuoka shortly followed them. The two groups lost several members to starvation and ill treatment before the Japanese government intervened to repatriate those who wished to return to Japan.

The early workers in Vancouver had lived in temporary quarters in scows in the harbor. By the late 1890s, Japanese labor contractors had also begun to buy or lease land along Powell and adjacent streets. They built and ran boarding houses for their workers, diversifying their interests to retail and other services, including bathhouses, barbershops, and grocery stores. They provided translation, banking, and travel services for their workers and their friends and relatives. Their activities soon expanded throughout the entire province, where they obtained contracts in logging, milling, mining, railway, and agricultural ventures in remote areas. Without this system of sponsorship, modeled strongly on the Japanese system of patronage, many Japanese would not have survived. At the same time, the *bosu* negotiated with the white-run companies, offering lower wages within a racially split labor market. They also benefited from a percentage of the profits on supplies delivered to the camps.

Although Victoria was usually the port of entry, most emigrants traveled straight on to Vancouver, where they were met at the dock by an employer/sponsor, most often a *ken-jin* (person from the same prefecture), and were taken immediately to a house that boarded others from

Japanese Canadians 151

Cars arriving at the Hiroshima kenjin-kai *(prefectural)* picnic, Vancouver, B.C., ca. 1920s. (Photograph by Shokichi Akatsuka. Collection of Japanese Canadian National Museum [92/20.008a-c])

the same area. In this way, even relationships that had already been established in Japan became stronger, and the *kenjin-kai* (prefectural association) became one of the most important building blocks of at least the first generation of Nikkei. Immigrants might return to the same boarding house many times in search of new work contracts or simply companionship.

ENCOUNTERING RESISTANCE

Immigration increased after the turn of the century. In Japan, the end of the Russo-Japanese War in 1905 had created unemployment, exacerbated by devastating crop failures in 1906. Although the extant records are contradictory, it is estimated that until 1905 some fifteen thousand men and a handful of women had worked in British Columbia for varying periods of time, often as short as one season. To maximize their earnings, they moved back and forth between Canada and the United States; others entered via the Hawaiian sugar plantations. Between 1905 and 1907, the number was augmented by more than four thousand, most of whom worked for short periods of time. In 1906, the United States, under political pressure, followed amendments to immigration policy with a "Gentlemen's Agreement" that served virtually to halt Japanese immigration. In 1907–1908, nearly eight thousand Japanese set out for Canada, where the boom of sawmill building was beginning to subside. The majority of these immigrants came from Shiga Prefecture, where the late-summer typhoon season had wrought particularly heavy crop damage the year before. Shiga Prefecture subsequently became the largest source of emigrants to Canada.

These laborers were deeply resented by other Canadians. From the turn of the century, various official and unofficial measures were aimed at limiting both the numbers and the civil rights of Nikkei and others of Asian background. Virulent racism, historically fundamental to Canadian society, climaxed on September 7, 1907. Bolstered by public clamor and "yellow journalism" that sought to deny the rights and the existence of Asians in

Broken windows of storefront where Chinese and Japanese immigrant quarters are attacked by a mob of white supremacists, Vancouver, B.C., September 13, 1907. (Collection of Japanese Canadian National Museum [94/85.012])

Canada, a mob of five thousand attacked the Chinese immigrant area of Vancouver and surged on to Powell Street, causing extensive property damage.

After the riot, Asian workers staged a general strike amid continued racist manifestations from the white public. A royal commission undertaken by W. L. Mackenzie King (later prime minister of Canada) recommended compensation for physical damages but maintained that the "problem" could be solved only by limiting the number of Asian faces on Canada's streets. The result was the Hayashi-Lemieux "Gentlemen's Agreement" of 1908, which limited further labor immigration to four hundred annually, except for returning immigrants and their immediate families, commercial and official travelers, clerics, and students.

ISSEI WOMEN AND THE START OF FAMILIES

Few Issei women entered Canada before 1907, and those who did played very specific economic roles. Those less fortunate were imported by unscrupulous operators who used them as prostitutes. Life was more honored, if just as difficult, for wives and relatives of entrepreneurs. They were required to support the family enterprise by running the boarding houses, stores, and camps, cooking and cleaning for large gangs of men. Many worked in remote camps where the luxury of female companionship found on Powell Street was not available. The first Issei woman was Yo Shishido, who arrived in 1887 and, together with her husband, Washiji Oya, ran a business on Powell Street for many years. In 1889 their son, Katsuji, became the first Nisei (second generation) born in Canada.

Before 1908, many of the men had moved back and forth between Canada and Japan, often on a seasonal basis. The new restrictions, combined with economic circumstances, made such movement difficult, and many, especially those without prospects of land ownership in Japan, made the decision to remain permanently in Canada. Thus began the "picture bride" system, a variation on the tradition of arranged marriage whereby prospective partners were introduced by an exchange of

Japanese prospective brides on board a ship, ca. 1905. (Collection of Japanese Canadian National Museum [97/200a-b])

photographs. The marriage would take place in Japan in the absence of the groom, thus allowing a legal wife to enter the country after a requisite period of six months. From 1908 to the mid-1920s, some five thousand young women entered Canada in this way.

The life of an Issei woman was always difficult. While adapting to marriage with a man she had possibly never previously met, she was expected to work either in a family enterprise or in waged labor. She had few choices. Domestic work in homes of wealthy white families or line work in canneries generally constituted the jobs to which nonwhite women had access. A few who joined husbands who had managed to save enough to purchase or lease farms were considered fortunate.

As the number of families grew, so did the need for schools. The largest group of early students consisted of teenaged boys, brought to Canada by fathers or older relatives; they worked during the day as apprentices or shop assistants and took English classes at night, initially from Methodist or Anglican missionaries. Concerned about

Opening celebration of Port Hammond Japanese School, Port Hammond, Canada, October 19, 1917. (Collection of Japanese Canadian National Museum [94/77.002a-b])

maintaining a connection with the Nisei children, the Japanese Ministry of Education provided teachers for the first Japanese-language school established in Vancouver in 1906. Although many Nisei children later attended nearby Strathcona Public School, ostracism on the part of the white population encouraged the view within the Japanese immigrant community that fluency in Japanese was necessary for Nikkei children. Some chose to send their children, especially firstborn sons, to Japan for all or part of their education, but most sent their children after public school and on weekends to the Japanese-language schools, which numbered over fifty by the 1940s.

COMMUNITY BUILDING

World War I hastened the community-building process. Smaller communities became established throughout the province, especially along the West Coast. Somewhat higher wages and demand for labor during and immediately following the war allowed many to become established in business, pay off fishing boats, or purchase agricultural land in the Fraser and Okanagan Valleys or on Vancouver Island. In particular, the Nikkei were instrumental in creating the successful berry farms of the Fraser Valley.

Some 196 Japanese Canadians fought in the Canadian contingent of the British armed forces during World War I. Fifty-four were killed and ninety were wounded. This loss of life testified to the fact that many Nikkei were by then Canadian in every sense. Yet it was not enough, for other British Columbians continued to speak of the "Yellow Peril" and to deny fundamental human rights, such as the right to vote or purchase Crown lands, hold public office or professional licenses, or be employed in the public service. Less official means of discrimination occurred in restaurants, theaters, and schools. When Chitose Uchida became the first Nikkei to graduate from the University of British Columbia in 1916, she was also among the first of many who would find that their diplomas did not assure them appropriate jobs.

During the 1920s, public resentment became more and

Graduating eighth-grade class at Strathcona School, a public school attended by many Nisei children, Vancouver, B.C., 1931. (Collection of Japanese Canadian National Museum [96/182.1.006])

Japanese Canadians

Japanese Women's Association Ocean Falls, B.C., July 1, 1937. (Collection of Japanese Canadian National Museum [94/65.3.002a-c])

more open. In 1923 and 1928 the government, yielding to public pressure, reactivated and amended the Hayashi-Lemieux agreement with a new annual limit of 150, of whom no more than half could be female. The Japanese Canadian population declined from that time, as many of the original Issei returned to Japan. Some had never intended to stay in Canada; others gave up hope in the face of a tide of racism.

The 1920s also saw increasing differentiation within the Nikkei community, particularly in Vancouver. Nikkei workers, denied membership in the mainstream unions, formed the Japanese Camp and Millworkers Union in 1920, following a particularly bitter labor dispute at a coastal pulp and paper plant. Differences surfaced between the elite *bosu*, aligned with the merchants, and the laborers. The laborers themselves were not in full agreement on the need for a union. Although many resented the injustice of having to accept lower wages and often being forced to act as strike breakers against mainstream unions, they were torn by *on*, or allegiance to their patrons, and by the *ken* ties. These tensions and differences were well aired in the several Japanese-language newspapers that had been established on Powell Street, representing the full political spectrum within the Nikkei community.

During the 1930s, the community became more firmly established, despite economic decline. Although many of the original immigrants returned to Japan during this time, natural increase outpaced return emigration. There were twenty-three thousand people in 1941, of whom twenty-two thousand resided in the province of British Columbia. Fully 17,400, or 80 percent, were Canadian citizens; the balance were immigrants of Japanese citizenship. Over 50 percent of the population was under the age of thirty. There were 8,300 people in the workforce, half in the areas of lumber production, fishing, and agriculture. This was an established community, the members of which were strongly committed to Canada, their home.

Parade at Vancouver Silver Jubilee at the corner of Powell and Templeton Streets, Vancouver, B.C., ca. 1936. (Collection of Japanese Canadian National Museum [94/71.003a-b])

UPROOTING AND DISPOSSESSION

Canada declared war against Japan on December 7, 1941, immediately after the bombing of Pearl Harbor by the Japanese. Few Japanese Canadians held any political allegiance to Japan, but they were anguished by the outbreak of hostilities between the two countries. Many feared that simmering resentment would break out into hostility and violence against them in Canada. The events of 1941 showed the depth of Canadian racism and the precarious nature of the Nikkei existence.

Years of pressure by politicians, journalists, and civic groups had preceded the war. British Columbia politicians—notably Vancouver alderman Halford Wilson, Premier T. D. Pattulo, member of Parliament A. W. Neill, and cabinet minister and member of Parliament Ian Mackenzie—had mounted a campaign to keep Asian Canadians from serving in the armed forces. Their goal was achieved in 1940, when a cabinet committee recommended against their eligibility, claiming that violence against them would occur if they were admitted. F. J. Mead, assistant commissioner of the Royal Canadian Mounted Police, charged that the politicians had been responsible for provoking fear and suspicion where none need have existed, an opinion that was to be upheld in the coming years.

Within hours of the Pearl Harbor attack, male Japanese nationals suffered a suspension of all civil rights. They were quickly detained, and most later sent to prisoner-of-war camps in northern Ontario. All Canadian property of persons residing in Japan (regardless of citizenship) was confiscated. Next, the government turned its attention to Canadian citizens. Some 1,137 fishing boats owned by Japanese Canadians were impounded, suffering incalculable and irreparable damage through subsequent neglect. With cold deliberation the government put into place a plan for the uprooting and dispossession of the Nikkei community, under the auspices of the British Columbia Securities Commission, supported by the powerful War Measures Act.

A children's dining room in the temporary detention center at Hastings Park, Vancouver, B.C., during World War II, spring 1942. (Collection of Japanese Canadian National Museum [94/81.002])

Makeshift tents of an internment camp inhabited by uprooted Japanese Canadians, Slocan, B.C., fall 1942. (Collection of Japanese Canadian National Museum [94/63.001a-b])

In February 1942, it was announced that all persons "of Japanese ancestry" must leave the "protected area" of coastal British Columbia, where more than twenty-one thousand resided. Motor vehicles, cameras, radios, and firearms were confiscated by officers who swooped through Japanese Canadian homes. A dusk-to-dawn curfew was imposed, and movement was restricted. Hastings Park, an agricultural exhibition ground, was designated a "transit center," where Nikkei from all the coastal communities were to be collected. Once behind the barbed wire, men were separated from women and children. The "prisoners" were housed in recently vacated horse stalls, reeking of manure, with rough straw mattresses upon which to sleep. This facility operated until September 1942, over a very hot summer, under crowded, unsanitary conditions and a complete lack of privacy. Psychological conditions were terrible as people faced fear and the separation from friends and loved ones, about whom they often heard nothing. Those who lived in the city of Vancouver were not immediately incarcerated but waited, hearing little, knowing neither their fates nor those of their families, hoping that the nightmare would end. They were surrounded with public hostility. Children were taunted, and young men were assaulted in the streets. Employees were summarily fired. Insurance policies were canceled. Organizations such as the Imperial Order of Daughters of the Empire began to organize hate campaigns for the permanent removal of Japanese.

Beginning in March 1942, trains began to roll, their shades pulled down, carrying thousands of Japanese Canadians to unknown destinations. About seven hundred men were sent to prisoner-of-war camps, the largest being Angler in northern Ontario, and about 2,100 to road camps, where they were used as forced labor for road-building

Mrs. Take Akiyama carrying water at a detention camp, Lemon Creek, B.C., 1943. (Collection of Japanese Canadian National Museum [96/182.1.002a-b])

projects. The largest group, about twelve thousand, which included the families of the men in the camps, was sent to concentration camps in the British Columbia interior. These were either reclaimed ghost towns or hastily erected camps, consisting at first of tents, then of shacks made of green lumber that shrank in the subsequent winter and so provided little protection against the mountain cold. About four thousand were sent in family groups to the prairie provinces, where they worked the sugar beet farms under severe conditions. There were also about 4,200 who maintained some degree of freedom: two thousand were already outside the designated area; 1,200 were wealthy enough to establish self-supporting camps in the interior; about a thousand managed to join family members in Ontario and Quebec; ninety-two, those married to whites and their children, were permitted to stay in the coastal area. Of course, all were subject to curfew and registration and had belongings confiscated; none were allowed free travel.

Thus dispersed, the Nikkei resolved to wait out the war, hoping that the end of hostilities would end their conditions of forced apartheid. But when the war ended, they still were not allowed to return to the coastal area. Those who could find places to relocate east of the Rocky Mountains were told to do so. A strong network developed within the Nikkei community to find places for its members. They were supported by a variety of mainstream religious organizations, including the YMCA. A group of concerned citizens, the Cooperative Committee on Japanese Canadians based in Toronto, lobbied the government, arranged for employment and schools, and gathered food and clothing. Their efforts were hampered, however, by restrictive covenants in many cities, including Toronto, that prohibited residence by Japanese Canadians. Some were smuggled into white homes to work as domestic servants.

Hope diminished as the Securities Commission began selling off Japanese Canadian property and possessions. In early 1945, those still in the camps were told to remove themselves permanently to the East or sign papers renouncing their Canadian citizenship and agreeing to "deportation" to Japan. Lacking knowledge, means of support and employment, and fearing what they would face in the East, about ten thousand signed. They were told that they could rescind their signatures once they had made alternate arrangements; signing was thus a means of buying time. Many hoped that the war would end and that the papers would become moot.

AFTER THE WAR

The war ended in August 1945, but its conclusion made little difference for the conditions of Japanese Canadians. On October 5, 1945, the Canadian Parliament enacted the National Emergency Transitional Powers Act, which continued the original provisions of the War Measures Act. Japanese Canadians were told that they would never be allowed to return to British Columbia; that they would not be given civil rights (to vote, hold public office, or travel freely); that they must accept a pittance for their confiscated property (most of the proceeds having been used for their "support" while incarcerated); and that those remaining in the camps would indeed be exiled to Japan.

Second uprooting of more than four thousand Japanese Canadians who were exiled to Japan after World War II, Slocan, B.C., ca. 1946. (Collection of Japanese Canadian National Museum [94/76.015a-c])

Exiled Japanese Canadians leave by train for Vancouver where they will board ships bound for Japan, Slocan, B.C., 1946. (Collection of Japanese Canadian National Museum [94/85.025a-b])

Until this time no Japanese Canadian had been charged with or convicted of any crime against the wartime interests of the nation. There had been no evidence of fifth-column activity and no overt expression of allegiance to Japan. Convicted of no crime, they were judged on the basis of their "race," so that British Columbia could become a province cleansed of people of Japanese ancestry. Meanwhile the property of Japanese Canadians was dispersed, primarily to returning white veterans and to civil servants.

The removal legislation was later rescinded, but not before more than four thousand people were exiled, of whom more than half were children born in Canada. Those not expelled were sent to other parts of Canada, where they were prevented from resettling in close proximity to one another. After 1946, the Nikkei were gradually granted the rights of citizenship. In 1947, they were permitted to purchase real property; in 1948, they were allowed for the first time to vote federally; in 1949, they were allowed to vote in British Columbia. On March 31, 1949, the last of the restrictions under the War Measures Act was lifted, and they were allowed to travel freely and to return to live in British Columbia, should they have the means to do so. This freedom was indeed a Pyrrhic victory.

JAPANESE CANADIANS TODAY

Since the 1940s, Japanese Canadians have rebuilt their lives and communities. About a quarter of those exiled managed to return to Canada, starting in the 1950s. New immigrants *(Shin Ijuusha)* have come in relatively small numbers and now make up about 25 percent of the current population of approximately seventy-seven thousand. Many of today's Nikkei—third, fourth, fifth and sixth generations, known respectively as Sansei, Yonsei, Gosei, and Rokusei—are the products of intermarriage with members of other ethnocultural groups. Most of the population today is centered in Vancouver and Toronto. In contrast to their Issei forbears, contemporary Nikkei are urban and highly educated.

During the 1950s and 1960s, Japanese Canadians were too busy rebuilding their shattered lives to worry much about redress for their experiences. The Nisei generation, in addition, felt ambivalent about speaking out and perhaps risking their newfound freedom. This situation began to change in 1977, when celebration of the centenary caused a coming-together of the community, and discussions of redress began to reach a wider audience. For the next decade, the National Association of Japanese Canadians worked on behalf of the Nikkei to negotiate a redress settlement, achieved in 1988 after a difficult struggle and tremendous effort that involved the coordination of many Japanese Canadians and supportive religious, labor, and human rights groups. The War Measures Act was revoked in April 1988. The redress settlement, announced in Parliament on September 22, included an acknowledgement of injustice, individual payments of twenty-one thousand dollars to approximately seventeen thousand people, establishment of a community fund of twelve million dollars, a purge of criminal records of those charged under the War Measures Act, restitution of citizenship rights to those exiled to Japan, and the creation of the Canadian Race Relations Foundation, established in 1997.

Over the past decade the community-building process has intensified. Under the aegis of the Japanese Canadian Redress Foundation, set up by the National Association of Japanese Canadians to manage and disperse the community settlement, there has been an unprecedented creation of social infrastructure, from community centers to cultural and artistic groups. Japanese Canadians are more diverse than ever before, separated by geography as well as by differences of class, background, culture, and ideology.

The signing of the redress agreement: (seated) Prime Minister Brian Mulroney and Art Miki; (standing, from left to right) Don Rosenbloom (lawyer), Roger Obata, Hon. Lucien Bouchard (Secretary of State), Audrey Kobayashi, Hon. Gerry Weiner (Minister of Multiculturalism), Maryka Omatsu, and Roy Miki, Otawa, Ontario, September 22, 1988. (Photograph by Gordon King. Collection of the Japanese Canadian National Museum [94/64.5.001a-b])

There are ongoing debates about the future of the community, about intermarriage (which occurs in over 95 percent of new marriages), and about the role of Japanese Canadians in human rights struggles. Communities across Canada are striving to mend and develop the community networks and facilities that were destroyed during the 1940s.

Japanese Canadian Bibliographic Essay

AUDREY KOBAYASHI AND MIDGE AYUKAWA

THE LITERATURE ON JAPANESE CANADIANS, MOST OF which has been produced from within the community itself, is rich in some aspects but extremely varied. There were few works in English for the period prior to World War II, while there is relatively little in Japanese for the postwar period. Historical works include those of amateur as well as academic writers, and there are a few useful histories written from an external perspective. In the past decade in particular, the volume of writing by and about Japanese Canadians has increased strongly, particularly among Sansei writers.

The few books written about the earliest Japanese immigrants to Canada were compiled by Japanese writers who wished to report on the situation for a Japanese readership that included potential new immigrants. The most comprehensive are two books compiled in 1917 and published three years later by Jinshirō Nakayama (J-12, J-13). They list the immigrants and their home villages, and give short biographies on the more prominent ones, including recollections of the experiences of early arrivals. Since some related what they had heard while others relied on their recollection of experiences of decades past, there are many inconsistencies, but given the lack of other sources, Nakayama's works constitute the most valuable and detailed source of information on the early years.

A number of English-language books written by Anglo-Canadians during the pre–World War II period present heavily biased observations of the social, commercial, and laboring activities of the Japanese Canadians and reflect their authors' conviction that the immigrants were unassimilable. One exception is the work by Young and Reid (E-90), which is filled with factual information personally gathered by Rigenda Sumida, a student from Japan who worked with the Canadian Japanese Association on a survey of Nisei in British Columbia. Sumida's study was presented as a master of arts thesis at the University of British Columbia (E-78).

The Nisei voice begins to be heard the late 1930s, when young men and women wrote short articles expressing their frustrations and their dreams in the Nisei biweekly the *New Canadian*. These works are full of passion, idealism, and a strong sense of the Nikkei as Canadian citizens. Notable is the voice of Muriel Kitagawa, whose works would not receive broader recognition until decades later, when her wartime letters to her brother, Wes, were published (E-24).

After a hiatus following the uprooting, through the 1960s and the 1970s, there gradually emerged a body of work written by and about the pioneers—in fishing (Hayashi: J-3), farming (Yamaga: J-30), and education (Satō and Satō: J-21)—who recollected the prewar years and wrote about their experiences and their communities. These works establish the retrospective autobiography as one of the most significant sources of historical and social understanding of the Canadian Nikkei community. Equally important, though more for their social than their literary significance, are the collections of *haiku* and *tanka* poetry (Shikatani and Aylward: E-73; Kisaragi Poem Study Group: E-23) that allow access to the experiences of a wide range of ordinary Issei women and men in the poetic medium with which they feel most comfortable. Writing poetry in groups had been a major social pastime of the Issei, both before and during the internment years. The poetry written in later years, when most were in retirement, has a retrospective tone that contrasts with the spontaneity found in the few surviving (unpublished) examples of prewar poetry.

The 1970s also saw the coming of age of a new generation of Sansei writers influenced by the social movements of the 1960s and by the arousal of community consciousness in the early redress movement. The early Sansei work was characterized by collective endeavors that produced a number of short-lived journals and a few significant anthologies. During the 1970s a Sansei collective in Vancouver worked to produce a photographic exhibition titled *A Dream of Riches* (E-21). This effort played an important part in the subsequent redress movement, as the members went on to play leading roles both as community activists and in the arts. The Powell Street Revue and the Chinese Canadian Writers Workshop produced an anthology of the earliest work of Sansei writers (E-66) who later became the major literary voices of their generation, establishing the tone of social protest that defines the Canadian Sansei genre.

The most informative, comprehensive history in English is Ken Adachi's *The Enemy That Never Was* (E-1), commissioned by the Japanese Canadian Citizens Association. This complete history of the Japanese Canadians addresses reasons for emigration, the history of institutional and social racism, the involvement of the Japanese government in the Canadian immigrants' lives, the prewar communities, and their wartime and postwar experiences. The book is limited by Adachi's inability to use Japanese-language sources, as well as by the unavailability of government records at the time, but his book is still the best source of historical information.

Beginning shortly after the publication of Adachi's book, World War II experiences were extensively recounted by Issei, Nisei, and Anglo-Canadians. The experiences of those interned at the prisoner-of-war camp at Angler are related in a number of books in both English and Japanese. The frustrations of a Nisei mother (Kitagawa: E-24), oral recollections (Broadfoot: E-10), and an academic study of the politics behind the expulsion (Sunahara: E-79) all provide information on that period. After the redress settlement in 1988, Kobayashi and Miki summarized the wartime events in their story of the struggle and final victory (E-36). Nisei writers like Toyo Takata (E-82), Roy Ito (E-17, E-18), and Yon Shimizu (E-74), to name a few, have also added to the sparse collection of Canadian Nikkei history, especially in terms of labor and military history. The work of Audrey Kobayashi (E-29, E-30, E-31) and Midge Ayukawa (E-5, E-7) addresses the equally sparse documentation of the early years of immigration linking Canada and Japan.

Anglo-Canadian academics such as Patricia Roy (E-68) and Peter Ward (E-85) have studied Japanese Canadians from a strictly external perspective. Their works are important not only in order for understanding Nikkei history but also for the ways in which Anglo-Canadian society construed the Nikkei community.

More recently, Japanese scholars such as Toshiji Sasaki (J-18, J-19, J-20), Norio Tamura (J-26, J-27), Mitsuru Shinpo (J-23, J-24, J-25), and Shin'ichi Tsuji (also known as Keibo Oiwa) (J-28) have added much to our knowledge of the emigration process, the Japanese Labor Union, and the Japanese Canadian communities, as well as the fractures within them during the early years. These writers are part of a growing body of Japanese scholars of whom many belong to a national group called the Imin Kenkyukai, which holds regular academic conferences on Nikkei studies.

Like other branches of historiography, Canadian Nikkei history has been written by men and has concentrated on the experiences and occupations of males. The contributions and the lives of the pioneer women were rarely mentioned until two Japan-born women, Tomoko Makabe (J-10) and Miyoko Kudō (J-6, J-7), wrote about the picture brides, using early Japanese-language sources and personal interviews. Their studies have been followed by those of Canadian academics such as Audrey Kobayashi (E-29, E-30, E-31), Midge Ayukawa (E-5, E-7), Mona Oikawa (E-62), and Yuko Shibata (E-71). These more recent writings differ from earlier histories in that in addition to providing historical insight, they adopt a strong social-justice perspective, addressing issues of both racism and gender as fundamental to understanding the Nikkei experience in Canada.

A beautifully illustrated children's book by Shizuye Takashima (E-81) and poetry and novels by Joy Kogawa (E-37, E-38, E-39) were among the earliest creative works by Canadian Nikkei to receive wide literary recognition. Kogawa's *Obasan* now ranks among the most significant of Canadian novels and is widely viewed as a pioneering work in multicultural literature. Another Nisei, Roy Kiyooka (E-25), has had a significant influence upon the world of Canadian free-form poetry. More recently, many Sansei writers are making their marks in the literary world (see Kobayashi: E-27, E-34). They include Roy Miki (E-48, E-50), whose poetry captures the significant impact of the redress movement, as well as such younger writers as Terry Watada (E-87, E-88), Sally Ito (E-19), Kerri Sakamoto (E-69), Hiromi Goto (E-12), and Rick Shiomi (E-75, E-76), whose plays are performed throughout North America. Although many have written about their own or their pioneer parents' and grandparents' experiences, they have in no way confined themselves to these personal stories. Canadian Nikkei are also making a great impact in the visual arts.

Japanese Canadians Annotated Bibliography

COMPILED BY AUDREY KOBAYASHI AND MIDGE AYUKAWA

ENGLISH

1. Adachi, Ken. *The Enemy that Never Was: A History of Japanese Canadians.* Toronto: McClelland and Stewart, 1976.

    The most comprehensive history of Japanese Canadians to date.

2. Adachi, Pat. *Asahi: A Legend in Baseball.* Toronto, Ontario: Coronex Publishing, 1992.

    A photo-history of the Asahi Baseball Club and its prowess in the pre–World War II era, in Vancouver, British Columbia. Text in English and Japanese.

3. Ashworth, Mary. "The Japanese." In *The Forces Which Shaped Them: A History of the Education of Minority Group Children in British Columbia*, edited by Mary Ashworth, 91–132. Vancouver, British Columbia: New Star Books, 1979.

4. Awmack, W. J. *Tashme: A Japanese Relocation Centre, 1942–1946.* Victoria, British Columbia: Provincial Archives, 1993.

    The memoir of a teacher at Tashme High School. Includes letters to her from students, those who went to Japan, as well as those who settled in Eastern Canada after the closure of the camp.

5. Ayukawa, Michiko Midge. "Creating and Recreating Community: Hiroshima and Canada, 1891–1941." Ph.D. diss., University of Victoria, 1997.

6. Ayukawa, Michiko Midge. "From Japs to Japanese Canadians to Canadian." *Journal of the West* 38, no. 3 (July 1999): 41–48.

    A readable short history of the Japanese in Canada told through the story of the author's family including brief comparison with the experiences of the Japanese Americans.

7. Ayukawa, Michiko Midge. "Good Wives and Wise Mothers: Japanese Picture Brides in Early Twentieth Century British Columbia." *BC Studies* 105–106 (Spring/Summer 1995): 103–18.

8. Ayukawa, Michiko Midge, and Patricia E. Roy. "Japanese." In *Encyclopedia of Canada's Peoples*, edited by Paul Robert Margocsi, 842–60. Toronto, Ontario: University of Toronto Press, 1999.

    The origin and experiences of Japanese in Canada told by two historians. It is part of an encyclopedia of "Canada's Peoples"—119 ethnic groups in Canada.

9. Bernard, Elaine. "A University at War: Japanese Canadians at UBC during World War II." *BC Studies* 35 (Autumn 1977): 36–55.

10. Broadfoot, Barry. *Years of Sorrow, Years of Shame: The Story of the Japanese Canadians in World War II.* Markham, Ontario: Paperjacks, 1977.

    Japanese Canadian recollections of the uprooting during World War II, as tape-recorded by Broadfoot. A pictorial and testimonial description.

11. Fujiwara, Alan. *Baachan! Geechan! Arigato: A Story of Japanese Canadians.* Toronto, Ontario: Momiji Health Care Society, 1989.

    A children's book on Japanese Canadians.

12. Goto, Hiromi. *Chorus of Mushrooms.* Edmonton, Alberta: NeWest Press, 1994.

    An award-winning novel.

13. Granatstein, J. L., and G. A. Johnson. "The Evacuation of the Japanese Canadians, 1942: A Realist Critique of the Received Version." In *On Guard for Thee: War, Ethnicity, and the Canadian State, 1939–1945*, edited by Norman Hillmer, and others, 101–29. Ottawa, Ontario: Canadian Committee for the History of the Second World War, 1988.

    A controversial article. Two historians argue that the Japanese consulate was using Nisei spies, and thus try to justify the internment. Written at the height of the redress movement.

14. Hoshizaki, Bill, ed. *The Vision Fulfilled: Historical Sketches of Central Okanagan Japanese Canadian Families & Community Organizations, 1894–1994.* Kelowna, British Columbia: Kelowna and District Association of Japanese Canadians, 1995.

    A regional history of Japanese Canadians in the Okanagan Valley. Predominant family histories.

15. Ichikawa, Akira. "A Test of Religious Tolerance: Canadian Government and Jodo Shinshu Buddhism during the Pacific War, 1941–1945." *Canadian Ethnic Studies* 26, no. 2 (1994): 46–69.

16. Ito, Roy. *The Japanese Canadians.* Toronto, Ontario: Van Nostrand Reinhold Ltd., 1978.

    A short history of the Japanese Canadians for use in schools.

17. Ito, Roy. *Stories of My People: A Japanese Canadian Journal.* Hamilton, Ontario: Promark Printing, 1994.

    Roy Ito has told the history of the Japanese who immigrated to Canada and their descendents as a series of short accounts of events and interesting individuals. His sources (both Japanese and English) are predominantly popular books and articles as well as personal interviews.

18. Ito, Roy. *We Went to War: The Story of the Japanese Canadi-*

ans Who Served during the First and Second World Wars. Stittsville, Ontario: Canada's Wings, Inc., 1984.

An account of the Japanese Canadians who served in the armed forces during World Wars I and II.

19. Ito, Sally. *Floating Shore.* Toronto, Ontario: Mercury Press, 1998.
20. Iwaasa, David. "Canadian Japanese in Southern Alberta, 1905–1945." In *Two Monographs on Japanese Canadians,* edited by Roger Daniels. New York: Arno Press, 1978.

    A thorough study based on oral interviews.
21. Japanese Canadian Centennial Project. *A Dream of Riches: The Japanese Canadians, 1877–1977.* Toronto, Ontario: Gilchrist Wright, 1978.

    A concise coverage with many photographs of the history of Japanese Canadians from the earliest days of immigration to the celebration of the hundredth anniversary of the arrival of the first Issei. It is significant as it brought together members of the community to work on a joint project to celebrate the centennial of the first immigrant arrival in 1977, and is therefore of crucial importance to the revival of the Nikkei community.
22. Kawano, Roland M., ed. *Ministry to the Hopelessly Hopeless: Japanese Canadian Evacuees and Churches during World War II.* Scarborough, Ontario: The Japanese Canadian Christian Churches Historical Project, 1997.

    A study of the part that Christian Churches played during the uprooting and resettlement of Japanese Canadians during and after World War II.
23. Kisaragi Poem Study Group. *Maple.* Toronto: The Continental Times, 1975.

    A collection of *tanka* poems by Issei writers. In English and Japanese. See also J-4.
24. Kitagawa, Muriel. *This is My Own: Letters to Wes and Other Writings on Japanese Canadians, 1941–1948.* Vancouver, British Columbia: Talonbooks, 1985.

    A passionate activist's letters to her brother Wes Fujiwara, and her essays written during World War II.
25. Kiyooka, Roy. *Mothertalk: Life Stories of Mary Kiyoshi Kiyooka.* Edmonton, Alberta: NeWest Publishers Limited, 1997.

    Roy Kiyooka, Japanese Canadian poet, painter, performer, died suddenly in 1994 while writing the story of his mother (1896–1996). Completed and edited by Daphne Marlatt.
26. Knight, Rolf, and Maya Koizumi. *A Man of Our Times: The Life History of a Japanese-Canadian Fisherman.* Vancouver, British Columbia: New Star Books, 1976.

    The life of a labor activist, Yoshida Ryuichi, based on interviews by Koizumi. A good account of the relationship between Japanese pioneer laborers, labor contractors, and unions.
27. Kobayashi, Audrey. "Birds of Passage or Squawking Ducks? Writing across Generations of Japanese-Canadian Literature." In *Writing across Two Worlds: Literature and Migration,* edited by Russel King, John Connell, and Paul White, 216–28. London: Routledge, 1995.

    Argues that the writing styles of different Nikkei generations reflect their different experiences and their relations with each other.
28. Kobayashi, Audrey. *A Demographic Profile of Japanese Canadians.* Canada: Department of the Secretary of State, 1989.

    A detailed analysis of Canadian Nikkei population and challenges to community development.
29. Kobayashi, Audrey. "Emigration from Kaideima, Japan, 1885–1950: An Analysis of Community and Landscape Change." Ph.D. diss, University of California, 1983.

    Analyzes the relationship between emigration and development in an "emigrant" village.
30. Kobayashi, Audrey. "Emigration to Canada and the Development of the Residential Landscape in a Japanese Village: The Paradox of the Sojourner." *Canadian Ethnic Studies* XVI, no. 3 (1984): 111–31.

    Examines the impact of emigration on housing and family.
31. Kobayashi, Audrey. "For the Sake of the Children: Japanese/Canadian Workers/Mothers." In *Women, Work and Place,* edited by Audrey Kobayashi, 45–72. Montreal, Quebec and Kingston, Ontario: McGill-Queen's University Press, 1994.

    Describes the experiences of early Issei women.
32. Kobayashi, Audrey. "The Japanese-Canadian Redress Settlement and Its Implications for 'Race Relations.'" *Canadian Ethnic Studies* 24, no. 1 (1992): 1–19.

    Argues that the redress settlement needs to be understood as part of the fight against racism.
33. Kobayashi, Audrey. *Memories of Our Past: A Brief History and Walking Tour of Powell Street.* Vancouver, British Columbia: NRC Publishing, 1992.

    Documents the development of the largest prewar Nikkei community.
34. Kobayashi, Audrey. "Structured Feeling: Japanese Canadian Poetry and Landscape." In *A Few Acres of Snow: Literary and Artistic Images of Canada,* edited by G. Norcliffe, and Paul Simpson-Housley, 243–57. Toronto, Ontario: Dundern Press, 1992.

    Argues that poetry writing was a significant means of emotional expression and cultural adjustment for the Issei.
35. Kobayashi, Cassandra, and Roy Miki. *Justice in Our Time: The Japanese Canadian Redress Settlement.* Vancouver, British Columbia: Talonbooks, 1991.

    A historical account of the struggle for Redress with many photographs and documents, focusing on the National Association of Japanese Canadians, the organization that negotiated the settlement.
36. Kobayashi, Cassandra, and Roy Miki. *Spirit of Redress: Japanese Canadians in Conference.* Vancouver, British Columbia: JC Publications, 1989.

    Transcripts of workshops at the "Back to the Future" conference, May 16–17, 1987, held in Vancouver and the Internment Camp Bus Tour, which followed.

37. Kogawa, Joy. *Itsuka*. Toronto, Ontario: Penguin Canada, 1992.

    A sequel to *Obasan*. The main character joins in the struggle for redress.

38. Kogawa, Joy. *Obasan*. Toronto, Ontario: Lester & Orpen Dennys Ltd. 1981.

    A moving story of the Japanese Canadians during World War II as seen through the eyes of a child. Also published by Anchor Books (New York) in 1994.

39. Kogawa, Joy. *The Rain Ascends*. Toronto: Alfred A. Knopf, 1995.

    A novel about family relationships.

40. La Violette, Forrest E. *The Canadian Japanese and World War II: A Sociological-Psychological Account*. Toronto, Ontario: University of Toronto, 1948.

    A thorough account of the events and the effect on the Japanese Canadians of the expulsion from the West Coast during World War II.

41. Lang, Catherine. *O-Bon in Chimunesu: A Community Remembered*. Vancouver, British Columbia: Arsenal Pulp Press, 1996.

    A prize-winning "creative non-fiction" book of the prewar Japanese community in Chemainus, British Columbia on Vancouver Island, based on oral interviews of many Japanese Canadians. The complete lives of a number of families have been carefully and honestly retold, from the complexity of community to the trauma of the uprooting and resettling elsewhere later.

42. Makabe, Tomoko. *The Canadian Sansei*. Toronto, Ontario: University of Toronto Press, 1998.

    A sociological study of Canadian Sansei. Makabe concludes that because of the World War II uprooting, the Sansei no longer have Japanese traits.

43. Makabe, Tomoko. "Ethnic Group Identity: Canadian-born Japanese in Metropolitan Toronto." Ph.D. diss., University of Toronto, 1976.

44. Makabe, Tomoko. *Picture Brides: Japanese Women in Canada*. Ontario: Multicultural History Society of Ontario, 1995.

    Translated by Kathleen Chisato Merken. A thoroughly researched study of five Japanese Canadian pioneer women based on personal interviews conducted with them in their senior years. Originally published in Japan.

45. Manitoba Japanese Canadian Citizens' Association. *The History of Japanese Canadians in Manitoba*. Winnipeg, Manitoba: Manitoba Japanese Canadian Citizens' Association, 1996.

    A complete listing of the Japanese Canadian community in Manitoba based on oral interviews and the records of Manitoba Nikkei societies.

46. Marlatt, Daphne. *Steveston Recollected: A Japanese Canadian History*. Victoria: Aural History, Provincial Archives of British Columbia, 1975.

    Based mainly on oral interviews conducted in Japanese by Maya Koizumi, in 1972, of ten Japanese and one white pioneer; the story of Steveston, a fishing community near Vancouver, British Columbia.

47. Merilees, Bill. "Salted Herring." In *Newcastle Island: A Place of Discovery*, 84–93. Surrey, British Columbia: Heritage House, 1998.

    Describes the Japanese salteries and boat-builders on Newcastle Island from the early 1900s to 1942. Photographs.

48. Miki, Roy. *Broken Entries: Race Writing Subjectivity*. Toronto: Mercury Press, 1998.

    A collection of essays written during the 1990s addressing issues of cultural and national identity, critical race theory, activism, and contemporary Asian Canadian writing.

49. Miki, Roy. *Random Access File*. Red Deer, Alta: Red Deer College Press, 1995.

    The poems explore the effects on language and subjectivity of dislocation, shifting identities, and internment, including a series composed during a trip to Japan.

50. Miki, Roy. *Saving Face: Poems Selected 1976–1988*. Winnipeg: Turnstone Press, 1991.

    The author's first book of poems with a selection of poems that probe personal and family history and memory, including the mass uprooting of Japanese Canadians from the West Coast of Canada and the struggle to seek redress.

51. Miyazaki, Masajiro. *My Sixty Years in Canada*. N.p.: Miyazaki, Masajiro, 1973.

    An Issei doctor's memoir of prewar Powell Street and Lillooet, where he moved to during World War II.

52. Morita, Katsuyoshi. *Powell Street Monogatari*. Burnaby, British Columbia: Live Canada Publishing Co., 1988.

    The reminiscences of an Issei of the prewar Powell Street community and the internment center of Greenwood. Translated by Eric A Sokugawa.

53. Mullins, Mark. *Religious Minorities in Canada: A Sociological Study of the Japanese Experience*. Queenston, Ontario: Edwin Mellen Press, 1989.

    History of the Buddhist Church of Canada and the United Church of Canada, their relationship with Japanese immigrants and the evolution over the years.

54. Nakagawa, Roy K. *Ocean Falls Recollection: Story of the Town Where I Was Born*. Toronto, Ontario: Roy K. Nakagawa, 1995.

    A personal recollection of Ocean Falls, British Columbia, a prewar Japanese Canadian community. Includes a 1995 list of former residents, and a sketch of the former community with each home identified.

55. Nakano, Takeo Ujo, and Leatrice Nakano. *Within the Barbed Wire Fence: A Japanese Man's Account of His Internment in Canada*. Toronto, Ontario: University of Toronto Press, 1980.

    A personal account of an Issei during World War II who was removed to a road camp, then imprisoned. His personal anguish is eloquently expressed in prose and in *tanka*.

56. Nakashima, Kimiaki. "Economic Aspects of Japanese Evac-

uation from the Canadian Pacific Coast." Master's thesis, McGill University, 1946.

Documents the economic impact of the uprooting.

57. Nakayama, Gordon G. *Issei: Stories of Japanese Canadian Pioneers.* Toronto, Ontario: NC Press, 1984.

Short biographies of over forty prominent Japanese pioneers.

58. National Association of Japanese Canadians. *Democracy Betrayed: The Case for Redress.* Winnipeg: The National Association of Japanese Canadians, 1985.

A historic document of great symbolic importance to the Nikkei community in Canada, this report presents the case for a redress settlement.

59. National Association of Japanese Canadians. *Economic Losses of Japanese Canadians after 1941: A Study Conducted by Price Waterhouse.* Winnipeg: National Association of Japanese Canadians, 1985.

The "Price Waterhouse Study" provides a thorough economic report on the losses of Japanese Canadians due to uprooting and internment.

60. National Association of Japanese Canadians. *Justice in Our Time: Redress for Japanese Canadians.* Winnipeg: National Association of Japanese Canadians, 1986.

A sequel to *Democracy Betrayed*, this report provides the political context for the redress movement.

61. Nunoda, Peter Takaji. "A Community in Transition and Conflict: The Japanese Canadians, 1935–1951." Ph.D. diss., University of Manitoba, 1991.

A study of the leaders of Nisei organizations in prewar, wartime, and immediate postwar years. He concludes that there was division among the Nisei, and later, subordination to white middle class liberals.

62. Oikawa, Mona. "Driven to Scatter Far and Wide: The Forced Resettlement of Japanese Canadians to Southern Ontario, 1944–1949." Master's thesis, University of Toronto, 1986.

A study of the government policies and the experiences of the Japanese Canadians who were forced to resettle in southern Ontario during World War II.

63. Oiwa, Keibo, ed. *Stone Voices: Wartime Writings of Japanese Canadian Issei.* Montreal, Quebec: Vehicule Press, 1991.

Memoirs and letters written by four Issei (three men and one woman) during the uprooting of the Japanese Canadians following the bombing of Pearl Harbor were translated by Oiwa. The voices of the Issei, their turmoil, and their divided loyalties to their families and their native country are revealed as they never have been before.

64. Okazaki, Robert K. *The Nisei Mass Evacuation Group and P.O.W. Camp "101," Angler, Ontario.* Scarborough, Ontario: Markham Litho, 1996.

This is a translation (by Okazaki's wife and son) of a book written in Japanese in 1994. It is an invaluable, well-researched book based on the author's personal prisoner of war diary and actual records of the camp. The appendices document minutes of camp meetings, the internees, letters, camp orders, and sketches of scenes.

65. Omatsu, Maryka. *Bittersweet Passage: Redress and the Japanese Canadian Experience.* Toronto, Ontario: Between the Lines, 1992.

Omatsu, a lawyer, relates her personal story and her involvement with the redress movement, interspersed with anecdotes of experiences of other Nikkei, based on oral interviews.

66. Powell Street Revue, and the Chinese Canadian Writers Workshop. *Inalienable Rice: A Chinese and Japanese Canadian Anthology.* Vancouver, 1979.

This collection brought activist writers within the Chinese and Japanese Canadian communities together to publish some of their earliest writings. Many of the writers featured here went on to become the major writers representing the community today.

67. Roy, Patricia E. "The Education of Japanese Children in the British Columbia Interior Housing Settlement During World War Two." *Historical Studies in Education/Histoire de la Education* 4 (Fall 1992): 211–31.

68. Roy, Patricia E. *A White Man's Province: British Columbia Politics and Chinese and Japanese Immigrants, 1858–1914.* Vancouver, British Columbia: University of British Columbia, 1989.

Historian Roy's first of two books on white attitudes and actions against Asians in British Columbia.

69. Sakamoto, Kerri. *The Electrical Field.* Toronto, Ontario: Alfred A. Knopf Canada, 1998.

A novel set in the pre-redress years of the 1970s. It explores the deep-seated emotional pain permeating the lives of some Canadian Nikkei.

70. Sasaki, Toshiji [佐々木敏二]. "The Japanese Association of Canada: Its Democratic Reform and the Destruction of its Democratic System by Vancouver Consul Kaai [*sic*]." *Kirisutokyō shakai mondai kenkyū* [キリスト教社会問題研究] 41 (July 1992): 63–90.

71. Shibata, Yuko. "Coping with Values in Conflict: Japanese Women in Canada." In *Visible Minorities and Multiculturalism: Asians in Canada*, edited by Victor Ujimoto, and Gordon Hirabayashi, 257–76. Toronto, Ontario: Butterworth, 1980.

72. Shibata, Yuko, and others. *The Forgotten History of the Japanese Canadians.* Vol. 1. Vancouver, British Columbia: New Sun Books, 1977.

Part II is "The Japanese Canadian, A Bibliography," by Yuko Shibata. Volume II was never written.

73. Shikatani, Gerry, and David Aylward. *Paper Doors.* Toronto: The Coach House Press, 1981.

A collection of some of the best Japanese Canadian poetry by three generations. In English and Japanese.

74. Shimizu, Yon. *The Exiles: An Archival History of the World War II Japanese Road Camps in British Columbia and Ontario.* Delhi, Ontario: NCC Printing and Publishing, 1993.

A thoroughly researched archival history of the politics, the legislations, and the experiences of the male Japanese Canadians who were uprooted and detained in road camps in British Columbia and Ontario after the bombing of Pearl Harbor.

75. Shiomi, Rick. "Rosie's Cafe." Stage play, 1987.
76. Shiomi, Rick. "Yellow Fever." Screenplay, 1988.
77. Sugimoto, Howard H. *Japanese Immigration, the Vancouver Riots and Canadian Diplomacy.* New York: Arno Press, 1978.

    A thoroughly researched book on the early immigration of the Japanese in Canada, the events leading to the September 1907 riot and its aftermath.

78. Sumida, Rigenda. "The Japanese in British Columbia." Master's thesis, University of British Columbia, 1935.

    An invaluable source of information on prewar Japanese Canadian communities. Based on a social and economic survey by the Japanese community and many interviews.

79. Sunahara, Ann Gomer. *The Politics of Racism: The Uprooting of Japanese Canadians during the Second World War.* Toronto, Ontario: Lorimer, 1981.

    A groundbreaking book based on newly declassified government documents on the expulsion of Japanese Canadians from the West Coast in 1942.

80. Suzuki, David, and Keibo Oiwa. *The Japan We Never Knew: A Journey of Discovery.* Toronto, Ontario: Stoddart, 1996.

    Two prominent scholars expose usually unnoticed aspects of socially excluded groups in Japan.

81. Takashima, Shizuye. *A Child in Prison Camp.* Montreal, Quebec: Tundra Books, 1971.

    A beautifully illustrated children's book of a young girl and her experiences in the internment camp at New Denver.

82. Takata, Toyo. *Nikkei Legacy: The Story of Japanese Canadians from Settlement to Today.* Toronto, Ontario: N C Press, 1983.

    A readable history, with many photographs. Thoroughly researched, but undocumented.

83. Tanaka, Tosh. *Hands Across the Pacific: Japan in British Columbia, 1889–1989.* Vancouver, British Columbia: Consulate General of Japan, 1990.

    Includes many photographs.

84. Wakayama, Tamio. *Kikyo: Coming Home to Powell Street.* Madeira Park, British Columbia: Harbour Publishing, 1992.

    A photo-documentary with oral interviews conducted by Linda Uyehara Hoffman. Powell Street was the center of Japanese town in pre-World War II.

85. Ward, W. Peter. *White Canada Forever.* Montreal, Quebec and Kingston, Ontario: McGill-Queen's University Press, 1990.

    Ward has focused on the hostility of the whites in British Columbia towards the Asian immigrants, its psychological and sociological causes.

86. Watada, Terry. *Bukkyo Tozen: A History of Jodo Shinshu Buddhism in Canada, 1905–1995.* Toronto, Ontario: HpF Press, 1996.

87. Watada, Terry. *Daruma Days: A Collection of Fictionalised Biography.* Vancouver, British Columbia: Ronsdale Press, 1997.

    Watada wove together Japanese folk tales and ghost stories to recreate stories of Issei and Nikkei in the internment camps.

88. Watada, Terry. *A Thousand Homes.* Stratford, Ontario: Mercury Press, 1995.

    "Snapshots" of Japanese Canadian life. Includes translations of his father's Japanese poetry.

89. Yesaki, Mitsuo, Harold Steves, and Kathy Steves. *Steveston, Cannery Row: An Illustrated History.* Richmond, British Columbia: Lulu Island Printing Ltd., 1998.

    An illustrated history of Steveston and the stories of the Japanese Canadian fishermen and their families who had lived there.

90. Young, Charles H., and Helen R. Y. Reid. *The Japanese Canadians.* Toronto, Ontario: University of Toronto Press, 1938.

    A sociological study of the Japanese in Canada in the 1930s.

JAPANESE

1. Amano, Mieko [天野美恵子]. *Chikara to kihin: Tagashira Masue fujin no kokuhaku* [力と気品: 田頭ますえ夫人の告白]. Vancouver, British Columbia: Tagashira, 1987.

    This story of a pioneer woman, her marriage, widowhood with two children, her survival, and remarriage is candidly shared with the author.

2. Gamō, Masao, Kazuko Tsurumi, and Ronald P. Dore [蒲生正男, 鶴見和子 and Ronald P. Dore], eds. *Umi o wattata Nihon no mura* [海を渡った日本の村]. Tōkyō [東京]: Chūō Kōronsha [中央公論社], 1962.

    Two Japanese scholars and a University of British Columbia historian describe the sociological history of Steveston, where fishers from Mio village settled.

3. Hayashi Rintarō [林林太郎]. *Kuroshio no hate ni* [黒潮の涯に]. Tōkyō [東京]: Nichibō Shuppansha [日貿出版社], 1971.

    A comprehensive history of Japanese Canadian fishers, with a second section which is Hayashi's personal impressions of various Steveston personalities.

4. Kisaragi Poem Study Group. *Maple.* Toronto: The Continental Times, 1975.

    A collection of tanka poems by Issei writers. In English and Japanese. See E-23.

5. Koyama, Shigeharu [小山茂春]. *Honma Tomekichi-ō no shōgai* [本間留吉翁の生涯]. Wakayama-ken Mihama-shi [和歌山県美浜市]: Koyama Shigeharu [小山茂春], 1995.

    Valuable information on the life of Tomey Homma, community leader, political activist. Poor editing.

6. Kudō, Miyoko [工藤美代子]. *Kanada yūgirō ni furu yuki wa* [カナダ遊戯楼に降る雪は]. Tōkyō [東京]: Shōbunsha [晶文社], 1983.

    The author has traced the stories and experiences of Japanese prostitutes in the early mining towns.

7. Kudō, Miyoko [工藤美代子]. *Shakonzuma: hanayome wa ichimai no miai shashin o te ni umi o watatteitta* [写婚妻:

花嫁は一枚の見合い写真を手に海を渡っていった]. Tōkyō [東京]: Domesu Shuppan [ドメス出版], 1983.

The story of thirteen pioneer Japanese immigrant women in Canada who were picture brides.

8. Kudo, Miyoko, and Susan Phillips [工藤美代子 and Susan Phillips]. *Bankūbā no ai: Tamura Toshiko to Suzuki Etsu* [版香坡の愛: 田村俊子と鈴木悦]. Tōkyō [東京]: Domesu Shuppansha [ドメス出版社], 1983.

The authors weave the story of the love affair between social activist, journalist, Suzuki Etsu, and Tamura Toshiko, a Japanese feminist author, and their contribution to the labor movement in the prewar Japanese Canadian community.

9. Kuwabara, Tom Sando, and Yumiko Hoyano [Kuwabara, Tom Sando and 穂谷野由美子]. *Toraware no mi* [囚われの身]. Edmonton, Alberta: Print Stop Inc., 1995.

Diary kept by a Nisei, educated in Japan, who was interned in a prisoner of war camp in Canada during World War II.

10. Makabe, Tomoko [真壁知子]. *Shashinkon no tsumatachi: Kanada imin no joseishi* [写真婚の妻たち: カナダ移民の女性史]. Tōkyō [東京]: Miraisha [未来社], 1983.

The oral history of five pioneer picture brides.

11. Morita, Katsuyoshi [森田勝義]. *Paueru-gai monogatari* [パウエル街物語]. Tōkyō [東京]: Live Canada Publishing Co. (Burnaby, BC), 1986.

Memoirs of a Japanese businessman.

12. Nakayama, Jinshirō [中山訊四郎]. *Kanada dōhō hatten taikan* [加奈陀同胞発展大鑑]. Tōkyō [東京]: Nakayama, Jinshirō [中山訊四郎], 1921.

Two hundred short biographies and history of Japanese immigration.

13. Nakayama, Jinshirō [中山訊四郎]. *Kanada no hōko* [加奈陀の宝庫]. Tōkyō [東京]: Nakayama, Jinshirō [中山訊四郎], 1921.

Lists of Japanese immigrants in Canada, their village roots and addresses in Canada.

14. Nikka Jihōsha [日加時報社]. *Kanada zairyū dōhō sōran* [加奈陀在留同胞総覧]. Tōkyō [東京]: Nihon Tosho Sentā [日本図書センター], 1993.

Contains short biographies with photographs and prefectural roots of approximately five hundred pioneers and a brief history of the Japanese immigrants in Canada.

15. Nishiyama, Hisakazu [西山久計]. "Kanada imin no chichi, Kuno Gihei [カナダ移民の父工野儀兵衛]." *Ijū kenkyū* [移住研究] 30 (1993): 170–84.

A well-researched biography of Kuno Gihei, the Miomura, Wakayama-ken emigrant reputed to be the one who influenced his fellow villagers to go to British Columbia to fish. The result was "Kishū's Amerika-mura."

16. Nitta, Jirō [新田次郎]. *Mikkōsen, Suian Maru* [密航船 水安丸]. Tōkyō [東京]: Kōdansha [講談社], 1982.

A chronicle of Oikawa Jinzaburō who brought eighty-two people from Miyagi-ken to Canada in 1906 without legal papers. They were allowed to immigrate and lived communally on Don and Lion Islands in the Fraser River, which they renamed Oikawa and Sato Islands.

17. Okada, Kiyomi [岡田きよみ]. *Michikusashū* [道草集]. Tōkyō [東京]: Keisō Shuppan [勁草出版], 1990.

An Issei teacher who emigrated in 1928 to Chemainus, Vancouver Island, expressed in poetry and essays her feelings and experiences up to the present day.

18. Sasaki, Toshiji [佐々木敏二]. "Kanada Yunion Tankō to Kōbe Imingaisha [カナダ・ユニオン炭坑と神戸移民会社]." *Han* [汎] 6 (September 1987): 164–88.

A thoroughly researched paper on the circumstances surrounding the experiences of one hundred Hiroshima men who were sent to work in the coal mines in Cumberland, Vancouver Island.

19. Sasaki, Toshiji [佐々木敏二]. "Meiji Imingaisha ni yoru jiyūtokōsha no okuridashi [明治移民会社による自由渡航者の送り出し]." *Han* [汎] 8 (April 1988): 156–81.

The unethical activities of the Meiji Emigration Company are discussed.

20. Sasaki, Toshiji [佐々木敏二]. "Yunion Tankō dainiji keiyaku imin [ユニオン炭坑第二次契約移民]." *Han* [汎] 7 (December 1987): 170–98.

The circumstances surrounding the sending of a second group of emigrants to the Union Collieries.

21. Satō, Tsutae, and Hanako Satō [佐藤伝 and 佐藤英子]. *Kodomo to tomoni gojūnen: Kanada Nikkei kyōiku shiki* [子どもと共に五十年: カナダ日系教育私記]. Tōkyō [東京]: Nihon Shuppan Bōeki [日本出版貿易], 1969.

An excellent account of the history of the Japanese language schools in Canada, in particular of the largest school, the Vancouver Alexander Street School. Written by its long-term principal and his wife.

22. Shikatani, Gerry, and David Aylward. *Paper Doors*. Toronto: The Coach House Press, 1981.

A collection of some of the best Japanese Canadian poetry by three generations. In English and Japanese.

23. Shinpo, Mitsuru [新保満]. *Ishi o mote owaruru gotoku: Nikkei Kanadajin shakaishi* [石をもて追わるるごとく: 日系カナダ人社会史]. Tōkyō [東京]: Ochanomisu Shobō [御茶の水書房], 1996.

Nikkei Canadian social history.

24. Shinpo, Mitsuru [新保満]. *Kanada Nihonjin imin monogatari* [カナダ日本人移民物語]. Tōkyō [東京]: Tsukiji Shokan [築地書館], 1986.

A thorough history of Japanese immigrants to Canada by a Japanese anthropologist who was one of the first to conduct research in this field.

25. Shinpo, Mitsuru, Norio Tamura, and Shigehiko Shiramizu [新保満, 田村紀雄 and 白水繁彦]. *Kanada no Nihongo shinbun: minzoku idō no shakaishi* [カナダの日本語新聞: 民族移動の社会史]. Tōkyō [東京]: PMC Shuppan [PMC出版], 1991.

A study of the Japanese language newspapers that were published pre-World War II. It is an especially interesting study of the Japanese Canadian society of that time, with a revelation of the lives of the laborers, their union, and how their newspaper had to struggle against the rest of the community.

26. Tamura, Norio [田村紀雄]. "Nikkan Minshū: shūkan jijō Nichi-Bei kaisen to Bankūba Local 31 [日刊民衆：週間事情日米開戦とバンクーバ Local 31]." *Komyunikēshon kagaku* [コミュニケーション科学] 3 (1995): 27–41.

   Study of the Japanese language newspaper, the *Daily People*, the voice of the labor union Local 31 and what occurred following the bombing of Pearl Harbor.

27. Tamura, Norio [田村紀雄]. *Suzuki Etsu: Nihon to Kanada o musunda jānarisuto* [鈴木悦：日本とカナダを結んだジャーナリスト]. Tōkyō [東京]: Riburo Pōto [リブロポート], 1992.

   A thoroughly researched biography of Etsu Suzuki, a Waseda graduate and social activist, who came to Canada in 1918 and played a major part in the unionization of the Japanese laborers.

28. Tsuji, Shin'ichi [辻信一]. *Nikkei Kanadajin: Redressing the Past: Self-Portraits of Japanese Canadians* [日系カナダ人：Redressing the Past: Self-Portraits of Japanese Canadians]. Tōkyō [東京]: Shōbunsha [晶文社], 1990.

   This book includes all the Japanese Canadian memoirs in *Stone Voices* by Keibo Oiwa, also known as Tsuji Shin'ichi. In addition, there are two of Nisei.

29. Tsurumi, Kazuko [鶴見和子]. *Sutebusuton monogatari: sekai no naka no Nihonjin* [ステブストン物語: 世界の中の日本人]. Tōkyō [東京]: Chūō Kōronsha [中央公論社], 1962.

   A Japanese scholar interviewed Japanese Canadians who had returned to Steveston to fish again after World War II and related their stories.

30. Yamaga, Yasutarō [山家安太郎]. *Henē nōkaishi* [ヘネー農会史]. Tōkyō [東京]: Henē Nōkaishi Henshū Iinkai [ヘネー農会史編集委員会], 1963.

   A history of Japanese Canadian berry farmers in the Fraser Valley and their relations with the mainstream community.

31. Yamagata, Takao [山形孝夫]. *Ushinawareta fūkei: Nikkei Kanada gyomin no kiroku kara* [失われた風景：日系カナダ漁民の記録から]. Tōkyō [東京]: Miraisha [未来社], 1996.

   The saga of a group of immigrants from Miyagi-ken who lived communally on two islands in the Fraser River in the early decades of 1900.

Supplementary Materials

COMPILED BY AUDREY KOBAYASHI, MIDGE AYUKAWA, KATHLEEN WILSON, AND MICHAEL PACEY

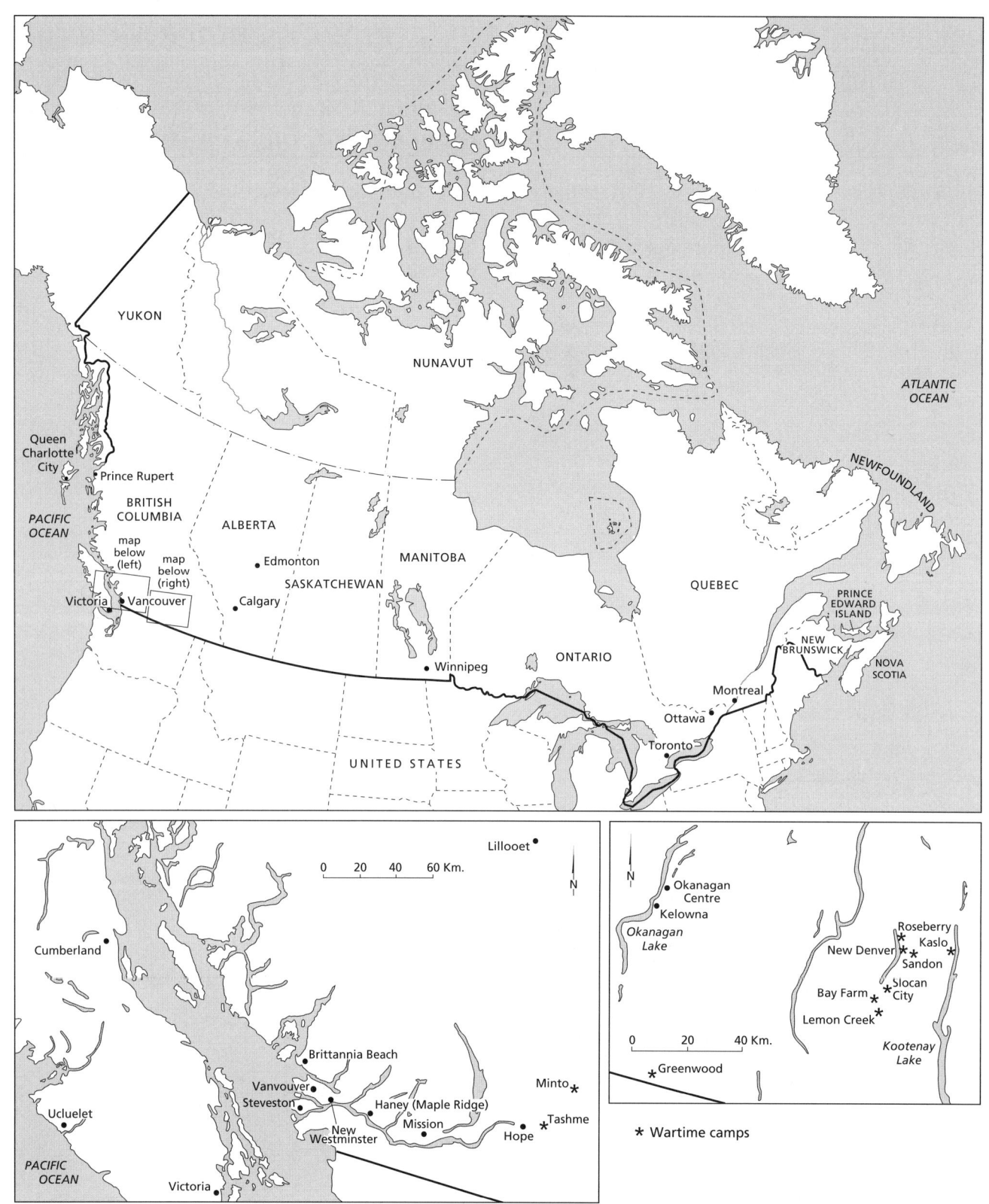

Map 5.1 Locations of Nikkei Populations in Canada

Japanese Canadian Demographic Information

Table 5.1 Japanese Emigration to Canada by Prefecture of Origin in Japan, 1899–1993

	1899	1900	1901–'05	'06–'10	'11–'15	'16–'20	'21–'25	'26–'30	'31–'35	Total
	1,726	2,710	568	4,615	5,177	7,196	4,915	3,688	457	**31,052**

	1946–'50	'51–'55	'56–'60	'61–'65	'66–'69	'76–'80	'81–'85	'86–'90	'91–'93	Total*
Tōkyō	-	-	-	-	-	180	197	32	9	**418**
Kanagawa	-	-	-	-	-	89	53	6	4	**152**
Ōsaka	-	-	-	-	-	58	59	5	-	**122**
Chiba	-	-	-	-	-	36	24	7	-	**67**
Aichi	-	-	-	-	-	27	40	-	-	**67**
Total*	27	168	843	759	2,511	647	610	92	18	**5,675**

Sources: Figures for 1899–1969 were taken from Gaimushō Ryōji Ijūbu. *Waga kokumin no kaigai hatten: ijū hyakunen no ayumi (shiryō hen)* (Tōkyō, 1971), 2–3, 144. Figures for 1976–1993 were taken from Japan International Cooperation Agency, *Kaigai ijū tōkei (FY 1952–FY 01993)* (Tōkyō, 1994), 38–39.
Note: *Total includes other prefectures.

Table 5.2 Total Population of Japanese Canadians (Showing Single and Multiple Responses by Sex)

	Male	Female	Total
Single Responses	23,600	28,200	**51,800**
Multiple Responses	12,460	12,870	**25,330**
Total	**36,060**	**41,075**	**77,130**

Source: 1996 Census—Statistics Canada—93F0026XDB96001.
  Category: The Nation: 1996 Census of Population.
  Note: The data in Tables 5.2 to 5.10 have been subjected to a confidentiality procedure known as "random rounding" by Statistics Canada, so that some of the figures do not add up to the totals. The difference is often +/– 5–10.

Table 5.3 Total Population of Japanese Canadians (Showing Age–Sex Distribution), 1996*

Age/Sex											
0–14		15–24		25–44		45–64		65 and Over		Total-Age/Sex	
M	F	M	F	M	F	M	F	M	F	M	F
8,485	7,655	6,130	7,615	10,200	13,250	7,270	8,100	3,975	4,450	**36,055**	**41,075**

Source: 1996 Census—Statistics Canada 94F0009XDB96010.
  Category: The 1996 Dimensions Series.
  Note: *The distribution shows combined Single and Multiple Responses.

Table 5.4 Regional Distribution of Japanese Canadians by Sex (Showing Single and Multiple Responses)

Province/Territory	Single Responses		Multiple Responses		Total Responses	
	Male	Female	Male	Female	Male	Female
Newfoundland	15	15	15	10	**30**	**20**
Prince Edward Island	0	55	20	30	**20**	**85**
Nova Scotia	125	120	85	90	**210**	**210**
New Brunswick	10	20	20	15	**30**	**40**
Québec	810	1,255	535	620	**1,345**	**1,870**
Ontario	8,930	9,960	4,535	4,400	**13,465**	**14,355**
Manitoba	410	515	380	550	**795**	**1,060**
Saskatchewan	135	110	170	120	**310**	**230**
Alberta	2,840	3,035	1,845	1,940	**4,685**	**4,975**
British Columbia	10,305	13,085	4,800	5,055	**15,105**	**18,140**
Yukon	10	30	20	30	**30**	**55**
Northwest Territories	10	15	25	15	**30**	**30**

Source: 1996 Census—Statistics Canada—93F0026XDB96001.
Category: The Nation: 1996 Census of Population.

Table 5.5 Total Population of Japanese Canadians (Showing Age–Sex Distribution), 1996*

Province/Territory	Age/Sex										Total Age-Sex
	0–14		15–24		25–44		45–64		65 and Over		
	M	F	M	F	M	F	M	F	M	F	
Newfoundland	0.0	10	20	0.0	0.0	10	10	10	0.0	0.0	**40**
Prince Edward Island	10	0.0	10	40	0.0	10	0.0	35	0.0	0.0	**105**
Nova Scotia	80	65	40	40	50	45	35	45	10	10	**425**
New Brunswick	10	10	0.0	10	15	15	0.0	10	0.0	0.0	**70**
Québec	390	330	175	400	375	625	235	280	165	230	**3,215**
Ontario	3,155	2,765	1,785	2,035	3,995	4,660	2,825	2,935	1,710	1,965	**27,825**
Manitoba	200	230	100	215	220	325	110	130	160	155	**1,855**
Saskatchewan	95	65	75	55	70	60	50	35	15	15	**535**
Alberta	1,285	1,080	810	815	1,360	1,740	800	945	430	390	**9,660**
British Columbia	3,240	3,075	3,105	3,985	4,085	5,730	3,185	3,670	1,485	1,680	**33,245**
Yukon	0.0	15	10	15	10	10	0.0	0.0	0.0	0.0	**90**
Northwest Territories	15	10	10	0.0	10	15	10	10	10	0.0	**65**

Source: 1996 Census—Statistics Canada—94F0009XDB96010.
Category: The 1996 Dimensions Series.
Note: *The distribution shows combined Single and Multiple Responses.

Table 5.6 School Attendance of Japanese Canadians, Ages Fifteen Years and Older, 1996

Level of Schooling	Age Group				Total Age Group
	15–24	25–44	45–64	65 and Over	
Total Population 15 Years and Over	11,830	20,845	14,665	8,240	55,590
Not Attending School	2,695	17,020	14,160	8,165	42,035
Attending School Full-Time	8,220	2,000	70	25	10,310
Attending School Part Time	920	1,830	440	55	3,240

Source: 1996 Census—Statistics Canada—94F0009XDB96003.
Category: The 1996 Dimensions Series.

Table 5.7 Highest Level of Schooling of Japanese Canadians, Ages Fifteen Years and Older, 1996

Highest Level of Schooling	Age Group				Total Age Group
	15–24	25–44	45–64	65 and Over	
Less than Grade 9	75	55	315	1,725	**2,175**
Grade 9–13	5,050	3,260	4,445	3,775	**16,525**
Without secondary school graduation certificate	3,490	1,160	1,865	2,390	**8,900**
With secondary school graduation certificate	1,560	2,100	2,580	1,385	**7,625**
Trades Certificate or Diploma	30	185	370	340	**925**
University	4,115	11,485	5,900	1,090	**22,590**
Without degree	3,065	3,400	1,755	470	**8,695**
Without certificate or diploma	2,520	1,235	565	200	**4,520**
With certificate or diploma	545	2,165	1,190	270	**4,175**
With bachelor's degree or higher	1,045	8,085	4,145	620	**13,890**
Other Nonuniversity Education Only	2,565	5,865	3,635	1,305	**13,370**
Without certificate or diploma	1,575	1,375	825	345	**4,120**
With certificate or diploma	985	4,490	2,815	960	**9,255**
Total Population 15 Years and Over	**11,830**	**20,845**	**14,670**	**8,240**	**55,590**

Source: 1996 Census—Statistics Canada—94F0009XDB96003.
Category: The 1996 Dimensions Series.

Table 5.8 Labor Force Activity of Japanese Canadians, Ages Fifteen Years and Older, 1996

Labor Force Activity	Age Group							Total Age Group
	15–19	20–24	25–34	35–44	45–54	55–64	65 and Over	
Total Labor Force Activity	5,045	6,785	11,850	9,000	8,595	6,075	8,240	**55,590**
Total Labor Force	1,580	3,895	8,930	7,415	7,135	3,795	905	**33,655**
Employed	1,270	3,370	8,345	7,115	6,845	3,605	870	**31,430**
Unemployed	315	520	580	300	285	190	35	**2,225**
Not in Labor Force	3,460	2,895	2,920	1,585	1,460	2,275	7,335	**21,930**
Participation Rate	31.3	57.4	75.4	82.4	83.0	62.5	11.0	**60.5**
Employment Population Ratio	25.2	49.7	70.4	79.1	79.6	59.3	10.6	**56.5**
Unemployment Rate	19.9	13.4	6.5	4.0	4.0	5.0	3.9	**6.6**

Source: 1996 Census—Statistics Canada—94F0009XDB96003.
Category: The 1996 Dimensions Series.

Table 5.9 Industry Divisions of Japanese Canadians, Ages Fifteen Years and Older Who Worked since January 1, 1995 (Showing Sex Distribution), 1996

Industry	Age Group 15–24	25–44	45–64	65 and Over	Total Age Group	Sex Male	Female
Total Population 15 Years and Over	6,700	17,520	11,555	1,310	**37,090**	18,595	18,495
Primary Industries	190	395	365	185	**1,135**	760	375
Manufacturing	430	2,170	1,770	155	**4,530**	3,250	1,280
Construction	245	475	480	110	**1,315**	1,050	260
Transportation and Storage	90	590	390	0	**1,070**	640	435
Communication and Other Utility	75	590	285	25	**975**	585	390
Wholesale Trade	185	1,180	920	80	**2,365**	1,545	820
Retail Trades	1,730	1,810	1,350	135	**5,025**	2,190	2,840
Finance and Insurance	145	1,090	300	35	**1,575**	550	1,020
Real Estate	65	340	270	70	**745**	290	455
Business Service	345	2,000	900	70	**3,305**	1,845	1,460
Government Service	205	865	550	50	**1,665**	885	785
Educational Service	370	1,505	1,540	85	**3,505**	1,355	2,155
Health and Social Service	235	1,570	825	115	**2,750**	745	2,005
Accommodation, Food and Beverage Services	1,485	1,310	600	75	**3,465**	1,535	1,930
Other Service Industries	905	1,625	995	130	**3,650**	1,375	2,275

Source: 1996 Census—Statistics Canada—94F0009XDB96003.
Category: The 1996 Dimensions Series.

Table 5.10 Japanese Canadians, Ages Fifteen Years and Older Who Worked since January 1, 1995, by Occupation (Showing Sex Distribution), 1996

Occupation Group	Age Group 15–24	25–44	45–64	65 and Over	Total Age Group	Sex Male	Female
Total Population 15 Years and Over	6,700	17,520	11,560	1,315	**37,090**	18,600	18,495
Senior Managers	15	260	385	45	**710**	620	95
Middle and Other Managers	120	2,015	1,400	120	**3,660**	2,435	1,220
Professionals	550	4,340	2,540	255	**7,695**	4,010	3,680
Semiprofessionals and Technicians	430	1,385	825	100	**2,740**	1,510	1,230
Supervisors	30	185	120	15	**360**	165	190
Supervisors: Crafts and Trades	10	320	270	100	**700**	600	105
Administrative and Senior Clerical Persons	150	1,100	810	70	**2,130**	360	1,175
Skilled Sales and Service	170	955	540	75	**1,740**	1,080	660
Skilled Crafts and Trades	145	640	695	85	**1,560**	1,435	130
Clerical Personnel	790	2,250	1,205	115	**4,365**	1,055	3,305
Intermediate Sales and Service Personnel	2,030	2,510	1,210	105	**5,855**	1,815	4,040
Semiskilled Manual	360	625	750	95	**1,830**	1,480	355
Other Sales and Service Personnel	1,535	675	515	75	**2,805**	1,265	1,540
Other Manual Workers	360	250	280	40	**935**	765	165

Source: 1996 Census—Statistics Canada—94F0009XDB96003.
Category: The 1996 Dimensions Series.

CHAPTER 6

Japanese Chileans

**DEVELOPED IN COLLABORATION WITH THE SOCIEDAD
JAPONESA DE BENEFICENCIA, "NIKKEI-CHILE"**

BETWEEN 1910 AND 1940, THE NUMBER OF JAPANESE IMMIGRANTS WHO ENTERED the country never exceeded nine hundred. Among those who came to Chile was a wide variety of individuals ranging from professionals and businessmen to laborers remigrating from neighboring countries. They tended to be dispersed in the nitrate-rich north and to be attracted particularly to the southern regions of Valparaíso and Santiago. They found employment in a variety of jobs as salaried workers and in small business pursuits, especially as barbers. The early Nikkei society was overwhelmingly male. The majority of Issei men married Chilean women. Their children, the Nisei, were raised in the belief that "if they are going to live in Chile, let them be Chilean." However, the Pacific War stirred up anti-Japanese sentiments and disrupted the Nikkei's process of integration into Chilean society. Starting in early 1943, several dozen Nikkei were forced to move from strategically sensitive areas (like copper mines) to the interior of the country. Meanwhile, the Japanese community gained greater unity, offering mutual support in the face of wartime hostility. These ties would resurface after the war with the organization of the Japanese Beneficence Society (Sociedad Japonesa de Beneficencia). By the 1990s, Chilean Nikkei enjoyed middle-class status, a high level of education, and employment in white-collar jobs. Unlike other Latin American countries with Nikkei populations, no more than 5 percent of the Nikkei population has gone to Japan for dekasegi work. The small size of the Japanese community, its lack of cohesion, and the predominance of mixed marriages call into question the future of the Chilean Nikkei.

Japanese Immigrants and Nikkei Chileans

ARIEL TAKEDA

INTRODUCTION

Any attempt to define the origins and development of Japanese immigration to Chile is filled with complexities. There is almost no recorded data, and in developing information there is great confusion between personal aims, circumstances, and historical facts. Early Japanese immigration to Chile was the result of a spontaneous migration undertaken by a small number of people who were driven by their own hopes and dreams. Japanese collectivism was scarce, due to the small number of immigrants that arrived in Chile; individuality played a very powerful role in the attempts of the Japanese to achieve their goals.

All Japanese who came to Chile were in search of opportunities; while some ended up returning to their homelands, some found refuge in other countries, and others decided to stay. Among those who settled in Chile, the majority, with silent stubbornness, almost always chose to live obscure lives in small, unknown communities. For this reason, unique landmarks or significant historical data that can be used to define the Chilean Nikkei[1] community are few and far between, waiting to be discovered in old family trunks and gathering dust in people's attics. Therefore, this study is not only a retelling of historical events but also a compilation of different people's recollections and interpretations—a personal/historical essay of sorts. We have chosen to present our history in this manner because it is the only way to establish a co-

Japanese ship, Rakuyo Maru, *leaving the port of Yokohama, Japan, for Valparaíso, Chile, 1928. (Collection of Sociedad Japonesa de Beneficencia)*

herent understanding of the immigration of Japanese who ultimately became the Chilean Nikkei.

MOTIVATIONS TO TRAVEL TO CHILE

The presence of Japanese in Chile began rather early. In fact, the 1875 census counted two Japanese; during the rest of the nineteenth century there were approximately twenty Japanese, despite the serious disturbances that affected the country—the War of the Pacific against Peru and Bolivia, 1879–1883[2], and the Revolution of 1891, which was a Chilean internal armed conflict that culminated in the suicide of President Manuel Balmaceda (1886–1891). With the dawn of the twentieth century, the numbers of Japanese increased with much greater speed, due in part to a number of events and factors.

Chile's Role as Victor of the War of the Pacific and the Peak of the Nitrate Industry

The end of the conflict gave Chile international prestige and unexpected prosperity, an economic boom that lasted until the second decade of the twentieth century.[3] These fortuitous conditions, combined with the freedom, beauty, and bounty of the Chilean territory and the air of freedom within, created a country very attractive to many foreigners.

Knowledge about Chile Acquired by the Japanese

In 1867, a Japanese ship arrived on Chilean shores in search of new commercial routes. In 1883, the military training vessel *Ryujo*, under the command of Ito Sikeyuki, docked at Valparaíso. Following these encounters there was an interchange of visits by merchant vessels, warships, and training vessels of both nations. In 1897, Japan and Chile signed a Treaty of Friendship, Commerce, and Navigation. In 1904, Chile sold to Japan the cruiser *Esmeralda III*.[4] In this same year, the Transoceanic Emigration Company began to discuss bringing Japanese migrants to Chile. In 1909, a Japanese consular office opened at the order of Ambassador Eki Hioki. In 1910, the Toyo Kisen shipping company began regular service to Valparaíso, and Japan participated in the inaugural exposition of the Museo de Bellas Artes (Museum of Fine Arts) in Santiago. In 1915, Japanese commercial goods were put on display in Santiago. In these first few decades the image and name of Chile gained a positive aura among the Japanese, who heard of the fortunate experiences of their countrymen who returned triumphant to Japan after a few years of living in Chile. Some of these migrants returned again to Chile to establish permanent roots.

Another factor that lead us to believe that Chile rapidly became well known among the Japanese in general is that

Estado Street in Santiago, Chile, 1916. (Collection of Sociedad Japonesa de Beneficencia)

Japanese immigrants came to Chile from all over Japan. Only three prefectures (Iwate, Kochi, and Shimane) were without representation in the Chilean national territory (see supplementary materials, table 6.1, "Japanese Emigration to Chile by Prefecture of Origin, Pre-1940").

Planned Migration of Japanese to the Americas

Planned migration began first to the United States of America, then to Mexico, Peru, Brazil, and Argentina. Unfortunately, Chile stayed on the fringes of migration to the Americas, due to the xenophobic attitudes of affluent groups of Chilean businessmen and Creole (descendants of the Spanish born in Chile) politicians. However, unaware of these anti-Japanese sentiments, some immigrants who went to Peru or Bolivia ended up settling in northern Chile. Their presence greatly influenced the solidification of the spontaneous Japanese immigration to Chile. In fact, Shozo Ota (one of the Japanese Chilean pioneers) recalls that when Ambassador Hioki traveled to the north of the country, he was greatly impressed by the large amount of commercial activity generated by the nitrate industry and by the Japanese who worked in Iquique, a northern port directly involved in the nitrate boom. In 1907 there were already 159 Japanese in the north. In addition, there were thirty-eight Japanese settled in the central region and twelve in the south.

Caricature of Ambassador Eki Hioki of Japan, appearing in the magazine Sucesos, *Chile, 1913. (Collection of* Sucesos)

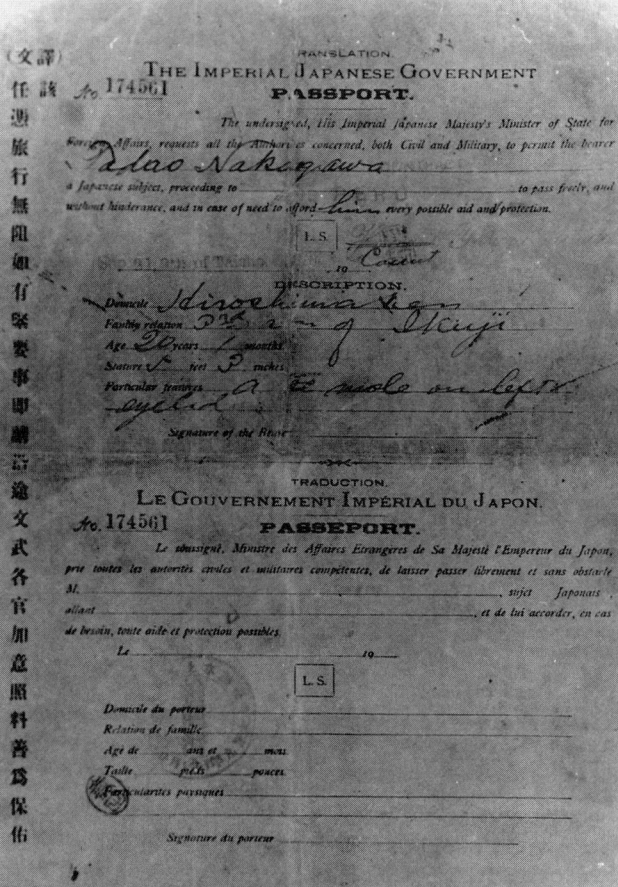

Japanese passport of Tadao Nakagawa, who immigrated to Peru, September 21, 1920. He later settled permanently in Iquique, Chile, in January 1921. (Collection of Sociedad Japonesa de Beneficencia)

View of the port at Valparaíso, Chile (V Region), 1905. (Collection of Sociedad Japonesa de Beneficencia)

THE WEAK MIGRATORY FLOW TO CHILE

There is no doubt that the decisive factor that explains the smallness of the number of Japanese that migrated to Chile was the lack of a planned migratory movement. A persistent negative attitude against the influx of Japanese lasted until the 1950s. Any situation related to their presence was labeled as "a grave danger to Chile." Furthermore, making one's own way to America, and to Chile in particular, was made almost impossible by poor Japanese economic situations. Such great hurdles meant that only a small number could even attempt the adventure. Among those who could were: (a) children of families with sufficient resources; (b) those who could count on special opportunities (e.g., seamen on ships traveling to the American continent, individuals called over by families or friends already residing in Chile, or people contracted to work as professionals); (c) those who for various circumstances changed their travel itineraries and ended up in

A group photograph of the Japanese residents of Iquique settlement, with the consul of Japan, the Hon. Horacio Mujica Mardoes, and his wife, seated in the second row, third and fourth from the left, 1929. (Collection of Sociedad Japonesa de Beneficencia)

Chile; and (d) those who were part of planned migratory movements that ended up close to Chile's borders.

Two international events (the global economic depression of 1930 and World War II) and one national event (the decline of the nitrate industry) completed the Japanese migratory pattern. The invention of synthetic nitrate during World War I forced Chile to wake up to a stark reality—the mainstay of its economy plummeted sharply. One by one, the Offices of the Pampa (nitrate processing and distribution centers) and the job centers they had generated shut down. The income of hundreds of families fell below the poverty line, and those of the Japanese who provided services for these families as well. The domino effect of the great economic crisis and later World War II forced Chile to break its relations with the Axis powers in 1943 and close its borders. Therefore, the somber panorama that loomed over Chile from the 1920s onward tarnished its special, dreamlike attractiveness and became another reason for the reduction in the influx of immigrants. It is certain that in the decade between 1910 and 1920 only 448 Japanese nationals arrived in Chile, and that only 391 did so in the decades that followed.

The exceptional living conditions evident in the first quarter of the century had disappeared. Copper began to take the place of nitrate, but six long decades had to pass before new opportunities leading to an economic revival could occur.

GEOGRAPHIC DISPERSION AND THE VARIETY OF LABOR SOURCES

One characteristic of the Japanese pioneers was their geographic dispersion and mobility. The mere two hundred Japanese who came during the first decade of the twentieth century settled down in at least nine different areas, spread over three thousand kilometers. Although the majority was concentrated in the nitrate-rich north, in Val-

Japanese Chileans 181

Ishikawa Hayashi, a Japanese immigrant who was a medical doctor in Japan, had to practice as a physical therapist since his medical training and title were not recognized in Chile, 1929. (Collection of Sociedad Japonesa de Beneficencia)

paraíso and Santiago, by 1920 they were already settled in twice as many places. In time the numbers of Japanese almost tripled, but this increase in numbers did not bring union. Surely, the tendency to disperse can be explained only by the lack of family ties or common goals that could otherwise have worked as unifying elements. Moreover, as these new immigrants filled their lungs with the fresh air of freedom, unknown to them before, they began to look for opportunities previously unavailable to them; as they followed their dreams, distances became less of an obstacle. By 1940, the areas in which they had chosen to settle down had increased to twenty-three provinces (see supplementary materials, table 6.3, "Distribution of Japanese Population by Province, 1907–1940").

The kinds of labor they took up are also noteworthy for their diversity. Almost forty different occupations have been documented. Independent labor accounted for a plurality (43 percent), within which the occupation of barber made up 30 percent. Commerce became the occupation of around 24 percent of the Japanese population, salaried labor of 15 percent, and land cultivation of another 15 percent. The remaining 3 percent did various other kinds of work.

Independent jobs were of many types: merchants, hatters, shoe repairmen, bakers, masseurs, and gardeners, among others. Barbers tended to be concentrated in ports (Iquique, Antofagasta, and Valparaíso) and their surrounding areas. This was a popular profession because it could be learned quickly, involved few overhead costs, could be practiced without necessarily knowing Spanish, and could be pursued independently. Those who followed this profession were able to form guilds; they gained the respect of their communities by their kindness, solidarity, and cultural contributions.

Merchants varied by field of interest and level of commerce—from street vendors to importers of Japanese goods. They were spread out all over the country and helped in the settlement of Japanese in the south, especially in Concepción, Temuco, and Valdivia.

Those hired as salaried workers also held diverse types of jobs. They worked for either well-established Japanese who had covered their travel expenses to Chile, or for people who received them as "scholarship recipients" *(becados)*.[5] Generally speaking, they worked for both Japanese and Chilean employers in a wide range of jobs. Added to these jobs were those provided by well-known Japanese companies that were starting to cast their eyes on Chile, positions available with diplomatic delegations, and jobs with technical teams from Japan that came fully staffed with personnel.

Finally, there were those who concentrated on farming. They cultivated rice and other grains, some fruit, and especially ornamental plants and flowers (which continue to have special significance today). There were also poultry farmers and beekeepers. They chose primarily the center of the country for their activities.

It should be noted that the Japanese who settled in mining regions did not work as miners but rather as providers of services to the miners; that the fishing industry had few followers among them; and that the scarce capital that arrived was invested primarily in commerce and agriculture.

FAMILY AND THE EDUCATION OF CHILDREN

The first immigrants were predominantly men who came alone; about 50 percent were less than twenty-five years old. More than ten years had to pass before the first five Japanese women entered the country. The disparity in

Japanese hatmaker Asazo Kodama (left) and his assistant seated inside his shop located in the center of Santiago, Chile, ca. 1930s. (Collection of Sociedad Japonesa de Beneficencia)

numbers between the sexes slowly decreased, but by 1940 women were still in the minority by a ratio of three to one (see supplementary materials, table 6.2, "Japanese Population in Chile, 1875–1940"). This reality strongly limited the possibility of marriage with Japanese women. It was also almost impossible to travel to Japan and ask for a bride's hand in marriage, because the meager wages available did not allow for much saving. The majority of Japanese men, after an average of ten years of living outside of Japan, not having fulfilled their original dreams, began to plant roots in Chile, marrying Chilean women and thus forming the Chilean Nikkei.

These mixed marriages[6] were subject to certain influences, whether great or little, that helped to shape their homes and future Nikkei generations. These factors included: (a) difficulties in communication between husband and wife; (b) the great cultural divide that existed between them; (c) the weakness or nonexistence of a nearby Japanese environment that might have provided support to the husband; (d) the great feeling of geographical and psychological isolation experienced by immigrants; and (e) the idiosyncrasies of Chilean woman, who, inside their homes, extended their own customs and values to those around them.

Under the weight of these factors, the Issei husband was forced to adapt quickly to his new cultural surroundings, which transformed him despite his wishes. He had to give preference to the Spanish language, accept his new culture's manners and customs, and adopt the Catholic religion.[7] This new reality made the mother and the surrounding cultural environment assume a more significant role in the development and education of the children born into the family. The Issei father was faced with the remoteness of Japan and the immediate exigency of his newly acquired responsibilities. He decided, regarding his children, "If they are going to live in Chile, let them be Chilean."

Furthermore, recognizing that it would be impossible to amass material wealth to leave to his children, he provided them with the legacy of a good education. In every

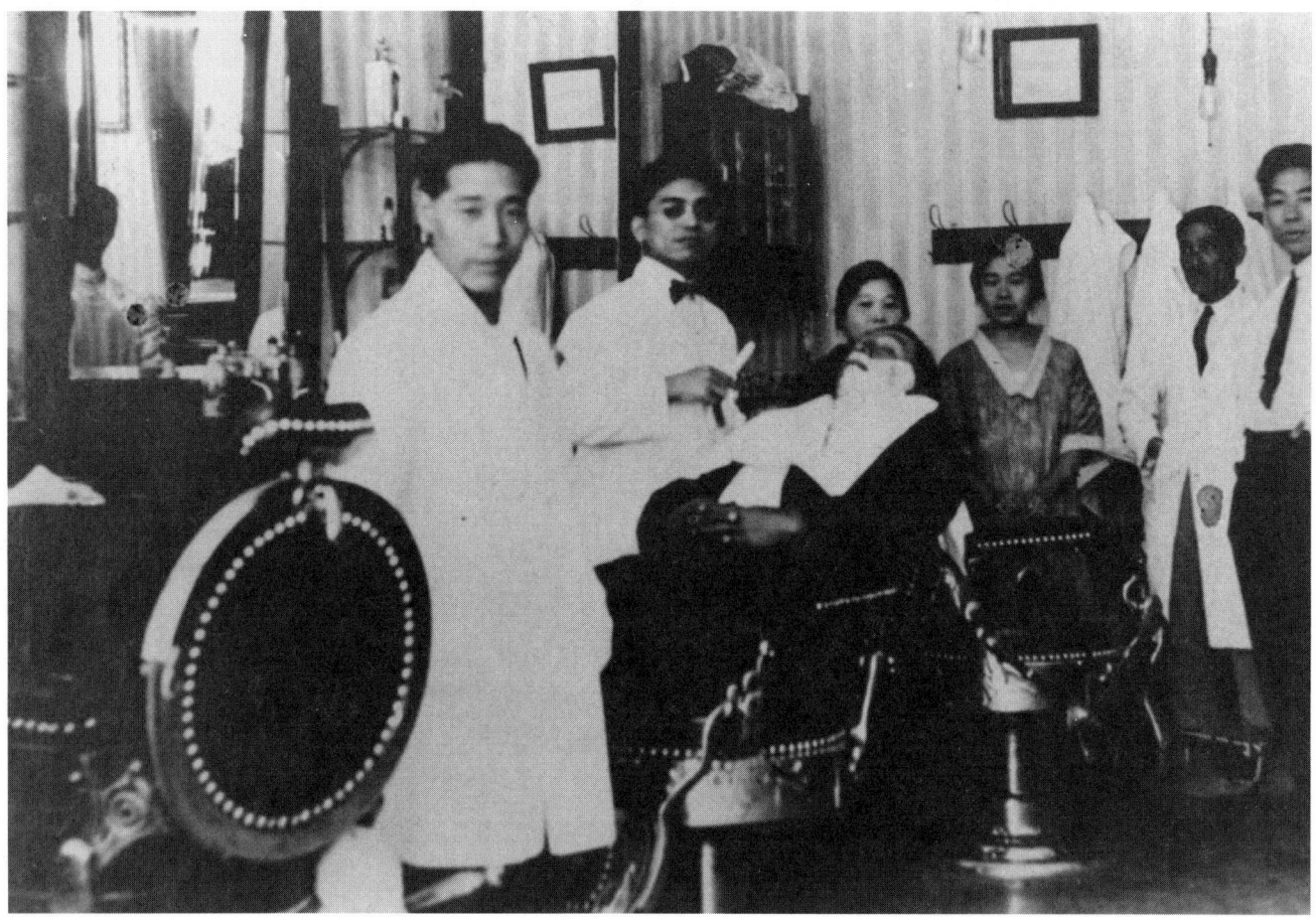

"El Sol" of Kiyoki Kataoka, a barbershop located in Chuquicamata (II Region) before World War II. (Collection of Sociedad Japonesa de Beneficencia)

home, the formal education[8] of the children took precedence over everything else. But this decision was made at the expense of relinquishing Japanese culture. According to a 1998 survey done for the Fourth National Nikkei Gathering, organized by the Japanese Beneficence Organization (Sociedad Japonesa de Beneficencia), the Japanese culture represented by the father tends to decrease to 50 percent in the Nisei generation (his children); by the Sansei generation (his grandchildren), the cultural loss is sometimes as high as 75 percent.

Immigrants who married Japanese women created positive environments within their homes that favored the retention of Japanese culture. However, at the same time, the Chilean cultural environment prevailed over these influences as the children grew up. Later unions between Japanese woman and Chilean men were to retain and transmit Japanese culture to a greater degree than those between Japanese men and Chilean women. (In these cases it is the Japanese woman who fights to preserve her culture.)

THE JAPANESE COMMUNITIES AND WORLD WAR II

Until the end of 1941, there were no obvious problems for Japanese immigrants due to the war being fought by Germany in Europe and by Japan in the Far East. On all levels, very harmonious relations were maintained—so much so that for the centennial celebration of the founding of Santiago, the Japanese community presented an enormous Chilean flag made of Japanese silk. It was flown for the first time in the center of Santiago on May 21, 1941. During this time, the Nikkei remained in close and permanent contact with Japan through the International Red Cross.

Japan's attack on Pearl Harbor in December 1941 and the immediate entry of the United States into the conflict led to complications. Chile was under diplomatic pressure to take sides in the conflict (copper was of great strategic importance). The Axis powers lost the support of the print media that had favored them, while their opponents increased the violence of their attacks upon them. Once

The interior of Casa Comercial Akita, an import business located in Coquimbo, Chile (IV Region), established by Yosokichi Akita, 1919. (Collection of Sociedad Japonesa de Beneficencia)

more, the "Japanese Peril" became a concern, and it was used to justify concentration camps, expropriation of properties, deportation, and exile. "Black lists"[9] arose and grew longer. Fear and apprehension among the Nikkei were widespread, and precautionary measures were taken (for example, switching titles of property to neutrals). Nevertheless, when Chile's relations with the Axis powers were broken off altogether, the ensuing repression was not as harsh as had been anticipated. It was only months before the end of the war in 1945 that Chile declared war on the Axis powers.

On January 27, 1943, the newspaper *El Mercurio* published a decree of the Ministry of the Interior exiling seventy-six Japanese to towns in the interior of the country, but by that date these Japanese had already been exiled. In Concepción, a large country estate called "Andalién" was expropriated, and several small businesses were closed down. Chuquicamata[10] became known for its particularly virulent treatment of Japanese residents. On the average, the period of exile lasted only six months, except for one family that was in exile until 1949.

During this period the Japanese "communities"[11] or "societies" showed great strength in their actions to achieve greater unity and provide mutual support. A large percentage of the affected families were forced to restructure their lives. The majority of the Chilean population did not participate in these political matters and continued to live alongside the Nikkei, without causing them any major problems.

THE POSTWAR CHILEAN NIKKEI

Once diplomatic relations with Japan were restored in 1952, life started to return to normal. In 1954, the Japanese community in Santiago (which had tried to consolidate even before the war) formalized its "Japanese Society" as the "Japanese Beneficence Society." In 1960, a census registered less than five hundred Japanese, but the few Japanese who were in Chile on a temporary basis fore-

Japanese immigrant Haruo Monma, age seventeen, a graduate of an agricultural technical school, who arrived as a scholarship winner in V Region of Chile, 1937. (Collection of Sociedad Japonesa de Beneficencia)

Suegorō Sone, an immigrant who arrived in Chile in 1917 and traveled back to Japan to marry his bride Kata Mizunuma in 1919. (Collection of Sociedad Japonesa de Beneficencia)

Yoshijirō Kimura and his wife Sako Hirahara, one of the first married couples to arrive in Chile, accompanied by their four children, 1911. (Collection of Sociedad Japonesa de Beneficencia)

shadowed the astonishing flourishing of economic activity that was to follow. Japanese venture capital started to flow into mining, commerce, fishing, banking, and forestry activities.

In 1963, the Japanese External Trade Organization (JETRO) arrived to Chile, and in 1980, the Chilean-Japanese Chamber of Industry and Commerce was created. In 1983, the Japan International Corporation Agency (JICA) began its operations as a result of an agreement on technical cooperation signed between Chile and Japan in 1978. In 1992, 761 Japanese appeared in the national census. In 1999, the Japanese embassy in Chile reported that the Japanese population totaled 1,237 (796 men and 441 women). Among them were 402 permanent residents (238 men and 164 women); the remaining 835 (558 men and 277 women) were only temporary residents.

Chilean national flag presented to the city of Santiago by the residents of the Japanese Association of Chile, commemorating the four-hundredth year of municipal government, 1941, Santiago, Chile. (Collection of Sociedad Japonesa de Beneficencia)

Sumiko Kawashima, Issei woman who contributed twenty-five years of her life (1971–1996) to the diffusion of Japanese culture in the community, Santiago, Chile. Deceased in 1996. (Collection of Sociedad Japonesa de Beneficencia)

In 1992, the Japanese Beneficence Society and JICA represented 1,614 Nikkei throughout the country, approximately 80 percent of the total Nikkei population. They were spread out over eleven regions,[12] and they mostly belonged to the middle class (see supplementary materials, table 6.4, "Nikkei Population by Gender and Regional Distribution, 1992," and table 6.5, "Nikkei Families by Income, 1992"). Altogether they numbered more that two thousand, and they tended to prefer the Chilean lifestyle over the Japanese, even while trying to fill the voids on the Japanese side.

In this respect, the Fourth National Nikkei Gathering in 1998 noted: (a) that Nikkei fathers lacked the time to relate with their children in an effective manner so that they might transmit Japanese feelings, experiences, and knowledge; (b) the smallness of the Japanese community and its lack of cohesion diluted its influence on the Nikkei;

(c) the predominance of mixed marriages increased the possibility of adopting Chilean lifestyles; (d) the lack of tangible motivational forces that might favor getting closer to Japanese culture; and (e) the inability in the Japanese community—considering its limited resources and size—to motivate people, bring them together, and increase the number of sponsored activities designed to educate people and make them more aware of Japanese culture.

WOMEN AND THE NIKKEI HOUSEHOLD

A survey conducted by the International Nikkei Research Project (INRP)–Chile Commission in December 1999, conducted among a sampling of sixty Nikkei households in the northern and central regions, confirmed the trends that have been described. This survey was conducted exclusively among households either directly or indirectly

Chilean residents send blankets to Japan during World War II through the Red Cross International, 1942. (Collection of Sociedad Japonesa de Beneficencia)

Newspaper headline refers to the "dangerous Japanese" and measures to be taken, 1942. (Collection of Sociedad Japonesa de Beneficencia)

Civil servant Yokichi Shinya of the Japanese legation (seated with child on lap) and his family, who were consigned to the interior of the central zone (Puemo) on January 1, 1943, and held there until 1949. (Collection of Sociedad Japonesa de Beneficencia)

linked to a Japanese organization, in Santiago or another region (some 100 to 150 families). The results of the survey represent approximately one-fourth of the "Nikkei universe" in Chile. Presumably an even greater tendency to drift away from Japanese roots can be found among the three-fourths of the Nikkei population who were not represented in this survey. Among the wives, 50 percent were non-Nikkei Chileans, 42 percent were Sansei or Nisei, and 8 percent were Issei. Among the husbands, 39 percent were non-Nikkei Chileans, 54 percent were Sansei or Nisei, and 7 percent were Issei. Therefore, in 89 percent of the marriages one of the spouses were non-Nikkei Chilean.

The wife's primary activity continues to be as a homemaker (67 percent). In 12 percent of the households, both the husband and wife speak Japanese; however, Japanese is spoken in the home only 3 percent of the time. The percentage of time spent speaking Japanese in the home increases slightly in the case of Issei families and in homes where Issei relatives live. In 13 percent of the cases, all or some of the children know Japanese, and in 17 percent of the cases the children have been to Japan (*dekasegi*-type work has contributed to this). Friendships with other Nikkei are scarce. The adults of the family customarily get together with other Nikkei in 30 percent of the cases, whereas only 12 percent of the children do the same. When the children marry, they choose other Nikkei in only 8 percent of the cases. Fifty-nine percent of the children are students; the rest work. Thirty-two percent of the students who pursue higher education show a preference for engineering, 18 percent go into teaching, and 14 percent choose health-related careers. Of those who work, 24 percent are in engineering, 21 percent are salaried employees, 10 percent are teachers, and 6 percent work in health-related services. Laborers make up 2 percent of the total. Among the wives, 25 percent say that they are involved in activities related to the diffusion of Japanese culture, and 34 percent believe their children will transmit this culture to their offspring, because the opportunities to do so will be better (see supplementary materials, document 6.1, "Survey of Nikkei Families, December 1999").

THE DEKASEGI IN CHILE

The dekasegi[13] comprise a little over a hundred Nikkei, are mainly from the Metropolitan Region (Santiago). They represent no more than 5 percent of the Nikkei population and are predominantly from families with limited economic means. For the most part, they have completed at least high school (twelve years of education); among them are some technicians and working professionals. About 20 percent returned to Chile after a stay of four to five years. Those who remain in Japan have established themselves there, either bringing over their families or starting families with other Chilean or Latin American dekasegi. Those that have returned consider themselves lucky, because they have improved their economic situations, have helped out their families, and have grown culturally. They long for Japanese culture and Japanese-style efficiency and the high economic compensation that they received. None of them complain about the treatment they receive at work or the work assigned to them. On the contrary, they yearn for new opportunities to return to Japan.[14]

CONCLUSIONS

The history of the Chilean Nikkei is similar to that of other Latin American Nikkei who could not count on the advantages of a planned migration movement. The cultural fruits gathered by the pioneers and enjoyed by their descendents are the products of hard, steady work by which they have reached beyond the family circle, despite their lack of resources. The concept of Japanese "community" has limited application to the Chilean Nikkei, because their collective efforts over the course of history have not contributed significantly to the preservation and transmission of the Nikkei cultural heritage. However, despite the tangible loss of their Japanese legacy, the Chilean Nikkei continue to cultivate the virtues that flow in their mixed blood. The main preoccupation continues to be the education of the children, and sleepless nights are reduced by knowledge of their children's growing academic achievement. Presently, it is very hard to find a Nikkei who has not finished high school, and all have plans for professional careers. More than approximately 75 percent of the young people over twenty years of age are studying to become

Family photo of Sansei Kimio Naito and his wife María Galleguillos, her mother Berta Guajardo, and their children Hasuko, Kimiko, and Takeshi in Antofagasta, 1999. (Collection of Sociedad Japonesa de Beneficencia)

Sansei couple Kenji Kodama and Alejandra Miura with their three children represents one of the few marriages between Nikkei, 1999. (Collection of Sociedad Japonesa de Beneficencia)

Nikkei delegates from throughout the Americas gather at the closing dinner of the Pan-American Nikkei Association's Tenth Conference held in Santiago, Chile, Saturday, July 31, 1999: (seated) James Hirabayashi (far right), Akemi Kikumura-Yano (second from right); (standing) Emilio Higa (second right). (Photograph by Marilyn Alquizola)

María Isabel Vergara Kimura is among other Nikkei Chilean dekasegi working in Nagoya, Seki, and other areas, who actively participates in the diffusion of Chilean artisan culture in Japan. Photo taken in Seki in 1994. (Collection of Sociedad Japonesa de Beneficencia)

professionals, and their way of life continues to resemble that of their ancestors: simple, silent, dignified, responsible, and positively involved with those around them.

NOTES

1. Chilean Nikkei: An Issei who decides to stay permanently within the Chilean territory and makes Chile his or her second homeland; all of the descendants of such a person.
2. The War of the Pacific, 1879–1883, pitting Chile against Peru, involved conflict over the nitrate concessions.
3. Having won the War of the Pacific, Chile took control of all the nitrate and became the only volume exporter of this product. Nitrate was highly valued, and likewise highly priced, because it was very effective as a fertilizer, and also a necessary raw material for gunpowder.
4. The *Esmeralda III* had state-of-the-art technology at the time that Chile sold it to Japan in 1904. It was renamed the *Itzumi* and played a leading role in the Russo-Japanese War. Russia protested against Chile's sale of the warship.

5. *Becados:* Japanese graduates of technical schools who came to Chile to work. The Japanese government gave them a salary for two years, which was paid through an *apoderado*. The *apoderados* were honorable persons who took the Japanese under their care and gave them work. The support given to these becados was the only concrete contribution that the government gave to the Japanese emigrants of Chile. This form of support still exists today, on a larger scale.
6. "Mixed marriages" during these times referred to an Issei male married to a Chilean female. Years later, there would be marriages between Issei females and Chilean males. Today in Chile, "Nikkei mestizos" (individuals with mixed Japanese and Chilean blood) predominate.
7. The Catholic religion was and is the most widely practiced religion in Chile and among Japanese emigrants. Presently, 72 percent practice the Catholic religion, 2 percent practice, other religions and 26 percent have no religious preference.
8. The formal education made available by the Chilean government through its educational institutions include: *prebásica* (kindergarten), *básica* (elementary), *media* (high school), and *superior* (higher education). Technicians and professionals begin to get their training in high school and continue to a higher education level.
9. These lists included the names of all the Japanese residing in Chile who supposedly posed a threat to national Chilean security (there were also lists of Germans and Italians). The state agency responsible for compiling these lists was Department 50 of the Chilean Bureau of Investigation.
10. Chuquicamata, the largest open copper mine in the world, began copper exploitation in 1913. As the mine was in the hands of North American capital investors in the 1940s, any Japanese working there was considered an enemy. All jobs were either taken away from, or denied to, Japanese workers. This happened in other mining centers where North Americans had the strongest voice.
11. The "Japanese communities" were informal organizations formed in cities with concentrations of immigrants. Their aim was to facilitate the unity of the Japanese locals as well as to foster joint actions and activities. But because numbers were small, it was not possible to achieve their objectives. Presently, these organizations continue to exist, with varying levels of efficiency. Santiago is home to the only legally established organization, the Sociedad Japonesa de Beneficiencia (Japanese Beneficence Society).
12. Regions: A political division of the country. Chile is divided into twelve regions and one Metropolitan Region (where the capital is located—Santiago de Chile). Each region is subdivided into provinces, and these in turn are divided into departments and communities.
13. Dekasegi are migrants who do dekasegi-type work (for example, work as migrant laborers) in Japan.
14. The data on Chilean dekasegi reality is based on surveys conducted by the INRP-Chile Commission in 1999, which included the families of dekasegi of the Metropolitan Region and the V Region.

Japanese Chilean Bibliographic Essay: General Historical Perspective

NAOMI HIROSE, MARÍA TERESA SENDA, AND ARIEL TAKEDA

INTRODUCTION

Currently, research and interest in the history and development of the Nikkei community in Chile are still in an embryonic stage. Consequently, bibliographic materials are practically nonexistent. The Japanese Chilean historical overview in this chapter discusses the reasons for this apparent lack of interest, including the notable geographic dispersion of the Japanese community, their diversity of occupations, their small numbers, and their accelerated integration into the environment. This reality has caused the Chilean Nikkei to turn inward and to center their aspirations on family life. Hence they are only loosely linked to the group, and the many efforts toward building community solidarity, both past and present, have been marked by difficulties.

What little has been recorded has been found in personal correspondence, in long-forgotten manuscripts dealing with observations on family life, rare newspaper clippings from different locations in Chile, formal records of certain Japanese organizations, the Nikkei census of 1992, few references in articles published by and for Japanese community organizations, and in the records of some national and Pan American Nikkei conferences.

In desultory efforts to salvage the hidden stories of the early Japanese immigrants for future generations, a few individuals preserved information, now decades old, of undoubtedly great value to students who are interested in this subject. A starting point is the centennial celebration of the Treaty of Friendship and Commerce between Chile and Japan in 1997, the year in which the first and only book to deal directly with the Chilean Nikkei experience was written by a Chilean commission (S-2).

PRESS AND SENATE RECORDS

Given that in Chile there is no Nikkei press, the first known references to Japanese, "Orientals," or "Chinese" (terms considered nearly synonymous) appear in the national press around 1906, before massive immigration was perceived as a possible "risk" to the Chilean people and economy. The topic is dealt with in a generic fashion and without reference to specific immigrants, since the few immigrants that were already settled and the trickle of new arrivals passed unnoticed. Perhaps the first known direct reference is a comment on Japanese working at the Collahuasi mine in 1907 that appeared in the newspaper *El Mercurio* in Valparaíso on August 2, 1907. Other news of the period is general in nature and limited to national or regional events, such as sightings of Japanese ships in Chilean ports, the activities of the Plenipotentiary Minister Hioki in Chile (always newsworthy), the participation of Japan in the expositions for the centennial of Chilean independence in 1910 or for the Quinta Normal in 1915. Other references deal with judo at the Escuela Naval de Valparaíso (Valparaíso Naval School), which appeared in *Sucesos* in 1915, and the curiosity aroused by Japanese baseball teams.

Until the 1940s, references pertaining to people of Japanese descent are hard to find. An exception is the anticipation occasioned by the arrival of the Japanese plane *Nihon-Go* in 1939 and the resident Japanese community's ceremonial delivery of a giant flag to the city of Santiago in 1941. However, from 1942 the comments of the press become more exaggerated as the Allies put pressure on Chile during the Second World War. In 1943, the names of seventy-four Japanese who were relocated to towns in the interior of the country were published in Santiago in *El Mercurio*, on January 27, 1943.

After the war, conditions returned to normal, and once again there was only sporadic mention of events concerning the Japanese, most of it dealing with Japanese business and capital as it found its way to Chile. In 1952, the reopening of the Japanese legation and the inauguration of a Japanese park on a hillside in Santa Lucia made news, as did the centenary commemoration of the Chilean-Japanese Treaty of Friendship and Commerce in 1997. In the provinces, occasional recognition is given to an elderly neighborhood Nikkei who have made cultural or athletic contributions to the community, or whose daily interactions with others have made them beloved by their neighbors. In addition, the descendants of Japanese immigrants have attracted the attention of the press and the public by some of their activities.

Lastly, the publications of the Chilean Senate should be noted. They record key moments in the Chilean experience but distort the truth when it is politically expedient, as in the case of Japanese immigration to Chile and alleged anti-Chilean activity within the Japanese community. In a similarly equivocal manner, they present informational publications prepared by influential voices in national politics and economics.

In conclusion, very few references to the Japanese presence or works in Chile have appeared in the press. Existing reports tend to be superficial or fallacious.

GENERAL LIBRARY RECORDS

As previously mentioned, there is practically no systematically categorized body of research available on people of Japanese ancestry in Chile. Any research must be based on interviews and the gathering of isolated data from different sources. Some of this data can be found in organizations dealing with the Japanese presence in Chile, such as the Japanese embassy, the Japan International Cooperation Agency (JICA), the Japan External Trade Organization (JETRO), and the Cámara Chileno-Japonesa de Comercio e Industria (Chilean-Japanese Chamber of Commerce and Industry), which publishes a bulletin in Japanese for its members. At the cultural level there is the Instituto Chileno-Japonés de Cultura (Chilean-Japanese Institute of Culture).

The only document that contains a general bibliography on Japanese in Chile is the 1997 publication *Chile y Japón, un siglo de amistad* (Chile and Japan: A Century of Friendship) (S-2).

SPECIAL COLLECTIONS

An organization directly related to people of Japanese descent in Chile is the Japanese Beneficence Society of Santiago (Sociedad Japonesa de Beneficencia de Santiago). However, it does not have an easily accessible collection of studies or written materials, past or present. (Recently efforts have been made to discover and analyze records pertaining to a reconstruction of the history of Japanese immigration to Chile and its outcomes.) The society does offer an informational newspaper and a registry of Nikkei professionals. Aside from these publications, there is the material contributed by Nikkei conferences at the national level and records compiled by the 1999 Pan American Nikkei Convention in Chile. Undoubtedly, the original and partially translated records of the first Japanese settlers, passed on to us by a couple of Issei pioneers (S-6), and the data of the 1992 national Nikkei census (S-11), are the most valuable sources of information available. In addition there are glimpses of history in letters and documents (S-4, S-5). Faced with this dearth of resources, the Chilean-INRP Committee had no choice but to interview members of the Japanese community in order to obtain the desired information. Within the Japanese society, different groups (Showa-kai, Sakura-kai, Andes-kai, Fujin-kai, Takeno-kai, and Taisho-kai) offered a wealth of experiences and knowledge that may be very valuable, depending upon one's research goals. The same can be said of the Nikkei Association of Valparaíso, which has undertaken its own research.

No other areas of interest in Nikkei literature have yet materialized in Chile. To date, one book, dealing with Nikkei in agriculture in Region V, has been published in Valparaiso—*Presencia japonesa en la región de Valparaíso* (The Japanese Presence in the Valparaíso Region), 1997 (S-3).

To this limited bibliographical material and to the sources of information on the Nikkei in Chile can be added the present study, with its global vision of the historic unfolding of Japanese immigration to Chile. The results of this study, with the International Nikkei Research Project (INRP), may be considered the basis for a broader, more in-depth, more localized research project.

Annotated Bibliography of Japanese Chileans

COMPILED BY NAOMI HIROSE, MARÍA TERESA SENDA, AND ARIEL TAKEDA

ENGLISH

1. Akagi, Taeko. "Japanese Chileans Historical Overview." Unpublished, written for International Nikkei Research Project. Los Angeles: Japanese American National Museum, 1997.

    Brief history, timeline, and summary of information on the Japanese settlement in Chile.

JAPANESE

1. Cámara Chilena-japonesa de Comercio e Industria. *Boletín mensual*. N.p., 1995.

    The objective of this work is to acquaint the Japanese resident or visitor to Chile with Chilean institutions, daily life, and regions.

2. Estrada Turra, Baldomero. *Presencia japonesa en la región de Valparaíso: un proceso de asimilación étnica y de desarrollo agrícola*. Valparaíso, Chile: Ediciones Universitarias de Valparaíso de la Universidad Católica de Valparaíso, 1997.

    Briefly deals with the settlement of Japanese immigrants in the region of Valparaíso, where the temperate climate makes it especially suitable for the cultivation of flowers. Summarizes migrational tendencies of settlers within the region, ethnic assimilation of Japanese families, and the passing on of customs to the next generation. Japanese-Spanish Bilingual Edition. See also S-3.

SPANISH

1. "Actas de las sesiones del Consejo Directivo: Sesión 891 del 17/06/1913." *Boletín de la Sociedad de Fomento Fabril* XXX, no. 7 (July 1913).

    Meeting minutes. Confronting the fears of a possible wave of Japanese immigration to Chile, a speaker reports on the advantages and risks that the presence of Japanese poses to the country and considers their characteristics and behavior in other American countries.

2. Comisión Chilena de Celebración del Centenario de las Relaciones Chile-Japón. *Chile y Japón: un siglo de amistad*. Santiago, Chile: Comisión Chilena de Celebración del Centenario de las Relaciones Chile-Japón, 1997.

    Topics analyzed are past and present Japanese culture, the path of Chilean policy with regard to external affairs, Chile's position on the Western Pacific and Japan's on Latin America, the development of bilateral contacts, and a description of economic connections.

3. Estrada Turra, Baldomero. *Presencia japonesa en la región de Valparaíso: un proceso de asimilación étnica y de desarrollo agrícola*. Valparaíso, Chile: Ediciones Universitarias de Valparaíso de la Universidad Católica de Valparaíso, 1997.

    Briefly deals with the settlement of Japanese immigrants in the region of Valparaíso, where the temperate climate makes it especially suitable for the cultivation of flowers. Summarizes migrational tendencies of settlers within the region, ethnic assimilation of Japanese families, and the passing on of customs to the next generation. Japanese-Spanish Bilingual Edition. See also J-2.

4. Kawaguchi, Y. "Notas del señor Y. Kawaguchi." Personal note, a copy in part held by the Sociedad Japonesa de Beneficencia "Nikkei-Chile," n.p.

    Pertains to the founding and achievements of the hacienda collective "Caupolican," established in 1943 by the Japanese community of Santiago during World War II to aid Japanese detainees.

5. Kokawamura, J. "Carta personal: de Japón a Chile." Letter, held by the family. A copy is held by the Sociedad Japonesa de Beneficencia "Nikkei-Chile," 1947.

    Recollections of the fate of early settlers who returned to Japan at the beginning of World War II and of the difficulties they faced in surviving there amidst the destruction and overcrowding.

6. Ota, Shozo, and Kyutaro Tsunekawa. *Antecedentes varios sobre la colonia japonesa en Chile: manuscritos y grabaciones*. Santiago: n.p., 1940.

    A collection of recorded memories, situations, personal concerns, and impressions of the development of the Japanese community in Chile. Authenticity is limited by the informal nature of the writings and recordings. Nevertheless, a work of great interest for any student of the subject since these are the recollections of people who lived the reality of Japanese immigration.

7. República de Chile. "Declara suspendidas las relaciones diplomáticas y consulares del Gobierno de la República con los Gobiernos de Alemania, Italia y Japón." Decretos relacionados con la Segunda Guerra Mundial Decreto N° 182, 1943.

    A declaration by which the Chilean government suspended diplomatic relations with Germany, Italy, and Japan.

8. República de Chile. "Decretos con diversos números que relega a extranjeros a diversos lugares del país." Decretos relacionados con la Segunda Guerra Mundial, 1943.

Various decrees regulating foreigners to different areas in Chile.

9. *Revista de Marina* (May-June 1983 and July-August 1986).

    Historical account. Pertains to naval links between Chile and Japan.

10. Servicio Nacional de Agricultura. *Boletín de la Sociedad de Fomento Fabril* 32 (1906).

    Taking into account the scarcity of labor in Chile, this article proposes that European immigrants should be favored instead of Chinese and Japanese immigrants, due to the social and genetic repercussions of Japanese immigration on the native population.

11. Sociedad Japonesa de Beneficencia. *Censo nacional Nikkei: conclusiones.* Santiago: photocopied material, 1992.

    Census includes eleven regions and 1,614 Chilean Nikkei. Completed by heads of household, collects private, family, and historical materials. Includes approximately 80 percent of the Nikkei community.

12. Sociedad Japonesa de Beneficencia. *Directorio de expertos y profesionales Nikkei.* Santiago: n.p., 1997.

    This publication of limited scope consists of an updated summary of the professional activities of ninety-six Chilean Nikkei experts and professionals.

13. Sociedad Japonesa de Beneficencia. *Informativo Nikkei Santiago.* Santiago: Internal publication, 1990.

    Report published by the "Society" with relative regularity since 1990. It offers its members local and national news pertaining to Nikkei activities, historical references to its early members, tidbits on Japanese culture, and the like. During the last few years there have been five issues annually.

14. Torres, Isauro. "Concesión de base ballenera a industriales japoneses." Minutes of Ordinary Legislature of the Senate of Chilean Republic: Sessions 9 and 13, 1957.

    On July 2, 1957, during the Ninth Session, Senator Isauro Torres shows the extreme national security risks of allowing the installation of Japanese whaling boats on the island of Santa María. On July 17, during the Thirteenth Session, Senator Jorge Lavandero effectively refutes his argument.

15. Villegas, Jorge. "A letter." *Boletín de la Sociedad de Fomento Fabril* XXXI, no. 7, June 1914.

    Attacks the idea of Japanese immigration. Bases its argument on the dangers of the overwhelming spirit of solidarity shown by the Japanese in their relations with each other and of their ability to rapidly make use of resources within their grasp.

16. Yanaguida, Toshio, and Dolores Rodríguez. *Japoneses en América.* Madrid: Editorial Mapfred SA, 1992.

    Contributes global information on the nature of Japanese emigration to the Americas. No references to Chile.

Supplementary Materials

COMPILED BY NAOMI HIROSE, MARÍA TERESA SENDA, AND ARIEL TAKEDA

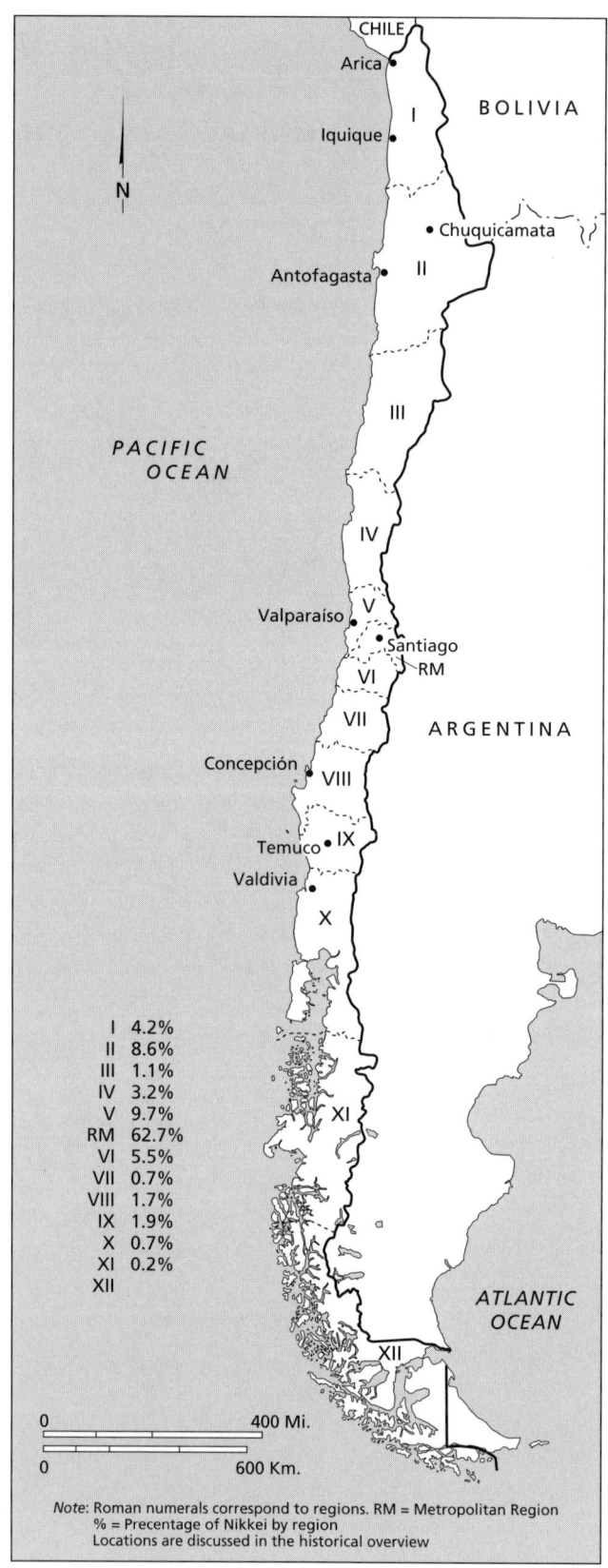

Map 6.1 Geographic Distribution of Nikkei Populations in Chile

Japanese Chilean Demographic Information

Table 6.1 Japanese Emigration to Chile by Prefecture of Origin in Japan, Pre-1940

Aichi	12	(3.1%)
Akita	1	(0.3%)
Aomori	2	(0.5%)
Chiba	9	(2.3%)
Ehime	5	(1.3%)
Fukui	4	(1.0%)
Fukuoka	13	(3.4%)
Fukushima	13	(3.4%)
Gifu	5	(1.3%)
Gunma	3	(0.8%)
Hawai`i*	3	(0.8%)
Hiroshima	32	(8.2%)
Hokkaidō	9	(2.3%)
Hyōgo	7	(1.8%)
Ibaraki	6	(1.6%)
Ishikawa	37	(9.6%)
Kagawa	1	(0.3%)
Kagoshima	18	(4.6%)
Kanagawa	25	(6.4%)
Kumamoto	35	(9.0%)
Kyōto	6	(1.6%)
Mie	1	(0.3%)
Miyagi	2	(0.5%)
Miyasaki	1	(0.3%)
Nagano	7	(1.8%)
Nagasaki	2	(0.5%)
Nara	3	(0.8%)
Niigata	2	(0.5%)
Ōita	4	(1.0%)
Okayama	3	(0.8%)
Okinawa	7	(1.8%)
Ōsaka	2	(0.5%)
Saga	2	(0.5%)
Saitama	4	(1.0%)
Shiga	7	(1.8%)
Shizuoka	23	(5.9%)
Shimane	1	(0.3%)
Tōkyō	43	(11.1%)
Toyama	2	(0.5%)
Tottori	1	(0.3%)
Wakayama	8	(2.1%)
Yamagata	3	(0.8%)
Yamaguchi	10	(2.6%)
Yamanashi	2	(0.5%)
Total	**386**	

Source: Compiled by the Sociedad Japonesa de Beneficencia, INRP-Chile Commission, December 1999, primarily based on the data gathered by the National Nikkei Census, 1992.
Note: *Hawai`i is included in this data, even though it is not a part of Japan since some of the emigrants originated from Hawai`i.

Table 6.2 Japanese Population in Chile, 1875–1940

Year	Male	Female	Total
1875	2	-	2
1885	51	-	51
1895	20	-	20
1907	204	5	209
1920	513	44	557
1930	554	116	670
1940	691	257	948

Source: Chilean population census: 1875 to 1940.

Table 6.3 Distribution of Japanese Population by Province, 1907–1940

Province	1907	1920	1930	1940
Tacna[1]	2	46	-	-
Tarapaca	98	89	89	50
Antofagasta	55	171	95	212
Atacama	1	16	13	11
Coquimbo	3	6	13	9
Aconcagua	-	8	206	88
Valparaíso[2]	24	75	-	146
Santiago	14	93	169	308
Cachapoal	-	9	-	12
Colchagua	-	2	38	5
Curicó	-	-	-	1
Talca	-	1	4	4
Linares	-	1	-	3
Maule	-	-	3	4
Ñuble	-	1	1	3
Concepción	11	8	17	18
Arauco	-	4	-	-
Bio Bio	-	4	6	4
Malleco	-	10	-	13
Cautín	-	6	4	24
Valdivia	-	2	10	16
Osorno	-	-	-	23
Llanquihue	-	5	-	4
Chiloé	2	-	1	-
Aisén	-	-	-	3
Magallanes	-	-	1	3
Totals	**210**	**557**	**670**	**964**

Source: Baldomero Estrada. *Presencia japonesa en la región de Valparaíso* (*The Japanese Presence in the Valparaíso Region*). University Editions of the Catholic University of Valparaíso, Chile, 1997.

Notes:
[1] As a result of the War of the Pacific, 1879–1883, Tacna was considered a Chilean territory from the beginning of the twentieth century until 1929.
[2] In the 1939 census, no population registry appeared for Valparaíso, as it had been absorbed by Aconcagua (which is why the Aconcagua population shows such a large concentration of Japanese).

Table 6.4 Nikkei Population by Gender and Regional Distribution, 1992

Region	Male	%	Female	%	Total	%
Metropolitan	534	33.1	478	29.6	1,012	62.7
V	76	4.7	80	5	156	9.7
II	76	4.7	63	3.9	139	8.6
VI	44	2.7	45	2.8	89	5.5
I	29	1.8	38	2.3	67	4.1
IV	27	1.7	25	1.6	52	3.3
IX	17	1.1	13	0.8	30	1.9
VIII	15	0.9	12	0.7	27	1.6
III	9	0.6	8	0.5	17	1.1
VII	4	0.2	7	0.4	11	0.6
X	8	0.5	3	0.2	11	0.7
XI	2	0.1	1	0.1	3	0.2
Total	**841**	**52.1**	**773**	**47.9**	**1,614**	**100**

Source: National Nikkei Census, 1992.
Note: The XII Region (comprising the Magellan and Antarctica Regions) did not register any Nikkei settlers.

Table 6.5 Nikkei Families by Income, 1992

Level	Urban Area	%	Rural Area	%	Total	%
Level 1	4	0.7	5	0.9	9	1.6
Level 2	28	4.9	2	0.4	30	5.3
Level 3	190	33.4	101	17.7	291	51.1
Level 4	132	23.2	69	12.1	201	35.3
Level 5	17	3	15	2.6	32	5.6
Level 6	1	0.2	5	0.9	6	1.1
Total	**372**	**65.4**	**197**	**34.6**	**569**	**100**

Source: National Nikkei Census, 1992.
 Note: Wage levels are calculated in the national currency ($) with the value in 1992.
 Codes: Level 1 = Less than one minimum wage salary
             Level 2 = 1–5 minimum wage salaries
             Level 3 = 5–10 minimum wage salaries
             Level 4 = 10–20 minimum wage salaries
             Level 5 = More than 20 minimum wage salaries
             Level 6 = Without any past historical data

DOCUMENT 6.1

SURVEY OF NIKKEI FAMILIES, DECEMBER 1999

1. **Racial Characteristics:**
   Wife: Issei: 5 (8%); Nisei/Sansei 25 (42%); Non-Nikkei Chilean: 30 (50%)
   Husband: Issei: 4 (7%), Nisei/Sansei: 32 (54%); Non-Nikkei Chilean: 24 (39%)

2. **Japanese Language Proficiency:**
   Wife: Perfectly fluent: 7 (12%); Knows a little: 2 (3%); None: 51 (85%)
   Husband: Perfectly fluent: 7 (12%); Knows a little: 9 (15%); None: 43 (72%); No answer: 1 (2%)

2.1 **Use of Japanese language at home:**
   Regularly: 2 (3%); Ocasionally: 7 (12%); Use only some words: 12 (20%)
   Only used by Issei family member or relative: 5 (8%); Never used: 34 (57%)

2.2 **Children's knowledge of Japanese language:**
   All of them speak: 0 (0%);
   Only the older children: 6 (10%);
   Only some words: 30 (50%);
   None of the children speak: 24 (40%)

3. **Relations with other Nikkei families:**
   Fathers: Relate regularly: 18 (30%); Only occasionally: 21 (35%); Almost never: 21 (35%)
   Children: Mostly relate with Nikkei: 7 (12%); Rarely relate with Nikkei: 28 (47%); Relate only with Non-Nikkei Chileans: 21 (35%); No answer: 4 (6%)

3.1 **Children's marriages:**
   With another Nikkei: 5 (8%); With non-Nikkei Chilean: 55 (92%)

4. **Consumption of Japanese food at home:**
   Regularly: 19 (32%); Rarely: 18 (30%); Never: 23 (38%)

5. **Japanese names given to children:**
   First name: 22 (37%); Second name: 13 (22%); None: 23 (38%); No answer: 2 (3%)

6. **Visits to Japan:**
   Wife: Yes: 17 (29%); No: 41 (68%)
   No answer: 2 (3%)
   Children: Some or all: 10 (17%); None: 42 (70%); No answer: 8 (13%)

7. **Relations with relatives in Japan:**
   Frequent: 18 (30%); Rare: 14 (23%); Have not located: 26 (44%); No answer: 2 (3%)

8. **Occupation held by homeowners:**
   Wife: Housewife: 40 (67%); Employed: 10 (17%); Independent professional: 8 (13%); Merchant: 2 (3%)
   Husband: Employed by Japanese company: 3 (5%); Employed: 19 (32%); Merchant: 5 (8%); Retired: 10 (17%); Independent professional/technician: 16 (27%); Agriculture: 3 (5%); Other occupations: 2 (3%); No answer: 2 (3%)

9. **Age of children in years:**
   0–10: 25 (17%); 11–20: 25 (17%); 21–30: 37 (25%); 31–40: 28 (19%); 41 and over: 33 (22%)

9.1 **Children's occupations:**
   Student (elementary – high school): 41 (31%); Student of higher learning: 28 (21%); Work: 63 (48%)

9.2 **Careers after higher studies:**
   Medicine: 4 (14%); Engineering: 9 (32%); Teaching: 5 (18%); Design: 3 (11%); Others: 7 (25%)

9.3 **Occupation held as members of the work force:**
   Engineering: 15 (24%); Medicine: 4 (6%); Design: 4 (6%); Secretary: 3 (5%); Teaching: 6 (10%); Entrepreneurs: 2 (3%); Agriculture: 4 (6%); Salaried employee: 13 (21%); Others: 12 (19%)

Source: Survey conducted by the INRP-Chile Commission in December 1999, of sixty Nikkei homes in five regions.
Note: The survey's objectives were to shed light on the behavioral tendencies inside Nikkei homes in relation to the preservation and transmission of Japanese culture, and to define some of the characteristics of the household members.

CHAPTER 7

Japanese Mexicans

**DEVELOPED IN COLLABORATION WITH
THE ASOCIACIÓN MÉXICO JAPONESA, A.C.**

ON MAY 10, 1897, THE FIRST JAPANESE IMMIGRANTS ARRIVED IN MEXICO TO start a coffee plantation in the state of Chiapas. Their venture eventually failed, but many of these immigrants married local women and established a base for future Japanese immigration to Mexico. Unlike these early settlers, the Japanese who came to northern and central Mexico between 1901 and 1907 were mainly dekasegi laborers. They found contract work in mines, railroad, and farms through the services of emigration companies. The majority of these laborers used Mexico as a stepping-stone to remigrate to the United States even after it prohibited the entry of Japanese from Mexico in March 1907. The following decade ushered in the emergence of stable Nikkei communities in the northern states, as well as in Mexico City. However, in early 1942, with the outbreak of the Pacific War, all Japanese living in Baja California were ordered to move to Mexico City and Guadalajara. Uprooted and disoriented, the resettlers were able to find housing and jobs with the assistance of the Kyoeikai of Mexico City. After the war, major shifts occurred within the Japanese Mexican community. Most of the Nikkei population remained concentrated in Mexico City and Guadalajara, and their occupations shifted from agriculture to urban small businesses. Mexico became their permanent home. The postwar Nikkei community experienced problems of factionalism and some degree of disunity, but after the mid-1950s the Japanese Mexican Association played a vital role in bringing the community together to build a Nikkei cultural center and later the Mexican Japanese Institute, under new Nisei leadership. Today, young Japanese Mexicans continue to build upon the legacy of their past while playing a more integral role in Mexico's multicultural society.

Japanese Mexican Historical Overview

JESÚS K. AKACHI, CARLOS T. KASUGA, MANUEL S. MURAKAMI, MARÍA ELENA OTA MISHIMA, ENRIQUE SHIBAYAMA, RENÉ TANAKA

THE BEGINNING

The history of the Japanese Mexican community begins around the end of the last century. On May 10, 1897, the first thirty-four Japanese arrived at Puerto Madero in the state of Chiapas, near the Guatemalan border. Dispatched by Takeaki Enomoto, the former minister of the exterior, who had headed the Colonization Society (Sociedad de Colonización) in Tokyo since 1892, these first Japanese Mexicans dreamed of establishing a prosperous coffee plantation in the coastal area of Soconusco. Despite their perseverance and struggle, however, the venture eventually failed due to the climate, rampant illness, financial strains, and a lack of necessary agricultural knowledge, among other reasons. Notwithstanding, they left a profound footprint on the future of Japanese immigration.

While many immigrants left the area in search of better work opportunities elsewhere, a core group of the so-

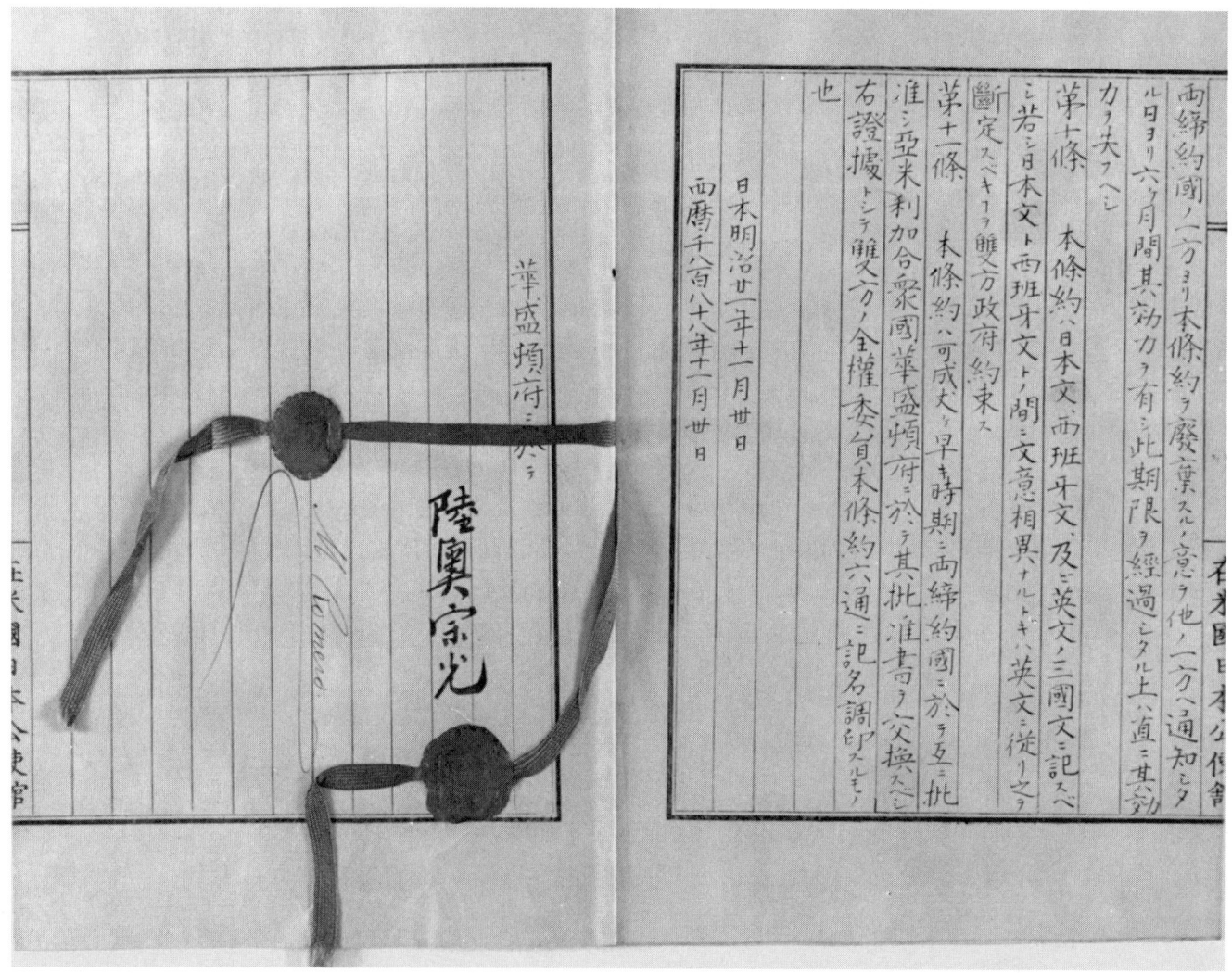

The Treaty of Amity and Commerce between Japan and Mexico, signed on November 30, 1888, between Japanese Ambassador to the United States, Munemitsu Mutsu, and Mexican ambassador to the United States, Matias Romero. This treaty was unusual in that it did not impose unequal conditions on Japan. (Collection of Ministry of Foreign Affairs Diplomatic Record Office)

Several Japanese families—Ismael Kajima, Dr. Shiba, Ricardo Arima (one of the first immigrants of the Enomoto Colony), Oscar Shibayama, Santiago Nimi, Isaac Nagaya—in Huixtla, Chiapas, a center of Japanese immigrant settlement, ca. 1930. (Collection of Asociación México Japonesa, A.C.)

called Enomoto Colony formed the Japanese Mexican Cooperative Society Company (Compañia Japonesa Mexicana Sociedad Cooperativa) in Escuintla in 1905. Possessing farms, general merchandise stores, and pharmacies, it brought additional immigrants from Japan and offered employment opportunities to the local Mexican workers. Under the leadership of Ryojiro Terui, the members of this cooperative attempted to realize the fundamental goal of the society, "to unify the Japanese and the Mexicans," by marrying Mexican women and creating truly Japanese Mexican families in Chiapas. Their contributions to the local society included daily distribution of free medicine to people who could not afford it, construction of bridges and schools, and donation of money for the construction of an aqueduct. The company continued expanding until the effects of the Mexican Revolution began to be felt in the area around 1914. Although some key leaders, including Terui, left southern Mexico after the company experienced financial problems at the end of the civil war, the foundation of the Japanese community was so firmly established in Chiapas that many others remained in the area operating businesses indispensable to the local economy.

LABOR MIGRATION: 1901–1907

Meanwhile, the mass immigration of Japanese laborers into other parts of Mexico began in 1901. Their main objective was to make their fortunes and return triumphantly to their native villages to improve the economic condition of their families. This practice was known as *dekasegi*. Until 1907, there were three groups of Japanese labor immigrants in Mexico. First, between 1904 and 1907, North American–operated sugar plantations lying between the states of Oaxaca and Veracruz attracted a total of 4,407 Japanese. Recruited by an emigration company, many came from the prefectures of Hiroshima, Okayama, Yamaguchi, Wakayama, Fukuoka, and Kumamoto, where dekasegi laborer emigration overseas was an established practice from earlier times. Second, in 1906–1907, the same emigration company arranged for the travel of over 1,400 laborers to the state of Colima to work in railroad construction. Combined with hundreds of other laborers who arrived the following year, some three hundred Japanese in Colima moved to the Montaña Negra mine in the state of Sonora after the completion of the railroad construction.

The third group of Japanese laborers consisted of over three thousand people who were sent to the Las Esperanzas coal mine in the state of Coahuila between 1901 and 1907 and some five hundred sent to the El Boreo coal mine in Baja California in 1904. As in other cases of dekasegi migration, emigration companies recruited contract laborers from rural villages in the southwestern areas of Japan. Upon arrival, these workers found themselves subject to extremely poor labor conditions, cruel treatment, and violation of their contracts, among other problems. Many refused to work, asking help from the Japanese government, while others fled northward to the United States. Those who remained finally found other lines of work. The town of Tampico became a hub of Japanese laborers who had left Las Esperanzas. They formed a community of two hundred residents with stores and a Japanese hall.

NORTHBOUND IMMIGRANTS: 1902–1907

The entry of Japanese contract laborers into Mexico ended in 1907. One estimate reveals that approximately two thousand to four thousand Japanese still remained in the country in that year, of a total of more than ten thousand laborers who had crossed the Pacific under the auspices of three emigration companies since 1901. This difference indicated the extremely fluid nature of the first

The farm managed by Copania Japonesa Mexicana Sociedad Cooperativa (Nichiboku Kyodo Kaisha), founded in 1905. Ryojiro Terui (far right), the man holding child, is one of the leaders, ca. 1910. (Collection of Asociación México Japonesa, A.C.)

Japanese immigrants to Mexico. While a minority of them returned to Japan after a few years of dekasegi labor, the majority crossed the northern border to work in the United States. In addition, the social chaos caused by the Mexican Revolution between 1910 and 1919 contributed to the volatility of the first Japanese communities in Mexico. Until the end of the 1920s, these two factors made it highly improbable for the Japanese to form a settlement in northern Mexico, despite the large number of immigrants who had entered the region.

In fact, many of the first immigrants considered Mexico a necessary step for entering the United States. Because the direct migration of laborers from Japan to Mexico's northern neighbor had become very restrictive after 1902, hundreds of aspiring dekasegi laborers claimed Mexico (for which passports were much easier to obtain from the Japanese government) as their destination. This method seemed to have been especially popular between 1906 and 1907, when the number of passports issued to emigrants

Early Japanese immigrants who worked at the mine of Kananea Company, Sonora, Mexico, ca. 1910s. (Collection of Asociación México Japonesa, A.C.)

The border of Mexicali, B.C., Mexico, and Calexico, U.S.A., ca. 1920s. (Collection of Asociación México Japonesa, A.C.)

Japanese Mexicans   207

Emiliano Zapata and his army, marching in front of Francisco Madero, 1911. (Collection of Asociación México Japonesa, A.C.)

Kisaburo Yamane, born in Yamaguchi prefecture in 1889, arrived in Mexico in 1907. He joined the army in 1911 and fought in the Mexican Revolution. In 1928, he moved to Monterrey and became a farm owner. (Collection of Asociación México Japonesa, A.C.)

Fukuoka Kenjinkai picnic, held by one of the six prefectural associations formed in Mexicali. Mexicali, Mexico, 1928. (Collection of Asociación México Japonesa, A.C.)

A float presented by the Japanese settlement won first prize in this festival in Tijuana, Mexico, September 1925. (Collection of Asociación México Japonesa, A.C.)

declaring Mexico as their destination increased drastically, from 346 in 1905 to 5,068 in 1906, dropping only to 3,822 in 1907. Since the mines and the railroad absorbed only a few thousand immigrants in these two years, one can assume that the majority of the immigrants who arrived in Mexico in 1906 and 1907 intended to go to the United States. While those who had money proceeded directly on land northward to the United States, others had to work in Mexico for a few years to collect the resources needed for that trip.

There were several routes available to enter the United States from Mexico. Among them were the points along the Rio Grande that linked Nuevo Laredo in Tamaulipas to Laredo in Texas; Piedras Negras in Coahuila to Eagle Pass in Texas; and Juárez City in Chihuahua to El Paso in Texas. One source of information indicates that over one thousand Japanese crossed the border through these routes in the course of a few months between 1906 and 1907, and that between five hundred and six hundred Japanese from Mexico stayed in San Antonio, Texas, before dispersing to other places.

As the United States tightened its control in the border checkpoints along the Rio Grande, other routes became more popular among the Japanese immigrants. After 1910, many Japanese migrants, along with those from Perú and Panamá, chose the Mexicali route, despite its more challenging climate. In Baja California, foreigners had either to pay a per capita tax of one hundred pesos at that time or engage in heavy labor at construction sites in the area. In order to avoid this financial burden, the Japanese usually had to hide in the daytime and refrain from taking public transportation, even on the Mexican side. Although many managed to cross the border with the help of Mexican guides and Japanese merchants in Mexicali, a number of others must have died on their way, since this method involved a long walk in a vast desert, where water and other vital provisions were difficult to obtain. Even so, by serving the desperate need of these im-

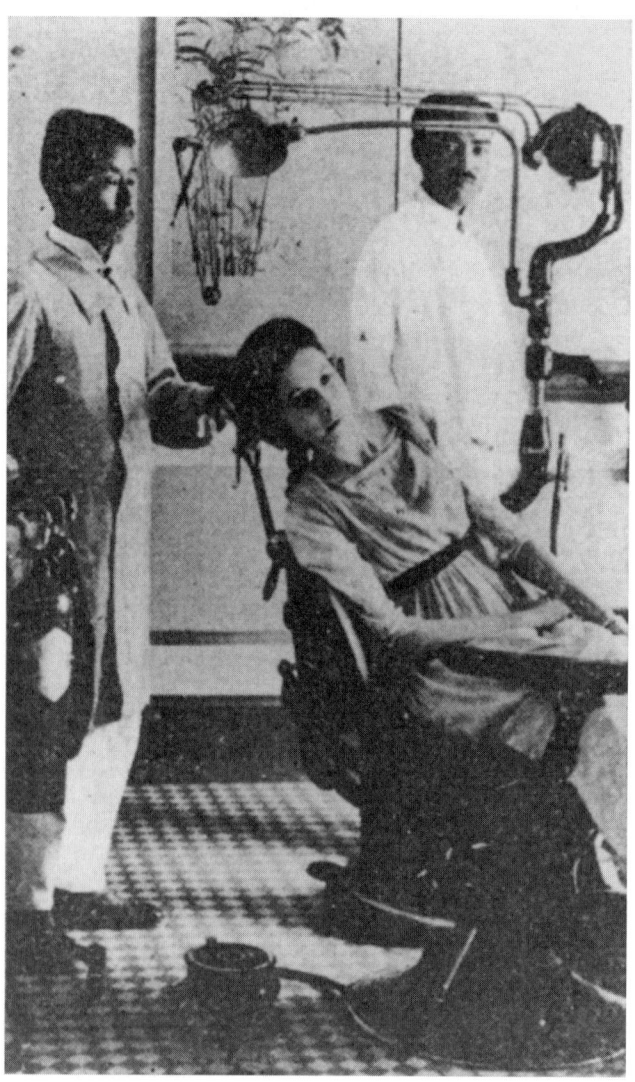

The Misawa brothers, Gihei and Ryo Misawa, went to dental school in Japan and moved to Mexico in the early 1900s. They later opened a Japanese hospital in Mazatlan, Mexico, ca. 1930s. (Collection of Asociación México Japonesa, A.C.)

Flamenco dance members of Guadalajara: (left to right) Emiko Matoo, Kimita Yamazaki, Lucila Yida, Hiroko Ueda, Kazuko Yika, and Gloria Kumazawa, in Guadalajara, Mexico, 1949. (Collection of Asociación México Japonesa, A.C.)

migrants, the Japanese businesses in the border towns of Mexicali and Calexico prospered after 1910.

THE MEXICAN REVOLUTION AND JAPANESE IMMIGRANTS: 1910–1920

On October 25, 1910, political émigré Francisco Madero declared the reelection of the dictatorial President Porfirió Díaz null and void, and began his struggle against the Díaz government. In other parts of Mexico, many other statesmen and military leaders rose up against the government, submerging the nation of Mexico in a turmoil that lasted an entire decade. Madero returned to Mexico from Texas and confronted the government forces. On May 26, 1911, President Díaz was forced to leave Mexico and take refuge in Paris, France; Madero, victorious, entered Mexico City on June 17. However, the new president did not meet the expectations of his followers and allies, because his new government established a policy favorable to the established landowner class. With the revolt of his right-hand general, the country again was engulfed in the storm of civil war.

In the midst of this confusion, the Japanese residents often found themselves subject to plundering and xenophobic attacks by both governmental and antigovernmental forces, as well as by common criminals. Tenant farmers who leased land from the Mexican elite who had fled to the United States found their crops confiscated by the military, while the merchants lost much of their stock

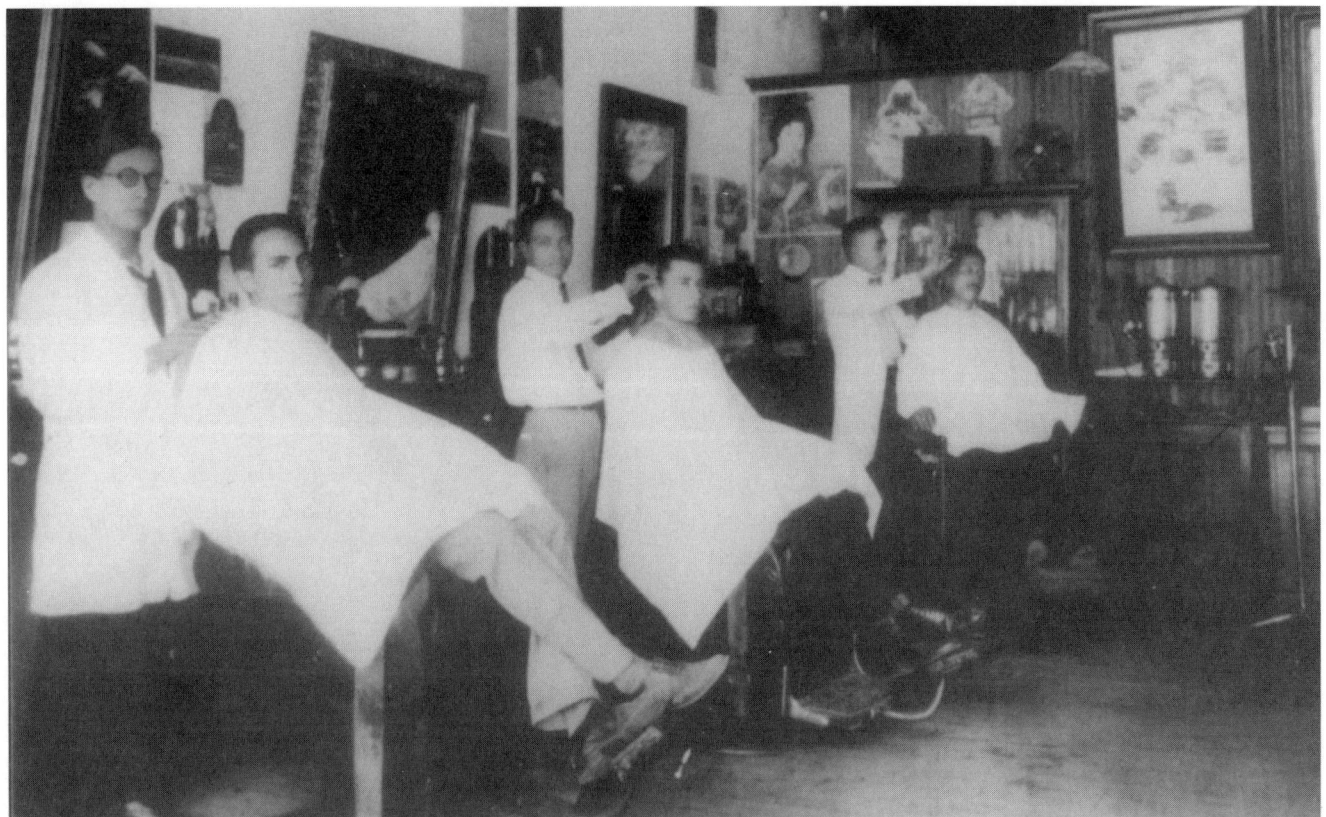
Typical barbershop owned by Japanese immigrant Kyōtarō Inoue, in Acacoyagua, Chiapas, Mexico, ca. 1940. (Collection of Asociación México Japonesa, A.C.)

to armed intruders. A considerable number of Japanese immigrants were murdered both accidentally and intentionally. The Japanese government demanded the safety of its citizens in Mexico, as well as compensation (about twenty-four thousand pesos) for the losses suffered by the immigrants, but the Mexican government did not meet either demand.

Some one hundred Japanese participated in the Mexican Revolution. Because mining and farm work ceased to exist for the Japanese immigrants during the social instability, some chose to serve in both antigovernmental and governmental forces, where they were paid a daily wage of one peso to 1.5 pesos and received free meals. No one particularly cared about the political ideology or interests that had divided the Mexican leadership; it was purely the simple necessity to survive that impelled them to risk their lives in military operations.

THE EMERGENCE OF JAPANESE SETTLEMENTS: 1920s–1930s

From the rigors of the Mexican Revolution emerged the prototypes of the Japanese immigrant settlements in Mexico, and the decades of the 1920s and the 1930s marked a radical transformation from the dekasegi social orientation to a permanent settlement one. In general, the major Japanese communities were concentrated in northern states of Baja California, Sonora, and Sinaloa and in the southern states of Veracruz and Chiapas, as well as in Mexico City and its vicinity. They generally had Japanese associations, which sprang up particularly after the late 1920s. According to one source, over 90 percent of Japanese Mexicans belonged to these community organizations in 1939, a statistic that reflected the accelerated cohesion of ethnic ties among Japanese Mexicans. Of all the states in Mexico, Baja California was the most populous during the decades of permanent settlement.

Baja California: Mexicali
From 1917 until the Great Depression, the Japanese community in Mexicali grew rapidly. The cultivation of cotton offered a lucrative business for many Japanese immigrants in the area. This sudden prosperity due to cotton production convinced many people to set aside their goals of en-

Japanese Mexicans 211

A Japanese school established by Mr. Inukai in about 1937, in Navojoa, Sonora, Mexico. (Collection of Asociación México Japonesa, A.C.)

tering the United States illegally. Gradually, many Japanese became tenant farmers for the Colorado River Company (Compañía del Río Colorado), owned by North American promoters, which monopolized land ownership in the Mexicali region. By 1925, approximately 70 percent of the total area cultivated with cotton was in Japanese hands. At that time, the local Japanese population in Mexicali exceeded one thousand inhabitants. Many farmers brought their wives and siblings from Japan, a practice that contributed to the formation of family-based settlements.

The prosperity of the Mexicali Japanese community was also closely linked with the enactment of the Prohibition in the United States, which forbid the manufacture, sale, import or export of alcoholic drinks, and created an increased demand among businesses catering to a North American clientele. While many Japanese immigrants opened small stores with the money they had saved, some people came from Los Angeles to establish a branch of the Tokyo Club, which was said to have offered gambling and prostitution. It was rumored that the murder of Saburo Mashiko, secretary of the Japanese Association of Mexicali (Asociación Japonesa de Mexicali), in December 1926 was the price paid for his strong opposition to the club's attempt to bring young women from Japan to practice prostitution.

Despite the existence of these social vices, a host of social, educational, and economic institutions characterized the healthy growth of Mexicali from the 1920s onward. Founded in 1917, the Japanese Association of Mexicali had a Japanese hall, a Japanese-language school, and a women's association. For the benefit of the residents, it played an intermediary role in processing necessary documents for the Japanese consulate in Los Angeles, which was responsible for the Japanese of Baja California. The Japanese Agricultural Association of Mexicali (Asociación Agrícola Japonesa de Mexicali) was organized in 1928 to defend the agricultural rights and economic interests of the Japanese cotton growers, who in 1927 found their lands subject to arbitrary confiscation.

Baja California: Ensenada
Located along the Pacific Coast, Ensenada became a hub of Japanese immigrant fishermen. Since the 1910s, Seiji Kondo, an immigrant living in San Diego, California, had brought Japanese fishermen to catch tuna and abalone along the Baja California Peninsula. By 1937, a total of nearly five hundred Japanese had come to Mexico to work as fishermen. They were based in Ensenada. At first many worked for wages, but after the mid-1920s, more and more immigrants owned their own fishing boats and were contracted by Japanese fishery firms in San Diego and Terminal Island, California. Near Ensenada were some Japanese agricultural activities that targeted the Los Angeles market. Ensenada, along with Tijuana, had a local Japanese association starting in 1926.

Sonora and Sinaloa
In the northern states of Sonora and Sinaloa, small Japanese immigrant settlements appeared in the 1920s. According to data gathered in 1925, the majority of Japanese residents were involved in small businesses. There were also Japanese doctors and dentists, who often assumed leadership positions in the local Mexican communities. Under the 1917 treaty, the Japanese medical license was accepted as legal in Mexico, making it possible for Japanese to practice medicine if they had received their degrees in Japan. This induced a small number of doctors and dentists in Japan to emigrate to Mexico. Many Japanese of Sonora and Sinaloa married local women, producing many interracial Nisei children, like in Chiapas. In total, Sonora had 449 Japanese Mexicans (209 Issei) and Sinaloa had 269 (131 Issei). The Confederation of Japanese Regional Societies of Northwest Mexico (Confederación de las Sociedades Regionales Japonesas del Noroeste de México), based in Culiacan, supervised the activities of the Japanese associations in the two states.

Veracruz and Chiapas
The southern states of Veracruz and Chiapas constituted another center of Japanese immigrant settlements. In Veracruz, the town of Minatitlán housed 35 percent of the total 353 Japanese immigrants and their families in 1930. With a total population of 276 the same year, Chiapas possessed the largest concentration of Japanese Mexicans in the areas around the former Enomoto colony, which encompassed the towns of Tapachula, Escuintla, and Huixtla, near the Guatemalan border. The Japanese Mexicans of this area participated in a wide range of occupations that ranged from farming to commercial ventures. In these two states, there were eight Japanese associations.

Mexico City and Its Vicinity
In 1939, Mexico City and its vicinity had 967 Japanese residents (295 families), consisting mainly of business owners and traders. The Mexican Japanese Circle (Círculo Japonés de México) offered a variety of services, including Japanese-language instruction, a Japanese hall, and the publication of the *México Shimpo*. In the realm of mutual support among Japanese business owners, the Union of Mexican Exporters and Importers (Unión de Exportadores e Importadores de México) played a very important role in fostering the trade relationship between Japan and Mexico. Established in 1931, the Japanese Sports Club (Club Deportivo Nippon) sponsored athletic activities among the Japanese residents, while the Mexican Japanese Youth Association (Asociación Juvenil Nippon Mexicana) offered a place of socialization for Japanese Mexican Nisei beginning in 1939.

THE PACIFIC WAR AND THE JAPANESE MEXICANS
The mounting tension between Japan and the United States seriously affected the Japanese residents of Mexico after the late 1930s. In December 1938, the United States took the initiative in organizing a series of "Pan American Conferences," where a network of economic and military cooperation was established between Latin American countries and the United States. The Mexican government deepened its ties with its northern neighbor, and in July 1941 it concluded a new economic treaty that banned the export of strategic goods to Japan. As a result of Japan's attack on Pearl Harbor, Mexico immediately severed its diplomatic relations with Japan and in May 1942 proceeded to declare war. Suddenly the Japanese Mexicans, a majority of whom were still Japanese nationals, found themselves in an extremely difficult situation.

As the Japanese diplomatic office in Mexico became defunct, the Society of Mutual Prosperity (Kyoeikai La Sociedad de Prosperidad Mutual), a wartime metamorphosis of the Japanese Association of Mexico City (Asociación Japanesa de la Ciudad de México), took charge of community affairs and attempted to ensure the protection of the residents. Because the Mexican government had frozen the assets of all the Japanese, they had difficulty surviving day by day, although the withdrawal of five hundred pesos per month was later permitted. Moreover, many Issei were arrested and detained in local jails for no specific reason. The Japanese associations were the only source of help for these people.

At the same time, Japanese Mexicans in the northern states were obliged to abandon their homes. Under pressure from the U.S. government, on January 5, 1942, the Mexican government ordered all the Japanese residents to

Sumo tournament organized by the Japanese settlement in Tijuana, Mexico, May 5, 1926. (Collection of Asociación México Japonesa, A.C.)

leave Baja California and to go to the interior of the country. They were given only ten days to report to local alien registration offices, sign "voluntary relocation applications," and clear out of the area. The Japanese of Mexicali, Tijuana, and Ensenada immediately organized an extraordinary mass meeting, where they collected ten thousand pesos to lobby in favor of the cancelation of the order, but they did not succeed. As a result, all the Japanese residents, except their Mexican wives and some Nisei who could stay behind, had to move to Mexico City and Guadalajara in several groups—a sad and difficult trip that took five long days. Soon, many Japanese from Sonora, Sinaloa, and Coahuila joined this mass movement southward. Before the war, approximately 2,800 Japanese had lived in the northern states, where the relocation orders were issued. Upon arriving in Mexico, many Japanese families were given refuge in the El Batan ranch, to the south of Mexico City.

Over five hundred of them relocated to a small town of Temixco, about fifty miles from Mexico City, where a loosely organized internment camp was set up. Meanwhile, other Japanese Mexicans joined their compatriots in Mexico City and Guadalajara. Combined with some nine hundred original residents of the regions, the influx of these relocated settlers increased the total Japanese population in the central region of Mexico to over 3,500 between 1942 and 1945.

In this chaotic situation, the Kyoeikai of Mexico played a central role in finding accommodations and employment for the relocated settlers. In some cases, the organization offered financial assistance to those who did not have enough money to make the journey from the north. Uprooted and deprived, many relocation settlers barely eked out a daily living, working on farms and in small businesses, but without assistance from the Kyoeikai and their fellow Japanese Mexicans they might have not have

Takugoro Shibayama, pictured here with his family, was the head of Temixco farm, a collective agricultural enterprise that included about 450 Japanese who were forced to move from the border towns of Mexico. (Collection of Asociación México Japonesa, A.C.)

survived. Although the war suddenly wiped out the thriving Japanese communities in the northern states, new communities and ethnic ties emerged in Mexico City in the midst of the wartime confusion.

POSTWAR YEARS: NEW START, NEW COMMUNITY

Although the Pacific War caused a myriad of devastating effects on the lives of thousands of Japanese Mexicans, it also impelled the people to make definite decisions about their future. They no longer thought of returning to Japan but of participating in Mexican life. Their decision to make Mexico their permanent home was perhaps an unexpected product of the international tragedy, but it transformed the shape and nature of the Japanese Mexican community in many different ways.

The first change occurred in the demographic distribution of the Japanese population. After the war, the majority of the settlers remained in Mexico City and Guadalajara. According to 1955 statistics, approximately 56 percent of the Japanese Mexicans resided in these areas. Meanwhile, Baja California had only 7 percent that same year, a decrease of 27 percent since 1927; Chihuahua had 9.5 percent, a 6 percent decrease, and Veracruz and Coahuila 3.3 percent, a decrease of nearly 7 percent. This general trend has continued; data taken in 1980 indicate that over half of the Japanese Mexican population in that year resided in Mexico City and Guadalajara.

Another change pertains to the general occupational shift from agriculture to small urban businesses before and after the war. In 1955, a comprehensive survey of 829 Japanese Mexican households showed their tendency to concentrate in such specific categories as general merchandise retailing, dentistry, food service, and floral businesses. Because most, if not all, of these stores and businesses catered to the general Mexican clientele, Japanese

Murakami and Kimura family picnic, Chapultepec National Park, Mexico City, ca. 1950s. (Collection of Asociación México Japonesa, A.C.)

Mexicans did not form geographically demarcated ethnic communities like "Little Tokyo" in Los Angeles or "Oriental Town" in São Paulo. Some consider that this situation, in which the individual families had to make their own way among the Mexican people, made Japanese Mexicans "more independent and less timid" than Nikkei in other nations.

This complete restructuring of the community also brought about new organizations that introduced a dispersed population throughout the central region of Mexico. Perhaps because the majority of the Japanese Mexicans were busy rebuilding their lives in new locales, the establishment of community organizations did not take place until the first half of the 1950s. The organizations quadrupled, from only four to twenty-two, in the four years between 1951 and 1955. In addition to key community institutions like the *Nikkeijin-kai* (Japanese Mexican associations) and *kenjin-kai* (prefecture associations), there were a number of sport clubs and art and cultural groups, which had rarely been seen prior to 1942. This trend illustrated the growth of the second-generation Japanese Mexican population and the economic recovery of many residents, which allowed engagement in activities other than everyday work.

Mexico City became the center of postwar community networks; over half of the Japanese Mexican population resided there. The frozen assets of the prewar Japanese consular offices were graciously returned by the Mexican government to Japan after the Peace Treaty of 1951. The local Issei leaders succeeded in convincing Japan to use the money for "the promotion of friendship and cultural exchange between Japan and Mexico." After accepting the proposal of the residents, the Japanese government nevertheless insisted on the conditions that the receiving agency consist of Nikkei and local Mexicans and that the project be a joint collaboration. This compelled the Nikkei leaders to overcome their internal differences and to discuss the possibility of establishing a new bilateral organization with sympathetic Mexicans. To this end, on July 30, 1956, a committee of ten prominent Mexicans resolved to form

Las Quinceañeras, a Mexican traditional ritual celebrating the fifteenth birthday of young girls and their debut into society: (left to right) Yoko Akachi, Junko Abe, Eiko Kumura, Setsuko Kawabe, Teruko Kimura; (back row) José Ichikawa, Pablo Yoshida, Roberto Okamoto, Alberto Hamabata, Jesús Takeda. This celebration was held by the alumni of the Tacuba School in Mexico City, September 1953. (Collection of Asociación México Japonesa, A.C.)

the Mexico Japanese Association (Asociación México Japonesa) in Mexico City. Their project was to build a Japanese cultural center.

Real collaborative efforts ensued, involving the cooperation of Japanese consular representatives, Mexican sympathizers, and Nikkei residents. The projected expenses exceeded the gift from the Japanese government; the association had to raise an additional three hundred thousand pesos. For this effort, the Japanese embassy offered an automobile, in which consular officials rode with Nikkei leaders when they went to solicit donations. As a result, over 1,130,000 pesos were collected from both Nikkei residents and the Mexican people. In addition, to reduce the financial pressure, Mr. Sanshiro Matsumoto donated ten thousand square meters of land for free and was paid a purely symbolic price for an additional ten thousand square meters, while a Nisei professor of architecture volunteered to provide his services for free to design and oversee the overall construction of the project. On February 1, 1959, after a collaborative effort among the Japanese of Mexico City, and between the Nikkei and Mexican people, the Japanese Mexican Cultural Center (Centro Cultural Mexicano Japonés) opened its doors to the public. The center became a focal point for the formation of the community and a symbol of intra-ethnic cooperation. The Asociación México Japonesa united the existing Nikkei associations of Mexico by taking charge of the operation and administration of the center for the good of the permanent community, as well as for the friendship between Mexico and Japan, in March 1962.

PRESENT SITUATION

As the immigrant generation overcame its internal divisions and began to share a vision of what it, as a group, wanted to strive for, the Mexican-born generation began to exert more and more influence within the community. As early as 1954, it was reported that many second-generation Japanese Mexicans had attained positions of prominence—as biologists, professors, lawyers, doctors,

Partial view of the Japanese Mexican Association (Asociación México Japonesa, A.C.) building in Mexico City. (Collection of Asociación México Japonesa, A.C.)

dentists, engineers, military officers, and government bureaucrats.

In 1965, Nisei (second generation educated in Mexico), *Kiboku* (following generation educated in Japan) and *Shin Issei* (Japanese who arrived after the Second World War) organized the Japanese Mexican New Leaders Society (Nichiboku Seinenkai), which lasted a short time but influenced the restructuring of the Asociación México Japonesa, A.C.

The Japanese Mexican Cultural Institution, Inc. (Instituto Cultural Mexicano Japonés, A.C.), founded by the Nisei Association of Mexico (Asociación Nisei de México), has been dedicated to the teaching and diffusion of the Japanese language and culture to Mexican adults since 1967. The institution published the first romanized books on the subject, *Basic Course* and *Basic Text of the Japanese Language.* More than five thousand students have passed through its classrooms, among them many scholarship recipients of the official exchange programs between Mexico and Japan. It has official recognition from the secretary of public education and maintains agreements with the secretary of foreign relations and the National Council of Science and Technology for the preparation of its scholarship recipients and active members. The institute is an organizing member of the official Japanese-language exam in Mexico and the Japanese-language speech competition in Mexico.

Beginning in 1974, the Japanese Mexican School (Liceo Mexicano Japonés, A.C.) merged five Nikkei-run schools and a preparatory school for the children of temporary residents and thereby became the first transnational educational venture of its first kind in the history of any Nikkei community. Accredited by the governments of Mexico and Japan, the school formally opened its doors in September 1977, offering regular classes, based on a Mexican curriculum, taught in Spanish for first grade through the fifth year of secondary school, and a separate program certified by the Japanese Ministry of Education for the children of Japanese business owners. In addition to the general courses, Mexican and Nikkei

Members of Nisei kai, *1969. (Collection of Asociación México Japonesa, A.C.)*

students receive instruction on Japanese language and culture to augment their knowledge of Japan. While Japanese pupils are fundamentally educated in the same way as those in Japanese schools, they must also study the Spanish language as well as the Mexican culture. Kindergarten children attend integrated classes in a multicultural environment.

In 1981, a group of Mexican Nikkei attempting to promote a mutual understanding of the unique but common experiences of the Nikkei in the Americas organized the first Nikkei conference in Mexico. The slogan of this conference, "*Seamos mejores ciudadanos en nuestro continente!*" ("Let us be better citizens in our continent!"), clearly demonstrated a vision that came to be shared by other Nikkei of the Americas. The conference led to the formation of the Pan-American Nikkei Association (Asociación Nikkei Panamericana).

In 1987, the ninetieth anniversary of the Japanese migration to Mexico was celebrated in homage to the Issei, amid many festivities and the construction of the Urasenke Tea House in Mexico City. In 1997, the centennial celebration marked a new phase of progress with the building of educational centers in Acacoyagua and Tapachula, Chiapas.

In the artistic arena, Seki Sano, maestro of cinema and theater, stands out among the best, with top artists training under his direction. In sports, Amalia Yubi, winner of the 110-meter hurdle at the Pan American Games and the Caribbean Games, has achieved international recognition for his accomplishments. Also, the work that Alfredo Atsumi has carried out throughout his lifetime is outstanding. However, the area where Japanese Mexicans most excel is education and professional fields. In almost all the universities of Mexico there are recognized Japanese Mexican professors and researchers, especially in the fields of medicine and dentistry. Japanese Mexicans doctors can be found in the principal medical centers of the country, occupying positions of great importance and responsibility. The first Nikkei in the important position of minister of health is Dr. Jesús Kumate Rodríguez. Another famous

President Luis Echeverria (third from right) and his family at the home of Carlos Kasuga, head of the Society of the Japanese Mexican New Leaders (Nichiboku Seinenkai), and his friends, 1971. (Collection of Asociación México Japonesa, A.C.)

Reception hosted by students at the Universidad La Salle attended by Prince Haruhito (center), June 30, 1993. (Collection of Asociación México Japonesa, A.C.)

Nikkei is Luis Nishizawa, who received the National Prize of Art in 1998 and has his own museum and school of art in his natal state of Mexico, Toluca City.

Privileged with dual cultural backgrounds, Japanese and Mexican, the Nikkei of Mexico have come a long way—as integral members of Mexican society, as the bridge between Mexico and Japan, and as leaders among the Nikkei of the new continents. Now the third generation has gradually come to inherit the work of their ancestors. Building upon the legacy of the previous generations, the young Japanese Mexicans continue to strive for better citizenship and community.

Japanese Mexican Bibliographic Essay

JESÚS K. AKACHI, CARLOS T. KASUGA, MANUEL S. MURAKAMI, MARÍA ELENA OTA MISHIMA, ENRIQUE SHIBAYAMA, AND RENÉ TANAKA

THERE ARE A GREAT NUMBER OF BOOKS ON JAPANESE IN Mexico, including tourist guidebooks, travel diaries, political and economic reference books, and their translations. However, with the exception of some relevant documents and research reports, there are surprisingly few books on Japanese immigration. Among these few resources are autobiographies, but most common are biographies written by Japanese authors who traveled and interviewed people on topics of interest. Some of the books discourage those who come to Mexico as *dekasegi* thinking it will be easy to make money, although those who have settled down permanently in Mexico deserve special recognition. Among these selections, there are some excellent works.

Language and marriage were the biggest concerns among the young Japanese who emigrated abroad alone. Those who arrived in Chiapas decided to settle down permanently and tried to assimilate into the host society. Difficulty in learning the Spanish language and educational concerns for their children gave rise to the first Spanish-Japanese dictionary published in Japan (1925: J-17); it took the compilers eleven years to complete. Both Chinese characters and Roman letters for the translated words were included.

Hisashi Ueno's book *Mekishiko Enomoto shokumin* (1994: J-21) describes the life conditions and characteristics of the early Enomoto Colony immigrants of Chiapas and their descendants who lived between the ideal and real worlds. The author draws the following conclusions: (1) the Japanese with high educational level held leadership positions; (2) the immigrants were idealists; (3) they conducted business, however, from realistic viewpoints; (4) they were self-reliant and did not expect financial support from others; and (5) by marrying natives they established foundations close to the local society.

Among the best works that focus on the lives of the Japanese immigrants are the books compiled by Masafumi Aoyama (1938: J-1) and Ken'ichi Murai (1975: J-10). Aoyama's treatise reveals the feelings of the Japanese settlers, who maintained their value of honesty, industriousness, and sincerity in Mexico. The author does not portray the grim picture of immigrant life that usually accompanies the Japanese term "immigrant" *(imin)*. Likewise, Murai's work vividly depicts the colorful life of a Japanese immigrant, who survived the chaotic social changes in his adopted land. Both books bear witness to the resilience and determination of immigrant settlers without the prevailing biases against them.

When the war between Japan and the United States broke out, the Japanese Mexicans were expelled from their hometowns and gathered in Mexico City and Guadalajara. Forty-five years later, Atsuko Yamamoto traveled three thousand miles throughout Mexico and the towns located near the U.S. border. She visited ordinary people and recorded life histories of the immigrants and their descendants, who recalled experiences of the Enomoto colony (the first Japanese settlement in Mexico), the Mexican Revolution, and the Pacific War. Her objective and accurate description covered a limited number of people but vividly reconstructed the conditions of those days, giving a voice to the interviewees (1988: J-25).

Most of these books are mainly descriptive, focusing on the lives of individual immigrants. Interpretation of immigration history through the analysis of economic and political processes of both sending and receiving countries is limited. One exception is the compendium of Japanese Mexican relations *Nichi-Boku kōryūshi* (1990: J-11), compiled by a group of community scholars in 1990. This is a history of the international and intercultural relations with Mexico, in the framework of which all Japanese Mexicans have lived.

The vast majority of the publications on Japanese Mexicans are written in Japanese. However, if one looks to the future, books written in the Spanish language will be indispensable if the Nisei are to know about their roots, or the Mexicans are to know about Japanese immigration. Currently, the only existing Spanish-language studies of Japanese Mexicans are the path-breaking studies by the late Dr. María Elena Ota Mishima (E-1, S-2, S-3, S-4). To continue her efforts is an important future task.

Annotated Bibliography of Japanese Mexicans

COMPILED BY JESÚS K. AKACHI, CARLOS T. KASUGA, MANUEL S. MURAKAMI, MARÍA ELENA OTA MISHIMA, ENRIQUE SHIBAYAMA, AND RENÉ TANAKA

ENGLISH

1. Mishima, María Elena Ota. *Destino México*. El Colegio de México, 1997, and *Siete Migraciones Japonesas en México*. El Colegio de México, 1982. Excerpts translated from Spanish to English in *Japanese Migration and the Americas: An Introduction to the Study of Migration*. Edited by Gary Mukai, and Rachel Brunette. Stanford, Calif.: The Asia/Pacific Project, SPICE Institute for International Studies (IIS), 1999, 55–56.
2. Watanabe, Chizuko. "The Japanese Immigrant Community in Mexico: Its History and Present." Master's thesis, California State University, Los Angeles, 1983.

JAPANESE

1. Aoyama, Masafumi [青山正文]. *Karera wa kaku no gotoku Mekishiko ni funtōseri* [彼等は斯くの如くメキシコに奮闘せり]. Mekishiko-shi [メキシコ市]: Aoyama Masafumi [青山正文], 1938.

    The author portrays in this book the honesty, industriousness, and sincerity of the early Japanese settlers of Mexico.

2. Ishida, Takeshi [石田雄]. *Mehiko to Nihonjin: daisan sekai de kangaeru* [メヒコと日本人：第三世界で考える]. Tōkyō [東京]: Tōkyō Daigaku Shuppankai [東京大学出版会], 1973.

    The author, a Japanese political scientist, conducts research on the Nichiboku Kyōdō Kaisha, the students of Kanzō Uchimura, the process of settlement and assimilation from Issei to Nisei, and differences between Mexican and Japanese viewpoints of immigration to Mexico.

3. Itō, Keiichi [伊藤敬一], ed. *Bokkoku o kataru* [墨国を語る]. Tōkyō [東京]: Itō Setsuo [伊藤節夫], 1956.

    The author, who arrived in Mexico as a foreign student sponsored by the Ministry of Foreign Affairs in 1897 and became the consul of Japan in Mexico, observes the conditions of Mexico and Japanese in Mexico from the viewpoint of a diplomat.

4. Itō, Keiichi [伊藤敬一]. *Kyūjissai kinen, omoide no ki* [九十歳記念・思出の記]. N.p., 1966.

    Memoir of a Japanese diplomat, Keiichi Itō. Written to commemorate his ninetieth birthday.

5. Kaibara, Yukio [貝原幸夫]. *Mekishiko ni hikari o mitsukete* [メキシコに光を見つけて]: Yamato Shobō [大和書房], 1982.

    The author, creator of Dentsū, describes the experiences with his family in Mexico, where he chose to permanently settle after his brain tumor operation.

6. Kasuga, Akane [春日あかね]. *Kushū Akane* [句集あかね]. N.p., 1985.

    A collection of Japanese poetry by the author who sponsors the gathering of poets.

7. Kasuga, Akane [春日あかね]. *Tanka Akane* [短歌あかね]. N.p., 1985.

    A collection of Japanese poems. Author was awarded the Excellency in the Imperial new-year poetry celebration.

8. Katō, Heiji [加藤平治]. *Mekishikan rapusodī: Chūnanbei bōeki ni kaketa otoko no ennetsu jinsei* [メキシカン・ラプソディー：中南米貿易に賭けた男の炎熱人生]. Tōkyō [東京]: Sōgō Rōdō Kenkyūjo [総合労働研究所], 1984.

    The author provides firsthand advice to immigrants, by analyzing national and social situations around him on how to understand the environment and use it for one's own advantage and to concentrate on work.

9. Meishinkai [明申会]. *Meishin* [めいしん]. N.p., 1996.

    A collection of essays written in celebration of the twenty-fifth anniversary of the Meishin Society, a socialization organization.

10. Murai, Ken'ichi [村井謙一]. *Paionia retsuden* [パイオニア列伝]. N.p.: Murai Shigeko [村井茂子], 1975.

    A record of interviews of 150 Japanese immigrants who are more than eighty years old and living all over Mexico. The author was inspired at the age of sixty-seven and used his own private funds to conduct these interviews.

11. Nichi-Boku Kyōkai Nichi-Boku Kōryūshi Henshū Iinkai [日墨協会日墨交流史編集委員会]. *Nichi-Boku kōryūshi* [日墨交流史]. Tōkyō [東京]: PMC Shuppan [ＰＭＣ出版], 1990.

    The main subject of this book is the history of Japanese-Mexican relations. The book contains essays written by a group of community scholars.

12. Nihonjin Mekishiko Ijūshi Hensan Iinkai [日本人メキシコ移住史編纂委員会], ed. *Nihonjin Mekishiko ijūshi* [日本人メキシコ移住史]. N.p.: Nihonjin Mekishiko Ijūshi Hensan Iinkai [日本人メキシコ移住史編纂委員会], 1971.

    A history of Japanese migration to Mexico.

13. Sekiguchi, Teiji [関口貞司]. *Nichi-Boku Kyōkai to watakushi* [日墨協会と私]. N.p., 1993.

    This book describes from a unified viewpoint the various incidents that took place at the Japanese Mexican Association since its establishment with abundant sources.

14. Taki, Yasutarō [瀧釟太郎]. *Sekai muhi no shinnichikoku daihōko Mekishiko* [世界無比の親日国・大宝庫メキシコ]. México D.F., México: Kōshinsha [公進社], 1927.

    More than half of its 750 pages are dedicated to the explanation of the national condition of Mexico, which the author defines as a country friendly to Japan and a treasure chest, and lessons for immigrants. It also introduces brief biographies of the Japanese in various areas in Japan. Also contains many pictures. This book shows the enthusiastic desire of the author to make the Japanese understand Mexico.

15. Taki, Yasutarō [瀧 釟太郎]. *Shinnichi no shinkōkoku Mekishiko kokujō taikan: shokumin shichijūnenshi* [親日の新興国メキシコ国情大観 ： 植民七十年史]. México D.F., México: Mehiko Shinpōsha [メヒコ新報社], 1968.

    A historical overview of seventy years of settlement in Mexico.

16. Tamagawa, Otosaku [玉川音作]. *Mekishiko no ayumi* [メキシコの歩み]. N.p., 1976.

    A collection of poems written by an author who lived in Mexico as a Christian.

17. Terui, Ryōjirō, and Nichi-Boku Kyōdō Kaisha [照井亮次郎 and 日墨協同會社], ed. *Seinichi jiten* [西日辞典]. Tōkyō [東京]: Yūbunsha Shuppan [右文社出版], 1925.

    This Spanish-Japanese dictionary, the first in Japan, uses both Chinese characters and Roman letters for the translated words.

18. Tōsha, Katsuji [当舎勝次], ed. *Zenboku Nikkeijin jūshoroku* [全墨日系人住所録]. México: Shimizu Yukio Shōten [清水幸夫商店], 1955.

    A directory of Japanese in Mexico with essays by the author on people he met during his travels.

19. Tsumura, Yoshinari [津村義就]. *Mekishiko nagoyaka ni utaishi sanga: Tsumura Yoshinari hanseiki* [メキシコ和やかに歌いし山河： 津村義就半生記]. Tōkyō [東京]: PMC Shuppan [PMC出版], 1991.

    The author believes that the success of the Japanese community in Mexico was due not to luck but to their challenging mentality when faced with difficulties.

20. Tsunoyama, Yukihiro [角山幸弘]. *Enomoto Takeaki to Mekishiko shokumin ijū* [榎本武揚とメキシコ植民移住]. Tōkyō [東京]: Dōbunkan Shuppan [同文館出版], 1986.

    Biography of Takeaki Enomoto, who implemented the first organized Japanese emigration to Mexico.

21. Ueno, Hisashi [上野久]. *Mekishiko Enomoto shokumin: Enomoto Takeaki no risō to genjitsu* [メキシコ榎本植民：榎本武揚の理想と現実]. Tōkyō [東京]: Chūō Kōronsha [中央公論社], 1994.

    This book describes the real conditions of so-called Enomoto Colony in Mexico organized by the former foreign minister Takeaki Enomoto.

22. Unno, Minoru [海野稔]. *Mekishiko Chūbei taikan* [墨西哥中米大観]. N.p.: Mekishiko Jihōsha [墨西哥時報社], 1941.

    Published in celebration of the 2600th Japanese year; half contains a community directory and advertisements. The author's background as a resident reporter of the Dōmei Tsūshinsha in Mexico is reflected in the detailed political and economic information provided about Mexico at the time.

23. Watanabe, Masako [渡辺正子]. *Kokoro no mado* [心の窓]. Vol. 1. Shinseisha [新声社], 1971.

    A posthumous collection of poems by Watanabe who was brought up as a Christian and lived a pure, warm-hearted life.

24. Watanabe, Masako [渡辺正子]. *Kokoro no mado* [心の窓]. Vol. 2. Shinseisha [新声社], 1978.

    A posthumous collection of poems.

25. Yamamoto, Atsuko [山本厚子]. *Mekishiko ni ikiru Nikkei imin tachi* [メキシコに生きる日系移民たち]. Tōkyō [東京]: Kawade Shobō Shinsha [河出書房新社], 1988.

    Author records life histories of the immigrants who lived through the Enomoto settlement, the Mexican Revolution and the Pacific War, and through these interviews, vividly reconstructs the conditions of those days.

SPANISH

1. Bonfil Batalla, Guillermo. *Simbiosis de culturas: los inmigrantes y su cultura en México*. México, D.F.: Consejo Nacional para la Cultura y las Artes, 1993.

    This book addresses questions about Mexican culture and the cultures of various immigrant groups living in Mexico. One main concern is how the host culture and the cultures of different immigrant ethnic groups affect each other.

2. Mishima, María Elena Ota. *Destino México: un estudio de las migraciones asiáticas a México, siglos XIX y XX*. México, D.F.: El Colegio de México, 1997.

    Demography of Asian migration to Mexico in the nineteenth and twentieth centuries and the social and economic characteristics of Japanese immigrants. In addition to Japanese, the Chinese, Arabic, Palestinian, Filipino, and Indian immigrants are also discussed.

3. Mishima, María Elena Ota. *México y Japón en el siglo XIX: la política exterior de México y la consolidación de la soberanía japonesa*. Tlatelolco, México: Secretaría de Relaciones Exteriores, 1976.

    This book is a compilation of many documents related to the first treaty ever signed between Japan and Mexico. It was a milestone treaty for Japan, in the sense that it was founded on the principles of reciprocity, unlike other treaties signed with Western powers, which were one-sided and for the most part not respectful of Japan's sovereignty or interests.

4. Mishima, María Elena Ota. *Siete migraciones japonesas en México: 1890–1978*. México, D.F.: El Colegio de México, 1982.

    Analyzes seven types of Japanese migrations in Mexico. Includes historical demography of Japanese immigrants in Mexico.

Supplementary Materials

COMPILED BY JESÚS K. AKACHI, CARLOS T. KASUGA, MANUEL S. MURAKAMI, MARÍA ELENA OTA MISHIMA, ENRIQUE SHIBAYAMA, AND RENÉ TANAKA

Map 7.1 Locations of Japanese Mexican Populations in the Historical Overview

Japanese Mexican Demographic Information

Table 7.1 Japanese Emigration to Mexico by Prefecture of Origin in Japan, 1890–1949

	1890–1940	1890–1949
Fukuoka	50	406
Hiroshima	36	279
Kumamoto	35	260
Wakayama	16	226
Yamaguchi	19	191
Okinawa	9	170
Kagoshima	17	136
Shizuoka	18	135
Nagano	20	126
Tōkyō	7	110

Sources: Figures for 1890–1940 were taken from María Elena Ota Mishima, *Siete migraciones japoneses en México* (Mexico City: El Colegio de México, 1982), 171–72 (cuadro 25); figures for 1890–1949 were taken from María Elena Ota Mishima, *Destino México: un estudio de las migraciones asiáticas a México, siglos XIX y XX* (Mexico City: El Colegio de México, 1997), 89–90.

Table 7.2 Total Japanese Mexican Population and Male/Female Ratio, 1950–1990

Year	Males	Females	Total
1950	1,425 (73.1%)	526 (26.9%)	**1,951**
1960	1,569 (71.2%)	636 (28.8%)	**2,205**
1970	1,089 (59.1%)	752 (40.9%)	**1,841**
1980	1,989 (51.7%)	1,856 (48.3%)	**3,845**
1990	2,625 (48.9%)	2,746 (51.1%)	**5,371**

Source: Registro Nacional de Población (National Register of Population).

Table 7.3 Regional Distribution of Japanese Mexicans, 1950–1990

Year	Region A	Region B	Region C	Region D
1950	483	213	986	269
1960	513	239	1,108	336
1970	286	124	1,163	268
1980	1,186	636	1,260	763
1990	1,645	873	1,760	1,063

Source: Registro Nacional de Población (National Register of Population).
Region A: Baja California, Baja California Sur, Sonora, Sinaloa, Chihuahua, Durango, Guanajuato, Jalisco, Nayarit, Colima.
Region B: Aguascalientes, Coahuila, Hidalgo, Nuevo León, San Luís Potosí, Tamaulípas, Tlaxcala, Zacatecas.
Region C: Dístrito Federal, Estado de México and Morelos, Michoacán, Guerrero.
Region D: Veracruz, Puebla, Oaxaca, Chiapas, Tabasco, Campeche, Yucatán, Quintana Roo.

Table 7.4 Educational Level of Japanese Mexicans, 1950–1990

Year	0–8 Years	9–12 Years	13–15 Years	16 Years or More
1950	178	147	156	1,470
1960	306	287	378	1,234
1970	287	193	262	1,099
1980	620	543	674	2,008
1990	813	484	533	3,541

Source: Registro Nacional de Población (National Register of Population).

Table 7.5 Educational Level of Japanese Mexicans by Primary, Secondary, and College Education, 1950–1990

Year	Primary	Secondary	College
1950	154	207	487
1960	352	234	618
1970	294	195	497
1980	615	407	1,076
1990	876	572	1,499

Source: *Registro Nacional de Población* (National Register of Population).

Table 7.6 Occupational Areas of Japanese Mexicans by Percentage, 1950–1990

Year	Agriculture	Industry	Commerce
1950	35	25	40
1960	26	38	36
1970	22	36	42
1980	15	40	45
1990	7	44	49

Source: *Registro Nacional de Población* (National Register of Population).

Table 7.7 Religion of Japanese Mexicans, 1950–1990

Year	Buddhist	Catholic	Other
1950	98	1,840	13
1960	59	2,135	11
1970	27	1,880	14
1980	35	3,780	30
1990	74	5,270	27

Source: *Registro Nacional de Población* (National Register of Population).

CHAPTER 8

Japanese Paraguayans

DEVELOPED IN COLLABORATION WITH THE CENTRO NIKKEI PARAGUAYO

THE OFFICIAL BEGINNING OF JAPANESE IMMIGRATION IN PARAGUAY CAN BE traced back to 1936, when the first immigrant group arrived as agricultural settlers. The first Japanese agricultural colony of 134 households was established in La Colmena. Many moved to other cities and countries in search of better jobs and opportunities, while others stayed to face the hardships of malaria epidemics, natural disasters, and wartime restrictions on social and educational activities. The next wave of Japanese immigration took place in the early 1950s, when Paraguay opened its doors to countries devastated by the war. In 1953, the Japan Paraguayan Colonization Corporation assisted a number of Japanese to settle in "Fedrico Chaves" colonies in the southern part of the country, while the Company for the Promotion of Japanese Immigration set up agricultural colonies in Itapua Department (Santa Rosa, La Paz, and Fuji) from 1959. As a result of their remarkable success in developing regional agriculture, both governments officially concluded an immigration agreement that permitted the entry of eighty-five thousand farmers from Japan between 1959 and 1989. However, only seven thousand Japanese actually entered Paraguay during the thirty-year period, due to Japan's economic recovery in the 1960s. The third group of treaty immigrants settled in the Pirapó and Yguazú colonies of southeastern Paraguay, where they have engaged in the production of soy beans, wheat, orchard fruits, and cattle farming. The settlements have received substantial financial assistance from the Japanese government—the enduring linkage that has made the Issei and also many Nisei more prone to identify with Japan and to maintain Japanese cultural values, practices, and the language.

Japanese Paraguayan Historical Overview

EMI KASAMATSU

INTRODUCTION

The first recorded history of Paraguayan-Japanese relations begins with the signing of a trade treaty between Japan and Paraguay in 1919, during the reign of Emperor Yoshihito of Japan and the administration of Dr. Jose P. Montero, president of the Republic of Paraguay. This treaty repealed the Paraguayan Immigration Law of 1903, which had prohibited the entry of "black and yellow races," and declared that Japanese were not to be included in the "yellow race" category. Thus, full freedom was granted to citizens of both countries to enter and remain in each other's country, to own property legally, and enjoy equal treatment as subjects and natural citizens. Since then, Paraguayan-Japanese relations have not been broken at any point. On the contrary, there are examples of solidarity, friendship, and reciprocity at crucial times in the history of both countries.

HISTORY OF JAPANESE IMMIGRATION TO PARAGUAY

Until 1934, Japan's Ministry of Foreign Affairs had no record of Japanese moving individually to Paraguay. In reality, since 1912, there had been Japanese in Paraguay, immigrants who had paved small paths in an isolated fashion. The first Japanese man recorded in Paraguayan history was Kanezo Sakoda, born in Maizuru, Kyoto.

Kanezo Sakoda was the first Japanese immigrant in Paraguay, shown here with his family in Japan, 1912. (Collection of Fernando Sakoda)

Portrait of Kanezo Sakoda, an accountant working in the tannin industry, 1930. (Collection of Fernando Sakoda)

Shotaro Fukuoka (bottom, right) may be considered the second Japanese to arrive in Paraguay, shown here with his family in Paraguay, 1933. (Collection of Raymundo Fukuoka)

Sakoda was an accountant who worked in the tannin industry for the firm of Carlos Casado, situated on the banks of the Paraguay River, north of Asunción, the capital of Paraguay.

The second Japanese to arrive in Paraguay was Shotaro Fukuoka, who resided in the capital from 1915 and became an important collaborator in the development of Paraguayan-Japanese relations. In recognition of his services, Fukuoka was invited to the celebration of the 2,600th anniversary of the Japanese Empire.

Paraguayan-Japanese relations did not become active until 1936, when the first group of Japanese immigrants arrived in the country under a previous governmental agreement between the two countries. One of the greatest promoters of Japanese immigration to Paraguay was Kunito Miyasaka, a man of vast experience in organizing the emigration of Japanese to Mindanao (in the Philippines), Peru, and Brazil. In 1935, Miyasaka, together with representatives of the Japanese government, reached an agreement with the Paraguayan president, Rafael Franco, to permit one hundred Japanese families to enter the country as part of an experimental program for agricultural immigrants.

In order to receive the immigrants in an adequate manner, offices of the Corporation for Japanese Immigration in Paraguay (Paraguay Takushoku Kumiai) were opened in the Paraguayan capital. One of its members, agricultural engineer Hisakazu Kasamatsu, selected appropriate land for agricultural purposes and drew up blueprints for the first Japanese colony, La Colmena. Kasamatsu was to be in charge of administrating La Colmena during World War II, when the other representatives of the Japanese government were sent back to Japan.

Between 1936 and 1941, 134 families entered the country. The increase in immigration exceeded the quota previously set by the Paraguayan government due to an amendment of the terms agreed upon by both countries.

Two men on horseback at the entrance to the first Japanese colony in Paraguay called "La Colmena," 1936. (Collection of Centro Nikkei Paraguayo)

However, many of the immigrants migrated to other cities or countries due to difficulties in communication, lack of access to national highways, malaria epidemics, locust invasions, and terrible weather that ruined the crops. Some families chose the capital and its surrounding areas so that their children would have access to higher education. Therefore, the original population was reduced by 30 percent. This minority demonstrated its strength, perseverance, and stoicism by respecting the agreement between both governments and remaining in the area as agricultural immigrants, thereby contributing to the growth of the country.

In 1941, the first official Paraguayan envoy to Japan, Manuel Ferreira, labored intensely to improve the ties between the two countries. However, his good intentions were frustrated when relations with the Axis nations, among them Japan, were severed during the Chancellor's Conference of twenty-one Pan American countries on February 28, 1942.

In spite of the adverse situation, the Paraguayan government respected the 1919 treaty accords with Japan and assured its Japanese immigrant population that they

Family photograph of Mr. and Mrs. Moriya and their six children, 1939. (Collection of Fujio Moriya)

Early immigrants of La Colmena Colony, Paraguay, 1940. (Collection of Centro Nikkei Paraguayo)

would not suffer any type of property expropriation or eviction. However, given the circumstances, there were certain restrictions to Japanese civic and educational activities; Presidential Decree 8,087 of April 11, 1945, established La Colmena as a "restricted zone." It is important to highlight, however, that no acts against human dignity were committed at any time.

The second stage of Japanese immigration to Paraguay started in 1953, when the government of Gen. Higinio Morinigo opened the doors of the republic to all types of immigrants as a gesture of solidarity with countries that had been devastated by the war. Thereafter, Japanese immigration to the country resumed. The Japanese, especially those who had been repatriated and overwhelmed by their difficulties, went to the few countries that opened their doors to them.

In order to receive the immigrants, the Nippo Paraguayan Colonization Corporation (Nippo Paraguaya de Colonización SRL) was established. It was headed by Hisakazu Kasamatsu and Tanji Ishibashi, who placed the newcomers in the fertile and forested southern region of the country. Kasamatsu and Ishibashi voluntarily offered their labor to settle hundreds of immigrants, who arrived in successive groups and faced extremely precarious conditions.

In 1956, a Japanese legation (later an embassy) was officially established in Paraguay with the arrival of Otoshiro Kuroda, minister plenipotentiary. This development gave hope to the immigrants, especially the 137 families who were hired by the American company CAFÉ, located in the northern coffee-growing region of the country.

In 1959, the Company for the Promotion of Japanese Immigration (Compañía Pro-Fomento de la Inmigración Japonesa, S.A.) was established in Paraguay, with 95 percent of the capital provided by the Japanese government and 5 percent from the private sector. It was founded to promote efficient settlement, on the basis of strong financial support and also aid from the United States. The company sent Yoshio Haneda to Paraguay with capital to pur-

First Paraguayan official mission to Japan in 1940 with Mr. and Mrs. Manuel Ferreira and their children (center). (Collection of Centro Nikkei Paraguayo)

chase land for the immigrants. The land was parceled into lots of thirty hectares (approximately seventy-four acres) for each family. The company was also in charge of constructing routes, bridges, and other infrastructure needed for the settlement.

In 1963, the Service for the Japanese Emigration Corporation (Servicio de Corporación Emigratoria del Japón) was established under the jurisdiction of the Japanese Ministry of Foreign Affairs. In 1974, the Japan International Cooperation Agency (Agencia de Cooperación Internacional del Japón, or JICA) was formed in order to promote international cooperation and socioeconomic development of underdeveloped countries and to provide assistance to the immigrants. The largest branch in South America was set up in Asunción.

Under the auspices of the first two companies, the La Paz and Santa Rosa settlements were established in 1956. Many of these immigrants were originally from the prefectures of Hiroshima, Kochi, and Saga. An agricultural cooperative was organized with the purpose of commercializing local products; soybeans produced in the region were exported to Japan for the first time.

Due to the exemplary behavior of the Japanese and their contributions to the development of agricultural exports and the cultivation of fruits and vegetables of good quality, both governments signed an immigration agreement in 1959 in which Paraguay made a commitment to receive eighty-five thousand Japanese within a thirty-year period. At the end of the treaty period, only seven thousand Japanese and Nikkei resided in Paraguay.

They had settled in the Pirapó colony, whose name is an indigenous Guaraní name that means "fish that can be caught with the hands," founded in 1960; and the Yguazú colony, also bearing an indigenous name, which translates as "big water," established in 1961. Both are located in the rich southeast region of the country. Unlike the other colonies, these settlements received substantial assistance from the Japanese government for the development of their infrastructure: the construction of roads, highways, bridges, community centers, and schools; the supply of

Wedding reception of immigrants, Mr. and Mrs. Sato, attended members of the sixth group of immigrants to Paraguay following the war, 1957. (Collection of Centro Nikkei Paraguayo)

machinery; and the support of agricultural cooperatives. The main production of these colonies is soy, wheat, fruit trees, and cattle. These two colonies are exemplars of development and prosperity today.

The successive immigration of Japanese, to Asunción starting in 1914, and then to other big cities, such as Encarnación (1937), Pedro Juan Caballero (1937), and Ciudad del Este (1958), was motivated by greater access to higher education for their children; the easy establishment of companies, such as dealerships and import of automobiles, machinery, and technology; and the growth of family businesses, such as hotels, restaurants, supermarkets, beauty salons, workshops, food processing facilities, and spinning mills. Among professionals, the most numerous are the Nikkei physicians, followed by economists, agricultural engineers, university professors, veterinarians, civil and electromechanical engineers, and architects. The Nikkei also run large vegetable and fruit plantations, and they raise chickens, pigs, and other animals.

The excellent and flourishing relationship between the two countries motivated the first visit of the Paraguayan chief of state, Gen. Alfredo Stroessner, to Japan on April 14–20, 1972, accompanied by 132 Paraguayan and Nikkei business people. Emperor Hirohito received General Stroessner with full honors and thanked him for the warm welcome and protection that his government had extended to the Japanese in Paraguay. After that, loans and grants, as well as technical and financial cooperation, increased for the well-being of the Paraguayan people. To reciprocate the state visit, Crown Prince Akihito and Princess Michiko traveled to Paraguay in 1978. The presence of such illustrious visitors brought renewed faith and hope to the Japanese Paraguayan community.

To celebrate the fiftieth anniversary of Japanese immigration to Paraguay in the year 1986, members of the Japanese imperial family were once again present; Prince Hitachi and Princess Hanako were accompanied by representatives of the Japanese government and special

The first marriage ceremony held in Chaves colony, August 1956, among the second group of Japanese immigrants to Paraguay after World War II. Between 1953 and 1956, 110 Japanese families had settled in Chaves colony, which was established by the government as an international settlement in 1953. (Courtesy of Centro Nikkei Paraguayo)

The inauguration of Centro Nikkei Paraguayo in February 1996, with the president of Paraguay, Juan Carlos Wasmosy (third from left), the ambassador of Japan (second from left), Emi Kasamatsu (fourth from left), and members of the Comisión Directiva of the Centro Nikkei Paraguayo. (Photograph by Japan Color. Collection of Centro Nikkei Paraguayo)

The first State visit to Japan of Alfredo Stroessner, president of Paraguay, greeted upon his arrival by Emperor Hirohito, April 1972. (Photograph by Kajima Projections Ltd., Japan. Collection of Emi Kasamatsu [Mrs. Desiderio Enciso, former ambassador to Japan])

The imperial highnesses of Japan signing official document commemorating the fiftieth anniversary of Japanese immigration to Paraguay, September 1986. (Collection of Emi Kasamatsu)

Two brothers on a pig farm in Paraguay, ca. 1961. (Collection of Centro Nikkei Paraguayo)

guests from neighboring countries. Also, the Paraguayan government, headed by the General Stroessner, participated in all the events. This celebration undoubtedly will remain in the memory of the Nikkei for many years to come.

In 1991, a total of 450 people participated in a very important Pan-American event that took place in Paraguay and was attended by the president of Paraguay (then-general Andres Rodriguez), representatives of the Japanese government, and outstanding Nikkei from Pan-American countries. This was the Sixth Pan American Nikkei Convention (VI Convención Panamericana Nikkei); its slogan was "To Be Better Citizens in Our Countries," and the its principal theme was "Nikkei Par-

Twenty-fifth anniversary celebration of the foundation of La Colmena Agro-Industrial Cooperative, Ltd., 1973. (Collection of Centro Nikkei Paraguayo)

ticipation in Panamerican Society." In 1996, the sixtieth anniversary of Japanese immigration was celebrated jubilantly in the Paraguayan capital, again with the presence and support of the representatives of the Japanese and Paraguayan governments.

CHARACTERISTICS OF THE NIKKEI IN PARAGUAY

Japanese who visit La Colmena discover how zealously the inhabitants of that first Japanese settlement have protected the values and customs of Meiji-era Japan (1868–1912). As if time has stood still, visitors are likely to observe behavior that is no longer practiced in Japan but remains distinctively characteristic among the residents of La Colmena.

The communities where Issei influence remains strong consist mainly of people who arrived after World War II. Customs are protected and transmitted by Japanese associations located throughout the colonies and grouped together under a Federation of Japanese Associations, which provides social and educational support. Among its activities are artistic exhibitions, festivities and *seijinshiki* (celebration of adulthood), *bon odori* (the Feast of Lanterns Festival dance), and *roojinshiki* (celebration of old age). The organization of the colonies is well structured, with Japanese-language schools. Also, *sakubun* (short stories) and *benrontaikai* (oratory) contests in Japanese are of extraordinary quality.

The Nikkei in Paraguay identify more with the Japanese than with the national citizens of Paraguay. Ninety-five percent speak Japanese fluently, and some prefer to adopt the Japanese nationality of their parents. Almost all of them feel great admiration for the country of their ancestors and are proud to belong to this distinct ethnic group. Continuous communication with Japan is maintained through trips, scholarships, books, newspapers, videos, and the Internet.

However, it would be very useful for the Paraguayan Nikkei to interact more with the Paraguayan nationals and to be more concerned with the problems and the con-

Delegation of Paraguayan baseball players, 1974. (Collection of Centro Nikkei Paraguayo)

crete realities of life in Paraguay. Already, most of the Nikkei among the first group of immigrants have reached a stage of professional success and economic and social satisfaction. Without a doubt, Paraguay has suffered many unfortunate trials, unwise policies, and economic calamities, and the country needs the participation of all its citizens alike. It is time to start combining Japanese strengths with Paraguayan abilities.

Bibliographic Essay on Themes of the Japanese and Nikkei of Paraguay

EMI KASAMATSU

THE FIRST BOOK WRITTEN ABOUT THE JAPANESE immigrants was a commemorative book entitled *20 Years of Japanese Immigration in Paraguay* in 1956. The book, compiled by various authors, discusses the history of the organizations in the various Japanese settlements, how the first group of immigrants to Paraguay migrated from Brazil, and the experiences of the original 132 families who immigrated to Paraguay directly from Japan. It is a thorough job, including the names of the immigrants, the names of the ships they boarded, and the dates of their arrival. The book also discusses the unfortunate experiences and the profitable ones of the immigrants, the great exodus that occurred during the first ten years, and the various difficulties that motivated so many to migrate to other countries. This kind of massive task cannot be attributed to only one author. Written in Japanese and now out of print, the book is a very important source for learning about the first period of Japanese immigration in Paraguay.

Since 1956, more Japanese have arrived as immigrants. The settlements in remote areas of the country have organized their tenth, twentieth, thirtieth, and fortieth anniversary publications. These commemorative books contain the dates of special events and interesting experiences of the residents. The works mainly provide a chronological narration of events and experiences in the community, the relations among leaders of different associations and cooperatives, the improvement in education, statistical data of the residents, and so on. Among these commemorative books, the following can be mentioned.

In 1970, the Japanese Association of Pirapó compiled a 358-page book recounting the ten-year history of their community; it was entitled *Hirakeyuku daichi* (J-7).

In 1975, *La Colmena Nokyo kinembi* commemorated the twenty-fifth anniversary of the first Japanese agricultural cooperative formed in the city of La Colmena. The publication includes a chronological history of the creation, development, and expansion of this agricultural cooperative.

In 1980, the Japanese Association of Pirapó published another commemorative book covering the ten-year history of the community—*Hirakeyuku daichi* (J-5).

In 1981, the Japanese Association of Amambay published a 370-page commemorative book for the twenty-fifth anniversary of their settlement, entitled *Yūhi: Amambai ijūchi 25-nen kinenshi* (J-1). The book contains detailed records of memorable experiences, such as the painful situation faced by the first immigrants who worked on the coffee plantation owned by an American company. The ultimate failure of the company led to the establishment of an independent Japanese settlement. Though their efforts bore fruit, some immigrants moved to other territories. The chronological development and statistical data in this book provide very useful information on the Japanese Paraguayans in Amambay.

In 1986, the Japanese Association of La Paz published a book for its members entitled *Midori no daichi* (J-3), commemorating the thirtieth anniversary of Japanese settlement. (La Paz was the first community created in the post–World War II period.) The book contains data on the poverty and prosperity of this early period, when the Japanese government had not extended its assistance to its emigrants aboard.

In 1990, the Japanese Association of Pirapó published its third book, *Hirakeyuku daichi* (J-6), in recognition of the thirtieth anniversary and founding of Colonia Pirapó. The continuity of the Japanese Association's membership and its goal to preserve the written testimonies of the immigrants in their community are admirable.

The Agro-Industrial Cooperative of La Colmena published another informative book for forty years of its foundation, published by Litocolor in 1990 (S-3).

Daichi ni susumu (1991: J-8) is the title that the members of the Japanese Association of Yguazú gave to their book commemorating the thirtieth anniversary of Japanese immigration to this settlement, located in one of the richest regions of Paraguay. The publication is a compilation of the positive experiences of the community, which include the visit of His Imperial Highness Crown Prince Akihito and Crown Princess Michiko of Japan, and the development and growth of cattle-raising and agricultural enterprises in the region. Also, the book describes cultural and recreational activities.

In 1995, *Midori no daichi* (J-4) was published as part of the fortieth-anniversary celebration of La Paz.

In 1973, Kiyoaki Okuhata, a Japanese journalist living in Paraguay, wrote a book that commemorated the first visit of the Paraguayan president to Japan in April 1972.

Its title is *Paraguai to Nihon* (J-12); it has 425 pages, including color and black-and-white photographs. This work is considered the first important book written in Japanese that examines the beginning of immigration, the experiences of the agents of the immigrant organizations, and the profiles of Japanese immigrants and their history. Also, Okuhata presents unique aspects of Paraguayan history in order to let Japanese readers know more about the country where Japanese have settled. The details of the presidential visit and the relationship and subsequent cooperation between the governments of Paraguay and Japan are useful.

In 1986, *Eikō e no ishizue* (J-11) was published in hardback to commemorate the fiftieth anniversary of Japanese immigration in Paraguay. The publication documents in minute detail the important events and personal experiences of the Japanese and Nikkei throughout Paraguay. Data include the place of origin, arrival dates, the number of family members, and the names of all immigrants who arrived in the country and of their descendants. The work is a collaboration of various authors who voluntarily offered their dedication and time in order to compile a commemorative book, which also features greetings from Japanese and local authorities.

In 1988, Dr. Desiderio M. Enciso, the ambassador of Paraguay to Japan from 1972 to 1976, wrote the first book regarding Paraguay-Japanese relations; it is entitled *Origen, evolución y perspectiva de las relaciones paraguayo-japonesas* (The Origin, Evolution and Perspective of the Paraguayan-Japanese Relations) (S-4). Dr. Enciso's work discusses the beginning of Paraguayan-Japanese diplomatic relations, the favorable relations that evolved between the governments, the opening of the country to Japanese immigrants, and the protection given to the Japanese residents in Paraguay. It is a short book, written in Spanish, but it is a substantial resource for researchers.

After the successful Sixth Pan-American Nikkei Convention of 1991, held in Asunción, all the discussions, conference reports, and panel discussions were compiled into one book of 223 pages with photographs, *Nikkei presente y futuro* (1992). The book offers a general overview of the Nikkei population's participation in Pan-American society.

In 1993, Chiyuki Taoka, a student at the Catholic University in the city of Encarnación, wrote a book as part of her course work in social studies entitled *Historia y evolución de la comunidad japonesa en su integración al Departamento de Itapúa* (S-6). Her study, which is written in Spanish, focuses on the historical evolution and contributions of the post–World War II Japanese immigrants in southern Paraguay.

Another important book, and the only one published by a local publisher—the Biblioteca de Estudios Paraguayos, Universidad Católica—is *La presencia japonesa en el Paraguay* (S-5), written by Emi Kasamatsu in 1997. The book covers detailed research on historical, anthropological, religious, and social themes of Japanese immigrants; Paraguay-Japanese relations; Japanese immigration in Paraguay and its characteristics; and Japanese cooperation in the development of Paraguay. This three-hundred-page publication, written in Spanish and illustrated with black and white photographs, is a good reference book for researchers.

The Japan International Cooperation Agency (JICA), with an office in Paraguay, has a series of publications that contains information on population, education, and Japanese cooperation in Paraguay. Some are written in Japanese and others in Spanish.

Regarding the subject of education, the Association of Professors of Japanese Language (*Nihongo Kyoiku Kenkyu Kyogi Kai*), in its elementary and secondary level, annually publishes its activities, projects, and achievements, as well as experiences of the professors in classrooms and their recommendations, in the annual magazine *Mihotsukushi* (1981–1998), under the direction of Professor Teruko Okamoto.

In the past decade, there have been brief research papers written in Spanish by Yoshiko Moriya Freundorfer about the education and identity of Nikkei. Also, Dr. Felix Kasamatsu, a resident of the United States, has written research papers presented at international Nikkei conferences regarding Nikkei in Paraguay.

In 1999, Yuichi Tanaka authored a 421-page book in Japanese entitled *Nambei no paradaisu Paraguay ni sumu*, with a prologue written by the ambassador to Japan, Miguen Solano López. Tanaka, who is a Japanese national, portrays Paraguay as a pleasant, peaceful, and secure country of greenery and beautiful women, where one can enjoy European modernity as well as the indigenous customs of Paraguay's mixed Spanish-Guaraní population. In addition, he mentions the country's relation with MERCOSUR (the Southern Cone common market). The best of Paraguay, the land where the Japanese also live, is presented through these pleasant themes.

In summary, little has been written about the Japanese community in Paraguay except commemorative books involving group endeavors and containing mostly descriptive information, experiences, and commentaries.

Annotated Bibliography of Japanese Paraguayans

COMPILED BY EMI KASAMATSU

ENGLISH

1. Kasamatsu, Emi. "The Nikkei's Education in the Japanese Language in Paraguay: Re-identifying with the Motherland." In *New Worlds, New Lives: Globalization and People of Japanese Descent in the Americas and from Latin America in Japan*, edited by Lane Hirabayashi, Akemi Kikumura-Yano, and James Hirabayashi. Stanford, Calif.: Stanford University Press, 2002.
2. Stewart, Norman R. *Japanese Colonization in Eastern Paraguay*. Washington, D.C.: National Academy of Sciences, 1967.

    A study of the colony of La Colmena established by Japanese pioneers, undertaken in 1958.

JAPANESE

1. Amanbai Nihonjinkai [アマンバイ日本人会]. *Yūhi: Amanbai ijūchi 25-nen kinenshi* [雄飛：アマンバイ移住地25年記念誌]: n.p., 1981.

    Contains detailed records of memorable experiences. The chronological development and statistical data provide useful information on the Japanese Paraguayans in Amambay.
2. Commemorative committee for 20 years Celebration. Federation of Japanese in Abroad. *History of 20-Year Anniversary of La Colmena: The First Japanese Colony in Paraguay*. Tokyo: n.p., 1958.

    The first book published in the Japanese language on the Japanese immigration in Paraguay. Contains chronology of events: arrival of the Japanese in Paraguay, search of adequate land and preparation, and arrival of immigrants, along with the impressions of principal organizers and pioneers of immigration.
3. Japanese Association of La Paz. *Midori no daichi: 30th Anniversary of La Paz Colony*. Asunción: n.p., 1986.

    Contains data on poverty and prosperity of the early period when the Japanese government had not extended its assistance to its immigrants abroad.
4. Japanese Association of La Paz. *Midori no daichi: 40th Anniversary of La Paz Colony*. Asunción: n.p., 1995.

    Published as part of the fortieth anniversary celebration of La Paz.
5. Japanese Association of Pirapó. *Hirakeyuku daichi: 20th Anniversary of Pirapó Colony*. N.p., 1980.

    Contains greetings of Paraguayan and Japanese authorities, lives of postwar immigrants who arrived in 1960, their efforts and development of the area with mechanization, cooperativization, social organization, and their success.
6. Japanese Association of Pirapó. *Hirakeyuku daichi: 30th Anniversary of Pirapó Colony*. Asunción: n.p., 1990.

    A continued attempt of the community to preserve the written testimonies of the immigrants.
7. Japanese Association of Pirapó. *Hirakeyuku daichi I: Tenth Anniversary of Pirapó Colony*. Asunción: n.p., 1970.

    Contains the chronology of the arrival of Japanese immigrants in the area southeast of Paraguay, and its foundation by the Companía Pro Fomento de la Inmigración Japonesa in 1960 as an agricultural colony. Introduction of new cultivation technology and efforts of the Japanese.
8. Japanese Association of Yguazú. *Daichi ni susumu: Thirty Anniversary of Japanese immigration in Yguazú Colony*. Asunción: Nippa Art. Grafic, 1991.

    A compilation of the fruitful experiences of the community. Also describes cultural and recreational activities.
9. La Colmena Nihongo Gakko. *Hachikko*. La Colmena: n.p., 1987.

    A textbook for Nikkei children of La Colmena, a Japanese settlement in Paraguay, in order to complement the shortage of educational materials.
10. La Colmena Nihongo Gakko. *Hachikko*. La Colmena: n.p., 1988.

    A kind of educational textbook for the children of the settlement to learn Japanese.
11. Organizational Committee for 50th Anniversary of Japanese immigration in Paraguay. *Fifty Years of Japanese Immigration in Paraguay: eikō e no ishizue*. Tokyo: n.p., 1987.

    Documents details of the important events and personal experiences of the Japanese and Nikkei throughout Paraguay.
12. Paraguai to Nihon Kankōkai [パラグァイと日本刊行会]. *Paraguai to Nihon* [パラグァイと日本]. Tōkyō [東京]: Rajio Nikkeisha: Paraguai Shinpōsha [ラジオ日系社: パラグァイ新報社], 1973.

    A special edition for the commemoration of the official visit of President Stroessner of Paraguay and his procession to Japan. Written by a Japanese journalist Kiyoaki Okuhata in 1972, by the commission of Edición Paraguay y Japón, Paraguay Shinpo, and Radio Nikkei. Contains greetings of the Japanese and Paraguayan authorities, short history of Paraguay, economic, social, and political aspects, and the situation and evolution of the Japanese immigrants in Paraguay.

SPANISH

1. Centro Nikkei Paraguayo, 6ta Convención Panamericana Nikkei. *Nikkei presente y futuro.* Asunción: Centro Nikkei Paraguayo, 1992.

    A comprehensive record of the sixth Pan-American Nikkei Convention of 1991. Offers a general overview of the Nikkei population's participation in Pan-American society.

2. Comisión de conmemoración del aniversario de la Cooperativa Agroindustrial. *25 años de la Cooperativa Agro-industrial de La Colmena.* La Colmena: n.p., 1975.

    Includes a chronology of the creation, development, and expansion of La Colmena agricultural cooperative.

3. Cooperativa Agro-Industrial de La Colmena. *40 aniversario de la Constitución de la Cooperativa Agro-Industrial.* Asunción: La Colmena Ltd.: Editora Litocolor, 1990.

    An informative book commemorating the forty years of its foundation.

4. Enciso, Desiderio M.. *Origen, evolución y perspectiva de las relaciones paraguayo-japonesas.* Asunción: n.p., 1988.

    Discusses the beginning of Paraguayan-Japanese diplomatic relations, favorable relations that evolved between the two governments, and the opening of the country to Japanese immigrants and the protection given to the Japanese residents.

5. Kasamatsu, Emi. *La presencia japonesa en el Paraguay.* Asunción: Universidad Católica, 1997.

    Biblioteca de Estudios Paraguayos, Vol. 55.

    Covers detailed research on historical, anthropological, religious, and social themes of Japanese immigrants; Paraguay-Japanese relations and Japanese immigration in Paraguay and its characteristics; and Japanese cooperation in the development of Paraguay.

6. Taoka, Chiyuki. *Historia y evolución de la comunidad japonesa en su integración al Departamento de Itapúa.* N.p.: Trabajo Práctico, Universidad Católica de Encarnación, 1993.

    Focuses on the historical evolution and contributions of the post-World War II Japanese immigrants in southern Paraguay.

Supplementary Materials

COMPILED BY EMI KASAMATSU

Map 8.1 Locations of Nikkei Populations in Paraguay

Japanese Paraguayan Demographic Information

Table 8.1 Japanese Emigration to Paraguay by Prefecture of Origin in Japan, 1921–1993

	1921–'25	'26–'30	'31–'35	Total
	1	-	520	**521**

	1952–'55	'56–'60	'61–'65	'66–'70	'71–'75	'76–'80	'81–'85	'86–'90	'91–'93	Total*
Kōchi	19	949	92	9	4	4	1	1	-	**1,079**
Hokkaidō	127	401	180	29	7	6	-	-	3	**753**
Iwate	-	150	374	46	9	6	-	3	-	**588**
Ehime	23	343	134	2	1	2	1	3	-	**509**
Fukuoka	39	348	105	1	1	7	1	-	-	**502**
Hiroshima	22	434	4	3	7	10	5	1	-	**486**
Kumamoto	58	231	-	13	12	9	1	4	-	**328**
Kagoshima	-	220	25	-	4	4	4	1	-	**258**
Tōkyō	33	65	19	26	50	34	2	10	2	**241**
Wakayama	79	97	7	-	1	-	-	1	-	**185**
Total*	**873**	**4,214**	**1,271**	**242**	**214**	**243**	**50**	**47**	**23**	**7,269**

Sources: Figures for 1899–1935 were taken from Gaimushō Ryōji Ijūbu. *Waga kokumin no kaigai hatten: ijū hyakunen no ayumi (shiryō hen)* (Tōkyō, 1971), 141. Figures for 1952–1993 were taken from Japan International Cooperation Agency, *Kaigai ijū tōkei (FY 1952–FY 1993)* (Tōkyō, 1994), 30–31.
  Note: *Total includes other prefectures.

Table 8.2 Nikkei Population in Paraguay by Ethnic Categories in 1991

Generation	Japanese	Mestizos	Total
Issei	2,278		**2,278**
Nisei	2,877	827	**3,704**
Sansei	939	109	**1,048**
Yonsei and later generations	44	12	**56**

Source: Japan International Cooperation Agency (JICA) of Paraguay, 1991.
  Note: In 1991, 70 percent of the Japanese population—Nikkei—had Paraguayan nationality. Among the actual data of the Japanese and Nikkei population submitted by the office of JICA in Paraguay (1998), 15 percent were Mestizos. In 2000, the Japanese consulate in Paraguay reported that 50 percent of the Nikkei in Paraguay have dual nationalities (Japanese and Paraguayan).

Table 8.3 Japanese-Language Education in Asunción

Year	Preschool	Primary	Secondary
1960	-	-	-
1991	24	90	36
1993	29	94	35
1998	17	84	29

Source: Teruko Okamoto, Nihongo Kyōiku Kenkyū Kyōkai, personal research, November 2000.

Table 8.4 Japanese-Language Education of Two Japanese Paraguayan Settlements

Year	Primary	Secondary	College	Total
1940	140	-	-	**140**
1981	1,671	190	-	**1,861**
1986	915	304	20	**1,239**
1998	755	350	14	**1,119**
2000	717	225	-	**942**

Source: Nihongo Kyōiku Kenkyū Kyōkai. Mihotsukushi, No. 18. Asunción, December 2000.

Table 8.5 Occupational Fields of Japanese Paraguayans by Percentage

Year	Agriculture	Business/Industry	Ranching	Other
1940	90	0.1	0	-
1960	70	8	0.2	-
1991	63	11	0.5	2
1999	60	30	1	8

Source: Centro Nikkei Paraguayo, 1999.

Table 8.6 Religion of Japanese Paraguayans by Percentage

Year	Buddhist/Shinto	New Religions	Christian	Other
1940	60	-	10	30
1960	20	20	6	58
1996	10	35	8	47
2000	7	30	4	59

Source: Emi Kasamatsu, "La presencia japonesa en el Paraguay." In Biblioteca de estudios paraguayos (Asunción: Universidad Católica, 1997), vol. 55.

CHAPTER 9

Japanese Peruvians

DEVELOPED IN COLLABORATION WITH THE FUNDACIÓN CULTURAL NIKKEI DEL PERÚ AND THE MUSEO CONMEMORATIVO DE LA INMIGRACIÓN JAPONESA EN EL PERÚ

THE STORY OF NIKKEI IN PERU BEGAN IN 1899, WITH THE ARRIVAL OF THE FIRST immigrants from Japan, who worked on sugar and cotton plantations in the middle coastal valleys. Many subsequently left for the cities of Lima and Callao, where they engaged in small business, like barbershops and restaurants, during the first half of the 1920s. Between 1924 and 1936 the second wave of Japanese immigrants headed for these urban areas rather than plantations, pursuing new opportunities as merchants and small suburban farmers. Toward the 1920s, community solidarity emerged markedly in Lima. However, the strength of the ethnic community made the Nikkei population a target of jealous discrimination that increased with Japan's military aggression in Asia, the termination of Japanese immigration in 1936, and the anti-Japanese riot of May 1940 in Lima. The Pacific War made the situation even worse, as the Peruvian government collaborated with the U.S. government in sending 1,800 civilians to North America, from where most of them were deported to Japan after the war. The Nikkei who remained in Peru suffered extreme restrictions and hardships, including the confiscation of personal property. With the lifting of wartime restrictions in 1947, the Nikkei community slowly rebuilt, reestablishing Japanese associations and schools. During the 1950s and 1960s, the Nikkei continued their course of economic recovery and assimilation into the mainstream society. Nikkei white-collar workers and professionals increased in number, and interracial marriage was no longer unusual. Perhaps the height of Nikkei assimilation was symbolized by the election of President Alberto Fujimori in 1990. The same decade also witnessed a large migration of Nikkei workers to Japan due to the economic challenges that gripped the Peruvian nation.

Japanese Immigrants and Their Descendants in Peru: 1899–1998

AMELIA MORIMOTO

AT THE TURN OF THE NINETEENTH CENTURY, MASS worldwide migration began due to the development of capitalism around the world. This was the start of Japanese overseas migration. South America became one of the destinations for the Japanese after legal restrictions were established in North America.

Japanese immigrants arrived in Peru between 1899 and 1923 as *braceros* (workers), hired by agricultural landholders. Between 1924 and 1936, the migratory process continued freely. The pattern of temporary migration discontinued with the outbreak of World War II. The consequences of this conflagration shaped the permanent settlement of the Japanese in Peru. Certain features continue to distinguish the Japanese Peruvian population as a collective entity; however, their integration into the national economy is accompanied by a gradual process of assimilation on various levels, reflected more clearly in the younger generations.

JAPANESE IMMIGRATION TO PERU

Before the War of the Pacific between Chile and Peru (1879–1884), the Peruvian economy was based mainly on the agricultural production and export of sugar and cotton. After the war, the sugar industry resumed its process of recovery and expansion, supported by foreign investments and the demands of the international market. The lack of manpower, ever present since the beginning of the republic (1821), emerged again. But this time, landowners

Japanese immigrants landing in Cerro Azul Port in Cañete, 1913. (Collection of Museo Conmemorativo de la Inmigración Japonesa en el Perú)

could not count on the Chinese, who had been first brought to Peru in 1849; that traffic had been cut off in 1874 by the Tientsin Treaty, signed by the Chinese and Peruvian governments.

After 1890, the old "hooking" systems of forced indigenous labor were put back into practice on the coastal plantations. Despite the diverse measures used by coastal landholders to secure this manpower, the labor shortage problem persisted; the landholders could not count on a permanent workforce. Indians captured and retained on the coast searched for ways to escape the plantations. The coastal landholders looked to recruit braceros from different countries. Between 1899 and 1923, 18,258 Japanese immigrants entered Peru, hired at first by sugarcane enterprises and subsequently by cotton growers. Among these recruits were 15,887 men, 2,145 women, and 226 children. Approximately 13 percent entered in 1908, and another 43 percent arrived between 1914 and 1929, with the start of World War I and the growth of international demand for sugarcane and cotton. In general, the greatest numbers came from the agricultural prefectures of Japan: Okinawa (20 percent), Hiroshima (9 percent), Fukuoka (8 percent), and Yamaguchi (7.5 percent). Less than 1 percent came from industrial prefectures, like Osaka or Tokyo.

Seventy-eight percent of the immigrants settled in plantations located in the middle coastal valleys. The Cañete plantations, located in the southern valley of Lima and operated by the British Sugar Company, hired approximately 33 percent, followed by the Negociación Agrícola San Nicolas, with 11.6 percent, and Paramonga with 8 percent, the latter two located in the northern valley of Lima.

The situation of the immigrants who entered after 1903 was analogous to those of the first group, with conflicts arising due to similar reasons. The immigrants who worked as contract laborers on the Peruvian plantations at the beginning of the century faced similar work conditions as the native workers and were subjected to the same oppressive measures of past Spanish colonial rule aimed at intimidating and quieting the laborers. The common response of the Japanese was to strike or escape. But the

Japanese women and children farmers working in the fields of Cañete, Peru, ca. 1900–1920s. (Collection of Museo Conmemorativo de la Inmigración Japonesa en el Perú)

Peruvian businessman Isataro Ura of Fukuoka prefecture and his family in his cotton field during harvest, in Huaral, Chancay Valley, Peru, ca. 1920s. (Collection of Museo Conmemorativo de la Inmigración Japonesa en el Perú)

main difference between the native worker and the Japanese immigrant was that for the latter, the situation would be temporary, lasting only until he could save enough money to change jobs and thereby earn sufficient money to return to Japan.

Even during the period when most Japanese were living in the *haciendas* (plantations), a significant number migrated to other regions of Peru. From World War I to World War II, the Chancay Valley attracted the largest concentration of Japanese. Because of its close proximity to the capital city, this valley was an intermediate zone for migration to the cities of Lima and Callao. Japanese attracted to these two cities became employees and merchants. Shortly afterward, they established small businesses, such as barbershops and restaurants.

Before World War I, there were thirty-two establishments, mainly grocery stores, owned by Japanese in Lima and Callao. After the war, the number increased to 243. The stores were often bought from earlier Chinese and Italians immigrants. In 1920, there were 2,386 stores of different kinds run by Japanese, their number increasing to 3,844 four years later. Hairdressing shops were most common, since few resources were necessary to get started. The first hairdressing shop owned by Japanese began in 1904; in 1924 there were 130, with a total of 176 located in Lima and Callao. By 1924, the number of immigrants that remained in Peru was approximately eleven thousand, and their property was valued between thirty-five and forty million yen. It was calculated that two and a half million yen was sent each year to relatives in Japan.

During the 1920s, the need for labor diminished, and the low wages offered failed to attract new immigrants. From the 1930s, forced labor recruitment and retention started to disappear, as did the practice of "mixed salary" (part money and part food). The emergence of a free labor market and the consolidation of rural property in the hands of few landowners were accompanied by the expansion of vast holdings of rural property and the expulsion of small landowners.

Monhachi Hara's store in Lima, Peru, ca. 1920s. (Collection of Museo Conmemorativo de la Inmigración Japonesa en el Perú)

However, Japanese immigration did not stop. On the contrary, between 1924 and 1936 a larger number entered the country. But the conditions of these immigrants differed from those of the earlier period. Their main destinations were the cities, where they became involved in commerce and service activities. Those who went to the rural areas worked as small farmers, landholders, and *yanaconas* (farmers who paid for the use of land in products or services to the owner). During this period, the migration of *yobiyose imin* (immigrants called from Japan by their relatives or friends) was greatly facilitated by those who had established themselves as merchants and small farmers.

COMMUNITY LIFE

The presence of family members, friends, and other Japanese in general, helped the Japanese immigrants to adapt to the their new environment. The practice of mutual support allowed them to cope with the difficulties of adjusting to life in their new environment.

Because of their poor knowledge of Spanish and the inaccessibility of credit from banks, the *tanomoshi* was instrumental to the start of many businesses. The tanomoshi, introduced by a Japanese immigrant, was a community-based rotating finance system whereby members of a group contributed a certain amount of money to a pool. Members could borrow money from this source. Those who withdrew their money last gained more interest. The success of the practice was based on mutual trust and a sense of community solidarity.

With the emergence of businesses also came the establishment of guilds. In 1907, the Barbershops Association started in Lima with a collectivity of twenty-five barbershops managed by Japanese, and in 1909 another association began in Callao. These associations and guilds served as defensive fronts and were the only formal Japanese institutions representing the interests of the Japanese immigrant community.

In 1914, the Association of Merchants of Home Articles was established. The Japanese Merchants Chamber

Yohichi Saito (second from right), laundry owner and cotton cultivator, with his family and agricultural laborers in Fundo Rosa, Huacho, Chancay Valley, Peru, ca. 1930s. (Collection of Museo Conmemorativo de la Inmigración Japonesa en el Perú)

began the following year with twenty-seven members, and in 1919, the Association of Restaurants Owners and the Association of Small Stores in Lima Markets were founded. The year 1917 marked the establishment of the Japanese Association, the one institution that represented all the Japanese immigrants in Peru.

For the immigrants, language difficulties made it hard to read the news. In the first decade of the twentieth century, the most important news source in the Japanese language was a handwritten bulletin (later mimeographed) titled the *Jiritsu* (Independence). In 1913, the first printed newspaper of the Japanese community, the *Andes Jiho*, was published, followed by four others; they were published until the beginning of World War II.

As the arrivals extended their stay in Peru, new priorities emerged; among these, the education of their children was the most important. With their enduring hope of returning to Japan, the immigrants educated their children according to formal Japanese standards and content. Therefore, until World War II, the children of the Japanese immigrants were educated in schools specially established for them. In 1908, the first one was founded in the hacienda Santa Bárbara in the Cañete Valley. In 1920, the Lima Nikko School was built; its modern facilities and advanced teaching methods were equivalent to those of the best schools in Lima.

WORLD WAR II AND THE POSTWAR PERIOD

During the 1930s and until World War II, the Peruvian government passed discriminatory laws directed against Japanese immigrants. Motives attributed to them included the high concentration of Japanese in Lima, the success of a few in agriculture and commerce, and after 1934, the military expansion of Japan in Asia. Local political and economic interests appealed to the government to consider the Japanese as a threat.

On May 13, 1940, Japanese were targets of a race riot, which resulted in the destruction of Nikkei properties. Some five hundred people lost all their belongings and took refuge in the Lima Nikko School. Eleven days later a violent earthquake hit Lima—some proclaimed it was divine punishment. (Collection of Museo Conmemorativo de la Inmigración Japonesa en el Perú)

Japanese Peruvian internees boarding ship in the United States for Japan in 1945. After the war, most Japanese Peruvians were refused reentry in Peru—only 5 percent were allowed to return. (Collection of the United States National Archives, Washington, D.C.)

When the menace of war began to expand in May 1940, rumors spread in Lima that the Japanese were planning to take over the country and had hidden guns in their stores and homes. Under this pretext, urban crowds, led by a certain political party, plundered Japanese properties, causing damages calculated at six million yen. Three hundred and sixteen persons, who lost all their property, decided to return to Japan.

On December 7, 1941, when Japan attacked Pearl Harbor, the Peruvian government imposed legal restrictions on the financial activities of Japanese individuals and associations. The following day, these orders became law. The implementation of these restrictive decrees began with the confiscation of the immigrants' properties, allowing only certain activities, like the operation of small businesses. Five Japanese schools were confiscated, including the Lima Nikko School.

In 1942, 342 Japanese decided to return to Japan. Also, from that year to 1945, 1,800 civilians were deported to the United States as prisoners of war on the basis of "military necessity," with the underlying intent of exchanging them for U.S. citizens held in Japan. Among the deported were immigrants considered "dangerous" and members of the Japanese consulate in Lima, including Nisei of Peruvian nationality. All were sent to Crystal City, Kennedy, Seagoville, and Missoula internment camps, in Texas and Montana. None of the deported was guilty of any crime. Many were sent to Japan, and about three hundred remained in the United States; only one hundred could return to Peru after the end of the war.

The defeat of Japan in World War II had a profound effect on the minds and attitudes of Japanese immigrants. The social and economic devastation of Japan at the end of the war destroyed their hopes of returning home. In place of that dream, they decided to settle in Peru and build a future for their descendants in this country.

In 1947, the restrictions against former Axis nationals were lifted. The Japanese associations resumed their activities, and new Japanese schools appeared, mostly with non-Japanese names, Peruvian personnel, and educational programs that taught Japanese as a foreign language. Also, new cultural, social, and sports associations were created to transmit the traditions of Japan to future generations of Japanese Peruvians.

Starting in the 1950s, the process of economic recovery gained momentum within the Japanese Peruvian community. Economic activities branched out into ventures such as *avicultura* (poultry keeping) and industry, and independent professionals emerged among the second generation. However, traditional activities like commerce and services still remained the most numerous, though larger in scale in some cases.

The concentration of the Japanese Peruvian population in the cities was accompanied by a process of assimilation toward other local cultures and also by an internal social and economical differentiation. In fact, the 1960s witnessed upward mobility by some families. However, the existence of community associations and the sharing of common values and traditions helped to obscure the differences and to show an image of homogeneity. Also, in

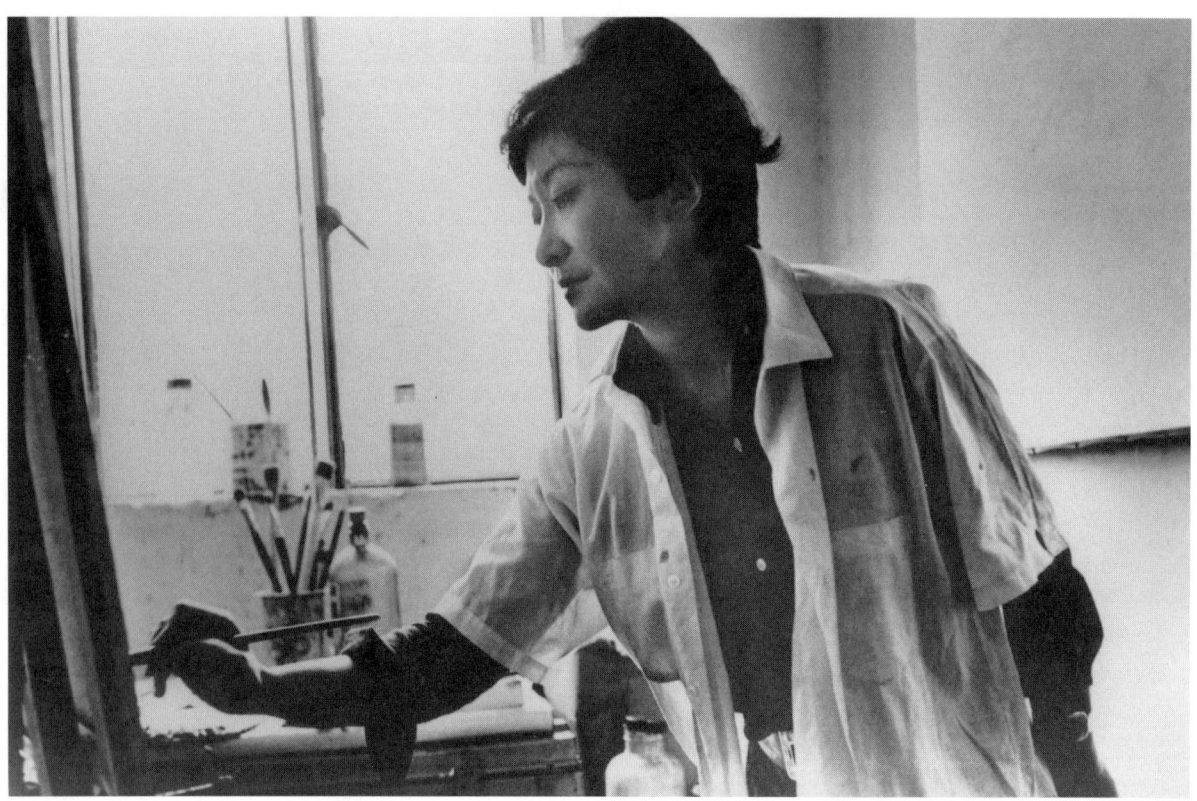

Tilsa Tsuchiya, Peruvian painter. (Photograph by Mario Pozzi Escot. Collection of Museo Commemorativo de la Immigración Japonesa en el Perú)

Jorge Hirano and Gerónimo Barbadillo, soccer players of the National Peruvian Team. (Collection of Hirano Family from Hural)

this decade, many Nisei names started to appear in national newspapers. Several Nisei distinguished themselves in fine arts and sports, winning international championships for Peru.

CURRENT POPULATION OF JAPANESE PERUVIANS

According to the survey census conducted in 1989, the population of Japanese origin was 45,644 individuals (50,303 to 55,421 by 1998). Their ages ranged up to ninety-nine, and they comprised five generations. The first generation, or Issei, accounted for only 5 percent of the entire Japanese Peruvian population; the second generation, or Nisei, were 33 percent; the third generation, Sansei, represented 47.8 percent; the fourth generation, Yonsei, 13.51 percent; and the fifth generation, Gosei, 0.35 percent.

As in the past, concentration continued to be high in the urban areas. Eighty-four percent remained in the *departamento* of Lima and 70.53 percent in the capital city. Other places with a significant Japanese Peruvian population were La Libertad, Piura, and Lambayeque (northern coast of Peru); San Martín, Loreto, Madre de Dios, Ucayali (jungle region); Arequipa, Ica (southern coast); Ancash (middle coast and Sierra); Junín and Cusco (middle and

President Alberto Fujimori (center) and Princess Sayako of Japan (left) at the inauguration of the Japanese Immigration to Peru Centennial Monument, Campo de Marte, Lima, May 1999. (Photograph by Denise Okuyama. Collection of Denise Y. Okuyama)

southern Sierra), and smaller numbers resided in Moquegua, Tacna (southern coast); Ayacucho (southern Sierra); Tumbes (northern coast); Cajamarca (northern Sierra), and Cerro de Pasco (middle Sierra and jungle).

An important change was an increase in mixed marriages to men and women of different racial origins. A third of the married persons of Japanese descent had a wife or husband of non-Japanese origin, and it was estimated that half of the entire Japanese Peruvian population was racially mixed.

The educational level of this population was relatively high. More than 63 percent of the total population had attended high school and university; 10,139 individuals were established in forty different careers. The most numerous occupational category was that of employees, followed by proprietors, independent professionals, and others. In a deviation from previous patterns, a significant number were employed in governmental institutions, mainly as physicians and schoolteachers. The proprietors or businessmen, who represented 33 percent of the economically active population, represented a wide range of endeavors, from small businesses to larger enterprises. Throughout Peru there were 4,828 businessmen of Japanese origin who were owners of firms in industry, commerce, and services. The professionals also occupied a prominent group in this population, making up a total of 1,754. The most numerous were engineers, physicians, public accountants, teachers, business administrators, pharmacists, dentists, architects, and biologists. At universities and scientific institutions there was also a significant number of professionals of Japanese origin. There

President Alberto Fujimori, Peru, 1998. (Collection of "Diario El Peruano")

were also people of Japanese descent, in smaller numbers, who were outstanding in fine arts and literature.

Though certain Japanese traditions are still observed, the racial mixture and the assimilation of other cultural practices are characteristically widespread. A common language spoken at home is Spanish mixed with Japanese expressions; 92 percent are Catholic, but 33 percent of families preserve Buddhist rituals; given names and surnames are mixed with non-Japanese ones; food is mostly local, and the Japanese cuisine prepared at home is often mixed with local seasonings. Nevertheless, the population and the processes of change are neither homogeneous nor identical. While some of the Japanese Peruvian population participates in its own social activities and traditions for the most part, other segments are integrating into the larger Peruvian society.

Almost a century has passed since the arrival of the first group of Japanese immigrants to Peru. Currently, their descendants are found in all levels and activities of na-

Chiyoteru Hiraoka and his wife Rosa Torres and their children: (left to right) Carlos, Vidal, Raúl, and Guillermo, 1949. Mr. Hiraoka, who was born in Kumamoto, Japan, became a prosperous businessman and community leader in Peru as president of the Japanese Peruvian Association and mayor of Huanta province in Ayacucho in 1959. His Peruvian wife and their children were all born in Ayacucho. (Collection of the Hiraoka Family)

Folk singer Angelica Harada, Peru, ca. 1960s. (Collection of the Harada Family)

tional life, and they are part of the social, cultural, and racial panorama of Peru. The 1990s held significant changes for the country as a whole and for Japanese Peruvians in particular. During this decade, thousands of Peruvians of Japanese descent migrated to Japan as workers, due to the general economic crisis inherited from the previous government. In 1990, Alberto Fujimori, an engineer and of second generation Japanese ancestry, was elected as president of Peru; he was reelected in 1995 and in 2000. His third period terminated less than four months after its beginning, in the midst of accusations of corruption. He left the country, sent his resignation from the presidency from Japan, and adopted Japanese citizenship. These two facts, especially the controversial government and scandalous end of Fujimori as president, and the effects of the episode on the Japanese Peruvians, are issues that will require further research and analysis.

César Ichikawa and Los Doltons, a popular Sansei musical group, Peru, 1966. (Collection of the Ichikawa Family)

Peruvian Japanese Bibliographic Essay

RAÚL ARAKI AND JORGE M. NAKAMOTO

REVIEW OF THE LITERATURE BY HISTORICAL TIME FRAMES

The publications on the Japanese Peruvians, although not numerous, have dealt with a great variety of themes, particularly from a historical point of view. These works primarily have been defined by the historical context and influenced by certain perspectives—especially political—and by different motivations. It should be emphasized that authors of different nationalities, professions, and expertise have produced the literature.

Writing on Peruvians of Japanese descent can be organized into the following historical periods: the 1930s and World War II, a product of international political confrontation; the 1960s, the defining period of Nisei identity; the late 1970s and early 1980s, which marked the beginning of publications with greater academic perspectives; and the 1990s, which produced a general interest in the origin of President Alberto Fujimori and people of Japanese descent in Peru.

Within these historical timeframes, special mention should be made to the celebration of the immigration anniversaries (seventy-fifth, eightieth, ninetieth, and hundredth anniversaries), which were accompanied by commemorative editions and many other publications, even outside the Japanese Peruvian community.

The 1930s and World War II
Like many other countries of the Western Hemisphere, the literature on the Japanese in Peru of this period was rife with deep racial prejudice, tacit and explicit arguments for their exclusion, and anti-Asian arguments that privileged white European immigration. The works of this period reflected the widespread ideology of the time, published with almost official character and "scientific claims" supportive of anti-Asian stereotypes, mixed with distortions of facts, arguments, and expressions of xenophobia and racism.

During the 1930s, an anti-Japanese campaign was instigated, promulgating various governmental decrees to limit the entrance of the Japanese into Peru and to reduce their expansion in commercial and agricultural activities. Some newspapers published xenophobic articles. For example, the daily *La Prensa* launched a campaign against "The Japanese Infiltration" and published numerous articles by noted intellectuals and politicians of the time. Victor Guevara articulated some of the arguments and ideas supporting this campaign in a thick chapter of a book titled *Las grandes cuestiones nacionales* (The Grand National Questions) (S-26), which framed Japanese immigration as a threat and a theme for national preoccupation.

The most negative and shameful demonstration of this extensive xenophobic sentiment occurred on May 13, 1940, when part of the population in Lima and Callao launched a political and press campaign, ultimately damaging and plundering many of Japanese businesses and households.

For contemporary publications that criticize this period from a new perspective, see the article by June Kodani (S-37). Kodani analyzes the impact of North American literature on Latin American thought of those years. She focuses her investigation on those works of prewar and postwar U.S. literature that are related to Japanese immigration. Some areas of her analysis include Japanese immigration as an extension of political ambition of Japan in the Western Hemisphere, and Japanese immigration as an expression of Japanese challenge against U.S. economic interest in Latin America and the "nonassimilability" of the Japanese. Amelia Morimoto (1979: S-51; 1999: S-52) reviews and analyzes Peruvian publications in these same years, as antecedents to the riot of 1940 and the government's anti-Japanese measures undertaken during World War II.

After the start of World War II, in May 1942, the Peruvian government began confiscating the property of Japanese immigrants, including their schools. The first deportation of Peruvian Nikkei was carried out on April 1942, as part of the U.S. program of Internment and Investigation for National Security, which was extended to Latin America for reasons of "military necessity." Between 1942 and 1945, about three thousand Japanese, Germans, and Italians were deported from Latin America to the United States. About two-thirds, or 2,300 people, were Japanese, and more than 80 percent were from Peru. Among them, not only Japanese nationals but also Peruvian citizens of Japanese origin were included. This topic is treated by Gardiner (E-6, E-7), Emmerson (E-5), Morimoto (S-51, S-52), Kodani (S-37), Nakamoto (S-59), Higashide (E-9), and Rocca (S-64).

The 1960s: The Nisei Period
In the postwar period, the majority of the Nisei studied in state schools, and many entered universities. The Nisei began to advance in the national academic and cultural fields and to realize the necessity of major participation in Peru's national life, especially in the field of politics. A demonstration of this trend was the emergence of a group called "The Generation of '64," formed by Nisei university students who got together with other progressive Peruvian intellectuals of the period at the legendary Cafe Palermo, located in front of the Universidad Nacional Mayor de San Marcos.

From the late 1950s to the 1970s, various works on Japanese Peruvians were published by descendants of the immigrants, including Arakaki (S-1) and Fukumoto (S-25). Some of their works are listed in the selected annotated bibliography. Almost all are essays written for bachelor's degree and the *Licenciatura* (a prerequisite for starting a professional activity). With almost no exceptions, the works are basically descriptive. They also reflect an increasing interest in the Japanese Peruvian experience among descendants of the immigrants and present a vision from within of a wide variety of subjects, such as history, education, religion, and health.

The Late 1970s and 1980s: A New Vision
In the 1980s, the magazine *Puente* (Bridge) began circulation under the direction of the Tamashiro brothers, Enrique and Alejandro. The magazine was a product of a matured new identity of Japanese Peruvians, namely Nisei and Sansei, an identity that manifested itself in a new, leftist attitude and vision of their country. In its time, the magazine was interesting, distinct, and controversial. One could find articles covering a great variety of topics and the participation of numerous renowned Peruvian intellectuals. Some of the authors were Pablo Macera, Rodrigo Montoya, Washington Delgado, José Watanabe (S-76), Marco Martos, Luis Gillermo Lumbreras, Wilfredo Kapsoli, Augusto Higa (S-29), Hildebrando Pérez, César Lévano (S-38, S-39), and Nicolás Matayoshi (S-42, S-43).

During this decade a more scientific and academic approach to the study of Japanese Peruvians emerged. At the end of 1979, Morimoto wrote the first book in Spanish that focused on the history and population of Japanese Peruvians—*Los inmigrantes japoneses en el Perú* (The Japanese Immigrants in Peru) (S-51). Written with methodological and academic rigor, this book is frequently cited in anthologies, historiographies, and bibliographies, and it is considered a pioneering work in the field of immigration and ethnic minority studies. The book's panoramic view of Japanese Peruvian history has influenced the majority of works written on the subject in subsequent years.

In 1986, the National Congress of Science and Technology organized the First Seminar on Immigrant Population in Peru. The Congress consisted of approximately thirty Peruvian and foreign specialists in international migration. In 1987 and 1988, the papers presented during the seminar were compiled into two books. Five of these papers are about the Japanese in Peru. The articles by June Kodani (S-37) and Jorge M. Nakamoto (S-59) are outstanding for quality and content.

The 1990s: The Fujimori Era
With the election of the Peruvian Nisei Alberto Fujimori as president of Peru, the Japanese Peruvian community attracted great attention. There was great media coverage, both nationally and internationally. There was a "boom" of publications, not only about the community but also about President Fujimori himself. Two books included in the bibliography, written by journalists, analyze Fujimori and his election: *Tsunami Fujimori* by José María Salcedo (S-70), and *Ciudadano Fujimori: La construcción de un politico* (Citizen Fujimori: The Construction of a Politician) by Luis Jochamowitz (S-35).

It is also necessary to emphasize the process in the 1990s of emigration to Japan of people of Japanese descent and of Peruvians in general, known as the "*dekasegi* phenomenon." The volume and the consequences of this phenomenon are discussed in numerous newspaper articles and other works, such as the university thesis of Brunette (E-4) and a novel by renowned Peruvian writer Augusto Higa (1994: S-28). This subject deserves more attention, due to its social impact and prevalence.

ANNIVERSARY CELEBRATIONS OF JAPANESE IMMIGRATION TO PERU

The anniversary celebrations of Japanese immigration to Peru (1974, 1979, 1989, 1999) have been important for the production of works on the Japanese Peruvians. Among the most important academic and cultural activities and publications derived from these celebrations, we can mention the book (written in Japanese) entitled *Zai Perú hōjin 75-nen no ayumi: 1899-nen–1974-nen* (J-5).

The Japanese Immigration Museum of Peru (Museo Conmemorativo de la Inmigración Japonesa en el Perú), dedicated in 1981 during the eightieth anniversary celebration, is significant for the collection and access of information it provides to Peruvian and foreign scholars. The national census of the Japanese Peruvians in 1989 was another contribution made during an anniversary celebration. Morimoto analyzes the results in *Población de origen japonés en el Perú: perfil actual* (People of Japanese Origin in Peru: Contemporary Profile) (1991: S-55).

With the centennial of Japanese immigration to Peru celebrated in 1999, the Congress of the Republic organized a colloquium titled "100 Years of Japanese Presence in Peru." Two edited collections resulted. One publication is a hundred-year photographic history of Japanese Peruvians entitled *La memoria del ojo* (The Memory of the Eye), by Watanabe, Morimoto, and Chambi (1999: S-77). Through the daily and private lives of families, this book captures a collective history of Japanese Peruvians. The photographs are accompanied with concise text. The other book, *Los japoneses y sus descendientes en el Perú* (The Japanese and Their Descendants in Peru), by Morimoto (1999: S-52), is a solidly documented analysis of a hundred years of history, written from an essentially political viewpoint and utilizing primary sources.

Various symposiums, expositions, and competitions were held as part of these distinctive celebrations. Numerous literary and institutional publications were sponsored, edited, and published by the Japanese Peruvian community to commemorate them.

REVIEW OF THE LITERATURE BY TOPIC

History
Research on the Japanese Peruvian community has been approached primarily from a historical perspective, which is similar to studies of other groups of immigrants who have settled in Peru. Many works are centered on global processes, such as studies that examine the causes or motivation of migration, periods of immigration, legal conditions, work situations, the lives of immigrants, settlement and economic activities of the community, conflicts, and World War II. However, there is still a lack of local and specific studies like the work done by Rocca about the Japanese of Lambayeque, in the northern part of Peru (1997: S-64).

In the bibliographies published to date, the absence of life histories or case studies is also noticeable. There are only short articles in books, newspapers, and magazines related to the life and work of Japanese individuals who live in small villages or towns (Bravo, 1981: S-10; Del Busto, 1993: S-19; Martínez, 1981: S-40; Araki-Ogata, 1981: S-3).

Even when Japanese Peruvians are mentioned in various works on culture, ethnicity, identity, religion, health, psychology, among others, they have not been developed in great depth, with the exception of some studies in progress that will be published soon. However, the themes of culture and identity as historical processes and contemporary issues have been documented and analyzed by Morimoto in her publications.

Demography
The Peruvian national census eliminated "race" as a category in 1940. Since then, it has been difficult to collect demographic and statistical data on minorities and the composition of the immigrant population and their descendants in Peru.

The Japanese Peruvian community conducted its own census twice, unlike other minority groups of foreign origin in Peru. The first census was conducted in 1966, and the results were published in 1969 (J-7). In 1989, the second national census was conducted, with more modern methods and techniques. Its results were published in 1991 (S-55). Both publications, the first in Japanese and the second in Spanish, are included in the bibliography.

Art and Literature
From the 1950s, Japanese Peruvians started to be recognized in the field of national art and literature. Tilsa Tsuchiya, one of the most important and distinct painters of contemporary Peru, held her first individual exhibition in 1959. Since then, her works have been well received by national critics. Two books are dedicated to the artist and her works by art critics Wuffarden (S-78) and Möll (S-47). Many articles have been also published in magazines and newspapers.

Regarding other distinguished artists of Japanese origin in Peru, commentaries of their works and exhibitions appear in the press on an almost daily basis. There are also significant studies and extensive publications dedicated to them, such as essays on painters Jaime Higa and Eduardo Tokeshi by the art historian and critic Gustavo Buntinx (S-11, S-12).

In regard to literature, it must be noted that writers of the Japanese origin have not focused much on the themes of immigration and related topics, with the exception of novelist Augusto Higa, who wrote about his experience as a dekasegi in Japan (1981: S-29). Nevertheless, there are abundant works and publications by poets and novelists of Japanese origin. Some of these works have been reviewed by renowned national and foreign critics.

The works of poet José Watanabe—considered as one of Peru's foremost contemporary poets—have attracted the attention of various specialized critics in Peru and abroad. Extensive published commentary has been dedicated to the evaluation of his poems. Some examples include the presentation by the university professor of literature Marco Martos during a colloquium on the Centennial of the Immigration in the Congress of the Republic (S-41), and the analysis of literature critics Miguel Angel Huamán (S-31), Ricardo Gonzáles Vigil, and Carlos Batalla, among others. The works of Watanabe are also included in various specialized anthologies.

Cooking

In the past few years, great interest in a new kind of cooking has emerged in Peru. "Nikkei cooking" could be characterized primarily by the use of seafood prepared with a combination of ingredients and styles of preparation that blend Japanese regional cooking with the local *criolla* (native Peruvian) cuisine. So far, there are many articles on this subject written in newspapers and magazines. In addition, two journalists have written well-known books: editor Jonathan Cavanagh (S-13) and Mariela Balbi (E-1; S-6), in bilingual English and Spanish editions.

ABOUT THE AUTHORS

Finally, it is important to briefly mention the authors who have written about Japanese Peruvians and other related topics and themes. Before World War II, mainly Peruvian and American journalists, politicians, and intellectuals developed works on this subject. Since the 1960s, professionals in academia, especially Japanese, Peruvian, and North American scholars, became interested in the Japanese Peruvian experience. With the election of Fujimori as president of Peru, Fujimori and immigration subjects attracted the attention of many Peruvians, both international academic researchers and journalists alike.

A selection of these studies, observations, and analysis appear in the annotated bibliography. Efforts were made to include the most representative works of each time period and topic. Due to space constraints, many deserving works could not be included. Surely the body of literature will increase in the near future, as many works are in progress or will start soon.

Books published in Peru and in Spanish are the main focus of this bibliography. However, some books published in other countries and languages, mainly in English and Japanese, are also included in order to show the global scope of the development of this field of study to date. Among these selections are works based on the author's firsthand experiences and fieldwork conducted in Peru.

Annotated Bibliography of Japanese Peruvians

COMPILED BY RAÚL ARAKI

ENGLISH

1. Balbi, Mariella. *La cocina según Sato: pescados y mariscos a la manera Nikkei.* Lima: Universidad San Martín de Porres, Facultad de Turismo y Hotelería, 1997.

    This book presents so-called Nikkei cooking as an important variant of the Peruvian gastronomy, with its influence in the use of fish and shellfish. Contains basic recipes of chef Sato. Includes a brief history of Nikkei cooking. Bilingual edition: English-Spanish. See also S-6.

2. Barnhart, Edward N. "Japanese Internees from Peru." *Pacific Historical Review* 31, no. 2 (May 1962): 169–78.

    Based on the information obtained from the declassified documents of the Departments of State and Justice of the United States, the author describes and analyzes the subject of deportation of the Japanese and their descendants from Peru during World War II. The negotiation of their civil rights and the expropriation of their assets are emphasized.

3. Bowen, Sally. *El expediente Fujimori El Perú y su Presidente 1990–2000.* Lima: Peru Monitor, 2000.

    Written by an English journalist, the book includes a selection of events most controversial during Alberto Fujimori's two terms. Uses as a basic source, a series of interviews conducted mainly with former collaborators and opponents of the regime. Published in two simultaneous editions, English and Spanish. See also S-9.

4. Brunette, Rachel. "Dekasegi Nikkeijin: Reflections on Japanese Immigration Policy and the Return Migration of Japanese Latin Americans." Master's thesis, Stanford University, Department of History, 1999.

    This study is based on the inspection of secondary sources, Japanese and Peruvian newspapers, and interviews with Latin American Nikkei and Japanese government officials. A major part of the collection of information was conducted in Lima. The thesis deals with Japanese immigration policies, the context, which produced the *dekasegi* phenomenon, and the labor and legal situation of these workers and their perspectives.

5. Emmerson, John K. *The Japanese Thread.* New York: Holt, Rinehart and Winston, 1978.

    The author was in charge of the implementation of the deportation program during World War II. This book that contains his memories of these events, describes detailed operations of the program and shows the injustice committed against the Japanese during those days.

6. Gardiner, Harvey C. *The Japanese and Peru, 1873–1973.* Albuquerque: University of New Mexico Press, 1975.

    Based on numerous Japanese, North American, and Peruvian sources, the author, a North American historian, reconstructs the centenary history of commercial, political, and cultural relations between Japan and Peru. Also includes the subjects of origin and development of the Japanese Peruvian community during this period.

7. Gardiner, Harvey C. *Pawns in a Triangle of Hate.* Seattle: University of Washington Press, 1981.

    The author describes and analyzes the politics of the Peruvian and U.S. governments that determined the deportation during World War II. Also filled with testimonies of the victims from the moment of their arrest in Peru to the end of the war, when they lacked the legal status to permanently stay in the United States, while at the same time they were prevented from returning to Peru.

8. Gerbi, Antonello. "The Japanese in Peru." *Asia and the Americas* 43, no. 1 (January 1943): 43–46.

    The author, a Peruvian economist at Credit Bank of Peru, maintains that the Japanese community remained separate and organized outside of the society and, above all, did not conduct its financial transactions with Peruvian banks.

9. Higashide, Seiichi. *Adios to Tears: The Memoirs of a Japanese-Peruvian Internee in U.S. Concentration Camps.* Honolulu, Hawai`i: E&E Kudo Publisher, 1993.

    An autobiography of a Japanese immigrant who had lived in Peru since 1930 and was deported to the United States during World War II. It is a testimony of a life filled with nuances and experiences, processed and written in his matured age. His memories and sentiments serve to reconstruct and transmit the complexities of this era.

10. Irie, Toraji. "History of the Japanese Migration to Peru." *Hispanic American Historical Review* XXXI, nos. 3–4 (August–November 1951): 437–52 (no. 3) and 648–64 (no. 4).

    Originally published in Japanese, these articles offer valid, objective, and detailed information about Japanese immigrants and their activities, from their early days in the Peruvian plantations until 1925.

11. Nakamoto, Jorge. "Middleman Minority, Acculturation, and Ethnic Persistence: The Case of the Japanese Peruvians." Ph.D. diss., University of California, 1994.

    The author revisits the literature on the Japanese in Peru in order to refute the stereotypes and confusions existent in such literature. As theoretical support, he utilizes the concepts of "middleman minority" and of assimilation and acculturation.

12. Normano, J. F., and Antonello Gerbi. *The Japanese in South America.* New York: The John Day Company, 1943.

    Provides a historical overview of Japanese immigration

in Latin America, mainly Brazil. In terms of Peru, it emphasizes the economic success achieved by the Japanese and how its organization, used as the strategy for such success, is at the same time an obstacle for their assimilation.

13. Press Secretariat of the Government Palace Republic of Perú. *Biography of Mr. Alberto Fujimori President of Perú.* Lima: n.p., 1994.

    Brief official biography of Alberto Fujimori and summary of some achievements of his first government, especially in the area of international relations.

14. Thompson, Stephen. "Survival of Ethnicity in the Japanese Community of Lima." *Urban Anthropology* 3, no. 2 (1974): 243–61.

    The author, through research conducted in Peru, focuses his interest on numerous institutions created by immigrants, which would explain their own resistance to assimilation.

15. Titiev, Misha. "The Japanese Colony in Perú," *The Far Eastern Quarterly* 10, no. 3 (May 1951): 227–47.

    Discusses the stereotypes existent about the Nikkei community from the prewar era, mainly with respect to its organization and economic activities. In the postwar period, Titiev maintains that, due to the suspension of the immigration and absence of contacts with Japan, the community oriented itself toward imminent assimilation.

16. White, John W. "Japan's Amazon Dream." *Asia and the Americas* 43, no. 10 (October 1943): 580–83.

    An article representative of the American fear during World War II, which saw the Japanese colonies in Brazil, Ecuador, and Peru as part of a Japanese politico-military plan for expansion, with supposed interest in establishing a communication line between the Pacific and Atlantic.

JAPANESE

1. Club Fukuoka. *Historia de la inmigración Fukuokana al Perú.* Lima: Gráfica Biblos, 1993.

    Contains a history of immigration from the Japanese prefecture of Fukuoka, history of the Fukuoka Kenjin-kai Association, and the result of a census of residents from Fukuoka and their descendants in Peru. Written in Spanish and Japanese. See also S-15.

2. Comisión Conmemorativa del 80º Aniversario. *80º aniversario de la inmigración japonesa 1899–1979.* Lima: Impreso en los talleres de Perú Shimpo, 1979.

    Written almost completely in Japanese, this publication is a recollection of the first eighty years of immigration history and the commemorative ceremonies, emphasizing the Issei experience and friendship between Peru and Japan. Includes a chronology comparing the history of the two countries (1844–1980).

3. Morimoto, Amelia [アメリア・モリモト]. "Nikkeijin no seiji ishiki [日系人の政治意識]." In *Rima no Nikkeijin: Perū ni okeru Nikkei shakai no takakuteki bunseki* [リマの日系人：ペルーにおける日系社会の多角的分析], edited by Toshio Yanagida [柳田利夫], 323–341 and 383–385. Tōkyō [東京]: Akashi Shoten [明石書店], 1997.

    This chapter presents a short Japanese translation of the results of the study about the political identity of the Nikkei, based on a questionnaire applied to more than five thousand people in 1989. A Spanish summary is included in the same edition.

4. Morimoto, Amelia [アメリア・モリモト]. *Perū no Nihonjin imin* [ペルーの日本人移民]. Tōkyō [東京]: Nihon Hyōronsha [日本評論社], 1992.

    This book, with updated information, is the Japanese version of the book titled, *Los inmigrantes japoneses en el Perú* (The Japanese Immigrants in Peru), by the same author. Translation was done by a Japanese sociologist Kon Sakimori.

5. Perū Shinpōsha [ペルー新報社]. *Zai Perū hōjin 75-nen no ayumi: 1899-nen–1974-nen* [在ペルー邦人75年の歩み：1899年-1974年]. Rima [リマ]: Perū Shinpōsha [ペルー新報社], 1974.

    A book edited in Japanese with a small section translated in Spanish. Contains a section dedicated to history with a listing of Japanese immigrants by name, date, and ship of arrival, and initial destination in Peru until 1923. This book is the one most referred to by researchers and descendants of the Japanese who want to know about their ancestors.

6. Yanagida, Toshio [柳田利夫], ed. *Rima no Nikkeijin: Perū ni okeru Nikkei shakai no takakuteki bunseki* [リマの日系人：ペルーにおける日系社会の多角的分析]. Tōkyō [東京]: Akashi Shoten [明石書店], 1997.

    This book is a collection of studies, conducted and written by various authors, on such subjects as Japanese linguistics, identity, aspects of history and culture, health, and physical anthropology.

7. Zai Perū Nikkeijin Shakai Jittai Chōsa Iinkai [在ペルー日系人社会実態調査委員会]. *Perūkoku ni okeru Nikkeijin shakai* [ペルー国における日系人社会]. N.p.: Zai Perū Nikkeijin Shakai Jittai Chōsa Iinkai [在ペルー日系人社会実態調査委員会], 1969.

    This book, published in Japanese, contains information about demographic and socio-economic aspects, compiled through a census among the Nikkei population, conducted in 1966. Includes also a brief interpretation of the history of immigration.

PORTUGUESE

1. Saito, Hiroshi. "Japoneses no Brasil e Peru." In *Assimilação e integração dos Japoneses no Brasil*, edited by Hiroshi Saito, and Takashi Maeyama, 521–30. Petrópolis, São Paulo: Vozes Ed. Da Universidade de São Paulo, 1973.

    This article written in the 1960s, compares the communities of Japanese origin in Brazil and Peru, mainly in relation to their levels of internal organization, which are determined by the socio-economic structure of the larger society.

SPANISH

1. Arakaki Oshiro, Lucía. "La educadora familiar y la situación del nisei." Bachelor's thesis, Pontificia Universidad Católica del Perú—Escuela Social, 1963.

    Based on personal experiences, the author reflects on the cultural and social problems of the young second generation of the postwar period and expresses the necessity of education as solutions.

2. Araki, Raúl. "Migración japonesa al Perú: 80 años, un largo camino." In *Ensayos de Integración*, Lima: Asociación Universitaria Nisei del Perú, 5–46, 1979.

    The author presents the immigration of Japanese Peruvians from an anthropological perspective. The author, a university student at the time, received first prize for this essay in the national competition José María Arguedas during the eightieth anniversary of the Japanese immigration to Peru.

3. Araki, Raúl, and Ogata, Ana. "De Okinawa a Río Tambo." *Puente* 1, no. 3 (1981): 48–49.

    This article makes known, for the first time, the life of Nisei Pedro Tomón Victoriano, a son of a Japanese immigrant and a native "*amuesha*" woman of the Iscozasin community (central forest of Peru), who became a mayor of the Río Tambo district in Satipo, Junín.

4. Asociación Femenina Okinawense del Perú. *20 años*. Lima: n.p., 1998.

    The first institutional magazine published by the above association. Contains several testimonies that demonstrate aspects of Okinawan women's lives in Peru. Includes greeting messages of authorities and dignitaries, as well as articles that reiterate the objectives of the association.

5. Asociación Femenina Peruano Japonesa. *40 aniversario de la fundación*. Lima: n.p., 1996.

    Contains a chronology of events and activities most important to the association, its statutes, and the directory of its members. Published in Spanish and Japanese.

6. Balbi, Mariella. *La cocina según Sato: pescados y mariscos a la manera Nikkei*. Lima: Universidad San Martín de Porres, Facultad de Turismo y Hotelería, 1997.

    This book presents so-called Nikkei cooking as an important variant of the Peruvian gastronomy, with its influence in the use of fish and shellfish. Contains basic recipes of chef Sato. Includes a brief history of Nikkei cooking. Bilingual edition: English-Spanish. See also E-1.

7. Basadre, Jorge G., and José Bustamante y Rivero. *Mensaje de dos patricios*, edited by Samuel Matsuda. Lima: Instituto Generación 64, 1993.

    Basadre, the most important Peruvian historian of the twentieth century, deplores the atrocities committed against the Japanese in Peru during World War II. Bustamante y Rivero, a famous intellectual and President of Peru between 1945 and 1948, emphasizes the Japanese contribution in Peru, especially in culture and art, and with their present mixed race.

8. Bedoya, Jaime. "Antiniponismo." *Caretas* 1104 (April 1990): 40–41.

    In this review article, the author refers to the racist manifestations against the Nikkei during the presidential elections of 1990.

9. Bowen, Sally. *El expediente Fujimori El Perú y su Presidente 1990–2000*. Lima: Peru Monitor, 2000.

    Written by an English journalist, the book includes a selection of events most controversial during Alberto Fujimori's two terms. Uses a series of interviews conducted, mainly with former collaborators and opponents of the regime, as a basic source. Published in two simultaneous editions, English and Spanish. See also E-3.

10. Bravo, José Antonio. "Mi amigo el Nisei: Suzumo." *Puente* 1, no. 3 (1981): 26–27.

    Bravo, a novelist and journalist, presents a biographical sketch of Suzumo Oshiro, his school friend in a state college in the postwar era, and tells us his experiences in the neighborhood and afternoons of playing soccer.

11. Buntinx, Gustavo. "Los signos mesiánicos: fardos funerarios y resurrecciones míticas en el arte de la 'República de Weimar peruana' (1980–1992)." In *Arte y violencia*, 525–52. N.p.: Instituto de Investigaciones Estéticas, Universidad Nacional Autónoma de México, 1995.

    An essay about the work of Eduardo Tokeshi that demonstrates his continuities and transformations, his testimony about the situations of violence that exist in the country, the contradictions that mark his unique experience as an artist, and his relation to the environment. According to the author, the work also represents the institutional deterioration of the country, the post modernity, the end of an era and the restoration of lost order, which is long-awaited but sometimes feared.

12. Buntinx, Gustavo. "Texto / Textura: Jaime Higa 1987–1990." In *Ponencia al coloquio Los cien años de presencia japonesa en el Perú*. Lima: Congreso de la República, 1999.

    Essay on painter Jaime Higa, his works and identity. The author contrasts the identity assigned by public opinion to the works of the Nikkei plastic artists with the opinion of the artists themselves, who emphasize more generational rupture, contradictions and internal conflicts, as characteristics of their works. This essay is based on a profound analysis of Higa's works and on interviews with him, as well as with other noted Nikkei plastic artists.

13. Cavanagh, Jonathan, ed. *Las recetas de Rosita Yimura: la cocina Nikkei y algo más*. Bogotá, Colombia: Peru Reporting, 1995.

    Nikkei cooking made Rosita Yimura one of the most famous exponents. This book presents sixty-four of her recipes and a small biographic sketch of her life.

14. Centro Cultural Peruano Japonés. "Autores Nikkei." In *El Japón en la literatura Peruana*, edited by Rumi Morimoto, 37–44. Lima: n.p., 1993.

    Description of Nikkei writers and reviews of their principal works.

15. Club Fukuoka. *Historia de la inmigración Fukuokana al Perú*. Lima: Gráfica Biblos, 1993.

Contains a history of immigration from the Japanese prefecture of Fukuoka, history of the Fukuoka Kenjin-kai Association, and the result of a census of residents from Fukuoka and their descendants in Peru. Written in Spanish and Japanese. See also J-1.

16. Comisión 90º Aniversario de la Inmigración Japonesa al Perú. *90 años: revista conmemorativa por el Aniversario de la Inmigración japonesa al Perú 1899–1989*. Lima: n.p., 1989.

    This magazine contains a description of the activities and works motivated by the ninetieth anniversary celebration, messages of authorities and officials, as well as various aspects of the history and character of the community, which emphasize the Issei spirit of overcoming difficulties.

17. Comisión Organizadora del monumento a Manco Cápac. *La independencia del Perú y la colonia japonesa*. Lima: Imprenta Eduardo Ravago, 1927?

    This book is a compilation of all the events related to the construction and inauguration of the monument of Manco Cápac that the Japanese community donated to the Peruvian nation as a centenary celebration of its independence. Includes discourses conducted by authorities and present officials in public acts related to the monument, and newspaper articles of the same period, as well as testimonies that demonstrate nuances of the Lima and Peruvian society in the 1920s, and the vision of Japan and the situation of immigrants.

18. Degregori, Carlos Iván, and Romeo Grompone. *Elecciones 1990: demonios y redentores en el nuevo Perú, una tragedia en dos vueltas*. Lima: Instituto de Estudios Peruanos, 1991.

    This publication analyzes the presidential elections of 1990 in Peru and the victory of Alberto Fujimori. Explores different dimensions of the process that constituted, according to the authors, a major surprise in the annals of Peruvian electoral history. The book is divided into two parts; a political-social approximation to the subject by Grompone, and an analysis of the ethnic-cultural aspects of the electoral process by Degregori.

19. Del Busto Duthurburu, José Antonio. "Kishimoto." In *Barranco. Personajes de Ayer*, 39–46. Lima: Editorial Brasa S.A, 1993.

    In this article, a famous historian of the day presents a biography of Jorge Kishimoto, who was his barber during his childhood and youth in the neighborhood of Barranco. This article is also a testimony about his relationship with Kishimoto and how he influenced the author's vision of Japan.

20. Diez Canseco Núñez, Luis. "La inmigración japonesa en el Perú." In *Ensayos de integración I*. Asociación Universitaria Nisei del Perú, 49–77. N.p., 1979.

    This essay won second place in the national competition "José María Arguedas" during the eightieth anniversary of Japanese immigration to Peru. Its contents are reflections on the subject of Japanese immigration and characteristics attributed to the Nikkei, based on his review of materials and publications related to these subjects.

21. Ex Escuela Japonesa de Lima. *Album de oro: recuerdo del cincuentenario de su fundación. 1920–1970*. Lima: n.p., 1970.

    This book, published in Japanese and Spanish, is a testimony of the activities realized during the celebration by the fiftieth anniversary of the foundation of Lima Nikko (Japanese School of Lima).

22. Ex Escuela Japonesa de Lima. *Bodas de diamante, 1920–1995*. Lima: n.p., 1996?

    Contains a short history of the education center, testimonies of some of its teachers, and photographs that show its environment and activities, as well as its graduation. Japanese and Spanish edition.

23. Figueroa San Miguel, Pedro. *Historia sintética del ruidoso proceso sobre 'Reivindicación del Tulumayo' en la carretera Huánuco—Pucallpa*. Lima: Imprenta Sagrestán, 1938.

    In 1919, an entrepreneur Hajime Hoshi acquired 300,170 hectares of land in Tulumayo north of Huánuco, in order to cultivate products for the pharmaceutical industry. This project created a controversy with most of the important newspapers of the day and a long judicial process. Its main opponent was Figueroa San Miguel, who questioned the possession of land in the above area by foreigners. In this publication he presents his point of view in detail.

24. Fukumoto, Mary. *Hacia un nuevo sol: japoneses y sus descendientes en el Perú*. Lima: Asociación Peruano Japonesa del Perú, 1997.

    This book, mainly based on secondary sources, demonstrates aspects of Japanese immigration history until the 1990s. The last section deals with the issue of culture and identity through testimonies.

25. Fukumoto, Mary. "Migrantes japoneses y sus descendientes en el Perú." Bachelor's thesis, UNMSM, Programa de Antropología, 1974.

    Based on secondary sources, the author presents an overview of Japanese immigration history. Her central focus is the problem of national identity among the Nikkei population.

26. Guevara, Víctor. "La inmigración japonesa." In *Las grandes cuestiones nacionales: el petróleo, los ferrocarriles, la inmigración japonesa, el problema moral*, 129–73. N.p.: Biblioteca de la Revista de Filosofía y Derecho, Cuzco. Talleres Tipográficos de H.G. Rozas, 1939.

    Compiles a series of articles published by the newspaper *La Prensa de Lima*, as part of a campaign called "The Japanese Infiltration." This publication is representative of the thoughts of an important sector of Peruvian politicians and intellectuals in the 1930s, when explicit racist and xenophobic expressions were abundant.

27. Hayasaka, H. *Los agricultores japoneses en el Perú*. Lima: n.p., 1933.

    As part of the explanation for the development of agricultural activities in Peru, the author emphasizes the contributions of Japanese farmers and presents various suggestions for the technical advancement of this activity in different regions of the country.

28. Higa, Augusto. *Japón no da dos oportunidades*. Lima: Editorial Generación 94, 1994.

    Based on his personal experience as dekasegi for eighteen months in Japan, novelist Augusto Higa constructs a history about daily life, the environment, and working conditions of Peruvian dekasegi in Japan.

29. Higa, Augusto. "'Vertiente japonesa del nisei' and 'Vertiente peruana del nisei'." *Puente* 1, no. 3–4 (1981): 54–55 (no. 3) and 50–52 (no. 4).

    In these two articles, the author analyzes the process of Japanese immigration to Peru, questions the role of organizations in the Nikkei community, reflects on the validity of Japanese customs and traditions, and approaches the transformation of the "Japanese colony" in the actual Peruvian Japanese community.

30. Hoshi, Hajime. *El Tulumayo*. Lima: Compañía de Impresiones y Publicidad, 1942.

    This publication contains the documents of the defense that Hajime Hoshi initiated in the Peruvian court of justice to recuperate the land that he had obtained in Tulumayo (rim of Peruvian forest). Reveals part of the controversy sustained with Figueroa San Miguel. See also S-23 for the same subject.

31. Huamán, Miguel Angel. "Poesía, modernidad y posmodernidad: dos poemas." *Socialismo y Participación* 85 (August 1999): 137–46.

    Analysis of the poem "La Oruga" by José Watanabe, comparing it with the poem "L'Albatros" by Baudelaire.

32. Iida, Juan K. "El primer contingente de inmigrantes japoneses contratados." In *Primer Seminario sobre Poblaciones Inmigrantes: actas: Lima, 9 y 10 de mayo de 1986*. Vol. 2, edited by Consejo Nacional de Ciencia y Tecnología, 223–51. Lima: Consejo Nacional de Ciencia y Tecnología, 1988.

    The publication presents a list of data regarding the first Japanese immigrant group that arrived in Peru in 1899. Based on a previous publication by the newspaper *Perú Shimpo* (1975), the author compares initial data with other sources in order to identify mainly the destination of each individual member of the group.

33. Iida, Juan K. *Los primeros inmigrantes: publicación de los datos referentes a los primeros inmigrantes japoneses contratados llegados al Perú*. Lima: n.p., 1999.

    Contains the list of the first 790 immigrants in Spanish and Japanese, detailing the date and place of birth of each one of them, the plantations where they completed their initial contracts, and subsequent destinations of the majority.

34. Jhoncon Kooyip, María. "Jóvenes limeños de ascendencia Japonesa y la persistencia de valores en las relaciones interpersonales asociada a sus antecesores." Bachelor's thesis, UNMSM, Programa de Psicología, 1976.

    Study about the patterns of behavior of the young Nisei in their interpersonal relations and the degree of Japanese values transmitted by the Issei.

35. Jochamowitz, Luis. *Ciudadano Fujimori: la construcción de un político*. Lima: Peisa, 1997.

    The author examines Alberto Fujimori in this biography, based on numerous testimonies of people who knew him in different periods of his life and written within the context of the most important passages of Japanese Peruvian immigration history in the twentieth century.

36. Kishimoto de Inamine, Elena. *Tradiciones y costumbres de los inmigrantes japoneses en el Perú*. Lima: Universidad Nacional Federico Villarreal, Centro de Investigaciones Histórico Sociales, 1979.

    The first part discusses Japanese immigration until the 1960s; the second part presents a description of some customs and ceremonies.

37. Kodani, June. "La 'amenaza' japonesa en los escritos sobre la inmigración." In *Primer Seminario sobre Poblaciones Inmigrantes: actas: Lima, 9 y 10 de mayo de 1986*. Vol. 2, edited by Consejo Nacional de Ciencia y Tecnología, 205–22. Lima: Consejo Nacional de Ciencia y Tecnología, 1988.

    This article analyzes numerous publications published by Americans and Peruvians in the U.S. regarding Japanese immigration in Latin America, mainly Peru, during the pre–World War II and also the postwar era. It emphasizes the influence of U.S. ideas on Latin American thinking during the four decades and its impact on the anti-Japanese measures adopted during the war.

38. Lévano, César. "Mi amigo el nisei: Nishiyama." *Puente* 2 (March–April 1981): 26–28.

    The author writes a short eulogical biography of Gonzales Nishiyama, whom he knew as a pioneer of Peruvian movies and as his vivid expression of Peruvian "*mestizaje*" (mixed race).

39. Lévano, César. "El samurai del huayno." *Puente* 4 (August–September 1981): 59.

    This article contains the life story of Juan Makino Tori, a Nisei, known artistically as "Samurai of Huayno (traditional Andean song)."

40. Martínez, Gregorio. "El fígaro de Nazca." *Puente* 1, no. 5 (December 1981): 56.

    A chronology about the life and work of Pepe Higashi, known as the best barber in the city of Nazca, south of Lima.

41. Martos, Marco. "La poesía de José Watanabe." In *Ponencia en el coloquio los cien años de presencia japonesa en el Perú*. Congreso de la República. Lima: n.p., 1999.

    The renowned poet, university professor, and literary critic analyzes the works of Watanabe and considers his poetry as among the best in Peruvian literature of all times. Also indicates that his works incorporate an Asian sensibility into Peruvian poetry in general.

42. Matayoshi, Nicolás. "El cajoneo." *Puente* 6 (1982): 60.

    An article about the custom of Nisei children taking small amounts of money from a family business box in order to cover their recreation expenses. It conveys the nuances of the daily lives of Nikkei families.

43. Matayoshi, Nicolás. "Tiempos de ira, tiempos de esperanza." *Puente* 4 (August–September 1981): 56–57.

    A testimony of the author about his preoccupations with the problems of the Andean peasant communities and with the preservation and diffusion of their folklore and traditions. The author was initially influenced by his own Issei father and motivated mainly by his provincial environment.

44. Matos Mar, José. *Yanaconaje y reforma agraria en el Perú.* Lima: Instituto de Estudios Peruanos, 1976.

    In a chapter of the book, the author emphasizes the contributions of Japanese immigrants to the agricultural development of Chancay valley and to the industrial cotton operation. Also emphasizes their role in the modernization of plantations and in Huaral City, mainly through commerce and urban activities in general. As a central figure, Ikumatsu Okada, an old immigrant, becomes the most prosperous entrepreneur of the valley in a few years.

45. Matos Mar, José, and Jorge Carbajal. *Erasmo Muñoz, yanacón del valle de Chancay.* Lima: Instituto de Estudios Peruanos, 1974.

    Life history of Erasmo Muñoz, a *yanacón* (a type of farmer in the coastal area of Peru), together with the Japanese in Chancay valley. In a chapter, the author demonstrates details of the relationship between the Japanese and the community of the valley.

46. Miyagi Kenjinkai. *Perú Miyagi Kenjinkai: 90 aniversario de inmigración, 25 aniversario de Perú Miyagi Kenjinkai.* Lima: n.p., 1998.

    A commemorative book of Peru Miyagi Kenjin-kai. Includes data of Miyagi prefecture, a description of the first immigrants (1908–1920), and messages from the officials, in addition to history of the institution.

47. Möll, Eduardo. *Tilsa Tsuchiya.* Lima: Editorial Navarrete, 1995.

    Its main contents are reproductions of the works of a great Peruvian artist of Japanese origin, Tilsa Tsuchiya (106 color reproductions). It also compiles some biographic information and interpretation by the author regarding her artistic production.

48. Morimoto, Amelia. "El Bushido en el espíritu Nikkei." *Quehacer* 117 (March–April 1999): 46–48.

    In this article, the author explores the persistence of old values among the present Nikkei community, the foundation of which could be found in the code of samurai ethics.

49. Morimoto, Amelia. *Fuerza de trabajo inmigrante japonesa y su desarrollo en el Perú: una exploración bibliográfica.* Lima: Taller de Estudios Andinos, Universidad Nacional Agraria, 1979.

    This is an examination of Japanese immigration, mainly based on secondary sources.

50. Morimoto, Amelia. "Inmigración y comunidad de origen japonés en el Perú." In *Europa, Asia y África en América Latina,* 291–322. México: UNESCO, 1989.

    The chapter presents an overview of history and the community of the people of Japanese origin until the 1980s.

51. Morimoto, Amelia. *Los inmigrantes japoneses en el Perú.* Lima: Taller de Estudios Andinos, Universidad Nacional Agraria, 1979.

    The pioneering book covers an overview of immigration and the community up to the 1970s, based on primary source research utilizing documents of plantations at the Archive of Fuero Agrario. Final section refers to the problems that the community faces in the 1970s.

52. Morimoto, Amelia. *Los japoneses y sus descendientes en el Perú.* Lima: Fondo Editorial del Congreso del Perú, 1999.

    This book covers one hundred years of Japanese immigration, analyzing the transformation of the community in its political thought and national consciousness.

53. Morimoto, Amelia. "Origen y destino de una inmigración en el Perú." *l'imaginaire* 2, no. 6 (November 1992): 72–78.

    This article presents an overview of Peruvian immigration history until the 1990s, when a Nisei, Alberto Fujimori, becomes president elect of Peru.

54. Morimoto, Amelia. "Población de origen japonés en el Perú: investigaciones y bibliografía." In *Primer seminario sobre poblaciones inmigrantes: actas: Lima, 9 y 10 de mayo de 1986.* Vol. 1, edited by Consejo Nacional de Ciencia y Tecnología, 105–40. Lima: Consejo Nacional de Ciencia y Tecnología, 1987.

    This article, initially a central presentation in the first seminar on immigrant populations, contains a brief summary of the immigration until the 1980s, and a commentary about the publications and other works on the subject to this day.

55. Morimoto, Amelia. *Población de origen japonés en el Perú: perfil actual.* Lima: Comisión Conmemorativa del 90° Aniversario de la Inmigración Japonesa al Perú, 1991.

    This book presents the general results of a census among the Nikkei population, conducted in 1989 and their analyses. Contains statistical information about demographic, socioeconomic and cultural aspects. It also includes a detailed description about the methodology employed.

56. Morimoto, Amelia. "Presencia Nikkei en la cocina peruana." In *Cultura, identidad y cocina en el Perú,* compiled by Rosario Olivas Weston, 257–70. Lima: Universidad San Martín de Porres, 1993.

    This article specifically deals with one of the activities that are mostly concentrated in the Nikkei population throughout its history—restaurants—as well as dealing with origins of different foods, prepared and consumed by the same population. So-called Cocina Nikkei (Nikkei Cooking) appears frequently in these contexts.

57. Morimoto, Rumi. "¿Ocha o café?: Un acercamiento al habla de los Nikkei." *Prensa Nikkei* (1992): 105–106.

    The author examines the use of certain expressions and words in the Japanese language used by the Sansei, and those that are used as a replacement for Spanish words within the family environment or with other Nikkei interlocutors. This linguistic analysis of Nikkei society provides a method of rediscovering a cultural specific community and understanding the transmission of values through the use of language.

58. Moromisato, Doris. *Okinawa Shi Kyoyukai del Perú: testimonios de vida y homenaje al vigésimo aniversario de vida institucional (1979–1999)*. Lima: Okinawa Shi Kyoyukai del Perú: Fondo Editorial OKP, 1999.

    A commemorative book, prepared by a study committee that is mainly formed by young professionals of the Asoshieishon Okinawa Shi (Association of Okinawan History). Contains brief personal history told by the members of different generations related to this association, a brief version about Okinawan immigration, general information on Okinawa and Peru, messages from authorities, and directories of professionals and families of Okinawan origin.

59. Nakamoto, Jorge. "Discriminación y aislamiento: el caso de los japoneses y sus descendientes." In *Primer seminario sobre poblaciones inmigrantes: actas: Lima, 9 y 10 de mayo de 1986*. Vol. 2, edited by Consejo Nacional de Ciencia y Tecnología, 175–203. Lima: Consejo Nacional de Ciencia y Tecnología, 1988.

    This article analyzes the determinants of ethnic persistence among the Japanese Peruvians and the maintenance of their community through a historical perspective, mainly in the prewar period, and discusses the assimilation and integration of this group within the context of the Peruvian social structure.

60. Ortíz de Zevallos Paz-Soldán, Carlos. *Iniciación de las relaciones diplomáticas entre el Perú y el Japón: 1872–1874*. Lima: Comisión Conmemorativa del 80º Aniversario de la Inmigración Japonesa al Perú, 1981.

    The author, ex-ambassador of Peru, chronologically gathers Peruvian documents about the first diplomatic contacts between Peru and Japan in 1872 and 1873, and includes biographic data of Aurelio García y García, who represented Peru in signing the first treaty between the two countries.

61. Padilla Bendezu, Abraham. "La inmigración japonesa." In *La inmigración en el Perú*, edited by Juan Arona, 222–28. Lima: Academia Diplomática del Perú, 1971.

    This article emphasizes some of the subjects related to Japanese immigration, reproducing arguments and perspectives of the prewar era. Includes a discussion of laws and decrees about the subject.

62. Prensa Nikkei. *90º Aniversario de la inmigración Okinawense al Perú*. Lima: Imprenta Cano, 1996?

    A commemorative edition of the ninetieth anniversary since the arrival of the first Okinawan immigrants to Peru. Summarizes the most important activities conducted for this celebration. The publication contains various articles on the history and customs of the Okinawan community, as well as information about the institutions.

63. Riveros, Jorge. "Heridas de guerra." *Somos* 605 (July 1998): 32–36.

    A chronology about the dramatic event that affected the Nikkei population during the 1940s with its central focus on detention, expulsion, and following incarceration of the Peruvian citizens of Japanese origin in internment centers located in the United States. Includes brief declarations of affected people.

64. Rocca Torres, Luis. *Japoneses bajo el sol de Lambayeque*. Lima: Universidad Nacional Pedro Ruiz Gallo, 1997.

    This book gathers the conclusions of the research conducted in the department of Lambayeque, in the northern part of Peru. The research focuses on community history of the people of Japanese origin. It is based on the inspection of local archives and various testimonies collected among the Issei and Nisei in the region.

65. Rose, Juan Gonzalo. "Los ahijados del sol naciente." *Puente* 4 (August–September 1981): 60.

    The famous poet dedicates testimony to the relations between his family and a Nikkei family, the Tsujas, who, by the influence of Mrs. Rose (the mother), baptizes their newborn son with Catholic ritual, establishing a spiritual bond between them.

66. Saito, Chihito. "Los periódicos de la colonia japonesa en el Perú." *Nikko* XXVI, no. 241 (September 1979): 44–45.

    This article covers approximately fifty years of history of the Nikkei community newspapers, starting from the first two that had been handwritten to those later printed, until the 1960s.

67. Sakata de Chang, Nancy. *Estadio La Unión: cuatro décadas de historia*. Lima: Talleres Santiago Valverde S.A., 1992.

    Presents history of Union Stadium, an important Nikkei institution in Peru. The book is mainly based on documents of the institution, newspaper articles, and personal interviews. Includes a discussion of the directive *juntas* (unions) (1953–1994) and the institutions formed around such a relation in order to broaden its activities, as well as other initiatives, such as the promotion of Pan-American Nikkei Association.

68. Sakuda, Alejandro. *El futuro era el Perú*. Lima: Esicos, 1999.

    The author, a professional journalist, mainly utilizes secondary sources to describe the events of the one hundred year history of Japanese immigration with many anecdotes. The last section describes the years of the Alberto Fujimori government starting from his election as president.

69. Salazar, Jorge. *La medianoche del japonés*. Lima: Editorial El Barranco, 1991.

    In this novel, the author, a professional journalist, presents an interpretation of the political case led by Mamoru Shimizu, a Japanese citizen who was accused and incarcerated in 1944 for the assassination of seven members of his family in Lima.

70. Salcedo, José María. *Tsunami Fujimori*. Lima: La República, 1990.

    The author, a renowned journalist, analyzes the reasons for the popularity of Alberto Fujimori and his surprising election as president of Peru in 1990. He analyzes not only

71. Shimazaki, Luis. "Anales históricos de la colonia japonesa." *Nikko* XXVI, no. 241 (September 1979): 116–26.

    Extensive and thorough chronology that includes the facts and events most relevant to Nikkei general and collective history. Covers the period between 1896 and 1977.

72. Thorndike, Guillermo. *Los Imperios del sol: una historia de los japoneses en el Perú*. Lima: Editorial Brasa S.A., 1996.

    A history of the Japanese and their descendants in Peru, which adopts a style between journalistic and literary, with chronological focus. Demonstrates the experiences of anonymous and well-known people and families, with great richness of detail and entertaining anecdotes. The book includes testimonies of other invited authors.

73. Tokeshi, Juan, and Mary Fukumoto. "Integración de los Nikkei a la nacionalidad peruana: 87 años después." In *Primer Seminario sobre Poblaciones Inmigrantes: actas: Lima, 9 y 10 de mayo de 1986*. Vol. 2, edited by Consejo Nacional de Ciencia y Tecnología, 253–71. Lima: Consejo Nacional de Ciencia y Tecnología, 1988.

    Examines the integration of the Peruvian Nikkei to the national life at different economic, educational, political, cultural, and social levels. Presents prior discussions about the issue of the Peruvian national identity through history.

74. Vega Pardo, Ricardo, ed. *Pioneros de un desarrollo corporativo*. Editorial Pacific Press S.A. Lima, 1992.

    This publication discusses the business trajectory of an immigrant group who managed to succeed in Peru, emphasizing their creative and entrepreneurial spirit.

75. Watanabe, José. "Elogio del refrenamiento." *Quehacer* 117 (March–April 1999): 49–51.

    Based on personal experiences and the work of painter, Tilsa Tsuchiya, Watanabe, a famous poet, penetrates aspects of Nikkei subjectivity, the origin of which would be encountered in the old philosophy of *bushidō* (way of the warrior), transmitted through the conduct and values of the Issei.

76. Watanabe, José. "Laredo, donde los japoneses se hallaban." *Puente* 1, no. 1 (December 1980): 52–53.

    Describes the world of a group of Japanese settled in Laredo plantation, north of Peru, with their first experiences of life and work on the plantation, and their efforts to save money in order to improve their future welfare. Also, testimony about the relations they establish with the people and the process of cultural mixing.

77. Watanabe, José, Amelia Morimoto, and Oscar Chambi. *La memoria del ojo: cien años de presencia japonesa en el Perú*. Lima: Fondo Editorial del Congreso del Perú, 1999.

    Captures through historiographic resources and photographic aesthetics and narration, the dramatic one hundred-year history of Japanese Peruvians.

78. Wuffarden, Jorge Luis Eduardo. *Tilsa. Serie: pintores Peruanos*. Lima: Banco Popular, 1981.

    The book contains reproductions of the work of painter Tilsa Tsuchiya, accompanied with an analysis by the author and art critic and some biographic data.

79. Yrigoyen, Carlos Alberto. *Setogiwa: tiempos difíciles*. Lima: Haruki Abe Production, 1994.

    The author, a Peruvian diplomat, is a knowledgeable admirer of Japanese culture that made him capable of writing this extensive novel. As a base, he takes real moments and events of Japanese immigration history until the election of Alberto Fujimori as President of Peru.

Supplementary Materials

COMPILED BY AMELIA MORIMOTO

Map 9.1 Important Locales in the History of Japanese Peruvians

Japanese Peruvian Demographic Information

Table 9.1 Japanese Emigration to Peru by Prefecture of Origin in Japan, 1906–1923, and 1989

	1899	1903	1906–'09	1910–'14	1915–'19	1920–'23	1989
Okinawa	-	-	375	396	2,015	939	5,180
Kumamoto	-	202	694	635	1,063	101	1,024
Hiroshima	176	293	574	329	774	110	600
Yamaguchi	187	30	387	118	517	35	418
Fukuoka	-	-	206	479	336	63	597
Fukushima	-	-	227	58	461	33	433
Kagoshima	-	-	280	316	139	15	362
Yamagata	-	-	3	260	486	15	63
Okayama	50	387	38	37	87	12	64
Miyagi	-	-	89	140	192	8	207
Niigata	372	-	47	1	81	9	67
Ehime	-	183	61	122	59	3	139
Total*	790	1,175	4,408	3,331	6,870	1,571	11,147

Sources: Figures from 1899 to 1923 were published by Mary Fukumoto, *Hacia un nuevo sol: japoneses y sus descendientes en el Perú* (Lima: Asociación Peruano Japonesa del Perú, 1997), 142, and are based on data previously published by *Perú Shimpo*, "Inmigración japonesa al Perú. 75 Aniversario, 1899–1974," 1–204, 1974. Figures for 1989 are results of the Peruvian Nikkei National Census conducted in 1989 and published in Amelia Morimoto, *Población de origen japonés en el Perú: perfil actual* (Lima: Comisión Conmemorativa del 90° Aniversario de la Inmigración Japonesa al Perú, 1991), 112.

Note: *Total includes other prefectures.

Table 9.2 Total Population and Gender Breakdown of Japanese Immigrants and Their Descendants in Peru

Year	Male	Female	Total
1914	4,917	218	5,135
1924	-	-	10,678
1930	-	-	20,433
1940	11,745	5,853	17,598
1966	16,550	15,451	32,001
1989	22,485	23,137	45,622

Sources: Figures for 1914, 1924, 1930, and 1940 were published by Mary Fukumoto, 193, 196, and 201. Figures for 1924 and 1930 are based on data previously published by the *Perú Shimpo* in 1974, 522–23. Figures for 1940 are from the Peruvian national census of 1949 and previously published in *República del Perú, censo nacional de población y ocupación* (Lima: Resúmenes generales, Ministerio de Hacienda y Comercio, 1944), vol. 1, 506–17. Figures for 1966 are based on the first Peruvian Nikkei National Census of 1966 and published in Zai Perū Nikkeijin shakai jittai chōsa iinkai. *Perukoku ni okeru Nikkeijin shakai*, 1969, 96–97. Figures for 1989 are based on the Peruvian Nikkei second and last national census of the same year and published by Amelia Morimoto, 47.

Note: According to Japanese Ministry of Foreign Affairs (MOFA), *Kaigai zairyū hōjinsū chōsa tōkei* (Tōkyō: Ministry of Foreign Affairs, 1974, 1981, 1987, and 1994), the total Nikkei populations for 1973, 1980, 1986, and 1993 were 60,962; 70,081; 58,173; and 55,472. These figures show that due to the methodological differences, the MOFA's figures have come out greater than those of Peruvian researchers. However, they are useful to show the recent tendency of decline in the Nikkei population due to the dekasegi phenomenon.

Table 9.3 Regional Distribution of Japanese Peruvians by Percentage

Year	Lima	La Libertad	Madre de Dios	Lambayeque	Junin	Ancash	Ica
1966	84.29	4.46	1.36	1.66	2.78	1.20	1.75
1989	84.33	3.58	1.87	1.66	1.59	1.48	1.00

Sources: Morimoto, 90. Figures for 1966 were previously published in *Zai Perū Nikkeijin shakai jittai chōsa iinkai,* 1969, 96–97.

Table 9.4 Educational Level of Japanese Peruvians by Generation in 1989

	1st generation	2nd	3rd	4th	5th+
None	113	165	1,165	1,911	71
Initial	2	46	704	656	20
Primary	1,123	4,449	4,139	2,057	45
Secondary	868	7,113	9,455	1,220	27
Superior	794	3,370	6,313	262	0

Source: Peruvian Nikkei national census of 1989 published in Amelia Morimoto, 107.

Table 9.5 Occupational Fields of Japanese Peruvians by Percentage, 1934–1989

Year	Agriculture	Livestock	Industry	Commercial	Services	Others Unknown
1934	28.00		8.40		(Combined: 63.50)	
1940	21.20	1.80	13.70		(Combined: 60.20)	2.90
1966	9.34	10.19	10.36	25.45	44.66	
1970	8.90	5.40	5.10		(Combined: 80.50)	
1980	11.80	2.90	11.30	32.20	35.00	6.70
1989	6.08	1.03	10.77	28.75	49.11	4.24

Source: Morimoto, 128–29.
Note: In 1989, industry includes industry and construction. Services include services, transportation, health, education, and federal agents and police officers. Figures based on studies conducted in 1980–1981 and in 1989.

Table 9.6 Religion of Japanese Peruvians in 1989

Religion	Number	Percentage
Catholic	47,678	92.41
Buddhist	1,507	2.92
Shinto	149	0.28
Evangelist	420	0.81
Protestant	62	0.12
Others	1,072	2.07
No Religion	705	1.36
Total	**51,593**	**99.97**

Source: Morimoto, 164.

CHAPTER 10

Japanese Americans

DEVELOPED IN COLLABORATION WITH THE CENTER FOR ORAL HISTORY AND SOCIAL SCIENCE RESEARCH INSTITUTE AT THE UNIVERSITY OF HAWAI`I AT MĀNOA AND THE ASIAN AMERICAN STUDIES CENTER AT THE UNIVERSITY OF CALIFORNIA AT LOS ANGELES

BETWEEN 1885 AND 1924, APPROXIMATELY TWO HUNDRED THOUSAND JAPANESE arrived in Hawai`i, and 180,000 immigrated to the continental United States. Most were from the southern prefectures of Japan, which were plagued by drought, famine, and overpopulation. In Hawai`i the early Issei worked on the sugar plantations; on the mainland the new arrivals were sent to salmon canneries in Alaska, mining camps in Utah, sawmills in Oregon, and the agricultural fields of California. Racism always played a part in the lives of Nikkei, eventually bringing a halt to the entry of new laborers after the U.S.-Japan Gentlemen's Agreement of 1907–1908. In the following decades, the composition of the Nikkei community shifted from single males to families, accompanied by achievements in Issei agriculture and renewed anti-Japanese attacks. The denial of naturalization rights in 1922 and the termination of immigration from Japan in 1924 (both effective until 1952) were severe setbacks. With the outbreak of the Pacific War, all people of Japanese descent living on the West Coast were subject to mass removal and incarceration. To prove their loyalty, many American-born males served in the army or military intelligence service. Their heroic contributions helped Nisei to break through racial barriers and gain rapid social mobility after the war. In Hawai`i, the Nisei war veterans became a major political force leading to statehood in 1959. In the 1980s, the third-generation youths joined the Nisei in seeking redress for the injustices suffered by the internees during the war. The lengthy struggle ended in the passage of redress legislation in 1988. Today, the Japanese American community is more diverse than ever before, with changing boundaries and self-definitions, with many new immigrants and multiracial Nikkei, but the bonds remain strong.

Japanese American Historical Overview, 1868–2001

EIICHIRO AZUMA

IMMIGRATION AND EMERGENCE OF COMMUNITY

In the year of the Meiji Restoration (1868), the first Japanese immigrants (Issei) entered the kingdom of Hawai`i.[1] They had been recruited to work on the sugar plantations of Hawai`i by an American trader who served as the Hawaiian consul in Japan. This group of 148 Japanese, known as the *gannen-mono*, or people of the first year of Emperor Meiji's reign, had left Japan without receiving permission from the new Japanese government. Without consular protection, these first immigrants were badly treated by plantation bosses and were forced to live under primitive conditions. Fearing that this might hurt the prestige of the new government, Meiji leaders dispatched a government envoy to Hawai`i to rescue the stranded laborers. While some returned to Japan, other gannen-mono chose to stay in Hawai`i.

It was not until 1885 that Meiji Japan allowed its subjects to leave the country lawfully as labor emigrants. Given the slavelike treatment of Chinese immigrants, Japanese leaders feared that the mass migration of "low-class" peasants would damage Japan's national image and cause serious diplomatic problems. However, a drastic deflation policy, which led to a severe agricultural depression during the early 1880s, compelled government officials to seek ways to abate the problem of rural unrest and earn concurrently foreign currency through remittances.

In 1886, Japan concluded the Immigration Convention with Hawai`i, by which it would send contract laborers *(kan' yaku imin)* to work on sugar plantations for three years. The actual recruitment of laborers, handled by a private firm, focused on selected prefectures in southwestern Japan, an arrangement that set a pattern of geographic concentration in terms of the origins of Japanese immigrants to Hawai`i, and later to the continental United States. Between 1885 and 1894, a total of approximately twenty-nine thousand contract laborers entered the Hawaiian Islands under this system. After the treaty

The family of gannen-mono *Matsugoro Kuwata, ca. 1899: (from left to right, front) Matsugoro, Seiichi, Meleana with baby Shiro, Lindo; (back) Umi, Ome, Kimi. (Collection of Bishop Museum)*

Kona men in sugar cane field of Hawai`i, date unknown. (Gift of Sukeji Yamagata. Courtesy of the Rev. Shugen Komagata. Japanese American National Museum [95.197.25])

Early Issei immigrants from Hotaka-machi in Nagano Pefecture, Japan, who started a cooperative farm growing lettuce, celery, and cauliflower in Pontiac, approximately five miles northeast of Seattle, Washington, ca. 1912: (front row) Mrs. Shoichiro Katsuno seated and holding baby (second right); (second row) Motoyoshi Hirabayashi (far right); (third row) Shungo Hirabayashi (second left), Toshiharu Hirabayashi (fifth left). (Collection of the Hirabayashi Family)

was abolished with the overthrow of the Hawaiian monarchy, emigration companies assumed the role of recruiting and sending laborers to Hawai`i and the continental United States. In order to oversee and regulate their activities, the Japanese government enacted the Emigration Protection Act in 1896. In 1900, two years after Hawai`i became a territory of the United States, the entry of contract laborers from Japan ended.

Meanwhile, a few hundred student-laborers and political activists headed for San Francisco and other cities on the Pacific coast. Many of them sought political asylum in the United States following Meiji government persecution in the late 1880s. Though advocating popular rights in Japan, many activists were also expansionists who called for the overseas development of the Japanese in the Americas. Some eventually returned to Japan to run emigration companies or to become politicians, while others became leaders of the Japanese immigrant communities. The student-laborers usually found domestic work in the homes of American families, where they did household chores in the mornings and evenings in exchange for room and board, and attended school during the day. With their knowledge of the English language and the American social system, many student immigrants became labor contractors, who for fees and commissions helped newer immigrant laborers to find work.

From 1894 to 1908, approximately 125,000 immigrants from Japan arrived in Hawai`i, and 76,400 entered the western United States. Most of them looked for temporary work *(dekasegi)* and had no intention of settling down in the new land. In Hawai`i, a majority of these dekasegi laborers usually toiled on sugar plantations even

Mrs. Mitsu Hirabayashi, née Suzawa (second row, second from left) and other "picture brides" on board ship bound for Seattle to meet her prospective husband, Shungo Hirabayashi, ca. May 1914. (Collection of the Hirabayashi Family)

Wedding photo of Shungo and Mitsu Hirabayashi, Seattle, Washington, 1914. The Hirabayashis had five children, Gordon, Edward, James, Esther, and Richard. (Collection of the Hirabayashi Family)

after their three-year contracts expired, while some started their own businesses in Honolulu and plantation settlements. Between 1901 and 1908 some thirty-seven thousand laborers remigrated to the continental United States, where they formed labor gangs and worked on railroads and farms and in lumber mills and canneries. As in Hawai`i, many saved their meager wages to move up the ranks from tenant farmers to landowners, or shop owners, although a large number of the laborers returned to their native villages in Japan with their savings. By the first decade of the twentieth century, the urban and rural Japanese communities in Hawai`i and the Pacific coast states already had established Japanese associations, vernacular newspapers, churches and temples, language schools, and various other social organizations.

Central to the process of community formation was the emergence of Japanese immigrant families after 1907, which turned the social orientation of many Issei from dekasegi to permanent residence in the United States. From the beginning, there was a tendency for more male immigrants than females to leave Japan. Many left their families behind in Japan, since they initially had little desire to settle permanently in the United States. Others were young bachelors, who intended to make fortunes in a foreign land and later live comfortable lives in their native villages. Hawai`i, however, had

Members of the Hotaka-machi Club at a picnic with invited guests from the community, Seattle, Washington, April 26, 1914. (Collection of the Hirabayashi Family)

more female immigrants than the continental United States, due to conscious efforts to bring families to plantations. Gender imbalance characterized the early immigrant communities, giving rise to prostitution and other related problems.

The Gentlemen's Agreement between Japan and the United States in 1907–1908 stopped labor immigration but allowed family members of bona fide Issei residents to go to the United States. As a result, large numbers of Japanese women began going to Hawai`i and the mainland United States to join their husbands. Many came as "picture brides," who entered into marriage by exchanging photos with their future mates. On the mainland alone, a total of 92,907 Japanese arrived between 1909 and 1920, of whom almost 39 percent were women. Nearly seven thousand "picture brides" entered through Seattle and San Francisco from 1912 to 1920. Therefore, during the 1910s, settled family life, rather than migrant bachelor life, became a norm in the Issei community, though simple economics and legal barriers still prohibited many laborers from establishing their own families.

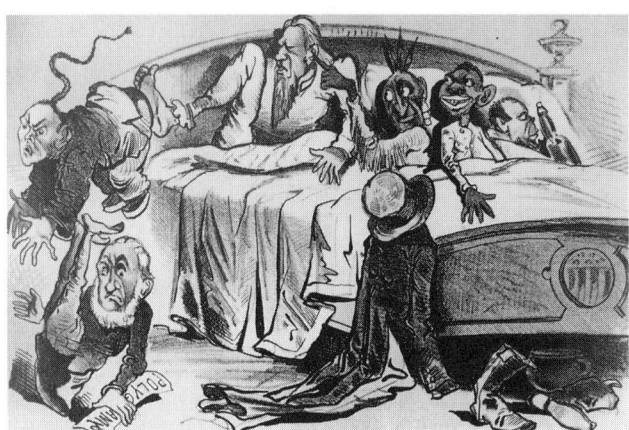

Political cartoon, ca. late 1800s. (Collection of Visual Communications Collection [NRC.1997.53.1])

Portrait of Takao Ozawa, October 6, 1916. ". . . I have all [the] confidence in myself that as far as my character is concerned, I am second to none. In name, General Benedict Arnold was an American, but at heart he was a traitor. In name, I am not an American, but at heart I am a true American." Takao Ozawa, undated brief. (Gift of Takeya Family. Japanese American National Museum [99.208.1])

Kayo Senda (mother) with her son Kazuo and daughter, Eiko, Kaua'i, Hawa'i, ca. 1919. (Photograph by W. J. Senda. Gift of the W. J. Senda Family. Japanese American National Museum [96.449.20])

THE IMPACT OF RACISM

American racism chronically influenced the everyday lives of Japanese immigrants. In Hawai'i, Japanese laborers tended to occupy the bottom tier of the racially constituted social hierarchy, a fact that benefited the white oligarchy. In 1887, when a handful of *haole* (white) elites captured the real political power with the proclamation of the Bayonet Constitution, the Japanese were deprived of the suffrage, which had been promised to them under the bilateral treaty between Hawai'i and Japan. Ten years later, the entry of Japanese into the islands was severely curtailed, as the white elite, which had completely taken over the political control in Hawai'i, began to fear their numerical increase in the local population. In 1898, Hawai'i was annexed to the United States and was incorporated into the American legal and social system.

In the continental United States, where sporadic attacks had tormented Issei laborers since the 1890s, an organized anti-Japanese exclusion movement led by white labor unions and opportunistic politicians gained prominence in San Francisco. The movement culminated in the segregation of Japanese pupils in the city's public schools in 1906. Since the U.S. government feared that such incidents would antagonize Japan, segregation was ended in exchange for agreement by Japan not to send laborers to the United States.

As the anti-Japanese agitation gained political momentum in local legislatures of the Pacific coast states and Hawai'i in the 1910s, many discriminatory laws were enacted using the racist definition of the Japanese as "aliens ineligible to citizenship" as their legal basis for racial exclusion. These laws included the alien land laws in California, Washington, Oregon, and other states, as well as restrictions on commercial activities. Along with the Japanese predominance in agriculture, Japanese-language

In 1920 Japanese and Filipino sugar plantation workers of O`ahu, Hawai`i, joined forces and struck for better wages and living conditions. The planters claimed victory after the six-month strike drew to a close, but three months later they increased wages and met other demands. (Gift of Honpa Hongwanji Mission of Hawaii. Japanese American National Museum [96.488.29])

education became another notable target of exclusionists, who accused the schools of turning Japanese American pupils into "worshippers of the Mikado." From the late 1910s to the early 1920s, various regulations against Japanese schools were put into effect in California and Hawai`i. The persistent demand for the termination of Japanese immigration finally reached Congress. In 1924, the Immigration Act was passed; it prohibited the entry of all Japanese immigrants, even family members of the Issei, until 1952.

However, Japanese immigrants did not merely sit quietly under these assaults. In their quest for self-determination, they often stood up and demanded better living conditions and appropriate compensation for their hard labor. In Hawai`i, not only did Issei plantation workers frequently protest low wages and abuse by *luna* (labor bosses), but they played major roles in the great plantation strikes of 1909 and 1920. In their everyday life, as in sporadic collective struggles, ethnic cooperation was a key to their social activities and economic advancement. In almost every Japanese settlement, Issei formed farming guilds, chambers of commerce, and other organizations in order to gain broader entry into rural agriculture and urban small business.

The Japanese associations served as the main vehicles by which the immigrants vigorously fought legal oppression in the early 1920s. One of the most important litigations was the Takao Ozawa case, which revolved around the issue of Japanese naturalization rights. In 1922 the U.S. Supreme Court denied Ozawa citizenship, ruling that "the intention [of the Constitution] was to confer the privilege of citizenship upon that class of persons whom the fathers knew as white, and to deny it to all who could not be so classified."

Other suits included test cases against alien land laws and language-school regulations. Much to the disappointment of the Issei, most test cases that reached the U.S. Supreme Court before 1923 were decided unfavorably. One bright spot in this history of struggle was an exceptional legal victory in Hawai`i of a group of Hawai`i Issei who fought for the right to send their children to Japanese-language schools after attending American public schools. After more than six years of legal battles, the U.S. Supreme Court ruled in their favor. From the mid-1920s

Japanese Americans 281

Nisei delegates at the Fifth Biennial Japanese American Citizens League (JACL) National Convention held in Los Angeles, California, September 1938. Patriotism and complete identification with American life were positions most clearly articulated by the JACL founded in 1930. (Jack Iwata photo. Gift of Jack and Peggy Iwata. Japanese American National Museum [93.102.287])

onward, the Japanese immigrant community placed a special focus on the education of their children, the Nisei.

TOWARD A NISEI ERA

While the U.S. government shut the door to new immigrants from Japan and the courts denied Japanese rights to land and naturalization, many Issei started to become more concerned about the future of their American-born children than about their own "success." Japanese-language schools flourished both in Hawai`i and the mainland, since the Issei believed that the language would play a role in bridging the generations and offer the Nisei new opportunities in a coming "Pacific" era. Community activities also revolved around the second-generation children; organized ethnic athletic leagues emerged, including such American sports such as baseball and basketball and Japanese martial arts like kendo and judo. Many Issei believed that certain Japanese qualities and values would help the Nisei become better Americans and hence benefit the American nation. In order for the Nisei to be truly bicultural, a number of parents sent their American-born children to Japan for secondary or higher education during the 1930s. These second-generation youths were often called the Kibei.

Starting in the mid-1920s, Japanese immigrant newspapers started to attach daily English-language sections to help mold the Nisei's political thought and to foster a sense of pride and connection to their ethnic community. Issei leaders encouraged older Nisei to take active part in American politics in order to integrate themselves into middle-class white America. At the urging of their parents' generation, Nisei leaders formed their own sociopolitical organizations by the end of the 1920s. High school and college Nisei established the Japanese Students' Association of Hawai`i; their mainland counterparts formed the Japanese American Citizens League (JACL). In Hawai`i, the New Americans Conference annually provided Nisei adolescents with an opportunity to discuss the issues that they faced as minority Americans. The JACL likewise held a national convention biannually. Beginning in 1930, some Nisei, notably those in Hawai`i, successfully ran for local offices.

With the backing of their immigrant parents, Nisei youths sought to expand the realm of economic and social activities beyond the boundaries of the immigrant generation. A number of Nisei men and women pursued higher and vocational education, acquiring college degrees and such special skills as nursing and teaching. At the same time, the structure of ethnic economy underwent a transformation. Plantation work became much less important in Hawai`i; the percentage of plantation workers in the total Japanese labor force had dropped from over 70 percent in 1902 to a mere 18 percent in 1931. Conversely, more and more of Hawai`i's Japanese, of whom many were Nisei, entered such occupational fields as truck farming, fishing, small businesses, and civil services, with an increasing rate of urbanization.

On the mainland, many Nisei found work in urban businesses, especially those associated with agricultural wholesale and produce retail sectors, although racial discrimination still continued to limit their opportunities and mobility. In spite of some positive changes, racism still plagued the lives of Japanese Americans. Its effects often manifested itself in the form of Nisei juvenile delinquency, poverty, and a racial inferiority complex. By 1930, the Nisei outnumbered the Issei in both Hawai`i and the mainland, at a time when international politics started to affect the lives of Japanese in America in direct and profound ways.

By its invasion of China, Japan put itself on a collision course with the United States during the 1930s. Out of concern for their troubled native country, many immigrants supported Japan's war effort in China. The Issei did not feel that helping Japan contradicted their loyalty to America. Believing that the American public was being misguided by anti-Japan propaganda, they engaged in a pro-Japanese publicity campaign with an eye to restoring friendship and peaceful relations between Japan and the United States. Nisei leaders also shared the conviction that explaining Japan's position could serve their generational mission by forming a bridge of understanding between

Konawaena High School Editorial Staff, Kealakekua, Kona, Hawai`i, 1927. (Gift of Shigeru Akamatsu. Japanese American National Museum [94.227.3])

their native country and their parents' homeland. U.S.-Japan relations rapidly deteriorated, however, and anti-Japanese agitators simply regarded the Issei's support for Japan before 1940 as "anti-American," arguing that Japanese Americans posed a threat to national security. This mentality helped to lay the foundation for wartime hysteria and the ensuing mass incarceration of Japanese Americans.

THE PACIFIC WAR AND JAPANESE AMERICANS

Japan's attack on Pearl Harbor in December 1941 put Issei and Nisei in an extremely difficult position. In Hawai`i, martial law was immediately proclaimed, and immigrant leaders, now categorized as "dangerous enemy aliens," were rounded up by the Federal Bureau of Investigation and sent to local detention centers, an event that caused a sudden shift of community leadership from the first to the

Soldier addressing 442nd Regimental Combat Team during World War II, ca. 1945. (U.S. Army photo. Courtesy of Harold Harada [NRC.1997.94.37])

second generation. On the mainland too, the federal and local law enforcement authorities arrested many key Issei. Combined with some 1,450 from Hawai`i, these people were separated from their beloved families and interned at detention camps for the duration of the war.

Meanwhile, the daily lives of Japanese residents became more and more restricted. The American government, backed by general public sentiment, moved quickly to enforce the mass incarceration of Japanese Americans. On February 19, 1942, President Franklin D. Roosevelt signed Executive Order 9066, authorizing the "evacuation" of the Japanese from military zones, both "enemy aliens" and citizens alike. Starting in late March, a total of 110,000 Issei and Nisei were shipped to temporary "assembly centers" and then to ten War Relocation Authority concentration camps built hastily on the wastelands in the interior.

While mass incarceration destroyed Japanese communities on the West Coast, the people of Hawai`i did not go to camps en masse. Selected ministers, Japanese-language schoolteachers, newspapermen, prominent businessmen, and other community leaders were incarcerated at Sand Island and Honouliuli on O`ahu. A number of these individuals were later moved to mainland camps, where a few were joined by their families. Other families in Hawai`i were ordered to vacate certain areas near the coastline or

Nishi Hongwanji Buddhist Temple in Los Angeles' Little Tokyo (currently the Historic Building of the Japanese American National Museum) became a roundup point for the Japanese Americans who were sent to "assembly centers" in 1942. (Jack Iwata photo. Gift of Jack and Peggy Iwata. Japanese American National Museum [93.102.102])

military facilities. Nevertheless, in order to demonstrate their loyalty to the United States, many Japanese residents cooperated in America's war effort in various capacities. Though initially excluded from military duty, thousands of Nisei youths volunteered to serve in the army, which formed the all-Nisei 442nd Regimental Combat Team in 1943.

Stripped of their civil rights and liberties as citizens of the United States, the Nisei who were incarcerated in camps on the mainland responded to their plight with complex choices. In the winter of 1943, the U.S. Army and the War Relocation Authority, in order to separate "disloyal" elements from loyal Japanese Americans for military enlistment, administered the infamous "Loyalty Registration." A minority of Nisei took issue with the apparent hypocrisy in American policy that incarcerated them but asked for their military service. In contrast, many Nisei enlisted in the military forces, sensing a need to show their loyalty. The majority who enlisted served in the European theater with the legendary 442nd RCT, which incorporated the 100th Battalion, from Hawai`i; others worked as translators in the Pacific as members of military Intelligence Service. Their heroic contributions helped to redeem the name of Japanese Americans and to ease the process of returning to mainstream American society after the war. Whatever their response, Japanese Americans

Death of a soldier. Family portrait at Poston concentration camp, western Arizona, 1942–45. (Gift of Eric Saul. Japanese American National Museum [96.314.21])

adapted to the most difficult situations to seek better futures for themselves and their families in the United States.

THE END OF THE WAR AND THE NISEI ERA
When the Pacific War came to an end, Japanese Americans had to start all over again. The second generation took the postwar lead in rebuilding their communities and becoming part of the American middle class, since many of the Issei were already too old to work. For the mainland internees, the release from concentration camps posed practical problems of how to eke out daily livings. Most internees eventually found themselves back on the West Coast, but they needed housing and jobs, which were not easily found in a postwar society still full of hatred and intolerance. Gradually they rebuilt their individual lives and communities. Many Nisei found themselves breaking racial barriers by entering occupational fields that had been closed to them in the past. Starting in the 1950s, Nisei increasingly took part in a wider range of sociocultural activities, producing literary works of their own, creating their own art pieces, and becoming visible in the performing arts. Their "successful assimilation" into the mainstream society even generated a new stereotype of Japanese Americans, that of a "model minority."

With a renewed sense of confidence as full-fledged, loyal members of the nation, Japanese Americans actively engaged in its social and political affairs. First and foremost, Nisei leaders confronted the survivals of past injustices, determined to win the repeal of discriminatory laws that had rendered them second-class citizens. They not only achieved the repeal of the alien land laws in Oregon and California but vigorously lobbied Congress for Issei naturalization rights and the resumption of Japanese immigration. In 1952, Congress passed the Walter-McCarran Act, which lifted the ban on Japanese immigration and allowed the Issei to become naturalized citizens.

Hawai`i's Nisei played a pivotal role in changing the

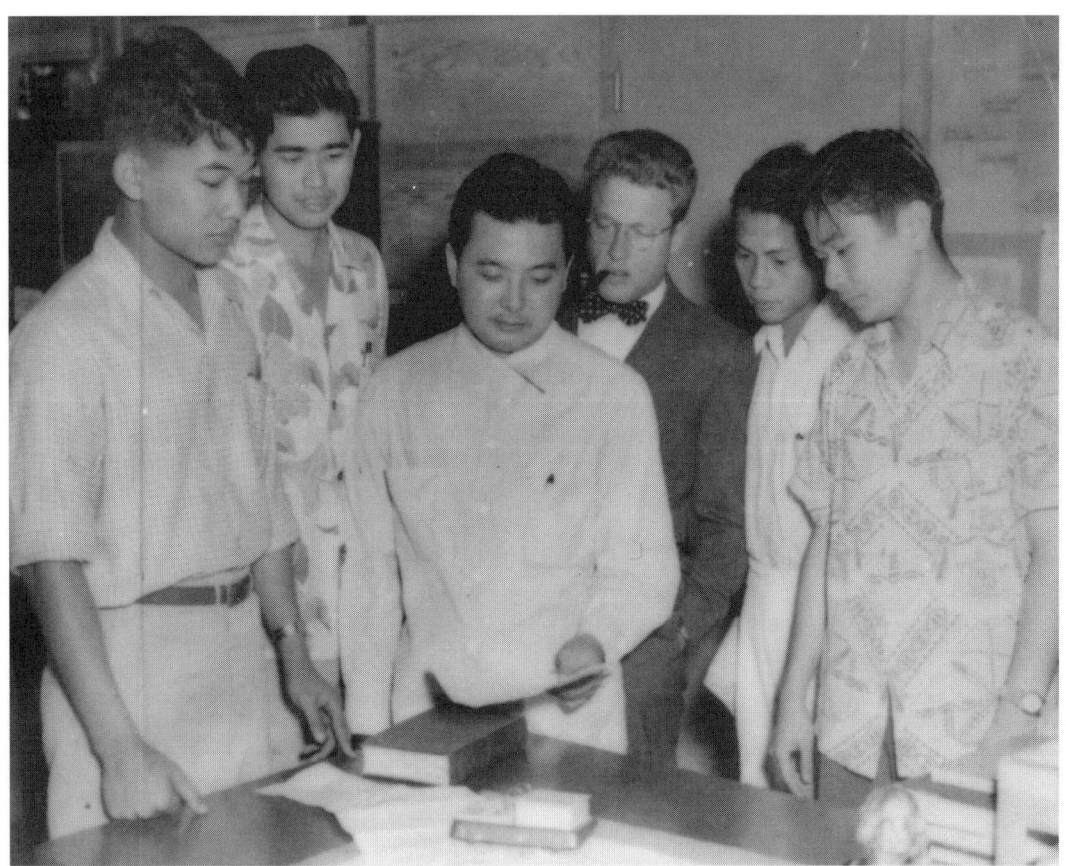
U.S. Senator Daniel K. Inouye as a University of Hawai`i freshman enlisting in the U.S. Army, 1943. (Gift of U.S. Senator Daniel K. Inouye. Japanese American National Museum [95.179.1])

Issei becoming U.S. citizens at a naturalization ceremony at Konawaena High School, Kona, Hawai`i, 1952. (Gift of Daisy Suezaki. Japanese American National Museum [94.237.5])

Asian American performance artist Nobuko Miyamoto Betserai (center) with her husband Tarabu Betserai (left), son Kamau Ayubbi, and granddaughter Asiyah Ayubbi. Los Angeles, California, November 29, 1998. (Gift of Nobuko Miyamoto. Japanese American National Museum [98.363.2])

political and social landscape of the islands. In 1946, union leaders, including key Nisei, mobilized over twenty thousand plantation workers to walk out in protest of low wages. The strike paralyzed the sugar industry for seventy-nine days and challenged the dominance of the haole business elite. Eight years later, Nisei war veterans formed with liberal whites a powerful coalition to bring down the islands' Republican oligarchy. Often characterized as the "bloodless" Democratic Revolution of 1954, Japanese Americans became a major political force in Hawai`i's territorial legislature and municipal governments. With the statehood of Hawai`i in 1959, Daniel K. Inouye, a decorated veteran of World War II, joined the U.S. House of Representative as its first Asian American; he was elected as a senator from Hawai`i in 1962. Patsy Takemoto Mink was the first Asian American woman elected to the House, in 1964.

Hawai`i also produced the first Asian governor of an American state, George Ariyoshi in 1973.

REINTERPRETING THE PAST, REENVISIONING THE PRESENT

The Sansei, third-generation Japanese Americans, joined the Nisei's quest for greater involvement in the larger society. While many Nisei basked in new suburban Japanese American enclaves and felt they had achieved the "American Dream," signs of problems associated with greater affluence and acceptance manifested themselves among the Sansei youth. For example, Japanese American youth gangs emerged in urban areas, while drug addiction became an issue. The Sansei started to question the past, often challenging, with youthful idealism, the quiet acceptance by Nisei of racial injustice. Influenced by the anti–Vietnam War and the civil rights

Anti–Vietnam War demonstration on Wilshire Boulevard in Los Angeles, 1972: (left to right) Kenji Kudo, Kiyoko Shibasawa, unknown, Mike Murase, unknown, Mike Yamamoto, Gary Uyekawa, Joy Yamasaki. (Collection of Visual Communications)

movements, many Sansei soon found a linkage between their collective experience of racial victimization and the larger social ills in America. Many began to commit themselves to social reform and the making of a better nation.

Within this historical context there emerged a call for redress and reparations, a movement that sought an official apology and acknowledgment by the government for its wrongdoing during the war. Responding to persistent lobbying by various Japanese American organizations, the federal government in 1981 set up a special "Commission on Wartime Relocation and Internment of Civilians," which subsequently recommended concrete ways of redress for the former internees. In 1988, after a lengthy struggle, the Japanese American community finally saw the passage of a redress law. The first redress payment of twenty thousand dollars and an official letter of apology,

signed by President George Bush, were delivered to the oldest Issei survivors in 1990.

At the same time, Sansei have aspired to go beyond their ethnic boundaries, to seek the understanding and cooperation of other groups of Americans. With a deeper understanding of shared experiences in American society, the young men and women have taken part in the larger Asian American movement, establishing various organizations that offer social, educational, and cultural services to Asian-Pacific Islander populations, as well as Asian American/Ethnic Studies programs in institutions of higher education both on the mainland and in Hawai`i.

Greater integration of Japanese Americans into American middle-class life has been accompanied by greater diversity and divergence in perspectives. In Hawai`i, as Nisei formed a political establishment of their own, some Sansei began to question whether Japanese Americans

On August 10, 1988, President Ronald Reagan signs the redress law, H.R. 442. (Gift of Norman Y. Mineta. Japanese American National Museum [96.370.16A])

had joined the "oppressors"—a charge often made by other minority groups in the islands as well. In fact, many Nisei preferred a more conservative approach to social issues, often opposing the progressive views of Sansei youths. A group of Nisei farmers in the agricultural heartland of California, for example, formed the Nisei Farmers League, which took a hostile attitude toward the farm labor movement. Similarly, a large number of Nisei were initially reluctant to support redress and other social reform agendas.

Nevertheless, the national politics of redress and its subsequent success have compelled Japanese Americans to reflect upon their collective past and position in American society and the overarching ties that overcome individual, generational, and regional differences. The redress and reparations movement was an act of political empowerment; it pointed to a new Japanese American community based on a common understanding of a shared past, present, and future. With a growing interest in ethnic culture and history, Japanese Americans have been engaged continuously in community building. The Japanese American National Museum, established in 1985, is but one example of this collaborative process and of the commonality and diversity within the Japanese American community.

The postwar community, with peoples of different generations and regions, and "nonconventional" populations, has been forced to grapple with the issue of its changing boundaries and self-definitions. The postwar years saw the entry of many new immigrants, often called *Shin Issei* (new Issei). At first, some were wives of American GIs, while others came as students and "refugees." The enactment of the 1965 immigration law did away with race-based requirements for immigrant status, enabling thousands of Japanese nationals to immigrate as investors, workers with specialized skills, and family members of American citizens or permanent residents. While these newcomers have added vitality to the existing

Students protest in support of Ethnic Studies at the University of Hawai`i at Mānoa, 1972. (University of Hawai`i, Ethnic Studies Program [NRC.1997.52.3])

A joyous birthday celebration for Ryan Hanami (six years old, seated on floor, center left) with a taiko drum demonstration held at the Japanese American National Museum, November 23, 2000. (Photograph by Clement Hanami)

Japanese American community, the community, in turn, has faced the challenge of accommodating them.

The concept of "community" has itself expanded beyond the conventional, monolithic notions of ethnicity and race. In recent years, a vast majority of Sansei have married persons of other races or ethnicities, reflecting dramatic changes in the larger society. Many of the fourth and fifth-generation children, the Yonsei and the Gosei, are thus multiracial, multi-ethnic Japanese Americans. Their presence has forced the community to redefine itself, often shedding light on its own ethnocentrism and racism. Lately, being a Japanese American is not solely an issue of "racial" or physiological characteristics, and shared "cultural" elements are no longer a central binding force either. For most people, being a Japanese American has increasingly become a matter of heart, self-identity, and individual commitment. Today, one can see in community activities many non-Japanese-appearing faces, many names of non-Japanese origin, and many people of heterogeneous backgrounds. Nikkei beauty queens no longer have to be "racially pure" Japanese. Nor must one any longer have had a grandparent incarcerated in a wartime concentration camp to join a Nikkei sports team. In the era of multiculturalism and globalization, the Japanese American community constantly reshapes itself in accordance with the transformations of the larger American society and of the world at large.

NOTE

1. Michiko Kodama-Nishimoto provided valuable input in the development of this essay. I would like to thank her for her insight and contribution.

Japanese American Bibliographic Essay

BRIAN NIIYA AND EIICHIRO AZUMA

This selected bibliography of important works on Japanese Americans has two distinct sections, one consisting of works in Japanese, the other of works in English.[1] These two types of works are very different in character, beyond the difference in language. For the most part, the selected Japanese-language works were written by Japanese immigrants themselves, mostly in the years before World War II. The selected English-language works are by both Japanese American and non-Japanese American authors and were mostly written in the last twenty years. An extensive Japanese-language literature on Japanese Americans has appeared in the last two decades; these works, most of which were written by contemporary Japanese authors, can be found in the "Japan" chapter of this volume. Because of the different character of the Japanese and English-language works listed here, different principles of selection were adopted for each section.

ENGLISH-LANGUAGE MATERIALS: BY BRIAN NIIYA

This bibliography of important English-language sources on Japanese Americans is by necessity a highly selective one, as a great number of works have been written on some aspects of the Japanese American experience. In choosing a short list of works, I kept the following criteria in mind:

Currency

Because this volume is intended for a general audience, I tended to favor works that represent the current state of thinking on whatever topic it addresses. The bibliography is thus heavily weighted toward works that have appeared in the last twenty years or so, at the expense of older works. For example, literally hundreds of works were written in the 1910s and 1920s in the context of the anti-Japanese movement. Given the heated political debate around Japanese immigration at the time, it is not surprising that nearly all of the literature on Japanese Americans from this period takes the form of either prosecution or defense, to borrow Yuji Ichioka's metaphor. While these works would be of value to historians as primary material documenting how people of that time thought, they would be of limited interest to general readers today and might even mislead them. Thus, none of these works are included in this bibliography. Instead, a single work on the anti-Japanese movement on the West Coast, Roger Daniels' *Politics of Prejudice* (E-13), is included, since it remains the standard work on this topic and incorporates much of what came before it.

Breadth

I tried to choose works that cover the breadth of the Japanese American experience. Thus, there are works on such subtopics as art and music; on different communities and regions of the country; and on specific subsets of the Japanese American community, such as Japanese Americans who trace their roots to Okinawa, and women. Sometimes, the best work on an important topic is an unpublished thesis or dissertation; sometimes it is a novel; sometimes it is a work that is not specifically on Japanese Americans. Whatever the case, that work is included in this bibliography.

On the other hand, a high percentage of works on Japanese Americans deal with just a few topics, especially the mass removal and internment of Japanese Americans during World War II. Rather than list works on these topics in proportion to the total number of works produced, I generally chose only a couple of the best. Thus, though there are dozens of works, for instance, on Japanese Americans in the U.S. armed forces during World War II, only one work, Masayo Duus's *Unlikely Liberators*, is listed here (E-17), since it provides the best overview for the nonspecialist.

Depth

Because there are so many book-length works on Japanese Americans, I choose to limit this bibliography to in-depth studies in the form of books, Ph.D. dissertations, or master's theses. Neither journal articles (popular or scholarly), pamphlets, conference papers, nor unpublished manuscripts are included. Government reports are included only if a nongovernmental publisher has reprinted them.

Accessibility and Frequency of Use

For topics where there are many works available, I weighed other factors besides those listed above. Chief among them was accessibility. Is the work in print or otherwise widely available? Is it written in a style that would be accessible to the general reader? I also took into account how often a given work has been used, both by teachers of Asian American/Japanese American Studies courses and by other scholars, judging by how often the work has been cited in others.

Like any bibliography, this one will no doubt be out of date the moment it is finalized, since new work continues to be produced all the time. The cutoff date for consideration for this bibliography was October of 2000; works published after that date will not be found here.

JAPANESE-LANGUAGE MATERIALS: BY EIICHIRO AZUMA

Japanese-language publications listed in this annotated bibliography include the significant works by the Issei or the Kibei-Nisei. Although there is a variety of such works, the compiler has chosen books that fit five categories. First, a majority of the works are histories of Christian and Buddhist churches, Japanese schools, certain prefectural groups, and specific Japanese communities in Hawai`i and the continental United States. These historical works usually take the form of a "*hattenshi*," or "a history of Japanese development," usually focusing on the "sufferings" and "triumphs" of successful Issei farmers, merchants, and community leaders, often accompanied by a Who's Who of "representative" Issei men. As such, a typical Japanese immigrant *hattenshi* is both gender and class-biased, in that it usually was written from the perspective of Issei men who "made it in America." By the same token, such works were designed to promote a positive image of immigrants, or "*imin*," among the people of Japan, who tended to have negative stereotypes about Japanese immigrants in the United States. In this respect, many historical works selected in this bibliography are as much valuable "historical" sources as they are reflective of Issei's current views at the time they were produced.

A second category of common Issei works comprises collections of newspaper commentaries and essays by immigrant journalists and intellectuals. These books can serve as good sources for understanding Issei's views on various social, political, and cultural issues that they faced at the time.

The third category consists of Japanese directories, yearbooks, Who's Whos, or any combination of these. Ever since 1904, when the *Nichibei Shinbun* of San Francisco published the first *Nichibei Nenkan* (yearbook and directory), many major Japanese immigrant newspapers have compiled their own publications of this sort in consecutive years, or at irregular intervals (see J-52). As the books often contain detailed historical and demographic data, they can be useful primary source materials for researchers.

The fourth category includes life histories, autobiographies, biographical accounts, and published diaries. These publications are useful for understanding the day-to-day experiences of individual immigrants. Readers, however, should be advised that these publications, like Japanese immigrant *hattenshi*, were often intended to illuminate the "successes" of particular individuals.

Finally, there are fictional and literary works produced by Issei. Although the compiler could include only a small number of the publications available, there are many more books in this category than in any other. In particular, books of poems and short stories are widely available, the vast majority of them published privately by the Issei poets and writers themselves. It is also important to note the prominence of Issei women in this area, as literary expression was among the few intellectual venues open to them in the male-dominated immigrant society. Anyone interested in the Issei female experience should consult this group of source materials.

NOTE
1. Eiichiro Azuma dealt with Japanese-language materials; Brian Niiya dealt with English-language materials.

Annotated Bibliography of Japanese Americans

COMPILED BY BRIAN NIIYA, MICHIKO KODAMA-NISHIMOTO, AND EIICHIRO AZUMA

ENGLISH

1. Adams, Ansel, Photographer. *Born Free and Equal: Photographs of the Loyal Japanese-Americans of Manzanar Relocation Center, Inyo County, California.* New York: U.S. Camera, 1944.

   Collection of photographs taken by the famed photographer Ansel Adams upon his visit to the Manzanar concentration camp.

2. Albert, Michael Daniel. "Japanese American Communities in Chicago and the Twin Cities." Ph.D. diss., University of Minnesota, 1980.

   Historical study of two midwestern Japanese American communities focuses mostly on the resettlement era.

3. Azuma, Eiichiro. "Walnut Grove: Japanese Farm Community in the Sacramento River Delta, 1892–1945." Master's thesis, University of California, Los Angeles, 1992.

   Community study based on Japanese language sources and interviews.

4. Boylan, Dan, and T. Michael Holmes. *John A. Burns: The Man and His Times.* Honolulu: University of Hawai`i Press, 2000.

   Biography of the Democratic Party leader and governor of Hawai`i.

5. Chan, Sucheng. *Asian Americans: An Interpretive History.* Boston: Twayne Publishers, 1991.

   Synthesizes existing literature on Asian Americans to build a general interpretive history.

6. Chang, Gordon H., edited, annotated, and bibliographic essay by. *Morning Glory, Evening Shadow: Yamato Ichihashi and His Internment Writings, 1942–1945.* Stanford: Stanford University Press, 1997.

   Ichihashi was a pioneering Issei academician at Stanford and author of one of the most important prewar studies of Japanese Americans. This work compiles his diaries, letters, and essays covering the internment years along with a biographical essay on his life before and after camp.

7. Chuman, Frank F. *The Bamboo People: The Law and Japanese-Americans.* Del Mar, Calif.: Publisher's Inc., 1976.

   History of laws pertaining to and fought against by Japanese Americans.

8. Coffman, Tom. *Catch a Wave: A Case Study of Hawaii's New Politics.* Honolulu: University Press of Hawaii, 1973.

   On the 1970 Hawai`i gubernatorial race and the role of Japanese Americans in the political process. Foreword by Stuart Gerry Brown.

9. The Commission on Wartime Relocation and Internment of Civilians. *Personal Justice Denied: Report of the Commission on Wartime Relocation and Internment of Civilians.* Foreword by Tetsuden Kashima. Seattle: University of Washington Press, 1997.

   Report of the Congressional Commission includes a summary of the removal and detention of Japanese Americans during World War II. The original was published by the Government Printing Office in Washington, D.C., in 1982.

10. Consulate-General of Japan. *Documental History of Law Cases Affecting Japanese in the United States, 1916–1924.* New York: Arno Press, 1978.

    Two volume compilation of legal cases involving Japanese Americans. Volume one contains naturalization cases while volume two contains land law cases. Originally published by the Consulate-General of Japan, San Francisco in 1925.

11. Cooper, George, and Gavan Daws. *Land and Power in Hawaii: The Democratic Years.* Honolulu: Benchmark Books, 1985.

    Examines the linkages between the Democratic Party, development, and real estate in postwar Hawai`i.

12. Daniels, Roger. *Asian America: Chinese and Japanese in the United States since 1850.* Seattle: University of Washington Press, 1988.

    General history of Chinese and Japanese Americans that incorporates much of Daniels' previous work on the topic.

13. Daniels, Roger. *The Politics of Prejudice: The Anti-Japanese Movement in California and the Struggle for Japanese Exclusion.* 1962. 2nd edition. Berkeley: University of California Press, 1977.

    Study of the anti-Japanese movement until 1924; developed from a doctoral dissertation (University of California, Los Angeles, 1960).

14. Daniels, Roger, Sandra D. Taylor, and Harry H. L Kitano, eds. *Japanese Americans: From Relocation to Redress.* Seattle: University of Washington Press, 1991.

    Papers coming out of the International Conference on Relocation and Redress held in Salt Lake City in 1983 covering many different aspects of the Japanese American World War II experience; the revised edition is the same as the earlier one with the exception of one short essay by Roger Daniels titled "Redress Achieved." The original was published by the University of Utah Press, Salt Lake City, 1986.

15. Dower, John W. *War without Mercy: Race and Power in the Pacific War.* New York: Pantheon Books, 1986.

295

Examines racial stereotyping on both the American and Japanese sides during World War II and how these stereotypes recur in different forms during times of peace.

16. Drinnon, Richard. *Keeper of Concentration Camps: Dillon S. Myer and American Racism*. Berkeley: University of California Press, 1987.

    Biography of WRA (War Relocation Authority) director Myer, who later became director of the Bureau of Indian Affairs.

17. Duus, Masayo. *Unlikely Liberators: The Men of the 100th and the 442nd*. Honolulu: University of Hawaii Press, 1987.

    History of the all-Nisei military units in World War II.

18. Ethnic Studies Oral History Project and United Okinawan Association of Hawaii. *Uchinanchu: A History of Okinawans in Hawaii*. Honolulu: Ethnic Studies Program, University of Hawaii at Manoa, 1981.

    Anthology of works on Okinawans in Hawai`i, along with oral histories of Okinawan Issei.

19. Fuchs, Lawrence H. *Hawaii Pono: A Social History*. New York: Harcourt, Brace and World, 1981.

    Landmark history that made explicit the nature of interracial relations in Hawaiian society.

20. Fujita, Stephen S., and David J. O'Brien. *Japanese American Ethnicity: The Persistence of Community*. Seattle: University of Washington Press, 1991.

    Examines the persistence of Japanese American identity and community in the face of structural assimilation.

21. Girdner, Audrie, and Anne Loftis. *The Great Betrayal: The Evacuation of the Japanese-Americans during World War II*. New York: Macmillan, 1969.

    General account of the World War II experience with an emphasis on the actions and thoughts of the Japanese Americans themselves.

22. Glenn, Evelyn Nakano. *Issei, Nisei, War Bride: Three Generations of Japanese American Women in Domestic Service*. Philadelphia: Temple University Press, 1986.

    Pioneering study of Japanese American women in domestic service both before and after World War II.

23. Grodzins, Morton. *Americans Betrayed: Politics and the Japanese Evacuation*. Chicago: University of Chicago Press, 1949.

    Examines the role of West Coast politicians and economic interest groups in the forced removal of all Japanese Americans during World War II. Research for this work was conducted by Grodzins as a staff member of the Japanese American Evacuation and Resettlement Study project, but it was published separately.

24. Hansen, Arthur A., ed. *Japanese American World War II Evacuation Oral History Project*, 1991–1994.

    Five volume compilation of oral history interviews in the Japanese American Project of the Oral History Program at California State University, Fullerton. Part I. Internees (Westport, Conn.: Meckler, 1991); Part II, Administrators (Westport, Conn.: Meckler, 1991); Part III, Analysts (Munich, Ger.: K. G. Saur, 1994); Part IV, Resisters (Munich, Ger.: K. G. Saur, 1993).

25. Hatamiya, Leslie T. *Righting a Wrong: Japanese Americans and the Passage of the Civil Liberties Act of 1988*. Stanford: Stanford University Press, 1993.

    History of the legislative aspect of the redress movement.

26. Hayashi, Brian Masaru. *"For the Sake of Our Japanese Brethren": Assimilation, Nationalism, and Protestantism among the Japanese of Los Angeles, 1985–1942*. Stanford: Stanford University Press, 1995.

    Study of three very different Issei Christian churches in Los Angeles prior to World War II. Adapted from a doctoral dissertation (University of California, Los Angeles, 1990).

27. Higa, Karin, ed. *The View from Within: Japanese American Art from the Internment Camps, 1942–1945*. Los Angeles: Japanese American National Museum, UCLA Wight Art Gallery, and UCLA Asian American Studies Center, 1992.

    Catalogue to a pioneering exhibition of art created by inmates in America's concentration camps.

28. Hirabayashi, Lane Ryo. *The Politics of Fieldwork: Research in an American Concentration Camp*. Tucson: University of Arizona Press, 1999.

    Examines issues in doing anthropological fieldwork through looking at the life and work of pioneering Nisei anthropologist Tamie Tsuchiyama and her work with the Japanese American Evacuation and Resettlement Study.

29. Hirose, Stacey Yukari. "Japanese American Women and the Women's Army Corp, 1935–1950." Master's thesis, University of California, Los Angeles, 1993.

    Pioneering study of Nisei women who served in the WAC (Women's Army Corp) during World War II.

30. Hohri, William. *Repairing America: An Account of the Movement for Japanese American Redress*. Pullman: Washington State University Press, 1988.

    Hohri was the key figure in the National Council for Japanese American Redress, one of three major groups in the Japanese American community fighting for redress.

31. Houston, Jeanne Wakatsuki, and James D. Houston. *Farewell to Manzanar*. Boston: Houghton Mifflin Co., 1973.

    Autobiographical account of life at Manzanar through the eyes of a child.

32. Hunter, Louise Harris. *Buddhism in Hawaii, Its Impact on a Yankee Community*. Honolulu: University of Hawaii Press, 1971.

    Pioneering study of Japanese American Buddhism in Hawai`i; adapted from a master's thesis (University of Hawaii, 1966).

33. Ichihashi, Yamato. *Japanese in the United States: A Critical Study of the Problems of the Japanese Immigrants and their Children*. New York: Arno Press, 1969.

    General survey of the Japanese American community of the time. Originally published from Stanford University Press, in 1932.

34. Ichioka, Yuji. *The Issei: The World of the First Generation Japanese Immigrants, 1885–1924*. New York: The Free Press, 1988.

    History of Issei in the western United States. The first to

use Japanese language sources to examine events from the perspective of the Issei themselves. Incorporates many previously published articles by Ichioka.

35. Ichioka, Yuji, edited and with contribution by. *Views from Within: The Japanese American Evacuation and Resettlement Study*. Los Angeles: UCLA Asian American Studies Center, 1989.

    Papers from a conference reassessing the JERS (Japanese American Evacuation and Resettlement Study) project held in 1987. Includes articles by Yuji Ichioka, S. Frank Miyamoto, Lane Ryo Hirabayashi, James Hirabayashi, Peter T. Suzuki, Robert F. Spencer, Charles Kikuchi, Dana Y. Takagi, and James M. Sakoda.

36. Inada, Lawson F. *Before the War: Poems as They Happened*. New York: Morrow, 1971.

    Influential collection of poetry by the Fresno, California-born Sansei poet.

37. Irons, Peter. *Justice at War: The Story of the Japanese American Internment Cases*. New York: Oxford University Press, 1983.

    Account of the effort to reopen the cases, which challenged the curfew and exclusion of Japanese Americans in the 1980s by one of the principals.

38. Ito, Kazuo. *Issei: A History of Japanese Immigrants in North America*, translated by Shinichiro Nakamura, and Jean S. Gerard. Seattle: Executive Committee for the Publication of Issei: A History of Japanese Immigrants in North America, 1973.

    A volume with over one thousand pages based on oral history data obtained from Issei in the Pacific Northwest in the 1960s.

39. Iwata, Masakazu. *Planted in Good Soil: A History of the Issei in the United States Agriculture*. New York: P. Lang, 1990.

    Sprawling two-volume survey of farming in the Issei era.

40. James, Thomas. *Exile Within: The Schooling of Japanese Americans, 1942–1945*. Cambridge: Harvard University Press, 1987.

    Study of various aspects of education in the World War II concentration camps, as well as the resettlement of Nisei college students outside of camp. Adapted from a doctoral dissertation (Stanford University, 1984).

41. Kadohata, Cynthia. *The Floating World*. New York: Viking, 1989.

    Coming of age novel set in the resettlement period centering on an adolescent girl whose father is a chick sexer.

42. Kanazawa, Toru J. *Sushi and Sourdough: A Novel*. Seattle: University of Washington Press, 1989.

    Novel about Issei prospectors in Alaska.

43. Kent, Noel J. *Hawaii, Islands under the Influence*. New York: Monthly Review Press, 1983.

    Historical study of Hawai`i focusing on the dominance of the Islands' economy by a succession of industries–sandalwood, whaling, sugar and tourism-operated for the benefit of forces external to Hawai`i. Adapted from a doctoral dissertation (University of Hawai`i, 1979).

44. Kikuchi, Charles. *The Kikuchi Diary: Chronicle from an American Concentration Camp*, edited and introduction by John Modell. Urbana: University of Illinois Press, 1973. Illini Books ed., 1993

    Diary of life at Tanforan Assembly Center kept while Kikuchi was a participant in the Japanese American Evacuation and Resettlement Study.

45. Kikumura, Akemi. *Through Harsh Winters: The Life of a Japanese Immigrant Woman*. Novato, Calif.: Chandler and Sharp Publishers, 1981.

    Widely cited life history of an Issei woman in Central California. Adapted from a doctoral dissertation (University of California, Los Angeles, 1979).

46. Kimura, Yukiko. *Issei: Japanese Immigrants in Hawaii*. Honolulu: University of Hawaii Press, 1988.

    Social history of the Issei in Hawai`i which incorporates many previous works on the subject by the author.

47. Kitano, Harry H. L. *Japanese Americans: The Evolution of a Subculture*. 1969. 2nd edition. Englewood Cliffs, N.J.: Prentice-Hall, Inc., 1976.

    Influential work mixes sociological methods with first person insights in recounting the development of the Japanese American community. Though it has a different title, *Generations and Identity: The Japanese American* (Needham Heights, Mass.: Ginn Press, 1993) is largely an updated version of the same book.

48. Kitayama, Glen Ikuo. "Japanese Americans and the Movement for Redress: A Case Study of Grassroots Activism in the Los Angeles Chapter of the National Coalition for Redress/Reparations." Master's thesis, University of California, Los Angeles, 1993.

    Study of NCRR (National Coalition for Redress/Reparations), one of the three major groups fighting for redress, by a key member.

49. Kiyama, Henry Y. *The Four Immigrants Manga: A Japanese Experience in San Francisco, 1904–1924*, trans., introd., and notes by Frederik L. Schodt. Berkeley: Stone Bridge Press, 1999.

    Collection of an Issei era comic strip that touches on many of the issues faced by the early immigrants.

50. Kotani, Roland. *The Japanese in Hawaii: A Century of Struggle*. Honolulu: Hochi, Ltd., 1985.

    Popular history of Japanese Americans in Hawai`i commemorating the one hundredth anniversary of large scale Japanese migration to Hawai`i.

51. Lind, Andrew W. *Hawaii's Japanese: An Experiment in Democracy*. Princeton: Princeton University Press, 1946.

    Study of the Japanese American community in Hawai`i during and just after World War II. Anticipates the "success story" literature to come. Reprinted in 1978 with Katharine Coman's *The History of Contract Labor in the Hawaiian Islands* (New York: Arno Press).

52. Lukes, Timothy J., and Gary Y. Okihiro. *Japanese Legacy: Farming and Community Life in California's Santa Clara Valley*. Cupertino, Calif.: California History Center, 1985.

Community history of Japanese Americans in the Santa Clara Valley in California.

53. Mackey, Michael R., edited and with contribution by. *Remembering Heart Mountain: Essays on Japanese American Internment in Wyoming*. Powell, Wyoming: Western History Publications, 1998.

    Papers from (and inspired by) a 1995 symposium on Heart Mountain.

54. Maki, Mitchell T., Harry H. L. Kitano, and S. Megan Berthold. *Achieving the Impossible Dream: How Japanese Americans Obtained Redress*, forewords by Robert T. Matsui and Roger Daniels. Urbana: University of Illinois Press, 1999.

    Overarching study of the redress movement.

55. Masumoto, David Mas. *Country Voices: The Oral History of a Japanese American Family Farm Community*. Del Rey, Calif.: Inaka Countryside Publications, 1987.

    The community is Del Rey, California.

56. Matsumoto, Valerie. *Farming the Home Place: A Japanese American Community in California: 1919–1982*. Ithaca, N.Y.: Cornell University Press, 1993.

    The community is Cortez, in Central California. Adapted from the doctoral dissertation (Stanford University, 1985).

57. McWilliams, Carey. *Prejudice: Japanese-Americans: Symbol of Racial Intolerance*. Boston: Little, Brown & Co., 1944.

    One of the first books on the internment which influenced much of what was to follow.

58. Mirikitani, Janice, and others, eds. *Ayumi: A Japanese American Anthology*. San Francisco: Japanese American Anthology Committee, 1980.

    Anthology of literature by Japanese Americans including sections on Issei, Nisei, Sansei/Yonsei, and Art. The pieces in the Issei section are presented in both Japanese and English.

59. Miyamoto, S. Frank. *Social Solidarity among the Japanese in Seattle*. Seattle: University of Washington Press, 1984.

    Early and influential study of the Japanese American community in Seattle. Based on a Master's thesis (University of Washington, 1938). Also published in *University of Washington Publications in the Social Sciences* 11.2 (Dec. 1939): 57–130, and by the Asian American Studies Program, University of Washington, Seattle, in 1981.

60. Modell, John. *The Economics and Politics of Racial Accommodation: The Japanese of Los Angeles 1900–1942*. Chicago: University of Illinois Press, 1977.

    Economic study of the pre-World War II Japanese American community in the Los Angeles area. Adapted from a doctoral dissertation (Columbia University, 1969).

61. Mori, Toshio. *Yokohama, California*. Seattle: University of Washington Press, 1985.

    Collection of short stories set in a fictional Northern California town. Also published with introduction by William Saroyan from Caxton Printers, Ltd., Caldwell, Idaho, in 1949.

62. Moriyama, Alan Takeo. *Imingaisha: Japanese Emigration Companies and Hawaii, 1894–1908*. Honolulu: University of Hawaii Press, 1985.

    A study of Japanese American emigration companies and their role in inducing Japanese emigration to Hawai`i. Adapted from a doctoral dissertation (University of California, Los Angeles, 1982).

63. Mura, David. *Turning Japanese: Memoirs of a Sansei*. New York: Atlantic Monthly Press, 1991.

    Memoirs of a Sansei visiting Japan.

64. Murayama, Milton. *All I Asking for Is My Body*. 1959. Honolulu: University of Hawaii Press, 1988.

    Novel set in the plantation camps of prewar Hawai`i. Also published by Supa Press, San Francisco, in 1975. Afterword by Franklin Odo.

65. Naka, Harry Maxwell. "The Naturalization of Japanese War Veterans of the World War Forces." Master's thesis, University of California, Berkeley, 1939.

    Examines the rocky road to citizenship of Issei World War I veterans.

66. Nakano, Mei. *Japanese American Women: Three Generations, 1890–1990*. Berkeley and Sebastopol, Calif.: National Japanese American Historical Society and Mina Press, 1990.

    Overarching popular study of Japanese American women.

67. Nelson, Douglas W. *Heart Mountain: The History of an American Concentration Camp*. Madison, Wis.: The State Historical Society of Wisconsin, 1976.

    Study of the American concentration camp at Heart Mountain, Wyoming. Adapted from a Master's thesis (University of Wyoming, 1970).

68. Niiya, Brian, ed. *More than a Game: Sport in the Japanese American Community*. Los Angeles: Japanese American National Museum, 2000.

    Companion book to an exhibition of the same name. Includes essays by various authors on different aspects of Japanese American sport and many photographs.

69. Nishimoto, Richard. *Inside an American Concentration Camp: Japanese American Resistance at Poston, Arizona*, edited by Lane Ryo Hirabayashi. Tucson: University of Arizona Press, 1995.

    Compiled out of wartime writings by Nishimoto, researcher for the Japanese Evacuation and Resettlement Study and internee leader at Poston.

70. Odo, Franklin S., and Kazuko Sinoto. *A Pictorial History of Japanese in Hawaii, 1885–1924*. Honolulu: Bishop Museum Press, 1985.

    Published on the one hundredth anniversary of the beginning of large scale Japanese migration to Hawai`i, this book augments pictures from the Bishop Museum collection with text and charts by the authors.

71. Ogawa, Dennis M. *Kodomo no Tame ni, For the Sake of the Children: The Japanese American Experience in Hawaii*. Honolulu: University Press of Hawaii, 1978.

    A rich collection of essays on the many aspects of the Japanese American experience in Hawai`i.

72. Okada, John. *No-No Boy.* Seattle: University of Washington Press, 1979.

    Intro. Lawson Fusao Inada. Novel centering on issues of Nisei identity and "loyalty" in postwar Seattle. Also published by Charles E. Tuttle, Rutland, Ver., in 1957 and by Combined Asian American Resources Project, Inc, San Francisco in 1976. Afterword by Frank Chin.

73. Okamura, Raymond Y. "The American Concentration Camps: A Cover-Up through Euphemistic Terminology." *Journal of Ethnic Studies* 10, no. 3 (Fall 1982): 95–108.

    Influential article arguing that contemporary readers should reject the euphemistic terminology the U.S. government introduced in referring to the "relocation center" experience.

74. Okihiro, Gary Y. *Cane Fires: The Anti-Japanese Movement in Hawaii, 1865–1945.* Philadelphia: Temple University Press, 1991.

    History of Japanese Americans in Hawai`i which makes the case that there was an organized anti-Japanese movement in Hawai`i as on the mainland.

75. Okihiro, Gary Y. *Storied Lives: Japanese American Students and World War II*, with a contribution by Leslie A. Ito. Photographs by Joan Myers. Seattle: University of Washington Press, 1999.

    On Japanese Americans who left the World War II concentration camps to go to college.

76. Okihiro, Gary Y. *Whispered Silences: Japanese Americans and World War II.* Seattle: University of Washington Press, 1996.

    Volume of Myers' contemporary photos of the former WRA (War Relocation Authority) camp sites accompanied by Okihiro's historical/autobiographical overview of Japanese American history.

77. Okinawa Club of America, comp. *History of the Okinawans in North America,* translated by Ben Kobashigawa. Los Angeles: UCLA Asian American Studies Center and The Okinawa Club of America, 1988.

    Anthology of works on Okinawans on the mainland.

78. Okubo, Mine. *Citizen 13660.* Seattle: University of Washington Press, 1983.

    Book of line drawings and text based on the author's experiences at Tanforan Assembly Center and Topaz. Originally published by Columbia University Press, New York, in 1946. Also published by Arno Press, New York, in 1978.

79. Ota, Shelley Ayame Nishimura. *Upon Their Shoulders.* New York: Exposition Press, 1951.

    Epic novel of a Japanese American family in Hawai`i.

80. Sakamoto, Edward. *Hawai`i no ka oi: The Kamiya Family Trilogy.* Anthology of plays (Foreword by Franklin S. Odo). Honolulu: University of Hawai`i Press, 1995.

81. Sawada, Mitziko. *Tokyo Life, New York Dreams: Urban Japanese Visions of America, 1890–1924.* Berkeley: University of California Press, 1996.

    Includes a chapter on Issei who traveled to New York. Adapted from a doctoral dissertation (New York University, 1985).

82. Shibutani, Tamotsu. *The Derelicts of Company K: A Sociological Study of Demoralization.* Berkeley: University of California Press, 1978.

    Uses a demoralization framework in a study of an underachieving Nisei company during World War II.

83. Shirota, Jon H. *Lucky Come Hawai`i.* Honolulu: Bess Press, 1988.

    Novel set in World War II era Hawai`i focusing on an Okinawan family in Maui. Originally published by Bantam Books, New York, in 1965.

84. Smith, William Carlson. *Americans in Process: A Study of Our Citizens of Oriental Ancestry.* New York: Arno Press, 1970.

    Looks at second generation Asian Americans both in Hawai`i and on the mainland. Also published from Edwards Brothers, Ann Arbor, Mich. in 1937.

85. Sone, Monica. *Nisei Daughter.* Seattle: University of Washington Press, 1979.

    Autobiographical account of growing up Nisei begins in Seattle, continues to Minidoka, and ends with college. Also published by Little, Brown and Company, Boston, in 1953.

86. Spickard, Paul Russell. *Japanese Americans: The Formation and Transformations of an Ethnic Group.* New York: Twayne Publishers, 1996.

    Overview of the Japanese American experience.

87. Stephan, John. *Hawaii under the Rising Sun: Japan's Plans for Conquest after Pearl Harbor.* Honolulu: University of Hawaii Press, 1984.

    Includes accounts of how Japanese Americans played a role both in drafting such plans and in the implementation of them.

88. Suzuki, Masao. "Japanese American Economic Achievement, 1900–1942." Ph.D. diss., Stanford University, 1994.

    Economist's study of Japanese American achievement prior to World War II.

89. Takahashi, Jerrold Haruo. *Nisei/Sansei: Shifting Japanese American Identities and Politics.* Philadelphia: Temple University Press, 1997.

    Examines Japanese American political styles from the 1930s to the present. Adapted from a doctoral dissertation (University of California, Berkeley, 1980).

90. Takaki, Ronald. *Pau Hana: Plantation Life and Labor in Hawaii, 1835–1920.* Honolulu: University of Hawaii Press, 1983.

    History of the multiracial sugar plantation labor workforce in Hawai`i of which Japanese Americans were a major part.

91. Takaki, Ronald. *Strangers from a Different Shore: A History of Asian Americans.* Boston: Little, Brown and Company, 1989. Updated and rev. ed., 1998.

    The most widely read general history of Asian Americans.

92. Takezawa, Yasuko Iwai. *Breaking the Silence: Redress and Japanese American Ethnicity.* Ithaca, N.Y.: Cornell University Press, 1995.

    Examines the redress movement as a catalyst for a revival in Japanese American ethnic identity. Largely based on oral histories conducted in the Seattle area. Adopted from a doctoral dissertation (University of Washington, 1989).

93. Tamura, Eileen Hisayo. *Americanization, Acculturation, and Ethnic Identity: The Nisei Generation in Hawaii.* Urbana: University of Illinois Press, 1994.

    On the various kinds of Nisei education in prewar Hawai`i. Adapted from a doctoral dissertation (University of Hawai`i, 1990).

94. Tateishi, John. *And Justice for All: An Oral History of the Japanese American Detention Camps.* New York: Random House, 1984.

    Volume of edited oral history transcripts with thirty former concentration camp internees.

95. Taylor, Sandra C. *Jewel of the Desert: Japanese American Internment at Topaz.* Berkeley: University of California Press, 1993.

    Study of the Topaz, Utah concentration camp.

96. Ten Broek, Jacobus, Edward N. Barnhart, and Floyd Matson. *Prejudice, War, and the Constitution.* Berkeley: University of California Press, 1954.

    Looks at how the evacuation and internment came about. The third published volume of the Japanese American Evacuation and Resettlement Study.

97. Thomas, Dorothy S. *The Salvage.* Berkeley: University of California Press, 1952.

    Looks at those who resettled in the East and Midwest; includes fifteen life histories. The second published volume of the Japanese American Evacuation and Resettlement Study.

98. Thomas, Dorothy S., and Richard Nishimoto. *The Spoilage.* Berkeley: University of California Press, 1946, 1969.

    Looks at the Japanese American community in camp with a special emphasis on the "disloyal" at Tule Lake. The first published volume of the Japanese American Evacuation and Resettlement Study.

99. Tomita, Mary Kimoto. *Dear Miye: Letters Home from Japan, 1939–1946,* edited by Robert G. Lee. Stanford: Stanford University Press, 1995.

    Letters written by a Nisei women caught in Japan during the war to friends in the United States.

100. Tsuchida, John Nobuya, ed. *Reflections: Memories of Japanese American Women in Minnesota.* Covina, Calif.: Pacific Asia Press, 1994.

    First person accounts by Japanese American women—both Nisei resettlers and postwar immigrants—in Minnesota.

101. Uchida, Yoshiko. *Picture Bride.* Seattle: University of Washington Press, 1997.

    Novel centering on an Issei picture bride. The original was published by Northland Press, Flagstaff, Ariz, in 1987.

102. Uyeda, Clifford I., and Barry Saiki, eds. *The Pacific War and Peace: Americans of Japanese Ancestry in Military Intelligence Service 1941 to 1952.* San Francisco, Calif.: Military Intelligence Service Association of Northern California and the National Japanese American Historical Society, 1991.

    Includes many photographs.

103. Uyematsu, Amy. *30 Miles from J-Town.* Brownsville, Ore.: Story Line Press, 1992.

    Collection of poetry.

104. Walls, Thomas K. *The Japanese Texans.* San Antonio: Institute of Texan Cultures, 1987.

    Study of Japanese Americans in Texas. Also includes a chapter on the three enemy alien internment camps in Texas during World War II.

105. Waugh, Isami Arifuku. "Hidden Crime and Deviance in the Japanese-American Community, 1920–1946." Ph.D. diss., University of California, Berkeley, 1978.

    Pioneering study of Japanese American crime in Los Angeles ranging from Issei gambling syndicates to Nisei youth gangs.

106. Weglyn, Michi. *Years of Infamy: The Untold Story of America's Concentration Camps.* New York: William Morrow & Co., 1976. Updated ed. Seattle: University of Washington Press, 1996.

    Influential study of Japanese Americans and the World War II concentration camps. The first to be written from the perspective of a former inmate.

107. Yagasaki, Noritaka. "Ethnic Cooperativism and Immigrant Agriculture: A Study of Japanese Floriculture and Truck Farming in California." Ph.D. diss., University of California, Berkeley, 1982.

    Sprawling study of pre-World War II floriculture and truck farming in both San Francisco and Los Angeles; also includes a chapter on Japanese American immigrant banking.

108. Yamamoto [DeSoto], Hisaye. *Seventeen Syllables and Other Stories.* Latham, New York: Kitchen Table Women of Color Press, 1988.

    Collection of short stories.

109. Yamanaka, Lois Ann. *Wild Meat and Bully Burgers.* New York: Farrar, Straus and Giroux, 1996.

    Coming-of-age novel centering on a young woman growing up in 1970s Hilo.

110. Yamauchi, Wakako. *Songs My Mother Taught Me: Stories, Plays, and Memoir.* New York: Feminist Press at the City University of New York, 1994.

    Anthology of works by the Los Angeles based Nisei artist, writer and playwright.

111. Yanagisako, Sylvia Junko. *Transforming the Past: Tradition and Kinship among Japanese Americans.* Stanford: Stanford University Press, 1985.

    Study of Japanese American kinship emphasizing the process of culture change; focuses on marriage, filial relations, and sibling relations. Adapted from a doctoral dissertation (University of Washington, 1975).

112. Yoneda, Karl G. *Ganbatte: Sixty-Year Struggle of a Kibei Worker.* Los Angeles: Asian American Studies Center, University of California, Los Angeles, 1983.

    Autobiography of a Kibei labor organizer and Communist.

113. Yoo, David. *Growing Up Nisei: Race, Generation, and Culture among Japanese Americans of California, 1924–1949*, foreword by Roger Daniels. Urbana: University of Illinois Press, 2000.

    Study of the Nisei generation through the World War II concentration camps. Adapted from a doctoral dissertation (Yale University, 1994).

114. Yoshida, George. *Reminiscing in Swingtime: Japanese Americans in American Popular Music: 1925–1960*. San Francisco: National Japanese American Historical Society, 1997.

    Encyclopedic history of the Japanese American jazz scene.

115. Zalburg, Sanford. *A Spark is Struck!: Jack Hall and the ILWU in Hawaii*. Honolulu: University Press of Hawaii, 1979.

    Biographical study of International Longshoremen's and Warehousemen's Union leader Jack Hall.

JAPANESE

1. Asano, Takayuki [浅野孝之]. *Ohai no kage* [オハイの蔭]. Honoruru-shi [ホノルル市]: Jitsugyō no Hawaisha [実業之布哇社], 1925.

    A collection of essays by a Japanese school teacher on educational matters.

2. Beikoku Seihokubu Renraku Nihonjinkai [米國西北部聯絡日本人會], ed. *Beikoku seihokubu zairyū Nihonjin hatten ryakushi* [米國西北部在留日本人發展略史]. Shiatoru [シアトル]: Beikoku Seihokubu Renraku Nihonjinkai [米國西北部聯絡日本人會], 1921.

    A historical survey published by the United Northwestern Japanese Association in Seattle.

3. California Flower Market. *Kashū Nihonjin kaengyō hattenshi* [加州日本人花園業発展史]. Sōko [桑港]: Kashū Kaki Shijō Kabushiki-gaisha [加州花卉市場株式会社], 1929.

    Published by the California Flower Market, Inc., of San Francisco.

4. Fujii, Sei [藤井整]. *Beikoku ni sumu Nihonjin no sakebi: zaibei yonjūnenkan no kenbun* [米国に住む日本人の叫び: 在米四十年間の見聞]. Los Angeles: Kashū Mainichi Shinbunsha [加州毎日新聞社], 1940.

    A collection of newspaper editorials and columns published by the *Kashū Mainichi* of Los Angeles. Many articles deal with the patriotic activities of Japanese immigrants after the outbreak of the Sino-Japanese War in 1937.

5. Fujioka, Shirō [藤岡紫朗]. *Ayumi no ato: Hokubei tairiku Nihonjin kaitaku monogatari* [歩みの跡: 北米大陸日本人開拓物語]. Los Angeles: Ayumi no Ato Kankō Kōenkai [歩みの跡刊行後援会], 1957.

    A collection of Issei personalities and anecdotes about events and communities from the beginning of Japanese immigration to the post-World War II period. Organized by regions, which includes Mexico, Alaska, and Canada. Based on information collected from Issei throughout the United States.

6. Fujioka, Shirō [藤岡紫朗], ed. *Beikoku Chūō Nihonjinkai shi* [米国中央日本人会史]. Rosu Anzerusu [ロスアンゼルス]: Beikoku Chūō Nihonjinkai [米国中央日本人会], 1940.

    A chronological history of the leading community organization in Southern California.

7. Fujioka, Shirō [藤岡紫朗]. *Minzoku hatten no senkusha* [民族發展の先驅者]. Tōkyō [東京]: Dōbunsha [同文社], 1927.

    This work traces the historical development of anti-Japanese exclusion movement in California and the Issei's struggle against it. Includes also a section on the Nisei problems.

8. Fukunaga, Torajirō, and Haruie Miwa [福永虎治郎 and 三輪治家]. *Hawai guntōshi. Kauai hen* [布哇群島誌. 加哇篇]. Hawai-ken Kauai-shi [布哇県加哇市]: Kawai Shinpōsha [加哇新報社], 1916.

    A history and general description of Japanese in Kaua`i, with statistical data.

9. Furukawa, Eiji [古川栄次]. *Minami Kashū to Kagoshima kenjin* [南加州と鹿児島県人]. Tōkyō [東京]: Nihon Keisatsu Shinbunsha [日本警察新聞社], 1920.

    A brief overview of Japanese immigration from Kagoshima Prefecture to Southern California, with an extended Who's Who.

10. Furuya, Suikei [古屋翠渓]. *Haisho tenten* [配所転々]. Honoruru [ホノルル]: Hawai Taimususha [布哇タイムス社], 1964.

    Record of a Hawaiian Issei's experience as a detainee at Justice Department camps during the Pacific War.

11. Gotō, Chinpei [後藤鎮平]. *Hawai Hōjin yakyūshi: yakyū ippyakunen kinen* [布哇邦人野球史: 野球壱百年記念]. Honoruru [ホノルル]: Hawai Hōjin Yakyūshi Shuppankai [布哇邦人野球史出版會], 1940.

    A history of Japanese baseball in Hawai`i, published in commemoration of the one hundredth anniversary of the sport.

12. Hawai Hōchisha Henshūkyoku [布哇報知社編輯局], ed. *Nihongo gakkō shōso jisshūnen kinenshi, 1927–1937* [日本語学校勝訴十周年記念誌, 1927-1937]. Honolulu: Hawaii Hōchisha [布哇報知社], 1937.

    A collection of documents pertaining to the victorious lawsuit against the territory of Hawai`i on the constitutionality of legal restrictions placed on Japanese language schools. It was published to commemorate the tenth anniversary of the legal victory.

13. Hawai Kyōikukai [布哇教育會], ed. *Hawai Nihongo kyōikushi* [布哇日本語教育史]. Honoruru [ホノルル]: Hawai Kyōikukai Shuppanbu [布哇教育會出版部], 1937.

    Includes a general history of Japanese language education, development of the Hawai Kyōikukai and its affiliated organizations, and the legal battle against discriminatory laws on Japanese language schools in the 1920s.

14. Hawai Nichinichi Shinbunsha [布哇日日新聞社]. *Hawai seikōsha jitsuden* [布哇成功者實傳]. Honoruru-fu [ホノルル府]: Hawai Nichinichi Shinbunsha [布哇日日新聞社], 1908.

Biographical accounts of Japanese immigrant entrepreneurs and professionals, who achieved success and prosperity. Covers the islands of O`ahu, Kaua`i, Mau`i, and Hawai`i.

15. Hawai Nihonjin Iminshi Kankō Iinkai [ハワイ日本人移民史刊行委員会史刊行委員会], ed. *Hawai Nihonjin iminshi* [ハワイ日本人移民史]. Honolulu: Hawai Nikkeijin Rengō Kyōkai [布哇日系人連合協会], 1964.
    History of Japanese immigrants in Hawai`i.

16. Hayashi, Saburō [林三郎]. *Hawai jitsugyō annai* [布哇実業案内]. Hawaitō Kona [ハワイ島コナ]: Kona Hankyōsha [コナ反響社], 1909.
    History and current conditions of Japanese economic activities in Hawai`i, with a special focus on those in the Kona district. Includes statistical data and information on Japanese organizations.

17. Hirohata, Tsunegorō [広畑恒五郎]. *Zaibei Fukuoka kenjin to jigyō* [在米福岡縣人と事業]. Los Angeles: Zaibei Fukuoka Kenjin to Jigyō Hensan Jimusho [在米福岡縣人と事業編纂事務所], 1936.
    A historical survey of Japanese immigrants from Fukuoka Prefecture, with sections on Nisei, kenjin-kai, and prominent individuals, like Kinji Ushijima, also known as "Potato King" George Shima. Includes an extended Who's Who and directory. A slightly shorter version was published in 1931 under the different title, *Zaibei Fukuoka Kenjinshi*.

18. Hirose, Shurei [広瀬守令]. *Zaibei Kōshūjin funtō gojūnenshi* [在米甲州人奮闘五十年史]. Los Angeles: Nanka Yamanashi Kaigai Kyōkai [南加山梨海外協會], 1934.
    An overview of the activities of Japanese immigrants from Yamanashi Prefecture, with an extended Who's Who.

19. Hokka Nihonjinkai [北加日本人会]. *Hokka Nihonjin hattenshi* [北加日本人発展史]. Chico, Calif.: Hokka Nihonjinkai Shuppanbu [北加日本人会出版部], 1922.
    A brief history of Japanese immigrants in the Chico area, published by the local Japanese Association.

20. Hokubei Jijisha Henshūkyoku [北米時事社編輯局]. *Hokubei nenkan* [北米年鑑]. Vol. 1–2. Shiatoru [シアトル]: Hokubei Jijisha [北米時事社], 1910–1911.
    The yearbooks include useful statistical data and directories, as well as histories of Japanese in the Pacific Northwest.

21. Imamura, Emyō [今村恵猛]. *Honpa Honganji Hawai kaikyōshi* [本派本願寺布哇開教史]. Honolulu: Honpa Honganji Hawai Kaikyō Jimusho Bunshobu [本派本願寺布哇開教事務所文書部], 1918.
    History of the Hongwanji mission in Hawai`i.

22. Itō, Kazuo [伊藤一男]. *Hokubei hyakunen-zakura* [北米百年桜]. Shiatoru [シアトル]: Hokubei Hyakunen-zakura Jikkō Iinkai [北米百年桜実行委員会], 1969.
    A collection of personal accounts and interviews by Japanese immigrants in the Pacific Northwest. Organized topically. There is an English translation under the title, *Issei*.

23. Kaibara, Sakae [開原栄]. *Kashū Hiroshima kenjin hattenshi* [加州広島県人発展史]. Sacramento: Yorozu Shoten [萬書店], 1916.
    Includes a Who's Who and statistical data.

24. Kanai, Shigeo, and Banshō Itō [金井重雄 and 伊藤晩松]. *Hokubei no Nihonjin* [北米之日本人]. Sōkō [桑港]: Kanai Tsūyaku Jimusho [金井通譯事務所], 1909.
    Descriptions of Japanese settlements in California with Who's Who of leading immigrants.

25. Kaneshiro, Takeo [金城武男], ed. *Okinawa imin no chichi, Toyama Kyūzō* [沖縄移民の父 當山久三]. Los Angeles: N.p., 1959.
    Biographical sketches of Kyūzō Toyama (1868–1910), who was considered by many to be responsible for massive emigration of Okinawan people to the overseas. Published in commemoration of the sixtieth anniversary of his death.

26. Kashiwamura, Ichisuke [柏村一介]. *Hokubei tōsa taikan* [北米踏査大観]. Tōkyō [東京]: Ryūbundō [竜文堂], 1911.
    An extensive survey of Japanese settlements in California with Who's Who.

27. Katō, Shin'ichi [加藤新一]. *Beikoku Nikkeijin Hyakunenshi: zaibei Nikkeijin hatten jinshiroku* [米国日系人百年史: 在米日系人発展人史録]. San Francisco: Shin Nichi-Bei Shinbunsha [新日米新聞社], 1961.
    A general history of Japanese in America. Divided into various topical sections, it relies heavily on *Zaibei Nihonjin-shi* for the prewar information. Includes an extensive Who's Who.

28. Kazahaya, Katsuichi [風早勝一]. *Minami Kashū Okayama kenjin hattenshi* [南加州岡山県人発展史]. Rafu [羅府]: Minami Kashū Okayama Kenjin Hattenshi Hensanjo [南加州岡山県人発展史編纂所], 1955.
    Focuses on the histories of the Okayama Prefectural Association and the Okayama Woman's Association in Southern California. Includes an extended Who's Who.

29. Kihara, Ryūkichi [木原隆吉]. *Hawai Nihonjin shi* [布哇日本人史]. Tōkyō [東京]: Bunseisha [文成社], 1935.
    History of Japanese in Hawai`i.

30. Kiyama, Yoshitaka [木山義喬]. *Manga yonin shosei* [漫画四人書生]. Oakland: Inhaku Doshikai, 1931.
    Satirical cartoons depicting the lives of four Japanese student-laborers in Northern California through the 1910s.

31. Kobayashi, Masasuke [小林政助]. *Nihon minzoku no sekaiteki bōchō: Kobayashi Masasuke ronbunshū* [日本民族の世界的膨張: 小林政助論文集]. Tōkyō [東京]: Keigansha [警眼社], 1933.
    A collection of essays and commentaries, which includes the author's past activities as a Major of the Japanese Salvation Army in California. Reflective of his strong nationalism, many articles deal with expansionist ideas and themes.

32. Makino Kinzaburō Den Hensan Iinkai [牧野金三郎伝編纂委員会委員会], ed. *Makino Kinzaburō den*

[牧野金三郎伝]. Honoruru [ホノルル]: Makino Michie [牧野道枝], 1965.

Makino Kinzaburō was the publisher of the *Hawaii Hochi* who lived a colorful life as a community leader in Honolulu.

33. Maruyama, Michiharu [丸山千曲]. *Agun dōhō taisei ichiran* [亜郡同胞大勢一覧]. Ōfu [王府]: Shin Sekai Shinbun [新世界新聞], 1908.

Description of Japanese communities in Alameda County, primarily in Oakland, Berkeley, and Alameda. Includes short biographical sketches of successful individuals and an address directory.

34. Merisubiru Chihō Nihonjinkai [メリスビル地方日本人会]. *Hokka yongun Nihonjin hattenshi* [北加四郡日本人発展史]. Marysville, Calif.: Merisubiru Chihō Nihonjinkai [メリスビル地方日本人会], 1932.

Description of Japanese in the counties of Yuba, Sutter, Butte, and Colusa in Northern California.

35. Mie Kenjin Hokubei Hattenshi Hensan Iinkai [三重県人北米発展史編纂委員会]. *Mie kenjin Hokubei hattenshi* [三重県人北米発展史]. Tsu [津]: Mie-ken Kaigai Kyōkai [三重県海外協会], 1966.

A brief overview of Japanese emigration from Mie Prefecture to North America. Includes descriptions of the Mie Prefectural Association of Southern California and an extended Who's Who.

36. Mizutani, Bangaku [水谷万嶽]. *Hokubei Aichi kenjinshi* [北米愛知県人史]. Sacramento: Aichi Kenjinkai [愛知県人会], 1920.

A detailed history of Japanese immigration from Aichi Prefecture to North America, especially the Sacramento Delta Region. Stresses their agricultural activities with statistics. Includes an extended Who's Who.

37. Momii, Ikken [籾井一剣]. *Hokubei kendō taikan* [北米剣道大観]. San Francisco: Hokubei Butokukai [北米武徳会], 1939.

A historical description of the Hokubei Butokukai, a leading kendo organization that quickly grew throughout the Pacific Coast states. Includes short biographical sketches of Issei leaders and Nisei kendoists.

38. Morita, Sakae [森田栄]. *Hawai gojūnenshi* [布哇五十年史]. Hawaii: Morita Sakae [森田栄], 1919.

This is an expanded version of the author's 1915 work.

39. Morita, Sakae [森田栄]. *Hawai Nihonjin hattenshi* [布哇日本人発展史]. Hawai-ken Oafutō Waipafu [布哇県オアフ島ワイパフ]: Shin'eikan [真栄館], 1915.

The earliest general work of Japanese immigrants in Hawai'i written by a local immigrant writer.

40. Murai, Kō [村井蛟], ed. *Zaibei Nihonjin sangyō sōran* [在米日本人産業総覧]. Rafu [羅府]: Beikoku Sangyō Nippōsha [米国産業日報社], 1940.

A comprehensive survey of Japanese agricultural activities organized by the kinds of crops. Includes an extended Who's Who that covers the Western states.

41. Murano, Takaaki [村野孝顕]. *Bukkyō kaigai dendōshi* [仏教海外伝道史]. Rafu [羅府]: Hokubeizan Zenshūji [北米山禅宗寺], 1933.

This book treats a history of Sōtō Zen mission outside Japan, including Hawai'i and the mainland United States.

42. Murayama, Tamotsu [村山有]. *Hawai Nisei: kutsujoku kara eikō e* [ハワイ二世: 屈辱から栄光へ]. Tōkyō [東京]: Jiji Tsūshinsha [時事通信社], 1966.

Historical sketches of Japanese immigration to Hawai'i and the experiences of the Nisei. Includes biographical essays on prominent Nisei, both in Hawai'i and Japan, before and after the Pacific War.

43. Nagai, Eiko [永井ゑい子]. *Nagai Eiko shibun* [永井ゑい子詩文], edited by Hajime Nagai [永井元]. San Furanshisuko [サンフランシスコ]: Nagai Hajime [永井元], 1929.

An anthology of an Issei Christian woman's writings. A leading figure in the Bay area's Japanese women, the author wrote for local immigrant newspapers and Christian publications. Compiled posthumously by the husband.

44. Nakajima, Yō [中島陽]. *Kona Nihonjin jitsujō annai* [コナ日本人実状案内]. Hawai Kona [布哇コナ]: Nakajima, Yō [中島陽], 1934.

A survey of Japanese residents in Kona, Hawai'i. Focuses on their individual and organizational activities, as well as coffee farming. Also includes brief Who's Who.

45. Nakamura, Masatoshi, and Katsuma Mukaeda [中村正敏 and 迎田勝馬]. *Zaibei no Higojin* [在米の肥後人]. Rosu Anzerusu [ロスアンゼルス]: Nanka Kumamoto Kaigai Kyōkai [南加熊本海外協會], 1931.

An overview of Japanese immigration from Kumamoto Prefecture to California. Includes an extended Who's Who.

46. Nanka Fukui Kenjinkai [南加福井県人会]. *Nanka Fukui kenjin gojūnenshi* [南加福井県人五十年史]. Los Angeles: Nanka Fukui Kenjinkai [南加福井県人会], 1953.

Stresses the activities of the Fukui Prefectural Association of Southern California.

47. Nanka Hanashijō [南加花市場]. *Nanka Hanashijō hattenshi* [南加花市場發展史]. Rafu [羅府]: Nanka Hanashijō [南加花市場], 1952.

A history of the Southern California Flower Market from 1912 to the early 1950s.

48. Nanka Nihonjin Kirisutokyō Kyōkai Renmei [南加日本人基督教教会連盟]. *Zaibei Nihonjin Kirisutokyō gojūnenshi* [在米日本人基督教五十年史]. Rosu Anzerusu [ロスアンゼルス]: Nanka Nihonjin Kirisutokyō Kyōkai Renmei [南加日本人基督教教会連盟], 1932.

Includes Hawai'i.

49. Nanka Nikkeijin Shōgyō Kaigisho [南加日系人商業會議所]. *Minami Kashū Nihonjin shichijūnenshi: Nichi-Bei shūkō hyakunensai kinen* [南加州日本人七十年史: 日米修好百年祭記念]. Rosu Anzerusu [ロスアンゼルス]: Nanka Nikkeijin Shōgyō Kaigisho [南加日系人商業會議所], 1960.

A comprehensive history of Japanese in Southern California from 1890 to 1959.

50. Nanka Nikkeijin Shōgyō Kaigisho [南加日系人商業會議

所]. *Minami Kashū Nihonjinshi* [南加州日本人史]. Los Angeles: Nanka Nikkeijin Shōgyō Kaigisho [南加日系人商業會議所], 1956.

A chronological history of Japanese in Southern California spanning from 1885 to 1918. The original manuscript was compiled in 1939, but never published due to the Pacific War.

51. Negoro, Motoyuki [根来源之]. *Meiji yonjūichi, ninen Hawai hōjin katsuyakushi* [明治四十一二年布哇邦人活躍史]. Honolulu: n.p., 1915.

    A detailed history of the 1909 Japanese strike on O`ahu, in which the author played a leading role. Written from the vantage point of a strike leader to justify why Japanese laborers had to stand up against sugar plantation owners. Includes the list of the people who donated money to the strike fund.

52. Nichi-Bei Shinbunsha [日米新聞社]. *Nichi-Bei nenkan* [日米年鑑]. Vol. 1–12. Sōkō [桑港]: Nichi-Bei Shinbunsha [日米新聞社], 1905–1918.

    A series of the Yearbooks compiled by the *Nichibei Shimbun*, which carry useful statistical data and directories divided by communities.

53. Nichi-Bei Shinbunsha [日米新聞社]. *Nichi-Bei taikan* [日米大観]. Sōkō [桑港]: Nichi-Bei Shinbunsha [日米新聞社], 1930.

    The first general history of Japanese in America, much of which was later incorporated into *Zaibei Nihonjinshi* published by the Japanese Association of America in 1940.

54. Nichi-Bei Shinbunsha [日米新聞社]. *Zaibei Nihonjin jinmei jiten* [在米日本人人名辞典]. Sōkō [桑港]: Nichi-Bei Shinbunsha [日米新聞社], 1922.

    Includes an historical overview of Japanese immigrant lives in America and a Who's Who in Canada and Mexico.

55. Nyūyōku Nihonjinkai, and Shōzō Mizutani [紐育日本人会 and 水谷渉三], eds. *Nyūyōku Nihonjin hattenshi* [紐育日本人発展史]. Nyūyōku [紐育]: Nyūyōku Nihonjinkai [紐育日本人会], 1921.

    Focuses mainly on the development of the U.S.-Japan trade and the activities of Japanese immigrant businessmen in the city. Includes biographies of leading individuals.

56. Ochi, Dōjun [越智道順], ed. *Minami Kashū Nihonjinshi, Kōhen* [南加州日本人史. 後篇]. Los Angeles: Nanka Nikkeijin Shōgyō Kaigisho [南加日系人商業会議所], 1957.

    A comprehensive history of Japanese in Southern California, which covers the period from 1919 to 1955. An extensive description of Japanese experiences during the war, including the internees in the Justice Department detention camps.

57. Ōhashi, Kanzō [大橋貫造]. *Hokubei Kashū Sutakuton dōhōshi* [北米加州スタクトン同胞史]. Stockton, Calif.: Su-shi Nihonjinkai [須市日本人會], 1937.

    Focuses mainly on community organizations, especially the Japanese Association of Stockton.

58. Oka, Naoki [岡直樹]. *Hokubei no Kōchi kenjin* [北米の高知県人]. San Francisco: Oka Naoki [岡直樹], 1921.

    A history of Japanese from Kōchi Prefecture with a Who's Who.

59. Okumura, Takie [奥村多喜衞]. *Hawai dendō sanjūnen ryakushi* [布哇伝道三十年略史]. Honolulu: n.p., 1917.

    Brief history of thirty-year Christian mission work in Hawai`i.

60. Okumura, Takie [奥村多喜衞]. *Onchō shichijūnen* [恩寵七十年]. Honolulu: Okumura Takie [奥村多喜衞], 1935.

    A collections of essays by an Issei Christian leader on his life in Hawai`i as a minister, teacher, and community leader.

61. Okumura, Takie [奥村多喜衞]. *Taiheiyō no rakuen* [太平洋の楽園]. Honolulu: n.p., 1930.

    A collections of essays on the general conditions and history of Hawai`i, the author's personal experiences, and second-generation issues.

62. Rakki Jihōsha [絡機時報社]. *Sanchūbu to Nihonjin* [山中部と日本人]. N.p. Rakki Jihōsha [絡機時報社], 1925.

    A history of Japanese in Utah, Idaho, Wyoming, and Nevada. Includes an extensive Who's Who.

63. Saka, Hisagorō [坂久五郎]. *Santa Maria heigen Nihonjin shi* [サンタマリア平原日本人史]. Gadarūpu [ガダループ]: Gadarūpu Nihon Kyōkai [ガダループ日本協會], 1936.

    Includes a history of the Japanese Association of Guadalupe and an extended Who's Who.

64. Sasaki, Sasabune [佐々木ささぶね]. *Yokuryūjo seikatsuki* [抑留所生活記]. Los Angeles, Calif.: Rafu Shoten [羅府書店], 1950.

    An experience of a Japanese immigrant writer in enemy alien detention centers and finally at Amache.

65. Satō, Yasuji [佐藤安治]. *Kashū to Fukushima kenjin. Nanka hen* [加州と福島縣人. 南加篇]. Kashū Rafu [加州羅府]: Kashū Fukushima Kenjin Hattenshi Hensanjo [加州福島縣人発展史編纂所], 1929.

    Includes the history of the Fukushima Prefectural Association of Southern California and an extended Who's Who.

66. Shishimoto, Hachirō [四至本八郎]. *Nikkei shimin o kataru: Amerika umare no Nihonjin* [日系市民を語る: アメリカ生まれの日本人]. Tōkyō [東京]: Shōkasha [章華社], 1934.

    This books deals with the general problems and characteristics of the second-generation Japanese Americans. A former Issei journalist, the author defines the Nisei as a bridge of understanding between Japan and the United States and gives a hopeful picture of their future. Includes biographical sketches of prominent Nisei individuals in various fields.

67. Sōga, Yasutarō [相賀安太郎]. *Gojūnenkan no Hawai kaiko* [五十年間のハワイ回顧]. Honolulu: "Gojūnenkan no Hawai Kaiko" Kankōkai [『五十年間のハワイ回顧』刊行會], 1953.

History of Japanese in Hawai`i, with which the author's personal experience is interwoven. Publisher of the *Nippu Jiji*, the author was one of the most prominent community leaders in the prewar Japanese community in Honolulu.

68. Sōga, Yasutarō [相賀安太郎]. *Tessaku seikatsu* [鉄柵生活]. Honolulu: Hawai Taimususha [布哇タイムス社], 1948.

    A memoir of wartime internment in Justice Department detention camps on the mainland. Publisher of the *Nippu Jiji*, the author was among the small number of Issei, who were taken away from Hawai`i to the mainland for incarceration during the Pacific War. Includes the list of Hawai`i internees.

69. Sogawa, Masao [曽川政男]. *Hawai Nihonjin meikan* [布哇日本人銘鑑]. Honoruru [ホノルル]: Hawai Nihonjin Meikan Kankōkai [布哇日本人銘鑑刊行会], 1927.

    A comprehensive directory of Japanese in Hawai`i, with a historical narrative of Japanese immigration to Hawai`i and their experience there.

70. Sōkō Bukkyōkai Bunshobu [桑港仏教会文書部], ed. *Sōkō Bukkyōkai kaikyō sanjūnen kinenshi* [桑港仏教会開教三十年記念誌]. Sōkō [桑港]: Kageyama Tetsujirō [陰山鐵二郎], 1930.

    A thirty-year history of the San Francisco Buddhist Church established in 1899. It was the first Buddhist institution in the mainland United States.

71. Suzuki, Hansaburō [鈴木半三郎]. *Nisei nenkan* [二世年鑑]. Honolulu, Hawaii: Nenkan Hensankai [年鑑編纂会], 1939.

    An extensive list of Nisei in Hawai`i, who were eligible for voting. Includes a Japanese-language section that gives a general account of Japanese experience and living conditions in the Islands.

72. Suzuki, Rokuhiko [鈴木六彦]. *Intāmaunten dōhō hattenshi* [インターマウンテン同胞発展史]. Denbā [デンバー]: Denbā Shinpōsha [デンバー新報社], 1910.

    Description of Japanese activities in the Rocky Mountain states, which include Colorado, Utah, Wyoming, Nebraska, and Kansas. Contains biographical sketches of successful individuals, especially labor-contractors.

73. Takeda, Jun'ichi [竹田順一]. *Zaibei Hiroshima kenjinshi* [在米広島県人史]. Rosu Anzerusu [ロスアンゼルス]: Zaibei Hiroshima Kenjinshi Hakkōjo [在米広島県人史発行所], 1929.

    An overview of Japanese from Hiroshima Prefecture in the Pacific Coast states. Includes statistical data and an extended Who's Who.

74. Takei, Nekketsu [武居熱血]. *Hawai ichiran* [布哇一覧]. Honoruru [ホノルル]: Motoshige Shinjudō [本重眞壽堂], 1914.

    General description of Japanese in Hawai`i, organized by each island. Includes residential maps and statistics on them.

75. Takeuchi, Kōjirō [竹内幸次郎]. *Beikoku seihokubu Nihon iminshi* [米国西北部日本移民史]. Shiatoru [シアトル]: Daihoku Nippōsha [大北日報社], 1929.

    A comprehensive history of Japanese in the Pacific Northwest with an extended Who's Who.

76. Takeuchi, Kōsuke [竹内幸助]. *Sanpidoro dōhō hattenroku* [サンピドロ同胞発展録]. Terminal Island, Calif.: Takeuchi Kōsuke [竹内幸助], 1937.

    Description of a Japanese fishing village in Terminal Island with an extended Who's Who.

77. Takoma Nihonjinkai [タコマ日本人会]. *Takoma shōkai* [タコマ紹介]. Takoma [タコマ]: Takoma Nihonjinkai [タコマ日本人会], 1922.

    A guide to the port of Tacoma and its vicinity, which also includes the description of Japanese settlements in the region.

78. Takoma Shūhōsha [タコマ週報社]. *Takoma-shi oyobi chihō Nihonjin shi* [タコマ市及地方日本人史]. Takoma-shi [タコマ市]: Takoma Shūhōsha [タコマ週報社], 1941.

    A general history of Japanese in Tacoma and the vicinity.

79. Terakawa, Hōkō [寺川抱光], ed. *Hokubei kaikyō enkakushi* [北米開教沿革史]. San Furanshisuko [サンフランシスコ]: Honganji Hokubei Kaikyō Honbu [本願寺北米開教本部], 1936.

    A chronological overview of the North American Buddhist Mission, with a history of each church.

80. Tōga, Yoichi [藤賀與一]. *Nichi-Bei kankei zai Beikoku Nihonjin hatten shiyō* [日米関係在米国日本人発展史要]. Oakland: Beikoku Seisho Kyōkai Nihonjinbu [米国聖書協會日本人部], 1927.

81. Tomimoto, Iwao [富本岩雄]. *Zaibei Wakayama kenjin hattenshi* [在米和歌山縣人發展史]. Wakayama-ken Susame-mura [和歌山縣周參村]: Tomimoto Iwao [富本岩雄], 1915.

    Includes an extended Who's Who.

82. Tomori, Mokuo [登森杢雄]. *Taigan no koe* [対岸の声]. Portland: Tomori Mokuo [登森杢雄], 1969.

    A collection of articles on Issei pioneers in the Pacific Northwest and the U.S.-Japan relations. The author wrote for the Oregon Japanese newspaper.

83. Tsutsumi, Takashi [堤隆]. *Sen-kyūhyaku-nijūnendo Hawai satō kōchi rōdō undōshi* [一九二〇年度布哇砂糖耕地労働運動史]. N.p.: Hawai Rōdō Renmeikai Honbu [布哇労働連盟会本部], 1921.

    A detailed account of the Great Strike of 1920 led by Filipino and Japanese laborers, written from the perspective of a strike leader. Includes useful discussion of underlying labor and economic factors that provided a background for the labor activism.

84. Tsuyuki, Sōzō [露木惣蔵]. *Shōwa seidai zaibei Kanagawa kenjin* [昭和聖代在米神奈川縣人]. Kanagawa-ken Sakata-mura [神奈川縣酒田村]: Zaibei Kanagawa Kenjinsha [在米神奈川縣人社], 1934.

    An extended Who's Who with a brief description of the Kanagawa Prefectural Association. A slightly shorter version was published in 1915 under the title *Zaibei Kanagawa Kenjin*.

85. Wakukawa, Seiei [湧川清栄]. *Jidai no senkusha Toyama*

Kyūzō: Okinawa gendaishi no issetsu [時代の先駆者當山久三: 沖縄現代史の一節]. Honolulu: Toyama Kyūzō-shi Denki Hensankai [當山久三氏傳記編纂会], 1953.

Biography of "the father of Okinawan emigration," placed within the context of the modern Okinawan history.

86. Washizu, Shakuma [鷲津尺魔]. *Zaibei Nihonjin shikan: fu zaibei zaifu Nihonjin rekishi no minamoto* [在米日本人史観: 附在米在布日本人歴史の源]. Rosu Anzerusu [ロスアンゼルス]: Rafu Shinpōsha [羅府新報社], 1930.

This contains essays, speeches, and commentaries on anti-Japanese exclusion and U.S.-Japan relations by Japanese immigrant leaders and white Americans. The appendix describes origins of various historical matters and Issei's social customs, as well as pioneering individuals and organizations in the mainland and Hawai`i.

87. Watanabe, Shichirō [渡辺七郎]. *Hawai rekishi* [布哇歴史]. Tōkyō [東京]: Ōtani Kyōzai Kenkyujo [大谷教材研究所], 1930.

Consists of two parts: the first deals with the general history of Hawai`i, and the second focuses on Japanese residents. The 1935 edition includes a history of Japanese language education in the Islands and Who's Who.

88. Yakima Nihonjinkai Sōritsu Sanjisshūnen Kinen Jigyō Iinkai [ヤキマ日本人會創立三十周年記念事業委員會], ed. *Yakima heigen Nihonjin shi* [ヤキマ平原日本人史]. Yakima, Wash.,: Yakima Nihonjinkai [ヤキマ日本人會], 1935.

A history of Japanese in the Yakima Valley, with an emphasis on community organizations. Includes an extended Who's Who.

89. Yamamoto, Iawao, and Satae Shinoda [山本岩夫 and 篠田左多江], eds. *Nikkei Amerika bungaku zasshi shūsei* [日系アメリカ文学雑誌集成] 22 volumes. Tōkyō [東京]: Fuji Shuppan [不二出版], 1997–1998.

This reprint collection consists of twenty-two volumes of eight different Japanese-language literary journals, many of which were originally produced in internment camps. Authored by Issei and Kibei writers, these volumes include: six issues of *Shūkaku* [収穫] (harvest), 1936–1939; three issues of *Wakōdo* [若人] (the Youth), 1943; six issues of *Dotō* [怒涛] (angry wave), 1944–1945; nine issues of *Tessaku* [鉄柵] (Iron cage), 1944–1945; seven issues of *Hāto Manunten bungei* [ハート・マウンテン文藝] (Heart Mountain literary works), 1944; thirty-two issues of *Posuton bungei* [ポストン文藝] (Poston literary works), 1943–1945; 11 issues of *NY bungei* [NY文藝] (New York literary works), 1955–1975; and thirty-five issues of *Nanka bungei* [南加文藝] (Southern California literary works), 1965–1985. As a compilation, the reprinted volumes of these obscure journals constitute valuable source materials for the study of Japanese immigrant and Kibei literature and the analysis of their minds and creative spirits inside the internment camps.

90. Yamasaki, Isshin [山崎一心], ed. *Amerika bungeishū* [アメリカ文藝集]. Tōkyō [東京]: Shinseidō [新星堂], 1930.

An anthology of literary works by Issei.

91. Yamasaki, Isshin [山崎一心], ed. *Hokubei bungei senshū* [北米文藝選集]. San Francisco: n.p., 1927.

An anthology of literary works by Issei.

92. Yamashita, Sōen [山下草園]. *Nichi-Bei o tsunagu mono* [日米をつなぐ者]. Tōkyō [東京]: Bunseisha [文成社], 1938.

A discussion of the so-called Nisei problems in the mainland United States and Hawai`i. Interpreting the second generation as a bridge of understanding between Japan and the United States, the author emphasizes their future contributions to the bilateral relations. Includes an account of Nisei students in Japan.

93. Yamashita, Sōen [山下草園]. *Nikkei shimin no Nihon ryūgaku jijō: fu Hawai kankeisha retsuden oyobi jūshoroku* [日系市民の日本留學事情: 附ハワイ関係者列傳及住所録]. Tōkyō [東京]: Bunseisha [文成社], 1935.

A detailed examination of Nisei studying in Japan. Describes the reasons and motives of their daily life in Japan. Offers information on Japanese schools and organizations that assisted Nisei's studying in Japan.

94. Yamashita, Sōen [山下草園]. *Ukurere no nageki* [ウクレレの嘆き]. Honolulu: Morishige Shosekiten [森重書籍店], 1933.

A collection of stories on the plights of Japanese in Hawai`i.

95. Yamazato, Yūzen [山里勇善]. *Hawai no Okinawa kenjin* [布哇之沖縄県人]. Honolulu: n.p., 1919.

A general history of Okinawan immigration to Hawai`i, and a description of their lives in the Islands. Includes statistical data with an extensive Who's Who.

96. Yatsu, Riichirō [谷津利一郎]. *Zaibei Miyagi kenjinshi* [在米宮城縣人史]. Rosu Anjerusu [ロスアンジェルス]: Zaibei Miyagi Kenjinshi Hensan Jimusho [在米宮城縣人史編纂事務所], 1933.

Includes an extended Who's Who.

97. Yoneda, Karl G. *Zaibei Nihonjin rōdōsha no rekishi* [在米日本人労働者の歴史]. Tōkyō [東京]: Shin Nihon Shuppansha [新日本出版社], 1967.

98. Yoshitake, Hachirō [吉武八郎]. *Kawai no kaori* [カワイの香り]. Tōkyō [東京]: Beifu Jihōsha [米府時報社], 1957.

Divided into two parts, the first describes a general history of Japanese in the Kaua`i Island with a focus on community organizations. The second part consists of the directory of Japanese residents with Who's Who.

99. Yuki, Shōjirō [湯木床次郎]. *Rafu Nihonjin Mii Kyōkai yonjūnenshi* [羅付日本人美以教会四十年史]. Los Angeles: Rafu Nihonjin Mii Kyōkai [羅付日本人美以教会], 1937.

100. Zaibei Nihonjinkai Jiseki Hozonbu [在米日本人会事跡保存部], ed. *Zaibei Nihonjin shi* [在米日本人史]. San Furanshisuko [サンフランシスコ]: Zaibei Nihonjinkai [在米日本人会], 1940.

The most comprehensive history of prewar Japanese immigrant society on the mainland United States. Compiled by the Japanese Association of America.

Supplementary Materials

COMPILED BY EIICHIRO AZUMA, MARIE MASUMOTO, TOSHIKO MCCALLUM, AND SHARON YAMATO

Map 10.1 Location of Sites of Incarceration during World War II

■ Numbers of people incarcerated in the War Relocation Authority (WRA) camps
● Justice Department camps

Japanese American Demographic Information

Table 10.1 Japanese Emigration to Hawai`i and the Continental United States

	Continental U.S.	Hawai`i	U.S. (Hawai`i included)	
1899	3,140	22,973	1946–50	1,168
1900	7,585	1,529	1951	3,212
1901	32	3,136	1952	4,436
1902	70	14,490	1953	3,614
1903	318	9,091	1954	3,945
1904	640	9,443	1955	5,002
1905	714	10,813	1956	7,308
1906	1,715	25,752	1957	6,686
1907	2,712	14,397	1958	6,794
1908	1,585	3,455	1959	5,901
1909	777	1,329	1960	4,980
1910	926	1,717	1961	3,904
1911	1,963	2,595	1962	3,763
1912	3,378	4,732	1963	3,790
1913	4,381	4,276	1964	3,265
1914	5,553	3,187	1965	2,850
1915	5,498	3,055	1966	3,152
1916	5,761	3,643	1967	2,845
1917	6,457	4,111	1968	2,964
1918	6,306	3,024	1969	3,005
1919	6,273	3,088		
1920	5,959	2,789		
1921	4,321	3,215		
1922	3,558	2,960		
1923	2,617	2,112		
1924	4,064	2,163		
1925	289	485		
1926	344	636		
1927	370	526		
1928	306	265		
1929	236	119		

Source: Gaimushō Ryōji Ijūbu. *Waga kokumin no kaigai hatten: ijū hyakunen no ayumi (shiryō hen)* (Tōkyō 1971), 1899–1929, 2–3; 1946–1969, 144–45.

Table 10.2 Total Japanese American Population by Decade and Gender Breakdown, 1900–2000

	Male	Female	Total
1900	70,849 (82.9%)	14,588 (17.1%)	85,437
1910	117,854 (77.6%)	33,978 (22.4%)	151,832
1920	135,351 (61.4%)	84,933 (38.6%)	220,284
1930	156,779 (56.3%)	121,686 (43.7%)	278,465
1940	154,787 (54.3%)	130,065 (45.7%)	284,852
1950	169,697 (52.1%)	156,279 (47.9%)	326,366[1]
1960	224,828 (48.4%)	239,504 (51.6%)	464,332[2]
1970	271,453 (46.1%)	316,871 (53.9%)	588,324
1980	328,703 (45.9%)	387,628 (54.1%)	716,331
1990	389,484 (45.9%)	458,078 (54.1%)	847,562
2000	-	-	796,700

Source: U.S. Census, 1900–2000.

Notes:

[1] Total population figures for 1950 in table 10.2 and table 10.3 differ due to discrepancies in the data provided by 1950 U.S. Census, General Characteristics, table 8, "Race and nativity, by Sex, for Hawaii, Urban and Rural, 1950, and for Hawaii, 1900 to 1950" and by U.S. Census, Special Reports, table 4, "Age of the Japanese Population, by Sex, for the United States, by Regions, Urban and Rural: 1950."

[2] The general statistics prior to 1960 did not include Hawai`i, because it was still a territory. Therefore, they are conflated with the separate Hawai`i figures by the researcher.

Table 10.3 Regional Distribution of Japanese Americans, 1900–2000

	Northeast	Midwest	South	West	Hawai`i	Total
1900	535 (0.6%)	349 (0.4%)	66 (-)	23,376 (27.4%)	61,111 (71.5%)	85,437
1910	1,915 (1.3%)	1,482 (0.9%)	610 (0.4%)	68,150 (44.9%)	79,675 (52.5%)	151,832
1920	3,613 (1.6%)	2,142 (1.0%)	973 (0.4%)	104,282 (47.3%)	109,274 (49.6%)	220,284
1930	4,014 (1.4%)	2,025 (0.7%)	1,126 (0.4%)	131,669 (47.3%)	139,631 (50.1%)	278,465
1940	3,400 (1.2%)	1,571 (0.6%)	1,049 (0.4%)	120,927 (42.4%)	157,905 (55.4%)	284,852
1950	7,438 (2.3%)	18,734 (5.7%)	3,055 (0.9%)	112,541 (34.5%)	184,598 (56.6%)	326,366[1]
1960	17,962 (3.9%)	29,318 (6.3%)	16,245 (3.5%)	197,352 (42.5%)	203,455 (43.8%)	464,332[1]
1970	39,125 (6.7%)	42,670 (7.3%)	28,504 (4.8%)	260,850 (44.3%)	217,175 (36.9%)	588,324
1980	46,913 (6.5%)	46,254 (6.5%)	47,631 (6.6%)	335,799 (46.9%)	239,734 (33.5%)	716,331
1990	74,202 (8.8%)	63,210 (7.5%)	67,193 (7.9%)	395,471 (46.7%)	247,486 (29.2%)	847,562
2000	76,350 (9.3%)	63,012 (7.9%)	85,180 (10.7%)	370,394 (46.5%)	201,764 (25.3%)	796,700

Source: U.S. Census, 1900–2000.

Notes:

[1] See notes of table 10.2.

Table 10.4 Japanese American Population by State, 1900–2000

State	1900	1910	1940	1970	1980	1990	2000
Hawai`i	61,111	79,675	157,905	217,175	239,734	247,486	201,764
California	10,151	41,356	93,717	213,277	268,814	312,989	288,854
Washington	5,617	12,929	14,565	20,188	27,389	34,366	35,985
Oregon	2,501	3,418	4,071	6,213	8,580	11,796	12,131
Colorado	48	2,300	2,734	7,861	10,841	11,402	11,571
New York	354	1,247	2,538	19,794	24,754	35,281	37,279
Illinois	80	285	462	17,645	18,432	21,831	20,379
Texas	13	340	458	6,216	12,084	14,795	17,120

Source: U.S. Census, 1900–2000.

Table 10.5 Educational Level of Japanese Americans, 1950–1990

	0–8 Years	9–12 Years	13–15 Years	16+ Years	Median School Years
1950	16,015	58,055	11,690	6,900	12.2
1960	86,502	179,998	36,596	29,164	12.2
1970	67,136	182,247	48,001	56,323	12.5
1980	53,119	273,226	133,650	137,792	12.9
1990	34,864	206,142	169,020	216,376	

Source: U.S. Census, 1900–1990.
Notes:
1. The figures for 1950 and 1960 include those fourteen years or older. The 1970 and 1990 statistics are taken from those over twenty-five years old, while the 1980 counterparts from those over fifteen years old.
2. The 1950 statistics do not include the Hawai`i data.

Table 10.6 Occupational Breakdown of Japanese Americans, 1920–1990

	Agriculture	Manufacturing	Professional	Commercial	Service	(Domestic)
1920	26,789	6,926	1,295	4,879	18,014	(12,723)
1930	25,193	3,977	1,970	8,693	14,397	(12,009)
1960	24,318	56,194	26,204	56,402	21,625	–
1970	10,203	77,612	50,083	92,109	33,965	–
1990	12,058	66,869	87,875	154,193	131,010	–

Source: U.S. Census, 1900–1990.
Notes:
1. Each census has slightly different categories with which to sort out the data. Therefore, the statistics are compiled sometimes rather arbitrarily. This is intended to show a general picture of occupational breakdowns among Japanese Americans in each year and a general sense of historical change over the period. For more detailed breakdowns, see the U.S. Census.
2. The 1930 statistics do not include Hawai`i.

Contributors

Akemi Kikumura-Yano is vice president for programs and director of the International Nikkei Research Project at the Japanese American National Museum, where she has curated exhibits, including *Issei Pioneers: Hawai`i and the Mainland, 1885–1924*; *In This Great Land of Freedom: Japanese Pioneers of Oregon*; and *The Kona Coffee Story: Along the Hawai`i Belt Road*. She is the author of several books, including *Through Harsh Winters: The Life of a Japanese Immigrant Woman*; and *Promises Kept: The Life of a Japanese Immigrant Man*.

Gary Y. Okihiro is professor of international and public affairs and director of the Center for the Study of Ethnicity and Race at Columbia University. He is the author of several books in Asian American studies, including *Cane Fires: The Anti-Japanese Movement in Hawaii, 1865–1945*; *Margins and Mainstreams: Asians in American History and Culture*; and *Whispered Silences: Japanese Americans and World War II*; and *Storied Lives: Japanese American Students and World War II*.

Masayo Ohara is a political scientist who received her Ph.D. from Columbia University. She is currently a research specialist for the International Nikkei Research Project at the Japanese American National Museum.

Eiichiro Azuma is an assistant professor of history and Asian American Studies at the University of Pennsylvania and specializes in Japanese American history, immigration/emigration, and U.S.-Japan relations.

JAPAN

Institutional Participants
Imin Kenkyukai, Masako Iino, President

Historical Overview
Eiichiro Azuma, History and Asian American Studies, University of Pennsylvania

Bibliographic Essay
Masako Iino, History and American Studies, Tsuda College
Kenji Kimura, Shimonoseki Municipal University
Tadashi Sugiura, Iwate University

Annotated Bibliography
Nobuhiro Adachi, Kansai Gaidai University
Taeko Akagi, Mejiro University
Ken'ichiro Cho, former JICA official
Tomoko Fukuda, Tokyo Metropolitan University
Kojiro Iida, Osaka University of Commerce
Masako Iino, History and American Studies, Tsuda College
Yumiko Imaizumi, Hosei University
Tomonori Ishikawa, University of the Ryukyus
Kenji Kimura, Shimonoseki Municipal University
Masaaki Kodama, Suzugamine Women's College
Shigeru Kojima, Japan International Cooperation Agency
Teruko Kumei, American Studies, Shirayuri College
Kunio Mamiya, formerly with Waseda University
Etsuko Maruyama, graduate school, Tsuda College
Naoko Masuda, graduate school, University of Tsukuba
Toyotomi Morimoto, Waseda University
Yukio Morita, Kanazawa Gakuin University
Yoko Murakawa, Keiai University
Yoshiaki Nakahata, high school teacher
Masako Nakamura, Graduate School, Tsuda College
Tatsuji Nakano, Asia University
Sugako Niikura, graduate school, Waseda College
Yuko Nishikawa, graduate school, University of Tsukuba
Rei Oiwa, JETRO
Yasuhiro Oshika, Chofu Junior and Senior High School
Noriko Shimada, Japan Women's University
Satae Shinoda, Tokyo Kasei University
Tadashi Sugiura, Iwate University
Mariko Takagi, Tōkai Women's College
Yasuko Takezawa, Anthropology, Institute for Research of Humanities, Kyoto University
Muneyoshi Togami, Ryukoku University
Shiro Umino, Ibaraki Christian University
Chikako Yamada, Nagasaki University
Hiroko Yagishita, The Diplomatic Record Office, Ministry of Foreign Affairs

Supplementary Materials*
Eiichiro Azuma, University of Pennsylvania, charts, maps, and timeline
Masayo Ohara, Japanese American National Museum, charts, maps, and photographs
*All maps designed by William L. Nelson Cartography

ARGENTINA

Institutional Participants
Asociación Universitaria Nikkei, María Angelica Nagahama, President; Jorge Higa, Advisor
Centro Nikkei Argentino, Emilio L. Higa, Past President; Gabriela Yoshihara, INRP Coordinator

Historical Overview, Bibliographic Essay, and Annotated Bibliography
Isabel Laumonier, Centro Nikkei Argentino

Supplementary Materials
Cecilia Onaha, Geography, University of the Ryukyus, demographic charts
Isabel Laumonier, map
Jorge Higa, photographs

BOLIVIA

Institutional Participants
Federación de Asociaciones Boliviano Japonesas, Guillermo Genshin Nema, President; Tomás Higa, Head Administrator; Keisuke Sakai, Advisor
Keio University, Presencia Japonesa en el Continente Americano, Toshio Yanaguida, Director

Historical Overview, Bibliographic Essay, and Annotated Bibliography
Iyo Kunimoto, Faculty of Commerce, History of Latin America, Chuo University

Supplementary Materials
Federación de Asociaciones Boliviano Japonesas, demographic charts and photographs
Toshio Yanaguida, Presencia Japonesa en el Continente Americano, map
Kozy Kazuko Amemiya, University of California, San Diego, photographs

BRAZIL

Institutional Participants
Museu Histórico da Imigração Japonesa no Brasil, Masato Ninomiya, Past Director and President of Administrative Commission and Celia Abe Oi, Director; Hironobu Kai, Researcher; Vivian Otsubo, Research Assistant; Aurea Christine Tanaka, Research Assistant

Historical Overview
Masato Ninomiya, Professor of Law, University of São Paulo

Bibliographic Essay and Annotated Bibliography
Masato Ninomiya, University of São Paulo
Naomi Hoki Moniz, Associate Professor of Portuguese, Georgetown University

Supplementary Materials
John Mizuki, Free Methodist Church, demographic charts
Masato Ninomiya, demographic charts and map
Hironobu Kai and Masato Ninomiya, photographs

CANADA

Institutional Participants
Japanese Canadian National Museum, Grace Thomson, Executive Director; Frank Kamiya, Past President; Reiko Tagami, Administration

Historical Overview, Bibliographic Essay, and Annotated Bibliography
Midge Ayukawa, Historian, Japanese Canadian National Museum
Audrey Kobayashi, Geography, Queen's University

Supplementary Materials
Audrey Kobayashi, demographic charts
Midge Ayukawa and Audrey Kobayashi map and photographs
Kathleen Wilson and Michael Pacey, map

CHILE

Institutional Participants
Sociedad Japonesa de Beneficencia "Nikkei-Chile," Mario Tsunekawa, Past President; Mika Toyao, Administration

Historical Overview
Ariel Takeda, Sociedad Japonesa de Beneficencia

Bibliographic Essay
Naomi Hirose, Sociedad Japonesa de Beneficencia
Ariel Takeda, Sociedad Japonesa de Beneficencia

Annotated Bibliography
Naomi Hirose, Sociedad Japonesa de Beneficencia
María Teresa Senda, Sociedad Japonesa de Beneficencia
Ariel Takeda, Sociedad Japonesa de Beneficencia

Supplementary Materials
Naomi Hirose, demographic chart, map, photographs
María Teresa Senda, demographic chart, photographs
Ariel Takeda, demographic chart, photographs

MEXICO

Institutional Participants
Asociación México Japonesa, A.C., Jesús K. Akachi, Past President

Historical Overview, Bibliographic Essay, Annotated Bibliography, Supplementary Materials, and Photographs
Jesús K. Akachi, Asociación México Japonesa
Carlos T. Kasuga, Asociación México Japonesa
Manuel S. Murakami, Asociación México Japonesa
María Elena Ota Mishima, History, Center of Asian and African Studies, El Colegio de México
Enrique Shibayama, Asociación México Japonesa
René Tanaka, Asociación México Japonesa

PARAGUAY

Institutional Participants
Centro Nikkei Paraguayo, Makoto Martín Nara, President

Historical Overview, Bibliographic Essay, Annotated Bibliography, and Supplementary Materials
Emi Kasamatsu, Philosophy, National University of Asunción

PERU

Institutional Participants
Fundación Cultural Nikkei del Perú, Ginyu Igei, President
Museo Conmemorativo de la Inmigración Japonesa en el Perú, Amelia Morimoto, Director of Research

Historical Overview
Amelia Morimoto, Museo Conmemorativo de la Inmigración Japonesa en el Perú

Bibliographic Essay
Raúl Araki, Museo Conmemorativo de la Inmigración Japonesa en el Perú

Jorge Nakamoto, Senior Research Associate, Aguirre International

Annotated Bibliography
Raúl Araki, Museo Conmemorativo de la Inmigración Japonesa en el Perú

Supplementary Materials
Amelia Morimoto, demographic chart, map, photograph documentation, and selection

UNITED STATES

Institutional Participants
University of California, Los Angeles, Asian American Studies Center, Don Nakanishi, Director
University of Hawai`i, Center for Oral History, Warren S. Nishimoto, Director
University of Hawai`i, Social Science Research Institute, Michael P. Hamnett, Director

Historical Overview
Eiichiro Azuma, History and Asian American Studies, University of Pennsylvania

Bibliographic Essay
Eiichiro Azuma
Brian Niiya, University of Hawai`i

Annotated Bibliography
Eiichiro Azuma
Michiko Kodama-Nishimoto
Brian Niiya

Supplementary Materials
Eiichiro Azuma, demographic materials and map
Marie Masumoto, Toshiko McCallum, Sharon Yamato, photographs

Index

Abe, Fumiko, 21
Abe, Junko, *217*
Adachi, Ken, 162–63
Agarie, Fumiko, 11
Agarie, Yuki, 10
Agencia de Cooperación Internacional del Japón. *See* Japan International Cooperation Agency
aging, Nikkei, 125
Akachi, Yoko, *217*
Akihito, Crown Prince, 235, 239
Akita, Yosokichi, *185*
Akiyama, Onatsu, 24
Akiyama, Take, *158*
Aliança Cultural Brasil-Japão, 121
Andes Jiho, 252
anti-Asianism, 25, 69; in Canada, 15, 35–36, 152–53, 155–56; in Chile, 17; in Mexico, 210–11; in Peru, 252–53, *253*, 258; riots and other violence against, 15, 35–36, 152–53, 210–11, 252–53, *253*, 258, 280–81; in the United States, 35–36, 280–81. *See also* discrimination, against Nikkei; immigration, restrictions on Japanese; World War II, effect on Nikkei
Anzai, Gizuke, 10
Aoki, Fujikuma, 97
Aoyama, Masafumi, 222
Arakaki Oshiro, Lucía, 259
Argentina: History, 9; Japanese migration to, 9, 10, 36, 44, 69, 71, 72, 79
Arima, Ricardo, *205*
Ariyoshi, George, 288
Asian American movement, 289
Asociación Agrícola Japonesa de Mexicali, 212
Asociación Japonesa Argentina, 77
Asociación Japonesa de la Ciudad de México, 213, 214
Asociación Japonesa de Mexicali, 212
Asociación Juvenil Nippon Mexicana, 213
Asociación México Japonesa, 216–17, 218
Asociación Nipona de Universitarios de La Plata, 80, 83
Asociación Nisei de México, 218
Asociación Universitaria Nikkei, 2, 83
Association of Merchants of Home Articles (Peru), 251
Association of Restaurant Owners (Peru), 252
Association of Small Stores in Lima Markets, 252
Association of University Nikkei, 2, 83
Atsumi, Alfredo, 219
Atsumi, Rafael Masahiro, 15
Australia, Japanese migration to, 33, 45, 68, 70
Ayubbi, Asiyah, *288*
Ayubbi, Kamau, *288*
Ayukawa, Midge, 163

Baja California, Nikkei in, 213, 214, 215
Balbi, Mariela, 261
Balmaceda, Manuel, 179
Barbershops Association (Peru), 251
Batalla, Carlos, 261

Benavides, Oscar R., 22
Beneficência Nipo-Brasileira de São Paulo, 125
Betserai, Nobuko Miyamoto, *288*
Betserai, Tarabu, *288*
Bolílvar, Simón, 11
Bolivia: History, 11; Japanese migration to, 11, 12, 36, 43–44, 68, 70, 96, 97, 99, 102–3
El Boreo coal mine, 206
Bouchard, Lucien, *161*
Brazil: History, 13; Japanese migration to, 13–14, 36, *42*, 43, 44, 69, 116–17
Brazil-Japan Cultural Alliance, 121
Brazilian Society of Japanese Culture, 121
brazucas, 128
Brunette, Rachel, 259
Bush, George, 289
business, Japanese, 117–18
businesses, Nikkei, 10, 73–75, 182, 215–16, 250; cafés, 75, 76, 79; dentists, 210, 213; doctors, 213; dry cleaning, *74*, 75, 81–82; nurseries, 75; retail, 98, 99

Cámara Chileno-Japonesa de Comercio e Industria, 186, 193
Canada, Japanese migration to, 15, 35, 45, 70, 150–51
Cardoso, Ruth C. Leite, 128
Casado, Carlos, 231
Catholics, Nikkei, 79, *80*, 191n7
Cavanagh, Jonathan, 261
Centro Cultural Mexicano Japonés, 217
Centro de Estudos Nipo-Brasileiros, 123
Centro Geriátrico Nipo-Brasileiro, 125
Centro Nikkei Argentino, 2, 80, 83
Centro Nikkei Paraguayo, *236*
Chaco, Nikkei in, *77*
Chaco War, 11, 98
Chambi, Oscar, 260
Chaves colony, *236*
Chiapas, Nikkei in, 213
Chile: History, 16–17; Japanese migration to, 17, 36, 68, 179–81
Chilean-Japanese Chamber of Industry and Commerce, 186, 193
Chinen, Seijitsu, 9, 10
Chinese immigration. *See* immigration, Chinese
Círculo Japonés de México, 213
Club Deportivo Nippon, 213
coffee farming, 13, 14, 116, 117, *119*, 204
La Colmena, 20, 231, 232, 233, 237, 239
Colonia Fram, 20
Colonia Okinawa, 102–3, 106
Colonia Presidente Chávez, 20
Colonia San Juan de Yapacaní, *96*, 102, 103–4, 106
colonialism, Japanese, 38–39, 68–69
Colonization Society, 34, 68, 204
Columbia, Japanese migration to, 69
Compañía Japonesa Mexicana Sociedad Cooperativa, 205, *206*
Compañía Nipo-Paraguayo de Colonización, 20
Compañía Pro-Fomento de la Inmigración Japonesa, S.A., 233–34

317

Company for the Promotion of Japanese Immigration (Paraguay), 233–34
concentraton camps, for Nikkei, 24, 102, 158, 285
Confederación de las Sociedades Regionales Japonesas del Noroeste de México, 213
Confederation of Japanese Regional Societies of Northwest Mexico, 213
Cooperativa Agrícola de Cotia, *125*, 129
Cooperative Committee on Japanese Canadians, 159
Córdoba, Nikkei in, 75–76
Corporation for Japanese Immigration in Paraguay, 231
Cortia Agricultural Cooperative, 125, 129
cotton farming, *123*, 211–12, *250*

Daniels, Roger, 293
Davao, Nikkei, in, 41–42
Dekasegi: definition of, 3, 7, 191n13; Japanese Latin Americans to Japan, 15, 22, 25, 47–48, 70, 81–82, 123–25, 128, 189, 255, 259; Japanese migrants to North and South America, 33, 35, 150–51, 205–7, 277–78
Delgado, Washington, 259
Díaz, Porfirio, 18, 210
discrimination, against Nikkei, 11, 14, 15, 22, 41, 78, 155, 158–60. *See also* anti-Asianism
Dom Pedro II (Brazilian emperor), 13
Dominican Republic, Japanese migration to, 44, 46, 70
A Dream of Riches, 162
Duus, Masayo, 293

Echeverria, Luis, *220*
education, of Nisei, 154–55, 252, 282–83
Eikō e no ishizue, 240
Elías, Domingo, 21
Emigrant Protection Ordinance, 33, 68
emigration companies, 13–14, 33, 68, 206, 277
Emigration Protection Act, 33, 68, 277
Emmerson, John K., 258
Enciso, Desiderio M., 240
Enomoto Colony, 34, 68, 205, 213, 222
Enomoto, Takeaki, 68, 204
Ensenada, Nikkei in, 213, 214
Las Esperanzas coal mine, 206

farming colonies, Nikkei, 24, 68, 103–4, 118, 204–5, 233–35, 236, 277
farming suveys, Nikkei, 121–22, *182*
Farrell, Gen. Edelmiro, 10
Ferreira, Manuel, 232, *234*
Fiji, Japanese migration to, 33, 68
Flores, Mr. (Bolivia), *98*
food, 19, 261
442nd Regimental Combat Team, 284, 285, *284*
Franco, Rafael, 231
Freundorfer, Yoshiko Moriya, 240
Fujiike, Tamotsu, *98*, *101*
Fujimori, Alberto, *255*, 257, 258, 259, 261
Fujita, Miyoji, 26
Fujiwara, Wes, 162
Fukumoto, Mary, 259
Fukuoka, Shotaro, 231

Galleguillos, María, *189*
gannen-mono, xi, 32, 68, 276
Gardiner, Harvey C., 258

Garuhapé Colony, 76, 80
"The Generation of '64," 259
Gentlemen's Agreement, 36, *37*, 68–69, 152, 279, 280
Germany, Japanese migration to, 70
Ginoza, Tsuruko, 14
Goto, Hiromi, 163
Guajardo, Berta, *189*
Guam, Japanese migration to, 32, 68
Guatamala, Japanese migration to, 68
Guevara, Victor, 258

Hamabata, Alberto, *217*
Hanako, Princess, 235–36
Hanami, Ryan, *291*
Handa, Tomoo, 119, 129
Haneda, Yoshio, 233
Hapa. *See* multiracial persons, Nikkei
Hara, Monhachi, *251*
Harada, Angelica, *257*
Haruhito, Prince, *220*
Hashimoto, Ryutaro, 125
hattenshi, 294
Hawai`i, Japanese migration to, 24, 32, 33, 68, 276–78
Hayashi, Count Tadasu, 37
Hayashi, Ishikawa, *182*
Hayashi-Lemiuex Gentlemen's Agreement, 36, 68–69, 153
Hidaka, Takeaki, *45*
Higa, Augusto, 259, 260
Higa, Emilio, *190*
Higa, Jaime, 260
Higa, Kajo, *102*
Higa, Riokichi, *102*
Higa, Sono, 12
Higa, Yoshi, 10
Higashide, Seiichi, 22, 258
Hioki, Eki, 179, *180*, 192
Hira, Magojiro, 10
Hirabayashi, Edward, *278*
Hirabayashi, Esther, *278*
Hirabayashi, Gordon, *278*
Hirabayashi, James, *190*, 278
Hirabayashi, Mitsu, *38*, *39*, *278*
Hirabayashi, Motoyoshi, 277
Hirabayashi, Richard, *278*
Hirabayashi, Shungo, *38*, 277, 278
Hirabayashi, Toshiharu, 277
Hirahara, Sako, *186*
Hirano, Umpei, 119
Hiraoka, Carlos, *256*
Hiraoka, Chiyoteru, *256*
Hiraoka, Guillermo, *256*
Hiraoka, Luís Nicho, 22
Hiraoka, Raúl, *256*
Hiraoka, Vidal, *256*
Hirohito, Emperor, 235, *236*
Hisaki family (Argentina), *76*
Hitachi, Prince 235–36
Horiuchi, Denjū, 100–1, 105
Horizonte, 80, 83
Hoshi, Seizo, 9
Huamán, Miguel Angel, 261

Ichikawa, César, and Los Doltons, *257*
Ichikawa, José, *217*

Ichioka, Yuji, 293
Ikoi-no-Sono rest home, 125
illegal immigration, 18–19, 68–69, 207–10
Imin Hogo Kisoku, 33, 68
Imin Hogoho, 33, 68
Imin Kenkyukai, 49, 163
Immigration: Chinese, 15, 18, 21, 23, 32, 248–49; Hawaiian, 23; restrictions on Japanese, 15, 25, 36, 41, 68–69, 116, 127, 152–53, 281, 286; Sikh, 15. *See also various destination countries for Japanese immigration*
Immigration Convention of 1886, 33, *34*, 276
Los inmigrantes japoneses en el Perú, 259
Inoue, Kyotaro, *211*
Inouye, Daniel K., *287, 288*
Instituto Cultural Mexicano Japonés, A.C., 218
intermarriage, 10, 76, 161, 183, 188, 255, 291
International Nikkei Research Project, 1–2, 187, 193
Inukai, Mr. (Mexico), *212*
Ishibashi, Tanji, 233
Ishibras shipyard, 118
Ishihara, Tatsuo, *120*
Ito, Hatsuko Kikuchi, 19
Ito, Hisao, 19
Ito, Roy, 163
Ito, Sally, 163
Ito, Sikeyuki, 179

JACL. *See* Japanese American Citizens League
Japan International Cooperation Agency, 4, 46–47, 70, 80, 106, 125, 186, 193, 234, 240
Japanese Agricultural Association of Mexicali, 212
Japanese American Citizens League, *282*, 283
Japanese American National Museum, *285*, 290, 291
Japanese Americans, 24, 50, 68, 275–311
Japanese Argentine Association, 77
Japanese Argentines, 9–11, 71–97
Japanese Association for Migration Studies, 49
Japanese Association of Mexicali, 212
Japanese Association of Mexico City, 213, 214
Japanese Associations, 211, 212, 213, 216, 237, 252, *254*, 281. *See also* Nihonjin-kai
Japanese Beneficence Organization (Chile), 184, 185, 187, 191n11, 193
Japanese Bolivians, 11–13, 95–114
Japanese Brazilian Beneficence of São Paulo, 125
Japanese-Brazilian Geriatric Care Center, 125
Japanese-Brazilian Studies Center, 123
Japanese Brazilians, 14–15, 50, 115–47
Japanese business. *See* business, Japanese
Japanese Camp and Millworkers Union, 156
Japanese Canadian Redress Foundation, 161
Japanese Canadians, 15–16, 149–76
Japanese Chileans, 17, 177–202
Japanese collective settlements, 118–19. *See also* farming colonies, Nikkei
Japanese Commercial Union (Bolivia), 98
"Japanese dry cleaner," 74, 75
Japanese Immigration Museum of Peru, 259
Japanese-Korean Exclusion League, 35
Japanese language schools, 119–20, 155, *212*, 218–19, 280–81, 282
Japanese Latin American internment. *See* World War II, effect on Nikkei
Japanese Merchants Chamber (Peru), 251–52

Japanese Mexican Cooperative Society, 205
Japanese Mexican Cultural Center, 217
Japanese Mexican Cultural Institution, Inc., 218
Japanese Mexican New Leaders Society, 218, *220*
Japanese Mexican School, 218
Japanese Mexicans, 18–19, 203–28
Japanese migration. *See the various destination countries*
Japanese Paraguayans, 20–21, 229–46
Japanese Peruvians, 22, 247–74; interned in the U.S., 253, *253*, 258
Japanese Society of La Paz, *97*, 98
Japanese Sports Club (Mexico), 213
Japanese Students' Association of Hawai`i, 283
Japanese Women's Association (Canada), *156*
JICA. *See* Japan International Cooperation Agency
Jiritsu (newspaper), 252
Jochamowitz, Luis, 259
Jujay, Nikkei in, 76

kachi-gumi, 120–21, *122*
Kaigai Iju Jigyodan, 45
Kaigai Kogyo, 36–37, *40*
Kajima, Ismael, *205*
Kamei, Joichi, 17
Kanazawa, Chiyoko, 21
kan'yaku emigrants, 33, 68, 276–77
Kapsoli, Wilfredo, 259
Kasamatsu, Emi, *236*, 240
Kasamatsu, Felix, 240
Kasamatsu, Hisakazu, 231, 233
Kasato Maru, 116
Kasuga, Carlos, *220*
Kataoka, Kiyoki, *184*
Katsuno, Mrs. Shoichiro, *277*
Kawabe, Setsuko, *217*
Kawamura, Yoshio, *98, 101*
Kawashima, Sumiko, *187*
kenjin-kai, 10, 73, 77, 152, *208*, 216
Kibei, 22, 282
Kikumura-Yano, Akemi, *190*
Kimura family (Mexico), *216*
Kimura, Maria Isabel Vergara, *190*
Kimura, Teruko, *217*
Kimura, Yoshijiro, *186*
King, W. L. Mackenzie, 153
Kinjo, Matsusuke, 12
Kishimoto, Kama, 10
Kishimoto, Kamezo, 10
Kishimoto, Kiho, 10
Kishimoto, Matsu, 10
Kitagawa, Muriel, 162
Kiyooka, Roy, 163
Kobayashi, Audrey, *161*, 163
Kobayashi, Cassandra, 163
Kodama, Asazo, *183*
Kodama, Kenji, *189*
Kodani, June, 258, 259
Kogawa, Joy, 163
Kokoku Shokumin Kaisha, 14
Komori Company, 98
Komori, Keiryo, *98*
Komori, Shinyemon, *101*
Komori, Tamiichi, *101*
Kondo, Seiji, 213

Koriyama, Mr. (Bolivia), *102*
Kudo, Kenji, *289*
Kudo, Miyoko, 163
Kugimiya, Mr. (Bolivia), *102*
Kumazawa, Gloria, *210*
Kumura, Eiko, *217*
Kuno, Gihei, 151
Kuroda, Otoshiro, 233
Kurushima, Eddy, *47*
Kuwata, Kimi, *276*
Kuwata, Lindo, *276*
Kuwata, Matsugoro, *276*
Kuwata, Meleana, *276*
Kuwata, Ome, *276*
Kuwata, Seiichi, *276*
Kuwata, Shiro, *276*
Kuwata, Umi, *276*
Kyoeikai La Sociedad de Prosperidad Mutual. *See* Japanese Association of Mexico City

labor contractors, 151, 277
labor organization, Nikkei, 156, 281, 296–97
Lévano, César, 259
Liceo Mexicano Japonés, A.C., 218
Lima Nikko School, 252, 253
Lopéz, Miguen Solano, 240
Lumbreras, Luis Guillermo, 259

Macera, Pablo, 259
Mackenzie, Ian, 157
Madero, Francisco, *208*, 210
Maeda, Alfonso, 15
Makabe, Tatsuo, 12
Makabe, Tomoko, 163
make-gumi, 121
Makino, Armando, *77*
Makino, Kinzo, 9, 75–76, *77*
Makino, Jose, *77*
Makino, Pedro, *77*
Makino, Roger, *77*
Manabe, Mr. (Bolivia), *102*
Manchuria, Japanese colonization of, 39–41, 69
Manchurian Colonization Company, 39, 69
Manshu Imin Kyokai, 39, 69
Manshu Takushoku Kaisha, 39, 69
Mardoes, Horacio Mujica, *181*
Martos, Marco, 259, 260–61
Mashiko, Saburo, 212
Matayoshi, Nicolás, 259
Matoo, Emiko, *210*
Matsumoto, Sanshiro, *217*
Mead, F. J., 157
Meiji emperor, *33*
Mendoza, Nikkei in, 76
mestiços, Nikkei. *See* multiracial persons, Nikkei
Mexicali, Nikkei in, 211–12, 214
Mexican Japanese Circle, 213
Mexican Japanese Youth Association, 213
Mexican Revolution, 210–11
Mexico: History, 17–18; Japanese migration to, 18–19, 68, 204–9
Mexico City, Nikkei in, 213, 214, 215, 216
Mexico Japanese Association, 216–17
México Shimpo, 213
Michiko, Princess, *118*, 235, 239

Micronesia, Japanese migration to, 69
Miki, Art, *161*
Miki, Roy, *161*, 163
military service, Nikkei, 155, 285
Ministry of Colonial Affairs (Japan), 37, 39, 69
Mink, Patsy Takemoto, 288
Minumo, Ryo, 13
Misawa, Gihei, *210*
Misawa, Ryo, *210*
Mishima, María Elana Ota, 222
Misiones, Nikkei in, 76
Miura, Alejandra, *189*
Miura, Yoichi, *74*
Miyagui, Ryoko, *73*
Miyamoto, Nobuko, 288
Miyasaka, Kunito, 231
Miyasato, Kamado, 25–26
Miyasato, Miho, 21
Miyazaki, Takeo, 97
Mizunuma, Kata, *186*
"model minority," 286
Möll, Eduardo, 260
Monma, Haruo, *186*
Montero, Jose P., 230
Montoya, Rodrigo, 259
Mori, Tatsuzo, *101*, *102*
Morimoto, Amelia, 258, 259, 260
Morinigo, Higinio, 233
Moritani, Fujio, 20
Moriya family (Paraguay), *232*
Mulroney, Brian, *161*
multiracial persons, Nikkei, 3, 128, 160, 255, 291
Murai, Ken'ichi, 222
Murakami family (Mexico), *216*
Murase, Mike, *289*
Museo Conmemorativo de la Inmigración Japonesa en el Perú, 259
Mutsu, Munemitsu, 204

Nagano, Manzo, *150*
Nagata, Mr. (Java), *41*
Nagaya, Isaac, *205*
Nagayama, Tetsu, *96*
Naito, Hasuko, *189*
Naito, Kimiko, *189*
Naito, Kimio, *189*
Naito, Takeshi, *189*
Nakagawa, Tadao, *180*
Nakamoto, Jorge, 258, 259
Nakamura, Pastor, *41*
Nakamura, Tami, 15–16
Nakamura, Toichi, *101*
Nakayama, Jinshiro, 162
Naruse, Kadori, *41*
National Association of Japanese Canadians, 161
nationalism, Nikkei, 283. *See also kachi-gumi*
Nawamura, Naoko, *47*
Neill, A. W., 157
Nema, Gensho, 12
New Americans Conferences, 283
New Caledonia, Japanese migration to, 33, 68
The New Canadian, 162
New Worlds, New Lives, 1
newspapers, Nikkei, 252, 282, 294

Nichiboku Kyodo Kaisha, *206*
Nichiboku Seinenkai, 218, *220*
Nihon Imin Gakkai, 49
Nihonjin-kai, 119–20. *See also* Japanese Associations
Nikkei Argentine Center, 2, 80, 83
Nikkei, definition of, xi, 1, 2, 3, 7, 190
Nikkeijin-kai. *See* Japanese Associations
Nimi, Santiago, *205*
Nippo Paraguaya de Colonización SRL, 233
Nippo Paraguayan Colonization Corporation, 233
Nisei Association of Mexico, 218
Nisei, education of. *See* education, of Nisei
Nisei Farmers League, 290
Nishikawa, Toshimichi, 103–4
Nishizawa, Luis, 219
Noda, Carlos, *102*
Noda, Monjiro, *98*
Noda, Ryōji, 97, 101–2, 105, 129
Nogueira, Arlinda R., 128

Obasan, 163
Obata, Roger, *161*
O'Brien, Thomas J., *37*
Oikawa, Mona, 163
Oishi, Tomisuke, *98*
Oiwa, Keibo, 163
Okamoto, Roberto, *217*
Okamoto, Teruko, 240
Okinawa Colony (Bolivia), 43
Okinawans, 9, 10, 12, 14, 33, *35*, 43, 45, 77, 102–3
Okino, Kishi, *40*
Oku, Kaneyoshi, *98*
Okuhata, Kiyoaki, 239–40
Okuma, Sadao, 14
Omatsu, Maryka, *161*
Omoya, Mr. (Bolivia), *102*
Ono, Hisashi, *98*
Ota, Shozo, 179
Ouchida, Shugo, *117*
Overseas Development Company, 36–37, *40*
Overseas Emigration Agency (Japan), 45, 46–47
Overseas Emigration Cooperative Federation, 37, 69
Oya, Katsuji, 153
Oya, Washiji, 153
Ozawa, Takao, *280*, 281

Pan-American Nikkei Association, 2, 190, 219
Paraguay: History, 19–20; Japanese migration to, 20, 43, 44, 69, 230–33
Paraguay Takushoku Kumiai, 231
Pattulo, T. D., 157
Pérez, Hildebrando, 259
Peru: History, 21; Japanese migration to, 21–22, 33, 36, 68, 248–49, 251
Peru Jiho, 22
Philippines, Japanese migration to, 33, 68
picture brides, 9–10, 15–16, 36, *38*, 153–54, *278*, 279
Pinto, Dr. (Bolivia), *102*
Pirapó colony, 234, 239
La Plata Association of Nipponese Academics, 80, 83
poetry, by Nikkei, 162, 260–61
Prado, Manuel, 22
Puente (magazine), 259

Reagan, Ronald, *290*
redress and reparations movement, United States, 289, 290
redress settlement, Canadian, 161
Reid, Helen R. Y., 162
Religion, 79
Riberalta, Nikkei in, 100–1
riots, anti-Japanese. *See* anti-Asianism
Rocca Torres, Luis, 258, 260
Rodriguez, Amalia, *77*
Rodriguez, Andres, 236
Rodríguez, Jesús Kumate, 219
Rodríguez, Juan, 21
Romero, Matias, *204*
Rosenbloom, Don, *161*
Roy, Patricia, 163
rubber growing, 99–100
Russo-Japanese War, 68

Saiki, Kikuko, 19
Saiki, Mario, 19
Saito, Fukuhei, 19
Saito, Hiroshi, 128, 129
Saito, Kishiro, *39*
Saito, Yohichi, *252*
Sakamoto, Kerri, 163
Sakoda, Kanezo, 230–31
Sakuragumi Teishintai, *122*
Salcedo, José María, 259
Sano, Seki, 219
Sasaki, Toshiji, 163
Sato family (Paraguay), *235*
Sawada, Teiryo, 18
Sayako, Princess, *255*
"school boys," 34–35, 277
Senda, Eiko, *280*
Senda, Kayo, *280*
Senda, Kazuo, *280*
senior citizens, Nikkei. *See* aging, Nikkei
seringero, 11–12
Shiba, Dr. (Mexico), *205*
Shibasawa, Kiyoko, *289*
Shibata, Yuko, 163
Shibayama, Oscar, *205*
Shibayama, Takugoro, *215*
Shimabukuro, Pamela, 22
Shimaru, Tokutaro, *98*
Shimizu, Yon, 163
Shimose, Pedro, 12
Shin Ijuusha, 160
Shin Issei, 47, 290
Shinpo, Mitsuru, 163
Shinya, G. Yoshio, 9
Shinya, Yokichi, *188*
Shiomi, Rick, 163
Shishido, Yo, 153
Shojima, Mr. (Bolivia), *102*
Shokumin Kyokai, 34, 68
Sinaloa, Nikkei in, 213, 214
Sino-Japanese War, 34, 68
slavery, 13, 23
Snell, Edward, 68
Sociedad Japonesa de Beneficencia, 184
Sociedade Brasileira de Cultura Japonesa, 121
Sociedade Paulista de Cultura Paulista, 121

Society for Manchurian Emigration, 39, 69
Society of Mutual Prosperity. *See* Japanese Association of Mexico City
Sokei, Chie, 9–10
soldiers, Nikkei. *See* military service, Nikkei
Sone, Suegoro, *186*
Sonora, Nikkei in, 213, 214
Stroessner, Gen. Alfredo, 235, 236
Suárez Company, 100
Suematsu, Kozo, *98*
sugar plantations, Nikkei workers on, 205–6, 276, 277, 281, 296–97
Sugimoto, Henry, *36*
Sumida, Regenda, 162
sumo, *214*
Suzawa, Mitsu. *See* Hirabayashi, Mitsu Suzawa
Suzuki, Teiichi, 121
Suzuki, Teijiro, 128

Takagi, Toshiro, 128
Takashima, Shizuye, 163
Takata, Toyo, 163
Takeda, Hidetoshi, *46*
Takeda, Jesús, *217*
Takeda, Satomi, *47*
Takumusho, 37, 39, 69
Tamashiro, Alejandro, 259
Tamashiro, Enrique, 259
Tamashiro, Masako, 12
Tamura, Norio, 163
Tanabata Festival, *126*
Tanaka, Masami, 14
Tanaka, Natsumi, 14
Tanaka, Teikichi, 97
Tanaka, Yuichi, 240
tanomoshi, 251
Taoka, Chiyuki, 240
Temixco Farm, *214*
Terasawa, Keiji, *98*
Terui, Ryojiro, 205, *206*
Thursday Island, Japanese migration to, 33, 68
Tigner, James, 103
Tokeshi, Eduardo, 260
Tokyo Club, 212
Toma, Yoshiko, 12
Tomii, Baron Shu, 78
Torres, Rosa, *256*
Treaty of Guadalupe Hidalgo, 18
Tsuchiya, Shinobu, *102*
Tsuchiya, Tilsa, 260
Tsuji, Shin'ichi, 163
Tucumán, Nikkei in, 76
20 Years of Japanese Immigration in Paraguay, 239

Uchida, Chitose, 155
Uchino, Mr. (Bolivia), *102*
Ueda, Hiroko, *210*
Ueno, Hisashi, 222
Uetsuka, Shuhei, 119

Unión de Exportadores e Importadores de México, 213
Union of Mexican Exporters and Importers, 213
United States: History, 22–23; Japanese migration to, 24, 34–35, 70, 276–79
Ura, Isataro, *250*
"Uruma disease," 12
Usinas Siderúrgicas de Minas Gerais, 118
Uyekawa, Gary, *289*

Van Reed, Eugene, 32, 68
Vargas, Getúlio, 13, 14
Vigil, Ricardo Gonzáles, 261

Wada, Tsunesaburo, *101*
Wakamatsu Tea and Silk Farm Colony, 24, 68
Walter-McCarran Act, 69
"war brides," 42, 69, 290
war vetearns, Nikkei. *See* military service, Nikkei
Ward, Peter, 163
Wasmosy, Juan Carlos, *236*
Watada, Terry, 163
Watanabe, José, 259, 260
Weiner, Gerry, *161*
Wilson, Halford, 157
women, Nikkei, 9–10, 12, 15–16, 24, 153–55, 163, 184, 187–89, 279
World War II, effect on Nikkei, 10, 14, 20, 26, 42, 69, 78, 120, 232–33; internment/forced removal, 16, 19, 24, 157–59, 184–85, 213–15, 283–85; Japanese Latin Americans interned in the U.S., 12, 22, 25, 102, 253, 258
Wuffarden, Jorge Luis Eduardo, 260

X COPANI, 2

Yagi, Sentei, 100, 105
Yamada, Kaoru, 17
Yamamoto, Atsuko, 222
Yamamoto, Mike, *289*
Yamamoto, Victor, *102*
Yamanaka, Shuzo, 20
Yamane, Kisaburo, *208*
Yamanuha, Senshu, 10
Yamasaki, Joy, *289*
Yamashiro, Seijun, 14
Yamazaki, Kimita, *210*
Yara, Chosho, *103*
Yguazú colony, 234–35
Yida, Lucila, *210*
Yika, Kazuko, *210*
yobiyose imin, 251
Yokohama, Kenkichi, *75*
Yoshida, Pablo, *217*
Yoshida, Yoshinori, *98*
Yoshihito, Emperor, 230
Yoshizawa, Yasukichi, 151
Young, Charles H., 162
Yubi, Amalia, 219

Zapata, Emiliano, *208*